WHAT IS THE THEATRE?

What is the Theatre? is one of the most coherent and systematic descriptions and analyses of the theatre yet compiled. Theatre is, above all, spectacle. It is a fleeting performance, delivered by actors and intended for spectators. It is a work of the body, an exercise of voice and gesture addressed to an audience, most often in a specific location and with a unique setting. This entertainment event rests on the delivery of a thing promised and expected – a particular and unique performance witnessed by spectators who have come to the site of the performance for this very reason. To witness theatre is to take into account the *performance*, but it is also to take into account the printed text as readable object and a written proposition.

In this book, Christian Biet and Christophe Triau focus on the practical, theoretical and historical positions that the spectator and the reader have had in relation to the locations that they frequent and the texts that they handle. They adopt two approaches: analysing the spectacle in its theatrical and historical context in an attempt to seek out the principles and paradigms of approaching the theatre experience on the one hand, and analysing the dramaturgy of a production in order to establish lines of interpretation and how to read, represent and stage a text, on the other. This approach allows us to better understand the ties that link those who participate in the theatre to the practitioners who create theatrical entertainment.

Christian Biet is Professor of Performing Arts, Theatrical and Drama Aesthetics and French Studies, University of Paris-Nanterre and the Institut Universitaire de France. He is also a regular visiting professor at NYU, and a member of the editorial committee of the French theatrical review *Théâtre/Public* and of *Littératures classiques*. Recent books include *Théâtre de la cruauté et récits sanglants (France XVIe–XVIIe siècle)* [*Theatre of Cruelty and Bloody Stories (France, from the End of the Sixteenth*

Century to the Beginning of the Seventeenth)] (2006), *Tragédies et récits de martyres (France, fin XVIe–début XVIIe siècle)* [*Tragedies and Martyrs' Tales (France, from the End of the Sixteenth Century to the Beginning of the Seventeenth)*] with M.-M. Fragonard (2009) and *Le Théâtre du XVIIe siècle* [*Seventeenth-Century Theatre*] (2009). He has recently worked on several issues of *Théâtre/Public* including topics covering Chinese theatre, "Penser le Spectateur" ["Thinking About the Spectator"] (no. 210, January 2014); Flemish performance, "Carte Blanche à Olivier Py" ["Carte Blanche for Olivier Py"] (no. 211, March 2014); and repertory, "Le répertoire aujourd'hui" ["The Repertory Today"] (no. 225, June 2017); "Théâtre et situationnisme" ["Theatre and Situationnism"] (no. 231, January 2019); and also an issue of *Communications* on the theoretical question of performance (no. 92, 2013).

Christophe Triau is Professor of Theatrical Studies at the University of Paris-Nanterre. He also works as a dramaturge. His PhD was on seventeenth-century French theatre, and his work now focuses mostly on contemporary theatre, especially dramaturgy and aesthetics of stage direction. He has edited many collective publications and issues of reviews such as *Alternatives théâtrales* (and is a member of its editorial committee) and *Théâtre/Public* (in particular, the biannual "Etats de la scène actuelle" issues, in collaboration with O. Neveux) and has written widely about contemporary stage directors, most recently a book on Joel Pommerat's *Cendrillon* (2013).

WHAT IS THE THEATRE?

Christian Biet and Christophe Triau

TRANSLATION JASON ALLEN-PAISANT
WITH THE COLLABORATION OF
JOANNE BRUETON

LONDON AND NEW YORK

This translation first published in 2019
by Routledge
2 Park Square, Milton Park, Abingdon, Oxon OX14 4RN

and by Routledge
52 Vanderbilt Avenue, New York, NY 10017

Routledge is an imprint of the Taylor & Francis Group, an informa business

Original edition © 2006 Editions Gallimard, Paris
English language translation © 2019 Routledge

All rights reserved. No part of this book may be reprinted or reproduced or utilised in any form or by any electronic, mechanical, or other means, now known or hereafter invented, including photocopying and recording, or in any information storage or retrieval system, without permission in writing from the publishers.

Trademark notice: Product or corporate names may be trademarks or registered trademarks, and are used only for identification and explanation without intent to infringe.

First edition published by Editions Gallimard 2006

British Library Cataloguing-in-Publication Data
A catalogue record for this book is available from the British Library

Library of Congress Cataloging-in-Publication Data
Names: Biet, Christian, author. | Triau, Christophe, author. | Allen-Paisant, Jason, translator.
Title: What is the theatre? = Qu'est-ce que le thâeãatre? / by Christian Biet and Christophe Triau ; translation Jason Allen-Paisant ; with the collaboration of Joanne Brueton.
Other titles: Qu'est-ce que le thâeãatre?. English
Description: London ; New York, NY : Routledge, 2019. | Includes bibliographical references and index.
Identifiers: LCCN 2018039380| ISBN 9781138701649 (hardback) | ISBN 9781138701656 (pbk.)
Subjects: LCSH: Theater.
Classification: LCC PN2037 .B5313 2019 | DDC 792—dc23
LC record available at https://lccn.loc.gov/2018039380

ISBN: 978-1-138-70164-9 (hbk)
ISBN: 978-1-138-70165-6 (pbk)
ISBN: 978-0-429-43713-7 (ebk)

Typeset in Bembo
by Swales & Willis Ltd, Exeter, Devon, UK

CONTENTS

Notes on contributors   xi
Cross section of the Opéra Garnier   xii

Introduction   1

Points of view   7

The spectator 7
The author 12
The dramaturg 14
The director 20
The set designer 22
The stage manager 26
The actor 30
The readers 33

PART I
What does it mean to go to the theatre?   41

Together with others or one among many? 42
Theatre and performance 43

1 Sites and spaces: definitions   51

Sites 52
The spaces 53
Text as site and text as space 56
Organising space through signs 56
The actor and their presence 57

2 The theatrical space: a concrete space   61

Theatre and urbanism 62
The open space 63
  The principle of the procession 64
  The infiltration principle 67
Locating the closed space 70
  Seventeenth- to eighteenth-century London 70
  The end of the Boulevard du Crime:
    nineteenth-century Paris 71
  La Cartoucherie de Vincennes in the 1970s 72
*Recycling and re-appropriating buildings in the
  twentieth century 74*
The evolution of places 76
Memory and repetition 78

3 Architecture   80

The illusion of creating illusion 84

PART II
The evolution of material and representational spaces   87

4 Some theatrical sites and spaces   89

The Greek skênographia 89
The scaena *and the Roman spectacle 92*
Medieval scenography: nowhere and everywhere 94
*The scaffold theatre and the trestle stage: integrative
  function versus critical function 95*
*Short digression: the amateur theatre in the
  contemporary moment 101*
A story of thresholds rather than of ruptures 103
Elizabethan theatre and the so-called "wooden O" 105
The "classic" French theatrical space: a rectangle 106
  At the courts 107
  In the cities 108
Italian-style theatre 110
Make way for the visible! 111
Scenography 112
Promoting attention 114

CONTENTS

5 The art of perspective and the social space   116

Italy, the "prince's eye" and Europe 117
The secularised space 119
The building and the session as spaces of socialisation 123
Line and circle: traditional double cone and multiple angles 126
Back to reality 128
The line and the circle: the depiction of infinity transcended by the infinity of words 134
Places, spaces, two spectacles and the distance effect 137
Reforming theatre from the building out: from d'Aubignac to Luigi Riccoboni 140
The experience of the fourth wall: dramatic theatre 146
The closed space instituted by dramatic theatre 152
The crisis of drama 154

6 Stage as place and stage as space   158

Rupture: the invention of the director, the total space of a total work 158
"Epic" theatre/dramatic theatre 164
The boundaries of the theatrical space 169
The dramatic space: a replica? 171

PART III
How to act at the theatre? How the theatrical space functions   177

The work of practitioners 180
Two senses out of five? 181

7 Description and vocabulary of the traditional theatre site   189

A traditional stage 191
The fly system 192
The proscenium 192
The curtain 192
The proscenium arch 194
The stage 194
The cyclorama 196
The trap room 196

CONTENTS

8 Other stages, other apparatuses — 198

Referential systems and innovations 199
Notes on bi-frontal staging 202

9 The coordinates of the stage — 205

A space more or less filled, more or less closed 207

10 The technical and material elements of the staging space — 210

The floor 210
Lighting 214
Sounds and silence 221
Scenery, objects and stage props 231
Costumes 240
Masks and make-up 248

11 On the danger of interpreting everything — 252

The pleasure of the audience 256

PART IV
Time, rhythm, tempo — 261

The time of the session 262
Stage time and dramatic time 265
The plasticity of time 266
The succession of sequences, the condensation of the 24-hour period and the transition to timelessness 275
Play, rhythm, staging 280

PART V
The body, the actor's play and illusion — 283

Where is the body? 283
Ostensible presence, exhibited communication 286
The handling and history of codes 289
The game of signs 290
When one body hides another: the virtual body of the character 297

CONTENTS

The dual utterance of the two bodies of the actor 300
From space, time and body, to representation 302
Illusion and identification 306
Continuity/discontinuity 311
Consecutivity, simultaneity: a necessary disillusion? 314
The blurring of the real and the virtual: delirium 315
Illusion and autistic performance 318
Theatrical illusion and cinematic illusion 324
The negative impact of theatre on the viewer and on the world 327
Seduction and utility of theatre: the thorny issue of "catharsis" 329
Spectacle, reading and judgement 335

PART VI
The reader of theatre texts   341

The appearance of the book and its pages 345
The oral text and the act of reading 348
Literariness, utterance and dramatic reading 355
Haphazard reading and the reading of a story 359
Places, spaces and the reader's time 362
The indexical reading of places, spaces and times 364
From reading time and space to the reading of a fable 369
Reading discourse and the constitution of characters 372
The test of the title 374
What is at stake here? 377
From general reading to reading of plot 382
From the plot to actantial narrative schema 393
From dramaturgical reading to dramaturgy 396

PART VII
Staging: traditions, concerns   403

Writing for the theatre today 406
Memory and forgetting 409

12 The age of all powers   415

The meaning mill 417
Re-reading the "classics": the issue of interpretation 420
The classics as a symptom: a prospective overview 425

ix

The image factory 436
The actor as a collective body 441
The actor as an individual body 444
Between tradition and invention: the play of forms 447
Triumphant theatricality 452
"A relative totality" 455

13 The experience of relativity   457

The "emancipation of representation" 462
Excess/void: Matthias Langhoff/Klaus-Michael Grüber 465
Collage, montage, hybridisation, performance 473
Kantor as an emblem 480
Armand Gatti, another emblem 484

14 Theatricality questioned: a theatre without illusion?   489

Contestations 489
Other aspirations, other practices 494
Crisis of representation, crisis of meaning 497
Showing writing: another relationship with the text 499
The actor exposed 505
From the legibility of crisis to the questioning of perception 509
The troubled perception 515
Theatre of presence and theatre of non-representation 516
Experiencing the theatrical relationship and the present-ness
  of the stage: theatricality unveiled 525
Choral aspirations 534
Decentring representation, diffracting reception: form
  as medium 542
Other distances, other presences 546
Deconstructing/reconstructing theatricality 549
The "postdramatic" 554

Conclusion   581

Index   587

NOTES ON CONTRIBUTORS

Jason Allen-Paisant is a scholar of African diaspora performance studies. He is currently Leverhulme Early Career Fellow in the School of Languages, Cultures and Societies at the University of Leeds.

Joanne Brueton wrote her PhD on Jean Genet and has published widely on his writing, as well as being the co-author of *Le Compas et la lyre: regards croisés sur les mathématiques et la poésie* (2018). She teaches French and English literature at the University of London in Paris and the Ecole normale supérieure.

Joseph Danan, playwright, dramaturg, Professor in Theatre Studies at Sorbonne Nouvelle University.

Scali Delpeyrat, playwright and actor.

Jean Jourdheuil, playwright, dramaturg, translator, Associate Professor in Theatre Studies at University Paris-Nanterre.

David Lescot, playwright, director, Associate Professor in Theatre Studies at University Paris-Nanterre.

Jeanne Piot, opera and theatre stage manager.

Anne Surgers, former set designer, Professor in Theatre Studies at Caen University.

CROSS SECTION OF THE OPÉRA GARNIER

It was on 29 September 1860, right in the middle of the Second Empire, that Louis-Napoléon Bonaparte announced the construction of the Opéra Garnier as a site destined for the public good, and an architectural tender went out around France. Although practically unknown at the time, Charles Garnier won the commission by unanimous consent and works began in 1862. The colossal building site elicited great consternation from critics, who maligned it as too expensive, too unsightly and too grand. Its construction endured many obstacles, such as the exorbitant cost involved in draining a subterranean reservoir, which has now been reduced to a small pond ironically called "Opera Lake", replete with its own myths and legends. By the end of the Second Empire, the building was yet to be completed. During the siege of Paris, it served both as a shelter for the Paris Commune and refuge for those displaced from Versailles. When the conflict had resolved, it became clear that the building must be completed, and on 5 January 1875, the inauguration took place to great pomp and circumstance.

Albeit just as expensive, but even larger, the Opéra Bastille was subject to just as much criticism, and never replaced the Opéra Garnier. Both buildings are now linked administratively, although preference is given to staging ballets and baroque operas at the Garnier, where the dance school is based (the original three-dimensional model of which can still be seen at the Musée d'Orsay).

This cross section of the Opéra Garnier identifies the general elements that constitute a theatrical floorplan (Figure 0.1). From Part III onwards, we will refer back to it when considering in more detail how the Garnier relates to the theatre more generally. This image offers an exemplar of a traditional Western theatre as it is perceived by the general public. Naturally, many other theatrical spaces exist and have done throughout the history of theatre. Exploring these is at the very heart of this book.

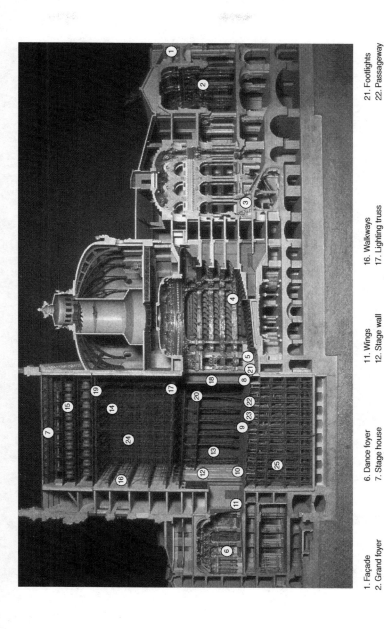

1. Façade
2. Grand foyer
3. Grand staircase
4. House or auditorium
5. Orchestra pit
6. Dance foyer
7. Stage house
8. Proscenium or forestage
9. Stage
10. Upstage
11. Wings
12. Stage wall
13. Lateral stage wall
14. Fly system
15. Machinery
16. Walkways
17. Lighting truss
18. Iron curtain
19. Batten
20. Mobile drapery (manteau d'Arlequin).
21. Footlights
22. Passageway
23. Trap doors
24. Chassis
25. Trap room

Figure 0.1 Cross section of the Opéra Garnier.

INTRODUCTION

Above all else, theatre is a spectacle, an oral genre, a fleeting performance, delivered by actors and intended for spectators. It is a work of the body, a vocal and gestural exercise addressed to an audience, most often in a specific location and with a unique decor. In that sense, it is not always linked to a previously written text, nor does it necessarily give rise to the publication of a written work. Because it is a spectacle, and because of its concrete, material and oral nature, theatre, which is always intended for a gathering of people, is an inherently collective activity. To attend a performance is thus to be with others at a particular moment, meeting in a specific location with the intention of participating in an event.

This dramatic event we call theatre relies on the delivery of that which is both promised and expected: a unique performance witnessed by an audience who have come to the site of the performance for that very reason. In principle, the theatrical space is divided into two groups of people that differentiate it from ritual practice: the practitioners who create the performance and the spectators who witness it (although the activities of these two sets of individuals may sometimes overlap or be interchangeable). The symbolic division by which observers are conventionally separated from those observed and that is, by and large, conceived of as a frontal, face-to-face dynamic, is thus systematically challenged, turned on its head, by all the partners who are literally *present* during a theatrical event. Our intention is thus to consider theatre as a dramatic *event*, with all of its interdependent activities, using the most coherent and systematic descriptive and analytical approach at our disposal.

Witnessing theatre means, first and foremost, taking into account the *performance* that it is. But it also means taking into account the printed text, provided that it is not considered as either the source of everything, or as absolute authority, and that it is approached as a specific element: a readable object and a written proposal. However, since it is claimed by a "writer" and is traditionally placed in the domain of "literature", the text is, in some respects, considered complete, as a "work of art", with its specific written quality and unique orality. What is written for the theatre is both a text awaiting staging and literary creation, both future event and literary, published work of art. This is the theoretical and historical paradox that the reader and critic must face. The result is that, particularly in Western theatre, the text is inscribed within the space and time of the dramatic representation. In other words, it is spoken by actors (imaginary or real) who are also characters, or themselves fictions or elements of fiction. The text written by an "author", interpreted using the bodies of actors, or simply recited, thus gives rise to the staging of a fiction that is imaginary for the reader, but that engages the spectator who "consumes" this staged drama with varying degrees of mediation and distance and who "buys into" a complex mechanism of illusion that, though relative, purports to be "absolute". Through his gaze, the spectator is thus ideally capable of willingly suspending the awareness of being in a theatre and in front of actors and of entering into the world of a story written beforehand (which may or may not be supported by characters). Through their imagination, the reader will be just as able to produce in his mind a world existing outside of it, transcending the specific presentation of the text, whose visual ordering constantly reminds him or her that it was written to be played by actors. And the spectator and reader, because they are in a real place, know that this story is an illusion. It is through this complex, paradoxical mechanism, which emphasises the mutual tension between concrete physical practice and imaginary stories, that the theatre *functions* and writers, actors, directors, but also readers and theatregoers, develop, innovate, share and carve out their own specific, individual roles.

Thus, one cannot overemphasise the complexity of this art, of its network of contradictions and of the profoundly social, yet particularly personal, nature of the experience. In any given setting, individuals, without any visible constraint, pay to assemble and collectively witness something other than what they are while observing *themselves*, so to speak. They decide to turn up at a given time, without really knowing what they will derive from this ephemeral experience. They play a strange aesthetic, psychological, political, philosophical, social and personal "game", each one vis-à-vis everyone else, and vis-à-vis *himself* or *herself*. Individuals – who have perhaps seen the staging of the text or who intend to see it – read a dramatic work, imagine (in their various ways) a setting and a space, use various reading strategies, think about the world constructed by the words printed in black and white, and about possible staging mechanisms, without necessarily choosing to be mere readers of fiction, authors, dramaturgs, actors, directors or the critics of their own imaginary production.

What does it mean to go to the theatre? What does it mean to read a dramatic text? How exactly should one approach these practical concerns? These are the questions we ask ourselves from the very outset.

Numerous books have been published on theatre, on its history, its aesthetic theories, its semiology and poetics, on the role of the actor, the director, the stage manager and on personal stories linked to the craft. It is our intention here to take a slightly different path. We have decided to underscore the fact that the theatre as an experience and an activity inherently and integrally involve the spectator and the reader. As such, the aim of our study has been to focus our descriptive efforts on the practical, theoretical and historical positions that such individuals have and have had in relation to the locations that they frequent and to the written text that they handle. This approach, while not profoundly novel, allows us nonetheless to better understand the ties that link the majority of those who participate in theatrical activity, the readers and theatregoers, to the practitioners who create the show. For in thinking that there is a homogenous reader, a homogenous theatregoer, or a homogenous audience, one neglects the fact that these individuals represent multiple groups, which are historically, socially, hierarchically and topographically distinct and varied. Above all, it is through these groups of people that the theatre lives or dies. We have thus decided to foreground this diversity, and to refuse any essentialism of the spectator, the reader or the practitioner (director, actor, decorator, etc.), in order to shed light on the behaviours that have governed and that govern the reception of theatrical performances and works, to classify them and to indicate various principles of operation.

Far from hoping to postulate or seek an absolute essence of the theatre experience, we have limited ourselves to the consideration of two experiences – both going to the theatre and reading a play – from a historical point of view. We do so in order to construct, if not a general theory, then at least a type of approach effective enough to aid in understanding them. For just as there is no homogenous (undifferentiated) spectator, there is no *one* essential theory of theatre, but rather a set of systematic questions and observable principles. And while, in order to "practise theatre", one must individually determine the criteria, choose the main theory (and this is often a matter of taste, or of aesthetic and ideological choice) or claim a particular essence (which then functions as a personal, subjective fiction, as a unique personal aesthetic, capable of grounding one's way of practising or experiencing the theatre), the long history of the craft shows us clearly that the choices of readers and theatregoers have varied considerably and have even been generally conflicting. We cannot speak of an eternal essence to the theatre, but rather of mechanism that produces characteristics that adopt certain traditional elements and various *practices*: a show, exposing the presence of bodies within an acted-out fiction, which organises individual perceptions, in a live performance amidst a collective framework. However, we can identify certain general notions, and especially conventions, which exist to be respected, overturned, transgressed, as the case might be, since theatre rests on the principle of *play*. The following are undoubtedly the essential constants: the rather evident fact that the spectacle and the spectators exist only by virtue of each other (theatregoers do not exist without the theatre, nor the theatre without theatregoers); and that there is *play* in all its forms, the play of bodies, spaces and times, play as amusement and as critical praxis, finally, play, as in the *interplay* between the different parts of a machine, where one little empty space prevents it from jamming and ensures its constant movement. And, indeed (we shall return to this point), if practitioners and authors play, so do spectators and readers, albeit in other ways and in respect of the game that has been suggested to them and that they assign themselves.

Therefore, with constant comparisons between old plays and more contemporary ones, we have sought to put our contemporary theatre into perspective. This is not merely to affirm that nothing new, or wholly original, is ever created, but rather to establish that some reflections, paradoxes, questions and behaviours recur systematically in the networks of complex, reciprocal interactions between theatre professionals (including authors) and their audiences. As we shall see, these interactions operate in both directions, so much so that performances, like the reading of texts, can be regarded as the product of a collective dynamic. These productions become shared, though not necessarily harmonious, entertainment operations. On the contrary, they can often seem rather contradictory, insofar as they imply differing and opposing appropriations and legitimacies with respect to a single event. Reading operations are based, for the most part, on one single object – the text – but with different systems of appropriation and, here again, contradictions and paradoxes.

And since our objective will be to examine certain notions in depth or, at any rate, to describe with some degree of precision the state of affairs, of space, of time, of bodies and texts throughout contemporary theatre and throughout the history that has forged it, we have adopted two approaches. The first, of paramount significance to the staged play, is the analysis of the spectacle or, at least, of its constituent aspects, players and categories, placed against the background of the history of the theatre, in an attempt to draw out certain principles and paradigms for approaching the theatre experience. The second approach, more closely linked to the relationship between the text and its staging, is the analysis of dramaturgy in order to better establish possible lines of interpretation, ways of appropriating the text to read it, represent it and (virtually or otherwise) stage it. Those will be our two objectives. And since it would be impossible not to consider the immediate interests of the contemporary reader, we have decided to outline the current landscape of certain tendencies and preoccupations found in contemporary theatre. In particular, those that relate to previously discussed theoretical and practical observations about the activities of spectators and readers.

This work is predominantly concerned with Western theatre. This is by no means a suggestion that other theatrical forms, from Africa, India and other important spaces, are not deserving of scholarly attention, but rather that these forms necessitate an entirely different set of critical and descriptive tools and entail a different definition of audience. Our study will nevertheless make references to the Nô, the Kabuki, to Balinese dance, etc., insofar as these repertories and theatrical manifestations, with their unique traditions of acting, naturally enhance critical reflection on Western theatre. Given that theorists, directors, writers and actors have continually drawn upon them since the dawn of the twentieth century, fascinated by what was first called non-European theatre before considering the diversity and specificity of each form (and of each civilisation) in its own right, we too shall "walk through" them in the manner of these practitioners – by forced entry, so to speak. In any case, it would have been dangerous to examine these forms wholesale or as "outside traditions", as one would run the gruesome risk of reducing them to one sole category, thus re-inscribing the Western-centric outlook of a bygone era. Each theatrical tradition must be analysed not as a function of its mere relationship to European theatre, that which we know and practice, but by observing its own specific functioning, and mainly with the tools of ethnography, a task that is beyond our purview. On that score, we direct the reader to other studies and critical works of far greater expertise concerning the modes of representation and of ritualisation specific to these genres and civilisations, for example the scholarship of Richard Schechner and Jean-Marie Pradier. And, of course, we direct you towards the discipline of ethnology itself, which should never be conflated with Theatre Studies, since it deploys its own unique methods and theories. This allows us to concentrate on our major objects of study – the position of Western theatregoers and readers – without losing sight of all the others who are, in fact, in the majority and that deserve our singular attention and a series of theoretical investigations specific to their different practices.

However, our first task will be to demonstrate that theatre is carried out, first and foremost, as an activity among several players. As such, spectators, directors, dramaturgs, scenographers, lighting directors, actors, authors and finally readers, will thus be allowed to have their say, giving us a specific account of their activity, fictionally set on an opening night. We will begin here with this series of multiple perspectives, which, perhaps more than all the contents of this book, depict the ungraspable essence of theatre.

POINTS OF VIEW

The spectator

Tonight I'm going to the theatre. The process is already in motion. First, I needed to "plan to go to the theatre", to get used to the idea of seeing actual bodies, listening to a text, sitting in front of a stage in a space specially designed for the show, alongside other spectators who one cannot ignore the way one would at the cinema, who one smells, hears and often sees. I needed to get seats (which are usually numbered) in advance. It's an absolute ceremony that ritualises one's evening out, an occasion one looks forward to. It is not trivial. And besides all that, I still needed to *choose*: the place, the building, its reputation, its manager (I do have my loyalties), the actors (they say that so and so is great in this play), the director, the author (a classic, a contemporary work that everyone is talking about?), the script (is there even one this time?). Oh yes! The script, that thing one goes to hear and judge, that thing mediated through a series of entities that claim it, a script interpreted through lighting, or set design, conveyed through diction, performed by the actors, magnified by the stage or swallowed up by it. Complicated. In going to the theatre, I feel compelled to make more choices than for any other show, with many more prerequisites. All in all, it is quite intimidating. To the point where there is now such a thing as "spectator schools" – I despair! So, tonight I decided to be curious, to reconnect with what theatre is in its essence: a show, which one has not seen and whose script one has not read, an altogether live spectacle. It's risky, perhaps, but I took the decision (yet another decision) to go see a contemporary play, by an author of which I know nothing. A play about which there has been a bit of talk in some newspapers (and even somewhat on the radio). What about the classics? It's often the same ones again and again (a limited selection: three plays by Racine, two by Corneille, four by Marivaux, a maximum of five by Molière), or, alternatively, Shakespeare, the undying, international, universal great. But I wanted a change. Let me be honest, I also wanted to avoid any idea of a performance specially put on for schools with their busloads of children. So there you go, I have my ticket, which I bought long ago, prepaid and received in the mail (I should look into subscriptions at some point) and I am approaching the building – a bunker in the suburbs, to make a change from the golden, very Parisian, proscenium theatres (which have their charm, I must admit). At least, I'll have a full view of the stage. From a distance, perhaps, but I'll be able to see it fully without having to lean, without having some other viewer behind me telling me to sit back because I am blocking their view.

I didn't go to the cinema. No. I won't be moved as much, perhaps. Surely, I won't cry – I have almost never cried at the theatre. But what I do know is that sometimes strange things happen inside me, which are very different from two-dimensional viewing. No screen, no close-up, it's not the same way of viewing images. None of that tonight, but something very interesting to feel and think about. And for once, I belie the statistics, I come alone. The experience is for me, as much as it is for all the spectators, very rare. Indeed, there is always, in the performance event, a collective aspect, a ritual group effect. And while it is considered the proper thing to be quiet during performances (a custom that is relatively recent) one does feel that, before and after the show, and during intermissions, people are here to talk, to comment on the actors, to appreciate the plot and the staging, as well as to talk about other things. Moreover, even during the show, the silence (mine as well as that of my neighbours) is almost alive, full of meaning, a testament to our collective presence.

So the event is already in progress. I approach, get closer, before the bell sounds to signal the real beginning. I see people in the main hall, the audience. As at an airport, these soon-to-be spectators are going on a trip, with no visible luggage, except for their cultural background, which is sometimes all too conspicuous. Some eat and drink, others do not. Some wait, others leaf through the mini-programme or a free newspaper. Most of them converse. A dense noise. I note in passing that one no longer dresses up (or perhaps just in black, in the style of "theatre people"). Also gone are the days of the bell. It has been replaced by a sound that covers the noise so that, with our tickets torn, we head inside, where we are greeted by an usher – almost certainly a performing arts student in one of the numerous university programmes open to these young people. No sooner have I sat in my seat that I begin to wonder whether I would not have been better seated elsewhere. Closer? No, since I'd hate to observe the actors' faces close up, to see the sweat on them and spittle from their mouths, and end up having far too close a view of their acting technique. Farther away? Yes, for the panoramic viewpoint but not for the sound, which may be too low at this distance; nor for the spaciousness of the room, the constant reminder of which I'd have from this viewpoint, and not for the rows separating me from the stage. More central? Yes, from this spot I'd have the so-called "prince's eye", but not a superb view of the actors' movements or the wide-angle view I like to have of the field of the stage. Anyway, I know I will always regret not being in another seat than the one I am in, I will always regret not being in two, three or even multiple seats all at once, to view the performance from all possible points of view. I'll probably have to come back (which I very seldom do). So I'm seated, and will soon be in the dark (maybe), silent (this has been the custom for less than a century), awaiting the arrival of "talking bodies". The bodies of actors and perhaps of characters, or specific entities who themselves live a double life while I remain motionless and mute. I wish that I were "physically engaged" a bit more, that I were called to partake with more than just my silence, my quiet attention, my boredom and drowsiness, my laughter or my applause. I sigh and dream, watching the other spectators turn off their cell phones based on the instruction of a recorded voice. We are in a modern rite: we lock ourselves away individually and collectively from the world as it is; we are here, alone, among many. But already I see that I'm not just here to observe a world that's radically "other" or "elsewhere", as is still the sensation one gets in some theatres: the stage is open, there is no separating curtain, and there will be no *trois coups* indicating a transition to an illusion. On the stage, a few, clearly visible actors are watching us. Are they waiting to turn into characters or are they just waiting for the moment when they will start acting? Here we go again. Before even hearing a word, I am summoned, taken aback, mentally engaged, and I must solve enigmas, be alert, shake off idleness and inanity (which, strangely enough, are precisely the attitudes that my role of silent sitting observer would seem to favour). Almost despite myself, I start acting silently, *I start wondering things*. I've come for the excitement, but I also know that much of this excitement will stem from my own faculties. In this great airport-supermarket-cultural centre, in this grey chair (red would be too conventional, too archaic), and before everything is set in place for several hours, I'm already wondering about my luggage. What have I brought for the trip? Useless things, as always: old references, an idea of the box of illusions, of character, of autonomous fiction, of the fourth wall, of conventions, in short.

But are these things so useless? I would like to be naïve; but I also know – in fact, "we" know – that I will not be. Now, as at the moment of an accident, when one sees images flashing before one's eyes, I see references flashing before me, though I do nothing and am unable to do anything. I imagine scenarios, I buy into the prolepsis, because the place puts me in a position to do so. And in my desire to know what will happen before the show begins, I gather every thread, every clue, without even thinking and form a whole.

I am in the suburbs, and thus removed from a certain tradition, but placed in another. I am in a modern building (which already has a lot of history) with its social and cultural connotations. I am in a room that allows everyone to see and hear, more or less, equally well; before a large stage, and within a particular audience (mixed tonight, different from the one yesterday and tomorrow). Today I paid to have my own space, my seat, for a few hours. In front of me, around me perhaps, there will be a space that I see momentarily, which will also change, thanks to the bodies and objects, the lighting and movements and the effort I make for it to change, for it to represent another space. It is not summer (I would not be in a place like this in summer), and it's not a Monday (a rest day for theatres generally). I'm here for an evening performance, and I know I'll get out at about 11 pm; I could have come for a matinee, on a Sunday, but I do not like matinees (I have dragged myself to them, but they are hardly my preference – and it seems to me, but it might just be me, that this is sometimes the case for actors too). Then I wait for the exchange to begin, for myself and the others to be given the gratification of a particular moment in exchange for the sum of money we have paid. I pay for my involvement in the hope of a transformation. I wait for time – my time – to change, for the few hours separating me from the return to reality to pull me into another time, one so difficult to define and that depends so much on what's on offer: will I be observing the past? Am I here to observe the future? Or a sort of present? Will I be in all three simultaneously and contradictorily, or in an erased time, one that's abstract, but of the now, contemporary? What fiction and what sensations will I get? How will I be *affected* by this experience? I do not know who exactly is next to me, but I know they are there, in space, time and in the posture that characterises us as spectators. And at the heart of this assembly, actors will come to life, framed by a stage design and inevitably forming part of the community.

And while, all dreamy-eyed, I summon all my knowledge, hoping to be an ideal spectator, the lights in the auditorium fade and the actors seem to come alive. All these questions – "Where am I, in what time am I, who am I and who are they?" – disappear as a recorded sound fills the room. The questions take a back seat, like a muting effect. I forget them and hope to forget myself for a moment, in this mixture of blurred knowledge and emotion that I seek after. I know all that, but still . . . I'm here. I am only one of many spectators, I don't represent that much in the larger scheme (and yet I do know that I *represent* everything). I wait expectantly for living bodies and the sound of words, illuminated objects, the space that I could almost take possession of if I wasn't me. I feel the presence of the present. I focus on the ephemeral. Here we go.

The author

I finished before the rest. I am the first to finish, before everybody else. I worked by myself, doubted, suffered alone. I have often thought of packing it in, but I didn't quit, I finished the job. I've turned over the script. It was read and I was there. I listened to it. I hoped that something would happen. Not all the actors had read the text previously. Some of them stumbled, as it was the first reading. And I wanted them to have it hard. Then they asked me not to come back. They told me, "Please, we'd rather not have you here, you understand". And I understood perfectly well and said, "OK, of course, better for me not to, when the author is present it's terrible when the author is there it's impossible". And for two months I had no clue as to what was happening, I saw nothing. Sometimes I called and was told that everything was going all right, going great, that it was difficult, that it was very hard, but that it was a treat and that things would have to be cut.

And I said, "Obviously, it makes sense, I expected that, we can't do everything, it makes perfect sense, so feel free to cut what you want, you decide, cut if you feel you must cut". And as soon as they told me what, as soon as they told what wouldn't be included I said,

> Really? *That*, really, *that*, you can't get that to work? I'm really surprised are you sure? That bothers me a bit actually because *that*. That's what I like most it's the most important thing. If you take out that . . . take out everything else if you must but leave that.

So they told me they'd have a look at it, that they'd try again but that they really weren't feeling it, that they didn't get it, that it was complicating things, that they had to make choices but they'd try again anyway and they'd see how it goes.

And tonight is the opening night we're going to hear and we're going to see. I'll be in the audience with everybody else, but I'll be a bit different from the others. Because I'll be the only one that the night belongs to. That's the author. He's the one that owns the opening night. This night happens to audience members. But opening night is the author's night — it's either his or it isn't his. For the director it's different. For the director the opening night is all about his powerlessness and him wanting to stop everything and start over but not being able to. On the opening night the actors are like firemen, they're on a rescue mission. They do what they can. They always need another week. If you like things premature, then come to the opening night, come to the hospital. Otherwise better wait a week then go see the child at home, at his home, when he's all settled and comfy.

I went to the invitation counter. First I asked how long the play would last. They told me two hours or two hours and five minutes. How could it be two hours and five minutes? I wrote a play for one hour and twenty minutes, they've turned it into a two-hour and five-minute performance. I know what I wrote. I know how long it lasts. I time things. And I'm strict about it. I act out the play for myself at home and time it. I also use the number of characters to help me gauge the time. Timing for me is no joke. And this play has 55,000 characters. And 55,000 characters is an hour and twenty minutes. Period. How did they manage to turn it into two hours? And with all that they still cut my favourite passage. Because they've definitely cut it I can bet on it.

And only then did I ask for my ticket, and they asked me what name. And when I said my name they all looked at me and said "Ah!" and smiled.

It's full. The real crème de la crème are here tonight. It's going to be a bit frosty, as usual. As I take my seat I think back to Heiner Müller answering a journalist who was worried that his plays wouldn't be understood by the audience: "That isn't my problem, that's the director's problem". And what about my director? What has he added? What story has he added to my story?

The next time I'll choose a Copeau-style director, if they still make them. The script, the actors, a bare stage. Then I'd be sure. Or I'll do what Valère Novarina does often, I'll do it myself, so I can be sure there is no director. I know I'll be asked, "Aren't you afraid you won't have the required distance?" The required distance. Distance isn't the only thing that matters. Not in the theatre, either, for that matter. Or I'll get a director like Langhoff, and he'll tear it to bits, rip it to pieces and like that it'll be settled once and for all. And we'll not talk about it any more.

They're dimming the lights. And everybody is silent now. I'm thinking, "The author isn't the last of the last after all". Who said that again? "The author isn't the last of the last". I should check it out but I do think it was Stanislavsky. What did he know anyway? What did he know?

David Lescot

The dramaturg

They call me the dramaturg, but I do not really know what I am, or if other dramaturgs do the same job as me. In France, we are a new category and each of us is unique.[1] From a theoretical perspective as well as from a historical and methodological one, "dramaturg" and "dramaturgy" have different meanings, all of which define me more or less. One can indeed observe that the term "drama" is used today in very different, even contradictory ways, depending on whether it appears in literary criticism or happens in theatrical practice. I am not, in any case, a "dramatic dramaturg-writer", nor a confirmed critic of dramaturgy. No, I intend to be fully on the side of art. But I'm finding it hard to move away from this academic function that I can't shake. I can't do anything about it, it's also part of my job.

I've read up on Eastern European practices. It was in Germany that the dramaturg (distinct in that respect from the *dramatiker*, the one who writes plays) emerged as one who sets in place a theoretical and practical activity capable of ensuring a link between the text and its staging, and who plays the role of practitioner-adviser in the interpretive reading of the theatrical text, the programming and choice of shows. The dramaturg also emerged as a historical and theoretical go-to person for those in charge of the staging. Now, in France, "dramaturgy",[2] my job, is now a theoretical and practical activity, a "reading" designed to determine how the text transitions to the stage: from the basic material, with its own economy, its semiotic and aesthetic system based on words, phrases and their sequence in a series of printed pages, to the production of a spectacle with a much larger organisational structure. This includes the performance space and stage (via the scenography), the bodies of the actors (and therefore their gestures, their voices, their acting, their characteristics and traditions), objects, lights, costumes, the moment of staging, the social and cultural nature of the audience, etc., all in the fleeting moment of the performance. As such, the work of dramaturgy, whether it's the act of a "dramaturg" (me), a director (my employer), or actors that are part of a decision-making group, and who, for the most part, wonder what I'm doing there,[3] consists of working out how the world of the text gets transformed into the world of the stage; how the semiological system founded on the ordering of words and sentences is transformed into the semiotic system of the theatrical event. And I try not to be too abstract, which sometimes costs me a little effort. In a nutshell, as a dramaturg, I read, I analyse and take structures apart. I try to understand all the meanings of what I read, and I tell the story or stories that the text brings to my mind, in more or less precise, more or less documented, ways. I am the storyteller who fills in the gaps of text and shines light on them for others, the person who uncovers problems and finds solutions. I inform, I motivate, I listen to what is beneath and beyond the text, I explore, I read and I make people read. I bring material not only to inform the director but also all members of the team. Besides this specific dramaturgical function, some of my "colleagues" (I envy them sometimes) are also co-responsible, with the theatre director,[4] for the cultural and aesthetic (even educational, when the space has a school[5]) policy of theatre itself. They look after this "theatre", which functions as a unique social institution (scheduling, outreach in the city, choosing public engagement activities; in short, participation in social life) in the city at large. All this is our lot, our margins and our centre. Being a dramaturg is making things relevant, engaging in every sense: I think of the past in the past and present; I speak in my name about the text; I provide the impulse needed to bring to life the story, the history, scenes, words and sentences of which the theatre is made. But I'm at a distance, behind, beside,[6] firmly confident in my knowledge and sensitive to emotions, wanting to get into the practice and perhaps, sometimes, whether consciously or not (because it's also frightening, and one exposes oneself to other vulnerabilities), I do fantasise about being the director,[7] but I know how to restrain myself. I'd also like it if many directors in France didn't do their own background work (the dramaturgy), but called on people like me. But I don't hold it against them – well, not really – and I do understand, when I see how some of them work, that they'd find it awkward to work with me. I understand that I'd just get in their way, since many of them do their own dramaturgy, in their *own* way. I understand that my role is justified only if it's part of an approach that embraces it, in whatever way that might be. Besides, I can be patient,[8] since, by all accounts, dramaturgy, as an approach to theatre, does seem to be here to stay.

I'm very eager to witness what will happen tonight. This project was conceived by the director and I; conceived in relation to this theatre, to its bill of specifications, to its own policies, to its "ideological line". And that's not to mention financial issues, which are ever so present. I can always claim that they don't fall under my responsibility, but everybody is affected by them ... But we've tried to convince ourselves that they must take second place, or that they must adapt to our desires, to our *need*. For there has to be a need in order for a play to exist. Otherwise, what's the purpose? And therein lies the real and constant object of my work: to help define that "need", and, indeed, to redefine it, when the conditions of the job seem to cause it to get sidelined or ignored. Issues or "stakes" that must carry or drive the project and the play, and that not only need to be explained but also need to be felt by all the other practitioners (it can sometimes be a steep climb, such as when an actor is struggling with his own doubts during the rehearsals and, while on our second post-rehearsal beer, he brings the conversation back to what he'd talked about with the director earlier, during the break, but he still isn't sure he agrees, etc.). Very soon after the director has crunched his figures (along with the theatre administration team and the stage manager), we had to think about conditions of production, whether or not this play can "tour", etc. From there, well before starting anything, we knew roughly the scale of what we would do. The only thing left for me to do was play my role as advisor on the interpretation of the text.

So, straightaway, I delved head on into the script and read, reread and read[9] again. I read a ton of things about the author, the play, its themes, just anything I came across. I then organised stuff, so as to be more structured, then gave the director things to read (and also distributed stuff to the actors, the lighting designer ... different things depending on their roles), but also images and even a recording, as and when I found things that seemed relevant to the project. Working closely with the director, I ended up deciding on a sort of stage-by-stage "assessment" of the interpretation of this play, offering a possible "reading", and with different choices. Not *a* story then, but rather stories, and finally a reading: what we could imagine at that point on a virtual stage, based on our research and a very specific, dramatic, reading of the play. The sequence of its spaces, temporalities, events, its composition, its structure, its unique movement. At this stage, what I'm doing amounts to a close assessment of separate scenes of the play, all linked to my analysis. An assessment of disjointed scenes this time, and all connected to my analysis. My work has not been, and must not be (though sometimes I get slightly carried away) to reconstitute the intention of the author: I've sought to put in place "an" author, a sort of imaginary author (or author-function), which has nothing to do with biographical, psychological or purely historical, expectations. And to bring to life the "world", the famous "relationship to reality" that seemed so obvious at the beginning and that was becoming so difficult to define, so unstable, at times. Finally, I've attempted ... After some lengthy formal and informal discussions, sometimes contradictory, often conflicting, we've agreed on some essential points concerning the dynamics of the show, how to use the stage, how to enlarge it or to reduce it, how to light it. In a way, we have worked out how to represent space and time, above all, from the indications provided by the script, as the director and I had read it. I know that some dramaturgs are far more punctilious than I am, so they write down their interpretation almost in the form of a novel; they even create, with their director, a book made up of drawings and text, a kind of prospective comic strip, a potential film of practical events. And they apply it. We don't do that. I prefer brief synopses or summaries rather than writing a *script*, I stick to the scenario of events, and that is probably even a big way of putting it. I do feel that the real *script* – the detailed, precise, yet evolving script – must, if it exists, be written during the stage rehearsals. (This is what they refer to as 'the Bible' at the Comédie-Française.) Or even during the performances, as was done by the prompters in the nineteenth century. But again, this idea of the Bible bothers me because the theatre should not be static or fixed, it must live, evolve with time, even a little, even in the margins. It is not a film; it is not the past. Obviously, like the director and the stage manager, I have my notebook, my leaflets and my sketches. And this use of multiple tools, this spreading out, keeps me on my toes, allows me the openness necessary for the development of this work that never ceases to be in progress, that is never finished, always ephemeral. Theatre is never printed once and for all; it is not a book. We've thought about the main things together, the distribution of roles, which is obviously the most important thing. Meetings, agreements, discussions. There again, my role was secondary, since in the end, it is the director who decides. Still, I had ideas that, despite all kinds of constraints and challenges, I was able to share with him.

Now we could move forward with the actors and the others involved, i.e. "rehearse" because in theatre, even in the midst of creation, one always rehearses. Obviously, I took part in roundtable discussions, in debates, and I "fed" the actors, taking into account their own food, what they also brought to the task, trying to maintain an overall dramatic mood. I love these moments of exchange; they are "my" moments. Between rehearsals, I reflect, I send notes and emails, I scribble, I pour my heart out and I absorb. Again, I organise, therefore I think. And I listen to others think – other people bring to mind questions, or ways of asking them, which I hadn't necessarily thought of, and that force me to reformulate, extend and re-focus. At times we've had guests, advisors more or less, whose observations, analyses and (sometimes very historiographical, abstract and short-sighted) proposals we've had to consider. Finally, since the room was free and the set was more or less ready, we acted everything out. We went from the table to the stage, and it was like going through the whole process again. In the end, we could have done without the discussion stage. Actually, some people have tried to do without it, have even made it their method to "bypass" this stage, as it were, "get straight into it". For me, it's just not possible, I feel like I lose out. In one go, I give over everything to my director, who then dismisses me, in a sense. And that is exactly the point where, little by little, I feel more or less erased. I contributed to the material production, giving my opinion, certainly, but my opinion only. I continued to note what was happening in my notebooks and made regular observations to my director, in the evenings after rehearsals.[10] I answered questions on the interpretation of specific points, and sometimes I got angry quite openly when I felt the show was spinning out of control. I acted as theoretical or ideological watchdog; indeed, that is one of my roles.[11] And then, my position in relation to the actors also changed, became more blurred, since I found myself in the very strange position of one who is both inside and outside of the creative work, which was now happening on the stage. A perspective somewhat offset from the various practical issues now being worked out on the rehearsal stage, one that focuses on the actors in a different way from the director, more like a kind, informed *spectator*, which will give the actors a sort of feedback on what they are currently developing. So, I provide a critical eye, an appraisal, but I am careful to do away with absolutes, to preserve *absolute* "faith" in the work being carried out, while paying attention to the coherence of what's being constructed and to what's no longer entirely how it was imagined. Even if at first I seemed a bit scary, and members of the team looked at me like a wild beast, a few beers have simplified relations – with some, anyway – to the point where, now, I'm regarded as a critical, but open, eye, who team members can ask, in a more informal way (than they would the director), "what their performance was like" this afternoon ... I'm also a mediator of sorts, someone who explains to them some point, which seems problematic to them, one who is always ready to explain and justify (again) the project that the director and I built. And I must also explain that if the director removes any aspect of the project, it entirely makes sense and I totally agree and that, after all, it's in line with the project as we conceived it ... Oh, the actors and I will talk about the director so often! I'll have to defend him, while at the same time telling them that they were right. In a nutshell, I'll be one more member of the team (gosh, sometimes I'll actually feel like – how I hate to say it – an *assistant*), but a bit on the sidelines, so that it's possible to discuss, exchange, debate with me about what is taking shape – and oh, how necessary such spaces are! I've thus seen it all, or nearly (I must keep the notion of distance, which is to set my perspective apart from those of the other practitioners), down to the last run-through, down to the costume designer yesterday.

Since then, I've been waiting, in full *effervescence*, like the rest of the team of the team, but not knowing exactly where my place is in all of it, from what angle to present myself. I too feel those terrible feelings tonight. I know that if I were a coward (but I'm not, I'm an absolute team player), I could use the notion of the text as absolute as a cover, in the theatre bar after the performance, to shirk responsibility for the things that went wrong but I know that what I can and must speak of (what it will be important to *justify*) now is the *show*. I was a facilitator, hopefully a discrete one, an active interface, a shooting star, gradually losing its light. So I took refuge in words and formulas, while watching the bodies, the objects, the space and the time that I helped create. I did go backstage just now with the intention of planting kisses and giving celebratory gifts, but they were now all in "their" rituals, it wasn't my world any more. All I am is a glance and a shadow, and it won't be until after the performance that the conversation will start again. That is why tonight I am literally offstage: I sit in the audience, at the back.[12]

With the kind (accompanying) notes of
Joseph Danan

The director

When he arrives at the theatre, on the day of the premiere, between 10 and 11 a.m. just like on previous days, a feeling of unease grips him. He says good morning to the technicians, the lighting man, the stage manager, who busy themselves with the finishing touches: adding a new coat of paint, hiding electrical wires, etc. The stagehands and engineers will then head backstage, from where they will no longer been seen. The audio and lighting technicians will go into the control booth, where each will run through his "routine" on his computer. Armed with pencil and crayon, each one will ensure that the details in his "stage management book", where positions at the start of scenes are noted, are clear and precise.

In the early afternoon, when he peeks through the door to the theatre, he immediately notices that his control station is not where it used to be. The cleaners are now in the auditorium with mops, brooms and hoovers. Only yesterday, he was giving directives from that control desk, showing his dissatisfaction, pouting openly. It was his own little theatre where he'd turn his little lamp on or off, write a few notes or have them written by an assistant, puff on a cigarette before putting it out right away, and express his discontent. The desk, placed at the "prince's eye" (as it's called in the Italian proscenium theatre, probably after the monarchy became a republic), was no longer there. It was evacuated, gone. Where it was before, a cleaning woman was now vacuuming. Yesterday, that desk was the centre of a military apparatus, a campaign headquarters from where the director, surrounded by a few assistants and technicians equipped with audio headsets, exerted an absolute power. The set designer, who is a painter in everyday life, would stand to one side and observe this pseudo-military activity with scepticism. Now without work, without a job and having no role to play, the director wonders who is now his enemy: the critics, the theatregoers, the actors, the theatre or himself? The notion of him being his own enemy is a consolation; it stimulates him. His mind darts quickly to a few of his colleagues. Patrice Chéreau was the equivalent, on a theatre stage, of Michel Platini on a football field: the actors, placed like French skirmishers (in the Great War), distanced from each other, so as to make possible a moment of "personal acting" when the time was right. As for Peter Stein, he has more in common with the German football strategist, Beckenbauer: he generally adopts a layout of attackers more closely positioned so as to reinforce confidence, discipline and coherence. Giorgio Strehler, after miming onstage the acting style of each of the characters, under the stupefied gaze of the actors, would wave from centre stage to the people attending the rehearsal, before going back to his director's chair; and the audience applauded. What's left to invent in the art of directing? Perhaps a paradox of strategy, a sort of football game where one would need to score goals against one's own team.

As the hours pass, the dark thoughts accumulate. He needs to slowly numb himself, prepare for the reaction of the audience and of the critics: indifference and insensitivity. He must have the same attitude towards success as the last hippopotamus at the Amsterdam zoo. The spectators are now in the room. Just now in the hall, they wouldn't stop kissing each other and licking each other's lips like those African wild dogs that bear the mythological name of "lycaons", who kiss and rub each other's mouths, though they do it while running in a pack as they go hunting. *Homo sapiens* is an unfinished creature. Now the director watches from the control booth. A sea of largely inexpressive backs, a static phenomenon. The play comes off fairly well. Moments from now, there will be applause, voting by acclamation, the honour of stars and dictators. The director is dreaming of the more than half an hour of applause with which mourners in the hall at the University of Venice greeted the body of Professor Mario Baratto, that great specialist of Goldoni's theatre and of Renaissance Italian drama. It didn't carry the same meaning as the applause in the theatre, not entirely, but a bit nonetheless, when theatre exceeds the boundaries of entertainment and concerns itself with the dead.

The director, behind the window, watches the drama, which has become foreign to him. He now thinks gloomy thoughts. The world is changing. He'll have to change careers, to do art performance, installations, adopt the Eurotrash aesthetic, become an interior designer, urban planner of intimate spaces, window designer, buy a PlayStation. What a life!

Jean Jourdheuil

The set designer

Tonight is the "opening night". But for me, is it really a "premiere"? That's just a matter of perspective. My time is always out of joint with that of the actors and the audience.

Wasn't my "premiere" the day when the mock-up was presented to the theatre director and when the designs were given to the technical director and the production designer? Indeed, that day, what had gestated over two years, during long planning meetings with the director, began to take shape and have a life of its own, to exist for the first time. That day, I presented what I had invented in the lonely silence of my workshop, while cobbling together pieces of carton and wood. That first work, teasing out the links between a text and a potential space, is a sort of translation. A translation of words into silences, into volumes, into substance, into (empty) spaces, into shadows. A translation awaiting the interpretation of the stage director and the actors. That day was really a "premiere" or "opening day" for me. Besides, the words suggest it: one "presents" his model, makes a present of it, offers it and, therefore, accepts, from that moment, that it now belongs to others.

And wasn't the night the set was put up onstage another "opening night"? Thanks to the carpenters' diligence and care, after a long period of labour in their workshops, the space imagined, invented, drawn, measured, built-in miniature model, finally took on life. Such a huge part of the success of my job as set designer, or "scenographer", is judged on whether the model lives up to expectations – whether it's free of distortions, so that the constructed space can resemble what was conceived in the imagination and that this space can be "inhabited". And based on that, the temporal frame I operate in is at odds with the director's and the actors' time, since, from that day onwards, nothing can be modified – or very little – if the scenographer has not had a clear vision of what his virtual image will look like in reality, if he has not foreseen the thing, then the faults and errors are there on a full scale, and he and everybody else will have to live with it. Despite that fact, the set, as much as it has a life of its own, remains a dormant space when it is installed – it is empty, hollow. To take on life, it must wait to be inhabited by the bodies of the actors, by their movements, the density and colours of their costumes, the resonance of their voices, the lights and the presence of the spectators. In the first half of the seventeenth century, an anonymous author and ardent defender of the theatre today known as baroque, used a very beautiful phrase to describe this, which he wrote in his *Discours à Cliton*: "The stage is in no way different from a tabula rasa".[13]

My "opening" is also the day when the actors see the set for first time and rehearse in that space what has been invented for the text and for them. That day is not always easy. The "opening night" is drawing closer, and the actors' nervousness is becoming palpable: they feel a bit clumsy in the costumes and with the set ... the set is still an empty, inexpressive, lifeless carcass, a body without soul or breath. Apart from the set designer, the costume designer and the lighting designer, nobody actually imagines what this vacant space can become. And yet, I have shown the model to the actors. They have rehearsed in the room where the layout of the set was drawn on the ground. They have gone around strips of adhesive paper indicating walls. They have crossed thresholds, indicated by a gap in the adhesive tape. But for most of them, all of that remains abstract. And one day, all of a sudden, the set is there, onstage. The strip of adhesive tape has become a wall, an obstacle. The actors walk about in an unknown place. Sometimes, they exclaim: "I hadn't thought of it like that!" Then one wonders how they had "thought of it" and, especially, what they had thought of, since the model is a faithful image of the set that is to come. But "not thinking of it like that" means, for me, "not seeing oneself in it". But just give it time ... Part of the job of a set designer and of a costume designer is to be a sort of collection point for fears and frustrations. In a sense, we must be an outlet for the natural apprehensions of the actors, linked to the rehearsals and all that goes into them and to the impending "opening night". Otherwise, the pressure from anxieties gets too high, and ends up causing an explosion (of fits, tempers, etc.), that brings everything to a standstill. So, even if the actors don't realise it most times, I become a kind of relief valve, a kind of outflow channel, for them. I can take on this role since my work is largely finished.

Sometimes the actors display their fears: "It won't be easy", said the lead actress upon seeing the set. And you feel a thinly veiled hostility, but that is her way of expressing her fear. The actors just need time to appropriate the space. I work along with the director in helping them do this. I watch the rehearsal from a seat in the auditorium. I move. I go up to first balcony, to the gods; I sit in the stalls (right or left), in the orchestra. I watch, I listen, in silence. I watch them slowly own this space that will eventually become a place. With the rehearsal finished, the actors quickly rush off the stage, which is still foreign to them on the first day. I get to confer with the stage manager and the stagehands: there's lots of work to do, in the shadows, to resolve problems with things exposed, raise a backdrop, adjust a canvas, fix paint jobs ... the stage design must be adopted, and adapted, for this stage.

Perhaps, there is yet one other "opening night" for me: it's not one specific evening, but a period of time, that begins the last night when what you might call "the technical team" takes over the stage for the last lighting adjustments, and ends after the costume session or the "dress rehearsal", the following evening. During that time, everything is set in place. Only details can be modified. If the communication with the lighting designer is good, the last night of lighting calibration is a pleasure: little nuances appear, aspects of the set gain density in imperceptible, but pleasing, ways, thanks to the light. The space is ready to welcome the actors, who have now become characters. Rays of light will be complemented and refashioned by bodies and their movements. Slightly brighter areas, hitherto unaltered by the shadow of any human presence, will become the bright ghosts of the future characters: for us, that night, the space receives its absent inhabitants.

The lighting designer works like a sculptor, except that he doesn't touch the sculpture. I watch him work. For me as a set designer, his art is the stuff of magic. I need to fashion, shave and work material so that what I imagine can take shape. The lightening designer, on the other hand, watches and acts from a distance.

So, this evening is the play's "opening night". I'm a spectator almost like any other. Besides, for some opening nights, I go and sit in the audience when relations with the director are not at their best. We just won't work together in the future, that's all. Mutual decision. But tonight, I'm in a calm mood (I'm probably the only one). The collaboration has been fruitful and my scenography has taken on a life of its own, independent of me. This afternoon, I'm probably the only one who has nothing special to do. I walk on to the empty stage, lit by the stagehand. The iron curtain has been lowered. Very dim light, long shadows. A stagehand is carefully cleaning the stage. We chat for a while. Then I go to meet with the dresser. Her den is a veritable treasure trove of fabrics, buttons, accessories and ribbons. A haven that is always calm and smells of freshly ironed linen, starch and lavender. I go with the dresser into the dressing rooms that are still empty, where she checks each costume, each detail. Then I stop in at the make-up artist's room. The stage and costume designer needs to have a good relationship with the make-up artist: we both sculpt, comb and paint, to help give birth to the right character. The brushes are carefully packed away, beside the powders and make-up. The little boxes of colour shine under the dazzling lamps above the mirror. The make-up artist, as well as the dresser, has a huge responsibility tonight, their tact, care and patience will help the actors face their enemy – stage fright. "I'm scared", a famous actress once said to me, in a slightly "altered" voice, absent-mindedly gripping my hands, just at the end of the corridor that leads on to the stage. She is great lady of the stage but, at that moment, she was a frail little girl.

The first actors arrive. Each expresses his or her nervousness in a unique way: some choose to be alone, others laugh with excess exuberance, some walk through the crossover without seeing or looking at anyone. Everyone is preparing. Everyone is elsewhere.

I say a few reassuring words, offer a few signs of encouragement, and I leave. I no longer belong here. I'm off to watch the premiere from the control box, at a distance, but for these people too it's the opening night. The curtains rise. The performance begins. For me, the adventure is over.

Anne Surgers

The stage manager

My job is to be the stage manager, and more specifically, the stage manager of this production, the conductor of the orchestra, so to speak. I am an actor who is invisible to the public. I conduct the performance and my job is to make sure that no one notices this. And to do that, to hide my presence, nothing works better than always being there. As such, from day one, I attend all rehearsals, I even participate in all the production meetings that take place before the first rehearsals, in order to formulate a clear idea of the vision that the director has for the work. There is no room for error. As a rule, I arrive two hours before each performance. It's a duty and a ritual. I visit all the changing rooms, check that each actor, and, as the case might be, each vocalist listed, is already there, that their hair, make-up and costumes are done, and I quickly check that there are no latecomers or whether anybody is sick. One always has to make sure. Besides that, I also try to foster a calm environment so that the apprehensions inherent in each performance may be forgotten for a moment. Therefore, I make time to say something kind to everyone, as a rule. And then, there are always last minute issues to solve. I reassure people. I smile. Actors, singers, orchestra conductors, the director, the technicians, I reassure them all – to reassure is one of my functions.

One hour before the start of the stage performance, I go on to the stage and speak into the microphone, notifying everyone that it is time to return to the dressing room. The "moment of truth" is here: "the performance will start in an hour". So the countdown begins, allowing actors and singers to go on to the stage, themselves, to check that their accessories are properly placed or hidden among the stage props. These simple checks help to calm them down: they get into position, get ready mentally, which, for them, means that they can concentrate a bit better and become their character. Meanwhile, I check on the stagehands and the fly crew,[14] on the stage, as they do a last inspection of the equipment and of the set. Finally, for security reasons, I roll the iron curtain,[15] to make sure that it works. We are now half an hour away from the start of the performance. The audience can now enter.

Tonight, the show is an opera, so I'll have more work than usual, with more workers, more lights, more technical controls, more difficulties also than for a play. Have I thought of everything over the last two months so that everything works properly and smoothly in half an hour? First, I organised the schedules for each day, devoted the utmost attention to fitting the costumes from the outset so that the costume workshops could finish them in time for the piano dress, then I ensured that the stage design would be set in place and synchronise with the act that we would be working on. I called on singers, choir directors, choristers, extras, rehearsal pianist, language coach, designers of accessories, stage hands and electricians as needed, and even checked that the piano had been tuned. And, while being constantly attentive and reactive to ensure the technical resolution of all artistic issues, whether they came from the director or the orchestra conductor, I always tried to foster a pleasant work environment, as much as possible. Somewhere between my authority (I need to command the respect of the entire technical team) and my patience, there lies what one may call my calm generosity, which is always very active.

The rehearsals for this opera took six weeks, as is often the case. And they were divided into several phases, as is also often the case: the first two days were devoted to musical rehearsals at the piano with the singers, the conductor, his assistant and a rehearsal pianist. These rehearsals enabled the conductor to set the different tempos[16] with the singers, which gave me an idea of the rhythm and the interpretation he wished to give to the work. I made note of everything. The four weeks that followed were devoted entirely to the staging. A pianist would play the work with a piano score extracted from the entire orchestral movement, and the rehearsals took place in a studio for two to three weeks (sometimes, if there is enough space, parts of the set are installed) with marks on the ground to indicate aspects of the set or represent the spaces. This was still a kingdom ruled by the director and it was at that time that I transformed his directions into precise, technical notes, based closely on the temporal progression of the performance. The fourth week was taken up with stage design, which took place onstage, up until the dress rehearsal of the work, with piano, and with make-up and costumes, as if it was the real performance. The singers also took their real positions, occupying a new space, and, looking at them, I noticed that a step or staircase portrayed in a studio does not entirely match the reality as it is on the real stage. We didn't have it all together but we made a lot of progress, to the point where I could see exactly what was left to be done. Once the lighting technician had sorted out the lighting with the director, we had numerous practical meetings to establish the timing of the lighting effects, some of which have only just been decided. The reason for this is that even though most of the lighting "cues" had long been written into our score, denoting changes in atmosphere at specific moments in the staging, we still needed to agree on a final session for doing last-minute modifications of a few effects at the end of the morning, right before this dreaded yet eagerly anticipated first performance. We also devoted a few rehearsals to the technique alone in order to find the right solutions for making the scene changes on time. This also gave the director more time with the singer, since our time is limited. I had to accept that things take time, but in a different way to usual: every rehearsal has a cost and opera budgets, whatever people say, are not unlimited. I was therefore keen on not exceeding the production budget, on perfectly mastering collective bargaining agreements governing the choristers, musicians and technicians, despite the unpredictable nature of rehearsals, which often requires adjusting schedules.

Obviously, I also read music and I also try to familiarise myself, as much as possible, with the language of the libretto, which allows me to note, on my score, the different staging indications, particularly the entrance and exit of singers, choristers or extras. But not just that, I've also made note of each movement in the scene changes, each new accessory that a singer brings, each new lighting effect, each audio or video effect. I also had to note changes of costume, hairstyle and make-up in order to establish transitions that allow the dressers and hairstylists to take their cues (some of these changes have to be done very quickly), since these teams arrive only on the day of the final rehearsal.[17] I've established very precise "cue sheets" of the performance for everyone: stagehands, accessory people, electricians, hairstylists, make-up artists and dressers.

Finally, the orchestra arrived for two "Italian" rehearsals (rehearsals without staging with just the orchestra, the singers and the choir), then four rehearsals onstage and with the orchestra. This was where the conductor took over as ruler of the kingdom since, whereas the rehearsals belong to the director up to the final rehearsal with piano, when the orchestra arrives, they become the inalienable domain of the conductor to the point where the director can no longer intervene, or even stop those rehearsals. He can only take notes, and give them to the singers at the end of rehearsals, and if they are agreed to, I take them into account in my "cue sheets". The arrival of the orchestra has made the atmosphere of the rehearsals tense in that way. Everyone needed to be present and on time. I was keen on ensuring that. The scene changes needed to come off problem-free so as not to slow the rehearsals down, and I made it a point of duty to prevent the conductor and the musicians (around a hundred) in the pit from having to wait at all; of if there was ever any waiting, it was minimal, indeed.

All of that in six weeks.

We're almost there. In a few minutes, as with all performances, I'll be giving "cues" to all relevant stagehands, very precise "cues" that correspond to all of the changes I've just described. It is then essential for me to keep the possible overall view of the staging and not forget anything from all those rehearsals. I now record each cue on my own score, giving a number to each effect. The show functions thanks to all these very precise rules. The rules also give me leeway to deal with unforeseen issues that might crop up: I not only follow my score to give "cues", I must take my eye off it sometimes to pay attention to what is happening on the stage. Therefore, I must simultaneously listen to the music, listen to what a technician is asking me through my headset, and keep an eye on the stage: check that a singer is entering with the correct accessory, that a stagehand is in place in front of a door in order to open it, that a dresser takes just the time necessary to change a singer's costume so the singer can make his entrance at the right moment. It's become second nature to me now to keep all parameters in mind.

The deputy stage manager who assists me and helps me control the entrance of the singers, choristers and extras on to the stage, is standing, like me, and is next to me. On the stage, the atmosphere is rather tense, as is always the case with opening nights. And like every time a performance is about to start, I get a little rush of adrenaline. It's inevitable but it's not unpleasant. In fact, it's what gives me that heightened level of concentration that I'll need over the next four hours. Just five more minutes. I'm now putting on my headset equipped with a microphone that will keep me in constant communication with all the technicians during the entire performance, and I call the singers with my microphone. They'll be the first to go onstage. I tell each of them something encouraging to help relax them.

So, here we go. The six weeks have come down to this one moment. I signal the cue for "half of the house in darkness",[18] then for "complete darkness".[19] The conductor heads to the pit, I put the light on him, wait for the audience to applaud him and then let the darkness come down over the auditorium. I give instructions for the curtain to be raised. The conductor raises his baton, and we hear the first note of the overture. I'm now the hidden person upon whom everything rests: a calm actor, that stays calm in every situation, an artist who must give himself the immense satisfaction of controlling time, space, all possible incidents; the director of a work never visible to the public. I'm not scared at all anymore, I'm just focused on this spectacle that I am now overseeing.

Jeanne Piot

The actor

I'm an actor in his dressing room. Someone's knocking. It's the stage manager. Without entering, he announces "*ten minutes*". "Ten minutes. Ten minutes". I know the danger lurking behind those harmless words. Six weeks have gone by since the first day of the rehearsals, 1,080 hours, and I always knew that this moment would arrive: the ten minutes before the opening performance. It's the first time that I'll be playing this role in public. In ten minutes. It was bound to become reality at some point. I'm going to have to leave my dressing room.

My dressing room is like a hotel room: I feel comfortable in it, but comfortable in the sense of "tolerated". All the dressing rooms of the world tell me the same thing:

> You can sing within my walls, warm up your voice, if you want to, rest on my little sofa, decorate me the way you like; but you know, you're not from here, you're made for out there, for the stage, and you must get ready to go. During your absence, I'm responsible for keeping your clothes, your watch, your bag and your lucky charms.

And, this evening, my dressing room adds: "I'm kind, but indifferent; I won't wish you good luck. Nine minutes". It's right, I need to go. In my mind is imprinted an image of the place I'm to go to, this lair where everything will take place, the scene of the crime – the stage. I get up. I'll have to cross thresholds.

First threshold: from the dressing room to the corridor, a long white corridor whose walls are decorated with posters. I become aware of my toes, of the arch of my feet, and of the word "*conspirators*" written on one of the posters. Second threshold: from the corridor to the staircase, a grey spiral staircase that smells of cold tobacco. I become aware of the muscles in my neck, in my legs and the weight they bare step after step. Third threshold: from the last step to the other corridor, a smaller one, equipped with a huge, bright red fire ramp. I become aware of my nostrils, my eyes, my jaw, my hands and the figure 9637 written on the pipe. Fourth threshold: from this little corridor to the big white door. I become aware of the opening of the door and the noise it makes when opening. There, a dimly lit double-door entrance. I forget my consciousness. A moment of *de-concentration*. Then the big black door. I gather myself at the fifth threshold: from the big black door to the stage of the theatre. I put my consciousness into my stomach, and my breathing, because I am afraid. The sixth threshold will be, in a moment, the one from the wings on to the stage. But for now, I'm still here, in the world of the living, the world of ordinary men. I'm in the wings.

I'm an actor in the wings on opening night, i.e. someone who doesn't know if he's ready. "Five minutes. Five minutes". The place is packed. Apparently, there are even people on the steps. The noise is growing. My fear gets me farther away from myself, makes me feel like sleeping. I must try to calm things down, come back to my centre, and concentrate on the last preparations: What time did I eat my complex carbs? Three hours ago, so that's good. Do you remember the objectives for the very first part of the performance? Yes: be very present, very passionate, totally absorbed in getting into the space. Perfect. And the character, has the character awoken, is he here? I think so, I hope so. Have you checked that the lighter is on the table to the left of the stage? Yes. Philippe A. is in the audience tonight!? Calm down. Hearing an announcement about cell phones, I realise we're starting in two minutes. I stare at the last threshold. This all feels very existential in my head: What do all these people in the room expect from a theatre experience? What do they expect from an actor? What does it mean to be an actor? Why are there people parts of every generation who dedicate their entire lives to this? Is it linked to the unconscious, to the human condition, to speech, to the body, to God, to singing? What's behind it, childhood, presence, violence, poetry, everything? Enough, calm down. The lights are going down. The performance is about to start.

And we start again. Since, once again, I'm going to face the mystic atmosphere of the theatre stage, this atmosphere so pregnant with listening and looking that it's hard to feel balanced in it. Once again, I will dig deep within myself to create the illusion that it is really I who speak the words that I speak. Once again, I shall enter into the fictional time of this performance, which does not flow the way time passes in my dressing room – I'll notice this later on when I go back there to get my things and put my dress back on, my dress that will have been sitting there for centuries. Once again, I will feel new things; tonight is the first monologue of my life. Once again, I will see that I am not a shrinking violet as I thought I was when I was small, since I will be speaking in front of people and they will be hearing me. Once again, I will feel overwhelmed when I think how much responsibility I have for transmitting the words of an author. Once again, I shall answer the irresistible call that a French teacher, twenty years ago, identified as my vocation. Once again, I'll be showing off. Once again, after doubting and after fearing, after working, I'll feel like that character from *Les Vainqueurs*,[20] who is *all right with just living* – I'll feel that I'm all right with just acting. Yes, acting is enough for me. I am an actor. It's time. The lights are on. I cross the threshold.

Scali Delpeyrat

The readers

FIRST READER: I like to read theatrical works, without necessarily wanting to act out or stage them, for pure pleasure. I know that this is a rare preference, and publishers, who, with the exception of a few specialist ones and others passionate about frequently sold classics, are aware of this too. I like to imagine my theatre, an ideal, potential one, which I sometimes visualise on my fictional stage and on which I ruminate in silence. In that sense, I follow in the line of illustrious figures: didn't the great theatre theorist, D'Aubignac, the author of *La Pratique du théâtre* (1657), finish his treatise by saying that the best place in which to appreciate tragedy was in one's study, alone with the text? I know that he was a theorist and a second-rate dramatist who complained about the practitioners and audiences of his time. But the reality is that I like the dramatic text. To put it another way, I love its literary, scriptural nature. But above all, I also like my own imagination. Therefore, I put my trust in the authors and in their power perhaps more than in the power of the actors, practitioners and those whose mission it is to translate on to the stage the text's poetry, elegy, thought and theatrical adventure. As a matter of fact, I naturally read plays as novels without a narrator. I read them as if they were a dialogue, complemented by a few indications to guide my imagination – as the unfolding of the story. My mind understands their function, their layout, the network of intertextualities; I can check the meaning of words and read notes. I imagine the world of the drama from my armchair, and I appreciate it better like that, since I appropriate it on my own terms. I have time, I can stop at any point during my reading, and so interrupt the spectacle. I am not bothered by physical bodies, the set, the staging, the lighting or by the noises, sighs and coughs of people in the audience and the various accidents that can happen to affect the moment. And then there's the fact that I don't need to go anywhere, literally speaking; I just need to travel with my imagination. I choose my seat, which is, ideally, at home. Many will say that reading theatre, in the way I describe it, limits or even nullifies the specificity of the theatre and automatically puts me in the frame of mind of certain literature professors. Perhaps, and so what? It is not that I hate actors, or that I hate directors, but that I find that their practice is by nature limited by time, space and the choices they are forced to make. As for me, alone in my comfy chair, I have no priorities or difficult choices to make. I am free to embrace all meanings, all contradictions; moreover, I am free to make all the dramatic, poetic, stylistic, historical and ideological observations I want, and to interpret everything my way. And when I do go to the theatre, I come away unsatisfied, as I find that the text is never "served" entirely, that the director and staging team are never entirely at its service, do not become invisible and erase their own selves from it. As Brasillach observed, theatre, if it wants to be legitimate, must be literary, must be an integral part of literature in the most noble sense of the word. Moreover, in the very act of publication, the text becomes lasting, eternal even, and in that respect, escapes the imperfect and ephemeral nature of the theatrical moment: it becomes a monument that I contemplate, that I explore, individually, when the opportunity presents itself.

SECOND READER: I also like to read theatre, but for reasons that are diametrically opposed to yours. I read it not from the perspective of an awed admiration, but for the paradoxical nature of the printed object. I do not think that a theatrical text can exist in isolation from its primary objective, which is to be staged. And the imagination you speak of, the study that you advocate, is merely an introduction, a preamble to the staging, to its being acted out, to the gathering of spectators, even if such spectators are virtual. It's a matter of principle, of design. Only a vain author would think otherwise, one who has not understood that drama consists in completing the unfinished nature of the text with the communal moment of a performance. Because theatre is not an individual sport, a meditation for the highly erudite, an academic's adventure, or an archival document; it is, rather, a place, a time, an audience, bodies, objects, lights, a set design – in a word, concrete objects on a stage, often with a text as starting, or reference, point. I understand that you respect authors and I understand that the authors themselves are still fighting to not lose control over their intellectual property, the text they have created: that is their prerogative and their fantasy. But if they print their work, is it not so it can be read and interpreted and so that they lose control of it? The more so since they write words that other bodies must speak and other ears hear, and since, by their imagination, they inscribe their text within a place and time and within gestures that they know do not belong to them. Mustn't they then know that their practice is only intermediary, taking place between the imaginary and concrete stage on which their text is set and the real stage, which will, perhaps, one day, receive it? That's why the imagination must, systematically, be transmuted into action, concretely and collectively. Hence what I notice first in a dramatic text: its incompletion, its empty space, its call for interpretation, its openness and readiness to be borne by a voice and a body, in the peculiar setting of a theatrical gathering.

FIRST READER: So you're no longer in the comfort of your armchair then?

SECOND READER: Yes, I am, of course, but my imagination allows me to be elsewhere too: in every place that the text I am reading resonates, which, you see, does not in any way impede the textual polysemy of which you boast. On the contrary, it enriches it. That is what is most interesting about reading theatre: looking at it, freely, from every perspective of creation and production, being able to ask all the questions. I also like to be the author and spectator of my own creation, journalist and critic, scholar, dramaturg, stage director and all that at the same time, if I happen to want to.

FIRST READER: You seem to be almost bulimic! Pardon the metaphor, my dear sceno-centrist. But in this confusion and despite the arrogance that characterises you, do you not need some method?

SECOND READER: Of course, I have *methods*, which become *my* methods, ones I adapt based on each text I read. I would say I have angles of vision. And I am always keen on preserving the coherence of each of my interpretations and on observing some elements in the texts, in order to think about the manner in which they are treated and the way in which they can be translated on to the stage, a space that I constantly need to define. One of my guiding principles is that the text must always find its time and place, that it implies characters (or the lack thereof), a story (or lack thereof) and a plot. In sum, a sort of thread that I need to describe. From that moment, after isolating, through my reading, a set of spatial, temporal and discursive signs, and after considering them in relation to the narrative and dramaturgical thread or observing, as the case might be, that there is no "narration" to be expected, I gather all of that into my mind to create my theatre, my representation, while being keen on making it coherent.

FIRST READER: That sounds highly post-structuralist and seems pretty abstract to me, coming from someone who preaches about live, speaking bodies!

SECOND READER: Well, I beg to differ. It is precisely because of the notation of these signs, of the way in which I elaborate these angles of vision, and follow the path of places, times and characters, held discourses, that I can "see" the play, that I can describe its essential movements, then consider each scene as a function of its own movement. From my sedentary, isolated position, I do the work of imagination, which consists in going virtually on to the stage, with all the comfort that that involves, since I am doing it just for me. However, while I am "constructing" *my* spectacle as the spectator of my own masterpiece, while I am being actor, director, lighting manager, scenographer, *if I want*, I also know how to take a step back and conduct a dramaturgical analysis (how to stage the text, even virtually, while creating for myself a narrative of the staging of the text). You see, in a way, it is as if I was taking over all the roles, including yours (which I enlarge considerably). As such, when I need to, or when I impose it on myself, I carry out "complementary readings": I try to understand the context and the meanings of the work; I read biographies and histories of the theatre; I investigate the meanings of words, the rhythm and prosody of the text, the structure of scenes. But I never lose sight of the stage. That is my rule, even if, in doing so, I have to deal with contradictions. To put it another way, I never lose sight of the fact that this text was made to be produced, embodied, spoken, vocalised, in a given space and time (which *I* create for myself based on what I read). And while this attitude leads me to find different or opposing solutions, I have the luxury, unlike the stage director and the other practitioners, of not necessarily choosing a lesson, or an acting style, but rather putting the whole thing into action, then seeking, at the very end, to find coherence. That is why, rather than going too quickly from text to interpretation, without going through one or several staging realities, I try as hard as I can not to skip stages. In so doing, I actually *avoid* being abstract. And I should also add that sometimes I momentarily lose sight of the stage and delve into the words and sentences of the text, carried along by the orality of the written work: it is my literary side, as you say, my happiness as a reader. Like you, you see, I can also be what you are.

FIRST READER: But isn't that work infinite? Doesn't it consist of endless mechanics and prevent you in the end from enjoying your reading and cancel the immediateness of the reading experience?

SECOND READER: Since when should one only be instinctive, since when does pleasure have to be immediate and since when is the marvellous pleasure of following a story, of being transported by it, not compatible with the joy of imagining one's own dramatisation of it? Moreover, I give you the absolute right to chronologically distinguish the different stages, if you find that too many things must be grasped during your reading. You have the time. You can come back to it in sum. As such, whether consecutively or spontaneously, you can add to your own sheer pleasure, concentrated as it is on the apparent deployment of the narrative, the thrill of imagining the story on whatever stage you choose, based on your observations and your perspective. You have to understand something: theatre is not an individual act as far as its reception is concerned. The reading of theatre, which is individual at first, escapes individualisation since its production implies a collective experience, one of infinite possibilities. When I read a play, I cannot help but locate myself within a collective field, and this is where I get the real pleasure of theatre. I set my pleasure in motion, so to speak.

FIRST READER: And my armchair? And my chair? *And my office?*

SECOND READER: I'll leave those all to you, because, you see, after all of this reading, I thoroughly enjoy actually going to the theatre.

Notes

1 Allow me to speak up in the name of this uniqueness. And, given that the dramaturg is, after a fashion, a man of endnotes – one that adds a second text to the first text of the *dramatist*, his namesake – that is indeed the mode of intervention I've chosen here. Nothing to say for now: I'm just marking my territory. Actually, yes (after all, we never change): the "novelty" of the "dramaturg" is relative (but I think that he, up there, the dramaturg-in-chief, talks about this a bit later on), so much so that one seriously wonders whether it is not on the decline, both the "dramaturg" and "dramaturgy" along with him. Let's just say that dramaturgy is no longer on the up.

2 In reality, it's *one* of my jobs. It's very rare for those who do this job to do *only* that. In cases where it's *the* job, it often gets camouflaged behind other functions: literary advisor, artistic advisor, even personal assistant.

3 Come on, don't be so defeatist!

4 Not me – it's not my job. I do intervene, however, when the aforementioned director asks me to, but in a private, unofficial way. In the shadows – I'm the brains behind it all. I do belong to a review panel, but my role as an advisor is often conducted one-on-one, tied in with my long-standing relationship with the director. The dramaturg is always a more or less covert figure.

5 Or even when it hasn't. There is also an educational role for the audience, not to mention for the pupils and students who constitute a significant quotient of that theatrical audience.

6 Underneath . . .

7 Or the author, for that matter. There are many illustrious examples, notably in Germany (Botho Strauss and, more recently, Marius von Mayenburg).

Sometimes, the director calls on a theatrical author to be a "dramaturg" (I don't think, however, that a director has ever asked another director to fulfil this role).

8 Doubtful, my friend (excuse me, I am getting a little forward): see note 1.
9 Yes: read, read and read again: it's all in the reading. Dramatic "reading" is like a limitless palimpsest, with no ultimate "truth". Always multi-voiced. It reflects the very nature of theatre, as you do observe a bit further, Sir.
10 I actually leave the scene, as it were, more radically, as most times I disappear after the discussion and planning stage and come back only for the first run-throughs with fresh eyes – the "eye of the outsider", who has the luxury of not having gone through the chaos, the trial and error and the remorse of the rehearsals.
11 The same role that Vitez referred to as "the policer of meaning". Thanks, but no thanks! But how to avoid it? Let's come back to the first run-throughs: it's always a case, more or less, of measuring the gaps within a project. I have to be open to these gaps, which sometimes throw me off-kilter, but that are the exact barometer of the theatrical work that has been accomplished, of the invention of the stage, the product of secondary annotations (or sometimes even tertiary annotations: but if they were my notes, then they were always secondary), so I've had to pick up the habit of being happily surprised by them. I no longer confront those gaps I notice from the initial project or, a little more abstractly, from what I guess might be the coherent reading of this new writing I've discovered – or that I recognise, that's the paradox: the previous work that we've done together, both me on my own, although mainly in conversation with others, those long conversations with a text in hand or from memory, then everyone round the table together. I recognise how the play has being transmuted, made tangible by the alchemy of the stage, passing through the body and the blood of the actors, in the materiality of the set design and the lights. I have also had to learn that if I recognise too much, that's not necessarily a good sign. (In a word, I no longer *check* that something has changed, but rather I simply notice it.)
12 That's what I really appreciated in *L'Illusion comique* [*The Comic Illusion*] staged by Brigitte Jaques, when Alcandre, the master of the theatrical ceremony, wasn't fulfilled either by her as the director or by Pierre Corneille, the author and main dramaturg, but by Francois Regnault, the dramaturg who wasn't credited in this role in the technical specifications of the show, an official covert dramaturg then (which further intensifies and endorses the hidden nature of this job). Francois Regnault fulfilled his role as conduit from text to performance, from scene to audience, and then disappeared into the pit. Where exactly was he? Everywhere and nowhere, pulling the strings but without anyone seeing. Coming to the surface and then disappearing again. Perhaps even writing more footnotes.
13 Anonymous [Jean Maiet], *Discours à Cliton sur les Observations du Cid, avec un traicte de la disposition du Poëme Dramatique, et de la Regle des vingt-quatre Heures* [*Speech to Cliton on the Layout of the Dramatic Poem, and the Rule of the So-Called Twenty-Four Hour Rule*] (Paris: Imprimé aux despense d'autheur, 1637), p. 72. See recent republication in N. Gougenot, *La Comédie des comédiens et le Discours à Cliton* [*The Playacting of Actors and the Speech to Cliton*], ed. François Lasserre (Tübingen: Gunter Narr Verlag, 2000), pp. 231–251. In the original quotation ("Le théâtre ne diffère en

rien d'une table d'attente"), theatre is to be understood in its seventeenth-century sense. The term stage would be used today. Translator's note: "table d'attente" is taken in the seventeenth-century sense as defined by Furetière: "Table d'attente: toile imprimée (c'est à dire préparée, n.d.a.) pour y faire un portrait" ["A canvas that has been imprinted (that is to say treated, or prepared), on which to paint a portrait"]. A. Furetière, *Dictionnaire universel* [*Universal Dictionary*] (Rotterdam: Leers, 1690), n.p.

14 The fly crew are stagehands with special responsibility for operating the fly system from its locking rail during the theatrical production. The fly system line sets bring the batten (a long pipe suspended above the stage from which lighting truss, scenery and drapes are hung) in and out, and the fly tower is generally raised to the same height as the stage proscenium, so as to "hide" the fixtures.

15 The "iron curtain" is a metallic screen placed before the stage curtain, to be used to block off the house from the stage in the event of a fire. Rolling it simply means to lower it.

16 Tempos or *tempi*, to use the original Latin, indicates the rate or speed at which a passage of music should be played, observing, in some instances, the author's explanations, indicated at the beginning of the piece (allegro, adagio, presto, etc.) or during the execution (slow down, accelerate, hurry, etc.)

17 Also known as the "piano dress": the final rehearsal with just the piano.

18 "Half of the house in darkness": the light is slowly dimmed and the house is in semi-darkness for a few seconds.

19 The light is slowly dimmed to create complete darkness for the duration of the performance.

20 A film by Olivier Py, produced by Carl Foreman and Harold Buck for Columbia Pictures and Open Road.

Part I

WHAT DOES IT MEAN TO GO TO THE THEATRE?

> *Theatrica* refers to the science of games, of theatre, where it was the custom of the people to gather to play; not that the theatre was the only place where one played, but it was more renowned than others. In fact, games took place in the theatre, or underneath the porticos, in gymnasia, in amphitheatres, in arenas, during banquets, or even at shrines. At the theatre, action was recounted in verse, using characters, masks and figurines. Under the porticos, Choruses were directed and people danced. In gymnasia, wrestling was practised; in amphitheatres, there was running and horse racing. Boxers fought in the arenas. During banquets, music was made with rhythms, instruments and songs, and people played dice. At shrines, during rites, praises were sung to the gods. These games were considered legitimate activities because the natural warmth of the body thrives on well-balanced movement, and because joy refreshes the soul. But there is another reason that is even more plausible: given that people needed to gather from time to time to play, the Ancient Greeks sought out specific places for this purpose to prevent people from gathering in dubious places where illicit, even criminal acts, would be perpetrated.
>
> (Hugues de Saint-Victor, 1096?–1141)[1]

"Going to the theatre" is the social and repeated experience of being *together with others*, the experience of participating in a community and in its story, *and* the personal experience of being *one among others*, and therefore alone, with one's own narrative. It is all these things at once. On the one hand, the spectator participates in an event peculiar to the society and to the link that this event creates among all its partners – in a sort of ceremony, therefore; on the other hand, she has taken the decision to be alone for an encounter with an Other, to isolate herself, to be face to face with this Other. As such, the performance she is witnessing (or in which she participates) is an expression of both the shared *and* the particular: it serves to reveal what she has in common with the world (humanity, inhumanity, passions, social behaviours, etc.) and to underscore her otherness (the fact that she is not the way she sees others represented, the fact that she thinks differently from others, both those on the stage and those around her, to be at a distance from them). This principle of simultaneity is essential, since it underscores what and who the spectator truly is: a social individual. And this principle engages her in several antithetical ways so that she must choose, or decide not to choose, one of them, based on what is being offered to her, where she is or the attitude that she decides to adopt.

Together with others or one among many?

Whether it is being together or alone among others, going to the theatre always means seeing what one does not ordinarily see in the world by oneself. This is due to arrangement proposed by others and in which one chooses to participate, or not. It means witnessing the unmasking of what is hidden, or imaginary, or what one does not normally see, due to a lack of time, means or special effort. It also means seeing someone separate themselves (for a moment or for the whole performance) from others, to be watched and listened to in a way that is different from what one might glean if this person had stayed among them. What the spectators then hear and see is a text that is acted or *performed*, that is organised in a specific manner distinct from the organisation, enunciation and speech of the day to day. It is a performance exhibited in a specific place and that establishes itself as essentially different from habitual modes of social action and speech.

Seeing theatre is therefore, literally, *seeing something else* from what one sees outside the theatre. But at the same time, these specificities must give the spectator the impression that they bear, more or less, a resemblance to the everyday life. In other words, the spectator must understand that they are similar to those who, nonetheless, are clearly and irreducibly different from them. Seeing theatre is therefore seeing in another way what one sees outside the theatre, or what one sees about others and about oneself. Thus, what the theatre unveils, thanks to, or through, the work of others – generally, the practitioners – is a figurative idea of a world, of the world, or a "representation" of the world, or of what the world can be, that one will consider (or not consider) legitimate or accurate, and that one will question, by oneself or among other people. The theatre is also a portrayal of the self, a figurative proposition of what one is, and that must also be debated or validated during and after the "session". Thus, the spectator has a normative expectation, while also expecting to be surprised by something: interested in seeing and hearing something, or something about someone or about themselves, which they ought not to have seen and that is perhaps not useful to have seen or heard. Finally, to go to the theatre is to escape the world and oneself in a spirit of entertainment, which allows for the creation of a space between the real world and that imaginary escape.

Thus, the person who goes to the theatre is one who simultaneously wishes to be joined to others, to be alone, to see the world as it is, to see the world as it is not ordinarily seen, to see both the resemblance and the difference between themselves and others, to see themselves as never before, to encounter both the expected and the surprising, and also to escape all of that, with (or without) the intention of entering a different world, which is substituted for the real world, for the self, for the session and for reality. All of that rests on a single, ephemeral event, which can be repeated, but never repeated and executed in an identical fashion, since at each performance (or at each representation) the conditions of action and reception change insofar as neither the audience, nor the acting, nor the layout of the location, nor the circumstances, can be strictly identical. Consequently, the practitioners and the audience are simultaneously aware that the performance has already taken place, but that it is new and living and thus different from the previous performance and from the next. We shall see further on that the position of reader is different, hybrid and that the reader is both in an imaginary scenic world of his own creation, as well as immersed in the act of reading, interpreting a text by simultaneously observing its physical structure and its layers of signification.

Theatre and performance

While the meaning of this expression "going to the theatre" has changed over time, and particularly over the last thirty years, we generally accept the idea that "going to the theatre" is an act that, in principle, consists of going to a place intended for this purpose, with a room and a stage, in a building that is conspicuously called a theatre. But, we also have to admit that it can also mean to go to a performance put on in the street, in a field of sunflowers (*Gilgamesh*, directed by Pascal Rambert in Avignon, 2001), in a quarry (*The Mahabharata*, directed by Peter Brook in Avignon, 1985), in a public square, in an abandoned hangar, in a kind of abandoned hotel (*Kafka-Théâtre complet*, by André Engel in Strasburg, 1979) or in any other space that was not designed specifically for any kind of performance. Indeed, theatre is first and foremost a place where one sees and hears bodies during a set amount of time, a place where bodies (the bodies of players, or rather of those being *watched*) make manifest to other bodies (the bodies of the *watchers*) words, discursive and physical signs. In this place, and in front of spectators who also are able to act, or who, indeed, can also be watched, the watched-players are in movement, speak, sing within a space constituting a system and that contains objects (a set, costumes, accessories) that themselves encapsulate a set of interactive relationships with all animate bodies present. This multiplicity of imbricated places and spaces is one intriguing aspect of the theatre. This present and this presence exert fascination and allow for the existence of a set of aesthetic, social, cognitive, sensorial and other practices and this is the complex organic mechanism that we seek to analyse here.

We shall therefore contend first of all with a present *performance*. *Performance* will thus denote the manifestation of a bodily action (gestures, voice, movement) in the framework of a specific place designed for observation. It is therefore in this specific place that the actor, or the performer, will play or carry out his practice, thanks to a set of conventions, which form the basis of the practice of both watched and watcher. We will thus take as point of departure Richard Schechner's minimalist definition of performance,[2] which distinguishes *being* (the existence of a body or of a thing in itself) from *doing* (the activity of that thing and of that body that exists). We will also call upon the concept of performance as "*showing doing*" (that which makes this activity so visible, organised, valorised), whereas the study of the *performing arts* will be to explain the activity of "showing doing" itself. Performance, from this point of view, will be considered as the event, the ostensible artistic manifestation in which the act (or the gesture of execution), whatever it is, has value for itself for the duration of time dedicated to the social exercise of theatre, gives rise to a distinct aesthetic and axiological judgement, is determined by a specific action and is also linked to multiple practices, to differing statuses (actors, author, practitioner and audience) and differing stakes.

Therein lies the basic definition of the performance and the performer: not just doing, but showing what one does, placing oneself in a place that immediately invites the partners in this unique communicatory relationship to involve themselves in a specific system of interaction that consists, first and foremost, in watching and listening to the activities that one shows that one is doing. Consequently, performance does not necessarily imply that there is a role to play, a dramatic space to form, but that there simply is a present action offering itself as an object to be contemplated. In that regard, the performer can be an actor, as well as a dancer, a singer, a painter, a narrator, etc., who manifests a staged presence in a special framework, distinct from (and located in) the general framework of the session. The performer is thus there for what he is doing and the performance is there to exist as a watched event. And if we look away for a moment from the theatre as a genre with all its unique conventions, the performer could very well be a sportsman, a priest, a politician or any other body that shows itself to be acting in front of another body. As such, the domain of performance includes theatre as a particular genre and exceeds it. And because the genre and the conventions are socially and aesthetically recognised by the partners in the relationship, because the places and times of performances are clearly distinct, it is hard to confuse (or one tries not to confuse) the type of performance of a head of state, a pope or Zidane with that of an actor on a stage (even if one might find resemblances between them, depending on the way things are staged, the attitudes of audiences, or the intentions of different actors).

Thus, we distinguish the term "performance" and "perform" from "representation", "actor" and "role". Yet they are not opposed, nor do we seek to oppose them. Indeed, the representation of a role by an actor is a (Western) instantiation of *performance*. Our argument is, rather, that performance contains the possibility of representation. We might also add that while working in contemporary theatre is about assessing an event in which the performer is defined by the activity that he shows to those who watch him, working in classical theatre involves taking into account the printed text *as well as* its performance. By establishing another methodological paradigm, by replacing the study of the text with the study of the theatrical session (which, temporally and spatially, reframes the theatre's *performance* as a function of its audience) and by substituting the "scientific" mode of observation of the object (the literary text) for an investigation into the relations between performance and text (which does not nullify the text but encapsulates it within a larger framework), we seem to be able to gain clarity. Additionally, one is able to better account for the theatre's specificity historically speaking and to promote a dynamic dramaturgical approach to the contemporary staging of the theatre of the past.

Indeed, if we speak of performance for the theatre that we witness in the twenty-first century, of theatricality, of bodies, of acting styles, of staging and of communication between audience, actors, the fiction represented and the text on which the whole dynamic often rests, it is perfectly legitimate to ask the same questions of the so-called "classic" texts with respect to the time when they were staged (and thus, also, with respect to the moment when they shall be staged again). Thus, it is by taking into account the *session as a theatrical event*, in other words the spectacle, the *mimesis* (which exists in relation to the real and not in servile imitation of it), the text and the material context of the spectacle (the practical production, the audiences, the reception and the physical architecture), that we shall find ourselves at the heart of the object that is theatre.

Nevertheless, when we consider recent contemporary theatre, we move away from a neutral notion of performance (which includes all that constitutes a spectacle, including the way bodies move and develop in space and the specificity of place as an observed space) to a current understanding of performance as *having to* exclude the idea of representation since, quite consciously, one is not playing the role of another nor is the set there just to represent another world. This is so much the case that the performer becomes *only* someone who acts and speaks, sings, dances, visibly, in an ephemeral time and in a particular place, all in their own name. The performer thus stages their own subjectivity through all the artifice available to them, offering their presence and addressing the bodies of those who watch, hear and, more rarely, feel and touch them. It is in this way that performers and spectators are both included in a phenomenon crystallised in the interaction between seeing, acting and conceiving, whose objective is, as Hans-Thies Lehmann calls it in *Postdramatic Theatre*,[3] a "synthesis" that brings together these different practices in a more or less coherent, structured and homogenous whole fashioned from perspectives and actions occurring within a specific space and time. The only exception to this is that, unlike in dramatic theatre, this space and time is no longer isolated and placed in representation, but appear generally devoid of causality, without hierarchy and caught in the very moment of the event.

However, if we understand *performance* in a way in which the staging can completely withdraw from mimesis if it does not convey a dramatic universe, does not postulate any other reference than that of the stage itself or consists only of a ostensible realisation of a gesture or an act, then theatre is still unable to rid itself of the question of representation, which is so anchored in the minds and conventions of Western spectators. If contemporary theatre performance can emphasise that the simple mobilisation of a body on a bare stage has no other apparent intention than to make this act visible, to the point where there is no longer any "elsewhere" represented — so no other space than the place of action — then it certainly has difficulty persuading its spectators to believe this. Western spectators are so used to thinking about moving bodies as representational, that they constantly look for information that proves a mimetic link to the real world. Of course, we imagine that this situation also applies to the reception of abstract painting, or of contemporary music, and one might suppose that, for a moment, the spectator, guided by the performance, may give up on trying to deploy a mimetic system at all costs (especially since it is deceptive and leads them nowhere). However, one must admit that this performance, which seeks to be only pure action onstage, would then function not only in counterpoint to the mimetic system, but also within a practical and theoretical critical reflection on the nature of what a spectacle is. Hence performance exists, not in the relationship between an imaginary referential reality and its representation, but in the analogous and meta-theatrical relationship between the action presented and the principle of representation itself. We will return to this question, of course, but will merely make these remarks for now, as we consider the different experiments that have contributed to the development of radical non-mimetic performance (such as those of the *happenings*, of the American avant-garde theatre, or of Bob Wilson, whose aesthetic is a truly abstract one backed up by choreography), and to the idea that theatre functions by *practically* exploiting the instability of the mimetic relationship, and also its uncertainty. The claim of reproducing another world totally (or exactly) is thus displaced, in favour of an attempt at evaluating the pertinence of possible analogies, or at introducing within the analogical principle distortions, which produce meanings. And it is thanks to these symbolic distortions, and to the theoretical and practical consideration of the mimetic and analogical relationship (i.e. the questioning of the dynamics of representation and of the referential system), that the theatre *plays*, and includes the spectators in this play, inviting them to doubt what they see and to reflect on the pertinence, lack of pertinence or impertinence of the mimetic system as it is displayed.

In sum, the dynamics of the Western theatre are most often suggestive of an underlying, but central, question: how does this concrete place, with physical and actual bodies, at a given ephemeral moment, transform itself into a dramatic space that one believes in, whereas everyone knows that this dramatic space is a mental construct, and fictional? How do bodies that act, speak and move also become other representative entities and function as roles and become characters, when we know full well that they are real bodies carrying out a performance and endlessly showing this fact? *We know it, but* (and this is Freud's principle of fetishism) ... we know that it is vain to marvel at this sleight of hand, but nevertheless, we believe in it. For a moment, often, on and off, the "mystery" is there.

Like all other performing arts, including dance, theatre therefore necessarily takes place in a concrete place, in a present moment and depends on the presence of living bodies. Cinema, on the other hand, always consists in displaying to living bodies images of places and bodies of the past on a two-dimensional screen: images of what were live, moving bodies now permeate, as it were, the actual bodies of the viewers, who are not in a position to interrupt their flow or to participate other than by suspending the viewing of this moment from the past. Conversely, as an attendee at a theatrical event, one that is as ephemeral as it alive, the theatregoer or the dance spectator, for example, knows, even if current conventions do not allow it, that they can, at any moment, affect these actual bodies, and exert an action on them with their own body. Legendary "accidents", as well as specific circumstances (the interruption caused by noise, an actor falling, an attendee fainting, etc.) thus prove that a small thing can change the fiction, since it is "live". Therein seems to lie the fundamental, and definitional, *fiction* behind the very concept of theatre: a representation that can be interrupted or disrupted, and whose quality of presence is defined in part by its vulnerability – the *possibility* that it can be affected by the potential risk (which the spectator may fear or hope for) – of an accident and of an unforeseen event that would modify its pre-established course. And this kind of disturbance is essentially one that any attendee could provoke on their own. Similarly, whereas cinema can easily rerun the same filmed event, theatre, because it is ephemeral and exists in a present moment, can only partially repeat the same actions, so that each performance, or the representation that is a variant thereof, is essentially different and each session carves out its own rapport with the fiction that is represented. And while we acknowledge that with film recordings, theatre can also make use of the screen, we recognise that theatre literally dies when film takes over, since it immediately loses its three-dimensionality, the presence of the body, the possibility of immediate interaction, its essential ephemerality. It thus becomes a past moment, fixed, once and for all. These recordings can be no more than a document, a film, but certainly not live theatre.

Nevertheless, theatre is also, by extension, an imaginary locus that is formed through reading. The only caveat is that such reading is complex and is based both on the historical conventions of its time and on equally temporally conditioned knowledge of places, bodies and time itself, which is essential to the spectacle. From a published text, the reader, generally, must be able to imagine the ideal place in which the fiction would take place, as he would for a novel, a place that we have defined as the dramatic space; but he must also imagine the place in which the fictional representation that he reads would be executed. As such, he imagines at once the fictional tale and its staged representation. As a result, he must also bear in mind the overall practical conditions, the habits and conventions, which he is meant to know. He must thus also imagine "his" story based on the text that is given to him (he is therefore a reader free of all material constraint) and, becoming a kind of practitioner himself, he has to envisage the manner in which he would render this story in a staged space that he must mentally create. Hence, somewhat confusingly, there is always the expectation that a reader of theatrical texts has the feeling they have created something.

"Going to the theatre" therefore involves moving physically within a space designed more or less for this purpose when one is a spectator. But, as a reader, it also involves travelling virtually to a place of ones choosing, which must be able to host a theatrical performance, imagining and updating the play to a current place and time. At any rate (we will constantly return to this), whether one is a spectator or a reader, one necessarily asks the same technical questions that practitioners ask themselves.

Therefore, in whichever way we approach it, theatre is first of all a place, or rather a complex set of places inhabited by bodies, whose characteristics one must know even before beginning the study of the stories represented. Thus, our first task is to explore those places.

1

SITES AND SPACES

Definitions

Theatre is, strictly speaking, a layering of different places, of different kinds of places and spaces, which we would do well to clearly define here. At the risk of making certain arbitrary distinctions in our effort to theorise the following elements, we shall draw on the major semantic distinction, first established by Anne Ubersfeld,[1] between the concepts of *scenic space* (a concrete and identifiable topological element) and *theatrical space* (an abstract, generic category by which the mind is prompted to see, feel and imagine a real or potential place). Consequently, we can then accept that scenic spaces that are visually and physically identifiable may become theatrical spaces from the moment they are no longer strictly thought of as topological elements, but rather as entities.

If we adopt this distinction, we can accept that the theatre has several sites: the *theatrical precinct*, which may vary materially and geographically over time, depending on fashions and traditions, and that is divided into the stage and then the place of acting (where the actor places his body). Furthermore, there are several spaces that are integrated into theatrical precincts from the start. The *stage space*, which represents the totality of signs laid out on the stage and lends them meaning; *the acting space*, which becomes a signifying element built around the material space occupied by the actor's body; and the *dramatic space*, which is the sum total of all the sites and environments formed within the theatre's physical spaces. This dramatic (or theatrical) space is therefore something to be distinguished from scenic space, since it exceeds the real place and frames it as representative and or imaginary.

Nevertheless, theatre is an art and theatrical practitioners will never cease to explore its potential. These spaces, which seem to be distinct in theory, may often be considered normative; but just as often, their alleged discreteness will be put into contention. We shall see this repeatedly, since the complex game of theatre is to locate influences in specific, distinct, places and to call into question the very distinction of these places. The basic premise of theatre is to play, after all.

Sites

The first site to consider is the *theatrical precinct*, which includes the actual spectators during a performance; the physical and concrete site of the theatre itself; the house and the stage; and all of the sites used by spectators, actors and theatre practitioners. It may often correspond to a more or less specific building.

Within the theatrical precinct is the *staging area* (or *stage space*), which is the real, material site of the stage, or the site on which the actors move. The stage space may or may not be distinct from the space of the spectators or the auditorium. Indeed, we know that numerous plays convert stage and room into one, in a way that allows actors to enter into the spectators' space, and it sometimes happens that spectators enter into the space designated mainly for the actors.

The acting space or *the physical acting space* is inhabited by the actor's presence, by his physicality and by the movements of his body, existing in a relationship both with other actors and with the organisation of the stage, or staging area.

These places are those that are easily identifiable in the theatre. Each one boasts a space within and without, and these topographies are clearly marked out. The physical space of the theatre is delineated by the building's walls, or by any physical extension added to it for the sake of the session. This theatrical place can thus become a "theatre", in the sense of a building, but it can also, once there exists an in/out crossover, be incorporated into any general location. Admittedly, some forms of theatre play with this spatial delimitation, transgressing it sometimes; however, all forms take it as the basic premise for a relationship between the practitioners and those who watch them. The performance space (the stage space) also has distinctions of what is within it and what is without; the space outside it can be the wings, the auditorium, what is on the other side of the curtain or, simply put, any space from which people watch. The actor's acting space is defined in relation to the body of the one who acts on the physical stage, who places watchers outside of this area, but who, from his acting space, can engage other bodies who, in turn, interact with him from near or far. Ultimately, these three places encompass a space, and open on to a space, which is that of the "world of the drama": the theatrical (or dramatic) space.

The spaces

The dramatic space, which some critics sometimes refer to as the *theatrical space*, distinguishing it from the theatre's physicality, is thus the space of the imagination, of the fictional story – a slice of the universe, which practitioners and spectators create for the play (or through reading it, based on the text's stage directions). Hence the space offstage, which is not another space in theatre (such as backstage), but an imaginary space suggested by the text interpreted by the actors, is a non-visible extension of the dramatic space. The dramatic space is thus an illusory space that the spectator is invited to believe in and imagine that is based on material, concrete elements (bodies, costumes, the set) and on a given discourse. By virtue of this phenomenon, a play creates a dynamic network of exchanges between the places described above and the fictional space in which the story lives.

The dramatic space is thus distinguished from the material space, or staging space, because of its literary, poetic nature: it provides the first impression of a space that is true to the fictional narrative or to its representation. Yet this space is constitutive both of the material place of the performance itself, thus of the stage (which, as we have said before, holds an infinite potentiality of space), and of the theatrical play as a textual space in its own right. Consequently, through a sort of contract that will affect his perception of the body of the actor and of the fictional narrative as a whole, the spectator enters an imaginary space, whereas the reader has a dual perception of space: on the one hand, the staging site (a theatre building) and the performance space (stage area) on which he is able to imagine the actors acting; on the other, the dramatic space that he forms based on stage directions (within the text itself, or external to the text) that he reads. The reader thus accepts the illusion suggested by the text, and accepts that the fiction he reads (whether it is actually mimetic or not) really exists, to a certain extent.

We will leave this key distinction for the moment and will return to it later. But, it is worth noting at this stage that the enterprise of reading involves an added degree of mediation since, as we have said, it forces the reader to imagine himself as spectator and practitioner when he reads the text to be spoken and the (internal or external) signposts marked in the text that he reads. While the spectator is thus able to imagine a fictional space from several real places – the fiction is thus informed by the signs on the stage – the reader must imagine, or suppose, a theatrical location, the material place of staging and a staging apparatus, which will then form the basis of the dramatic space that he will create. Consequently, in reading his text, the reader must construct a sort of representation, imagine the means of staging capable of moving him, while being moved by the fictitious tale he is reading, based on the impact of the potential staging effects suggested to him by his reading.

Be that as it may, the spectator, from their very first contact with the stage area can imagine another place than the one they see directly in front of them. When given the chance, which is not always the case, they are able to envisage somewhere else because of the theatrical conventions on site (objects, set, lights, costumes, for example). And as soon as they read the initial stage directions of the "classics" (such as "the scene takes place in ...") the reader also subscribes to a specific fictional pact and is transported to another place from the two they already know: the actual place where they read and the imagined theatrical space. In other words, they create the space in which their reading takes place. Thus readers, practitioners and spectators are meant to imagine that the plot will take place elsewhere, in a virtual space, which orients the interpretation of the play even before the actors appear on the stage or on the page and the first lines are said. From the first moments of the play, an imaginary space is thus set up, as is a spatial framework, which reflects a world that the relevant parts of the play must depict in some way or another.

When, at the very beginning of *Ubu roi* [*King Ubu*], Alfred Jarry indicates that the scene takes place "in Poland, that is to say nowhere", he takes on this code, parodies it and ruins the standard effect. From that moment on, *King Ubu* – which pokes fun at *Œdipus Rex* simply by virtue of its name – confirms the incongruity suggested by its title, by offering an ostensibly undetermined and clearly farcical place while playing on the reputation of a nation widely known to be torn apart and annexed by neighbouring countries. Similarly, choosing to set a play on a bare, empty, stage puts the spectator in the difficult position of not being able to imagine a specific, referenced site capable of leading the imagination to a possible "elsewhere". The use of the naked stage, of a staging space devoid of any referential signposts, simply reinforces the fact that one is on (or in front of) a stage, at the theatre, and that what one will be seeing is therefore just that – theatre and the artifice of performance. Alternatively, it may establish a sort of universal decontextualisation, which frees the imagination of the spectator, who will then be able to conceptualise the dramatic space they desire or are able to (and in that respect, the spectator becomes rather like the reader).

The plot of a play, in the classic sense of the term, therefore generally begins by situating itself in relation to a poetic, imaginary space, which reflects what the reader might assume the referential space to be; whether historical (Rome, Thebes), mythical, commonplace (a crossroads, the city, the interior of a house), or even minimal (the bare stage, as we have seen). The dramatic space thus brings the fiction to life, it stages the story that the reader reads and the spectator witnesses in a time and framework whose references are, in theory, shared with the author of that story. As such, the dramatic space constitutes an essential part of the world suggested by the text, and serves as a framework for the acting situations and the fictional situations that will take place.

In the context of reading then, depending on the initial composition of the dramatic text, this space is at once referential and singular: by nature, the play always promises a physical manifestation through the stage design, the particulars of acting, costumes and plot. However, the imagination that one may have of this dramatic space is constrained by the limits and customs specific to representation: one will not imagine Rome or Thebes, or a pastoral landscape, in the same way depending on one's constraints, say, the theatre of the seventeenth century, or a twenty-first-century theatrical site. On the one hand, one will have to take into consideration the narrow and badly lit stage of the Hôtel de Bourgogne in the seventeenth century, the declamatory style of its actors, the type of scenery that is used there, the spectators of the time and their conception both of Thebes and of theatre in general. On the other hand, one must take into account, for example, the very large stage of the Théâtre des Amandiers in Nanterre, or of the *cour d'honneur* of the Palais des Papes in Avignon, their modern stage mechanisms, their sophisticated lighting, the techniques of modern actors and, of course, the culture of theatregoers of the twenty-first century. And that is saying nothing of how relative cultural constraints are when given any specific period: one does not imagine seventeenth-century Rome and twenty-first-century Rome in the same way.

Conversely, the dramatic space tends to modify the customary technical and cultural constraints in order to foster the evolution or renunciation of traditional performance practices. The lengthy opening stage directions of the tragedies or dramas of the eighteenth century or of Beckett's plays in the twentieth century, while often remaining faithful to the customs of theatrical space, also imply the need for a spatial reorientation or rearrangement so that the action, plot or situation may be depicted in a different way to what general convention tends to permit.

Consequently, a theatrical representation must allow for the staging of the image suggested by the initial text through its stage layout and design, its costumes and the acting. The initial image that is envisaged by the author and made manifest by the stage directions, is based on the staging constraints and conventions of his time. So if theatre practitioners always have the latitude to accept, refuse or more or less interpret the directions in the text, dramaturgs can also write or rewrite the staging space by creating a specific metaphorical and semantic field, and can decide on ways of filling existing scenes, to adopt them, jettison them or try to modify them so that they fit their own authorial objectives.

Text as site and text as space

Finally, the *text as site*, essentially distinct from all others, denotes the materiality of the text, with its notation of all that must be spoken and of all that should be represented (as recommended primarily by the author, and sometimes by the publisher, in the stage directions within the text or external to it). It appears on the page and becomes an embodied space, rightly or wrongly, when spoken by the actor. We may speak of textual space as that which starts to take shape in the imagination of the reader as he reads – a complex staging (that is at once personal and informed by the habitual staging constraints of the reader's time) and an individual representation of the fictional story. We will come back to this when we consider the theatrical text.

Organising space through signs

Let us return to the theatrical event as our main focus. The original, physical, geographical, concrete, scenic site of the theatre, is one that, during a performance, is organised through signs that possess a multiplicity of visible meanings that are open to unexpected and individual interpretation that provide a pathway into a dramatic space. As long as those who decide to be actors create a world to be displayed, and their spectators accept the principle or convention of that world, the different elements that make up the performance area, be it a stage setting (the ground, the arch, the actors and their costumes, the objects on the stage, the set, etc.) or any other place, will bear a meaning or meanings that go beyond what they were before the start of the performance. Unlike the "real" world, which lacks a precise structure and is not fictional, a theatre world is presented as a world placed in a particular order that is ostensibly full of signification. In other words, around the body of the actor, the performance space organises the signs of another world, imbues them with meaning and forms an imagined (other) topography, a dramatic space, which strives to provide an enhanced understanding of the signs of the real world. As such, it can become an absolutely imaginary world. The theatrical space is thus not the identical copy of a place, and is not simply a real place, but the *representation* of a place of reference (a royal court, or a bedroom in the theatre is not a true royal court or a true bedroom, even if the scenery is a realist one).

Furthermore, through the use of other places besides traditional theatrical places, contemporary performance has built on other, older conceptions of performance and dramatic space and of the relationship between the spectacle and the audience (as in farce, Elizabethan theatre, the Spanish theatre of the seventeenth century, etc.), by including the spectator in the spectacle, sometimes despite himself or herself. Contemporary performance – renewing links with other forms of representation – has, in this way, had the effect of creating an original space around the actor and of including the spectator in increasingly significant ways in each show. The way in which the spectator looks, along with their physical relationship to the performance, often displaces their status as external viewer or attendee to allow them to feel a sense of interpenetration or inclusion in the spectacle. The spectator is thus often addressed, challenged or engaged directly; the room is sometimes lit; actors sometimes move between rows of seats, and sometimes touch spectators physically in order to break the illusion of the theatre. The body of the spectator is sometimes brought into the shared space of the performance, participating in the acting, the fictional story, the ceremony and the celebration. It was Ariane Mnouchkine's actors in *1789* who brought the spectators into the action of their circle of revolution (the revolution of 1789 and the possible, desired revolution of the 1970s) by placing them in the middle of the stage.

The actor and their presence

One should never forget that the staging area, whatever it might be, is always occupied and transformed by the gestures, body and voice of the actor. Through the actor's performance, the performance area becomes a performance space: a world of imagination available to the actor and the practitioners, most often through a text to be voiced and interpreted (in both senses of the word). It is important then to be aware that the actor's performance is inextricably linked to their appropriation, preservation, limitation or loss of place and space, all mediated physically through the use of the body and voice: where should the voice go? What area must the actor occupy? What degree of sound and gesture must the actor impose in relation the other actors and the audience? Those are the first questions that must be resolved from the reading of the text, and those are the first signs that the spectator must perceive during the performance – consciously or not, they must be able to interpret them.

It is thus possible to better understand the performance style of the actor through the organisation and handling of the performance areas and spaces. Upon each entry, the actor must appropriate his playing space, his area, and mark his presence, i.e. the function he has onstage. Often, the text written for the theatre makes explicit the function of this entry onstage. In Roman drama, for example, the actor, playing a given role, enters the stage with a unique dance step accompanied by a specific type of music; the slave, for example, runs in all directions; the *senex* (the sage) enters slowly, etc. In the pastorals of the seventeenth century, shepherds enter saying lengthy lines describing their characters and conjuring up the references needed to enter the imaginary world of the play. By so doing, the actor finds their position, establishes their presence, their fictitious self and performance onstage, sometimes in ways that vary depending on the actors who are already present. The *commedia dell'arte* does just that when Harlequin enters with his specific acting style, whereas, for example, Pantalon stands in the middle of the stage, in a static posture. Molière systematically insists, from his first scene, on the fact that a character wishes either to remain onstage or to leave as soon as possible: Alceste, in *The Misanthrope*, for example, patently wants to leave the stage or hopes that others will leave, to such an extent that the audience wonders what keeps him there. Dom Juan is a young newlywed who, according to Sganarelle, wishes to leave the stage that he has not even entered and flee the bonds of matrimony for an adventure. The spectator will always see him wandering, until the earth finally opens up, swallowing him in flames. In *The Imaginary Invalid*, Argan, who is seated and talking to himself, cries for someone to come and rings a bell, to the point where his sickness takes centre stage both literally and in his own imagination. Tartuffe makes everybody wait for him so he can revel all the more in his triumph, etc. In scenes where characters are opposed, the actors, while following the text, must manifest their superiority through their words or their body language, fight both with their bodies and their voice, and take part in the *agon* that the text invites them into. It all comes down to how the actor occupies their territory onstage. The construction of physical and auditory space is endowed with signification, and it bears immense symbolic importance as we shall see this further on when considering Beaumarchais' *The Marriage of Figaro* and the way he measures out his place and space from the first scene.

The staging area and the performance space are thus elements that are determined by the body of the actor based on the stage reality he has carved out for himself. Theatre is a space that the actor travels through, changing it into a dramatic space and, simultaneously, changing himself. The procedure of "forming a dramatic space" consists of entering into an ordinary place, or sometimes going on to a sort of platform, transforming this commonplace site into a theatrical stage through one's presence, remaining on this stage for a fairly long time, attempting to represent a different world, and often becoming a "character", then leaving the stage *and* the fictional space – which becomes, again, just another ordinary place, while the character, or the actor, turns back into just another everyday citizen. At any given moment, from a split second to a few hours, a real place can be transformed into a site of representation.

By entering into the performance area (perhaps a street corner chosen for a theatrical event, a theatre stage, etc.), and moving through this space, the actor thus creates an imaginary space, filled by words and the body. It hardly matters that the theatrical space is recognised as such. Whether it is a street, public square, proscenium theatre or modern bunker, any place can become a "theatre" so long as the bodies of actors go into it and transform it. All that is required are spectators and participants.

One can therefore transform an underground coach, a political rally, a classroom, or any other physical place, into a theatre stage provided that the usual function of the place is changed so that another slightly or absolutely different world can come into existence. The only requirement is that this space is watched. Consequently, a chalk quarry or a street in Paris might become the court of a prince's castle rather than places whose primary purpose is the extraction of rocks or the movement of people: the theatrical space that these places would form contains simultaneously the traces of the original place and another form of words, gestures, an organised discourse, if the bodies and voices of the actors decide it and if they obtain enough power over their audience for the spectators to "believe in it" or, in other words, subscribe to the fundamental pact that we described earlier on.

Theatre is thus organised within the framework of a place in which several bodies move. Around the body of the actor an "ideal space" is created that corresponds more or less to a sort of performance area, which in a standard staging configuration (an average-sized stage) is around 1.5 metres. If an actor is alone on the stage, in their specific "area" or "bubble" as it is sometimes called, they are always isolated in relation to the rest of the performance area. They must always establish their own space by moving across the surface of the stage, filling up the physical space of the stage, or remaining isolated and static in one area, so as to be perceived to be alone. If several actors are onstage, each with their own space, and if one moves a distance of more than 2 metres away from the others, a gap is created, which must be interpreted. If two actors get to within less than a metre, their closeness becomes intimacy, struggle, shared emotion, etc. Every physical presence on the stage thus has a meaning, based on the location of the actor on the stage (in his relationship to the other actors, or to the whole of the stage if the actor is alone), and based on the positioning of the actor in his relationship to the audience (close, far away, back turned, facing, in motion, moving among it, etc.).

We can thus see straight away that the material space of the theatre determines not only the acting and how the performance is received by the spectators, but also the theoretical and practical conditions of all the spectators and practitioners, their roles, their status and their relations. The evolution of staging that, in the twentieth century, increasingly hopes to do away with the traditional "frontal dynamic of theatre" and the boundary between the performance and the spectator, has thus moved towards a sort of democratisation of the principle of representation and an inclusion of the spectator in the spectacle. In that respect, it is reconnecting with the performance conditions of theatre of the not so distant past. We must now direct our attention and our analysis to the theatre's physical space, which determines the conception and aesthetic presuppositions specific to the theatre of a given period and that, in turn, testifies to the ever-evolving meaning of representation.

2

THE THEATRICAL SPACE

A concrete space

The theatrical space is above all a concrete space, generally urban, within which bodies are deployed and objects are placed. As with every place, it has dimension, depth, height and width. And these dimensions are as important for the theatre as a whole as they are for the make-up of the staging area and the dramatic space. What is specific to the theatre is that these categories, beyond the material constraints that they involve, immediately take on signification and it is imperative for a director and for a spectator to simply be aware of this in every action and in every analysis of theatrical performance (both during the session itself and at the show in which performance takes place). Perhaps by asking the first questions about the elements that determine this space and about the role played by the actor in this space, the spectator has an opportunity to enter the performance in a different way – at any rate, not through identification with the character or through the illusion that a real world appears before them. Furthermore, we know that during the spectacle, as is the case for many collective social practices, the space doubles topographically: the space of the performer differs from that of the spectator. This is then further refracted insofar as the staging area is not the same as the dramatic or imaginary space, which, as we have pointed out, are qualitatively different.

Scenography is the manner, the technique and the art of organising this place and space, but before describing the dramatic space, which implies beginning with the analysis of the theatrical text meant to give form to it, it seems more natural to begin at the beginning: to discuss the physical space in which so many people gather. In other words, we should consider theatre, first of all, as a social space, that is more or less integral to the society, and understand where, in the city, or in what type of building this meeting takes place.

Theatre and urbanism

The first question thus concerns the place where one gathers and the people with whom one gathers. Directors know this very well: when they intend to stage a work, they must first know where, and therefore for whom (which leads to aesthetic issues linked to financial, social and political issues), before even thinking about the way they will do it (with which actors, with what stage manager, according to what dramaturgical principle, etc.). The play thus depends on the place in which it is produced, which is closely tied to the financial conditions and the aesthetic possibilities of producing such a play. And it is worth remarking straightaway that the theatrical space is what frames the spectacle. This space is determined by its physical, geographical, urbanistic and architectural relationship to the society – the overall social group to which individuals belong, which is often a town or city. Theatre is therefore a place where one assembles, often for the sake of assembling.

However, what distinguishes this space from other social spaces is the fact that, on the one hand, the individuals who assemble do so under the pretext of watching, or uniting for the purpose of watching. That some are watched and others watch, or that the roles are interchangeable, is not crucial for now; what matters is that people gather and that they direct their attention towards something: towards a space where bodies are present and in movement and speak (and or sing); or, alternatively, towards bodies meant to be silent and attentive – which is certainly not often the case. Consequently, as with dance and opera, theatre is considered a live spectacle, as distinct from cinema that, as we have shown, also brings people together for the purpose of watching, but that shows a past event, images fixed on a screen and bodies that cannot see that others are observing them – it is thus an altogether different type of relation. And if the dramatic arts can sometimes use filmed material (cinema and videos), it characteristically mixes them with the material presence of bodes in the irreducibly present time of the performance, under the principle of a reciprocal physical exchange.

Thus, people gather for the purpose of watching living bodies or of being watched by living bodies. And even if in certain forms of theatre the audience does not seem extremely attentive to the speaking bodies who are there to be watched, even if this audience sometimes forgets their presence, preferring instead to converse or engage in other activities, including people-watching, it is undeniable that this gathering of people has its reason for being not in the fictional story, or in the plot, but in *the spectacle*. Yet neither the principle of watching, nor the fact that live bodies move and speak, is enough to define theatre's relationality. Because while one gathers, it is important to know where and with whom. Indeed, the fact that there is a specific building located at a specific location changes many things and determines the type of gathering and the type of performance that will take place. Consequently, one must immediately distinguish plays that take place in open spaces, particularly in public city spaces, and plays staged in a building, whether designed for that purpose, or appropriated and converted into a staging space.

The open space

Producing a play in an open, public space means changing the usual function of that space and, most often, capturing the attention of those who happen to be there and turning it towards the show at hand. In a word, it involves distracting people from their primary occupation. As a consequence, the conditions and forms of social and aesthetic activity are entirely unique and are less inclined towards the creation of a dramatic, literary, autonomous space. Indeed, streets, public squares, crossroads are there largely to allow for the movement of people from one point to the next, to allow people to randomly meet, stop and converse and perhaps even to set up a stall to sell things. And when a dramatic spectacle is set up in those spaces, often without any prior notice, it automatically strikes the onlookers as out of the ordinary, unusual, foreign. It thus must strive to be tolerated in that space, deploying ultra-spectacular forms meant to attract and hold the attention of those who move about, if it is to momentarily change the perception that the onlookers have of that space and gain their spectatorship for the duration of the show. It is a battle between the traffic, the place as a means of communication and the need to attract the attention of people who, by definition, are simply passing through and doing other things. The strength of the impact, the need for effect, expansive forms of acting, the use of provocation, visibility are thus essential, since at any moment the audience can easily choose to get on their way. Moreover, since the show is being put on in an open (even hostile) space, any attempt to close off that space is risky (as is the wishful thinking of requesting payment for providing such an impromptu theatrical service). In other words, the economic and aesthetic transaction that allows those who put on performances to continue their trade, does not find any favourable circumstances in this environment. Hence the fact that these theatrical performances are generally put on for free. They may be celebrations commissioned by some person in authority, performances in the name of activism, or instances of rare generosity. Alternatively, they may be used as opportunities to attract people in order to sell them something, in which case they are free of charge, but in a different sense.

The principle of the procession

The first principle of urban theatre consists in travelling through the city to stamp one's mark on it. Entrance processions in medieval theatre and modern animations function in the same way: after determining the performance areas in advance and announcing the route and the date of the ceremony (except if it is part of a ritual and set on the festive calendar), one travels through the city, proceeding according to a specific plan and, instead of the random flow of passers-by, substituting a very orderly procession of floats. Even if this kind of procession captivates the interest of onlookers, given the fact that this moving spectacle is more interesting than the flow of people, it is difficult to include in it the spoken word. The essence of it will thus be the scene, the posture, the easily recognisable symbolic or emblematic gestures allowing the audience to quickly identify what the procession is about and to be led to follow the procession, if necessary. The processions that go before the Spanish *autos sacramentales*, or the medieval passion processions follow this pattern, until they finally stop at a square or in a large forecourt where a different spectacle, a more sophisticated one with dialogue and songs, begins.

That is the reason why when dramatising the stages of the Passion of the Christ in the fifteenth century, one had to stop at every station to voice and stage the words of the story, before arriving at the final station, where the crucifixion would take place in the church's forecourt. And it was the same principle for the Spanish *autos sacramentales* in the sixteenth century: after processing in illustrative floats and depicting the virtues and vices, one would stop for a moment, or at the end, to dramatise the fable of the passions and virtues, *The Great Theatre of the World* or *The Process of Separation of the Soul and Body*, in a square designated for this purpose.

By contrast, the ceremonial entrances of princes and royals, which, in France, lasted until the seventeenth century (but that can be seen again under Louis XV before being renewed, recycled and used for other purposes during the Revolution and the Napoleonic Empire), are often mere pageantry. In that respect, they only serve the purpose of display, in all the ways possible and with all the most symbolic and emblematic scenery possible, the might and power of the one parading: coming from outside the city's walls, where he has received, from the hands of its officials, the keys to the city, and going from the periphery to the centre, the sovereign prince, the conqueror or the young royal bride and groom, ride through the main places of the city, contemplate the arcs of triumph, the statues of Hercules and the painted frescos that celebrate their valour. They sometimes stop at a designated square to watch a comedy sketch or a small, generally encomiastic, play, before entering into the most central place: the palace, the town hall, or the cathedral. The entire city becomes a spectacle, thoroughly dramatised and staged, to form the backdrop of sovereignty itself (as was the case in Florence under the House of Medici), and the citizens come to see the prince reflected in their dramatic representation of him.

We clearly see that the religious and political spectacle, filled with the strongest pedagogical and persuasive qualities, becomes mixed with theatrical representation, which is only there, in principle, to support it. This sort of theatre is one of integration, meant to achieve harmony in society. Nevertheless, street plays meant to be totally controlled sometimes fail to meet their intended purpose to the extent that the passers-by, who generally form a mixed crowd, do not necessarily react as they should, or according to the authorities' rules. In these cases, the official narratives speak of "popular outbursts" or "violent emotions" as they realise that the processions have been mocked and diverted from their purpose, and the official sources try to erase these events from the written archive. Yet we know how much Passion mystery plays performed in public spaces, before a heterogeneous crowd, have been greeted with irreverence, blasphemy and mockery, as much from audiences as from "actors" in the hope of currying favour with them. Even Florence under the Medicis or Paris under the Bourbons were not spared these sorts of reactions. If they were spared trouble during the processions, they were certainly not sheltered from the irreverence displayed in their wake. For when the city changes appearance to turn into a living theatre, when the daily pattern of life is upset, citizens start to let their hair down, drinking and carousing in squares becomes more abundant and it becomes easier to become a different person, to cross boundaries as one might during carnival, to forget the reasons for the celebration and, by the same token, to forget the monarch in whose name the spectacle is taking place.

The same configuration can be found in the contemporary period, in the militant processional performances of the American Bread and Puppet Theater. This theatre functioned primarily in the years 1968–1970 by marching in the street like demonstrators, and often joining in with actual demonstrators, dressed as large puppets depicting military or capitalist power, the oppressed people of Vietnam or the proletariat. The procession would stop at certain points, where the actors would dramatise scenes and sketches depicting the struggle. The people in North American and European streets would be symbolically offered the bread of egalitarian harmony and exchange, meaning they could then go from silent observation to inclusion, by lending a hand to the puppets and marching with them up to the final victory. Other such forms of processional theatre have arisen, based on the same principle, to the point where one might speak, perhaps wrongly, of a theatralisation of political demonstrations. However, while the dynamics of watching and performance are clearly present in this kind of art, and while spectators can join in with performers, if they so desire – which is the very objective of this kind of operation – these performances lack the kind of dramatic interpretation (at the different "stations") that could convince other collaborators to partake. It is rare for those police charged with shutting down such a procession to actually join in. Rather than being focused on dramatic action, this type of performance either ends up being a kind of party or it leads to non-theatrical political action (which is often the objective). And when the Bread and Puppet Theater came back to Paris the last time (in 2003), they attempted something novel, albeit in vain: marching and acting in a theatre (the Théâtre-Artistic Athévains) and pretending to put on a kind of dramatic spectacle in a conventional space without giving up the idea of the procession, the festive atmosphere and the desire to promote political action. The shared bread, the oversized appearance of the puppets and the nostalgia were the main pleasure of this event.

Nowadays, when modern street theatre companies such as the Royal De Luxe, travel through the streets of a city with their puppets, their stilt walkers, their giants and their performance, they do so within a certain framework (determined by public authorities) and according to a specific mode of action. What matters is, on the one hand, the public exposure that comes from showing different scenes in certain major parts of the city, and on the other, the dramatic action that takes the form of fantasy tales represented in a political manner, reminiscent of the medieval mysteries, but with other ambitions and another social functions. Therefore, while modern processions are generally more restricted and there is less room for flexibility, the context still allows artists to create a performance apparatus in the form of a narrated fictional story with dialogue. The audience, most of whom have had prior information, thus come to watch an open-air theatrical performance that is free of charge (the companies are paid by municipalities, regional councils and the state). It is a compromise between traditional theatre and performance that seeks to go into the city.

The infiltration principle

The second principle is to make oneself very conspicuous and attempt to set up an imaginary or real performance space in the middle of the crowd, or in a strategic, central place.

As with storytellers or ritual performances, the easiest solution is to create a *circle*, or a semicircle around the actor(s). The place most emblematic of this arrangement at the moment is, no doubt, the Jama'al Fna Square in Marrakech. If you take the time, you notice that behind the shorts and sun hats of the myriad tourists are a series of circles in the centre of which are storytellers, snake charmers, acrobats, showers of monkeys, musicians, jugglers, poets, charlatans and herbalists. Between the Medina and the royal palace, surrounded by buildings of different kinds, the square has for eight centuries been an almost permanent place of urban spectacle that provides Moroccans with an economic, mercantile and cultural place of meeting. The performances put on there are thus filled with dialogues between artists and spectators of all kinds, and despite the mass tourism and regardless of (or thanks to) the UN's designation of the square in 2001 as an "oral and intangible heritage of humanity", the real and fake storytellers, the supposed charmers and the passers-by paint a multiplicity of circles. Regardless of whether what one witnesses at any given time is folklore, authentic popular art or watered-down celebrations, the essential thing to note here is the principle that governs the performance: the circular principle, for rituals, performances or theatres, whereby the performer is simultaneously surrounded and distinguished from the spectator, but that allows for dialogue at any moment and even for spectators and performers to enter each other's space. And when Western trainee actors first begin their acting onstage, in the absence of an audience, the initial principle they must follow is to form a group onstage by establishing a circle: sufficiently separated one from another (the equivalent of a stretched out arm), but linked by the geometrical figure, they simultaneously see what they are and, at the centre, what they must conquer. They are thus spectators and actors at the same time and, through their positioning, compose the quintessential image of the spectacle.

Aside from the circle (which does not necessarily imply elevation), the platform is the most typical type means of staging a performance. The audience is in front of a floor area that is raised up, a *scaffold* that forms a staging space allowing an audience to easily see what is being shown to it. The scaffold at once denotes a place of torture (the bloody scaffold of public squares), the area of a stage and the ritual altar.

In its original sense, the torturer and his victim play their roles and, as Furetière puts it in his 1690 *Dictionnaire universel*, it is "the small theatre set up in a public square, on which criminals are beaten and gentlemen beheaded".[1] In that sense, it is a space upon which a very real "tragedy" is played out. Its final meaning comes from the place on which a sacred ceremony is carried out, a mystical liturgy that represents the mystery of transubstantiation: the sacred transformation of the host into the body, or *corpus*, of Christ. Between those two is located the stage, used both to carry out sacrifices and represent the transformation of the body of the actor into the entity of character. Because of this, the stage on which actors played was for a long time referred to as the "scaffold". In this way, the scaffold never lost its initial meaning, that of an elevated, easily observable place, a tribune or platform, and that, by its very existence, is distinguished from those who watch and distinguishes the viewing area from the performance area or the place of sacrifice. And this ritual, scenographic place, at once social, judicial and ceremonial, offers a real elevated spectacle and a series of effects that serve the purpose of moral edification (punishment as a means of convincing, for example), the ennoblement of the condemned (who becomes a hero), the perverse gratification of those who take pleasure in the sight of blood and in the suffering of their fellowmen, and even the most grotesque humour. In other words, and to quote Corneille, we see on this raised space the "undisguised face" of crime, as well as sorts of comic performances. And just as the performance area becomes the space of a sort of performance sacrifice on a raised platform and in front of an audience, the theatrical space itself represents the same space observed in the same way, but on a stage whose stated purpose is to represent the world: a decaying and comical world for farce, a heroic world for tragedy. But while bloody scaffolds and ritual altars are, in essence, free for their "spectators", the scenographic scaffold must feed those who work on it.

Hence, when Tabarin and his master set up stage on a platform on the Pont-Neuf, at the beginning of the seventeenth century, their primary aim was to be seen by a crowd able to stop and watch. It was not mainly to perform a play straightaway, and so not to gratuitously attract attention, but to use grotesque, parodic sketches of medical scholasticism in a way that would then facilitate the sale of their charlatanry. Even if the Pont-Neuf were a good choice, because it is simultaneously used to allow passage from one bank of the Seine to the other, for ambling and for commerce (it is quite large and has a square in the middle, on l'Ile de la Cité), the fact still remains that theatre first has to capture the interest of the passers-by in order to con them out of their money by selling them medicine.

Little by little, and with the emergence of other showmen, this method started to gain a purpose of its own that eventually superseded charlatanism, and achieved a certain aesthetic autonomy. However, it was also necessary to collect money either during or after the spectacle, or to try to close off or hide the area to prevent people from watching without paying.

It is as if to become an aesthetic object, one needed to create a boundary — to close off space. Prior to this, medieval pranksters had attempted to mark out their territory by setting up their performance stage in the market places, and in Spain, the birth of the *corrales* came out of a desire to fulfil the same demands: if it was easy to show a performance outdoors in a public forum, one had to, if only for economic reasons and social and aesthetic concerns, delimit the theatrical space based on the idea of the *patio* or on the concept of a sort of rectangle closed off on three sides. From that point onwards, all one needed to do was to close the entrance and set up a ticket booth so that the actors could be remunerated and the audience, settled in its place, could focus its attention on the performance with a modicum of attention. As we will see further on, the same phenomenon existed in England when the usually closed inn-yards began to be equipped with theatres.

For theatre to exist as more than just a communally inspired or imposed ceremony of integration that illustrates the harmony of the city, it must hold a certain mystique, a desirability even, set to inspire people to pay to attend. It must stimulate people's desire to enter, and pay (or to be so privileged as not to pay) and obtain the immaterial pleasure of the spectacle. Even after one passes through the open door there are curtains and partitions that all serve to pique the audience's curiosity. It is in the same vein that acrobats appear in front of the closed curtain and extol the wonders of what is to come, that posters inform and attempt to attract and "promoters" of all kinds whet the appetites of potential customers. It is for all these reasons, both aesthetic and economical, that one must create in future spectators the desire to enter, in order to watch what others cannot see; to enter, with other spectators, the secrets that the actors can deliver, or to be entertained and obtain pleasure, unlike those who remain outside. This is the point, therefore, at which we move from the outdoor, open space to the interior, closed space of the theatre: from the open ceremony or ritual to the paid theatre performance.

Locating the closed space

We have seen above that the location of the theatrical place within the city is of the utmost importance in determining the specificity of what one can do in that space. A platform on a bridge will not be conducive to silence and to the concentration of the audience; pranksters who overact have a far greater chance of being watched than dramatic actors whispering their text. It is purely a question of circumstance, even if one does attempt the impossible and sometimes succeeds. The specificity of an urban place has everything to do with its topological role in the geographical space and with its architecture. These give a sense of the type of people who frequent it, of its social role and of the aesthetics of the place. Of course, none of these prevent the subversion of what we may expect from this site. Indeed, for centuries, the matter of the location of theatres – in the centres and on the peripheries of towns – has been a subject of social interest.

As we shall see shortly, it is significant that during the Elizabethan era, London theatres were located at some distance from the city on the other side of the Thames, adjoining disreputable areas, such that they were considered amoral places. As a consequence, London actors and theatregoers, whether from the lower classes or the aristocracy, had to go there with the full awareness of this fact. It is significant that the first victory of the Confrères de la Passion, in 1548, was to have been able to play within Paris *intra muros*, i.e. within the gates of the city, and be legitimately classed among respectable – and central – activities of the city, and thereby attract an audience of citizens free of the shame of attending their performances. Lastly, it is significant that the public theatres constructed in the 1970s in the name of the democratisation of theatre and in a break from what city centre theatres represented, were built in Bobigny, Gennevilliers, Nanterre or Villeurbanne, regardless of the results ultimately obtained. Therefore, not only is place marked by political will, it also determines the aesthetic and function of performances.

Putting on a show somewhere, converting a place into a theatre, or more significantly, building a theatre, is thus always a social issue. The social function at stake can be anything from public praise (or flattery) of a sovereign or other power, entertainment, or critique, but there are always social stakes. Besides the issue of the content itself, the mere fact of bringing people together and creating an "assembly" carries with it certain risks.

Seventeenth- to eighteenth-century London

Whereas London theatres of the Elizabethan period were located on the south bank of the Thames, after the revolution and the closure of the theatres, they moved to the centre of the city to inaugurate a veritable theatre district. From Drury Lane to Haymarket via Covent Garden, although this is an area of London still famous for its theatre activity, at that time, it was considered to be a debauched, social melting pot replete with street performers and prostitutes who had also moved into the area. As such, the area was under constant surveillance by the authorities. However, at the same time, with the increasing success of the theatres and despite the police surveillance, this new district managed to attract crowds and became a focal point for all sorts of freedoms, including the plays themselves, which came to represent the atmosphere of liberty that prevailed in the area. Indeed, when reading John Gay's *The Beggar's Opera* (1748), it would be hard not to realise that the theatre personnel, the pimps, the women with loose morals, the thieves, the recipients of stolen goods and the corrupt policemen all represented actual characters in the crowds around the theatres at that time (much to the audience's delight). It was as if the theatre had espoused the notion that criminals, the underworld and the police were now fully part of the social system rather than being simply outlaws who were excluded from the city. In allowing theatres to be built in the centre of the city, one could hardly be surprised that the stories, which they staged, were inspired by the space around them. Thus, while the link between the physical space surrounding the building and the dramatic space is not a given, the location of a theatre is never a matter of chance.

The end of the Boulevard du Crime: nineteenth-century Paris

It cannot be said that the plays staged in the theatres of the Boulevard du Temple[2] in Paris at the beginning of the nineteenth century were mainly political, or even that they contained bitter critique of the social situation during the Bourbon Restoration or the July Monarchy. They consisted rather of entertaining, playful, musical shows and sometimes of maudlin dramas, but they attracted a mixed audience (and one hard to control). Outside, rotten apple vendors offered spectators the wherewithal to express their disapproval of actors; circus artists and three-card trick players shared the street space outside; and all sorts of people, from pickpockets to the bourgeois, went from one theatre to the next and from one stall to the next. In this way, the Boulevard du Crime – as the Boulevard du Temple was then known – became a major social issue that was not easy to control wherein real or supposed criminality and performance existed side by side. Consequently, as theatres (more selective ones that controlled attendance) were constructed along more socially reputable boulevards a bit further away (such as Boulevard des Capucines and Boulevard des Italiens), and as the need arose to construct larger avenues through which troops could pass, marching on to a large square (the future Place de la République, where the great East Paris barracks was built), the Boulevard du Crime and its theatres were almost all destroyed except the Théatre Déjazet, which was located on the opposite site of the street and still exists today. What this anecdote shows is that, as a place, the theatre is problematic in part because it leads to a gathering, but mainly because going to the theatre also means participating in an event laden with social connotations. It means taking a step that goes in a certain direction and indicating one's active participation in collective action, whether one intends to or not.

La Cartoucherie de Vincennes in the 1970s

The example of the Cartoucherie de Vincennes is significant in this regard. Equally, it demonstrates how a place that is not built for the theatre can be converted and how this conversion can itself take on new meaning. In this instance, the theatre is established on the outskirts of the city, resulting from a squat inside abandoned military buildings in a relatively inaccessible area. Transforming a disused military area into a theatre that is vibrant and socially useful would prove to be a fine tactic and a masterful effort, which was eventually, and not without effort, legalised, then recognised. The very identity of this recycled theatrical creation thus speaks volumes: it required a political effort on the part of both actors and audience. Going to the Cartoucherie de Vincennes at the beginning of the 1970s meant supporting the occupation even before supporting the (clearly political) plays staged there. It also meant ensuring that the popularity of the operation would lead to a point of no return that might prevent the authorities from reversing the state of affairs; that a military ammunition factory could become a place of culture and discussion. It is also entirely evident that the presence of theatre practitioners as well as theatregoers in these premises, which, little by little, became a series of theatres, was highly significant and proved that the very space of the Cartoucherie now had social stakes attached to it. Going to the Théâtre du Soleil, to the Aquarium or the Théâtre de la Tempête therefore meant participating knowingly and in a different way in social and artistic life; it meant sharing, at least outwardly, the same alternative and thus to accept another form of acting, of staging and of behaviour for spectators, one revelatory of another mode of political behaviour. This allowed for the representation in 1971 of a new French Revolution, which the audience did not yet know but with which it identified: *1789* was staged at the Cartoucherie de Vincennes (after its world premiere in Milan, at the Piccolo Teatro, a few months earlier) by the Théâtre du Soleil. On the outskirts of Paris, in front of spectators who had made the effort to come out east of the city, after having crossed the enclosed plot of land and met the actors, the Revolution, their revolution, was there on show. It was on the platform and wooden gangplanks, welcoming a crowd that could choose to remain standing in the pit, or to sit on risers on the outside of the rectangular performance space, or to move from one spot to another. Then, right in the middle of the session and of the spectacle, the Bastille Day celebration transports the eyes of the spectators up to the five raised performance areas and the footpaths linking them, in a large round, blending past, present and the hope of a future happiness. *The Revolution That Should Have Ended with the Perfection of Happiness* (*La révolution qui devait s'arrêter à la perfection du bonheur*), as the play was subtitled (and as the published version with the Édition du Stock was called), is thus celebrated in a moment of shared utopia, in an illusion of harmony and movement, until the historical and fictional events take over in the second part and the mood of happiness is challenged by the narrator who recalls the events of July 1971. Thus, faced with Barnave and the return of bourgeois theatre, a Marat emerges from the crowd in the pit, as if coming from among the people, and pronounces the revolutionary speech of Gracchus Babeuf, which closes the play. After staging the dramatised narrations, with the use of multiple platforms, celebration and declamatory speeches, *1789* ended on the hope of happiness *and* on martial law. In other words, there was a tension, after everybody had *almost* played, dialogued and danced with each other (characters, practitioners, acrobats, storytellers *and* the audience), *apparently* united by the performance and the spectacle, during the fleeting episode of festive social cohesion and the union of theatrical bodies. After all that, you had to leave the Cartoucherie to return to the centre of Paris and try to relive the effusion of the whole experience.

By the following year (1972), it had become more difficult to get to the middle of the Bois de Vincennes, and the troops posted there seemed less threatened. In the building, the staging mechanism had very slightly, but fundamentally, changed: *1793* developed a more distant representation, and used artificial daylight (the projectors were arranged behind the glass walls to create a diurnal effect), to engage the audience in a completely different way, in the style of a history lesson, teaching a great epic in a reflective argument. The utopian celebration was now replaced by the representation of a process. The corporeal bond of shared performance was now replaced (as was the audience's ability to go on to the boards) by a mediated spectacle. As if to show that the revolutionary society, momentarily affected on 14 July 1789, had been a political and theatrical utopia, which needed to be reconstructed in order to become real in the contemporary moment. It was thus the actors' duty to speak to us, to show us the way, to build the conditions in which the revolution would be possible; and it was the duty of the supposed chorus of actors and spectators to respond to that call. The initial parade had thus ensured the transition between the two dramatic systems: that of the past – represented as post-medieval – and that of the utopia of festive dialogue and of the union of institutions. The play's action had led towards an epic and political modernity filled with awareness and with the promise of future political action, outside of the Cartoucherie. The urgency, in 1972, was to clarify the complexity of history in order to convince the people (the spectators) that a 1793/1973 was perhaps possible, via 1871 and 1917. The urgency was to represent these past calls to revolt, these testimonies of the past, in order to provoke in spectators a desire to reformulate them in the present once the play was over. Something had thus essentially changed, since even though it was still conceivable for the spectators to move within the theatre, and even to speak or stand, the manner of convening and the mode of enunciation were no longer the same: there was now a separation of roles within the general atmosphere of a modern epic. In one year and two productions, Ariane Mnouchkine and the Théâtre du Soleil troupe had thus told the story of our theatre: the history of the dialogue between society's different entities, of the dialogue between the audience and the performance, with, at the centre, the spectacle's irreducibility and the productive need for the acknowledgement of boundaries between the spectator and the theatre. At the same time, it became clear that the theatrical space had changed without there being a change of location. It had already become institutionalised while remaining peripheral, and had become a theatre rather than an abandoned military building, a place for fictional stories rather than for direct political action.

Recycling and re-appropriating buildings in the twentieth century

If buildings in the twentieth century and all that went along with them became a social issue, and if the building of a theatre is significant, in all respects, for cities and for society, it is also possible to transform a place originally intended for other purposes into a theatre. The second part of the twentieth century is hardly lacking in examples of this phenomenon, neither are previous centuries, for that matter. Real tennis (*jeu de paume*) courts in the 1600s became places of spectacle, a fact that has influenced our typical staging apparatus (a long rectangular room, with dressing rooms at the sides). We are also aware of how much the "reclamation" of the great courtyard of the Palais des Papes in Avignon allowed the theatre to dramatically move into the town, before any institutionalisation of this phenomenon. It came as a huge surprise to a town that had never requested this transformation, and who, moreover, were not particularly welcoming of Jean Vilar's festival from the outset. And we have seen, from the 1980s onwards, that as the industrial crisis deepened and as factories closed down, abandoned factories were converted into theatre buildings. Each place, though re-appropriated, retains a trace of its past, which changes both the technical layout (no fly system, no trap room, no fire exits, a bare and often extremely large stage), which alters the idea that one often makes of stagecraft, and also allows one to place a set of different meanings on to the staging of a work. Staging a play right at the edge of Hagondange (Jean-Paul Wenzel's *Far from Hagondange*) and on its industry in a disused factory does not carry the same meaning as staging it in a proscenium theatre.

Similarly, showing *Kafka-Théâtre complet* (André Engel, 1979) in a deserted building in Strasbourg and making the spectators move from one place to another then locking them into a bedroom, letting them know that they could be kept there until the following day, produces very different results from staging the plot of Kafka's *In the Penal Colony* on a classic stage. For this performance, the spectators, who arrived in front of a sort of old hotel and entered in in small groups, were welcomed at the end of the red carpet by grooms (eleven "brothers" whose names were tattooed above their eyes) of the "modern hotel". Once there, they waited in a hall where a pianist – chained to his piano – played what they requested, while a singer broke down in tears or a shy young man spoke about his relationship to Yiddish. After a long wait, they were led individually, or in small groups, into bedrooms – narrow ones with a prison-like iron bed – in which the groom would lock them while he told them the narrative of *In the Penal Colony*, the only interruption being the noise from the courtyard, at which time the curious tourist-prisoners would look out the window and watch the spectacle below, where a homeless person was being violently and noisily chased away. The time would thus lengthen, and the audience became incapable of judging the duration, until a kind of Charlie Chaplin, after being bitten by a German shepherd, was thrown into a garbage skip. It is at that point that the spectator-tourist-prisoners discovered that all was finished and that they could leave though the basement.

Finally, when Luigi Ronconi decided to stage a play (*Infinites*, 2000) on the notion of infinity in Milan, he did not use either the Piccolo Teatro or the Strehler Theatre, but an old factory, so that the spectators could grasp the notion while going from play to play, from experience to experience, after having been surprised that they were being taken out into the Milanese suburbs. In fact, new theatres built after these experimentations contain not only a classic room, with a frontal mechanism, flys, trap room, a room and a stage, but also one or several other rooms, resembling lofts or hangars. These rooms are transformable and have the rudimentary appearance of industrial places transformed into theatres. And only lately, when the Odéon moved some of its operations to the Ateliers Berthier (which, before, was used to store stage sets), we saw how much going from a traditional location to one that is non-theatrical created possibilities for innovative stagings. What this suggests is that "recycling" the use of abandoned buildings or simply moving to a place not originally intended for theatre allowed not only a certain freedom of invention but also a different way of engaging the spectator, an easier or more convenient way of making them accept something other than the classic proscenium once they were transported to another place in the city and to an unexpected building.

The evolution of places

Within the last decade, there has been a move towards "recognisable" theatre locations, whether old or relatively modern. Old locations have been transformed into prominent buildings regarded as new monuments to modernity: hangars are now institutions, their ruins preserved in their current state. They become classified and highly respected locations, and large concrete edifices that served the purpose of decentralisation have had their appearance enhanced by the addition of a few symbolic glass structures. They are new additions in the panorama of Italian style theatres and celebrate the unity of a somewhat forsaken art. The precincts of the contemporary theatre celebrate the art unobtrusively. Theatre companies founded on the principle of the "event" in the 1970s and 1980s have now given way to more entrepreneurial ventures, with their backers, their professionals and the need to produce and to establish themselves.

THE THEATRICAL SPACE

In the 1970s there was an attempt to abandon classic theatre buildings in favour of more "true", less ostentatious and identifiable buildings in towns and suburbs. The directors and scenographers who led this move towards factories and disused places, have now returned – perhaps by choice or out of necessity – to the frontal perspective or in proscenium style theatres: Engel and Rieti at the Théâtre de Gennevilliers, Grüber at the Théâtre de Bobigny and at the Comédie-Française. Once advocates of the ephemeral, of the fleeting event in "real" locations momentarily converted into theatres, these scenographers now link their art to the buildings, even if they constantly try to alter their identity. Guy-Claude François, at the Cartoucherie, tries to fight against the institutionalisation of his hangar, by trying to imagine all the arrangements that might surprise him. And, despite the "retreat" back to centralised theatre buildings, they all hope to maintain the central idea of the previous decade: that ephemeral architecture can create modes of contact, relations and physical links between actors and the audience, in ways that transcend the limits of the mere visual. But how does one go back to conforming when one has known the most secret parts of a city, when one has played in the darkest and best-lit places, when one has taken over streets and squares? Might we concede that the theatre has taken revenge for all such diversions by re-imposing its own sacred space, its precincts and its docile, distant audience? Perhaps we have to do a little playing ourselves, in a disenchanted fashion, turning the building into a place of passage, or parodying the fact that it can also be a place where texts go to die.

In recent years, the re-occupation of theatre buildings by the vast majority of directors and scenographers who were previously "outside the walls" has become a remarkable phenomenon. Alongside this, however, we have witnessed other movements that seek to maintain something fleeting about them, not only within the body of a monument, but also in marquees and "wooden shacks" that derive from post-Brechtian and contemporary Germany. These shacks are often found at a slight distance from typical theatre buildings, and provide a complementary space that can host less orthodox performances, one that combines cabaret, choreography, singing, circus theatre or experimentation.

What is certainly interesting in this new phenomenon that combines age-old theatres, storage sheds (at the Odéon and at Thionville, for example), shacks (first at the Schaubühne in Berlin and now more and more often in Germany), marquees, hangars and even street theatre (which is always live), is that all sorts of texts and plays, including "classic" ones, can be performed in any of them. One example of this is the Footsbarn Theatre, a touring company that uses short-lived stage designs. In the winter of 1998 to 1999, this troupe performed Molière's *Dom Juan*, in French, in the proscenium-style Théâtre de l'Athénée, followed by Shakespeare's *The Winter's Tale*, in English, under a tent close to Gare d'Austerlitz. The Footsbarn Theatre nonetheless maintained its own style of "play": its characteristic audacious acting style inspired by circus shows and comic musical fantasies. All in all, theatrical performance, whether indoors or outdoors, under tents, in orthodox buildings or even in shanties, whether based on contemporary texts or "classic" ones, are now heavily invested in the practices of diversion, disruption and shifting.

Memory and repetition

By virtue of the widespread return to orthodox performance spaces, "short-lived staging mechanisms" have now become a feature of theatre buildings, causing much disenchantment by being instituted sceptically in age-old edifices. Directors and scenographers have abandoned utopian notions that their craft had somehow become "more real", and have returned to an embrace of doubt, lucidity, demanding complexity and even derision. At the same time, while no longer seeking an impossible break with orthodox theatre spaces, they have renewed their interest in memory and thus in play and repetition.

Theatre cannot escape from repetition, no more than the society it portrays and represents. In order to survive, it must now utilise its inherited framework and its history to engage in productive critical processes. Perhaps therein lie the best potentialities of this period, which seek to transcend stasis. If, on the one hand, theatre's survival at the start of the twenty-first century is largely linked to its status much more than to the events it produces, its survival should be unambiguously portrayed as such by being placed at the centre of discussion at each performance. Any desire for escapism, for forgetting, for playing in a transitory world and witnessing an ideal version of reality, have been replaced by the practical necessity of being actually, solidly anchored in the city or its suburbs. And this necessity must be spoken, not just so that the building might survive and receive some kind of funding, but also so there is debate and critical thought. In other words, theatre today will need to speak for itself, to justify its presence, put on a show, poke fun at its own self (in the best sense), to narcissistically (at the worst) observe itself acting and, at the same time, one hopes, question itself. Hence self-referentially re-focusing its energies on its own space. Theatre must fearlessly display its signs, defend the curtain, the pit, the arch and from its obsolete constraints, play, disrupt and shift meanings while remaining in its space of memory. Set design and costumes accompany this evolution while being shown as true and false, true sand and fake bank, fake beach and true wave, as we saw in Luc Bondy's staging (*Phèdre*, 1998) or, with more precision of colour and of strength, that of K. M. Grüber (*Iphigenie auf Aulis*, 1998). The theatre's memory, the portrayal of reality and the representation of scenes become inserted into the performance so that the performance space oscillates indefinitely and testify to the ambiguity of that which it represents. Although theatre is changing, it still seems imprisoned within a realm of conventions: thus, it recycles. Theatre portrays and calculates itself and, in that regard, exposes itself while deepening the definitions of its exercise and of its identity. It is hardly surprising that theatres stage classic texts and infinitely repeat the same plays, regularly exploring their meanings and ambiguities that directors feel duty-bound to represent. Theatre is re-reading itself, replaying and re-contradicting itself; it means endlessly innovating to generate new meanings within its own field.

3
ARCHITECTURE

Once we acknowledge the stakes attached to the theatre's presence in the social fabric of the city, and recognise that the stakes of such presence can be complex, it then follows that architecture becomes a means by which theatre buildings define their function and their social role. Theatre buildings reveal certain notions about the aesthetics produced within them. Just standing in front of the Opéra Garnier in Paris, or going to the rue d'Aurillac in the south of France during the street theatre festival, immediately makes you aware of these issues. And while at the turn of the seventeenth century, theatre spaces were more often than not just real tennis courts or multifunctional sites turned into theatres, it is clear that very quickly, during the same century and in the following one, the construction of a theatre building goes hand in hand with a series of particularly ostensible social and aesthetic actions. Drury Lane in London, the Odéon in Paris, the theatres of Metz and Bordeaux, all embody a major and essentially political intention of portraying the theatre as a recognised social activity, of affirming the need to locate it in the centre of the city, and of giving to its exterior (which resembles that of the courthouse – and in the eighteenth century, the same architect designs both) a monumental appearance. This is in order to distinguish it from other, less official theatre places, to which would be added a particular appendage – *théâtre de la foire, théâtre de société, théâtre de boulevard*, etc. – or that would be called by another name – *ambigu-comique, vaudeville*, etc. However, officially consecrating a place by making a monument of it, obviously means being selective about the type of people who can go there, even if this means forbidding access to valets and other unwelcome people, as was the case throughout the eighteenth century for the Opéra, the Opéra-Comique and the Comédie-Française – valets could not, in principle, approach to within 200 metres of these places. Thus, the architecture speaks for itself, without the need to even consider the stage or the arrangement of the room and of the spectators (other social delineators, as shall presently be seen). Steps or no steps? Peristyle and colonnade or not? Pediment or no pediment? A square in front of the building or just a street? These are the questions and answers that show what, socially speaking, spectators and actors do in these spaces.

It is thus clear that, from the eighteenth century to the beginning of the twentieth century, the theatre is portrayed as a social temple. Whether theatregoers head to the Odéon or to the ancient Masonic buildings at the theatre in Bordeaux, the audience that matters, those in the boxes and later in the pit, play a role in a ceremony that suits them and that fits with the idea they have of theatre. And the ceremony is immutable: walk through a public square, go up an initial flight of stairs, pass through the colonnade, push open a heavy door, be welcomed, go up another flight of stairs, leave the clothes that cover one's body and protect one from the streets, enter into a space that has already been reserved, see one's peers without having to see the hoi polloi from the tiers above, finally be seated, motionless, to admire the proscenium stage. In these places, one celebrates something: beauty, utility, art, the freedom to gather in peacetime, values of reference and conformity. But in the West, and mainly in France, there is nothing egalitarian about this temple, despite the dreams and utopia of the revolutionary architects: the theatre house displays a hieratical class structure, which the very cost of entry intends to demonstrate and reinforce.

Consequently, theatre and the art of representation are themselves representative (somewhat ironically, from the spectators' point of view) of a fundamental social hierarchy. While the upper classes have no advantage as spectators in their relationship to the performance, such advantage is based on their own visibility: an important aspect of theatre spectatorship is the need to be seen, and indeed, to be seen watching both the other spectators and the actors. It was this social visibility, rather than having a good view of the stage, that determined the price of seats in the seventeenth century and by extension the hierarchy of the spectators in open playhouses. Even today in Italian-style theatres, this sociological and economic sectoring still exists, always dividing the auditorium based on the cost of tickets. The latest trend to want to see and hear the performance from the best seat in the house, the "prince's eye", or as near to it as possible, has hardly supplanted the importance of the social visibility determined by your choice of seat.

Conversely, in the case of contemporary playhouses with frontal stage mechanisms, these distinctions referred to now as "seating categories", are based on the centrality of one's proximity or perspective in relation to the stage. This has long been the case in English playhouses, such as those at Drury Lane. Spectators still have the interval for socialising (when there is one), and the foyer, which previously would have remained open throughout the entire performance. It is hardly insignificant that a foyer exists within the theatre, and that it was traditionally reserved for certain people (which is no longer the case). A similar principle applies to the staircases (large ones for the first boxes, while the inconspicuous ones led to the others) and to the entrances (the Opéra Garnier based its grandiose design on welcoming the important personalities who arrived in horse-drawn carriages, and particularly for the Imperial family). The renowned "artists' entrance" only exists since the nineteenth century. This whole apparatus underscores the fact that from the seventeenth to the nineteenth centuries, and sometimes beyond, the theatre has been a place where the observed and the observers assess one other, gather together for the show, without considering that viewing the fiction itself was the main objective. And if one sometimes got close to the actors and actresses, it was in an effort to be seen by them, or to appreciate their performance, rather than to be caught in the net of the theatre's fiction. The result was that this social temple functioned as a mirror: a mirror of those present, a mirror of the society and, consequently, a mirror that often emphatically reaffirmed the dominant tendencies and values of society.

It is easy to understand why the architectural institution of these "mirror" changes based on the prevailing habits of the reception and consumption of art. It is not by accident that Garnier and the architects of the second half of the twentieth century conceive of theatres alongside the new department stores (*grands magasins*) through the ostentation of aesthetic and social codes that turn these buildings into temples of consumption reserved for an elite. The urban location, the design and appearance of their buildings and the large staircase of the Opéra Garnier and the Galeries Lafayette thus resemble each other. It is hardly accidental either that the new theatres built at the end of the 1960s were boxes erected on suburban grounds, that they were depicted as "open" to all, like supermarkets in a narrow radius. At the same time, it was good that they could become places where one came to consume shows or, at worst, cultural supermarkets isolated in an open landscape that was itself "discontinuous". Thus, the location of the theatre building within the urban space, like its architectural exterior, reflects the role that a society accords to the theatre, indicates the uses to which it can be put, and determines the audience that is considered welcome there. And it is by taking into account these realities that it becomes possible to play with or subvert these architectural or urban functions of the building in the service of a specific artistic purpose.

It is thus necessary, and not solely from the perspective of theatre history, to take these elements into account and to recognise that not all plays are equal, whatever the period to which they belong, and despite being faced with a general abstract staging mechanism. Authors knew this when composing their texts; as did actors while playing them and fine-tuning their effects; and this is one of the major givens for decorators and scenographers. And if the critical tradition has adopted the attitude that the text is a text in itself, as if abstracted from the moment of its first staging, or extricated from the conditions of its production, one must consider that it is not a mistake (who can prevent a critic or a director from doing this anyway, so long as he demonstrates the coherence of his project?), but a particular aesthetic decision that erases a certain consciousness of what a play meant in any given period.

The architectural enterprise of scenography has thus systematically sought to construct buildings that are able to account for the different categories of reception within the audience. As a result, when the democratisation of theatre got underway, it seemed the natural thing to do away with the proscenium apparatus in which divisions were based on class, to move towards the tiered seats of classical antiquity and to a single price. This is what the dramaturge and director Jean Jourdheuil ironically and aptly terms "the military perspective" (on the model of the parallel perspective of views from an aeroplane or from a fortress), in an overall conception of the theatre building "à la Le Corbusier", founded on rationality, functionality and, ultimately, on profitability (Jourdheuil highlights the fact that such an architecture implies sets conceived as "play machines" and perceived by the audience through its measurability and comfortability), and where the spectators, presumed to be equal in nature and before the law, have a panoramic view of the spectacle, caught in a utopia of the equality of perspective. As we have already said, this did not prevent the rows closest to the stage from being generally more expensive in a number of theatres, but the intention was there, and was realised more often in an effort to make the audience a sort of classless whole, an undivided assembly where each spectator's worth was that of a simple individual whose reception of the show was not defined essentially by his or her economic power. Again, that was of the ideal, as we are fully aware that the critics and guests are generally seated in the fifth and sixth rows directly facing the stage.

The illusion of creating illusion

Nevertheless, to describe a theatre building only through the lens of how the audience is seated is certainly not enough to account for what it really is, even if this organisation seems an essential point of consideration for authors composing their texts as well as actors and practitioners. Because actually – and this is another constant of scenography – we have been fixed on the illusion of the spectacle or, at least, fostering an art of staging that privileges the ideal perspective. Indeed, dramatic scenography systematically seeks to focus the eyes and ears of the spectators on the actors who are tasked with occupying and entertaining them; beyond the stage set, on the practitioners; beyond the text, on the author.

However, it is very difficult to satisfy everybody in a place that is also arranged so that the audience members can observe and meet each other and that generally does not allow for the vast majority of spectators to observe the whole of the stage in its full height, breadth and depth, and from a point of view corresponding exactly to the supposed "prince's eye".

Thus, theatre is not, and has never really been, an illusory scene void of consciousness, nor a box separated from reality. If the actor's body determines a fictive space, the spectators are also imbricated in that space. Their presence, their movements and their utterances are also assimilated by the actor's play as well as into all the readings and interpretations focused on it. If the set is there to create a theoretical illusion – which is suggested by the performance and recognised as such by the spectator – then a "real" place is indeed depicted in a sort of three-sided box. The referential system has always been played with, as has theatrical illusion and the distance enabled by the architecture and scenography of the building when staging a performance. Theatre is thus truly a place where something concrete and imaginary happens, for the actors as well as for the spectators.

Centred on the acting method, voice and body of the actor, the stage space is always a *proposition* to the spectator who, based on modes of play and representation, considers and interprets this proposition. The spectator, who is assigned to the position of the passive observer, is associated from the seventeenth century in England, Spain and also in France, with the performance and thus is caught in the imaginary transformations of objects and bodies that the choice of staging and acting imply. The experience, the very event, the session of theatre is thus played out on the stage, in the body of the actor-character, in the world of the fiction portrayed by the staging techniques, but also within the theatre building, amid the relationship between the fictive world and the bodies of those who are supposedly in the world of reality – the different sorts of spectators – and the roles they occupy in relation to the fiction represented and the world that surrounds them, which is, itself, beyond the theatre building.

Today and as in previous centuries, rather than depicting another radically different stage, theatre questions the spectator's relationship to representation and the ways of speaking about the concrete and abstract space that structures the continuity between the fictive world and that of the spectator. If man's body is always onstage, it is not because he is the centre of the universe; it is because he founds a human, aesthetic, political and philosophical relationship with those who play onstage with him (the other actor-characters), with those who watch him (the spectators) and with the worlds that surround him (set, building, city). In other words, the body of the actor, the voice he carries and the speech he projects, determines an interaction in the space of the theatrical precinct as a social space represented as such. Theatrical fiction thus becomes a pretext projected into the space of those who enter the precinct where it is carried out: a pretext to observe the sum of spatial, temporal and ideological relations that the theatre building contains for the duration of the session (and not just of the performance). Consequently, modern theatre, at the dawn of modernity, seems more like the means of representing a space of relationships (particularly those between fiction and reality) than a way of depicting a world radically different from reality. It is therefore this space of relation, replete with all of its complexity that now deserves our consideration.

Notes

Part I

1 "On appelle Theatrica la science des jeux, du théâtre, où le peuple avait l'habitude de se rassembler pour jouer, non que le théâtre fût le seul lieu où l'on jouât, mais il était plus renommé que les autres. En fait, les jeux avaient lieu dans les théâtres, ou sous les portiques, dans les gymnases, dans les amphithéâtres, dans les arènes, lors des banquets, ou encore dans les sanctuaires. Au théâtre, l'action était racontée en vers, au moyen de personnages, de masques, de figurines. Sous les portiques, on dirigeait les chœurs et l'on dansait. Dans les gymnases, on faisait de la lutte. Dans les amphithéâtres, on pratiquait la course à pied, à cheval. Dans les arènes, les pugilistes se combattaient. Dans les banquets, on faisait de la musique avec des rythmes, des intruments et des chants, et on jouait aux dés. Dans les sanctuaires, au moment des rites, on chantait les louanges aux dieux. Ces jeux étaient comptés au nombre des activités légitimes parce que la chaleur naturelle

du corps se nourrit d'un mouvement bien équilibré, et que la joie restaure l'esprit. Il y a une autre raison, plus vraisemblable: puisqu'il fallait bien que le peuple se rassemble de temps en temps pour jouer, les Anciens voulurent qu'il y ait pour le jeu des endroits déterminés, afin d'éviter que les gens ne se réunissent dans des endroits douteux pour y perpétrer des actes condamnables, voire criminels." Hugues de Saint-Victor, *Didascalicon de studi legendi, Lib. II, Cap. XXVII, septima, "Theatrica"*, édition Offergeld (Freiburg: Verlag Herder, 1997), n.p. Translated from the Italian by the authors. See *L'art de lire, Didascalicon* [*The Art of Reading, Discascalicon*], introduction, notes and translation by Michel Lemoine (Paris: éditions du Cerf, 1991). Reference provided by Michaël Desprez.
2 Richard Schechner, *Performance Studies: An Introduction* (New York: Routledge, 2003).
3 Hans-Thies Lehmann, *Postdramatic Theatre* (Oxford: Routledge, 2006).

Chapter 1

1 Anne Ubersfeld, *Lire le théatre I* [*Reading Theatre*], ed. J.-P. Debbeche and P. J. Perron, trans. F. Collins (Toronto, ON: University of Toronto Press, 2017). A summary of her methodology can be found in A. Helbo, J. D. Johansen, P. Pavis and A. Ubersfeld, *Approaching Theatre* (Bloomington, IN: Wiley, 1991), pp. 152–164.

Chapter 2

1 A. Furetière, entry "Scaffold", in *Dictionnaire universel* [*Universal Dictionary*] (Rotterdam: Leers, 1690), n.p.
2 The Boulevard du Temple in Paris was nicknamed Boulevard du Crime in the nineteenth century because of the many crime melodramas that were shown every night in its many theatres. It is notorious in French history for having lost many theatres during the rebuilding of Paris by Baron Haussmann in 1862.

Part II

THE EVOLUTION OF MATERIAL AND REPRESENTATIONAL SPACES

Over time, the spaces and areas of the theatre have changed. Nevertheless, as we have just seen, there are two constants that remain: first, the theatrical precinct is generally inscribed in relation to the society, be it in the centre, or at the margin; second, the dramatic space that it contains serves to represent the story of society, or a story in a social context, by spatialising the relations (political, psychological, private and philosophical) that exist among "the citizens".

4
SOME THEATRICAL SITES AND SPACES

It is helpful to run through a few points of reference here. Several spaces of theatre history thus immediately loom large: the theatres of antiquity, medieval theatrical spaces, Elizabethan theatre precincts and classical ones.

The Greek *skênographia*

Inside the theatre of ancient Greece, the actor was sustained by his voice and the role attributed to him within the staging apparatus: the actor-character is defined above all by the sound he makes through his mask and by the place from which he speaks. In these Greek theatres, the spectators were seated in a *theatron*: often a very large semicircle of wooden terraces that could be disassembled (theatres built from stone were not constructed until after the classical period), sometimes a rectangular area. The chorus moved, sang and sometimes danced in the orchestra (a circular area in the centre of the theatre that included a round alter dedicated to Dionysus) and formed a bridge between the spectators and actors. The heroes generally did not enter into the orchestra, and the characters of the chorus were considered to be independent from the action under way. They commented on this action in a lyrical way, gave advice, encouragement or admonition to the heroes. The Coryphaeus, leader of the chorus, spoke with characters without resorting to song or psalm, unlike the other characters of the chorus, who were always restricted to lyrical metre. The characters moved around the stage, separated from the orchestra by only a few feet. This stage, called the *proskenion* (a space that was usually about 50 metres by 3 metres), was located in front of the *skene*. The *skene* backed on to the stage or on to a sort of shack that held a balcony on which actors playing gods could appear (it was the god's space after all), as well as a few doors below that led to a fictional offstage world. The *parodos* was the narrow passageway by which the chorus made its entrances and exits, and was located between the *theatron* and the *proskenion*. The action of the plays generally took place outside, at the door of a place and a few signs hung on the walls of the *skene* would be used to attract passers-by. Albeit rarely, a theatre machine (*eccyclema*) would sometimes be used to reveal an interior or a scene that represented an action occurring offstage (such as something happening within the palace, for example). Greek tragedy thus depicts several spaces. We might outline three dramatic or representational spaces: the space of the gods, the space of the heroes and that of the chorus. Plus the real "theatrical" space: the audience. However, one can understand how much the chorus functions as a bridge between the world of fiction and of real society, establishing a complex interplay that allows for dialogue between both worlds.

The art of scenography was thus set in place when Greek theatre became established as an essential social practice, quickly becoming a trade tantamount to that of a painter. The *skenopoios* is the one who designs the decor – while the *poietes* is the person who crafts the story and the verse – and, therefore, the one who produces stage effects that were in no way rudimentary. The creation of the spectacle, decorations and machines thus resulted in considerable expenditure.

When in the fourth century BC, Athens put on theatre contests, witnessed the tragedies of Aeschylus, then of Sophocles and Euripides and was entertained by the comedies of Aristophanes. The first richly ornate painted panels appeared on the façade of the *skene* (the wooden shack directly behind the stage and built for the festivals of Dionysus). This is where hidden things were held: the interiors of temples and royal palaces, the main backstage area, access to the exterior and to the religious precinct dedicated to Dionysus. The *skene* thus represented the main space in front of which the plot took place (the palace of kings for tragedy, a marine cave or forest clearing for satirical drama, a house for comedies). Spread over about 12 metres – for the theatres that we know about – on either side of the central porch, the painted panels of the *skene* have a secondary door on each side that could then be lengthened into screens called *paraskenia*. Because of their optical illusion, they could allow for the depiction of two other places for the fiction onstage. More than a century later, the first stone screen walls appeared, with their two lateral wings, which continued utilising the principle of the painted panels. The end of the fifth century BC saw the appearance of the *periaktoi* (in the *paradoi* or walls of the mobile lateral scenery) – large upright triangular prisms that depicted three different sceneries by the simple effect of rotation. At least in some theatres, from the second century BC, it became possible to change these panels from a distance by means of rails that allowed them to be slid from the accessory house to the middle of the stage.

We can legitimately determine that an initial foray into perspective and the painting of drop shadows, crucial for producing an optical illusion onstage, was a widespread phenomenon in the majority of theatres as the techniques of architectural design continued to evolve. We might also suppose that the recourse to painted signs was as much for the *skene* as for the *proskenion* (at the bottom and top), and for the *thyromata* (in the upper story and the *skene*). However, from a scenographic point of view, the essential thing, for the Greeks, was not the effect of perspective, but the spectacle and the imagined representation of actions, with decorations, accessories, operations and machines. The accessories themselves were sparse and closely associated with essential scenes (mainly, there were tombs, statues and altars), and machines served the purpose of depicting yet another place, often an interior one (the large central door of the painted scenery would open, providing access to the *eccylema*, the low platform that rolled on wheels outside, and the audience "saw" the tragic bedroom or the domestic place that the frontal wall hid), or to allow for the guards and the heroes to move through the space. This latter phenomenon was due to the flying machine and the *mechanê* of the *deus ex machina*.

There was thus a real spectacle seen from the audience, or *theatron*, and organised around a religious ceremony. The event was depicted as an assembly of citizens and the spectacle was meant to be impressive. The spectators were generally south-facing, and were therefore exposed to the blinding sunlight that came from another world outside of the specific location of the representation. Additionally, when elevated they could see all the religious buildings behind the theatre that surrounded the specific ceremony. Therefore, rather than play on the modern opposition between reality and fiction, the Greek theatre session topologically and temporally imbricated the spectators and practitioners of the theatre in a ceremony spectacle where the visible and the invisible, the world of the divine and the human world, were at once distinct and porous, each existing in a visible and hidden space.

Finally, when Aristotle, in the fourth century BC made, in the *Poetics*, a clean distinction between poetics, the theatre as text to be read and pondered, and the *opsis*, theatre as art of the visual and of sensual appeal, it is merely to point to the essential duality of theatre, as both text and representation; intimate pleasure, critical reflection and pleasure of assembly. The problem that emerges is that Aristotle desires to privilege the poetic over the *opsis*, which was less likely to line up with the normative will and with the notion of the primacy of fiction and the author's absolute control (and, evidently, with the philosopher that he is). Theatre is, of course, less controllable than fiction, since it is more sensitive to the circumstances and the reactions of the audience. The importance of the spectacle and the place is therefore lessened for the sake of the text's constitution of the imaginary dramatic space that the reader, following the author's indications (who, himself, conforms to the principle of dramatic unity – an agonising action, with a beginning, middle and ending, which constitutes an organic "whole"), must create. From that point onwards, the attention of the theorist, and of those who espouse his positions, became focused on the textual apparatus, more then on the scenic one; on the story (or *fabula*) more than on the spectacle. The scenographic apparatus, the staging process and the *opsis*, became the business of the *skenopoïoï*, the decorators, and the *khorêgós* (choir leader), those who technically organise the spectacle, with the result that, for a long time, roles were allocated: the author attending to the construction, execution and composition of the *fabula*; the practitioners taking care of the machines, the scenography and the way of representing the text. And yet, a century earlier, as we have seen, the tragedies of Aeschylus, Sophocles and Euripides, and the entire Greek theatre, seemed to have achieved a sort of compromise between the practical and artistic manifestation of the text and the organisation of the event of the spectacle. Not in the spirit of denying spectacularisation, or denying the text its reflexive power, but rather to link these elements that were in no way considered opposed, since the theatre was a representation of society. As such, Aristotle has long been a filter appended *a posteriori* on to social, aesthetic and political spectacles that had, in fact, arrived at a meaningful equilibrium between what authors put forth, the representation of a story taken from an epic narrative, and what citizens saw – a duly scenographic action that they watched and of which they were a part.

The *scaena* and the Roman spectacle

Unlike in Greek theatre, as Florence Dupont has shown,[1] the Roman audience was seated with their back to the sun, which had the effect of shielding the spectators from its dazzling light and of shedding light, literally, on the spectacle. A new place of entertainment and comfort, the Roman theatre did away with the sacred and civic dimension of the Greek theatre. Therefore, the Roman theatre precinct, though inspired by the Greeks, was transformed in that it presented itself as theatre, as an absolute spectacle. The orchestra was a semicircle now filled by seats, the walled scenic backdrop (the *scaena*) was taller, and bronze or terracotta vases used as resonators were placed under the seats in the terraces (the *cavea*) to improve the acoustics. Everything was therefore done and organised so that the actors could be seen and heard perfectly: the theatres had smaller dimensions than in Greece, and the cover of the proscenium, the *cavea* and the *velum*, placed above the building (and that also provide provided shade and the sensation of a closed space), made listening particularly easy. The width of the *cavea* (the Greek *theatron*) was reduced and the stage, the *proscenium*, which overhung a reduced and increasingly neglected orchestra, took up all the width of the theatre and gained more depth, so that the actors acquired all the space necessary for their acting. The towering stage wall (the *scaena*) had three doors, as in Greece, and was painted and ornamented as an optical illusion: it was the scenery. Painted canvases placed on triangular panels resembling the Greek *periactes* formed moving backdrops. Additionally, the stage curtain was invented and placed between the stage and the benches of the orchestra. As the temporary wooden theatres became wider stone theatres and stages began to be made from hard materials in the first century BC, the statues, the pediment and columns moved to the scene wall at the back, where three levels could be distinguished. The painted scenery (of three types: palace, city, and the country, which symbolised, respectively, tragedy, comedy and satirical drama) was placed on movable devices, canvases fixed on turnstiles with three panels (*periactes*), as in Greece, or on painted canvases that slid one after the other and that could be attached to the roof of the proscenium (these inspired the future fly system). The essence thus lay in the clear distinction between reality (the spectators) and the self-referential world of the fiction, which might simply reflect the convention of the spectacle (that of monstrosity, in particular). Everything is profanity, everything is spectacle, everything is sensual pleasure for the ears and eyes, in a building closed on itself.

It is from the middle of the first century BC that stone theatres were constructed. These quickly became public monuments that were indispensable to the Roman polis. Between 10,000 and 20,000 people were in attendance at each performance. In these vast spaces, the actors had to accomplish vocal exploits that were an extension to their coded physical acting, while wearing buskins that elevated them. Theatre performance then began to take on its full meaning, which also explains why, apparently, theatricality was more important in the Roman theatre and less attached to the importance of speech. This theatre seems to move away, at least in part, from a theatre bound to the text or to Aristotle's poetics by giving all its power to the *opsis*. However, critics also note that tragedies, particularly those of Seneca, also establish a balance between scenic effects and discourse. For our part, we might suggest that Seneca was not necessarily played at that time, nor that the effects were performed to the point where there would have been a spectacular theatre to be seen, distinct from a theatre that was recited, read or imagined. How do you respond to that when the distinction had not struck European authors who, much later, had their minds set on pursuing an enterprise that was, for them, Senecan and Shakespearean, and who thus mobilised all their art in an effort to link the spectacular effect and the literary demands? It is as if they could not except that theatre could be simply textual, or only a spectacle bedecked with a sort of tragic insignificance.

The inventions of the Greek and Roman theatres, although seeming to disappear during the Middle Ages, were revisited, examined, evaluated and developed during the Renaissance. As we shall see later on, the distinction between theatre as text and theatre as spectacle was revisited in the Renaissance, just as Aristotle's arguments, and the classical Greek tragedies and those of Seneca, were renewed, discussed, corrected, interpreted in various ways and endlessly rewritten. However, with regards to the organisation of theatre spaces and the craft of scenography, the knowledge of ruins and especially the reading of Vitruvius' treaties, as well as those of Democritus and Anaxagoras on perspective, led to a renewed interest in the physical organisation of theatres in the sixteenth century. Vitruvius (first century BC), a Roman architect and author of a *De Architectura* dedicated to Augustus, whose fifth volume deals with the construction of theatres, is thus an important reference point. He describes the theatre in very precise terms as a place located within a complex of public monuments, where everything is made for the comfort of the spectator, and where one must devote attention to the laws of acoustics so that a huge audience can hear. Because of how explicit he was in his notations, Vitruvius was read, re-read, translated and commented on by Italian architects from the fifteenth century onwards to such an extent that he became more of an inspiring figure than a precise reference. Moreover, he was considered – falsely, it seems – to be the precursor of the laws of perspective. Theatre was practised throughout the Middle Ages without the knowledge of Vitruvius or, at any rate, without references to him; and medieval theatre invented an art far removed from the scenography we might recognise today.

Medieval scenography: nowhere and everywhere

Admittedly, no theatres were built during the Middle Ages, but spaces were turned into theatres: churches for liturgical dramas, market places for urban performance, courthouses for *sotties*, or farces, acted out by the

Basoche,[2] the taverns and in chords for profane theatre. Short-lived shows were common. Theatre did not appear in any specific place and therefore could be played anywhere: to play all that was needed was a "scaffold" of a decent width, suitably decorated and sufficiently grandiose and sometimes terraced seats. The remarkable thing about these seats, which sometimes had stalls placed in them, furnished by houses in the vicinity, was that they could hold up to several thousand spectators and that the scaffold could contain galleries dug in the ground and superstructures for incredible flying machines. There would sometimes be a bit of masonry so that the fireworks caused by other impressive machines would not get out of control. Finally, the scaffold could also be transported by pageant wagons in England and Spain (for the *autos sacramentales*) and be taken through the city, to the point where they became extremely elaborate machines made for Italian celebrations and solemn parades in all of Europe, including France. In a certain way, medieval scenography used physical space as it was, but lent it a new symbolic value and transformed it by embracing it, sometimes like a contemporary theatre. This place could be anything from the quire of the church to its main entrance for liturgical dramas and mystery plays. Multiple stage sets were laid out around the performance area, allowing actors to move between them in order to suggest scene changes. As for the spectators, they view the play or enter into the representation to exercise their role: this continuity, this close relationship between audience and spectacle, fosters a proximity and an imbrication that was either followed, stigmatised or sought after either as the scandalous or ideal heritage of popular theatre.

But the medieval scenography that was produced by master craftsmen did not limit itself to a frontal dynamic in its relationship with the audience. It was also circular (prefiguring the Elizabethan "wooden O") or rectangular (like the Spanish *corral*), as the conditions of the spectacle were invented. Plays could even be performed on trestle stages or on stages mounted on barrels and "open" in the sense of being surrounded by spectators standing on three sides, who the actors would address directly. There was no stage/audience division in the medieval theatre, evidently no fourth wall, no total illusion, but rather a porous communication between the observed and the observers; a hyperrealist theatricality for the pleasure of the spectacle and the carrying out of the sacred representation.

The scaffold theatre and the trestle stage: integrative function versus critical function

We can think of this theatre as a non-homogeneous whole and divide it into two theatrical spaces that correspond to two traditional functions of art: on the one hand, the artistic function of instituting a social space, fostering cohesion in the society; on the other hand, a critical function and, later on, a radical and a transgressive one, which poses major questions that are difficult to resolve. To establish this distinction with respect to medieval theatre, we will refer to the anthropological and historical analyses of Elie Konigson. According to Konigson, the dramatic function, which portrays the world in a given space, takes shape between the fourteenth and sixteenth centuries in two different ways and in two types of places: by an urban and religious theatre played by citizens within the social space, or by courtesans in the courts who were chosen according to their social statu, and that represented, for the city dwellers and men of the nobility, religious and mythological scenes. This is what Elie Konigson refers to as "scaffold theatre" (*le théâtre de plateau*).[3] Konigson also identifies a mobile "trestle stage theatre" (*le théâtre de tréteaux*), played by professionals or semiprofessionals trained in a specific art. The trestle stage theatre that performed texts was produced outside of the cities and towns, and it gave rise to the professional practice of theatre as we know it. It broke away from the social theatre of the *polis*. On the other hand, the theatre practised by "amateurs" would become the theatre of social inclusion, maintaining order and acknowledging common values.

As such, the distinction between modern professional theatre and amateur theatre seems to originate with the fact that very early on, there were not simply two different ways of doing the same thing (one free of charge, the other not), but rather two distinct modes of carrying out the dramatic function. There were two modes of dramatic representation: the mode of scaffold theatre that was deeply rooted to society and thus became known as "amateur" theatre. This activity did not cause the actor or viewer to lose his social status, just as the dramatic function was concerned with social harmony. The actors are rooted in the social structure and are caught in such a relationship of homogeneity with their audience that there is sometimes a kind of transferability between actors and spectators within a sort of social ceremony. As a result, this theatre is defined much more by the links it forges between the partners of the session as a theatrical event and by the close relations between them and society, than by the aesthetic forms that it adopts. In effect, the city stages and watches itself. Additionally, the "scaffold mode" is more focused on the discursive representation of forms of dramatic stories than on the specific craft of dramaturgy. In contrast, the trestle stage mode takes a step back from the business of the city, utilises artists and craftsmen that the city does not acknowledge or that it finds it hard to incorporate: this is the mode of professional theatre. It considers the city, questions and problematises it so as to be considered in turn by it. Formal questions, related to the organisation of the text and to scenography, are thus essential to this mode, so that the society can go to this peculiar place where strangers, entertainers, citizens from another place, portray it while creating spaces of reflection, satire, escape, dream or thought. Both modes then have their place, their space, their types of interpreters, their types of relationship to the text and to fiction and their types of acting.

We might take note of the fact that this dual model distinguishes amateur theatre from professional theatre without resorting to any negative labelling such as *un*paid or *non*-institutional. Instead, it valorises the social protocols that bring partners together and connect to them in a sort of fraternity, in the broad sense of the term. Consequently, considering "amateur" theatre through this prism links it to urban ceremonies (solemn entrances, festivities, for example) much more than to for-profit theatre events, since it systematically seeks to link the performance and the attendees (the observed and the observers), even to the point where they can exchange roles within the unifying moment of the shared space. Unlike professional actors who struggle to achieve status, audience and recognition within society, citizen actors, or citizens tasked with acting, portray their characters in the communal acting space without renouncing their own state and the status. They play to an audience that is perfectly aware of, and even in solidarity with, the ceremony; one that is aware of both their social standing and their role in performance. Therefore, while professional actors have no social status, or at most a marginal one, amateur actors must have a recognised social status.

Konigson's idea offers a strong platform on which to base a broad theoretical model. His hypothesis that the scaffold theatre is located within the social structure, is produced by citizen delegates who present themselves as such. The fact that it functions as a system of integration and harmony within the social body, suggests the construction of a breach in the symbolic nature of the theatre of integration, which sees itself as one internal to the life of society; and professional and semi-professional ("trestle stage") theatre, external to the common life of society, situated in the beginning outside of the cities and seeing itself as operating in the margins. One is essentially the restorer of social harmony, which can appear to be conservative, and speaks to the social body via actors from that same social body. The other offers either an aesthetic, entertaining, burlesque and marvellous "night out" to citizens who pay for it, or a problematisation of the social structure seen from the outside perspective of playwrights and actors.

In the Middle Ages, theatre in society can therefore seem predominantly "popular" and the places where it is produced seem also available to the greatest number of people. Mysteries and farces represent a multiple space, open and flat, that plays on the discontinuity of spaces and allows the spectator, located in the street or in a non-specific room, to witness, before scenes or stages erected for the occasion, a spectacle that transport her closer to God and the saints (the mysteries) or who bring her back to her comical reality (in the farcical mode). But beyond this representation of the religious and social link that produces a sort of shared recognition among the different parties present, we see itinerant troops outside of cities who do not operate within the framework of those ceremonies and who create two different groups (the watchers who pay directly for the spectacle or for products touted by the spectacle, and performers, whose job it is to be watched). They create special spectacles and, little by little, get into fairs, get closer to the walls and finally enter the city. In a sense, the spectacle produced by citizens for citizens made way slowly for the spectacle of the professionals for citizens. Significantly, moreover, the famous banning of mysteries in Paris in 1548 was intended not as a decree forbidding the staging of religious plays, but one against the transition from one dramatic mode to another: the theatre of citizens celebrating a moment in religious history was being competed against, then replaced, by the depiction in a given place of religious (or non-religious) plays by particular individual artisans. As a result, the famous *Confrères de la Passion*, who up to that time, played outside of the city walls and obtained a staging space within it. Significantly, there was no clean break with established practice and the spectacle of the city by the city for the city and produced by citizens continued, not just because mysteries were produced until the end of the seventeenth century in provincial France, but also because solemn ceremonies (entries, for example) and social ones (festivals, carnivals, processions) incorporated into their productions the whole of the citizenry (in a hierarchical manner).

Mysteries, the Passion plays all around Europe, and the *autos sacramentales* of Spain, disappeared little by little, as popular, sacred and city theatre was replaced by closed artistic theatres, solemn processions and popular festivals of different kinds, and very little is left of this kind of spectacle. A few processions in Spain, particularly in Seville during Holy Week, ceremonial marches in Italy during the same period, a few Breton "pardons", among other ambulatory ceremonies of sacred theatre art. However, even up to the present day, in Oberammergau, in Bavaria, a Passion play is still dutifully celebrated every ten years.

At the beginning of the seventeenth century, during the Thirty Years' War, while the city had been struck with the plague and after months of suffering, the inhabitants of Oberammergau made a vow that every ten years they would perform the *Passion of the Suffering, Death and Resurrection of Our Lord Jesus Christ* if the disaster was lifted. Consequently, at Pentecost 1634, for the first time, they fulfilled their vow by performing this Passion play in the cemetery in which the bodies of those who had succumbed to their illnesses had just been buried. Since then, the inhabitants of the city have never ceased to repeat this decadal ceremony, and, while now they are aided by actors, singers, players of instruments and technicians, they continue to perform this post-medieval Passion play for six hours. The last performance took place in 2000, when the passages judged to be most anti-Semitic were removed. When Hitler went to Oberammergau in 1934, he was enthused by this Passion and remarked that it was a "precious tool" for the fight against Jews and Judaism. With the help of its international success, the Passion's renewal took place in 2010, with tickets going on sale in 2008. Thus, besides the fact that the Spanish and Italian processions, the Breton "pardons" and the Bavarian Passion often gave rise to tourist events, the fact remains that the main participants and, in the case of the Oberammergau Passion, the actor-performers, are citizens for the most part: amateurs, even if they have specialised in their roles and rehearsed for a long time, but above all, volunteers representing corporations from their society, chosen and commissioned by their city. As such, we see in Bavaria one of the last vestiges of the medieval "scaffold theatre".

But we also know that, in other forms and with different content, similar systems still exist around the world. It is not within our scope to examine all cases, but here we might single out the example of the Iranian Tazieh (or Ta'siyè, which means commemoration of mourning), of which we have seen a few representations exported to the 1991 edition of the Festival d'Avignon (which Peter Sellars saw and from which he took inspiration for his play *Perses*). It has also been performed at La Villette in 2000, at which time it was filmed by Jerzy Grotowski and Peter Brook.[4] The Tazieh originated at the beginning of the sixteenth century and is a sort of Passion mystery performance, a popular and sacred ritual ceremony specific to Shiism. During the month of Muharram, a period of mourning for the Shiites, since it is linked in the collective memory to the Battle of Karbala (the betrayal of Imam Hussein, the massacre of Hussein and of his comrades, and the imprisonment of his wives in 661), Iran goes into mourning. Processions travel through the streets, the penitent whip themselves to the point of bloodshed, funeral chants are heard everywhere. And at the heart of this collective sharing of suffering, amateur actors re-enact the death of Imam Hussein, grandson of the Prophet Mohammed, third Imam of duodecimal Shiism. The actors are artisans, shopkeepers, workers, who, having rehearsed for a long time, play their roles for more than four hours to a fervent and often hysterical audience, before parting ways until the following year. The texts are generally in rhymed verse and are passed down orally, but certain plays of the Tazieh (or rather several versions, based on different regions and traditions) have been transcribed and anthologised by anonymous authors. Depending on the place of performance, on the communities' means and the quality of the amateur actors, these can range from short scenes with two or three characters, to large spectacles with horses, camels, extras, battles scenes, enchained prisoners, and all of this accompanied by drums and *sorna*, the Persian bugle. The spectacle ends with a long lamentation, repeated by the audience, announced by the sound of the *karna*, a long wind instrument, when the Imam Hussein is stabbed in front of his children. From its beginnings, the spectacle has been played in Iran (except for a certain disaffection during the Westernisation carried out under the Pahlavi dynasty) in village squares, streets or in vast open-air arenas called "takieh" capable of seating crowds of several thousand spectators.[5] The costumes are often basic: green for the followers of Islam, red for the assassins. The former, who sing and kill openly, are allowed to go on to the stage; the others speak, remain on the ground and kill from behind. The scenery and accessories are generally minimalist (banners citing the Koran, flags), metonymic and symbolic: a basin of water represents the Euphrates; a bit of cut straw the sand from the desert; cotton sprinkled with sheep's blood, or sometimes meat quarters, representing mutilated bodies. In the same way, the dramatic codes are typical of this sort of spectacle: a 360-degree turn means that there is a change of place, going around the stage one or several times indicates that one has travelled long distances and slaps of the thigh show that the character is stupefied or angry. Like the medieval Passion, the Tazieh, a representation of the martyrdom of Imam Hussein, is, in contemporary Iran, a scaffold theatre played by a fervent and sometimes hysterical community, depending on one's perspective. It is an aesthetic means of bringing solidarity to the community as a sacred object, and an aesthetic that has everything to do with what all of Europe experienced several centuries ago. Contemporary theatre perceives its roots in these practices and in a certain modernity that links distances, performance, spectacle, collective participation in the event and in the sacred, despite the passage of time. Hence an interest for these forms in contemporary theatre.

Short digression: the amateur theatre in the contemporary moment

What Élie Konigson has called "scaffold theatre" has not died away but has in fact developed even into the contemporary era. It manifests itself in festivals of all kinds, but also in the operations of amateur theatre, even if it has had to adopt different aesthetic forms.[6] As such, some of its traits and in particular those related to staging, are still observable today: community, sharing, interaction of different parties; movement, procession, itinerary through the city; aesthetic and social function of integration and harmonisation. It could be argued that contemporary amateur theatre, much like sporting events, religious ceremonies or popular and municipal festivals (which are on the rise today), functions as a stabilising non-institutional institution to foster social calm. The citizens' platform provides a buffer against the infernal aesthetic machine from the professional "trestle stage" that comes from outside and goes against the harmony and cohesion of the social body. This platform is one of integration, promoting peace and reconciliation – a machine for forging social links. Based on this schema, professional theatre is the space of transgression, of complexity and critique. However, in actuality, this is far from the case, especially given that it is often the model preferred by amateurs who only see their practice as a gateway to professionalism or star power. For such individuals, neither form of theatre is the object of an aesthetic or political reflection. In order to establish its difference, amateurism must reject the individualism that plagues professional theatre. Professional theatre must also be a precise reference and not play the role of a sort of pop idol or be confused for being a type of training course. For its part, amateur theatre must not be linked to either.

However, it can be seen today that a large number of amateur practitioners are able to loosen themselves from the grip of the spectators, directors, star power, television, careerism and the entertainment industry. Such practitioners can bring together a semi-public audience and organise synergistic efforts. It is also a fact worthy of note that in its structure, its reception and its very aesthetic (and no theory is ostensibly needed to observe this), amateur theatre can innovate and reconnect with its past. In this sense, it is not limited to worn-out lines and repetition, or, for that matter, to a facile celebration of the world. But the fact that contemporary theatre, festive and/or amateur, fosters links between citizens does not necessarily signify an intention to either celebrate existing political power or to conform to aesthetic practices. And while it is seen as symbolically different from professional theatre, it is worth considering the ways in which the symbolic functions of both forms can intersect: forming a theatre that is simultaneously platform (scaffold) and trestle stage, amateur and professional, internal and external to the social structure? The issue seems to lie there. Not in an enterprise of harmonisation, or pacifying synthesis, but in a practical effort and bridging contradictions.

In light of this, we could consider the case of militant theatre as a point of departure. Such theatre, as Olivier Neveux's doctoral thesis dissertation points out,[7] though apparently focused on struggle, is not different in principle from scaffold theatre. It too stages the harmony specific to a particular social body, the oppressed, while representing either in a traditional or non-traditional way narratives or dramas, which, via the struggle in question, can lead to the ultimate struggle of the oppressed and thus to a definitive harmony, seen as the triumph of the proletariat. The social body speaks to the social body, the oppressed to the oppressed, the proletariat to the proletariat – at least in principle – from within. In this mode of operation, strictly amateur militant theatre is seen as one of the instruments of the struggles led by citizens desirous of finding other forms of action (the train operators in Avignon in 1975, for example) to bolster the cohesion of the struggles, explain political issues to those who can be rallied and, in doing this, convince the more reticent.

However, because such a situation is very rare – the proletariat are not enticed to go to the theatre – the idea is then to deploy non-oppressed individuals into action, who work in the service of the oppressed and the Revolution and, also, to move beyond the amateur/professional dichotomy by mixing amateurs and professionals (such is the case of the Z theatre group). One key aspect of finding such a solution, therefore, is to do away with the notion of the "profession of acting", replacing it with the "function of being an actor". As such, the actor (from outside) enters into the social struggle on an equal footing, without giving up his particular skills and without instituting them as necessary elements of his performance (since art is at the service of the struggle and not the other way around). This amounts to advocating the recognition of a new figure, capable of bearing the "very stigma of amateur practice (weakness of acting, the predominance of the individual over the actor)" and of making it "one of the forms of his singularity".[8] This new figure would also take the necessary steps to equip themselves with techniques from professional acting. As such, it becomes possible to foster a dialogue between social insiders and outsiders, since their status and skills would come together within the same political performative action. This could set in motion formal innovation effects both within the performance as well as within the session itself. Though the individualist and careerist social mentality has always wanted to take back the reins of the professional actor in the theatre (even if it's a militant or political one), it is hard to ignore attempts at this aforementioned action.

If we want to move past the idea that grant-aided professional theatre "helps" amateurs become "true actors" (and thereby humiliate them under the guise of helping them), another way must be found: both professionals and amateurs can work side by side, with the knowledge that their styles and approaches are different. Similarly, by blending the traditional theatre audience with the "semi-audience" from social groups who have come to see their representatives onstage, we open the way for a heterogeneous, problematic and perhaps even contradictory audience since expectations differ wildly.

This hybridity can be a way of forcing the scaffold and the trestle stage to (violently?) co-exist without proclaiming their harmony, or without suggesting that either should be displaced by the other. Thus, the question will no longer be whether amateur dramatics can serve to regenerate theatre life as a whole, as this would amount to institutionalising it. Amateur actors do impromptu cost-free experimentation, which lead to official performances later on. Instead, the issue will be how to create the conditions necessary for the interaction between these two symbolic functions and the dramatic modes described by Konigson, both within the theatrical space and during the session. This practice of heterogeneity and hybridity might serve to re-establish the fact that the participants in a theatrical session, or gathering, be they "actors" or "spectators", come into the building for different reasons, behave in different ways, play in their different ways, and represent all together the contradictory facets of the social structure of which they are a part.

A story of thresholds rather than of ruptures

To return to the evolution that we began to trace before branching off to consider an old and new form of theatre, we must underscore one additional point: the arrival of a "trestle-stage theatre" produced by artisans dedicated to this crafts, constitutes the official origins of a modern theatre that clearly distinguishes those who watch and pay to watch from those whose trade it is to be watched, to play and to make a profit from this exercise. Furthermore, theatrical sites and spaces owe their development to the elaboration of this new structure in the architecture and urbanistic sense of term, and to the establishment of this new, closed and for-profit place. As we have mentioned, medieval and post-medieval spaces relied on a fragmentary, open and eclectic scenery, and this scenery was seen as a series of symbolic and emblematic representations meant to provide a non-illusionistic frame for the speech and actions of the players. The new medieval and post-medieval theatre, on the other hand, without immediately abandoning this type of stagecraft, gravitated slowly towards the feigned representation of a space. In other words, it discovered the usefulness of perspectivist techniques.

Thus, due to this invention of perspective, both in the Renaissance and the sixteenth century, dramatic performance was centred on the image of the hero at the centre of the universe, and at the same time, it turned the house into a fictive "reality" that was both possible and that corresponded with a great, promised future. The spectator, seized by the technical marvels of perspective, witnessed a dramatic space that pointed to a different world where other represented men, characters in other words, seemed to experience stories both familiar and strange. But once again, it is key to remember that there is no rupture in history, least of all in the history of theatre and stagecraft: the Elizabethan space and the space of the Spanish Golden Age are simultaneously based on medieval drama and the re-emerging classical theatre. The spaces portrayed are multiple, or triple, in England – the platform for fights, the stage for negotiations and trials, the bedroom for intimacies – and the spectacle in those cases had to play to a generally popular audience: the entire society and its mode of operating are represented. The compartmentalised stage backdrops that are emblematic, symbolic or simply indicative, continue to be used in France until the 1640s, without dissatisfying audiences (unlike the theorists). Therefore, before the stage became unitary and fixed, in the 1640s in a number of theatrical genres, and for a short time only (since in the eighteenth century, there was a renewed interest in the stage with three backdrops and perspectives) the practice of compartments was a widespread one. All that was needed was a curtain that could be opened, or a beam in the distance to provide the illusion of a cave, apartment or prison, all of whose emblematic signs were displayed, often without any real need for perspective.

But beyond this overlapping of forms and thresholds that pleasingly problematise a too often schematic history of theatre, it becomes clearer, after our rapid examination of the theatres of antiquity and the middle ages, how much this "referential stagecraft" has informed and shaped the major tendencies of contemporary theatre: theatre as ceremony, spectacle and entertainment, a 180-degree system, auditorium, single-focus perspective, linear, circular, trestles, physical movement with scene changes. All these elements already exist as archetypes to be "reinvented", displaced and appropriated in the twentieth century.

Elizabethan theatre and the so-called "wooden O"

The Elizabethan theatrical space is just as instructive from this point of view. If, in terms of stagecraft, it derives from medieval theatre, it is also a major space in which modern apparatuses are invented. Indeed, between the middle of the sixteenth century (from 1576, when James Burbage, actor and Count of Leicester, built a permanent theatre with actors and resident musicians) and 1642 (when theatre was banned by the Puritans), a theatre that was attended by aristocrats, the bourgeoisie and the masses developed in England. Marlowe, Shakespeare, Ben Jonson, John Ford and other actors known in France, were among those who were featured in this theatre. Born in the courtyards of inns, played outdoors and in daylight (which explains why it was then surrounded by galleries), it moved very quickly to privately owned buildings located on the outskirts of the city and reserved for entertainment. Initially, the actors would set up their boards against the side of gallery and the wealthiest spectators would be found in the three other galleries. The poor attendees would stand in the yard. The first theatres near London were, at the outset, built from light wood, before later being constructed out of hardwood (like the Globe, Shakespeare's theatre, recently rebuilt on the banks of the Thames by a wealthy American) based on the same model – their often, but not always, circular or elliptical shape was reminiscent of that of medieval theatre.

An overhanging stage leads from a side stage adjoining the galleries to the middle of the courtyard (of the theatre or inn) and allowed the actors to truly "come into contact" with the standing audience, composed of people from the lower classes. The stage was protected by an awning, which was often masked by a curtain, and two doors provided access to the wings (and the offstage space). It was on this inner stage that the most secretive moments of the drama were played, and where characters hid. Above this stage, beside the benches of the wealthy theatregoers (who were there to be seen and admired and who thus saw the actors up close but from the back), the first balcony functioned as another space (upper stage). This is the balcony from where Shakespeare's Juliet and the pompous Brutus speak. Additionally, an orchestra plays on the second balcony from behind the stage, and often are a part of the play and the fiction.

Because Elizabethan theatre is played in several distinct places and in a close relationship with the audience, it becomes a place that represents a whole world, seems astonishingly modern and serves as a model for numerous performances in the twentieth century. However, while Shakespeare's "wooden O" is a reality that existed, there were theatres at the time, which were neither circular nor elliptical and were organised around the trestle stages, especially in courtyard or in a rectangular room.

Last but not least, this theatre that brings together artists capable of playing and writing a text (and the two are sometimes one and the same), which operates outside of the city. Sometimes it was *extra-muros*, such as the South Bank in London, located quite literally on the margins, watching the city and welcoming those citizens who decide to cross the bridge and go beyond the city walls. In so doing, it was also on the margins in an urbanistic sense: fragile and vulnerable to being banned, but special also, since it was not seen as ceremoniously depicting the harmony of the social body, but rather problematising it (even if that meant providing, at the end of the play, a moral and political "happy ending" through fictional representation in a particular space, and in a place that is away from the city. This theatre is not an outlaw but existed on the margins of the law, allowed by it but not indefinitely. Theatre precincts and troupes therefore urgently invent stories that speak of what happens within the walls of the city; stories that speak of this "real" society that they seek to portray.

While medieval theatre was performed in the streets – or outdoors, at any rate – sixteenth- to seventeenth-century theatre continued to be performed in public squares, as well as in the streets and on bridges and often in the courtyard of colleges and of private residences (in England) or at the courts of kings and popes in France and Italy. However, theatre of this period began to orient itself more and more to specific places. Theatres became buildings and it is in the eighteenth century that this process was solidified in Paris as well as in the French provinces, in London and all of Europe.

The "classic" French theatrical space: a rectangle

It was in the sixteenth century in Italy and the seventeenth century in the royal courts of France that the standard stagecraft began to model itself on two centuries of theatre history. Practitioners now aimed for an ideal illusion at odds with the actual conditions of life. They aimed for a clear separation of house from stage and for the creation of a fictive world through stagecraft. These centuries saw a growth in the number of practitioners, for example Sebastiano Serlo (1475–1554), a sculptor and theorist known as Francis I of France who came to the court of Fontainebleau and who revisited Vitruvius in the light of discoveries made in the Italian Renaissance. In the *Second Book on Perspective* of his treatise on architecture devoted to the stages and theatres, he assessed the possibility of representing depth on a flat surface (the backdrop) and applying it to the staging area.[9] The symbolic and emblematic "reading" that the audience easily perceives had never been called into question, yet there was a desire to minimise or do away with the "emblematic stagecraft" in favour of a perspectivist illusion. And to avoid the problems of scale,[10] the stage was divided into two parts: the back part of the stage would be fitted with the scenery placed in an oblique manner to create the single-focus perspective of the vanishing point picture plane; the front part was reserved for the actor, and its floor was not subject to perspective. For several centuries, scenographers sought to resolve this opposition in order to make it more fluid.

Therefore, the sixteenth century in Italy (especially in Rome and Florence) and the seventeenth century in France, witnessed a transition from the medieval symbolic, emblematic and indicative scenography, with its "mansions", to a system of perspective. It is within this perspective staging system that actors, authors, technicians, decorators and future scenographers end up carving out their roles. Since that time, staging, having become a much more impressive affair, has benefited from this division of tasks.

At the courts

In the royal and papal courts[11] of the sixteenth and seventeenth centuries, it became a custom to set up wooden stages in large rooms with generally hosted ceremonies, balls and court ballets or to construct garden houses for the occasion. Little by little, in Europe – and especially in Italy – the courts became equipped with prestigious rooms and machines. To run them, the courts hired a plethora of stage managers skilled in the art of perspective having studied Vitruvius and, especially Serlo, as well as teams of engineers, often previously trained in the techniques of naval construction. It would be an appropriate metaphor to say that the theatre site is a ship with a naval machinery that controls the scenery and creates illusion through the deployment of a scenic apparatus, an army of sailors tending to the pulleys, tightening the halyard, hoisting and lowering the sails, so that the vessel of the spectacle can move, leave the port of reality and go on to the high seas of the staged fiction. In this wooden building, one runs certain risks (such as that of starting a fire and burning down the theatre, which actually happens). A team spirit is necessary for smooth manoeuvres, so that on the bridge (the stage), the main protagonists, the most visible people, take passengers on (entrance onstage), take care of the journey (the performance) and then the return (the curtain call).

Consequently, for a long time, until the 1640s in France, the stage and the auditorium at court were one and the same space, a large staircase linking both and allowing an aristocratic audience to go to dance during ballet intermissions or the actors to do down and dance with the audience. Large chandeliers, containing costly white wax candles, hung above the proscenium and the room. Mirrors were used to reflect the bright objects placed onstage, such as candles and oil lamps, and the back of the stage. The machines indispensable to these sorts of festivities were also equipped with lights. Chinese lanterns and various light effects were widely used. Additionally, the actors would don lavish costumes in order to shine and dazzle the audience. Actors very often cross-dressed and gold, crystal, silk ribbons, feathers and flowers were required by custom.

All of this was meant to provoke stupor and admiration and create a portrait of spectacular glory: the ideal was *marvel*, and for this all the resources of science and craftsmanship were mobilised, to dazzle attendees with these productions commissioned and closely observed by the prince in Italy, or the king in France. The king, placed at the centre of the single-focus audience, was the eye of the spectacle; hence, the term used by Italian stage decorators to describe the best seat in the audience: the "prince's eye". The king could thus fully enjoy the Italian innovations in perspective as he was placed at the very centre: the origin of the vanishing point in the image plane of the scenery based on a colonnade infinitely receding or a window opened on to a view that appears to extend infinitely far. The stage floor also formed part of the optical illusion: it was built at a slight incline and in a checkerboard pattern, to create the illusion of depth.

In the cities

By contrast, the playhouses in the French cities (Paris, Rouen and Lyon, for example) were managed by a few craftsmen. They were shoddy places in which the actors also had to double up as painters and decorators. The stage would be poorly lit by a meagre row of candles, which were decidedly inferior to the court productions that everyone tried to imitate. The candle lighting forced each act to last only around twenty-five to thirty minutes. The wicks of the candles would then be trimmed so they could keep burning.

The Hôtel de Bourgogne, like the Théâtre du Marais, were "French-style theatres", long rectangles with lateral booths, and their width was merely approximately 12 metres. The Palais-Royal and the Hôtel des Fossés Saint-Germain were the first theatres to acquire the round basic shape of the Italian proscenium arch theatre. The stage, which became less wide, was at head height for the standing spectators in the pit. The backdrops consisted for the most part of geometric perspective effects that would artificially give the overall picture greater depth as well as an air of pomposity. The spectators would thus enjoy the magical effects of perspective, which exerted such powerful fascination at the time. They would virtually experience the so-called "prince's eye" and feel "at the centre" of the representation, even if they were far way, since the perspective scenery tended toward infinity. For all these reasons, the compartmentalised scenery of the Middle Ages, based on symbolism and suggestion, was abandoned.[12] The space became unified and often represented, at the end of the century, no more than a "general palace", a pompous antechamber, a temple or a military camp where anything could take place (a wood or a clearing for a pastoral, the interior of a house of a public square for comedies). These sceneries were veritable crossroads, places where characters met, whether they came from "outside", an exterior place where an action took place, or from other rooms in the "palace", where other threatening intrigues took shape.

Moreover, this scenery was closed off on top, since the fly system was hidden by a large strip of canvas on which a sky and clouds are painted. The spectators therefore saw only a "box" of which only one side was open, through which they perceived characters, surrounded by lateral walls and by the horizontal effect of the sky. Transported by the depth represented by the perspective scenery and by the floor that angled upward toward the vanishing point of the backdrop, they would take in the show as if watching scenes from another, distant world. This world was a noble and heroic one that gave the semblance of being absolutely elsewhere and different from reality, but that, nonetheless, maintained a certain physical resemblance with this reality, since the stage was, in another sense, close and clearly filled with the physical presence of the spectators themselves.

Indeed, from 1637 onwards (since the success of *Le Cid*), the Théâtre du Marais rented seats on the stage itself, initially on the sides, and sometimes at the back of the stage. Consequently, the stage had on it about a hundred spectators who became a group of silent watchers and voyeur characters whose reactions were closely watched. This practice became widespread throughout the seventeenth century and, in the context of the theatre, the words "bench" and "seat" came to define this new category of spectators. The stage would only be cleared when there was major spectacle, and the practice of "stage benches" continued until 1759. It is interesting to note that these spectators were, in a sense, part of the show since their reactions could easily be observed. The meaning or importance of these reactions could also be assessed. The "theatre benches" placed on the stage were often filled with young, boisterous and unruly socialites. Their faces were turned towards the auditorium and the stalls, which were mainly filled with women and aristocrats. Nevertheless, the benches and the stalls provided the ideal audience while the standing spectators of the parterre (nowadays known as the orchestra) consisted of a mixed group of people who talked incessantly. Whistling was a common practice in the 1680s, and though there were attempts to reduce the number of valets and truculent musketeers, the parterre was used to heckle actors and sling insults. The bourgeois spectators, whether they were robins or artisans, would sit side by side and glance behind them at the terraced seats of the amphitheatre filled with scholars and authors who were either fans or critics of the play. It was particularly difficult to satisfy three such audiences – the ideal audience, the parterre and the scholars – all at the same time. As such, playwrights aligned themselves more and more to the "regular people", thereby excluding the pedants in the amphitheatre and the ostentatious socialites of the "benches", in an attempt to unite the parterre and the stalls around a shared aesthetic.

Italian-style theatre

During this same period, changes in theatre design determined the move away from the elongated rectangular form of the *théâtre du Jeu de paume* – theatres set up on tennis courts that, as we have seen, was a significant cultural and social phenomenon of the time – towards the Italian proscenium arch theatre characterised by a round auditorium. The auditorium was built in the eighteenth century as an enlarged form of the classical "horseshoe" semicircle: as a "truncated" ellipse that allowed for the seating of the largest number of spectators possible in a limited space, with a parterre filled essentially by spectators from the lower classes and with boxes occupied by spectators from different social strata, with the richer below and the poor above. At the end of the eighteenth century, however, the orchestra became a place that was no longer for the lower classes, as the poorest attendees were now seated in the gods (the upper balconies). While the spectator was trained to be silent and sit still, the apparatus that became part of the nineteenth century was set in place: when staging *Clytemnestra*, the Count of Lauraguais bought the "theatre seats" in 1759 and cleared the stage of spectators, an act that elevated the fiction to a higher degree of prominence, reinforced the illusion of the "theatre box" and allowed for a more expansive scenography to the point where the stage could now be divided into several places. In the theatre, acting was no longer merely a question of voice; one also had to show, even if this lead to a form of hyperrealism. Voltaire proposed a tripartite scenery, as if to return to the compartments of the beginning of the seventeenth century, in a more sophisticated form, which allowed for three different places alongside the front stage: actors would thus act out the fictional story in front of backdrops appropriate to the places in which it took place. In other words, one now had to attempt to resemble reality as much as possible – at least the reality suggested by the play. What was said had to be visible and theatre professionals, particularly stage managers, had to be brought in to give the audience an illusion of reality, thanks to their technical expertise. This is how Lemierre had huge success with his *Guillaume Tell*: by asking his stage managers to arrange the superb special effect of the apple pierced by an arrow. It still has us shuddering with delight.

Make way for the visible!

All these changes work together to augment the proportions, real and perceived, of the stage; to emphatically underscore the separation of the house from the stage through the effects of the curtain; to compose sumptuous and moving scenes for the audience; and also, to the extent possible, to focus lighting (through the use of oil lamps and mirrors). From then on, the practice of filling the stage with furniture, objects and massive sets will be a widespread one during the nineteenth century. Playing with entrances also became a common thing: from the sides of the stage, the back, beneath and the fly system, as in the last act of *Ruy Blas*. As a result, the spectator became witness to a sort of reality or hyperreality in which they would project themselves. The painter-decorators, spurred on by the excessive and sometimes utopian stage directions of the romanticism,[13] excelled at representing multiple sites with one single set design, within the unifying framework of Italian-style theatrical representation. Action in the romantic era thus found an apt theatrical scenery to support it: no more elliptical spaces or voids, fewer offstage speeches; these were the new rules.

The realist drama that ensued, as well as melodrama, followed the same path: everything that was performed had to be commented on by the text, and the stage had to be faithful to the text so as to give the impression of a reality, which the spectator could validate. Distance, so intimately linked to the theatre up until then, tended to be effaced and the mechanisms of staging were employed to satisfy the spectator's supposed desire for reality. As a result, the actors onstage essentially had characters, which pre-existed their roles: the dream of theatre was now to become an exceptional reality for those who watched it.

Faced with an audience ready to appreciate the performance and the brilliant craftsmanship of the set design from a distance, and to display their enjoyment, the actors and set designers tried their best to be sufficiently visible in order to be sufficiently appreciated. However, since the conditions of representation are by nature imperfect, these attempts at pure realism and perfect illusion had to be reassessed to a considerable degree. Paradoxically, the theatre of realist illusion faced its most robust challenge at the moment when electricity was invented. Despite the fact that it became possible to bring darkness down over the house and direct light with greater precision, thereby creating an effect through the atmospheres created by lighting, the notion of a total illusion was increasingly brought into question. The fact that innovations in staging techniques allowing for easier movement of objects and sets in large, well-equipped theatres were at their peak, did nothing to prevent this.

Scenography

Modern "scenography" makes its appearance under these circumstances. A mysterious word, "scenography", when used nowadays, immediately marks its user as a professional or an informed amateur. This "serious" word, which is reminiscent of the Greek (*skene*, the stage; *graphein*, to write, to note, to paint; and hence *skenographia*, painting in the theatre and art of painting scenery), now covers cognate domains and evokes the notion of a theatricalisation of social practices. One now speaks of the scenography of a place from the moment it begins to call attention to itself, the way a spectacle does. Consequently, the term is frequently associated with the layout of exhibitions, but also with the organisation of court sessions, with political gatherings and speeches, with religious ceremonies and for all sorts of *representation*, a complex, laden term that we will later analyse.

However, since our objective at this point is to replace this term with its theatrical context, we consider *scenography*, a word that denoted the craft of theatre painters and designers in antiquity, to have appeared in the French language in the fifteenth century, with the rediscovery of Vitruvius, a Roman architect of the first century BC. In this context, it was a technique specific to the art of perspective and thus linked to the aesthetic of painting, architecture and urban design. This technique, adapted to the new (or reinvented) art of theatre in the sixteenth century, allowed for the creation of scenery for the performance of plays in a given place. Theatre could thus be theoretically and practically based on a framework, with scenery and machines, inside a building, which was at first perfunctory, but later conceived specifically by a scenographer for this purpose. It was thus normal for theatre to evolve along with the changes occurring in the techniques of pictorial perspective, particularly in the way it sought to make stage decor effective and improve illusionistic effects. It was also inevitable that the theatre would take its cues from advances in machinery (which came primarily from the field of naval construction). Such advances became a necessity: pulleys, riggings, various mechanisms for moving objects across spaces, architecture and its techniques of organising buildings based on their usage.

During the eighteenth and nineteenth centuries, theatre practice was oriented towards a fine-tuned perspective technique, close to that of an optical illusion, and towards a profusion of decorations. The illusory field of the "three-sided box" was never questioned. However, at the instigation of directors, modern stage designers supplant the routine and the subterfuges of naturalism. The end of the nineteenth century saw widespread reflection on the theatrical space, on the translation of time on the stage, and on the presence of the actor. In opposition to romantic and naturalistic decoration, active space and, indeed, space *as* actor, were the alternative phenomena by which stage designers and directors sought to establish a signifying point of on the world as it was staged. What resulted was a self-critical approach to the division of space, time and action, which was meant to give back a symbolic, signifying and poetic value to the drama being staged. Space became a metaphor and a representation of itself, which acquired artistic dignity and legitimacy.

Consequently, the art consisted of organising the stage, the theatrical space and the layout of the stage design itself, became the *art of critical reflection on, and translation of, space*, in concert with the other practitioners of the theatre art. As the art of manipulating space and fashioning representation, scenography therefore came to include the art of set design, but also that of the physical arrangement of the theatre building itself and of all its intermediary spaces. This was, of course, understood in very diverse ways. The job of the scenographer is thus to *transcribe* space, or to write in space, using his own signs. Working with the director, this visual artist writes a coherent system that frames both acting and the spectator's interpretation of the drama. As such, it is no longer a matter of mere decoration or pure illustration of a text based on stage directions, but of a manipulation of space, a set of technical and artistic mechanisms that orient the meaning of the staged fiction through a close synergy with the material conditions of staging, and that has an artistic independence of its own.

Therefore, contemporary scenography has a tendency to break the frontal dynamic of spectatorship, and to open the so-called "proscenium box" by arranging the seating of spectators in ways different to the single-focus perspective; to restructure sets by consciously bringing space to life through the use of theatrical emblems, such as lighting, objects and scenic architecture.

Promoting attention

Evidently, this craft aims to focus the spectator's attention on the spectacle, to guide their gaze and their ability to listen, and even, sometimes, to underscore the instability and uncertainties of their perception. The aim of the scenographer is thus to aid all practitioners in orienting the audience *towards* the performance and *to* the fiction represented.

These assertions may seem self-evident; however, they do not go without saying, since the session of the theatre has resulted from a struggle between professionals to reduce the audience to silence – admittedly, for its own pleasure, or for the intended pleasure – and to capture its attention through marvel, spectator involvement or surprise, so that actors can play and be watched, and so that the fiction can be performed without (too many) obstacles. The motive of theatre as social event and as a gathering of people around the staging of a fiction has thus often been displaced by the practice of an art representation given as the absolute centre and *raison d'être* of the event.

In light of this, scenography now occupies a central role both in the architectural apparatus of the building itself, and in the operation of surprising and capturing the attention of the spectators, thereby allowing them to project a degree of imagination into the actors' space. As we shall see, little by little, scenography endeavoured to represent a division between fiction and reality, between actors and spectators, a division that encourages what is known as the "fourth wall". However, at the same time, since it also constitutes a critical artistic reflection in action, the practice of scenography also calls into question this "wall", supplanting its illusion in the representation of the spectacle itself, which is self-reflexively shown to be a machine, or a clearly material work of art. Indeed, scenography functions on an essential contradiction: the first "movement" of this dialectical process is to orient the spectator towards a fiction illusion by means of a scenic and architectural apparatus, the second is to show them the art of the illusion so that they can become simultaneously aware of "being at the theatre" and of witnessing a crafted artistic production from the very first moment they enter the fiction.

5

THE ART OF PERSPECTIVE AND THE SOCIAL SPACE

An issue that remains unresolved is the much-discussed concept of stage illusion, which rests on the sacrosanct principle of perspective. The fact that it is at once a reality, a technique and a sort of myth will form the basis of this chapter. As we have seen, the art of perspective was well known in the sixteenth and seventeenth centuries, to the point where it became institutionalised, structuring staging and scenery. From that period, the theatre represented the space mankind occupied with a precise technique that depicted the world by means of a mathematical and geometrical system of illusion, which suggested an infinite extension of space that the style of the actor and the imagination of the practitioners and spectators would appropriate and modify. The stage was filled with geometrical signs, which gave it the structure necessary to form an image, and thus show through fiction what mathematical science made available to the mind.

As we have seen in the previous chapter, perspective techniques in the theatre, since the sixteenth century at least, have allowed practitioners to represent the world within a system that places the body of the actor against a geometrical plane that represents a faraway place and conjures up a feeling of infinity. This materialisation of infinity in perspective creates the illusion of a fictional space that is represented on the backdrop, either on a part of it or forming the entirety of the scenery (as suggested by the structures located on either side of the stage and by the stage's framing systems). This then appropriates the actors' bodies to transform them into bodies of characters within a spatial fiction into which the ideal spectator, located in the "prince's eye", may project herself. As such, the representational space, oriented toward infinity, is framed by precise delineations and is made available to the actors' bodies, to their voices and to the text they interpret. The end result is that a dramatic space is constituted, and a fiction is created where man is, in the true sense of the term, an actor. The stage and the dramatic space are, therefore, essentially human spaces.

Italy, the "prince's eye" and Europe

One key issue is the question of the person to whom this image of mankind is addressed, and of what kind of man and woman is depicted. Evidently, in the sixteenth century, at the Florentine court of the Medici, the main spectator of perspective is the one who commissioned it, paid for and produced it, all in the service of the prince. This is how the invention of perspective became so politicised. The apparatus of illusionistic staging of *court theatre* – whether it was the court of Florence, that of papal Rome or later that of the king of France and his ministers – afforded a special place to the prince as the spectator par excellence of the action onstage. Consequently, the spectacle, which the prince attended, became one of power. The explicit symbolism of rites and ceremonies – coronations, entries, funerals – is, based on this design, supported by the quiet or implicit signs of calculated focusing of attention, to the extent that this phenomenon saw the emergence of a new regime of the symbolism of power, as a result of the attention placed on the positioning of the prince within the representation.

The instruments of perspective, the organisation of this mechanism of self-representational power, and the *apparently* theological nature of the princely gaze were shaped by techniques conceived by Vasari in 1565 (at the Palazzo Vecchio) and by Buontalenti in 1586 (at the Ufizi). The stage has the ideal point of vision, which places itself at the service of this "total gaze". In this sense, the arts, and particularly theatre, function as *instrumentum regni*: a rhetorical machine used for persuading the subjects of the prince, by depicting the elevation of the pontifical or princely power to become an absolute one. It could be said therefore that such developments in the field of optics in the Italian court theatre, the creation of the theatre house, of a stage and of a certain kind of scenery, enabled the theatre of the Medici dynasty to effectively promote a political power that portrayed itself as an essential "eye" that controlled places, times and the social structure. This all-seeing eye was central and constituted *in theory* the ideal spectacle of an attention oriented toward a theatre that demonstrated the organisation of the organisation and government of Florentine society. It is by virtue of this eye that the spectators assembled in a collective enterprise of belief in and idealisation of the prince that governed them. The analysis of theatrical perspective in Renaissance Italy, and particularly its attempt at reformulating and redefining the theatrical space itself as a space of human action and of the society given in a contemporary social and historical moment, shows that the spectator is *theoretically* subjected to the point of view of the prince, to its gaze and to its will to control. The gaze of the prince attends to all the effects of which it is the cause: the vanishing point does not lead to an opening, but to a sort of mirror held up to the gaze of the prince, who contemplates it (and thus himself) and masters all of its signs.

In the midst of the robust variety of Italian experiments in the sixteenth century,[1] the Florentine court theatre thus exhibits the central and dominant position of the prince, master of illusion and reality, of nature and the society.

But the mechanism that governed this court theatre, which was very different from the theatres in the cities, was above all a rhetorical *theoretical* one: the seat of the prince was a place saturated with analogies, and was the only place from which the spectacle was sensually complete and significant, since it was, by nature, different from the *practical* viewpoint of the spectators. But, here again, other points of view exist besides that of the prince: the oblique points of view of the spectators reveal to them the visual deception of the machines and the scenery, through a sort of Brechtian alienation effect *avant la lettre*. This effect revealed, additionally, that the prince was himself not totally absorbed in this illusion, which rendered him master of reality, of nature and of the society. This political perspective seems simultaneously capable of creating other, less theoretical and less optimal, vantage points. Indeed, given the dynamic of the theatre, any performance allows spectators other than the ideal spectator to see and to have themselves seen. Performance also allows actors to "come out of perspective" with or without their text, and permits other practitioners and spectators to exist within a given precinct that is, in principle, "confiscated" by a theoretical illusion. As a result, while perspective becomes a convenient means of materialising infinity itself through a phenomenon created by art, it also closes in on itself, and thus becomes instrumentalised for the purposes of illusionistic representation and for the political designs that control it.

The Medici dynasty's sixteenth-century illusionistic theatre was more of a paradigm than a strict model adopted by the theatres of the other major courts of Europe. There were some essential differences: in Paris and Madrid, court theatre was considered as an auxiliary to real power. For the House of Valois and for Felipe IV of Spain, it compensated for a relative loss of authority. French theatre of the sixteenth and seventeenth centuries was thus able, in part, to utilise this mechanism. And as we have previously outlined, theatres within cities and towns functioned differently. Nevertheless, the change from a feudal monarchy to an administrative one in France also meant a transition to the customs and practices of the court of Rome and that of Florence, due to the accession to the French throne of two Florentine regent queens, and then of two cardinals of the Roman church. Additionally, from the moment theatre started to be considered as more than the dramatic text, the architects, scenographers, machinists and painters, which provided "spectacles of the Italian court" to the court of France, and "theatre of the Italian court" under Richelieu, were almost all Italians. However, this Italian theatre imported into France was initially considered as a sign of weakness and of vulgar taste in the eyes of Parisian theatregoers. Richelieu's contempt for the Florentine entourage of Marie de Médicis also contributed to the disfavour of the "Italian illusion", which held that representation and power were necessarily linked. The political government through the arts, possible in a society like Italy's, deeply bound together by a government of ecclesiastic minds, liturgy, preaching and baroque processions, was not, by itself, credible in France. By contrast, Richelieu's political theatre consisted, in the beginning, of a public and hyperreal staging of the beheading of his enemies. Only later emerged the "dazzling visibility" of the spectacles of the Palais-Cardinal,[2] which were intended to display to the diplomatic corps the immense authority that Richelieu's military victories and the defeat of the great feudal lords of the interior conferred upon him and on the king.

The secularised space

Alongside these changes, the evolution of science caused the notion of indefinite and infinite space to break the ecclesiastical boundaries originally assigned to it. Space became an element allowing for the institution of operations of knowledge and was eventually characterised as a space of relativity, of representation and of method. The great displays of Italian perspective theatre left a major imprint on the sixteenth century, on the Roman court and on that of the Medici. Copernicus' beliefs spread rapidly in Europe, even if his theory was not wholly embraced. From the 1640s onwards, no scholar or philosopher believed anymore that the earth was motionless at the centre of the universe, and the vast majority of writers adhered to the idea that the sun and the planets do not rotate around the frame where God had chosen to create man. The heliocentric model therefore began to hold sway, bringing ruin on the idea of the immutability and perfection of heaven, which also meant that the laws of physics were now considered to be the same on earth as in heaven and that the laws of movement here and above were the same. Scholars of physics began to explore the laws, which presided over a differently conceived earth and heaven.

For scholars who continued to link physics and metaphysics in their work, mathematics was thought to be the appropriate language for finding answers to the structure of the cosmos, to the question of the finiteness or infiniteness of space and to that of the existence or non-existence of the ether. It was particularly pertinent to the question of whether space was consubstantial with God. In effect, the great problem was to know whether space was still the domain of God, whether it was only natural, or human, or whether one should, at least provisionally, distinguish between what one can affirm mathematically about space and what one must leave to metaphysics. Whatever their attitudes and responses to this question, philosophers sought to create an abstract, mathematical space capable of accounting for a natural, physical space, which, as it was thought, could not, in principle be excluded from metaphysics. At the same time, this constitution of this abstract space implied a sidelining, if only a provisional one, of the idea of God, and necessitated a human formalisation that could allow the building of a geometry given as a human, abstract and intellectual activity. Space, or the space that mathematics can provisionally define, was now extracted from the orb of the divine. As Cartesian geometry spread in Europe, the whole of observable space was now identifiable in nature, and could thus be perceived, theoretically elaborated and penetrated by man. The question then emerged as to whether it could be represented by means of an abstract discourse (mathematics), a figurative discourse (that today we call literature) or even by a metaphorical system (representation).

This point of view of the theoretical and mathematical mastery of space, regardless of its dimensions, had consequences not only for science, but also for representation. Indeed, if we provisionally disregard the fact that representation must not and cannot, by nature, represent infinity – which belongs to the domain of God and that moreover, is an abstraction difficult for the mind to conceive of, and therefore also particularly difficult to represent with words and objects – it becomes clear that modes of representation, including the theatre, can surpass boundary lines with the aid of geometrical techniques. Further, by virtue of the impact of their own arts, these modes of representation (which include theatre) can attain other limits, which may themselves, in turn, be further extended by the dynamics at work in them and by the evolution and progress of their techniques. And even if we admit that these arts can never truly represent the infinite, and will merely convey that which is material, we must also admit that that they also allow artists to push the boundaries of the representation of space. This tension underlines the fact that while it was not possible to represent that which was not natural space, i.e. the infinite, it was no longer impossible to strive to represent it, to the extent that the infinite could be made to become natural. Consequently, the principle of representation, frustrated by the qualitative boundary, which separated material, geometric space from infinite space, which belonged to God, immediately gained an extended reach. If previously representation did not concern itself with showing or speaking of what existed in the divine realm (since this would not only be blasphemous, but that the art of representation was deprived of access to the signs, discourse and mode of language needed to carry it out), this same art was now able to explore the totality of a secularised world, deepening, moreover, its discourse, at a time when the infinite began to be viewed as something attainable by, and even because of, geometrical science.

The problem was thus a dual one. On the one hand, it was essentially impossible to extend the reach of geometry and mathematics into the conceptual realm of infinity because it grappled with the nature of God and was thus forbidden by Catholic dogma. Consequently, it was equally impossible, and even transgressive, to try to represent it. On the other hand, each scientist, philosopher and mathematician grappled with the question of the boundaries and the dimensions of space: at what point does infinity, and therefore the forbidden, begin? Where does it end? As scholars sought to determine and define the limits assigned to space, the domain of God became more distant. And as far as representation was concerned, it became possible, if not to truly represent infinity, then at least to grasp its limits (through the vanishing point, for example) or to suggest the principle through a metaphorical portrayal of the notion in speech, itself represented through the medium of art.

Therefore, by pushing the limits of the divine, and by encroaching geometrically, philosophically and artistically upon the domain of God and on his most sacred attributes of the infinite and the unrepresentable, it became possible to extend the sphere of matter and of its representation by expanding the category of the physical body and its artistic representation. By the same token, it became less possible to represent the divine world as *truly* sacred: religious representation, particularly in city theatres rather than Jesuit and Oratorian colleges, was no longer credible. This was not because it pointed to a lack of belief, but because it highlighted the impossibility of representing belief onstage. In "secularising" the bodies represented, the theatre now perceived them as an extension of matter. Hence, the evolution, at the end of the seventeenth century and at the turn of the eighteenth, into a sort of religious psychagogy and towards a reasoned analysis of religious belief, or towards a historicisation of faith, through theatrical performance. The representation of belief through theatre could no longer be considered a self-evident practice in the same way as it had been in Roman religious tragedies or in the Spanish *autos sacramentales*. The bodies of actors, the techniques of performance and the theatre's effects all created a screen that meant that the individual could no longer play the role of saints and martyrs in a self-evident way.

The notion that infinity was, if not manageable, then at least signifiable and comprehensible to man, implied that the boundary that had been imposed by religion and that (at least in theory), Descartes had attempted to maintain, started to be erased. The symbolic and the metaphorical gave way to the human, so much so that theatre could no longer have the appearance of a sacred ceremony because it was considered to be material. It accounted for space as defined by humans, which it represented materially or discursively, whether finite or infinite. As Beaumarchais observed in a manifesto in the first scene of *The Marriage of Figaro*, theatre has the exact dimensions that enable humans to represent a human story. The first scene must unveil the plot, but, simultaneously, the hero takes the exact measurements of the staging space (19 feet by 26 feet), and evaluates his strategic situation in relation to the spaces offstage. Nearly two centuries later, it is the same principle that Beckett uses in *Endgame*. Hamm, the blind and paralytic master, asks his servant Clov to take him on a "little ride" in his wheelchair, which is as much "a journey around the world" as a ride around the stage. By ordering Clov to make his body brush against the walls before taking him back "to the very centre" of the stage, Hamm seeks to determine a measurable centre and expresses a fear of not achieving this: like an actor lost on the stage he occupies, Hamm, overwhelmed by his loss of strategic bearings, moves through the space of the stage in an attempt and retrieving them. The theatre's space is thus measurable and palpable, and organised based on human proportions – and what was evident for a comedy like Beaumarchais' *Figaro* was already the case for the tragedies of the early seventeenth century.

From the sixteenth and seventeenth centuries, physical space thus became a relationality built around a human project: it was a space of *work* determined by *a* point of view, which could itself change. However, in a human space, the characters can only be human. And when they explore the unrepresentable, the world's infinity, they do so through their own speech, referring only to their human knowledge of it. As such, more than representing a world that is "other", of a kind that encourages dream or religious belief (except in operas, where the divine is presented merely with the aura of the marvellous), theatre establishes a system of representation built on the relations between different partners of this multiple space taken in its totality. At the very end of the ideal vanishing point, and behind it, infinity opens out on to a discourse, which pushes the limits of representation. At the other end of this line of infinity is a human relation founded on the multiplicity of the spectator's gaze, each of whom has a point of view that effectively decentres the "prince's eye". Theatre thus rejected the limits that had been previously imposed on it, because it constituted through its own language, a new discursive infinity that transcended representation since it diffracted the ideal point of view into a numerous subjective points of view. *Relation*, rather than strict depiction, was now the defining concept; *mimesis* being considered as only one of the components of the genre. Critical thought, or the discourse of relationality between the stakeholders of the genre and the theatrical session, became its guiding aesthetic, social and philosophical principle.

The building and the session as spaces of socialisation

In the seventeenth century, theatre thus slowly became a defined social space and a specific genre: the theatrical space was slowly transformed from re-used tennis courts, reconverted banquet halls and places of entertainment into a few specific places constructed or converted based on an interior architecture that, progressively, became specifically associated with the theatre. The Palais-Cardinal, inaugurated in 1641, was abandoned for 20 years, before being refurbished to host a city audience and Molière's theatre troupe in 1661. The Théâtre du Marais was renovated after a fire in 1644, the Hotel de Bourgogne (the only one to have been a theatre from the beginning) revamped in 1645 and the Petit-Bourbon (former chapel and function room) was destroyed in 1660. And in the second half of the century, the theatre house of the Tuileries (which proved to be unworkable) was inaugurated and the construction of the Hôtel des comédiens du roi, on rue des Fossés-Saint-Germain,[3] was completed in 1689.

Rather than a series of innovations or constructions from scratch, this period witnessed a set of modifications: the plain rectangle was transformed into a house rounded at the back, then later into the opening of the so-called "Italian-style" theatre. Progressively, during the following century, the spectators (or a part of the audience, initially) began to sit and be quiet (at the beginning of the eighteenth century). Eventually, each part of the audience came to have its assigned seating, from which, as it would happen much later, it would not be allowed to move. The institution of a hierarchy and of a specificity of precincts of theatre, of the hierarchy and specificity of troupes, audiences and genres, became increasingly refined and totally ingrained in the eighteenth century. The birth of the "writer", and a specific group of authors who were no longer necessarily leaders of troupes and who became professionals, publishing their works and living off them, witnessed the emergence of a respectable social position for the theatrical crafts. It decreased accusations of prostitution and of the marginalisation of practitioners. The autonomy of the theatrical practice as an aesthetic capable of speaking about itself, led to a proliferation of writings that sought to comment on and define this art.

During the seventeenth and eighteenth centuries, the theatre building also became more specific. The theatrical genre gave rise to truly legitimate crafts and to an art made up of particular systems, which were then theorised by practitioners, such as Corneille, and by authors, such as d'Aubignac. In this sense, theatre became a new art, a new way of representing the world on a particular place (the stage) for the duration of a particular social time (that of the performance, or rather, of the session – a social practice that exceeds the narrow duration of the spectacle, since it includes also a time of socialisation). This place and time are fixed in a determined space within the social structure.

Theatre, as the place of a discourse within the social body and on the social body, affirmed its singularity inasmuch as it had codes of representation that became increasingly distinct; social roles that were debated but recognised; and a series of *social actors*, the existence and usefulness of which had to be recognised by the *society*. This new art, designed to speak about the world and about humans in the world, became less contested in its right to exist, after a struggle whose outcome was continually questioned (by the Church, then, in the eighteenth century, by Rousseauian philosophy). Therefore, the seventeenth century saw the establishment of a theatrical space, as well as the establishment of a set of professions and a specific art that was theorised and hierarchised. At the same time, the slow evolution of the social system also started to recognise the autonomous, distinctive existence of the theatrical genre within the social and political space. Likewise, a specific discourse of representation was brought into being.

Placed at the heart of the city (whereas, at court, they were merely a complementary part of the representation of royalty), theatre sites were organised into social spaces, which represented the city itself in a particular building and at particular moments (the year's calendar, days, hours and performance times became fixed). The city theatres themselves (such as the Hôtel de Bourgogne) divide their buildings into different areas of social standing.

No longer on the margins of the society, theatre was now at the heart of the city's social practices. Geographically, it also occupied a central location where urban society played out its own hierarchical divisions according to the seat allocations of spectators, and where the discourse of representation was staged at the very centre of this centre: onstage. However, the stage was not actually the centre of the centre: it was neither the best-lit place nor the only place where attention was directed. The theatre was primarily an assembly of people who gathered in a "session" for an "event", the motive being to witness a fiction, and who, themselves, witnessed an assembly in the distance of fiction – "the play" – and, in the building, an assembly that was a mirror held up to them.

While, in principle, the theatrical moment was the moment where fiction was played out on the stage under the guise of representation and illusion, there were many other moments during the theatrical session, which made the exercise of theatre a practice not necessarily, or uniquely, focused on the representation itself. Admittedly, the theatre was no longer a place where spectators participated in the fiction; moreover, the spectators were absent from the performance of the spectacle and the principles of illusion and distance dominated the show to the point where one may speak about the theatrical space specific to the fiction. However, as Georges Forestier has remarked, "the spectator is like a secondary actor".[4] Spectators made themselves visible to each other, showed off, watched each other and what was at the centre of the theatre's space, and that was the most clearly lighted within the building, was the parterre; in other words, the largest portion of the spectators, representing the largest portion of the city. Admittedly, spectators came, in principle, to see a fiction that was distinct from their world. However, they also came to the theatre to see the city and its social divisions and categories, lighted by the central chandeliers as they watched each other, spoke, commented, watched each other watch the show and, as the case might be, watched the fiction and listened to the discourse that it proposed.

It appears, then, that the evolution of spaces should be considered as a function of the transition from a non-specific location to a specific one: from a largely standing, noisy and unruly audience to a seated, silent and motionless one; from a rectangular room to a curve shaped house; from a narrow, elongated stage, crowded with spectators (from 1637 onwards), to a more open one, known as the "proscenium stage", from which, as of 1759, the audience was excluded. Up to this point, much of our attention in this section has been devoted to issues of points of view, perspective and scenery (in other words, to the ways of staging fiction in the theatre); to the manner in which theatre buildings become specific places, structurally and architecturally conceived for the practice of theatre; and to the emergence of the theatre professional: actors, writers and other scenographers. However, we have given relatively little consideration, up to now, to the space of the audience and on its attitudes of reception. Yet, it seems that this would bear consequences for the theatre's aesthetic and its discourse; that the question of whether a self-observant, heterogeneous audience is standing or seated, motionless or moving, in boxes, in the parterre or on benches in the back of the room, is silent or noisy, would have major consequences for the organisation of theatre.

Line and circle: traditional double cone and multiple angles

From 1637 to 1759, there seems to be a specific space that determines a particular kind of reception, a conception of a theatrical aesthetic, which one must examine from the point of view of the audience. Such a study allows for a better understanding of the social, ideological and juridical impact of the fiction represented. Whereas so-called *Italianstyle* theatre is defined by a separation between the audience space and that of the fiction,[5] based on the notion that the spectators are "under arrest" and that the presence of a frame defines the spectator's visual field and what is out of its scope, one must admit that French theatre is clearly distinguished from the canonical "Italian theatre" as it is ideally presented in manuals and that, by all appearances, has never truly existed. The adoption of Italian perspective occurred late in France. The stage directions, including accessories, and the sketches designed by Mahelot, the decorator of the Hôtel de Bourgogne, in his precise and descriptive *Mémoire* written during the first half of the seventeenth century, reveal the awareness the French had of this sort of perspective. However, up to then, practitioners confined themselves to a perspective envisaged as a simple mode of organising or distributing objects in space, in autonomous units, without a perceived need for continuity between them. It was not until the arrival of Italian scenographers in France who produced highly mechanised "*pieces à machines*" (Torelli, Mariani) that there was an interest in geometrically unifying the staging space, not in an attempt at giving it an appearance of "reality", but, rather to make it an illusory place of unreality, of Italian *meraviglia* or French "merveille" or "merveilleux".

Indeed, the first essential point is that the so-called "classic box" (a term forged much later and that was as idealistic as it was inexact) became concerned with stage seats and could not totally claim to be illusionistic or to have one sole point of view. The spectators, and particularly those on the theatre benches, were a part of the spectacle and physically depicted the fact that there existed another point of view, other than a frontal one, in relation to the frame of the stage. It was as if it was evident that the fiction could be seen obliquely and from the point of view of the actors (or even of the characters), and could be directly commented on by a performing audience. Furthermore, the movement of spectators in the parterre and, indeed, the movement of their gazes (from top to bottom) on to the spectacle of fiction, on to the seats onstage, into the secret spaces of the boxes, to the authors and critics seated at the back of the house – who were also noisy – clearly illustrated that point of view was that of several categories (which were spatially, socially and even aesthetically *marked* and in contradiction one with another). It also implied that the principle of illusion, necessarily centred on the ideal vanishing point, was diffracted or multiplied, with several vanishing points suiting (or not) the different modes of watching (one vanishing point for the frontal-focused boxes, two others for those on the sides, etc.); and was largely contested by the principle of distance that integrated the presence of the audience and its reactions – in other words, by the simultaneous presence of a *performed* reception.

We can distinguish the performance of plays that require no elaborate scenography – and that therefore allowed spectators on to the stage – and those that required a more complex staging – and thus did not allow spectators on to the stage. Rotrou, for example, explains in his *Dessein de la Naissance d'Hercule* (1649) that "it is expedient that the use of machines should chase the socialite off the stage".[6] Thus, simultaneously, there existed a tendency to integrate audiences into the representation within a theatre session and, on the other hand, an interest in foregrounding the fiction of illusion, spectacular captivation and marvel, which also sought to unify points of view around a single one. Consequently, when a maximum of illusion and bedazzlement was to be combined with the centralisation of the audience's vision around the supposed "prince's eye", the stage would be cleared of spectators. The "piéces à machines" and the lyrical tragedies were, at once, great moments of illusion and special effects and beautiful encomiastic objects accompanied by prologues that underscored their political content. As such, when these were staged, the stage was emptied of spectators and the prince (whether he was actually or symbolically present) was offered a mirror, which his eye was supposed to contemplate.

Therefore, perspective soon became a question of an audience's multiple points of view rather than the singular "point of view of the prince", or of an intermediary system that implied that the prince's point of view, originating in courtly theatrical performances, could be complemented, or contradicted, by the perspectives of the spectators themselves, represented by their active presence within the moment of the social practice of theatre. Perspective then became a matter of *assembly*: a sum of different, distinct audiences, each having their topographical, social and interpretative point of view of the fiction and the whole of the theatrical session as a spectacle in its own right.

Rather than a cone that originates in the "prince's eye" and ends onstage, one must imagine, in three-dimensional geometric dimensions, a double cone, or, in plane geometry, a rhombus. The first theoretical double cone functions in a traditional way: it goes from the eye to the vanishing point, spreads from the seats at the back of the theatre, opens on to the parterre, then on to the stage, before homing in on the perspective scenery and ending in the "nail", which suggests a space extended infinitely far. In plane geometry terms, we thus have a rhombus whose two most distant points represent the eye of the prince and the vanishing point, and whose two bases are determined by the width of the stage. That is the ideal theory and phantasmatic reference: the "prince's eye" opens on to the stage and hones in on the backdrop.

Back to reality

This theory of "perspective staging", at once political and aesthetic, appears to constitute a "marvellous" phenomenon. But we must bear two things in mind. First, the illusionistic scenery is put in place while the symbolic, emblematic and indicative one is still there: the compartments, painted canvases and author depictions that are not necessarily within the perspective framework remained in use, as we have said, until the 1640s, and retained their importance in the interpretive framework of the spectators. Second, the stage set does not have one, but several vanishing points (at least two) and that the effect of perspective, when actors must go into the distance and not remain on the *proscenium* as in Serlian perspective, is significantly modified, or even extremely restricted. As soon as the actors move, in comedies for example, the perspective effect is eroded; hence the eventual inclusion of a sort of crossroads or an apartment room with a few openings, which can depict a distant place.

Moreover, and most importantly, the hierarchical organisation of city theatres, which correspond more to the way in which spectators are seen by other spectators than to the comfort of their position, makes this theory all the more relative. One must examine the hierarchical organisation of these theatre houses in order to better understand the functioning of city theatre in the seventeenth and eighteenth centuries (distinct, as we have seen previously, in its organisation, from court theatre). In this theatre, the audience was divided into four groups. Two rows of boxes above and on the side contain an aristocratic audience or the wealthy bourgeoisie. On the tiered seats in the back of the auditorium, artists, learned men and "connoisseurs" would sit. As we have already said – but this is a point so crucial that it bears repeating – the theatre benches, on the stage, seat wealthy spectator-characters who wish to be seen watching the play. In fact, they were sometimes mistaken for the actors themselves insofar as they were allowed to wear the same garments, happened to speak loudly, entered and exited the stage at times and, indeed, exhibited themselves in very deliberate ways.

> But the thing that will immediately determine the failure or success of the performance is whether the stage is kept clear and only actors are allowed on it. The crowd that is there, or that appears, during the play, creates disorder and unbearable confusion. How many times, on the utterance of these lines: "but here he comes, I see him", these lines that our authors, in their miserable obsession with their so-called rules, fail to use when linking their scenes, how many times, upon hearing these words, has one mistaken for an actor for a good man with good intentions, but who enters at that moment upon the stage, searching for seats even after several scenes have already been performed?[7]

Then there is the parterre,[8] standing below the level of the stage. These "people" on the "ground below", also express themselves, move and look around them, towards the stage and the stage benches, towards the boxes, towards the seats at the back, showing that their mode of viewing is decidedly circular.

During this time, the most expensive seats were often bought on a yearly basis and were therefore the first gallery, followed by the stage seats, then, respectively, by the tiered seats located at the back of the room, the second gallery, and finally, the parterre, where the spectators stand below stage level. When the stage, which was occupied by tens of spectators, was emptied of the benches in 1759 and the parterre seated in 1782, things changed. The most expensive seats continued to be the balcony boxes. However, little by little, the tiered seats placed in the parterre (which came to be known as the orchestra) occupied the front of the room. Their prices increased, while the less affluent spectators moved up to the third and fourth balconies that were eventually constructed – "paradise" as they were called. Meanwhile, the habit of leaving the balcony boxes or of moving in the parterre, or of going from box to box, or from the boxes to the parterre to meet people, slowly died out, resulting in a relative silence within the theatre house. Progressively, behaviour took on a sense of uniformity, as what happened onstage came to be considered as essential, and eventually, as the only motive for gathering, despite the fact that social distinctions persisted.

Given the fact that in the seventeenth and eighteenth centuries there was not one single, static point of view that was located at the back of the parterre or in the tiered sections for "professionals" at the back of the house, but rather several moving ones where spectators moved around balcony boxes, the stage benches, the parterre, the tiered seats at the back, the notion of a rhombus-shaped pattern of viewing became a contested one. Instead, one needed to accept that a set of optical systems were set in motion that were more or less in keeping with the perspective system as it was initially conceived. The multiplicity of points of view therefore resulted in significantly different angles of vision that affected the interpretation that one would have of the show. In other words, the line-based prescription of perspective illusion was unsettled and subverted by people who watched from the "wrong place": who watched the show in a different way and who were authorised to do so based on the topographical layout of the theatre house. The result was that the multiplicity of points of view with respect to the staged fiction had far more in common with a series of parallel lines oriented towards infinity, as theorised by Gérard Desargues and Blaise Pascal (projective geometry) around the same period.

It was already a given that the theatrical precinct of the house and the stage was not only a place of fictional representation, but, now that the concept of perspective had evolved from the single-focus line to embrace the notion of circularity, the proliferating multiplicity of the audience's points of view led to a panoramic, circular conception of the theatre, also a network of shifting optical relations. Nevertheless, depending on the theatre, certain areas of the usable space remained more or less out of sight for the majority of spectators, for reasons of pure geometry, but also for reasons of lighting.

In the physical space of the theatre, the public space and the space of fiction were no longer perceived based on the concept of the ideal vanishing point, but rather on a circular point of view that encompassed the totality of the visual field and included, during the theatrical event, both the fiction and the other parts of the assembly. From then onwards, the city's theatres no longer determined points of view from the perspective of an ideal individual spectator (for example, the "prince's eye" is defunct), but from a sum of different points of view oriented towards all the others, a point that the show itself can only confirm. The illusion of the spectacle, which was considered up to then as being at the centre of vision, was then marginalised, or at the very least, diminished under the effect of the social dynamic at work within the theatre's space. At the same time, the discourse of those on the receiving end of the representation was recognised as being a part of the spectacle itself. The multiplicity of points of view thus acted on the spectacle and transformed it not into an illusion, but into the motive of a discourse around the fiction proposed by theatre professionals (actors and the author). Each spectator, from their viewing place (which can certainly change to the extent that they move), could perceive differently what was being shown and during the play, the intermission and between both plays (most often, in a theatrical session, there were two), but also before and after the staging of the fiction, can talk with others about their point of view.

And in a wider sense, the authors were fully aware of this and were thus able to play with the real complexity by composing texts that allowed both for a continuity in the illusion and for elements that would arrest the spectators' attention, provoking thereby a discontinuity with respect to plot. In other words, they used "moves" that could provoke a momentary sensation of disquiet, the effect of which was to throw the main action into relief. Consequently, the overall construction of the dramaturgy highlights the fact that all perspective illusion allows for the interplay of images and distortions. To better grasp the ways in which dramaturgy engages with this aspect of perspective illusion by unsettling it, we can consider the way the character of Matamore functions in Corneille's *Illusion comique*. However, in order for our demonstration to be effective, it will be useful to provide a synopsis of this comedy, described by Corneille as a "strange monster", a "caprice" and an "extravagant invention".

The play functions on several levels, including the metadramatic. In Act 1, the secluded cave of a magician from Tours, Pridamant, the authoritarian father, comes to see Alcandre, the magician, trying to discover the cause of the disappearance of Clindor, Pridamant's son. The second level, Acts 2, 3 and 4, through the use of a "talking spectre", Alcandre shows Pridamant the life of his son. Clindor is living the life of a *picaro* since his disappearance and is now in the service of a captain of soldiers (Matamore) in the region of Bordeaux. At the beginning of Act 2, Clindor is listening to Matamore brag about his impossible feats, but we learn about his love for Isabelle, who is also being pursued by Adraste, whose advances she rejects. Clindor loves Isabelle and is loved by her, while Adraste, his rival, apprised of this by the servant of Isabelle, Lyse (who loves Clindor), decides to avenge himself. The reader/spectator witnesses a pastoral, in which love is met with obstacles and the chain of feelings (Lyse loves Clindor who loves Isabelle who is loved by Adraste and by Matamore) threatens the fate of the lovers. Pridamant, who "witnesses" all of this, fears for his son.

The third act begins with the reproaches of Isabelle's father, Géronte, who wants her to marry Adraste. Alone, Géronte decides to force her to do his will. This leads to the daughter's resistance, the anger of the father, and the help offered by Matamore: this is a true comedy.

Lyse then appears, her stated aim being to lead Clindor to his mistress; however, Clindor tries to seduce Lyse, pretending that he only loves Isabelle for her money. Such duplicitous characters are common in Corneille's comedies. Lyse, who knows everything, devises a plot against the lovers, while Matamore arrives to demand that Clindor end his pursuit of Isabelle; Clindor, who knows his master well, refuses and manages to have Matamore "give" him the young girl. The play now teeters on the edge of farce and Matamore flees, and is thereby "removed" from the plot. Clindor kills Adraste in a tragic-comic duel and ends up in prison, which worries his spectator-father.

Act 4 continues in a tragi-comic vein. Isabelle vows that she will die. She is rejoined by Lyse who reassures her: Isabelle and Clindor can flee that night with Lyse and the jailer, who is now Lyse's lover; thus, a first, happy ending. However, Alcandre indicates that the "performance" is not over. Hereupon begins the third level of illusion: Act V changes place, tone and style. Lyse, who accompanies the noble Isabelle, warns her to beware of the love that Clindor has toward the wife of Prince Florilame. In the darkness of the theatre, the duplicitous Clindor declares his love to Isabelle, who he takes for the princess Rosine. When Isabelle reveals her identity, reproaching him for his infidelities, Clindor reaffirms his love for her. However, suddenly, the play takes a tragic turn: Florilame's people murder Clindor, and Isabelle dies of grief. Witnessing this bloody end, Pridamant is beside himself. At this moment, Alcandre begins laughing. He reveals that Clindor and the other characters are alive and in the process of dividing money. Clindor and his friends have become actors and what Pridamant observed was their performance of the final act of a tragedy. Alcandre struggles to make Pridamant realise that the drama has captivated, enchanted and overwhelmed him, and that his actor-son has chosen a marvellous profession, which pays well, moreover, and that Clindor, given his talents, is well poised to obtain success in the city. Pridamant, confused but happy, pardons Alcandre and accepts the arguments of those who think that theatre is useful, moral and entertaining.

What was played out in front of spectators was a pastoral, a comedy, a farce, a tragicomedy and a tragedy, coupled with the representation of a play within the play, organised to theoretically and rhetorically demonstrate the necessity and instructiveness of the social art that is theatre. All in one: the theatre event, generally divided into comic play and serious play is celebrated here as harmonious, to the delight of the audience and for the greater benefit of the actors of the Theatre du Marais, and their author, Pierre Corneille.

If we go back to the depiction of Matamore, what do we see? That the presence of this Spanish Capitan represents a "spectacular moment", an artifice recognised by everybody, and that is already presented as such, moreover, and able to function as a disjointed dramatic sequence. One quickly realises, however, that Matamore is integral to the overall plot and represents an obstacle anamorphically and through a decentring effect. It also helps the young couple, and depicts a theatre that they play on one plane of reality. It stages, in sum, an initial generic marker of the farce from which the story gradually moves (Matamore eventually serves no more purpose on the stage), transforming itself into comedy, then into tragicomedy and finally into tragedy. In an even broader sense, one realises that on the scale of the play in its entirety, Corneille, far from adhering to the classical theoretical criteria of homogeneity of representation, deploys a constant play of deformations and anamorphic shifts. He inserts a tragedy not only in the fifth act, played by the heroes without the character-spectator, Pridamant, knowing that they have become actors and that what is taking place before him is another level of representation, but also within previous acts, built upon an ingenious montage of heterogeneous elements and registers that are ostensibly spectacular and conventional and that impose shifting generic imaginaries (from the comic to the tragic, to put it simply). It is thus significant that, far from the model of a regular central perspective, we witness a "moving discontinuity" in Corneille's play that is presented as an apology for the theatre, and that allows for the establishment of the play of visual illusion. Through shifting registers and displacing points of view, he creates an unstable perspective, which thrills the spectator. However, this pleasure depends on the fact that the real spectator, contrary to the character-spectator of Pridamant, is not unaware of the fiction that is being shown to them. And Corneille knows that the benefit of an anamorphosis lies not only in the revelation of a single and established meaning that would be visible only when the right "vanishing point" is found, but is situated, rather, in the permanent play between the "normal" image and its deformations, in the ambiguities that this play of deformations and mutations engender and maintain.

We are therefore faced with an unstable, perverse, troubled and troubling perspective. Theatre is thus conceived not as the site of a central perspective, which would organise everything around itself, but as that of an anamorphic deformation and of the play of multiple points of view, specific to the stage and to the fiction. This anamorphic perspective that reaches into the depths of the psyche and of inter-human relations, can utilise their content and effects to reveal the desires, fears and pleasures of both the characters and the spectators, by seducing them into its traps.

In this way, theatre seems to offer the possibility of a perspective on perspective itself, and even multiple points of view on the ideal point of view (and, consequently, on the issues that emerge from the plot, for example, and on their ostensibly unitary meaning), to the extent that it decentres, makes mobile and irregular the ideal regularity of the perspective and linearity of the plot. Against the twinned articulation of theatrical discourse is thus pitted, on the one hand, the complex dialogue between the fiction and different groups of spatially defined spectators, as well as the dialogue of groups of spectators among themselves based on the fiction (but not solely) and, on the other and, the necessary awareness that authors, scenographers and actors have of this multiple communication that modifies the illusory principle of an ideal and normative point of view.

The line and the circle: the depiction of infinity transcended by the infinity of words

As with any art, theatre tackles dogma, science and laws, searching for flaws within them and finding material to produce unpredictable projections from them. By seizing perspective, it channels it towards one sole individual, the Florentine or Roman prince, for whom it constructs a world; but at the same time, it adds to this ideal, global and rational other eyes, which do not see the same thing, and it transcends the vanishing point at the other end of the perverted rhombus, making it the point of origin of a multiple imaginary, essentially undefined and itself diffracted by gazes capable of envisaging infinite interpretations.

We have seen that perspective enables the representation of the world within a fixed system that moves from the foreground, where the bodies of actors are located, to a second field oriented towards the representation of a vanishing point that goes towards infinity, and that indicates that these real bodies of actors become bodies of characters. The materialisation of infinity in the field of perspective thus creates an illusion and a qualitative change of bodies into characters, and actors into fictional beings. A space of fiction that is continuously extended, coherent and autonomous, and in which the ideal spectator can project herself. Of course, this system is theoretical, ideal and contingent, decentred and transformed, if one takes into account the multiplicity of points of view. But, to come back to the ideal space of representation, structured by perspective, one notices that, there too, the closing–opening of the vanishing-point principle provides for an exceedance and for a particular imaginary space.

The space of representation, when oriented towards infinity and framed by precise limits (the constructions that determine the opening of the stage), allows for a distribution between the stage (the shown) and the offstage (the recounted). From the point of view of the fiction and the illusion, offstage is thus what is transmitted through discourse and what originates in the mouths and bodies of actors, as well as in the voices of actors transformed into characters. In a sense, it is what creates the infinite illusion of the stage set, an imaginary world that is contiguous with the fiction represented, which allows the audience to cross over the frontiers constituted by the scenery. Through the actor's voice, this discourse represents an exterior metaphorical world. Offstage offers a glimpse into what is metaphorically situated "behind" the vanishing point, or behind the framing of perspective on the stage. The constitution of this offstage gives rise to the imaginary representation that the sum of audiences can produce (therefore, to an infinite number of imaginary representations shaped by speech and by the play of actors).

Consequently, the separation between representation and recounting breaks down insofar as what is narrated is enlarged through discourse and takes control of the stage by imposing the imaginary thus created. The line depicting space is thus undone by a multiplicity of imaginary spaces, which come to life within the voice, rather than in the representation; within discourse, and no longer in action, the infinity that was the referent of the scenery is now the referent of the fiction of words. In this way, theatre achieves the infinite field proposed by the vanishing point. It gives rise to an imaginary representation of scenes evoked by the voice of the actor-character, as if the vanishing point opened on to a world that is no longer under the role of the line (i.e. of the visible space organised through perspective), but that moves away from the vanishing point towards necessary consequences: the transition to an imaginary space, starting from a central point but leading to a space without circumference. More rarely, the offstage space was metonymic insofar as what this space represented was generally not the practical extension of the stage, but another space constructed by discourse. Indeed, it was in the eighteenth century that characters systematically appealed to this sense of metonymic extension and broadened the conception of the "stage" in a system that highlighted the continuity of the represented and the imaginary: Beaumarchais' characters could then look out of the window (overlooking the backstage area) and describe the very specific offstage area that they "saw" in front of them – the garden, the trees, the animals running, etc.

But offstage, from the material point of view specific to the staging area, is also all that is not the fiction represented or relayed by voice. In other words, it is the wings (where they exist), the space behind, above and to the side of the stage, the house occupied by the audience, but also what is outside of the theatre building, i.e. the city, the "real" world. This second offstage, complementary to the first, which does not necessarily depend on the fiction and illusion, brings to bear on the performance a referential system organised around the "lived experience" of the performance and the spectators, a reference to the social and political world outside the theatre, in the city and in the world that surrounds the building. Consequently, this referential offstage space, *practically* located on the fringes of the performance, becomes a sort of actualisation of the fiction taking place onstage, and of the imaginary discursive offstage located, ideally, behind the vanishing point.

As such, both offstage spaces, when added to the fiction represented, lend to the theatre experience a total and infinite representation of the world, via the mediation of the audience and actors and the mediation of discourse. Therefore, the conscious, evident presence of these offstage spaces make linear perspective and the mere fact of having the "prince's eye" inadequate for describing the principle of representation. The line that goes from the ideal eye to the point that symbolises infinity, with, in the centre, the transformed body of the actor drawn into the fiction, is no longer the sole vector of perception. There is a continuity between the vanishing point upon which perspective illusion rests, the offstage depicted by voice (the actors' discourse), and the offstage space outside of the actual, material site where the play is staged.

Places, spaces, two spectacles and the distance effect

The presence of the other, as we all know well, removes us from the fiction (so does the awareness of our own presence, sometimes). The visible presence of others who watch and who observe us watching, implies distance with respect to the illusion and the fiction represented. The theatre session thus becomes, essentially, a public space where points of view and discourses criss-cross based on the aesthetic proposition given onstage in the form of a depicted speech, itself diffracted into a space of representation (the shown play-act), an imaginary discursive space (the offstage space verbally relayed and bodied forth) and the space given as within the real world (the offstage space that the theatre attendees know). To the infinity located behind the stud that represents it, is the undetermined multiplicity or the infinity of interpretations found behind the eye of the prince. So much so that the pattern that structures the representation, the vanishing point, is totally eclipsed by representation's world beyond (the offstage, lived experience and the imaginary) but also by the representation itself (the multiplicity of the audience's points of view).

What is interesting here, in this diffraction of space into imaginary spaces, real spaces and individual hermeneutic spaces and places, is that the supposed reason for assembly, the play itself, bodied forth by actors, is no longer a pure material of projection, nor an element apt to develop some monosemy (the dream of a theatre responding obediently to a specific command has never been made reality). Instead, the play is the scene of a generalised debate, coupled with an art of distance apt to reflect one's notions of theatre aesthetic itself, refined into a specific art and the discourse that the theatrical medium holds about the world.

Organised as a plural aesthetic space open to interpretation, theatre is also organised into spaces that open on to one another. An aesthetic space of generalised vision where, from the foreground to infinity, each participant sees and is seen, even in her apprehension of lived experience or the imaginary. A juridical space in which each point of view, involving its own rules of thought and analysis (based on its place), assesses the fictional case presented according to the individual's knowledge, but also to the extent to which the case corresponds with lived reality and with the imaginary. A social space divided into optical solidarities, which all contemplate each other, oppose, exchange and share points of view. Given the distance effect on the one hand, and the recognition of the others in the room, on the other, each spectator can embrace the whole case and the infinite number of its extensions within this assembly of which they are but one of the constituents. Consequently, moving from the aesthetic to the juridical, from the juridical to the political and from the political to the philosophical, each point of view, different but participating in a whole, forms the space of the theatre.

Therefore, there are simultaneously and consecutively (before and after the representation of the fictions as well as during the intermissions) several plays existing contiguously in the theatre building: the play that the city performs for itself; the play of gazes that meet; the play of fiction represented onstage and interwoven with the social play (the house always makes its voice, more or less, heard). The boundaries between what is represented (the story, the fiction) and what gives itself in self-reflexive representation (the audience's reception) are far from fixed. The barriers are infinitely porous, not only in texts like *La Critique de l'École des femmes* [*A Criticism of the School for Wives*], where the actors address the various categories of spectators, but systematically and structurally in all the plays played in the city, given the configuration of the spectacle.

While there exists a sort of theoretical separation between the fiction and the audience's reception, which make for essential differences between plays, it is difficult to observe a practical separation within the room. Despite what theorists and authors might wish, theatre is not a fiction box that an audience observes, projecting itself into it, seated, passive and in silence, but a place in which the limits are often in flux. While the theatre clearly has frame, depth, a scenographic vocabulary and the awareness of a possible illusion of the spectacle for those who watch (defined in all its complexity and magnified by Corneille's *Illusion comique* [*Comic Illusion*], among other plays), there the audience's domain sometimes penetrates the very enclosure of the fiction (the stage benches), so that there is a constant address to the spectators by the actors, throughout the play-act. Additionally, there is a systematic transgression of the boundaries of the spectacle of fiction in the world beyond the human imaginary, or in the world-within representations of lived experience. In sum, the boundaries of the fiction box are porous, like those within the audience, and the frontier between the "lived experience" of the spectators and the "fiction" of the spectacle are also hard to narrowly fix.

Even when the text claims an absolute autonomy and a break between the world of reception (silent, contemporary and of a "real" social essence) and that of the fiction (filled with characters who act and speak in a mythical or ancient time, in a different, virtual place), the conditions of representation prevent this break from being entire. The spectacle is thus situated in an intermediary space and time; at crossroads, meeting points and intersections that are neither entirely the time and space of the fiction, nor the time and space of the spectators. Consequently, even when the fiction being staged belongs to ancient space and time, the constitution of the representation (including its costumes, objects, furniture and scenery weaves contemporary references into the ancient ones and informs the whole in an unending interaction. The allusions to contemporary facts allows the spectators to interpret, for themselves and for the society in which they live, the ancient fiction whose characters are caught in an ancient fable as it is represented to them. At the same time, "Hellenism", "Romanism" or exoticism, for example, provides distance. It is based on this dual referential game that classical tragedy, among other genres, functions (i.e. based on distance), and on the calibration of this distance with respect to the lived reality of the spectator.

Nevertheless, the theatre cannot represent just anything, nor does it say just anything; and the spectators, despite the plurality of their points of views do not judge and think just anything.

The expansion of the theatrical space and the principle of proliferation notwithstanding, theatrical representation does not stage the undecidable. On the contrary, the production of these intersecting spaces and differing of points of view during the theatre session is moored in the expression of a discourse, which is the "case" that these points of view examine. Consequently, by virtue of a formulated discourse, crafted into a story played by contradictory characters, and constituting a case to be assessed, theatre finds an irreducible point of focus and spectators find a reason to be present. It is the relevance of this discourse that constitutes the relevance of the play, its capacity to transform and enlarge physical place into space, and its claim to a point of view with regard to this very act of enlargement. Because the theatrical space (the fiction, its representation and the physical precinct) contains numerous qualitatively different spaces, because it is filled with different points of view (contradictory characters in the story, multiple modes and vectors of judgement among the audience), theatre depicts and realises the aesthetic, juridical and social scene of the world at large, based on a complex example. Therefore, because it establishes spatial relations of judgement, it is concerned with examples of behaviour (in its stories) and offers to spectators opportunities to exert their points of view under the gaze of other points of view. Such opportunities are provided in a poetic, aesthetic and seductive way to the spectators, who are cognisant of the space and of their own perceptions.

Therefore the centre of theatre is discourse; not the discourse of the story alone, but the sum of all discourses fashioned, during the moment of assembly, from, or under the pretext of, the represented discourse of this story. And while, based on the code of representation, one version or one lesson is highlighted by the text, by the actors or by a majority (or hierarchically superior set of persons) of the audience, the configuration of place and spaces makes it always possible and, indeed, necessary — actors and practitioners expect this — for other judgements and other points of view to emerge freely from the case laid out, and based on the expectations of those who judge. Thus, from the discourse that emerges from the voice and in the body of the actor, carrying the text and relayed by the discourse of those who observe it, the moment of the spectacle, the theatrical session, becomes a circular public scene, exceeding the mere interpretative illusory line and giving way, literally, to small hermeneutic affinities and finally to an individual interpretation.

Reforming theatre from the building out: from d'Aubignac to Luigi Riccoboni

The problem may be summed up as follows: an audience gathers in a place to witness a performance of actors, their virtuosity in declaiming a text and their use of body language. Simultaneously, this audience also gathers so the people in it can observe each other, express themselves and be seen. So what do the actors, decorators and dramaturgs do to make the audience consider them as the focus of this gathering? In other words, what do the practitioners — including the author — do to make the gathering, the session, become mainly and, eventually, totally, a proper spectacle, with perfectly distinct groups of watchers and watched? They place their art in the centre and minimise, as much as they can, gazes and attitudes that interfere. Scenography, the art of discourse and declamation, the crafting of costumes, the art of story and plot, virtuosity acting come together to create maximum interest and capture the attention of the audience. However, the game is complex and each party plays his own role, and nothing says that the text (and therefore the author), the play-acting (and thus the actor) or the arrangement of the stage (and therefore the set designer), direct the whole thing, or that the audience can suddenly be trained and made silent and attentive to the performance.

To the extent that the discourse and the text take on an obvious importance in the functioning of the theatre event, first of all the game will be played between actors and authors. The former are already members of troupes and know the ins and outs of their art. They know that they are esteemed for their artistic skill and are persuaded that the audience has come to see and listen to them for that very reason, more than for appreciating the text, which they use for playing. The author is, from this point of view, a mere servant of the text, employed and paid by the troupe. But in the seventeenth century, the authorial position changed and authors took on an essential role, aided by the literary and dramatic theory that developed among them or by others close to them. At the same time, texts were also read, published, discussed in salons and newspapers, debated in correspondences, prefaced, reprinted, republished, so much that writers were no longer considered employees that wrote texts, but central figures of theatrical activity. Practitioners, and particularly actors, therefore had to alter the role, without totally giving up their prerogatives. It was then that they truly became actors *of* the text: if, before, they could have been considered to *utilise* the text, they now were thought of as *serving* to the best of their abilities according to the desires or indications of the authors and/or the theorists. Their virtuosity was now placed at the service of what was written. And this has been the tendency since then, a heavy, intractable one, despite struggles to go against it.

While we can agree that discourse, story, plot and dramatic space are now at the centre of the aesthetic machinery, the problem remains that the different parties involved in the construction of this machinery are all in the same place, the same building. The question of how, for whose benefit and with what constraints the machinery functions becomes an important one. As such, it becomes easy to appreciate that when authors, theorists and sometimes actors mindful of theory and recognition sought to confer social legitimacy on their art in the name of a social and moral good, it became important to propose a reform of the theatrical space as a whole (while seeking to elaborate a proper poetics around the production of a text in line with aesthetic, moral and political norms accepted or needed by the society).

From d'Aubignac (*La Pratique du théâtre* [*The Practice of Theatre*], 1657)[9] to Voltaire, via Luigi Riccoboni, to the eighteenth century, there was no shortage of attempts to define a precise role for all partners of theatrical representation: for the actors, on the one hand, preferably situated in the centre of things and served by scenography, and the audience, on the other hand, whose attention was to be focused exclusively on following the play. As for the authors, they had to be present before the event (they imposed the text), during the event (the imposed service to the text, since they gave ever more precise indications that functioned like orders given to the actors) and after it (they comment on it, validate it or withhold their validation). As a consequence, the actors (who were now actors *also* in the sense of *enacting* the author's wishes), in order to maintain some authority and keep their position on the stage, were forced to kowtow to the text, even while trying to maintain the usage of their building. While following the wishes of the authors and trying to find benefits in them for themselves, they were also forced to take part in the great effort at training the audience. Silence! Remain seated! Refrain from moving! Pay attention to the text and to our acting! These are the marching orders of the new theatre. Orders that, nonetheless, took a very long time to take root.

The very first significant attempt to ensure that the audience was respectful and attentive was that of the Abbé Hédelin d'Aubignac, who, in 1657, added to his *Pratique du théâtre*, a proposal for reform (*Recovery Plan for the French Theatre*) in the form of a series of proposed rules. These aimed at reforming the audience, their traditions, their excesses and their lack of attention. In order for the theatre script to get the attention it deserved and for there to be a sense of illusion, d'Aubignac proposed that the spectators in the parterre be seated and made to be silent, even if this meant calling the police. These proposals came up against what d'Aubignac felt were the multiple causes of the French theatre's lack of progress: the first was the common belief that going to the theatre was a sin against Christianity; the second was the stigma of ill fame attached to the profession of acting; the third consisted in the flaws and failures that one observed in performances; a fifth problem was that bad poems and good ones were being given the same exposure; in addition, stage sets were of poor taste; and finally, there was the problem of the unruliness of the spectators. Consequently, precise rules had to be determined. Due care had to be taken to not confuse religious ceremonies and pleasurable, entertaining shows and to do away with base and dishonest farces as well as everything related to good morals. This would allow actors to perform their legitimate function, since one could no longer assume that they espoused the flaws depicted by their roles or in plays in which they acted. Additionally, they themselves, if they wanted to be good actors, needed to master the French language, know literature and understand the nature of the passions they played onstage.

It was also necessary for the king to make a declaration in support of theatre, attesting to its public value as honest entertainment, played by decent subjects to an upstanding audience.

> In the interest of good morals, girls shall not go up on the theatre stage, if they have not their father and mother with them. Widows will be obliged to remarry no later than six months after the death of their husbands, and shall not be allowed to play in the year of their bereavement, except if they are remarried.[10]

This implied the appointment of a

> capable person of probity as Director, Manager, or Grand Master of the Theatres and Public Playhouses of France, who will see to it that theatres remain places where good conduct prevails, who will oversee the behaviour of actors, and who will give account of this to the King, so that order may be maintained.[11]

This same steward would oversee the appointments of new actors and the morals of plays by existing authors, and would propose changes to the plays of new authors if needed. As a result, what took shape was a theatre that galvanised actors and authors in the hope of new earnings and honour. Decorations would be made by this overseer (the *intendant*), who would employ skilful people paid from the public purse (and not from that of the actors, who paid the decorators in the seventeenth century: now "their only expense was to be that of their costumes and the honoraria they give to the poets").[12] The other important group of people were the spectators, who needed to be controlled and managed, since, as was well known, they used to make constant outbursts in the theatre. D'Aubignac recommended that they be trained and separated in various ways: first, by preventing so-called troublemakers from entering: "in the interest of the safety and comfort of the spectators, the king shall forbid all pages and valets, as well as all persons bearing swords or other arms, from entering theatres, on pain of death".[13] That was an initial step to prevent the violence and thefts about which d'Aubignac had previously complained.

Even more interesting were the reforms he recommended for the auditorium:

> [F]or the comfort of the spectators, the parterre must be elevated, and filled with chairs so as to be completely reorganised, which will prevent the spectators from fighting, in

that they will have no space to do so. But to perfect the magnificence of the theatre, the Master [*l'Intendant*] will find a comfortable and spacious place and turn it into a room on the model of the ancient theatres; so that its length and depth could accommodate all large performances. The seats of spectators must be separate, though people of the upper classes should not be mixed with those of low birth. On the outside of this theatre house, rooms will be built to house two troupes of actors necessary for the city of Paris, completely free of charge.[14]

Here, then, was a well-supervised, structured and centralised theatre project, which, d'Aubignac hoped, would give the kingdom all the lustre it required. Less than a century later, it was an actor who would relay these demands. When Luigi Riccoboni, head of the Italian troupe, actor and theorist, published his book *The Reformation of the Theatre* in 1743,[15] there emerged, as Sarah di Bella has shown in her doctoral thesis,[16] the ideal programme of a socially regulated future theatre, where the actor would adhere to the *desiderata* of classical and modern theorists, down to the fine detail. Theorists won practitioners over: to defend the theatre, despite its imperfections and dangers, it was necessary to control it. Not only from the point of view of the texts that were played there, but also by overseeing its entire machinery and the multifarious spectators that attended. Since, according to Riccoboni — who merely echoed the severe judgements of theatre opponents who preceded him, and of the zealots of a convenient, useful and reasonable theatre — theatres are spaces of disorder where "the lazy and the licentious" lead the audience away, and spend their time watching and entertaining women (be they spectators or actors). Therefore, it was time that "the public authorities protect the Theatre".[17] However, the actor and head of the Italian troupe somewhat tempered his censorship. In his eyes, one should not be excessive, but should also be careful not to only show moral and reasonable plays lest one ends up with empty theatre houses. In order for the art of theatre to be entertaining, useful and adequately attended, a building, financed by the city and larger than the customary theatre precincts, should be constructed and managed by the "Government, which alone can order and ensure the execution of the reformation, despite the opposition of a great many people lacking in awareness of their own true interests".[18] In these large premises apprenticed actors were housed as per Riccoboni's plan. They were trained on the very sites of their theatrical practice, in close contact with their teachers, with the working acting troupe, and with retired artists. Spaces were also created for the meeting of a Council of Censorship and Control, presided over by the king, and composed of a representative of the chief of police, two doctors of theology, two poets and one or two former actors. All parties were thus fully convinced of the need for order, and were capable of sniffing out possible transgressions in texts sometimes placed there by unaware authors, and staging mechanics able to produce dangerous effects. Additionally, these theatres were commercial spaces exempted from taxation.

While for Riccoboni the stage must also be sufficiently large and emptied of spectators so that the machines can operate effectively and the actors appear alone, the house also had to be reconsidered. Women were separated from men and spectators were seated according to their social status. The first balconies were reserved for the nobility, the second for the bourgeoisie, the remaining two or three (since Riccoboni imagined a house with more vertical volume than usual) for the people and

> for those who, before, would be in the parterre. There are two advantages to be had from such an arrangement: the nobles, often inconvenienced by the whims of the parterre, would be placed far away from it; secondly, the makers of mischief would be brought under control more easily, without disturbance to the performance.[19]

The parterre, the space of transgressions, would therefore be removed, elevated into an amphitheatre by a system of tiered seats from the orchestra to the back of the house, and would thus become a socially "treated" space, as comfortable as the boxes, to the point where the aristocracy would come to prefer it to the boxes on the first balcony. What this modern actor defined in this process of transformation was, to some extent, a disciplinary panopticon, where each cell was perfectly indicative of the society that occupied it. A panopticon whose function was to represent texts inspected by the Council that monitored acting and writing. And the spectators' capacity to appreciate the play would be defined based on their perceived ability to appreciate acting, text, staging apparatus and the fiction that they were shown: the best point of view belonging, of course, to the most honest and best-trained audience.

This example of a theatrical ideal formulated in the first part of the eighteenth century would be revisited and adapted by Voltaire, La Harpe and thinkers of aesthetics, architecture and scenography of the time. However, it had the benefit of being infinitely clear since it revealed the major principles that preside over the traditional conception we have of the place in which the "magic of theatre" is staged: a regulated, disciplined and controlled social space.

The experience of the fourth wall: dramatic theatre

Given the evolution of the theatrical genre, the logical tendency at this stage was to separate the space of fiction from the social space of reception, the stage from the house. The spatial boundaries became more and more solidified and clearly marked, to the point where the notion of a "box" and a "fourth wall" came about, and stage benches disappeared in the eighteenth century. In the Romantic era, the space of fiction took ever-increasing precedence over all others and, with the help of lighting, the house was placed, little by little, in darkness, which left the stage as the only place lit up. Moreover, the main role of scenery, costumes and props became increasingly to direct attention, *in principle*, only towards the fiction.

D'Aubignac's "classic" ideal did not only consist in regulating place. In order for the aesthetic to be centred on the fiction during a performance, the audience that occupied that space had to be trained, and made to be attentive. As such, for D'Aubignac, the spectators should ideally be captivated by the plot by means of dramatic techniques, on the one hand, but also through the use of scenery, acting and machines, on the other, which all came together to turn the performance into the true-to-life unfolding of an action whose artifices would be invisible to the spectator. To show an art that was so perfect that its artifice was invisible: what could be more specific to this than a classic aesthetic perspective? And, in this context, it became essential that the representation be a closed box of which one transparent wall could be penetrated by the gaze of the spectator. This is the theoretical origin of the *dramatic* theatre. During the century that was to follow, the theatre was at pains to put in place the practical means for its operations.

Indeed, during the eighteenth century, scenography made a great deal of progress. The stage was divided lengthwise into several *tableaux* (at least three) and, from front to back, into several zones of play. The stage sets and machines, having perfectly integrated the rules of perspective, created an effective illusion. Specific sounds added realism so that there was a whole host of special effects capable of creating a credible dramatic space. The authors, well versed in the technical functioning of the theatre, proposed both in their stage directions and in the paratextual material, which they produced in abundance (Diderot, for example), staging techniques capable of concretising the spaces they imagined. Voltaire, the most famous writer of tragedies of his time, would always indicate to practitioners which devices he envisaged. Lemierre achieved remarkably wide success by requesting that the apple in his *William Tell* be actually pierced by an arrow during the performance itself. Simultaneously, the expressive acting style of English actors, which coincided with the overall anglomania of the mid-eighteenth century, enlivened declamation and radically altered body language: Garrick would come onstage with bloody hands, making spectators shudder. As people had forgotten the special effects of the early seventeenth century, they started thinking that France was finally discovering a British specificity of which it was previously unaware. Forgetting, recycling, borrowing, invention – that is the rule. But this time, it became clear that the scene and dramatic space produced onstage with its action, scenery, acting methods, effects, story and discourse, had become the priority. And while one continued to go to the theatre to be seen and to see others, the representation most often took on the value of something stronger than a pretext for being together. The illusion box was well and truly there. Authors could finally write *as if* their characters were perfectly isolated from the audience in this other space that they imagined for them, and the actors themselves, discovering the new joy of being alone on the stage, took advantage of the oil lamps and ramps to get fully into character. As for the audience, still often standing and boisterous, observers tell us that they calmed down, "forgetting" others who might interrupt the illusion, to enter the story through their sole conduit being their eyes. Everyone could then play as if the fiction acted out onstage was so separated from the audience's physical space that the spectators felt like witnessing, as if hidden behind a transparent curtain, a plot so believable that it could pass as being real. Dramatic theatre thus came into existence and, with it, the fourth wall.

In reality, however, the idea of the fourth wall originated elsewhere, in a sort of theatre script salon. Indeed, in his *Entretiens sur "Le Fils naturel"* [*Interviews on "The Natural Son"*][20] and in *The Natural Son*, Diderot imagined both a scenario and a staging device. The idea is of a hidden narrator who witnesses, in the privacy of a living room, the staging of a "real" plot, i.e. one previously experienced by a family. Simultaneously, the representation of this narrative by the family itself is supposed to "bring back to life" the dead father, since in the final scene, Lysimond, the father, enters onstage in the midst of the actors playing their own selves, and evokes pathos. It is a curious thing to witness theatre and, what is more, a theatre retracing a real and very recent story, with actors playing their own roles and knowing that only one actor is playing the role of a real dead person. What a curious thing to witness all of this without being seen; to witness these quasi actors being moved by the return of the father figure, and to be also moved by their emotion and their tears. And what is also unusual is the fact that, in the eyes of the hidden narrator (behind whom is the reader) – the spectator of this intimate scene, isolated from the dramatic space by the fourth wall and swept up by the emotion – the ("amateur") "actors", under the weight of the pathetic event (the return of the deceased father embodied in *another*, an actor), are forced to interrupt this representation. It is to share in the effusion of Dorval, one of the "real" characters who have presided over this memorial theatre performance, that the voyeur-spectator eventually comes out of his hiding place. The narrator testifies to Dorval of the feeling of truth that he has experienced during this private theatre ceremony. The result is that during this magnificent illusion manipulation, whereas no one is unaware of the artifice at work, the actors are overcome with real emotion. In this societal theatre, typical of the eighteenth century, the novelty consisted in determining strict boundaries, then purposely pushing them via the emotion that their structure produces. What makes this specific event distinctive, however, is the fact that it is both social theatre and a domestic, private and intimate plot that is taken to be real. Therefore, if one forgets for a moment the fictional framework of the *narrative* into which the theatre is inserted, the watcher does not exist as an audience (he is "truly" hidden from the "actors"). As such, the subjects who are viewed, rather than the objects of viewing, are part of ceremony of mourning and memory. What is highlighted here is the trace of these theatrical events shared by private citizens who are not acting in order to be seen, but rather to practise a ritual that will unify them. It is thus the traces of a theatre of integration we encounter, which takes place not within the social structure, but in a house, within the precincts of a family's private space. It is the movement that the dramatic plot and drama, transmuted into reality by narration, makes from the house into another space. At the heart of the matter, for Diderot, is that he makes this experimental ceremony, played by amateurs and framed by narration, a theoretical model capable of being figured on a theatre stage, in the space of professionals. Indeed, whereas the hidden narrator was in a position to see without being seen, and the actors playing their own roles were able to act as if they were really living their adventures, thereby hiding the fact that they were performing a spectacle; while the impression given to the hidden-narrator-audience was that it was witnessing something entirely different from theatre – life via the theatre, in a word – the challenge that was posed was the question of how to compose dramas that could transpose this narrative-dramatic model on to the stage, with an ostensibly present audience.

There needed to be, by a reliance on new staging devices and on a clearer separation of house and stage, dramas that represented the image of the world of the spectator by ensuring that the framework of the action would tend to mirror the real world, not just from the point of view of writing and dramaturgy, but also from that of the stage sets. It was thus thanks to the practical separation between watched and watchers, and specifically, the location of the performance in an isolated space upon which all gazes are concentrated, that the search for a stronger resemblance between house and stage could be undertaken, with the aim of achieving a heightened degree of realism. Such realism needed to evoke the present time, and the actuality and realness of human dramas. The aesthetics of the fourth wall that were forged in large part to Diderot's *Entretiens sur "Le Fils naturel"*, functioned both as a dramatic tool in the hands of the author and a guide for acting as far as the actor was concerned: an effort was required by both author and actor to forget the presence of the audience. Consequently, it seemed necessary to totally close the stage off with a curtain when one was not playing,[21] so that upon raising it, the practitioners – and particularly the actors, whose play was of critical importance to Diderot – could create the conditions for a yet more effective theatrical illusion: "only imagine the spectator as if he did not exist. Imagine, at the edge of the stage, a large wall separating you from the orchestra: play as if the curtain did not rise".[22] This was to lead to a double paradox: first, that of the actor, devoid of all sensitivity but capable of rendering "scrupulously the outer signs of feeling" and mobilising her art in the service of the spectator's identification with the character; and second, that of the spectator who is considered absent, or absorbed in a game of identification that allows her to recognise the real world onstage. Yet, this spectator is also privy to the whole operation of the theatrical illusion. Theoretically, the whole operation is superb. However, as Diderot admits, by distancing itself from the audience and appearing to take place that is absolutely elsewhere, the performance loses the warmth that unites spectators and actors, and erases the confused energy of the theatre session that allows both parties to communicate in a single place. Once again, Diderot highlights a paradox within his dramatic proposition: either the spectator is subdued and separated from the fiction so as to be able to empathise with it on an individual level, the result of which is the erasure of the perception of a shared, communal, infinitely social, if sometimes erratic, event; or the effect of the animated warmth of the session is achieved and the spectator is not clearly separated from the dramatic space such that the relations between place and space become porous, and the individual finds it difficult to "enter the fiction". Rousseau's response to this dilemma was to eliminate representational theatre, and thus remove the vice inherent in identification, in favour of ceremony and festivity, whose sole function was the political representation of the perhaps naïve, revolutionary or rediscovered happiness of assembling to create a more virtuous social body. This would produce the conviviality Diderot so desired, but this time without danger.

The theatre of the Romantic era, perfectly aware of the paradoxes articulated by Diderot and investigated by German theorists and dramatists (particularly Lessing, in his *Die Hamburgische Dramaturgie* [*Dramaturgy in Hamburg*]).[23] Taking advantage of the technical advances of the previous century, the scenery became more and more realist and filled with objects, furniture and all kinds of accessories. The use of rough perspective, research into optics and gas lighting allowed decorators to foster illusion and even imagine special effects: with optical illusions, three-dimensional objects and views that enlarged the framework of the usual scenery, the scenography of the nineteenth century was so impressive that the audience came for it as much as for the actors and to listen to the text. At the beginning of his career, Daguerre was the one who adapted the technical innovations in optics at the Ambigu-Comique, such as panoramas, much in vogue since the beginning of the nineteenth century, and dioramas, which were also to become very popular. The audience rushed to showrooms devoted solely to special effects and then saw such effects recycled in the theatre. Panoramas represented a whole landscape, a specific site or a scene through a realist painting on the curved interior surface of a rotunda. This allowed the spectator to grasp a whole landscape or scene, all the more since they were engulfed in semi-darkness, while the painting was lit in various ways and accompanied by objects in relief in the foreground. Originating in the United Kingdom (Robert Barker, 1787 and Germany (Johann Adam Breyzig, 1794), this technique was introduced by the English painter Robert Fulton in 1799 and displayed as an attraction at the picturesque Theatre of Monsieur Pierre, at the beginning of the century, and at the Panorama dramatique of Baron Taylor and the decorator Alaux, in 1822–1823. The diorama, invented by Daguerre and Bouton, went even further: it was a tableau painted on both sides with a mixed material, partly opaque, partly transparent, so that the projection of light ensured an illusion effect thanks to the game by which various parts were lit up differently by reflected and refracted light. An additional effect of movement was achieved thanks to partial or total changes of transparent canvases sliding on a chassis. With Pierre Cicéri in particular, such an effect was realised by means of a painted canvas uncoiled over a drum: this was the moving panorama of *Sleeping Beauty* in 1829. The prevailing idea was to create the perception of a concentration of visual effects that impressed the viewer through its sheer immensity.

The audience is thus caught up in the illusion and, at the same time, comes to see the performance for the sheer magnificence with which the decorators carry out the illusion (like the spectators who, nowadays, go to see the Geode at La Villette, or to Futuroscope). They want a taste of spectacle and of invention, not so as to believe that the other side of the fourth wall exists, but to appreciate the way in which the practitioners utilise their art to make another place appear and enchant the spectator. Authors were delighted by this technical godsend, and would demand so much innovation in their stage directions that it became impossible to carry it out. Consider Musset, for example, in his theory of the "theatre à lire", which was meant to be read in an "armchair" as manifested by *Lorenzaccio*. Kleist, in *Penthésilée*, thus aspires to create an "invisible theatre" that was judged harshly by a much dismayed Goethe. Others, like Victor Hugo, described their staging apparatus with the utmost precision and technicality even down to the most minor accessories. They did this based on their own conception of the drama. As a result, the scenography of the twentieth century would revisit the romantic dramas, making them scenographically possible, thanks to the development of techniques of lighting and staging. However, though illusion generated much fascination, it remained, as always, a game, which would never be complete or continuous: the local colour, the optical illusion and natural acting were tricks that everyone – authors, audience and scenographers – played with. As such, it was within this gap between the illusory and the real, with its vibrant interplay space and the machine, that the theatres of the time would represent *apparently* realist, and actually metaphorical, spaces. Indeed, it was out of this metaphorical movement that structured the romantic stage that realism in the theatre emerged.

This realist or naturalist theatre endeavoured to represent onstage a slice of life considered as real, down to the smallest detail, and no longer in a sort of general, grandiose vision: every object, every stage set, every form of acting had to appear as if it existed or as it was possible to view it in the world. It was in naturalist theatre that the fourth wall triumphed; and in a movement of reaction towards it, the symbolist movement strove to abolish it.

The closed space instituted by dramatic theatre

As explained above, the closure effect from the eighteenth century was what would characterise a part of the theatrical representation later associated with so-called dramatic theatre. This theatre encloses the story (the *fabula*) while opening up to the mute gaze of the audience, and is based on the theory of "the absolute", to use the words of Peter Szondi.[24] It aims to embody a "self-contained dialectic" in which the actor disappears behind the character he creates and works towards a self-contained representation. The practitioners endeavour to render the dramatic space believable and to make the spectator forget the stage, and the author attempts to erase all the signs that could reveal his own implication. Dramatic theatre thus recuses every visible sign of its (secondary) (re-)presentational character to portray itself as "primary". It removes any ostensible communication with the spectator and does not theoretically practice metatheatricality or exhibit its conventionality: on the contrary, it plays on the two poles of separation between stage and house and of any potential identification. Its principal vector is dialogue, the time it imposes is a succession of pure presents, organised in a dramatic tension, which is the only thing capable of captivating the spectator through the representation of conflicts leading to the moment of their resolution in the final catastrophe. Dramatic theatre, historically outmoded, thus aims to be *theoretically* and *practically* illusionistic: it is meant to construct a dramatic space onstage; a closed, self-contained and self-sufficient world into which the spectator can enter emotionally – a world that, for the duration of the representation, they can hold to truly exist before their eyes.

This principle eventually became the very definition of traditional Western theatre. So much so that the adjective "dramatic" in everyday language is now used as a synonym of "theatrical", and no longer defines a clearly defined theatrical aesthetic. However, as we have seen, this aesthetic, while it has imposed itself in the common imaginary, remains nonetheless something quite specific: it embodies a certain conception of theatrical *mimesis* that, re-emerging in the modern age, relies on the distinctions and definitions of Aristotle's *Poetics*, later reformulated by Hegel (*Lectures on Aesthetics*, 1832).[25] It is also a spatial apparatus linked to the emergence of perspective scenography followed by a "training" of the audience.

To sum up, the establishment of the dramatic model or, rather, of a notion of the dramatic in the theatre, coincides with the use of perspective and, from a theoretical and poetic point of view, with the rediscovery of Aristotle's *Poetics* in Italy then in France in the sixteenth century.

Dramatic mimesis is based on the duality formulated by Aristotle between imitation by narrative (specific to the epic, and claimed by an author or narrator) and imitation "in acts", specific to tragedy. Hegel, in his *Lectures on Aesthetics*, defines theatrical mimesis in relation to the genres of the lyric and the epic, between which it is located. The principle of dramatic theatre is thus that of an "imitation carried out by characters in action and not by means of narration",[26] carried out in the present, and made up of a complete, harmonious and coherent "whole": the Aristotelian "beautiful animal". As its etymology indicates (*drama*: action), dramatic theatre concentrates on the primacy of action: its principle is unity and its action is often centred on an interhuman conflict (*agon*). This action is then offered to the spectator in a performance that seeks to make them forget that it is produced by virtue of them being there. In other words, the action is (re-)presented as having its own autonomy, and even an autonomous reality.

During the Renaissance, in the wake of a resurgence of dramatic writing, rules seeking to create mimesis and allow for the use of illusion were gradually established (in particular in France during the seventeenth century). To create this illusion, from a material or practical standpoint, the framework of representation was tightened and, as we have seen, practitioners took advantage of perspective. Because it was based on the spectators' acceptance of the conventions engendered by the systematic use of perspective, the so-called "classical" dramaturgy of seventeenth-century France would see the establishment of rules of unity (time, place and action) and of propriety that aimed to foster this new kind of mimetic representation. These rules were based on the very coded and conventional genres of tragedy and comedy.

In the eighteenth century, with the emergence of drama [*le drame*], a new intermediary genre between tragedy and comedy, a new dimension was achieved with respect to dramaturgy. The drama was a serious genre, which nevertheless involved actors who struck the spectator as being human, close to her in nature, and who, therefore, were individuals with whom she could identify. It was a genre that foregrounded the representation of virtue and of common moral values. Displaying a tendency toward sentimental effusions, the drama sought to present to a bourgeois audience a realist mirror of its world and values. The notable practitioners of the time included Diderot (*Le Fils naturel* [*The Natural Son*]) and *Le Père de famille* [*The Family Man*]), Beaumarchais (*Eugénie* and *Les Deux Amis* [*The Two Friends*]) and Louis-Sébastien Mercier.

To be effective, this mirror had to be held up within a tight construction of dramatic tension that favoured captivation and identification.

The notion of the "fourth wall" (officially defined by Diderot in 1758) was a case of imagining representation *as if* the audience was not there and did not have to be taken into consideration. It was the manifestation on the stage of this aesthetic ideal.

It was this French (and later German) model that gradually came to hold sway in Europe up until the nineteenth century. As a result, the dramatic aesthetic could benefit from various technical evolutions; give up, in certain cases (romantic drama, melodrama), certain unities, so long as it preserved the unity of action; and find its most typical form in the "well-made play", characterised by a very tightly woven plot, an ideology that was perfectly in tune with that of its audience and a rigorously organised construction of suspense.

The crisis of drama

However, it was at the turn of the nineteenth and twentieth centuries that the dramatic form encountered resistance from new forms of representation, leading to what Peter Szondi called the "crisis of drama".[27] In the illusion box, the sphere of intersubjective conflict immanent to the drama is disturbed from within, be it with Ibsen's analytic dramaturgy, the crisis of communication and dialogue in the work of Chekhov, Strindberg's experiment with a subjective form of drama, or the need to represent social forces (Hauptmann). Or, indeed, the presence of death and the symbolist drive to represent other "dimensions" – those of the unformulated, the unconscious and of the untapped powers of the soul and of the world – such as those we find in the work of Maeterlinck.[28]

Indeed Maeterlinck sought to turn the stage into a place that would allow you to feel "the mysterious song of the infinite, the menacing silence of souls and of the gods, the eternity that rumbled on the horizon, the destiny or fate which one perceived inwardly, without outward identifiable signs", as he notes in the *Treasure of the Humble* (1896).[29] And it appeared necessary that "the march of time and many other secret marches become finally visible" allowing access to

> deeper realities than the stabbing deaths of ordinary dramas [. . .] Isn't it when a man thinks himself sheltered from death that the strange and silent tragedy of being and of the infinite truly opens up the doors of its theatre?[30]

The dramaturgy of the invisible, openness to the strangeness of the soul (and of the cosmos), and not merely pseudo-objective representation of interpersonal conflicts for their own sake, dramaturgy or *situations* and no longer simply of action, the "tragedy of the everyday" that Maeterlinck speaks about in his plays (*Intérieur* [*Inside*], *Les Aveugles* [*The Blind*]) and the apparently paradoxical notion of "static drama" radically challenge the stakes and principles of traditional dramatic representation.

> It is no longer a question here of the determined struggle of one being against another, of the struggle of one desire against another desire or of the eternal struggle of passion or duty. What matters, instead, is the will to highlight what is strange in the very fact of living, to put into focus the existence of a soul in and of itself, in the middle of a cosmos that is never inactive. What matters is to open our ears to hear, not just the ordinary dialogues of reason and sentiments, but the more solemn and uninterrupted dialogue of the human being and his destiny.[31]

From the primacy of action to the purely mimetic conceptions of dialogue and temporality, all the foundations of dramatic representation were thrown into crisis, by the will to turn the stage into a space of the experience of other categories of perception and other aspects of lived reality.

Both the theoretical presuppositions of the "absolutes" of drama and its canonical form could not withstand the necessity of bringing other dimensions of "reality" to the stage. There was now an interest in representing other relationships to time, other conceptions of action and of human relations, but also other understandings of the subject and, therefore, of the character, and, indeed, other forms of perception and of representation of lived experience onstage. As the stage's present became the crucial moment when buried secrets and unprocessed traumas are revealed and old scores settled, the crisis of drama was tantamount to the need to resolve issues that belonged to another time (issues whose linear representation might have been suited to a novel, rather than to a drama, in the conventional sense of the term). Given this context, the drama's present tense constantly harked back to the past, a past that it would unearth and analyse and from which it would draw consequences: it would be absolutely informed and determined by that other, seemingly non-dramatic time. This "presence" of the past thus invaded most of Ibsen's plays, such as *The Wild Duck* or the very aptly named *The Ghosts*. Here was another significant consequence of the emerge in the theatre of a *repressed* past that coincided with the emergence of psychoanalysis: the outer, visible life of the dramatic character, displayed in its relations with others, was replaced by characters plagued by unspoken resentments, undermined by the repressed aspects of their psyche, or haunted by the ghosts of their pasts. In the work of Anton Chekhov, the very notion of dramatic *action* is challenged by inner lives that refuse dialogue, and via a breach in the principle of an absolute (dramatic) present tense. Chekhov creates characters whose attempts at a harmonious relationship with their present time and space are thwarted, and who take refuge in the memories of a happy childhood (in Moscow) and in the utopia of a new beginning (in Moscow) that would give meaning to their lives (e.g. Chekhov's eponymous three sisters). Other Chekhov characters try to convince themselves that their lives will find meaning in work and in future generations: for example, Tuzenbach and Verchinin in *Three Sisters*. Others try to live in a happier past and, when confronted with an urgent situation, merely postpone essential decisions: Madame Lyubov Andreievna in *The Cherry Orchard*. And for all these characters trapped in their dreams and inner melancholy, communication, and thus the fundamental principle of the dramatic system that is dialogue and interhuman exchange, fails to function normally: conversations become merely quasi-exchanges that are false or partial, and each character follows his whims and thoughts in dialogues that, in many cases, might just as well be an intertwining of monologues. Dramatic conflict is thereby *relegated* or *marginalised* by what is being witnessed in the exchange of dialogues.

Naturalism seems to take issue with the medium of theatre. On the one hand, it rejects the theatre, and on the other, it proposes a different kind of theatre (such as in Zola's *Naturalism in the Theatre*[32] and certain works by Antoine). In France this fails. The success of Chekhov, Ibsen and Hauptmann in other countries suggested that the works that were branded naturalistic were not purely so. Given the desire of authors and dramatists to faithfully and "realistically" represent the human being, its behaviour and its relations on the stage, with all the complexity that such representation implied, the dramatic form found itself faced with an entire set of problematic dimensions (the complexity of the experience of time, the inner aspects or the interiorisation of the perception of action, the destabilisation of the efficiency of dialogue, etc.). These new dimensions introduced by dramaturgy exceed the boundaries of its conventional categories and undermine from within this theatre's claim of being "absolute".

With increasing attempts to abandon the representation of interpersonal relations and focus instead on the journey of one single character, often a projection of the author – as is the case in Strindberg's later productions – there was a shift towards a fundamentally *subjective* dramaturgy (for example with *To Damascus*). Strindberg went as far as choosing an oneiric model (that of the *drömspel*: "dream game"), in which "the author attempts to imitate the incoherent but apparently logical form of dream", where "anything can happen, everything is possible and plausible" and where "time and space no longer exist". Consequently, Strindberg "gives free rein to his imagination, which creates multiple places and actions in a mixture of memories and lived experiences, of free fantasy, absurdity and improvisations". A space, time, action and text would thus be created, in which "characters were split or multiple, disappeared or became effaced, came apart or were reshaped".[33] The death knell of absolute drama had been tolled.

This short review alone helps us to understand how the death of dramatic theatre, seen as "absolute drama", was foreshadowed at the turn of the twentieth century. Since then, it agonises every evening on stages that seek to prolong its life. But, while it has had an ending, can it truly be said to have had a beginning other than in theory and in the myth of its existence? For it is evident that even in works that endeavour to strictly apply its principles, the dramaturgy of absolute representation is shown to be simply an ideal and a theoretical goal in the real context of the theatrical stage. Faced with the principle of "dramatic theatre", the concrete representation of such plays unfailingly produces an essentially "anti-dramatic" theatricality that undermines their presuppositions and that, paradoxically, is necessary for their effectiveness as theatre. In the strictest sense, it may only be in the act of reading that dramatic theatre ends up being a faithful reflection of its theoretical bases, which uphold aesthetics of realist, rational and illusionistic *mimesis*. It is as a result of this that the entire dramaturgy of the twentieth century, in keeping with the scepticism towards the notion of an illusion box, saw theatre rebuilding itself based on either the outright rejection of dramatic postulates, such as in Brecht's "epic theatre", or on the deconstruction of its fundamental components (character, action, dialogue, narrowing and continuity). It has been faced with the weakening purchase of ideological-aesthetic presuppositions, and particularly that of the autonomy of the work of mimesis, which unpinned that dramatic conception of theatre and its scenographic organisation under the fourth wall.

6

STAGE AS PLACE AND STAGE AS SPACE

Indeed, at the end of the nineteenth century and the beginning of the twentieth century, the dominance of the pictorial perspective started to be challenged. The theatre endeavoured to go beyond the idea of the decorator as mere painter who created painted canvases that conventionally depicted a real scene, to aspire to the ideal of a theatrical space as a space in its own right, active and in real interaction with the actor's body and the dynamics of the drama, and participating wholly in the general organisation of the representation, which could now suitably be called a *mise en scène*.

Rupture: the invention of the director, the total space of a total work

This movement takes place first of all amidst an approach that sought a deeper experiment with stage realism – a naturalistic approach. The figure of André Antoine, traditionally considered as the first true "*metteur en scène*" of French theatre, is, in this regard, essential.[1] Antoine, who created the Théâtre-Libre in 1887, sought to carry out onstage the naturalistic aesthetic, which Zola had theorised in *Le Naturalisme au théâtre*. It was an attempt to reproduce, in the most exact fashion possible, "slices of life",[2] and to represent the concrete social environment that the play referred to through the use of scenery. This environment was considered fundamentally central, and it has a great influence on the actor who would show that his character was the very product of it. This environment was therefore not only decorative or illustrative, but rather it was essential to (and in) the action, since it determined it, and because it guides the reach of what is played onstage. It was thus the intention of Antoine to create a more realist space, not so as to create a picturesque environment, but to represent the characters' interaction with their social environment.

Following this "verist" mindset, it stood to reason that theatre would have to be freed of its conventional paraphernalia – that of painted canvases, ornaments, bourgeois salons and "theatre costumes" – but also that of declamation or of "exaggerated", larger-than-life acting. Everything had to be "true": the objects, the costumes, the furniture, but also the tone and the acting style. As legend would have it, Antoine went so far as to have bloody meat onstage! Thus the Diderotian principle of the "fourth wall" was not only reaffirmed but pushed to the extreme, and the space intended as a reconstitution-reconstruction of lived experience. The realist *aesthetic* implied a reconstruction of space rather than a naïve transposition of fiction on to the stage. It thus endowed this space with a structuring role that was fundamentally important, as in the novels of Émile Zola. It was essential to reconstruct a completely new framework: behind the fake doors of a room represented on the stage, Antoine's ideal would be, for example, to be able to represent the entire house, so that one could see it. Equally important was handling accessories and small objects with infinite care, as they were considered essential:

> [T]he profusion of small objects, the diversity of small accessories. Nothing creates a greater feeling of home in any interior. It is these imperceptible things that give a sense of the intimate, the deep character of the environment that one has desired to represented.[3]

Antoine thus brings together within the same principle the whole its small details, in his sets as much as in the naturalistic acting style of the actor, which was meant to be "natural" and "true", emphasising the autonomy of the stage: so true that the actors could play with their backs turned (and with the house in darkness). But what also contributed to the realism of Antoine's *mises en scène* – and to the possibility of acting with backs turned to the audience – was the value placed on the body of the actor, the foregrounding of his movement ("the most intense means of expression of the actor"), of his physical presence and concrete expressivity in the conception of play ("his entire physical person": "at certain moments of play, his back and his feet can be more eloquent than a soliloquy").[4]

At the turn of the twentieth century, the symbolists were also considering these elements of space imagined as a whole, movement and the body, but from an entirely opposed perspective to that of naturalism. We could go so far as to say that it was even a marked reaction towards it. While other arts were moving away from realism, theatre wished to free itself from the illusion of the real and of traditional mimesis, to make its space an aesthetic one in its own right. "Art theatre", the "art of theatre", or the idea of the stage as a site on which different arts were synthesised, in line with the Wagnerian idea of the *Gesamtkunstwerk* (the total work of art).

Indeed, Wagner's work, and the representation of his lyrical dramas in the Festspielhaus constructed in Beirut, had a profound impact on European artists. Wagner was the first to darken a room during a performance in 1876. He also played with stage lights and their variations, generating magnificent effects for the technique of representing time. While, in practice, he remained absolutely within the framework of an illusionistic perspective, his affirmation of the autonomy of the stage as the site of the most ideal and expressive art was a defining moment. Even more so, perhaps, was his conception of an art that would bring together poetry, music, mimetics, architecture and painting. It was in appropriating and critiquing Wagner that the Swiss and English theorist-practitioners Adolphe Appia and Edward Gordon Craig worked out their own vision of staging, which would have a huge impact in Europe at the beginning of the twentieth century. Appia, a musician by training, created his "rhythmic spaces" after the staging of an opera, in a radical rejection of painted canvases and flat surfaces. It is both revelatory and hugely notable that Appia regularly collaborated with Émile Jaques-Dalcroze, the inventor of "rhythmics", a science applied to the human body, and particularly that of the actor. Rhythm is fundamental in Appia's conception of space: it is conceived around the living, central presence of the actor. The stage was envisaged as plastic and dynamic. It was felt that it needed to be freed from the two-dimensional framework implied by the proscenium stage, and be organised in a three-dimensional way, in volumes (stairs, horizontal and vertical lines, tilted planes and raised surfaces), and using lighting (the precision of which was now greatly enhanced by electricity). Lighting itself was to convey movement and the expression of feelings – in a word, it was to be musical. It was Appia's intention, then, as a *scenographer*, to animate the *space* around the dynamic body of the actor, to favour a sensitive kind of acting in stylised, rhythmic forms. His approach (real, and virtual in numerous ways) embraced a stripped-out aesthetic that bordered somewhat on geometrical abstraction, resulting in a stage infinitely conducive to gestures, movement, lighting and sound.

For Craig, theatre would also be a stage stylised for the art of space, forms and lines, lighting and movement. Practising the art of the sacred and the invisible in an almost devout way, he sought to rediscover "an art of theatre that came before the degradation that, for Craig, is constitutive of the mimetic image", according to Monique Borie.[5] Realism, and, in particular, its naturalistic variant, is the enemy. In a passage from his 1905 work, *On the Art of Theatre*, Craig declares that it is the "blind" who praise theatre, whereas the "clairvoyant" praise "Beauty": "the aim of theatre considered as a Whole is to re-establish its Art, for the art of theatre has nothing to do with the representation of the real".[6] "Whole" implies that it is not a mere interface for other arts (and that it must, therefore, affirm its individual nature) and, second, that it combines several components, forming an essential unity ("the unity essential for every work of art").[7] From this understanding comes the need for a director, supreme designer and absolute creator who is the guardian of this unity. Here again, the idea of music would be significant as a guiding principle for Craig (who, after his early beginnings as an actor, launched into directing by first staging lyrical works). Music would be placed on an equal footing with plastic arts, painting and particularly sculpture, and perhaps even more particularly, dance. Craig was particularly fascinated with Isadora Duncan. In a dialogue in *On the Art of Theatre*, the "stage manager" remarks to the "lover of theatre" that the "father of the dramatist" is not the dramatic poet, but the "dancer".

Instead of only using words in the manner of a lyrical poet, Craig the dramatist, crafted his first play with the aid of gestures, words, lines, colours and rhythm, appealing to the eyes as well as the ears through a skilful use of these five aspects. Craig thus aimed to provoke a sentience of forces, to transform the actor's art and the art of staging by suggesting a play of "uber-marionettes" on a "fifth stage" (emerging after the theatre of antiquity, the medieval theatre, the *commedia dell'arte*, and pictorial theatre *à l'italienne*). The expression "uber-marionette" referred of course to the actors and the director, but also to the statues of antiquity reaching towards the gods; between the organic and the inorganic, like masks. Craig's was an "architectonic" stage design: a single stage but consisting of panels and screens without pictorial motifs, and using lighting to transform stage setting. The whole stage could be transformed under the viewer's eye ("a hundred stages in one"!). It was a plastic and rhythmic space, a symbolic and potentially ritual one also, that would open the mind to the dimension of the invisible. It was a space for "the exaltation of belief, not of pretence".[8]

Whether from a symbolist or naturalist point of view, a desire for reform took hold in the theatre at the end of the nineteenth century and near the beginning of the twentieth. Other than those we have already named, many others may be cited: Lugné-Poe (in the symbolist camp) at the Théâtre de l'Œuvre in Paris, Georg Fuchs in Munich or Max Reinhardt in Berlin. Stanislavski and Danchenko of the Moscow Art Theatre were also key figures; so was Meyerhold (also in Moscow) with his inexhaustible work on forms of theatricality. This fully artistic desire for reform led to the establishment and centrality of the figure of the theatre director and to the reconception of theatrical space, which was now considered to be an organic space characterised by a harmonious relationship between various dimensions and components that needed to be ordered and organised to achieve aesthetic coherence.

From this moment on, a set of technical aides would need to ensure the proper running of theatre: a specialist of space – the scenographer – acoustic effects, costumes, lighting, then eventually computer technology, video, etc. A whole host of professions was consequently established with the aim of ensuring the success of the performance. Alongside the professions that focused on the text (author, dramaturge), they would become the professions focused on the event. The actors, duly supported, could now engage with the resources made available through the director, who was meant to control the whole apparatus and foster interaction.

Consequently, the relationship between theatre performance and text was changed in this process, such that the elements that were considered secondary up to now (objects, scenery and bodies) were then re-evaluated. Moreover, the very idea of the theatre performance as event, as well as its effects, became an object of reflection: the theatre building was freed of its supposed architectural specificity, particularly as it related to the proscenium. Additionally, the idea that there had always been theatre "elsewhere", rather than solely at the theatre, was now strongly emphasised. Above all, the frame effect created by the proscenium arch set and offered to the gaze of the spectator like a classical painting was eliminated or diminished. Jacques Copeau, by adapting the principle of the trestle stage, completely reworked the stage at the Vieux-Colombier. Peter Brook used a quarry for his staging of the *Mahabharata*. There was a renewed interest in ancient sites (courts, streets, scaffolds). The Roman ruins in Orange were put to use and so were the courts of palaces, such as in Avignon. The Globe in London was "reconstructed" and Spanish *corrales* (Almagro) were "rehabilitated". Directors would take over an abandoned theatre, making visible the traces of its former state of abandonment (Peter Brook at the Bouffes du Nord in Paris). Halls and courtrooms, factories in the north-east of France, but also near Paris (the Manufacture des Œillets in Ivry), military warehouses (the Cartoucherie in Vincennes), were put to unconventional use as theatrical spaces. It was a period, then, that witnessed many endeavours of diversity approaches to representation based on careful study of the history of theatre (ancient, Elizabethan, theatre of the Italian Renaissance) and of theatre phenomena and rituals from spaces outside of Europe (the Noh, the Japanese kabuki, Balinese theatre, African ceremonies, etc.). The theatrical site (since one could now make theatre everywhere and from anything) was now considered an empty space where any form could appear, but also as a place into which theatre penetrated, taking from this unconventional encounter a set of visible meanings.

From a slightly different perspective, Jacques Polieri in France is a symptomatic example of such a process, insofar as this director-scenographer has consistently reflected on movement, play and the fictional act in both his theory and practice since the end of the 1950s. His thought process challenges the notion of boundaries and of the separation of genres, to create theatrical events such as having an audience placed on a revolving platform surrounded by the performance (1960 in Paris), dissymmetrical theatre at the Maeght Foundation (1969), electronic plays on giant screens, multimedia plays, digital images, etc. These are in no way isolated phenomena and, more and more in contemporary plays (e.g. Peter Sellars, the Wooster Group), one witnesses a theorised interaction of virtual elements, digitalised images, computerised instruments, architectural techniques, principles of bodily movement and acting and vocal techniques carried by actors. It shouldn't be forgotten that scenography, like all performing arts, is a generally self-conscious DIY practice between artistry and technicality. It is a practice that mixes the precarious and the technical in the service of a concept of representation, as we shall see in the final overview we will do of contemporary staging.

Consequently, the director who is helped, and even sometimes replaced, in his function by the scenographer-artist (so much that the two professions sometimes merge), becomes the one who proposes "installations" that emphasise the play of the actor, the actor's play with the stage and with the audience, or the scenographic machinery itself. As a result, from theatre, scenography has now spilled over into all sorts of domains of performance (opera, circus, television sets, cinema, but also exhibitions, museums, urban spaces). It bears repeating that scenography is not, or not merely, the specific work done on a stage set, but a *dramatic* organisation of the space of the stage, *and* of the "natural" social and urban space for imaginary, metaphorical or symbolic purposes. It is the manifestation of a tension between place and event.

Nevertheless, it would be remiss to forget that the theatre, even when emptied of its spectators, even when the house is darkened, remains an assembly made up of intersecting gazes that can appreciate, often despite the effect of illusion and the desire to separate the house from the fictional world, the play of distance. For even with the most intense illusion, when attempts are made to transport the spectator into another world or to make them step into the intimate lives of the characters, the actors are always aware that they are being watched. Likewise, the spectator will always be aware that others are watching and appreciating the play in a different way. We could say that twentieth-century scenography, as if dismayed by the trap of illusion into which the theatre had fallen, and questioning the separation and rupture between fiction and reception that had been theoretically determined, was reconnecting more clearly, more consciously and more boldly, with the porosity of places and times, between fiction and representation. It set off in search of that art of alienation and that pleasure of distance from which it had drifted.

"Epic" theatre/dramatic theatre

We might understand the history of theatre if we reconsider the links between theatrical representation before the advent of dramatic theatre and contemporary scenography today, and between the distance effect in theatre at the dawn of modernity and the "estrangement effect" in contemporary theatre.

Beyond the experience of illusion, identification and projection (all of which are completely relative), theatre reveals another constant: that of distance and reflection, founded on awareness and analysis, in action and representation. At the moment when modern theatre was founded, in the seventeenth century, there was a play on the porosity of the boundaries between reality and fiction, and on their interpenetration, within a building in which gazes intersected and converged, in which scenery and costumes functioned as intermediaries and referential doubling, and in which the different aspects of staging played with the boundaries between the real and the virtual, between the time and the place of reception, the time and place of fiction and the visible space and infinity.

In other words, it seems possible to think of theatre through the lens of self-reflexivity and self-interrogation, both of which are constant features of our contemporary era. The art of theatre that was practised before dramatic theatre, and more particularly within a *practical* and *theoretical* enquiry on time and space, questioned itself: it engaged in an internal artistic self-critique, and in a dialogue fraught with quarrels between theoretical and practical standpoints, between dramaturg-theorists and theorist-dramaturgs. And while this dialogue and these interrogations take on different forms between the seventeenth and eighteenth centuries and in the twentieth century, they remain, nonetheless, fundamentally similar, and form the basis of a particular reflection on aesthetics. The notion of "epic theatre", elaborated from the 1920s onward by Bertolt Brecht, can be a great help to us here. This notion was defined in opposition to the "dramatic" conception of staging, scenography and the text to be represented. "Non-Aristotelian dramaturgy", according to Brecht, lays claim to a theatre that embraces its narrative dimension (whereas the dramatic form of theatre claims to be a representation purely in "acts"). In fact, the German *epische* could equally be translated, as Irène Bonnaud has done, as "narrative". Instead of captivating the spectator through illusion, it attempts to turn her into a lucid and relaxed observer (with "the posture of a smoker"). It thus strives to break the principle of the "fourth wall" and to create effects of distancing, to show the world and events represented, not as natural and unchangeable, but as contradictory and debatable. It gives pride of place to montage, rupture and interruption, heterogeneity, contradiction and discontinuity – in contradistinction to the principles of narrowing and continuity, which guarantee dramatic efficacy and, more broadly speaking, the presuppositions of naturalistic representation.

However, it is clear that in doing this, Brecht does not invent the potentially epic nature of theatre. Even if only through the presence of the chorus, Greek tragedy contained epic traits (if we take the Aristotelian definition, which provided the theoretical basis for dramatic theatre). Medieval theatre, whether in the form of strolling players or mysteries, featured an ostensibly narrative theatre (in the frontal nature of comic dramatic monologues, or the mysteries' symbolic regime or representation and their nature as "spectacle-journey" or their use of simultaneous scenes). Elizabethan dramaturgy such as that we see in Shakespeare, for example, is also often characterised by discontinuity (both temporal and in terms of register), in addition to its use of allegorical characters such as "Time" (*The Winter's Tale*) to narratively indicate a temporal jump of several years. Yet more broadly speaking, it is a fact that the so-called "dramatic" theatre, as it takes shape theoretically and textually in the seventeenth, eighteenth and nineteenth centuries, once approached from the point of view of the material conditions of its representation, ended up functioning based on narrative principles, in that the theatricality of the period ostensibly took the spectator into account, as we have seen, and was never based on a continuous production of illusion and empathetic tension. Western theatre, then, never took leave, concretely speaking, from the epic traits of staged demonstration, even when the dramaturgy (built around the text) strove to hide them. As for oriental techniques of performance, their ritual and/or coded nature has always been part and parcel of a non-dramatic conception of theatre – they were, moreover, used by Brecht as models (particularly the style of the Chinese actor Mei Lei Fang, witnessed while on tour in 1935, and that would be a catalyst for a number of Brecht's reflections on the epic actor and on the *Verfrumdungseffekt*).

Therefore, the Brechtian revolution did not come out of the blue. Formally, it inherited certain traits of agit-prop theatre, as well as new models of representation (involving the notion of montage in particular) that emerged with the literary avant-garde, but also with the advent of new artistic media such as cinema. The influence of more quotidian models is also undeniable: Brecht often cited the "street scene" of a narrative, along with its accompanying gestures, in the same way as a witness would recount an accident. In the domain of theatrical spectacle, the means that Brecht put in place were often an extension of those that had been invented by his contemporary, Erwin Piscator. This director from Berlin, under whom Brecht served as a dramaturg, had in fact put into practice some new technical innovations capable of sustaining the principle of epic theatre: rotating stages; conveyor belts; platforms for simultaneous actions; hemispherical stage divided into several compartments (invented for a staging of *Rasputin* in 1927, which had as its subject the fate of Europe from 1914 to 1917); the projection of films, whether it be a documentary or even a cartoon (for example, *The Adventures of the Good Soldier Schwejk* in 1928, which was an adaptation of Hašek's work and for which the cartoonist Georg Grosz created no less than 300 drawings). For Piscator, there was a need to bring the world to the stage via this proletarian, political theatre. This was a world that belonged to the masses and to history, which implied "moving beyond the autonomous division of scenes, the purely individual nature of characters, and destiny in the form of chance".[9] In other words, moving beyond the dramatic. A theatre of montage, of narration and of lengthened time, of the multiplicity of scenic elements, of the examination of history that made it also a "documentary theatre" (hence *Despite All* in 1925, a "sort of review of the period which went from the beginning of the war to the assassination of Liebknecht and Rosa Luxemburg"[10]); a theatre that was, in a sense, already epic by virtue of its subject matter. Piscator used the term in the 1920s, seeing in his play *Flags* (text by Alfonse Paquet, 1924) "the first consciously epic drama".[11]

But the Brechtian approach that contributed to establishing what we have called here epic theatre, was distinctive in its systematic nature and in its political and theoretical associations (already significant with Piscator). For Brecht, the fact that the dramatic system, insofar as it aims to depict conflicts between individuals, was incapable of representing the way these individuals are caught up in larger economic and political systems in the twentieth century, mandated the creation of a theatrical form able to represent a larger sphere, while dis-alienating the spectator in her relationship to representation, to show her a lived experience that is transformable and not immutable. The techniques of epic theatre, like its theory, were gradually elaborated and constantly revisited by Brecht throughout his entire career.

Man for Man (1925) is a play that takes place in British colonial India, whose main character, Galy Gay, is a man without character or individuality, and hugely malleable since he cannot say no. Contrary to the dramatic character who has a specific personality, Galy Gay is a burlesque character who can be dismantled and reassembled like a machine. He literally becomes another. This is also the play in which Brecht introduced commentaries and *songs* for the first time that would interrupt the action. In the *Caucasian Chalk Circle* (1945), the entire performance is framed by the *mise en abyme* device of the theatre within a theatre. A chorus of kolkhoz farmers led by a singer, and performing a narrative function, tells two different stories one after the other: that of the escape of the servant Grusha and that of Azdak, the writer turned judge. These two stories are linked at the end of the play when the judgement and the test – the "probe" – of the chalk circle come together. This play, as is the case for many others, borrows many of the theatrical methods found in the music hall – *The Caucasian Chalk Circle* was initially written for Broadway after all! It is also important to note that in the last phase of his career, Brecht preferred the concept of "dialectic theatre" to that of "epic theatre": this shift in terminology was a means of foregrounding the tension between dramatic elements and epic elements, manifesting, therefore, in the heart of the performance "the contradiction between playing ('giving a demonstration of') and living ('identifying with')".[12] Consequently, the Brechtian "narrative" theatre does not constitute a totalising system, but is an endlessly self-renewing enterprise of play on montage and theatricality that seeks to turn the stage into the site of an *experience*: making manifest the contradictions of the world to a spectator who is made all the more alert during the process.

Though the dramatic tradition remains alive and vibrant, it can also be said that the notion of an epic dimension has become widespread in the vast majority of contemporary theatre. Since cinema and television have dethroned the stage as the site of realist representation, and indeed, of the production of direct emotions, the theatre of the last few decades has not ceased to display the conventions and the necessary involvement of the author and of the artistic team (director, actor, etc.) behind the fiction represented, even if this dis-illusionistic display takes on varying and often less ostensibly political forms at the moment (formalism, image theatre and the treatment of the stage as a mental landscape, performance, the model of the storyteller). In a sense, the contemporary theatre that follows on from this Brechtian heritage, continues to play with the awareness of its own theatricality, thus acknowledging the spectator as the sole judge and ordering mind of the signs offered by the stage – a fundamentally epic principle, if not a founding principle of the theatre.

Despite the invention of the fourth wall, the "taming" of the audience and frontality, theatre spectators have always had a circular gaze with respect to the complex site in which the fiction is represented, which points to a fiction outside of the stage (like at the stadium, as Brecht would say). In doing so, they look up, down, around, and find "partners" who share their vision, debate, judge and gauge.

> The obsession with shoving the spectator into a one-way dynamic, where he can look neither to the left nor to the right, neither up nor down, is, from the point of view of modern dramatic art, to be recused. [. . .] One must get used complex viewing. Consequently, thinking about the course of action is almost more important than thinking during the course of action.[13]

At the same time, the emergence of a clear social and aesthetic specificity for the theatrical precinct, the professions attached to it, and the audiences that attend, implied an awareness of the nature of the representational space. It was not only a question of mimesis on a site intended for fiction, but also of the representation of a space of fiction by craftsmen, artists and professionals for audiences capable of instantly transitioning from the representation to the actual present of the social spectacle in which they participate and that they collectively form. Without sidestepping its larger social and political function, the theatre session, with all its different players (actor, spectator, character, author) is presented in an ostentatious manner as an aesthetic world that closely links the world outside the theatre's doors (in the city) and the virtual world of the fiction. The doors of the building, like those of the stage, thus provide access to all places and spaces whether they are considered real or imaginary, so that they may communicate with one another regardless of whether they are in opposition or in synergy and so that theatre can have an impact, both in the imaginary realm and in the social structure. Through this distance effect, through the institution of all these spaces and types of spaces, theatre becomes a place, a time and a discourse to be interpreted and judged, based on the discourses articulated onstage and the discourses articulated around the stage. The stage of the world and a stage that transcends the conventional limits of the world, an intermediary site, and a space specifically conducive to debate among an audience that gathers, of its own volition, to consider a case presented to it: this is theatre. The entire enterprise is therefore a discourse machine and a space of expanded consciousness. Thus discourse, space and time are opened up, deployed, refracted and extended to infinity from the cases presented: the isolated points of representation in the space of a session.

Composite and intermediary, pathway and conveyor and therefore infinitely conscious, theatre cannot help but be self-reflexive and problematic, even when it is presented as dramatic, if only because it is played in a place. It carves out a virtual space that forms a pathway to a limitless circularity, enabling a diversified, indefinite and particularised sum of the many points of view that are exercised during the performance event and which formally bring together aesthetic pleasure and critical positions.

It is in this sense that theatre becomes beyond all else a gathering of *capable* assembly: it observes itself while it observes; it touches the infinity towards which it tends; it is attached to the pleasure of understanding and evaluating the set of discourses articulated within it. It is in this sense that this *conscious assembly* that we call theatre is fundamentally social and thus by extension fundamentally human.

The boundaries of the theatrical space

We can confirm that the form and status of the theatrical space determine the type of spectator and the type of spectacle, which can be hosted there. Moreover, the dimensions of the stage determine the type of play possible (static, dynamic, choreographed, etc.), the possibilities of staging, the number of objects possible onstage, the effect of a void that one can create and therefore the overall staging space that one can put in place to create a dramatic space. The shape of the stage space also determines the type of play: whether in a round with spectators in a semi or complete circle; in a ring, as a traditional stage but with footbridges for acting that overlook the spectators and jut out into the space of the auditorium; as a more or less elongated rectangle around which spectators sit; or as an open-air stage or a stage in a closed room. Above all, it dictates the type of communication and relation to the audience that the actors can have, and the action and implication that the spectacle demands of the spectators. The depth of the stage is also a crucial factor at play: certain theatres in the Far East, like the kabuki, for example, play on lateral space since their stages have little depth. A director may opt for a scenography purposely constructed on the mode of the panoramic image (as Daniel Jeanneteau, among others, has recently done for this staging of Sarah Kane's *Blasted* in 2005). Conversely, some modern Western theatres allow for acting that uses the depth of the stage and for the construction of staging based on a play of receding planes, thanks to which one can imagine the movement of characters in time or in space, for example; or simultaneous presences; or even the succession and play of movement between these different planes of the staging space. This succession or play of movement is what we see produced by the potentially oneiric strangeness of François Tanguy's spectacles, which often depend on the depth of the stage achieved thanks to differing planes. The awareness of depth, which can be reinforced by variations in dimension between the staging space and a reduced audience space, specially rearranged for a particular play – as Daniel Jeanneteau would often do as set designer for Claude Régy's plays – allows us to determine the sensory effects of diving space up into planes, or, conversely, of presenting a enormous space in which the actor is isolated. Of course, the awareness of the height and width of the stage can allow for the same effects. The play of empty and filled space thus becomes most important in scenography. By emptying the stage one offers an "experience" in itself (a visual, phenomenological one, as in the work of Claude Régy), and one also insists, of course, on what remains and, therefore, becomes extremely significant: the actor or a few rare objects. In ostensibly filling the stage, one endeavours on the contrary to provoke infinite interpretations through the multiple means that can be drawn from objects, set design, costumes and the number of (speaking or silent) actors.

Consequently, despite the artifice of illusion, spectators and practitioners alike are always aware that the theatre is a theatre: an actual place designed to facilitate the creation of a virtual space, but that also plays with the boundary lines between place and space (the concrete and the virtual) that are always visible – *all the more* when theatre embraces its own theatricality.

We should note in passing that theatre has never ceased to pose these questions, that it has never ceased to play with the frontiers between staging space and the dramatic space and has never ceased to represent everything while also representing itself. In fact, one notable phenomenon at the beginning of the seventeenth century was to create in the body of the staging space a dramatic space that itself represented the stage, through the principle of theatre within the theatre. As a result, as the spectator witnesses actors moving across the stage, they also subscribe to the fact that they represent characters in a fictional world. But the spectator also realises, gradually or suddenly, that this fictional world is the site of a theatre and that these characters have become actors again. One therefore finds in Rotrou's *Le Véritable Saint Genest*, in Corneille's *L'Illusion comique*, or in a number of Spanish and Elizabethan plays, such as those of Calderon, Lope de Vega, Shakespeare or Philip Massinger (*The Roman Actor*) this type of play that consists in ensnaring a spectator caught up in the illusion of a fictional world, i.e. who is taken by the dramatic illusion. This is therefore a method of *mise en abyme*, a metatheatrical device, but also, practically, a materially effective principle of internal focalisation: indeed, the staging experience frequently shows that the presence onstage of character-spectators (of an inserted representation but also, simply, of an action proposing an intra-scenic gaze), produces a framing effect as well as the concrete sign of self-reflexivity which generally reinforce the audience's concentration.

To conclude this line of reflection, the technical word "discovery" encapsulates the idea of theatre. Indeed, a "discovery" is, first and foremost, what the spectator sees in the wings when her seating position allows it. A discovery is what the scenery does not hide. But a "discovery" quickly becomes, in the scenographic vocabulary, what hides the wings. Discoveries are constructed just like theatre drapes and stage curtains. Consequently, the discovery in the theatre is both what is seen (by mistake, or by design) and what hides that which must not be seen. And one can play indefinitely on that dual meaning to signify distance, the fiction separated from the physical place of theatre or the theatricality of the *mise en scène*.

The dramatic space: a replica?

Because we are in the habit of thinking about it, the dramatic space seems to us a replica of an actual world in which the represented fiction is inscribed: the stage set serves to create the illusion – proposed by the representation and agreed to by the spectator – of a real place being depicted. That is the first step of a theatrical play in any given space. If we take the case of traditional European theatre, the theatre is depicted by a sort of three-sided box that offers a perspective view – with the techniques linked to pictorial art – of the image, the illusion of a real place of reference to which the dramatic space testifies or that it "represents". This is so that it can depict the place in which a fictional being expresses itself – a fictional being whose definition is that she *could* belong to a real referential world (the Parisian bourgeoisie from the middle of the seventeenth century in the case of Tartuffe, Rome for Augustus, etc.). The condition for the success of this depiction is that the spectators must understand this reference, and that the objects, the set and the costumes must easily speak to them.

However, one can *play* with the reference and transcend the illustration: by quite faithfully representing a place as the apartment of Orgon (an invented character), Augustus' place (for *Cinna or the Clemency of Caesar Augustus*), or a modern salon (for a Boulevard theatre play, for example). We can remain at the level of banality too (the typical modern salon), while also evoking irony (too typical) or adding objects and elements that create an interpretive distance (Rome in the first century, but also Rome as it was represented in Corneille's seventeenth century, or perhaps even Roman as one sees it in the twentieth century, for *Cinna*). Just by looking at the scenography, even a realist one, we can immediately see that a relationship has been created that enables another thing to come to life within a mimetic framework whose abstraction calls out for interpretation. Because there is exposition and ostentation, representation, realist objects and scenery give place to the questioning of the imitation of real life by the *play* that consists in *representing* a place of theatre and in surpassing the plane illustration of a real place through meanings which give rise to other interpretations. All the elements of the *mise en scène* (scenery, objects, costumes) can thus vary: there can be substitutions, additions and interweavings that, for each of them, will provide new elements of signification for the interpretation of the spectator.

Additionally, the practitioners can choose to only represent a single object on an empty stage: a lone, real-life object that can serve, throughout the play, to depict several fictional or symbolic objects. Often in Peter Brook's *mises en scène*, we might see strips of wood, for example, turn into swords, prison bars, signs indicating the geographic boundary of place, standards, etc. In other *mises en scène*, like those of Claude Régy, a sole object placed on an empty stage acquires a symbolic status via metonymy and the use of over-determination, while retaining its material and illustrative appearance. A sword can simultaneously be the sword of the hero, a plastic object for the aesthetics of the staging, the symbol of power and emblem of cruelty and violence.

All in all, then, the modern dramatic space takes roots in the illusion of the real (of lived reality) only to take distance from it and to aim for abstraction. In the staging space is inscribed an abstract space indicating the particular meanings, which the director intends to give to the play. Consequently, the task of the director and of the scenographer is to put in place and organise a coherent network of signification with all these objects and these stage sets so that the spectator may draw from them one or several coherent interpretations, and that the actor may incorporate them into his play. Alongside the play of the actor, we may also speak of a play of objects, of stage sets and of the entire staging material, which is capable of guiding the spectator in their intellectual construction of a theatrical space of signification specific to a particular reading that one might give to the play. Almost in its very essence, theatre therefore has the ability to show the signs of its own theatricality, while at the same time representing a fiction. Not only in the scenes or plays that have as subject the theatre within the theatre but in all plays, including the comedies of Labiche and of Feydeau, which, through their use of asides, play on the divisions between the fictional world and that of the spectators: at each moment, the actor and the director have the possibility of exhibiting their art while, at the same time, expressing a fiction. Consequently, the mechanism of the box, with its fourth wall and its illusion system, is much less unproblematic than one sometimes thinks, and not only nowadays. Theatre is not, and has never truly been, a stage of illusion unaware of its own artistry.

Notes

Chapter 4

1 Florence Dupont, *L'Acteur-roi: le théâtre à Rome* [*The Actor King: Theatre in Ancient Rome*] (Paris: Les Belles Lettres, 2003).
2 A guild of legal clerks of the Paris court system
3 Élie Konigson, *L'Espace théâtral médiéval* [*Medieval Theatrical Space*] (Paris: Éditions du CNRS, 1975).
4 Brook also comments on the performance in *The Slyness of Boredom*, references it in *The Conference of the Birds*, where he examines Iranian poetry and theatre, and also deploys it in his staging of *A Midsummer Night's Dream*. The Tazieh has also been staged lately by Abbas Kiarostami in the form of a "theatre/video performance" at the Théâtre de la Bastille in 2005.

5 The main "takieh" in Teheran, which held 20,000 spectators, was destroyed in 1946.
6 For more on this, see the most recently published reference guide by Marie-Madeleine Mervant Roux, *Du Théâtre amateur, approche historique et anthropologique* [*A Historical and Anthropological Approach to Amateur Theatre*] (Paris: Éditions du CNRS, 2004).
7 Olivier Neveux, *Esthétiques et dramaturgies du theatre militant: L'exemple du theatre militant en France de 1966 à 1979* [*Aesthetics and Dramaturgies of Militant Theatre: A Case Study in France from 1966 to 1979*] (PhD, Université Paris 10 Nanterre, 2003), *Théâtres en lutte. Le théâtre militant en France des années 1960 à aujourd'hui* [*The Theatre of Struggle: Militant Theatre in France from the 1960s to Today*] (Paris: La Découverte, 2007).
8 Neveux, *Esthétiques et dramaturgies*, n.p.
9 Sebastian Serlo, *The Five Books of Architecture: An Unabridged Reprint of the English Edition of 1611* (London: Dover, 1982).
10 The actors needed to avoid getting too close to the canvas lest they ruin the illusion effect.
11 Particularly the Italian courts of Florence and Rome.
12 However, this sort of scenery was still practised until the 1640s. Corneille's *Cinna* is proof of this.
13 As in Kleist's *Penthésilée*, whose stage directions include elephants moving across the stage.

Chapter 5

1 The theatre of Venice or of Vicenza was not linked to a court but to academies. The *commedia dell'arte*, a theatre of artisans and troupes was vastly dissimilar to the Italian proscenium theatre. And in Florence, the *Camerino*, or secret theatre of Francesco I of the House of Medici was an alchemical, compartmentalised theatre where the prince withdrew to reflect on the discordant social harmony that he himself imposes via a supposed art of ruling.
2 The Palais-Cardinal was inaugurated in 1641 and was not designed to be a public theatre.
3 This theatre replaced the Hôtel Guénégaud, the opera house of the former *jeu de paume de la Bouteille*, and on the site of the old *jeu de paume de l'Étoile*.
4 "Le spectateur est encore physiquement présent aux côtés de l'acteur". Georges Forestier, *Le Théâtre dans le théâtre* [*The Theatre in the Theatre*], 2nd ed. (Genever: Droz, 1996), p. 23 (original work published 1981).
5 Which, nonetheless, is modified by an out-of-frame space known as the *proscenium*, and sometimes by the presence of playing actors within the audience space.
6 "Il est avantageux que le privilège des Machines chasse le Courtisan de dessus le Théâtre". Jean Rotrou, *Dessein du poème de la grande pièce des machines de la Naissance d'Hercule* [*Sketch of the Poetical Part of a Drama on the "Birth of Hercules"*] (Paris: René Baudry, 1649), p. 8.
7 Translation ours. Abbé Michel de Pure, *Idées des spectacles anciens et nouveaux* [*Thoughts on Old and New Entertainment*] (Paris: M. Brunet, 1668), p. 175.
8 On the subject of the parterre, consult Jeffrey S. Ravel, *The Contested Parterres: Public Theater and French Political Culture (1680–1791)* (Ithaca, NY and London: Cornell University Press, 1999).

9 François Hédelin, d'Aubignac, *La Practique du théâtre* [*The Practice of Theatre*] (Paris: Antoine de Sommaville; Hachette Livre BNF, 1657).
10 Ibid., p. 510.
11 Ibid., p. 513.
12 Ibid., p. 512.
13 Ibid.
14 Ibid., p. 513.
15 Louis Riccoboni, *La Reformation Du Theatre* [*The Reformation of the Theatre*] (Whitefish, MT: Kessinger, 2010) (original work published 1743).
16 See Sarah di Bella, *L'Expérience théâtrale dans l'œuvre théorique de Luigi Riccoboni: Contribution à l'histoire du théâtre au XVIIIe siècle* (Part III: "Histoire de l'expérience dans la théorie théâtrale") [*Theatrical Experience in the Theoretical Works of Luigi Riccoboni: A Contribution to Eighteenth-Century Theatre* (Part 3: "A History of Experience in Theoretical Theatre"] (Paris: Champion, 2009).
17 Riccoboni, *De la Réformation Du Théâtre*, chap. IV, p. 42.
18 Ibid., p. 68.
19 Ibid., pp. 330–331.
20 *Paradoxe sur le comédien, précédé des Entretiens sur le fils naturel* [*The Paradox of The Actor, Preceded by Interviews on "The Natural Son"*]. Chronology and preface by Raymond Laubreaux (Paris: Garnier-Flammarion, 1967).
21 Denis Diderot, *Œuvres de théâtre de M. Diderot, avec un Discours sur la poésie dramatique* [*Diderot's Plays, with a Discussion on Dramatic Poetry*] (Amsterdam: M. M. Rey, 1772).
22 Ibid., p. 231.
23 Gotthold Ephraim Lessing, *Hamburgische Dramaturgie, Volume 1* (Cambridge: Cambridge University Press, 1950) (original work published 1769).
24 Peter Szondi, *Théorie du drame moderne* [*Theory of Modern Drama*] (Lausanne: L'Age d'Homme, 1983) (original work published 1956).
25 Stephen Halliwell, *Aristotle's Poetics*, with a new introduction by the author (Chicago, IL: University of Chicago Press, 1998); Georg Wilhelm Friedrich Hegel, *Aesthetics: Lectures on Fine Art. Vol. 2*, trans. T. M. Knox (Oxford: Clarendon, 1998).
26 Aristotle, *Poetics*, ed. Frank L. Lucas (Oxford: Oxford University Press, 1968), p. 50.
27 Szondi, *Théorie du drame moderne*.
28 On this last point concerning Maeterlinck, see no. 15–16 of the journal *Études* (1999), devoted to the "crisis of the dramatic form" ("la mise en crise de la forme dramatique") and edited by Jean-Pierre Sarrazac.
29 Maurice Maeterinck, "*Treasure of the Humble*", in *The Routledge Drama Anthology and Sourcebook: From Modernism to Contemporary Performance*, ed. Maggie B. Gale, John F. Deeney and Dan Rebellato (London: Routledge, 2010), pp. 120–125.
30 Ibid., p. 158.
31 Ibid.
32 Émile Zola, "Naturalism on the Stage", in *Playwrights on Playwriting: From Ibsen to Ionesco*, ed. Toby Cole (New York: Coopers Square Press, 2001), pp. 5–14 (original work published 1881).
33 August Strindberg, Foreword to "*A Dream Play*", in *Les Ecrivains Célèbres: Oeuvres* [*Famous Writers: Works*], Vol. 56 (Paris: Mazenod, 1968), p. 183.

Chapter 6

1. See the anthology edited by Jean-Pierre Sarrazac and Philippe Marcerou, *Antoine, l'invention de la mise en scène* [*Antoine: The Invention of Stage Direction*] (Paris: Actes Sud-Papiers/Centre national du Théâtre, 1999).
2. This phrase was not invented by Antoine but by author and theorist Jean Jullien, around the same time.
3. Conversation about mise-en-scène, 1903, in Sarrazac and Marcerou, *Antoine*, p. 116.
4. Sarrazac and Marcerou, *Antoine*, p. 79.
5. Monique Borie, *Le Fantôme ou le Théâtre qui doute* [*The Phantom or a Theatre of Doubt*] (Arles: Actes-Sud, 1997), p. 226.
6. Edward Craig, *On the Art of Theatre* (London: Browne's Bookstore, 1912), pp. 268 and 98.
7. Ibid., p. 98.
8. Edward Craig, *The Theatre Advancing* (London: Little, Brown, 1919), p. 35.
9. E. Piscator, *Le Théâtre politique* [*The Political Theatre*] (1929), trans. A. Adamov (Paris: L'Arche éditeur, 1962), p. 65.
10. Ibid., p. 64.
11. Ibid., p. 57.
12. Bertolt Brecht, "Addendum" (1954), in *Petit organon pour le théâtre* [*Short Organon for the Theatre*] (Paris: L'Arche, 1978).
13. Bertolt Brecht, "Notes sur *L'Opéra de quat'sous*" [*Notes on the Threepenny Opera*] (1941), in *Écrits pour le théâtre* [*Writings on the Theatre*], vol. II, trans. Jean Tailleur and Edith Winkler (Paris: L'Arche, 1979), p. 312.

Part III

HOW TO ACT AT THE THEATRE?
How the theatrical space functions

It is now possible to highlight a few of the key characteristics that relate to the general functioning of the theatrical space. This space can be divided into two qualitatively different elements: the physical places (the theatrical precinct, the staging space and the specific space in which the actor plays) and the dramatic space in which the fiction takes place (and that is inscribed into the physical spaces). It is because of this very distinction that the dramatic space can attempt to depict a given space as real and sociocultural. For example, the space of *Tartuffe* is the house of a bourgeois family in 1664. The space of boulevard theatre is the modern bourgeois living room. The space of naturalist theatre is the nineteenth-century café or street. Any attempt to transform a dramatic space into something else, however realist it might be, by definition tends to be self-exhibiting, ostentatious, *represented*. While it is inscribed into the space of theatre and representation, it can never be a single, real space. It thus becomes possible to affirm something *other* than the simple illustration of reality by placing stage objects and bodies, which transcend the real and cause the notion of illustration to become unstable. Realist depiction is supplanted by other depictions that are linked not to a real, practical world inscribed in a mimetic relationship, but to ideas, to abstract interpretation that hang on iconic signs placed on the stage and to a sometimes autonomous plasticity. The dramatic space can thus be the depiction of totally imaginary spaces (the psychic mechanism of a character, for example), the spaces of dream, symbolic spaces, plastic spaces, etc.

A *mise en scène* can consequently use a sort of rhetoric based on the images inscribed into that *mise en scène*, as well as its particular semiotic system, to produce an interpretation of the play, which the spectator can understand. Such an actor or such an object becomes a symbol (the colour of the clothing, white for example, expresses purity or virginity), or a metaphor (a piece of wood depicting a prison), or metonymy (a sword depicting an entire army); in a word, the image of an idea that one wishes to transmit. We can even see a set of rhetorical figures as part of one single object: a chair becomes a throne (metaphor), which itself then depicts the space of a court (metonymy) and thus becomes the emblem and the symbol of royalty, of the struggle for power and, for example, of the violence of the State. And based on the decisions of the *mise en scène*, the elements that are represented onstage might actually be superfluous to the text that indicates them (for example if a character says "I am going to have a drink" and the actor picks up a glass) or perhaps non-redundant, but symbolic, metonymic, metaphorical and, at any rate, different. Either it is not a glass that they pick up, or it is a particular glass that will signify something other than a simple glass, or they pick up nothing at all, or something completely else entirely, etc. We might note, however, that one of the principles of contemporary *mise en scène* is a general tendency towards the "non-redundant" so that an additional textual signifier can be added that unsettles the text, or that fits (or attempts to fit) coherently into the general interpretation.

But, for all that, one should not make lists of loose elements that are organised according to an ancient and, indeed, ambiguous classification (animate/inanimate, object/subject, human/non-human, for example). When we speak of signs arranged into a *mise en scène* (and we are obliged to distinguish them in our analysis, if only for the sake of clarity), we emphasise at the same time the fact that they function as a network: they are to be seen systematically as operating in a unified relationship for each *mise en scène*. Consequently, the actor's play must be realised and understood in relation to the scenery, the objects, the music onstage, the costumes worn, etc.; in relation to time (including the time taken up by the theatre session itself), and also in relation to the text and its dramaturgical interpretation. Bodies can be objectified, materialised as objects; objects can signify a human presence; sounds and lights can take one to the fringes of the immaterial, of the invisible and of the most concrete actuality. These lists (that are only considered as such because they facilitate the procedure of observation and analysis) should be revisited and reassessed in any in-depth investigation of the *mise en scène*, not only because of the dynamic interaction between apparently disjointed signs and the signifying networks created throughout the theatre session (that is to say *not only* in the performance played by the actors), but also in one's memory and one's interpretation of the event. The specific textures and characteristics of individual elements of the spectacle must thus be placed within the general coherent framework of the spectacle. Moreover, the *mise en scène* (on what interpretative and dramaturgical lines is this based?) should also take into consideration the place that houses it (the building and its location) by appreciating the sensual experience of the spectator in their cultural and aesthetic context. These are some of the imperatives we can easily establish with respect to the analysis of a theatre spectacle, but they are also reflexes that any spectator can have, so long as they are attentive to what is in front of them.

Consequently, dramaturgy − which is supposed to precede the work of any *mise en scène*, and that provides a series of dynamics and interpretive approaches capable of being actualised by practitioners when they come into contact with the audience − can be tasked with envisaging the transition from the fragmentation of signs (text, bodies, objects, lighting, scenery, etc.) to a dynamic signifying system. But at the same time, it cannot be tasked with everything, nor be accountable for all the effects produced. Since, as we have seen and shall constantly see, theatre is not able to reproduce an identical copy of any given project or re-actualise it through the same signs, if only because the audience, the conditions of representation and the exterior referential system change each evening. Moreover, because the system also produces meaning *sensually*, the *mise en scène* constantly struggles with the inability to fully determine or conscribe the spectator, the director and the actors. This also has to be taken into account. This is why, rather than producing lists of signs, which become immutable from the moment they are fixed by the practitioners, and simply stopping there, we prefer to underscore the fragility of a signifying dynamic (or of a series of signifying dynamics), composed by a network of signs, exhibited through a series of relationships between different aspects of the theatrical event, and offered as particular event, so that a polysemic, ephemeral spectacle is produced and, if possible, inscribed as a trace in the memory of those who are present that day.

Consequently, we deem it necessary to identify here the material elements of the spectacle and to isolate them for a moment for reasons of clarity. But we shall constantly emphasise the fact that they are not disjointed, since they function in relation to each other *and* in relation to the two major poles of interpretation, which are the practitioners and the audience (and that can overlap), in order to produce a specific dynamic of meaning. Such a dynamic can be encapsulated via a single dramaturgical enterprise, and is actualised during the moment of the session to produce unforeseen meanings, which may diverge largely from the dynamic initially intended.

The work of practitioners

The signs displayed by the spectacle are generally engendered by the text. They provide a basis for the production and guide the spectator's interpretation. From the moment the *mise en scène* establishes a signifying network, and with enough repetition for it to be understood, the signs become decodable. It is from this network of signs that the play of theatre can devote itself to asserting the distinction between the site of the stage and the dramatic space of the representation: the audience will move between one world and the other so that they are aware that what is played on the stage is actually theatre.

In the current configuration of theatre, the job of practitioners is primarily to create a lasting imprint on the spectator's memory during the ephemeral moment of the performance. The key is to capture their attention, move them, and offer them the possibility at each moment of the performance to witness *and* feel a series of sensations and significations that are impacting them without anyone being fully aware of the process or having to consciously identify them. The team of practitioners in contemporary theatre creates a network of signs, in the staging space and on the entire theatrical site (stage, house, buildings), capable of producing a series of coherent meanings from different elements (sounds, decor, lights, costumes, voices, objects, bodies, play, movements, etc.) implemented by different entities and professions (decorator, scenographer or artist-designer, musician and sound technician, lighting technician, costume designer or dressmaker, accessory designers, actors) and regulated by a director assisted by a stage manager for the technical aspects, and, as the case may be, by a choreographer and a conductor, for the musical part; by a dramaturg, if necessary, for the interpretation of the text. This diversity has restricted itself to the creation of one, or even several, coherent meanings so that the spectator can understand that the practitioners are addressing and working for them. Since all these professions, all this know-how and all these categories of signs do not necessarily work in tandem, the director has taken on the role of ensuring the smooth running of the system, and, sometimes, of imposing his point of view, taking into account the suggestions of each person and ensuring the coherence of the entire project.

Not that a theatre project requires a tyrannical commander; we often observe a division of tasks, a production being led by several people, a *mise en scène* conducted in a collective way and even performances composed by the actors themselves (this is the case for the Belgian group tg STAN and was for a long time the case for theatre troupes before the twentieth century). This entire process can be considered as the result of a dynamic relationship of forces, which would allow us to consider the history of theatre or theatrical institutions from the point of view of the decision-making powers of the different professions (and how these are bound up within issues of aesthetics, economics and politics). It is for this reason that the arrival of Italian decorators in seventeenth-century France changed many things and the ascendancy of dramatic actors in the same period transformed players into actors. But the most notable fact for the modern era (from the end of the nineteenth century to the beginning of the twentieth) has been the transformation of the head of theatre troupe/manager into a director, a veritable orchestra conductor who is in charge of the coherence and signification of the representation. Consequently, the audience, at the end of the twentieth century and at the beginning of the twenty-first, has gradually stopped only following the fortunes of text, authors and actors, but also the renown of the director and even of the scenographer or stage designer. The size of the typographical characters on notices and billboards, and the importance that critics have given to them, testify to this fact.

It is Patrice Chéreau's *Phèdre* that theatregoers came to see at the Odéon-Berthier, which they compared to the previous *Phèdre* of Antoine Vitez and Luc Bondy and to the contemporary *Phèdre* of Christian Rist at La Tempête; whereas before, one would talk about the *Phèdre* of Sarah Bernhardt, of Marie Bell or of Sylvia Monfort; or in the nineteenth century, about Racine's version, which would be compared to Pradon's.

When one considers a production from the point of view of space, and more particularly, from the angle of the use of the stage and the creation of a dramatic space from it, practitioners must produce (and spectators must interpret) a series of signs designed to function in a coherent semiotic network and that only take on meaning as a series of differences, through the signifying rapport that they have with each other, but also that they all have in relation to the referential system shared by the audience and the practitioners.

Two senses out of five?

In the three-dimensional staging space, one must first and foremost deploy visible and audible elements that are either static or alive, including speaking and moving bodies. Olfactory signs are rare in contemporary theatre and even rarer in classical repertoire; so are signs relating to touch and taste. Therefore, when they exist, they create a highly unusual effect and bring an element of surprise to the theatre experience. What distinguishes these senses is that they appear to be infinitely "real" and produce strong and radical emotions in the spectators, which separate them from the fiction and its illusion, or which allow them to identify with the situations portrayed to the point where these appear as "real" situations.

Smells in the theatrical session exist as much as touch (one must sit close to one's peers) or taste does (snow cones or that drink that it is so hard to purchase during the intermission, the sandwich before, the dinner afterwards). But smell can also be a product of the scenery when the natural elements laid out onstage replace artificial scenery, or when experiments are tried onstage. These sensations then appear as infinitely "real" and finally allow the spectators to personally identify with a dramatic situation. For odour does not represent: *it is*. Thus it does not function in the system of illusion, first, because it is not diffused at the same time as the action, the discourse or the plot and, second, because it brings the spectator back to their own materiality, in one sense, and to the memory of their own olfactory sensations, in another. Hence why smell interrupts the principle of representation by the emergence of a concrete reality, which, evidently, creates an element of surprise. While courtly festivities in the sixteenth and seventeenth centuries included glass lanterns full of odoriferous and multi-coloured oils; while in Bordeaux in 1789, Dauberval's *Le Ballet de la paille ou la fille mal gardée* [*The Ballet of Straw, or the Wayward Daughter*] placed at the centre of the staging apparatus a meal (a very flavourful cabbage soup shared by harvesters); and while Paul Fort, in staging at the Théâtre d'Art (1892) *Le Cantique des Cantiques* [*The Song of Songs*], combined text, music, colourful projections and perfumes, one cannot speak of an olfactory theatre. It is a fact that there have been a few successful productions in recent years that have featured food – a soup or risotto (Politecnico de Rome) – during the representation, with all the odours that can come from such things, and ended naturally by the sharing of a dish with the audience (the display of smell in time coincided, then, with the time of the representation and the preparation of the meal). We also know that real fish placed at the front of stage by Langhoff, in Gogol's *The Government Inspector* (1998), remained in the memory of the spectators seated in the first rows. But those are very rare examples of transgression of the code, which, generally, does not allow for smelling and tasting, even when there is no fourth wall.

Sharing taste with those who occupy the stage means being linked to their actual bodies rather than with a character. The spectator thus becomes part of the dramatic space, breaking its autonomy and entering into a symbolic and referential figuration of communion. Therefore, whether during or at the end of their performance processions, when the Bread And Puppet Theatre shares bread with the spectators, the desired effect is precisely that of communion, and particularly an environmental and political one between actors and the people, and the referential system can then also be moored as much in the Christian ceremony as in the native American one, which functions based on the same religious principle that is appropriated and used for the theatrical performance.

We should emphasise again, however, that these examples from contemporary theatre are neither the first, nor the most radical of innovations: there have been previous experiments with taste in theatre where practitioners have played with conventions and transgressed the codes that limit its effects with respect to hearing and sight. Such experiments have included the integration of feasts into theatre and theatrical representations within large royal festivals. This was the case, for example, for the *Plaisirs de L'Île Enchantée* [*The Pleasures of the Enchanted Island*] in May 1665 in Versailles, when Molière's troupe, besides the other plays that it performed (which included *La Princesse d'Élide* and the scandalous *Tartuffe* at the end), included in its processions the games and great theatricalised feasts performed by a veritable team of entertainers. It was a first step. But let us take a clearer example more reminiscent of the contemporary productions we have already cited. Take Thomas Corneille's *Berger extravagant*, for example, performed to great applause in 1652 at the home of the Countess of Fiesque, and then at the Hôtel de Bourgogne. In Act 5, three actresses appear disguised as wood nymphs "with tree branches at the end of which are attached a few dried fruits" and invite a shepherd, Lysis, himself disguised as a tree, to share their food. And at the same time, as the critics of the time tell us,[1] two "vendors" in the room (one close to the galleries, another to the parterre) stand ready to serve dried fruits and drinks (wines, liqueurs, tisanes) to the spectators. The actors simultaneously regale themselves with the same food and drink. There is then a strange overlap between fiction and reality when the pastoral fully coincides with the reality of the audience at the Hôtel de Bourgogne, and the text goes so far as to incite the spectators into buying beverages and delicacies and even more so to participate in the fictional action. While the act of consuming dried fruits and drinks during the seventeenth century was nothing new (a "vendor" being one of the small trades in the theatre), it is interesting that here it is absolutely linked with the play of the actors, which was rare. We can conclude, nevertheless, that the recourse to sight and touch can, in certain cases, and not only in the twentieth and twenty-first centuries, be complemented by a sort of shared sense of taste between the stage and the house that becomes all the more meaningful.

Touch is also a part of the forbidden practice of theatre; or rather, it stands outside of theatrical convention. To touch an object onstage or the body of an actor is to immediately break the autonomy of the dramatic space, and also, evidently, to rupture the system of the fourth wall and often to transgress the principles of representation. By inventing small barriers that separated the spectators seated on the theatre benches from the actors in the eighteenth century, practitioners did not only prevent the irritating movements of the spectators, but also their attempts to touch the actors and thus interrupt the illusion of the play. By preserving their own space, the actors were able to emphasise the creation of a sort of dramatic space. We also know that a certain number of theatrical performances opted to project objects (often liquid ones) from the stage into the audience, with an immediate implication being that the spectators would try to protect themselves from these objects, and, at the same time, from anything that could come out of dramatic space to which they did not have access in principle. This was the case with the fake blood at the Grand-Guignol at the end of the nineteenth century and at the beginning of the twentieth, and since then, of the panic effects of a number of spectacles (including those of La Fura dels Baus) where all sorts of liquids could reach the audience. However, all over the world, other forms of spectacle also appeal to touch, including the "happening", Richard Schechner's American experimental or environmental theatre. This introduces the idea of the flesh into theatre with the aim of turning representation into a collective interaction, a sensual communication between two groups of humans, so that this art becomes a veritable "art of sensation". Save for a few very isolated efforts (for example Castorf's effects in the Schaubühne in Berlin, which played on the extreme heat one year in *Forever Young*, an adaption of T. Williams, 2004; or on the cold the following year by projecting snow on to the first rows in *Meine Schneekönigin* [*My Snow Queen*], after Hans Christian Anderson in 2005), generally speaking touch creates a real sense of frustration for the spectator of Western theatre. There is a sense of isolation when this sense is represented onstage without this watcher-listener being able to associate themselves with it, to the point where a number of spectators dream of exchanging place with such a character, performer or actor.

HOW TO ACT AT THE THEATRE?

Lately, when the group tg STAN gave an interpretation of Diderot's *Paradoxe sur le comédien* [*Paradox of the Actor*], the play encouraged the spectator to touch an actor lying down, even if this meant forcing them to do so, and then, immediately afterwards, forbidding them to carry on by showing them that they were transgressing one of the principles of traditional theatre.

It is more unusual to hear of taste, touch and smell within the dramatic space as providing a physical link between the characters themselves. That is to say, objects that are eaten onstage tend to have a particular meaning; performers touch each other *as characters*; sometimes, more rarely, there is mention of what the actors can smell, but nothing, we could say, transpires from the point of view of the spectator, who cannot touch, taste or smell, except by entering into the system of relation between actors, characters or performers. When, in the *Cherry Orchard*, Madame Ranevskaya (Lyubov) asks "who has smoked detestable cigarettes in this place?" neither contemporary directors not Stanislavsky himself foresee that spectators will smell the odour. Likewise, it is not their desire that the coldness of the dramatic space should encompass the site where the spectators are seated. When Jan Fabre's dancer-performers sweat or urinate in *The Crying Body*, in theory, the spectators do not do the same because, usually, what concerns the dramatic space of theatre does not smell, has no taste and cannot be touched. All of this contributes to the spectator's frustration. Indeed, if the audience can "move across" space to render transparent the effects they hear and smell, it is nonetheless impossible for them to share the tastes, touch and even the smells to which the actor-characters refer. Consequently, the spectator knows that they are always missing three out of the five senses required to *act as if*. Or they must accept that the theatre has established a very specific *as if* founded on viewing and hearing (that is, the two senses of observation or of the observer and not the senses of the intruder).

When Sganarelle in *Dom Juan* takes a piece of chicken to put it into his mouth, we view the action, we hear that he can no longer articulate words because his mouth is full, but we cannot taste the chicken. As such, the spectator can desire to taste also, can desire revenge for being excluded from the sensation and be happy to see Dom Juan make the gluttonous valet confess his theft. And they may tell themselves that, while the characters can eat onstage, it is a pity that the spectators must refrain from eating, even if hunger makes them dream of their dinner once they leave the theatre. Similarly, if the characters of Eduardo de Filippo's *Sabato, domenica e lunedì* cook an extremely good *ragu*, so much that the spectators are dying of hunger, this same audience, which smells the odour from the kitchen, will be frustrated at not being able to taste any of it. Before the performance of *Tambours sur la digue* [*Drums on the Dike*], when an actress of the Théâtre du Soleil, already dressed in the costume of a Chinese businesswoman, in a passageway of a fictional Chinese marketplace – the audience awaits expectantly to enter into the real room where the performance will take place – offers the spectators the possibility to eat the Chinese noodles that the character of Madame Li will sell during the play and on the stage to the characters. Something unusual happens: the smell and taste of the dish have moved through the spaces to become memorialised by the space and time of the fiction. Conversely, the fictional taste and smell have gained a reality that the spectators (at any rate, those who have chosen to eat the Chinese noodles before the spectacle) still have "in their mouths", so that Madame Li is no longer merely a character, but also a woman encountered in the theatre building, a real one, a fictional one, an actress and a businesswoman. The effect thus lies, as in previous examples, on the emotional participation of the spectator, on the activation of their sense of taste, touch and smell, so that they can be simultaneously transported away from, and brought back to, what is most intimate to them. It is not classic frustration that is acting in this case; on the contrary, a link is established and all parties can activate, within a complex relation, in which reality and fiction are interwoven and in which the experience of the senses, usually excluded from theatrical representation, plays its role. Admittedly, as we have seen, some of these explorations and experiments take place within the principle of representation-frustration of taste, smell and touch, and this throughout the history of theatre. But broadly speaking, it is true that the stage space is given as functioning in two ways: sight, which creates the reality of watchers or spectators; and hearing, which determines the reality of "auditors" as Corneille names them in his prefaces to distinguish them from readers. These two senses are, moreover, at least since the time of Plato, considered to be the two noble senses available to man. The relation between bodies of actors and the scenery that surrounds them must then be considered in a complex manner, but based on these two principal aspects, save in the case of a unique approach to the production that amounts to a transgression of the conventional use of senses. However, while it is true that Western theatre emphasises two senses out of five, it is necessary to point out that many other theatrical practices do not supress touch or, indeed, taste and smell.

The famous way in which Western theatregoers appreciate theatre through their passions and their imagination, is further endorsed by the three other senses, and touch in particular. By watching without being able to touch, the spectator has every latitude to imagine that they are touching, or that they are silently replaying the movements of bodies they have observed, without even moving themselves, or that via the imagination, they are taking part in the gestures and body language of the actor. Despite the fact that it is forbidden to actually act on certain behaviours, the spectator is fully capable of exerting a sense of touch, getting up and speaking, feeling or tasting just like the actors do. And while they might realise that they are unable to break these conventions, the spectator imagines them based on what they see and hear. Therefore, the spectator's pleasure consists both in respecting the formal restriction of the representational protocol and in breaking it through their imagination. And when the *mise en scène* itself allows conventional boundaries to be crossed, in moments when actors touch a spectator and include them in their play, the spectator is immediately *arrested*, which surprises them because they do not, in principle, touch the actor. Hence the idea that this apparent separation between the visual world and the tactile world is less fundamental than one might generally consider, because it can evolve and can be transgressed. Furthermore, a continuation and a link between one and the other are often imagined by the spectator themselves. Indeed, it is pleasing to think that one can break the code that one has accepted, or involve oneself in a site and space into which one has not been invited, but into which one projects oneself.

7

DESCRIPTION AND VOCABULARY OF THE TRADITIONAL THEATRE SITE

Traditionally, at the centre of this space are the bodies of actors, with scenery and other supporting objects around them. Yet while their movement around one another appears to be the central concern of the stage, because these bodies are what actually *represent* through choreography, figures and mobile architectures, there are fringe cases in which the objects are no longer in a supporting role, but become characters themselves. Objects might create a performance of sorts, which then can be opposed to the bodies of the actors, threaten them and even replace them. In *The Chairs*, Ionesco plays on this principle by filling the stage with chairs, creating an obstacle for the characters and actors to the point where they can no longer move, where they are literally unable to move, because their dramatic and scenic space is invested with objects that limit their action. In so doing, the elements of the stage have been transformed into elements of dramatic space and, at the same time, take on both the concrete meaning they intrinsically have (these are the literal chairs that prevent the actors from moving) and the "dramatic" meaning that they acquire and that Ionesco stages. As a result, this stage, taken to be a volume of space to be filled by stage sets, objects, moving and speaking bodies, makes room for interpretable images whose details we must now try to better understand in order to describe them.

Since we have already seen how important the urban architectural space is – in particular based on its relationship with the audience and the specific aesthetic it promotes – we must now closely consider the stage and space of play from the point of view of its own scenographic techniques: scenery, lighting, sounds, music and silence, the objects it contains, the costumes, masks and make-up and also the performance of the actors.

We shall begin by describing the site of the stage. Like all space to be filled, the space of the stage should be measured according to its surface and volume. This is how Beaumarchais begins when he has his character Figaro say how many feet he has in which to play his role, and when he describes the area that he will have access to in order to install the "dramatic chamber" he will share with Suzanne. The dramatic situation depends on this very awareness of space, because at the Comédie-Française and on its precisely measured stage, the chamber is situated in an interstice: between two wings, but also between two major fictional poles. Dramatically situated between the private rooms of the count and those of the countess, the stage will thus always be threatened by the offstage space depicted and represented by the wings. It should be noted that classical theatre itself plays with this double meaning, as in *Bérénice*, for example. The very narrow space in which the tragedy is performed (tragic in a real sense, because it is destined to disappear) is the dramatic space in which Titus and Bérénice are located. This is a space so clearly observed by the spectators of the theatre benches, and yet it is also the private and intimate chamber of their love life that is rightly depicted as fragile, impossible, caught between Rome and Bérénice's rooms: a Rome whose menacing noise Racine will depict for the spectator and an apartment that is no longer a refuge.

Before continuing, it seems necessary to calculate, measure, fix and describe a few techniques from a typical example of Italian theatre, and to describe a few elements of staging vocabulary. We will describe the traditional machinery in the staging space, as well as the scenery, which is generally possible in this sort of configuration. We shall also speak about the transverse section of the Opéra Garnier, very apt to depict this set of features (see Figure 0.1 at the beginning of this book).

The transverse section of the Opéra Garnier offers a good model for an excursion into scenographic vocabulary, and we shall concentrate on the framework of the stage. But before this, we should point out that the stage occupies only a small part of the building. Indeed, a prestigious place such as the Opéra, from the eighteenth century, is above all a place of ostentation and of meeting.

To describe this image, we will imagine, first of all, that the extreme right depicts the façade of the building, in front of which is an imposing exterior staircase directly overlooking the Place de l'Opéra, and located at the end of a long avenue, the Avenue de l'Opéra, and at the intersection of two of the Grands Boulevards. As such, the place is perfectly chosen and corresponds to an urbanistic project in which the edifice is inscribed as a "great monument", while at the same time being at the centre of a district. The Opéra Garnier is a prestigious, luxurious building that is one of the highlights of the city. It was built in a new district that was created in the Second Empire in order to link the centre of the capital to other districts that were up until then far away or peripheral, and to a small town, Montmartre, which was absorbed into Paris. The size of the building is imposing: at 172 metres long, 101 metres wide and 79 metres high. Just behind the façade (1),[1] which is superb, lined with statues (mostly by Carpeaux), designed according to the tastes of the day and complemented by a loggia with Corinthian colonnades, is the grand foyer (2) that is 54 metres long, 13 metres wide and 18 metres high. And the galleries made to hold the audience during intermissions and receptions. On the first floor, lit by windows that overlook the square and decorated with mural paintings, the galleries and the grand foyer are places where theatregoers can see one another, admire each other and play a social spectacle, which partly accounts for their attendance at the theatre. The main entrance is through the foyer. This foyer and the theatre house are accessed via the grand staircase (3), over which an enormous ornamented clearing creates a space of large volume. The house or auditorium is a third space (4) over which a great crystal chandelier is hung (the chimney used for the evacuation of smoke before the advent of electricity can still be seen) and that is covered by a painted ceiling (by Chagall, at the moment). In red and gold, with five levels of galleries, seats in the stalls and larger, ornate seats in the dress circle (in total, 2,156 seats), the room was built to symbolise luxury, which, conventionally, attends the performance of lyrical spectacles and dance in a place of prestige. Between the stage and the house, the orchestra pit (5), sloping (with a raised platform for the orchestra conductor, who the audience sees from behind) allows the music, turned towards the audience, to spread out and flood the room. Finally, behind the stage and leading to it, the dance foyer (6) was a place where dancers, choirs, as well as those who wished to see them while the singers were onstage, would gather.

A traditional stage

At the Opéra Garnier, the stage house (7) is 26 metres wide, 52 metres deep and 60 metres high. The "stage", such as we tend to imagine it and on which most of the theatres of the eighteenth, nineteenth and twentieth centuries are built, is distinguished from the auditorium and consists of the playing area and the service area. The stage itself contains several parts: downstage (the proscenium or forestage) (8); the stage proper (9); upstage (10); the wings (11) and backstage. Based on the spectator's point of view, the right side of the stage is called "court side" and the left side is "garden side". The French appellation comes from the machine room of the Tuileries, between court and garden. In England, "prompt side" is used for the court side (on the same side as the prompter) and "opposite prompt side" for the garden. The back part of the stage is said to be the farside and the foremost part of the stage is called "the front". The stage house on its three sides is delimited at the front by a proscenium, at the back by the stage wall (12) (in front of which one can find scenery and the stage backdrop), and laterally by stage walls (13), which can be masked by moveable stage sets.

The fly system

In the nineteenth century, the fly system (14) became an essential space for machinery (15) with a height at least equal to that of the height of the proscenium arch. It is composed of corridors or walkways (16) – for loading and for service – of the flying bridge (above the stage), the lighting truss and of the stage lighting fixtures running from one side of the stage to the other (17). It is also composed of stage curtains and iron curtains (18) and of the batten (19), an iron structure above the stage house on which the stage backdrop, lights and machines, bridges and other accessories are placed.

The proscenium

The proscenium forms the key performance zone: the separation, contact or link between the house and the stage. Conceived in the sixteenth and seventeenth centuries in Italy and derived from the necessity to hide the machinery and hide the effect of perspective, the proscenium arch has given rise to various different permutations: from the Arch of Triumph to the majestic colonnades and the forestage boxes within the space of the proscenium itself. During the second half of the eighteenth century, the proscenium became a division depicting the fourth wall theorised by Diderot. Systematic curtain, iron curtain (to preserve the whole of the building from fires), the *manteau d'Arlequin*, mobile drapery or a more or less translucent Brechtian half-curtain: everything is done to insist on the essential difference between the fiction and the spectators.

The curtain

The curtain hides then unveils the space of fiction constructed through perspective. From the sixteenth century in Italy and the beginning of the seventeenth century in France, the curtain exists to reveal the scenery to the spectators and to insist on the stupor that the illusion wishes to provoke. During performances, it does not appear and changes of scenery, when they exist, are often done in full view of the audience. The curtain that one raises or lowers, which encloses the stage at the beginning and at the end of the spectacle, but also during the intermission, at the end of each act and sometimes to signal a change of place and time during the fiction, dates from the nineteenth century. It is usually made from hard canvas, painted red and gold, and may be complemented by a decorative frieze, which remains fixed at the upper part of the curtain (a sort of *manteau d'Arlequin*). Nowadays, it is a real drape curtain (40 per cent more material relative to the opening of the stage or the width of the proscenium arch), often in black velvet, midnight blue or red and heavy, to insist on the separation of the real from the imaginary, to mute sounds and absorb light. Technicians have even invented a "flap" (that also comes down on the stage when the curtain is lowered to hide from the audience any visible interstice). Finally, a limited space is left between the curtain and the stage to allow lighting from the forestage (the footlighting, 21), and to give the actors the possibility of using these spaces for their entrances and exits. This intermediary space is often delimited at the back by a second frame (a mobile drapery or *manteau d'Arlequin*) (20), which also seeks to re-centre the gaze of the spectator.

However, as we will later discover, contemporary productions often forego the use of the curtain and leave the stage open to the view of the spectator, from the moment of their entry into the auditorium. The effect of the fourth wall is thereby countered, as the practitioners suggest that the play will not construct an illusionistic dramatic space, but will be, above all, a performance intended to be viewed as such. This exclusion of the curtain that coincides sometimes with the total baring of the stage (neither scenery nor cyclorama) also has the effect of minimising the effect of framing, of no longer delimiting the time of the representation to the sole moment in which the drama is played in order to distinguish the staging from the traditional convention (we would be hard-pressed to speak of transgression since the procedure has become so common).

Finally, the curtain can also be used in another way: this time as backdrop, in full knowledge that it still keeps its original referential meaning. We are at the theatre after all, so there is a curtain that shows, hides and separates. Peter Stein in *Kleist: Prince of Homburg* used curtains in this way. The curtains would rise and open to show the actors in such a way that they became a part of the scenery and ended up becoming accessories depicting catafalques. It thus became possible, contrary to the usual mode of entrances and exits from the stage, for the actors to be unveiled when the curtain opened, showing them and the light of the cyclorama located behind them. They then became apparitions in both a literal and literary sense. Klaus Michael Grüber, in his second production (1982) of Goethe's *Faust* (one of the first productions to mark his return to the theatre after several plays performed "outdoors"), played ostensibly with the presence of a large red stage curtain. He played on its referentiality as framework and sign of theatricality, as a boundary between two worlds. The curtain itself sometimes became a heavy and imposing veil, which draped the frail and aged body of Bernard Minetti, a German actor who played the title role.

The proscenium arch

The proscenium arch, thus named because the character made his entrances through the wing situated between the stage curtain and the mobile drapery (20). It is made up of two vertical columns and of one horizontal frieze, which are generally painted draperies.

The stage

In the case of this traditional Italian stage, the height of the stage house allows for the installation of scenery at the back of the stage or in the space between the proscenium and the back wall. The spectator's vision is, in principle, framed and limited above by the *manteau d'Arlequin*, and on the sides by curtains that hide the tabs, or other flats at prompt side and opposite prompt side in traditional theatre. However, in reality, the spectators seated in the front see the fly system that is above and can observe the batten. And the spectators who are on the sides can see into the wings, etc.

The stage is the scenic space where actors move, and where the staging apparatus is set up for play. It is located between the wings (11) on the sides, the back stage wall (12), and the footlights (21) that separate the stage from the house or the orchestra pit. Its forepart is called the "proscenium arch", and in front of this is situated the "prompt box", masked from the point of view of the house by "tormentors" (or "side maskings"). From the front, the stage is divided into several planes (sort of bands), with passageways at the end of them (the intervals between the stage and the wings) (22), where immobile trap doors are located, giving access to the trap room. Trap doors, also called *costières* (23), are also located in the floor behind the proscenium arch, and allow the scenery to be removed and slid into the chassis behind the stage.

The suspended chassis on which parts of the scenery are painted (24) are also secured from underneath these trap doors and from the fly system by the use of brackets. These canvases hanging from bars are, in fact, the simplest staging technique: a painted panel that falls from the fly system and depicts a place. These canvases are therefore attached to poles and, with the help of pulleys, can then be lowered on to the walls at the left and right of the stage. This mechanism allows for the canvases to rise and come down so long as the batten is sufficiently high. This is the main reason for which the stage house has a much greater height than that of the house. When the batten is not high enough, one can slide the canvases on the side or fold them (a more difficult art). The machinists, who are on these sides, must oversee, like sailors, the proper manoeuvring of this apparatus, and when the scenery changes in full sight, must work silently, subtly and rapidly.

The spacing of the chassis, which are on the sides, makes it possible for actors to leave the stage, going through the intervals, which separate the stage from the wings. It is on these side canvases that flats are painted, which sometimes depict, through anamorphosis, a complete perspective that directs the eye toward the central background. In other cases, the chassis are uniformly painted canvases that can change based on the intensity of the colours and lighting projected on to them. For the audience, these ornate panels represent a structure leading to an offstage space (for example a house with doors and windows).

Naturally, the stage space is also made up of unmoveable elements (hence the importance and versatility of sliding canvases) to carry out changes of scenery (during intermissions; during the performance, by putting the house in darkness, or through operations in plain sight) so that another scenic space can appear. Likewise, this stage must contain openings that are sufficiently large, on the sides but also above, so that machines can also be arranged or moved, drawn by cords or pulley mechanisms, pushed by hidden machines or even remotely controlled by the control room. Full sceneries can also be created with openings – doors, for example – allowing for entrances and exits. Finally, the director can also have a totally bare stage (neither sliding panels, nor stage backdrop, nor cyclorama), which has the impact of showing ostentatiously that the play is in a theatre and on a stage. By making the back wall appear, the sidewalls and their machinery (pulleys, bars, electric sockets, etc.), one openly shows the materiality of the theatre, a practice that contemporary productions often resort to, to dispel the effect of illusion.

The cyclorama

This is a stage backdrop, which hides the wall at the back. It is a curved screen with large dimensions and no stitching: it is unified, has a neutral tint, or is clear, opaque or translucent. It is designed to receive light from projections. Although it is usually a vertical half-cylinder, its shape can vary and can even form a flattened background. But by extension of meaning, the cyclorama is now considered to be any taut background of neutral colour (or of a sky effect, for example). It creates the atmosphere, a notion of time that passes (morning, midday, evening) or of the weather (storm, clear skies, etc.) or the symbolism of a particular scene (red and violence, blinding white, etc.). It can be hung between two poles or connected to the batten, wound around two drums (like the panoramas in ancient Greek theatre) or even fixed on to a rigid frame. The cyclorama, very convenient to install and useful for creating an atmosphere, is widely used in contemporary productions, and is also an artistic, plastic element, such as in the work of Bob Wilson, who systematically uses this artifice to make it a central and essential component of the play of modulations and of the "sculpting" of light, which are foundations of his work. The cyclorama is therefore used by Wilson to colour the spectators' vision and place them in a sensual "bubble" that links them to the work onstage.

The trap room

There can be up to eight floors below the stage (here there are five) (25), but most often theatres are equipped with three levels. Poles uphold the floor of the stage, which can contain trap doors (23) for allowing objects, scenery and even actors to emerge. The floor also contains grooves for the movement of the sliding panels of the stage set. A trolley is sometimes placed on the first floor below for smooth manoeuvring with the aid of a pulley. While the trap room is invisible to the audience, if the technical apparatus of the stage allows it, certain productions might draw the spectators' attention to the existence of an unsuspected and therefore mysterious underground depth beneath the stage, for example, by making an actor enter from below, by means of an elevator, just as Strehler did with *Le mage Alcandre* at the beginning of his production of *L'Illusion comique* at the Odéon in 1984. The trap room (25) is not shown but its existence is suggested and left to the imagination of the spectator, opening another offstage space, which can be an inferno, such as the one in which the damned Dom Juan is engulfed; a stygian dungeon, or simply an intriguing underground space.

All this technical description paints the idea that theatre, from the point of view of stage design, is animated by a sort of craftsmanship where pulleys, capstans and masks occupy a crucial role in the movement and organisation of scenery, a fact that testifies to the nautical training of the Italian decorators. It also shows that, more and more since the invention of electricity (for machinery as well as for lighting), the systems become more fine-tuned and give rise to extreme precision in the practitioners' intentions (with respect to lighting, in the case of Bob Wilson, for example, and before him, with Svoboda). Finally, the recourse to computer technology and to the combined automated effects (sound, lights, changes in full sight, etc.) engenders phenomenal and spectacular possibilities.

Lastly, it should be highlighted that in this place where everything is made to create an effect of ideal illusion, it is entirely possible to recuse this principle by denouncing the use of machinery, so to speak, and exposing it. But we also know that when productions use the available machinery, it can opt voluntarily and ostensibly to not engender an ideal illusion in the scenic space, since it can utilise this technology in order to break down realism in the space.

Even when faithfully following the technical rules of illusion, the effects of a traditional *mise en scène* on the spectator do not necessarily result in the production of an illusionistic dramatic space or in the creation of a different place, which could be perceived as real. This is because what the spectator also sees is perhaps another world, but ultimately it is the *mise en scène*. In other words, the technical efforts, the perfection and the overabundance of tools that are there for the spectators to be transported elsewhere and that they appreciate sensually and visually. Consequently, the spectator naturally judges, sometimes with pleasure and admiration, the interest of the enterprise, which consists in the representation of an ideal world through the objective and infinitely visible utilisation of appropriate scenographic techniques.

8

OTHER STAGES, OTHER APPARATUSES

Nowadays, the Italian-style theatre building and its stage tend not to provide the sole model for the theatrical precinct. The stage may slide, turn, be elevated or dispersed, through an indeterminacy between the actors' spaces and that of the spectators. It may even be integrated into the house itself. In some cases, it is no longer isolated and therefore has no framing mechanism. The audience may walk about and the play itself can be spatially dispersed. While the so-called "retracted" stage, which puts the spectator at a certain distance from the action, as in the proscenium theatre, remains the most common model, there have been many experiments with all sorts of stages and spatialities (central circle stage, as at the circus; ring-shaped stages, stages encircling the audience, spherical stages, bi-frontal stages and thrust stages, as in Elizabethan theatre).

We are able to clearly distinguish ancient *mise en scène*, where the apparatus is conventional and forms part of the code, from modern *mise en scène*, where the apparatus is the result of a choice by the practitioners. That is why, while the open thrust stage organisation goes without saying for an Elizabethan actor, and while the central circle or plank is nothing surprising for a clown or for the audience at a classic circus, the choice of one or the other indicates a particularly creative act for contemporary staging. It is thus necessary for a contemporary critic to be aware of the effects produced by ancient staging mechanisms while being careful to consider that these mechanisms were regarded as conventional at the time. Conversely, the use of these mechanisms in contemporary theatre must be understood and analysed as signs, and even staging intentions, given the possible choices that practitioners have nowadays. Admittedly, these practitioners may have specific constraints due to the building that hosts them and the habits of the place.

We can thus affirm that the open thrust arrangement with a stage jutting into the audience and a perpendicular stage at the back is traditional for Shakespeare's Globe Theatre and that this layout also engenders particular types of reaction from the contemporary audience. It also engenders particular types of reaction from the contemporary audience, as well as a form of play, type of scenery and a writing style that takes this arrangement into account. But while it is necessary to possess this information when one wants to encapsulate or understand the synchronic particularities of this theatre, one must still interpret this mechanism today as distinguishing itself from the frontal staging apparatus of the Italian proscenium theatre, and conditioning the spectator's reception of this specific action: it is perhaps a reference to Elizabethan theatre but it is also a desire to enter into the space of the audience, to break illusion or some other thing that the spectator will be able to interpret. We can see that, from this point of view, the place that one attributes to the audience is evidently indicative of the role that one wants to give to it in the execution of the theatre performance.

In other words, whether the spectators are aware or not of the referential mode implied by the staging arrangement in which they find themselves, whether or not the practitioners are responsible for the organisation of the space, of the stage and of the audience, one must always consider that the arrangement is significant, and therefore has effects in terms of reception and interpretation. And while, in a certain way, a director chooses to not use a proscenium scenography when he stages a play at the Comédie-Française, he subscribes nonetheless, by the fact itself, to the principle, is meant to master it, carry it out, or undermine it and problematise it, to establish his own scenography and confer meaning upon it: a meaning or a set of meanings that the spectator will then be able to decipher, from their point of view and based on the coherence that they perceive in it.

Referential systems and innovations

Everything therefore works as if, for each period of theatre, the staging design has dominated the referential system, so much that any diversion becomes significant in relation to the conventions accepted by practitioners and audiences. Admittedly even if the type of play, the audience or the genre represented, can themselves demand their own conventional principles. As we have already seen, at the royal courts in the seventeenth century, the point of view of the house is quite particular: the king occupies the "prince's eye"; the stage is better lit and emptied of spectators; the machines are more numerous and more technically capable, etc. In the cities, on the other hand, the organisation of spaces was different, and the stage was less capable of exhibiting great technical feats. For each place, the audience and practitioners act in relation to the conventional prerequisites, and, as such, one may have been surprised to see grand machines in a city theatre. (Moreover, this was what led to the success of the Théâtre du Marais and of the Théâtre du Palais-Royal, which imitated the layout and organisation of the courtly staging space without entirely achieving this.) One might have also been surprised to observe trestle-stage actors design a sophisticated scenery, but a key feature of the transition to *mise en scène* was the refusal to strictly observe the habitual conventions and, therefore, the embrace of novelty and inventiveness in the creation of new staging mechanisms. And little by little, based on the interventions of Antoine, the influence of Craig and Appia and the stage experimentations of the first half of the twentieth century, theatre moved away from the self-sufficiency of the proscenium arch theatre and the frontal mechanism to find other modes of scenography. In other words, scenography inscribed itself in a language of rupture, in a refusal of tradition and convention in favour of creating the element of surprise; displacing stage, actors, audience, objects and technical apparatuses (including lighting) to create a world different from the one that any practitioner or spectator is supposed to occupy when they enter a theatre. Even if, nowadays, the modes of investment of space really are diverse, one always ends up positioning themselves (whether they mean to or not) in relation to a tradition of "frontality", facing the Italian box. In other words, while the decision to not respect the frontal perspective was considered a creative transgression up until the 1950s, it is now simply an artistic choice, but one that, still in France, stands in opposition to the dominant and referential frontal convention. Tradition ingrained in the mind dies a hard death.

In the 1980s and 1990s, there was even a return to the frontal proscenium theatre by some artists who had moved considerably away from it to invest in atypical theatre spaces (e.g. Grüber or Engel), and this return certainly has significance. A significant question is whether this was a matter of choice (returning to a "state" of the theatre deemed to be fundamental) or an economic constraint and or one linked to the politics of theatre.

As such, all the non-frontal organisations of space immediately seem to be more innovative or more modern, even if the productions themselves are sometimes poor or incoherent. Making the audience walk about;[1] placing them all around the stage, as if they were at the circus; placing them in the centre while the actors play around them, as in certain productions of the Catalan troupe *La Fura dels Baus*;

providing exciting scenographic productions that are particularly well adapted to certain performances and productions, insofar as they make sense or are coherent with respect to the general overall project. To cause the audience to get lost or anxious in an abandoned building transformed into a theatre makes sense when one is representing the world of Kafka. Playing Shakespeare's *A Midsummer Night's Dream* on a walkway covered with fur, that of the Médrano Circus (at the very beginning of the Théâtre du Soleil) also makes sense: the audience seated in a circle (or what is almost a circle) observes a world that is at once marvellous, troubling and circus-like, where savage clowns dressed in animal skin perform their number. Because the principle of the circular stage generally – and in this case, clearly – allows for the avoidance of any orientation (and therefore to disorient the audience in a magical world), and implies that one can enter it from different angles, so that, in the case of *A Midsummer Night's Dream*, all the secrets are always seen simultaneously as intriguing things and as objects of theatre. Thanks to this "circus-like" theatre, the audience has the impression that they are attending a ritual, in communion with the actors; yet the fact that everything is seen and all the mysteries are visible renders the whole process factitious, by virtue of the fact that they are theatricalised. Utilising the principle of the "open thrust stage" to depict the vision of St Antony in the middle of the audience of the Odéon on a raised platform (Jean-Louis Barrault, *La Tentation de St. Antoine* [*The Temptation of St. Anthony*], 1966) allows the saint to be isolated at the foot of his cross (aptly placed where the thrust stage and the transversal stage meet). This empties the traditional stage for the choreographic movements of Béjart and arrests an audience who are literally and topologically caught between tempting visions and virtuous suffering. However, it seems useless to make the audience move around for nothing, or to pretend to innovate or transgress convention, or to seat the audience in a sort of circus if nothing in the referential system actually warrants it. Yet again, taking some distance from the conventional system necessitates an act or an operation in accordance with the performance or the reading of a text. Likewise, borrowing precise staging devices from the past or from other theatrical codes (like the cabaret in Germany and, later, in France, for example) implies that one is doing it on purpose and based on a scenographic intention that coheres with the project. Although in Japan, the mechanisms and devices of the noh and of the kabuki are fixed, conventional and immutable, Western theatre appears innovative when it places the spectators directly in front of the stage – the musicians opposite prompt side, or far away, the chorus at a distance from the stage – and installs a sort of trestle-stage bridge in the auditorium.

Finally, where visible wings are concerned (which are rather frequent in the theatre of the last few decades),[2] actors who are not meant to appear either onstage or in the dramatic space, are nevertheless present on generally bare platforms. This device creates a sort of cohesion, and even an evocation of ancient theatre troupes, as in *Arlecchino servitore di due padroni* [*The Servant of the Two Masters*], so often staged by Strehler), but also a feeling of distance. These are, indeed, actors that are playing and who can become characters, under the eye of their acting partners and of the audience. Illusion is thereby minimised, even if at times the very force of play is supposed to conquer the spectator's impulse for identification,[3] while insisting on the fact that all this is "only theatre". Through the endless oscillation between the presence of actors and the manifestation of dramatic fiction, all sorts of effects become possible, even a porosity between two worlds that places the audience in a state of observation, in their own sort of *mise en abyme*, in which they behave in a way that is unique to the theatre: simultaneously believing in the fiction while recognising its artifice.

Notes on bi-frontal staging

There is a particular spatial organisation that is less charged with historical references, called the bi-frontal arrangement. This allows one part of the audience to see the other part, above the actors or through the spaces between them, to create empty spaces on each side. This bi-frontal arrangement was used during the 2002–2003 season to stage two tragedies by Racine: *Phèdre*, directed by Patrice Chéreau at the Odéon-Berthier; *Phèdre* directed by Christian Rist at the Théâtre de la Tempête; and *Andromaque* by Jean-Louis Martinelli at Nanterre-Amandiers, and contributed in various ways to making the spectators witness a sort of ceremony, while at the same time allowing them to observe one another over and above the actors, the characters and the text. It directed their gaze towards the edges of the theatre; in other words, towards the places that were cleared of spectators and that depicted the divine, the society or the wings. "Racine and/or ceremony", as Jacques Schérer formulated it.[4] And each one of these productions explores this strong assertion through the bi-frontal stage arrangement. The short, narrow, tight and rectangular stage is thus stretched in front of spectators who face each other, witness and watch each other. The tragic world of language and desire is thus ostensibly observed by several rows of silent gazes, and there is no frontal scenery for them to forget the fact that they are there, together, to spy on the ravaging fire that consumes, enflames and destroys the speakers of the poem.

Martinelli, who, at the Amandiers, revisits an older work already performed at the TNS, with the same set design, turns the spectator literally into a witness and simply plays the game: the conflict in the sand in the middle; on one side, the society; on the other, there is Troy, a divine place, an elsewhere, the site of the arrival and departure of Orestes. Everything is there so that everything can be played there, in the here and now, in a few hours, in a space that no longer has purpose at the end of the play. In a certain sense, this production adapts the code of bi-frontality to adhere to classical rules, so that the tragic conflict can loom large in full sight of everyone, being illustrated through verse. While the staging arrangement implies a departure from the regular frontal stage, with its specific denotation, it stops there and gives place to the actors' play. In that respect, it comes close to the staging techniques of Chéreau.

The way in which it differs from Chéreau's work, however, is that the spectators overlook the stage from higher up (the tiered seats rise from the stage all the way to the ceiling). They represent a large assembly, generally located in a theatricalised hangar, who witnesses the fall of *the others*, those who verbally express the exasperation of passion. Sometimes the character-actors enter through the rows, sit beside the seated spectators, and arrest the gaze of the watchers. The sounds and recorded music illustrate situations, reinforce essential moments, and connect the world of representation to the past and to the immediate future of those who are present, and who have taken a moment to witness the spectacle of desire and to feel that all this is still relevant. On the one hand, the set created by Richard Peduzzi recreates the ancient entrance of an imposing palace emerging from the sands of Pétra – which is linked to the stage by a precarious and almost improvised walkway on which Phèdre almost stumbles. On the other hand, the playing area loses all distinctiveness in the Atelier Berthier: a few ordinary chairs, as if to suggest something of an absent chorus (according to Georges Banu's expression); a large opening revealing a freight elevator; the doors of a building; the Boulevard Berthier; and the highway. Racine's verses are positioned within this tense in-between: between antiquity and the present.

Rist's spectators are very few (only four or five rows on the same level). Overlooking them is a walkway-altar-scaffold, a stage (which is a platform at the middle of which is placed a glass panel, out of which comes the light of the gods). This time, the gazes are not looking down, but rather they are looking up, and in this movement, they sometimes meet other eyes that watch in a state of enthralment. The sounds come from within; they are made from bamboo flutes and tympanum (by Jean-Michel Deliers), blending into the tempo, stilted by the movements of the tightrope walkers, they regulate the flow of the prosody to foster a kind of symmetric unity, while reinforcing the rupture of unity and the overall disequilibrium. These sounds accompany the Fall. On each side of the stage layout, two T-shaped bars are placed creating an equivocal space between stage and offstage, and all around, a sort of tent, which clearly creates a rupture with the real work: the play and its spectators take part in a particular ceremony, that of images, sounds, sensations, language and emotions produced by the enunciations of verse.

As we shall see shortly, Rist and Chéreau propose contrasting functions of lighting within this same bi-frontal stage layout, so as to be fully coherent with the different readings that they do of the play. But through this initial description, based on a rapid analysis of bi-frontality, it will be understood that this staging decision (which may simply be guided by the circumstances of production, a series of chances or, on the contrary, be a real decision)[5] always appears essential. By choosing bi-frontality, the open thrust stage, circularity or semi-circularity, itinerancy or a multiplicity of staging arrangements and spatialities, the directors lend a distinctive meaning to a production and a reading. It is a question of whether to conform to the norm (frontality) or to ostensibly move away from it. And, above all, it implies giving the audience immediate signs that fulfil or destabilise their expectations, signs that are clearly open to interpretation.

9
THE COORDINATES OF THE STAGE

Our objective is thus to take into account the fact that staging spaces and designs are not fortuitous, even when they are conventional, and that they carry meaning, even if circumstances lead practitioners to maintain conventional arrangements. The issue for practitioners as well as for spectators thus becomes how to master these architectural and technical arrangements by making them adhere to a coherent theory, an aesthetic project or a specific interpretation.

Therefore, a staging site must be considered from the point of view of its height, depth and width, which implies a negotiation between its horizontal and vertical dimensions. This negotiation, enacted via the bodies of the actors and through the scenery, takes place in the spaces between openness and closure, and between bareness and density of the stage. To stage a work of theatre thus involves a systematic relationship to all these variables, and it is the awareness of this relation, of this interplay of factors, that allows both the realisation of the *mise en scène* and the audience's interpretation of it. The practitioners, stakeholders (and these include the spectators) must endeavour to coordinate this set of signs, take them into account (whether they are intentional or not), know that every movement, every object, every sound has meaning. Additionally, one must choose one's own interpretative pathway in all of this and endeavour to achieve an artistic coherence of the object that is constructed. While one must attempt to find a common ground for all – the issue of coherence is important – it is based on this common ground that the spectator, "alone among others", and nevertheless sensitive to the others (spectators, actors, practitioners), also has to chart their own unique path.

We therefore have a "stage" that is fairly large, often slightly inclined (in the case of traditional stages, to enhance the effects of perspective) and generally flat. It is on this stage that signs (whether mobile or not) will be inscribed: above, in front, behind, on the sides, below.

Each element that one can notice, contributes to an effect, which is interpretable, so long as it functions in a network (complementary, the effect of repetition and emphasis, opposition, etc.).

What looms up first and foremost is the scenery (or its absence), or a simple platform (but it is always a sort of scenery), that is already there. This scenery, conceived of with a meaningful structure, as a *space*, is what confers meaning upon the horizontal and vertical dimensions of the platform, and on its depth: objects, bodies, painted canvases, cyclorama, platforms, lights. From here, we can determine a means of describing the scene by taking into consideration a number of key criteria: from the horizontal plane, we can see the scenery at the back that stands at a vertical and forms a more or less symbolic or illusionistic canvas. We can also determine all sorts of technical elements that allow one to raise or lower objects, lateral apparatus that open on to fictional spaces, other stages raised or placed opposite to the main one or on the sides (or in the space of the spectators); pits or openings in the stage floor; and, last but not least, bodies and objects. On the platform, there will also be a play of spaces based on depth: the proscenium or front of stage that is close to the audience and amplifies the reach of the voice; the back of the stage, which, evidently, hides and creates distance; the middle, which places any object into sharp focus. Moreover, it is possible to assign separate constraints to different sections of the stage, and to divide it into different spatial zones that confer special meaning to objects and actors, depending on their positions on the stage. Special meaning correlated with variables of height, depth and width. In so doing, one can have different spaces on one platform – fictional spaces, "psychological" spaces, strategic spaces, symbolic spaces, etc.

Likewise, the play between foreground and background can force spectators into creating a hierarchy, or into choosing their point of view, as when there is simultaneous play on the left side and right side of the stage, above and below, etc. The spatial relationship between the platform and the auditorium can also generate specific phenomena. The most seasoned actors at the Comédie-Française know that certain positions on the stage are acoustic dead spots and that at these points their voices will not "carry", and, as such, barring an instruction to the contrary by the director, it is better for them to remain in other places. Consequently, the spaces occupied by the actors do not only correspond to an effect of meaning of the *mise en scène* but also precise technical reasons. We can add that an actor downstage with their back turned will have less of a chance of being heard and will have to force his voice more than if he were at the front and facing the audience. Likewise, an acting troupe will be better heard if the auditorium is full than if it is empty and the actors' voices bounce of the empty seats. Finally, the primary vertical element that overlaps with the major principle of the horizontality of the staging mechanism is the body of the actor. Although this may seem obvious, it is worth re-emphasising.

A space more or less filled, more or less closed

Moreover, if one considers that a platform is first and foremost a space filled by theatrical signs, one will analyse the extent to which it is filled and the quality of its *fullness*. If the romantic and realist theatre of the nineteenth century, like boulevard theatre of today, tended to fill the stage with signs, even at the expense of a certain superfluity,[1] modern scenography since Copeau (and his ideal of the bare stage) endeavours to leave the stage empty.

Peter Brook is not the first director to have advocated the empty space of the stage and the minimalist or reduced scenery in order to foreground play and the polysemic effect of rare objects utilised. All this therefore fosters maximum mobility, a certain ease with respect to transformation and greater liberty in the spectator's imagination as well as in the director's. It also emphasises the void, as we have seen with Meyerhold and the Russian constructivists of the 1920s, and implies refusing illusionistic figuration, bourgeois theatre and building an intellectual and modern stage from a simple non-decorative stage design. The mimetic depiction of the fictional world thus gives place to the performance of an autonomous space in which characteristic signs, architectural figures, masses and planes allow actors to deliver through their bodies without superfluity or redundancy, and in such a way that the spectators have the leisure of interpreting this reduced mass of information and of filling the void through a work of the imagination. At the same time, this empty space becomes, above all, the space of the actor's work. Nowadays, it is even demonstrably so for all of those directors who foreground this notion of the use of space. In the 1950s and 1960s, Jean Vilar also harnessed the empty stage to produce a neutral and harmonious link between practitioners, text and spectators in a sort of unifying space where only a few platforms served as a basis for the movement of bodies and for the imagination of the spectators. However, the prevailing tendency in contemporary theatre is not to consider, like Vilar sometimes did, the stage as a site conducive to social harmony, destined to render the external world legible. As such, nowadays there is no shortage of techniques to divide the stage, to create the effect of montage suggested by texts or by the contradictory structure of plays.

Consequently, the stage, empty or filled, has been utilised in contemporary theatre to represent a field of contradictory, disharmonious forces that are reminiscent of the world of which it speaks. This is where lighting, and the immense technological progress that has transformed it over the years, has had significant impact: spotlights, follow-lights, illumination of a portion of space or body, particular colours, zebra lines and various filters not only make it possible to divide the stage, but also instantly change the set by a mere lighting adjustment. However, for all that, the tableau has not gone out of use in the twentieth century as a means of producing, on the one hand, a framing effect, and therefore the reality of a vision, of an *opsis*, and, on the other hand, a reference based on which the spatial functioning and interpretation of the play can shape. Though contemporary sets are often designed by painters or by decorators who sometimes have pictorial tableaux as their references, the modern principle of scenery does not necessarily impose the use of perspective as it has done in the past. Consequently, the image serves as much to produce the spectacle as the play of the actor who must blend into this image: the stage is formed by a series of signs, which are not necessarily subsumed by the body.

The other criterion that may be used to describe the platform of the stage is the principle of opening and closure. While dramatic theatre was supposed to present a closed world offered to the gaze of the spectator, we have seen that this supposed closure was in no way concrete or perfectly closed. And more generally, we have seen that theatrical practice prior to the era of dramatic theatre, like contemporary practice, did not cease to question the principle of the fourth wall. It did so, on the one hand, by challenging the supposed impermeability of the space of fiction (the dramatic space), in relation to the staging space, and in relation to the theatrical precinct taken as a whole, including the house. On the other hand, it highlighted the fact that the dramatic space is essentially a space of a performance, and not only that in which a fable and/or a true-to-life or credible plot were represented. As a result, the space of the staging platform became open to the audience, because, in a certain way, it already was open to them without them realising it.

As such, one can explain the principle of opening/closure through two tendencies (which, naturally, can then overlap and interpenetrate each other): a theatre that is closed and thus insists on the representation of a world of fiction absolutely separated from that of the spectator; and a theatre that plays on the relationship between the spectator, the play of the actors and the dramatic space, while envisaging all these dynamics as elements that interfere with each other.

Furthermore, the scenery, equipped with a certain number of apparatuses, can also play its role. Indeed, even though the platform space is given the role of representing a precise world-space cut off from the house, with an interior (what happens on the stage of fiction) and an exterior (what happens outside of the depicted dramatic space, which we have already termed the "offstage space" [*le hors-scene*]), one can perfectly conceive of open and indeterminate figurations on either side of the stage, above and below, or at the back of the stage, in the distance, which counter the notion of strict boundaries and allow the spectator to dream or imagine an indefinite and even abstract offstage space. The cyclorama, for example, that curved and lighted canvas, places the representation of the dramatic space against a coloured background that can free the fiction from its strict closure. Conversely, an opening on to a place depicted as being beyond the dramatic space may bring the spectator, mentally, back to the theatre building, i.e. to real offstage spaces: the wings, the walls of the stage, the pulleys and cords and even the outside of the theatre, when its back door opens on to the actual street (a device now widely used, for example by Georges Lavaudant in his production of *La Mort de Danton* [*The Death of Danton*]).[2]

There is therefore no purely empty theatrical space and no purely filled space; no true closure, no absolute horizontality, verticality or depth, but rather a series of oppositions and interplays that involve these criteria. Rather than describe an infinite number of cases that all depend on the inventiveness of practitioners, we will try here to establish the criteria of observation necessary to identify the games at play in theatre and, if possible, the linkages and references and thus sketch out an initial reading.

One must also have some criteria that are directly linked to canonical architectural descriptions (horizontality/verticality, near/far, void/volume, depth/width, closure/openness, static/dynamic, etc.) based on which one can categorise, if possible, the type of usage of the theatrical space as a whole and of the staging space (circular/rectangular/bi-frontal/ambulatory, etc.). Also integral to the use of theatrical and staging space are the technical and material elements, which compose these spaces (floors, lighting, sounds, scenery, objects, costumes, etc.) and bodies, on which the entire dynamic of staging is based.

10

THE TECHNICAL AND MATERIAL ELEMENTS OF THE STAGING SPACE

The floor

In ancient Italian theatres, the platform[1] is slightly inclined (3–4 cm per metre) toward the house to facilitate viewing from afar and to create perspective. In contemporary theatres, the platform is flat, without an incline, all the more so in cases where they were not officially designed as theatre buildings. But this stage, presumably, will always have a floor – in other words, a geometrical space that can be covered. The floor is indicative of the general intention of the production: dark fur for *A Midsummer Night's Dream*, staged by Mnouchkine; white fur for *Bérénice* staged by Planchon; sand for Martinelli's first production of *Andromaque*; as well as sand for the back left-hand side of the stage in *Phèdre* staged by Bondy. And when Langhoff, with his *Gloucestor Time – Matériau Shakespeare* (adaptation of *Richard III*, 1995), fills the floor with obstacles of all kinds and divides it up into several planes, he clearly seeks to create an interpretative effect, to denote the complexity of the world, the complexity of the actors' play, and the multiplicities of the spaces in which such play can be applied (the Elizabethan world, the modern world, the medieval world and all this in several layers. This is all contrary to the waxed floor that Vitez used for his *Phèdre* [*Phaedra*] and that was meant to evoke the harmonious, planned, shining and spectacular court of Louis XIV, as well as provide a context for the type of acting that he intended. The floor then becomes a theatrical object in the fullest sense.

The floor, which tends to be largely static, thus takes on a life of its own through the dynamic of bodies, their verticality and their movement and sometimes through objects themselves. The floor can also come to life via a machine that puts it into action, a phenomenon that always produces an effect: the floor can be opened slightly to lead to the space beneath the stage, so that Dom Juan can fall into hell or into the secret bowels of the theatre. It can also be changed through the use of mobile boxes, so that characters can scale obstacles. It can be transformed, reconfigured, split into several spaces, when the scenographer covers it with objects that are more or less mimetic (a pool of water by Chéreau in *La Dispute*, the bank of a river in *Iphigenie auf Tauris* by Grüber). As such, the floor can be adjusted and contains hidden compartments beneath it, trap doors allowing for characters to emerge or fall, mobile crates that mount and descend, adding to the verticality, a technical component on which scenographers rely to create new effects (the fall into hell or into a raging sea, an obstacle course, the creation of a heterogeneous landscape, etc.). Consequently, the verticality of the stage, which encompasses the entire space between the fly system and the underpart of the stage is thus thrown into relief. Nevertheless, one should note that vertical effects, whether they come from above (a machine coming down from the fly system or moving across the upper part of the stage's frame) or from above (the opening of a space in the floor) are always more remarkable than horizontal effects because they are more unusual. And it is not by chance that, for a long time, they have represented a sacred passage: the fall from heaven to earth; the fall from earth to hell; the upward climb from hell to earth; or the ascension to heaven. Indeed, the European spectator, even one relatively uninformed about theatrical conventions, will easily decipher vertical symbolism since it is clear that heaven and the gods are above (even since the theatre of the ancient Greeks), the world on the staging platform and the underworld below. As a result, all ostentatious depiction of this verticality will necessarily refer to the dual (heaven/world) or triadic (heaven/world/underworld) universe that the spectator imagines in cultural terms. It therefore becomes the very prerogative of the director to perform or upset this signification through his work.

And in cases where the floor is not covered with anything (in other words, when it is left bare), which is often the case, it is not an insignificant decision because all theatre represents a choice of some sorts. The bare floor is that of the staging platform (wooden or made from cement, depending on the building), and when one chooses not to alter it this is a decision to accept it, all the while downplaying its signification (in other words, it is evident and not highlighted as significant), and/or that one is showing it as it is. Likewise, by baring the stage and exhibiting its walls and the entire stage house, there is a decision to emphasise the very fact of being in a theatre. Indeed, the minimalist stage, with bare floor and walls, is one of the major current trends in France. Thus, when the stage floor is theatrically exhibited, that is to say it is bare but signifying theatricality, it becomes an act of hypersignification to cover it with lights, as we shall presently see, or to place on it an object that thereby becomes all the more remarkable. What these instances show is that simply by showing a key differentiating element in the staging space, one can create a transition into a specific dramatic world.

Peter Brook, for example, who generally works in the bare playing area of the Théâtre des Bouffes du Nord, systematically utilises mats and tapestries to construct a series of dramatic spaces and thereby change the sites of the fiction in full view of the spectator. In this "total space" as Georges Banu describes it,[2] a worksite-place where "different models of historical theatrical places overlap in multiple ways" (the actualisation of an ancient time that is re-constituted and a present time that is in the process of construction), Brook plays with all the functions of the carpet object, and especially with how this allows him to create a dramatic space. When, in his first production of *Hamlet* in English (2000), Horatio, standing at the edge of the mat, asks the most central question in the entire *mise en scène* ("Who's there?"), a lateral light illuminates the floor and an actor who has emerged from among the spectators. Guided by the sounds and rhythms of oriental music, he enters into the ceremony, stops, slowly stretches out his leg and places his foot on the bright red mat. With the stroke of a gong and in one full stride, the empty and neutral space suddenly takes on a new function: that of representing the arrival of the actor at his place, of Hamlet in a bloody theatrical space and of giving an initial response to the question posed. The fable, the ceremony and the theatrical experience can begin, since the actor has stepped on to the mat and since Hamlet is born theatrically. From then on, the mat, a spatial and geometric solution that condenses and delimits the space of play, designates above all, with utmost economy of means and expression, the frontier between place and space: "Where there is a mat, there can be theatre. Nothing else needed to announce it besides this temporary, carved out space of play in which the actor hides nothing".[3] And it is from that moment that it can signify something totally different, a plural space: the ceremony in general (the mat is an instrument of prayer, in a temple designed for this purpose); the magic of theatre (it can be transformed, it can travel); the suggestion of an atmosphere; the link between scenes and spaces (since it allows one to pass over ramparts inside the palace, to get into Gertrude's room, etc.); and also the blood in which one walks (the court of Elsinore).

Therefore, the floor must be empty in order to lend significance to the thing that fills it. That is why, in most cases, the floor is cleared after being filled with objects, particularly after each scene or each tableau. During the action, actors bring signifying objects on to the stage and, purposely or not, drop objects that their play does not necessarily allow them to pick up afterwards. Machines arrive, platforms are placed. In order to resume play and begin a new scene or tableau, and even without seeking a realist effect, it is generally considered useful that the ground be cleared and bare. Such changes may happen in plain sight or while the stage is dimmed, to allow the platform to be cleared of all encumbrances.

Mnouchkine always insists on this clearance of the stage in *Le Dernier caravansérail* [*The Last Caravan Stop*] or in her last play, *Une Chambre en Inde* [*A Room in India*]. It even becomes a sort of professional dogma of hers as she performs, in the truest sense, the preparation of the platform at each scene change via actors who regularly come onstage with objects, leave carrying those objects and then sweep up after themselves. In other words, whose duty it is to ensure that the play takes place within a proper and specific space: the space of theatre, that which fixes the gestures and words of the errant figures and that which, through the intervention of actors and objects, is transformed into a space of representation. Conversely, Langhoff, as we have seen, Castorf and now Rodrigo García, constantly fill the platform with all sorts of objects. García (*Jardinage humain* [*Human Gardening*], Théâtre de la Cité Universitaire, 2004) adds edible products and debris that remain on the stage like common rubbish until the end, and that can then be used again for another scene, so that the effect produced is that of a large garbage dump in which man lives and plays. The space of the theatre thus becomes the dramatic space that it denotes, a wretched global garbage heap that is full and cannot be cleared. Brutally, García confronts the spectator with her own reality, that of a postmodern hyperconsumption: her reality is laid bare by the performance (*After Sun*). Besides the blatant condemnation of the pollution of plastic and the general ecological scandal of our times, this scenic accumulation once again depicts a memory of the near past (in García's work, all the moments of the play thus remain onstage and become debris, as it were, of the past). The accumulation depicts a moment in the not so distant past of history itself (Langhoff), which testifies to time and of the material traces of this time with which the staged production seeks to engage: the vestiges (the ruins or traces) of the representation that has taken place and of the time that it evokes.

These examples therefore illustrate the need to understand that the staging space is shaped by a deep awareness of its horizontal and vertical coordinates, as much as by the issues of closeness and depth. Consequently, in a scenographic system in which one of the major principles is the horizontality of the platform, any staging effect that highlights its vertical dimensions will appear surprising, charged with signification, ostensibly designed by the practitioners, and therefore a feature that is to be interpreted by the spectator. In such cases, the viewer mentally creates a link between the verticality of the bodies of actors and that of the objects onstage, which, together, interrupt the conventional horizontality of play. In that regard, the arrival of Tartuffe in Act 3, Scene 2, is more important than initially thought, because this arrival happens via a very conspicuous staircase. This vertical entry, from above, parodically depicts a descent from the world of the gods (hidden, false or true) into that of men. Jean-Pierre Vincent's production (Amandiers, 1998) of *Tartuffe* makes this fact clear by providing much space for this large, useless yet troubling staircase until the third act, when one finally sees an actor descending it. Jean-Marie Villégier's staging of the play in 1995 (Athénée) plays with this effect by hiding the staircase, so that Tartuffe arrives on tiptoes as the hypocrite that he is. But both these scenographic and symbolic passageways are foregrounded in the production of the play in a way that allows the spectator to decipher their signs. It is also for this reason that all the trapdoors imagined by Romantic theatre are crucial, because they show that men do not cease to move to space at will and to play the role of the iniquitous and devious while remaining, irreducibly, men, or talented actors, since it is their duty to show that the world that they occupy no longer has boundaries or vengeful gods.

Lighting

As long as the performance is not held during the day, lights are used to light up the platform, to craft the space or to contribute to crafting it, by complementing other devices. As we have seen previously, lighting (from large tallow candles and oil lamps) was not versatile or easily manipulated before the advent of gas, and later of electricity and, eventually, of the technologies of guided lighting. We know that in the seventeenth century, the light provided by the tallow candles used in the cities was dim and gave off smoke, and that wax candles, which were costlier, were mostly used in court theatres. Actors at the Hôtel de Bourgogne thus had to rely on the brilliance of their costumes, on play that turned the proscenium to its advantage, on their carriage and on their vocal talents, to foreground the signs of the representation in relation to the scenery and stage design. As we shall see later, once it became possible to direct and control lighting, it would accentuate this process of exhibition of the character. In the eighteenth century, thanks to the new oil lamps equipped with mirrors, certain parts of the staging space (more than others) were now able to be illuminated during theatre productions and the first stars of theatre were thus able to be the object of greater focus. But it was later, once the direction and intensity of lighting were able to be controlled, that major effects were produced.

First, the stage could be placed in darkness (Wagner), i.e. all the lights could be turned off before being turned back on, and it was possible to illuminate only the platform (or the staging space). As such, the dream of classical theorists (d'Aubignac) and those of the eighteenth century (Voltaire and La Harpe) was finally being realised: the represented fiction was now totally highlighted and the dramatic space was now depicted, majestically, as being absolutely separated from the space of the spectators. And as these same theorists had predicted, this also gave rise to fears about possible public disorder. Indeed, whereas at the beginning of the twentieth century, the American National Legion of Decency was outraged by the idea of placing playhouses in absolute darkness and by the likelihood that theatregoers would be able to scream, shout, engage in kissing and all sorts of other immoral acts (so that American cinemas continue to this day to only dim the lights rather than plunge the room in full darkness), a few critics in France claimed that placing the audience in darkness would result in a lack of attention and even in screams and boisterous shouting under the veil of anonymity. But the desire for spectacle was too strong and the effects proposed too convincing, since the principle of illusion was evidently more magnified. The theatre houses were thus placed in darkness during the performance; the lighting in them had already begun to be dimmed throughout the nineteenth century. Consequently, leaving the lighting on in the house, even slightly, as Peter Zadek did for his production of *Hamlet* in 2000, proves to be troubling for the spectators, who thereby see themselves watching the spectacle and reacting to it. They then find themselves placed in a process of alienation from theatrical illusion, a process that is sometimes experienced as a desecration of representation and that is all the more provocative when the play being staged is a great classic produced by a well-known foreign director (as was the case for Peter Zadek's *Hamlet*, staged in Strasburg at the TNS, then at the MC93 in Bobigny).

One can therefore use adjustable lighting to create an atmosphere (based on warm or cold colours and their intensity) and to create the illusion of moments or periods of time (from morning to midday, from midday to evening), by playing on changes in light. And faced with an excess of hypersignifying effects linked to the enthusiasm of practitioners for these new technologies and with an increase in the use of expressionist lighting techniques (the play of light and shadow and the effect of backlighting), Brecht responded by neutralising the staging background to promote a uniform lighting that would denaturalise the character and focus the critical reflection of the audience on him. As a result, the art of lighting in the theatre became a veritable practical and theoretical issue, shaping the aesthetics of the spectacle. Therefore, as the job of lighting director was being created as a profession in its own right, the technical shaping of lighting and of colour (cold or warm, varicoloured, spotlighting, figurative or abstract) became central for theatrical productions. The choice of the background also became an entirely conscious act and one essential for controlling the way the performance would be received by the spectators. The background could be a uniformly lit neutral one (Brecht's Berliner Ensemble), a dark one (which gives an inward looking feel to the performance and can connect it to a psychic world with bodies and elements of set design standing out in unusual ways against a non-mimetic and rather indeterminate background, and creating the impression of emerging from a space whose depth cannot be fathomed or apprehended by the spectator's rational consciousness[4]) or a clear cyclorama at the back of the stage (which gives an expansive feel to the *mise en scène*, one of exteriority, making the spectacle more "objective").

Additionally, rays of light could now be made to focus on a specific place on the stage, and this focalisation could be made to move, creating different degrees of intensity at different points of the stage and, therefore, modifying the perception and the dimension of space through the light projected on to certain zones. Lighting thus became a crucial means for the orientation of the spectator's gaze and an essential narrative element. But lighting is also a particularly sensual device, and we know that the play of different luminous intensities produces affects, sensations and impressions that the spectator experiences consciously or unconsciously. Spotlights and profile spots also tend to carve out spaces of play when they are projected on to the floor or directly centred on an object, a body or a part of one or the other. Profile spots, for example, can thus be projected on to the theatrical scenery and on to the floor abstract elements or concrete elements and are capable of dividing up the stage in a patent manner. Precision lighting was dear to Bob Wilson, and can be used for tasks as various as lighting a hand, or even what is being held in that hand, so that the gaze of the spectator is focused on the plastic and signifying effect decided on by the director. This was exactly what Bob Wilson did both as an actor and director in *Hamlet*. In *A Monologue* of 1995, Wilson takes hold of the book object that is *Hamlet*, to divide it, interpret it and glorify it on a platform, as he saw fit. In *The Temptation of St. Anthony* in 2004, Wilson transformed the story of the saint into a veritable gospel music hall, where the entire purpose of the performance lay mainly in the music (each number or each temptation was narrated through a gospel song) and in the mastery with which all sorts of lighting effects were used. He therefore imagined an almost bare stage surrounded with walls painted white, on which he projected, based on the particular instance and the temptations depicted, warm or cold lights, varying colours as the music changed, turning lights off or alternating them based on movement and dance, so as to complement discourse with the rhythms of gospel music. Using profile spots, he also created geometrical figures on the floor that unified or separated his actor-singers or that grouped them together in rectangles and rounds of light. Finally, he focused the gaze of the audience on a bouquet, a face, a posture or a raised finger, which would arrest the spectator, thanks to the technical virtuosity and the pictorial quality suggested by such a framing device and by the play on an often static image. Wilson thus draws the spectator to appreciate *details*, and they must interpret and determine what each of these details signifies, by taking into account the devices and techniques of spotlighting and montage that preside over the production of the Wilsonian scenic image. At the intersection of entertainment spectacle, of Broadway revue,[5] of modernised medieval mystery, of or postmodern *auto sacramental*, the coherence of the *mise en scène* consists in harmonising, in the musical sense of the term, the lyrics of gospel songs, the sounds, objects, postures and lights, with the rhythm of the performance. Consequently, the meaning of the visions emerges from these "harmonies" that are largely created in the spectator's experience of watching, an experience that fully entails the internalisation of a series of discontinuous musical and choreographic numbers "blended" with the aid of lighting, within the linearity of a brilliant spectacle that illustrates the experience of the saint.

The invention of the follow-spot, to take another example, allows technicians not only to light up one actor in particular, but to follow a specific performer moving around the stage, while leaving the rest of the stage minimally lit or without lighting. This not only modifies the dimension of the space and extends infinitely far the boundaries of the dramatic space (since the scenic space becomes indeterminate), but also concentrates the gaze of the spectator on the possible play that the actor makes between the lighted halo and what is outside it. Indeed, lighting has a unique potential for isolating the actor's performance and making it expressly theatrical, such as in the delivery of a showman who commands attention – this is the merciless focalising light of the circus and of the music hall. Patrice Chéreau in his staging of *Dans la solitude des champs de coton* [*In the Solitude of Cotton Fields*] by B.-M. Koltès isolated both protagonists through the use of such follow-spots, and then used lighting to narratively illustrate their entanglement in a great epic combat, as if the scene became a ring and a dance floor. Through the violent light placed upon them, the production zoomed in on two opponents who became the ostensible spectacle of two horizontal entities in movement, as though in a combat and a *pas de deux* under the glaring light coming from the fly system.

We can return to the comparison of the productions of *Phèdre*, which we began earlier, with respect to the bi-frontal staging arrangement, developing it here from the point of view of the arrangement of light. In his staging of *Phèdre*, Chéreau revisits the same principle used in *La solitude des champs de coton* but this time developing it. His characters are literally *followed* by the light, frozen when they are not followed, always called on or forced to escape the freezing blue of the gelatine filtering the light of the projectors. The three follow-spots from the mechanism used to stage Koltès' text, divide up the actors' space of play and mark them as prey, and force the machinists to be intensely active (they become the gods of this spectacle). As a result, Phèdre tries in vain to escape the scenographic destiny, which encircles her and tries unsuccessfully to sidestep a role, which is ineluctably hers. However, she is then seized by a cold light: the quivering or trembling prey has no other solution than to be the object of the silent kill by the spectators seated on either side of the bi-frontal stage. Hippolytus in the distance, offstage, has met the monster and the goods-lift of the Atelier Berthier can bring back his bloody corpse. The halo that guides this funereal entrance triumphs at the same time that Theramenes' tale is being told. Since the "pursuit" has ended, the light then becomes warmer, as if tinted by cries and compassion: in a depiction that is somewhere between the living Christ painted by Philippe de Champaigne and Benetton's controversial *Pieta*[6] (1991) or "dying Christ", the young naked man is taken into the arms of a guilty *pietà*. The tragedy of the light is therefore not that of the brilliant Phèdre, as one may have thought, but is woven around Hippolytus, who is the point of intersection of all flames and passions.

Christian Rist's staging, produced in the same season (2002–2003) at the Théâtre de la Tempête, adopted an entirely different approach. The lighting did not limit the field of observation: it enveloped the whole, as in the canvases of Poussin, then blinded the actors and spectators, when Phèdre's father, the sun-god, finally emerges from the underworld through the trap doors of the stage. And turning toward the projectors located under the stage, the actor-characters witnessed the violence of the light, literally, face to face, looking into the dazzling face of their destiny. And at no time did the characters hide, at no time did they escape this bright place: the canopy of a white sheet spread over bamboo sticks and under which we all sat (spectators included), imprisoned with its fires. In Rist's *mise en scène*, lighting therefore presided over the execution of verse and of the characters' destinies. As a result, the costumes, the warm colours tinted with exoticism, could reveal bodies as much as they could uncover the sensuality of the skin and radiate under the sun created by lights – the sun of Troezen – and prevent any of the actors from disappearing from the enclosure: even when Œnone leaves the platform and stands alongside it, beside the spectators, or when the characters leave the walkway when their scene had ended. Since no one could disappear from view, each person silently witnessed the action of words.

Albeit a very brief example, this comparison proves that lighting techniques are necessarily integrated into the dramaturgical and theatrical apparatus, and that certain essential signs are constructed through the particular context of the staging arrangements (bi-frontality). By harnessing the spectators' perception of the play of colours and lighting, the director, the scenographer and the lighting technician control the immediate sensations of the audience (cold or warmth, for example), to impose their devices, their reading and the ideas that they intend to depict. As such, the entire *mise en scène* is sustained by lighting, since it orientates the gaze of the spectator on the scenery or the actor who must play with it and know how to "attract" it: it is often said of a given actor that he or she "uses light very well". And because lighting can change the appearance of scenery and of an actor (green and blue cause the colour of a face to tend towards grey, and orange enhances the skin's appearance). Furthermore, based on where projectors are placed and how they are focused on a particular object or on a particular actor, the impact of staging will change and give way to different perceptions and meanings. Side lighting tends to favour a relationship between the actor and the audience, whereas frontal lighting and, even more so, a line of projectors, will help to separate the actor (who can no longer see the auditorium) from the spectators. Similarly, a warm frontal lighting tends to erase the most salient physical features of the actor, whereas a lateral light will highlight them. An actor on the proscenium facing the audience, lighted with a low-angle light, will seem isolated. As a result, one tends to use this system for monologues. (At the same time, this isolation will provide time for changes to the scenery of the stage left in the dark or behind a curtain. The same thing could be said of cross-sectional lights.) The idea behind such isolation is to dramatise situations and to produce an impact through this lighting that thus sustains the theatrical production and that is synchronised with the rhythm or even creates it, in the sense that it helps to punctuate scenes, colour them and give to each one a specificity with respect to the others. Moreover, because lighting can both be radically marvellous and totally absent, it has the capacity to challenge one's vision or perception and thus the very foundation of a representation. To end a play or interrupt a representation by creating sudden darkness elicits anxiety from the spectator who is brutally plunged into darkness. However, it is a disquiet that makes them think and perhaps wonder if there has been an incident. This is the case in some of Engel's productions, and particularly in *The Last Judgement* (2003) with the scene of the derailment of a train. Conversely, the final spectacular moment that Koltès indicates in the last stage direction of his *Roberto Zucco* (*"The sun comes up, becomes blinding like the explosion of an atomic bomb. Nothing else can be seen"*), and that the productions of Bruno Boeglin (1991) and of Jean-Louis Martinelli (1995), for example, have interpreted by shining on to the audience a line of projectors of maximum intensity, actually blinds the spectators through an excess of violent light. This effect, by jolting the senses, makes one no longer able to calmly interpret the signs of the stage, and the blazing light thereby created exceeds both theatrical representation and one's rational ability to apprehend it.

On a stage designed in principle to be a site of images and, more broadly speaking, of representation, an excessive use of light can be the physical embodiment of moments that escape the spectator's powers of sensual apprehension. The writer Heiner Müller was thus able to write a letter to Erich Wonder (a German scenographer) in 1986 in which he stated that

> at times, we will be forced to put on the mask of Gorgon, the light that dazzles, the shadow that has devoured the light (the sun melts on the tongue): no eye should see everything. And every Sunday, we will show the invisible.[7]

Therefore, rather than the light of a scene, or the light of a stage, we will observe lighting in the succession of scenes and of tableaux that correspond to the intention behind the *mise en scène* (the English "light design"), to its temporal unfolding (morning, midday, night), to its atmosphere (warmth, coldness, shadow) and to its dramaturgical deployment. We will observe it in its functionality, given that lighting in the theatre (at least, in contemporary theatre) can be the thing that conditions the way one sees as much as the thing that challenges. One must also bear in mind that lighting is a plastic element that can also be utilised to destabilise the habitual categories of perception: through over-exposition; through under-exposition (and here, one could mention Claude Régy's plays again); through the play of dissonance, which can function like the counterpoint in music; or even through the intensity or physical violence that can sometimes characterise some of its usages.[8] In those cases, lighting becomes a key device used for questioning the spectator's mode of viewing and what they see, and also a key component of representation or performance as an experience, not only of showing, but of troubling and of questioning what is seen. In that respect, Georges Didi-Huberman's statement, initially applied to the plastic arts, is entirely apt: "to show is to always trouble what is shown, in its act, and in its perceiving subject. To see is always a subjective operation, and therefore a fissured, troubled, agitated and open one".[9]

Sounds and silence

Another dimension of place, but that calls upon the other major sense that inheres within the theatre, hearing, is that of sound. Sound is part and parcel of the category of space: when the spectator hears a sound, they identify it, and, for that reason, searches for the location from which it comes. This is evidently the case for spoken words where one immediately searches for who produces them and from where. Of course, this creates an effect of movement, of *mise en scène*, and of play between presence and absence, between the hidden and revealed. But this is also the case for noise and music. A sound that comes from a precise place, be it onstage or beyond the platform, commands the attention of the spectator (because it is not speech, and therefore appears to be distinguished from the specific conventional articulated sounds of the actors' play) and demands to be deciphered. Similarly, sound can depict a movement, by being transmitted from one loud speaker to another, and even depicting the real movement of a noisy object (the galloping of a horse, a car, the metro), without the stage designer having to represent the object. To do so, one can express it, represent it, through a play on lighting. When Nicky Rieti, in André Engel's production of Horvath's *Le Jugement dernier*, needs to represent the derailing of a train, he does not need a train, or even the design of a train or an object representing it: instead, he "spatialises" the sound of the train by playing on the transmission of a noise that seems near initially and gradually becomes farther and farther removed, suggesting the movement of the object. Then he introduces a loud collision to suggest the derailment. This sound has been previously recorded, and the director orchestrates the whole thing through his use of light (e.g. a harsh glare in the faces of the spectators) that is then enhanced by a real fire, the darkening of the platform and a sudden silence, so much that the spectators begin to wonder if the theatre itself might not be burning. By using the dynamics of sound, its force and its spatialisation in this way and by complementing it with the effects of lighting, Rieti creates an impression of reality while, simultaneously, highlighting the theatricality of his effect. But, inversely, sound and music can envelop the entire platform and, therefore, be equally distributed by several loud speakers placed at cardinal points of the stage and of the auditorium. An overall ambience is thereby created, since the spectator is unable to know from where exactly the sound is coming. And between these two extremes, all manifestations are possible, all effects and meanings, based on the spatial combinations that the director introduces (near/far, stage right/stage left, above/beneath, here/elsewhere), and how these work in synergy with other staging tools (lighting, objects, machines).

Additionally, in the theatre, sound is also the absence of sound: silence. We know that for a long time, the silence of the audience has been a major convention in theatrical performances and one of the theoretical imperatives necessary for the predominance of the dramatic space and the manifestation of the story transposed into fiction. If one accepts the ideal principle of dramatic theatre, it can also be said that the staging of an *other* place necessitates the silence of the platform and of the audience, in order for there to be a *transporting* of the spectator that originates in the silent moment of waiting. It is no surprise then that one waits for the audience to be quiet, that one tells the spectator to be silent (in France, by the famous curtain call known as the "*trois coups*", which is hardly practised any more) by the raising of a curtain or when the auditorium darkens. Moreover – actors know this – the house is noisy, deafening sometimes, even after a request for silence: the audience's attention and its more or less silent agreement with the performance is always sensitive, so much so that these same actors know perfectly how to gauge, in the course of their acting, the intensity of the audience's silence – in other words, the quality of attention and of involvement of the watchers. That is the first point relevant to the principle of the theatre session and that has major consequences on how audiences experience theatre productions.

But the second point has to do with the way in which the stage, and by extension the dramatic space, integrate silence in order to produce an effect. If one considers that the theatre experience consists in producing something out of nothing, it also becomes a way to transmit sound, whether articulated or not, from a silence that then appears to be essential or fundamental, given that it necessarily precedes the action that takes place onstage. It is charged with signification when it interrupts the flow of words and sounds of the performance. In such cases, silence becomes embodied; it highlights a particular moment that focuses the spectator's attention, as well as emphasising an emotion that the practitioners wish to make the audience feel. It offers a moment of sharing of passions, which incorporates the indications given by the actor, the sentiments attributed to the character and their impact on the spectator all at the same time. But this concentration and this effect of silent sharing are not limited to the shaping of an emotion — which, as one always knows, is artificial at the very moment when the actors conceive of it and feel it — to the extent that they still leave a moment of latency and freedom that, beyond stupor or emotion, can engage the spectator in an act of reflection: a gap for thought, in a sense, as in the moments in the cinema when Antonioni films clouds. This is when the spectator can hear, understand, feel and, at the same time, notice herself understanding and feeling.

Klaus Michael Grüber's *Bérénice* (Comédie-Française, 1984) is a superb example in this regard. From the very stage direction that asked actors to render audible "the noise of Racine's pen scratching the paper", Grüber does something quite different from destabilising his actors: he incites them to be silent, to weave sighs and tears into their recitation of three verses, but maintaining a certain distance that is manifested through the noticeable gaps in the discourse. Similarly, by installing a gauze-like curtain that was floating stage left, because of the wind coming from the wings (this imagined offstage space representing Bérénice's apartment), but also through the breathy diction of the alexandrine, he introduced an effect of suspension that could be felt by the audience. This moved the spectators as much as it encouraged them to muse on the silences of the text, of the characters, of Racine and of Grüber's interpretation itself. In this transitory place and space, which is on the brink of disappearing in the performance, and on which Gruber places the great round and massive (and enigmatic) stone of unsurpassable reality (at the back of the stage), the words seem to move through the silence and are overpowered by it, right until the final sigh of Antiochus ("alas"). Everything was orientated towards making the silence infinitely present, filling the minds of the spectators so that it could be interpreted as part of a ceremony of regret, where all was already consummated, written and, in a word, tragic. In this silence, what resonates is the simultaneous manifestation of emotion and reflection on a tragic element, which has no other action than that of irreparable loss.

We now know to what extent the theatre space is impacted by all sorts of sounds, noises, ruptures of silences and music, without even mentioning the impact of the words and the sung music that feature in the author's list of instructions. Generally, one hides these sonic phenomena as if they were outside of a play – the stage music literally masked, and that is called "incidental music" or "*música incidental*" in Spanish. However, and this has been the case since antiquity, the sound of an actor is essential since his very step moves at the pace of the music that characterises it. Yet, since our concern here is to consider the sound elements that are essentially part of the theatrical event, we should emphasise the fact that the sound-space goes beyond the music designed or intended to underpin or characterise the play of actors. Theatre incorporates within it the noises of the audience and of every staging apparatus, which seem so audible that at a certain point in history the orchestras of lyric tragedies would be made to play *fortissimo* so as to hide the noises made by the movement of machines. That is the same noise that we try to minimise nowadays by lowering the curtain so that an actor can speak very loudly at the forestage while the scenery is being changed, if this noise is not quieted through the abundant use of oil and various techniques.

As a result, we can distinguish noises that are said to be involuntary or contingent (because they derive from what one cannot prevent) from sounds, conventional or voluntary music, intentional and specific to the performance. Contingent noises are those of the audience (coughs, mobile phones, various movements, the late arrival of people, etc.); those that come from outside the theatre and that one cannot control (police sirens, the metro that passes below, the rain sometimes and all sorts of other undesirable elements). There are also those that come from the platform itself and that one tries, often in vain, to filter out. In the majority of theatre auditoriums nowadays, these noises appear quite irritating because they are perceived as interrupting both the ceremony and the spectator's self-projection into the dramatic space. This stands in sharp contrast to street theatre, where such noises must be tolerated, tamed and "domesticated", and played with, through their incorporation into the production.

But, for all that, let us not forget that this convention of general silence, which, in actual fact, never exists, is an extremely recent one. Up to at least up to the end of the nineteenth century, performances have always been seen and heard through a flow of sounds that never fitted properly into the notion of silent reception of the representation deployed in the dramatic space. Not only because the theatre was a place of socialisation, which allowed people to meet and speak to each other, but because the representation itself give rise to noisy reactions that were often far more than just laughter. And when commentators of the very early part of the eighteenth century indicate that the audience began to be silent, it is generally to observe that it no longer whistled so often or that the jeers were less frequent. It was later, when the parterre became a seated place and when the audience was trained to concentrate on the performance, that the idea of a relative silence became possible. And while, nowadays, the tacit expectation is for the audience to be quiet, for the building to filter out noises from outside and for the machines not to make noise, there are practitioners who make conspicuous the existence of noise, sometimes to the point of provoking it or adapting the *mise en scène* to the situation and to the circumstances.

The problem returns, but this time with regard to the sounds from inside the theatre. Must we isolate the stage at all costs from the house in such a way as to create an apparent dramatic space whose noises and sounds only aid in the depiction of the space represented? Or can we connect two worlds to allow the noises from the platform, from the building and from the city to be incorporated into the dramatic space? Or can one play with this interpenetration that is so difficult to strictly control, to establish surprising and productive connections?

To take only one example of noise and of meteorological circumstances, everyone knows that a staging of a play in the courtyard of the Palais des Papes in Avignon is, at least one out of three times, subject to the *mistral* and that one must prepare for this. Is this a non-controllable event that one must regret, or is it interesting to modify the production as a result, even if this means moving away that evening from the intended dramaturgical and scenic markers or the pre-arranged acting indications? Similarly, a representation will not be the same when it is played in front of an audience of connoisseurs (an audience accustomed to conventions) as when it is performed to secondary school children. This is what theorists often prefer to disregard but that practitioners cannot overlook. Consequently, instead of regretting that the audience, the weather or machines do not always conform to what one would ideally like the theatre to be – or instead of lecturing uninitiated spectators before a representation – it seems more interesting and, indeed, more in line with the history of theatre, to take these factors into account during the representation itself, even if this means pre-empting the thing and putting in place strategies capable of adapting to changes to meet an apparent dramatic ideal.

But one can do even more (or perhaps even better), and seek the noise from the audience, to inscribe it into the performance, thereby reconnecting with ancient practices or simply by being provocative. Bob Wilson, by representing continuously and for long hours *Einstein on the Beach* practically forces spectators to enter and leave the room, to move around in the theatre building, as one does during a baseball match or in the Japanese kabuki. As for provocation, the history of this is an ancient one. Even without mentioning Molière who calls out to the audience in *La Critique de l'École des femmes* through the laughter and the applause from the orchestra, and the loud noises from the stage benches (Molière even plans for and orchestrates such fights). We know that the Romantics were perfectly aware of provoking the spectators. During the representation of *The Moor of Venice* in 1828, Vigny translated exactly and ostentatiously the word "handkerchief" in his adaption of *Othello*, for he knew very well how to elicit booing from a post-classical audience that would not tolerate attacks on good manners. One only need read Théophile Gauthier to realise that the scandal of *Hernani* had been orchestrated with precision. Closer to the current day, surrealist theatre in the 1930s freely exploited the noise and furore of the auditorium by provoking the spectators. And from Ionesco to Romeo Castellucci to Rodrigo Garcia, via Blin and Genet or living theatre and Kantor's *happenings*, to cite only a few, we know that noise from an engaged or outraged audience is an excellent acting partner, so that efforts at provocation became one of the essential aspects of performance. Consequently, the notion of contingency has been redefined, since these noises became intentionally produced and, since it became sometimes a primary necessity for the audience not to be silent and for the machinery on the platform not to be oiled. A storm was then sometimes even desired. Conventional or intentional noises can belong to the theatre gathering, i.e. to the context of the representation, as much as to the representation itself.

The sounds of the session are a part of the organisation of the performance, of its ceremonial aspect and fit into conventions known to the audience. The bell (or the famous trumpets of the TNP-Chaillot or any other sound that indicates that one must enter into the auditorium) comes after the hubbub that characterises the arrival of the audience. The curtain call, coupled with the act of switching off lights, serves to summon the spectator's attention and to request silence from the audience while the curtain is rising. The intermissions that, before, would lead to around ten minutes of music (violins), are now a time for leaving the auditorium and for conversing, whether in the auditorium itself or in the foyer. They end with a sound (the bell, for example) or an instruction from outside inciting the spectators again to be silent. From classical antiquity, the most familiar sound has always been that of applause. Practitioners can decide to accept these conventions wholly and simply, which places the performance within an accepted norm, or to emphasise or parody them by exaggerating given moments of the "ceremony", which makes theatricality ostensible. They can, however, break certain rules, eliminate certain conventions or even play on their meaning. All of these choices alienate the spectator from a normative theatre session. It is noticeable that while the first sound conventions are often avoided or eliminated (and this includes the intermission) in theatre nowadays, for reasons that, each time, are perfectly justified and theoretically explainable, it is very rare to do away with the curtain call and therefore with the possibility of applause. If the actor were to not return at the end of the performance (and this is in fact the rule in certain Eastern theatres, such as Japanese Noh), and thus explicitly offer the spectator the opportunity, through her applause, to respond audibly to the representation and to mark its closure, this would be considered exceptional in Western theatre. Moreover, it would provoke a feeling of extreme awkwardness in the audience, since it breaks one of the fundamental codes of modern theatre sessions and denies the recognition of what had just been seen as a performance and a factitious and *appreciable* representation.

As such, when Yann Boudaut, the actor who had just played in Claude Régy's production of Charles Reznikoff's *Holocauste* (1998), a documentary text about Nazi extermination of Polish Jews transposed into poetic form, did not come back out for the curtain call, the awkward silence of the auditorium underscored and amplified the very evident malaise provoked by the ambiguous status of the representation that had just been witnessed. Indeed, one finds it inappropriate to applaud the account of the Holocaust, and it is not possible to take cover behind the notion of appreciating the actors' "play" and of recognising the work carried out by the practitioners in the construction of a fiction. The spectators were thus deprived of this traditional manifestation of the conventional demarcation between the fictitious side of theatricality and real lived experience. They were deprived also of the auditory sign of fulfilment, conclusion and the possibility of a return to the "normal" world that are all represented by the applause.

But the impossibility of applause can also arise when the performance refuses to end, taking on the appearance of a cyclical repetition. The actor never seems to leave the stage (that is to say, to not leave it until the last spectator has left the theatre precinct, is out of his sight, preventing the fictional pact from being ostensibly broken). This is the case in the mechanical imprisonment in an absurd and terrifying system (Martial di Fonzo Bo at the end of *L'Ile du salut* [*Salvation's*

Islands], based on Kafka's *The Penal Colony*, directed by Matthias Langhoff, 1996) or in that of grotesque madness (Valéry Dréville, at the end of Heiner Müller's *Médée Matériau* [*Medea Material*], directed by Anatoli Vassiliev in 2005). In these cases, the audience is deprived of the symbolic rupture that applause represents, deprived also of the re-appropriation of the whole of the theatrical space (to be able to leave normally) through the daily social life that such an auditory social ritual concretely manifests.

Sounds, noises and music attached to the performance will be the last point that we shall examine, insofar as they fully cohere with the intention of the practitioners, barring accidents. Platform music, composed specially for the play or borrowed from pre-existing compositions, is generally an accompaniment that functions in close relationship with the *mise en scène*. But it can also be an autonomous musical work that manages to go beyond or replace the text, to the point where one attributes to it a generic name (in opera, where music is produced and driven by the fiction; a musical interlude, in which the music inscribes itself into the theatre session as a break vis-à-vis the representation; an overture or finale, in which music metaphorically designates the framework or the conclusion of the play.

The theatre thereby positions itself at the outer limits of musical art and dance. This is more and more often the case. If *Le Bal* [*The Ball*], directed by Jean-Claude Penchenat in the 1980s pleased and surprised theatregoers so much, it is because he played on the theatrical and choreographic depiction of a popular ball in the 1930s and limited himself to music, without words, to signify both the postures and discontinuous plot. This theatrical spectacle of actor-dancers thus had the freedom of continuing to be a theatre of representation, and even a political theatre, while systematically borrowing from all the categories of choreography. And when Alain Platel's Belgian theatre group represented a choreography of bumper cars with very few words and much traditional music, which depicted the Fourth World in *Bernadetje* (1997), what the spectators witnessed was the production of a hybrid play that, despite the music used and the surprising choreography, did not fail to deliver a political message by combining all these elements. We can agree that this blending of genres and disciplines (song, dance and acting) is nothing new and that music has often been a means of combining effects and generating new aesthetics. When in seventeenth-century London John Gay wrote his *Beggar's Opera*, he combined the comedy of thieves, popular at the time, with opera (which he used in a surprising and unusual way) and ballet. Through the use of song and dance and parodic music, he created a new genre, which was to inspire Bertolt Brecht centuries later in his composition of the *Four Penny Opera*. However, in new attempts at musical theatre (those of Georges Aperghis or Heiner Goebbels, for example), there is an attempt at treating musical and spoken elements in a non-contradictory, non-differentiated way, which contributes to producing the idea of an overall performance that does not give all of its power to the text, as in the *Four Penny Opera*, and does not necessarily amount to an attempt at representation, as happens in *Le Bal* or in *Bernadetje*.

Here, we will limit ourselves to the subject of sounds and stage music, which have become increasingly important within the theatre since the invention of sound diffusion. The source can then be present and visible, which reinforces the impression of a fabrication of spectacle and excludes (unlike in traditional opera where singers sing their fiction and where the orchestra is hidden in the pit) all effects of illusion, but, increasingly, the source is invisible, since it is emitted off-stage, recorded and/or transmitted prior to the performance. The zero degree of sound intervention is, in this case, the use of sound effects, which illustrate or complement an action or an expression spoken by the actor, by giving to it a degree of probability or of truth (thunder, collisions, the noise of swords, etc.). We might note that added to these realist sound effects was a musical illustration most capable of creating an atmosphere suitable to the dramatic situation. This sort of sound or music is termed accompanying music, and might nowadays seem useless or redundant. Sounds and music that punctuate the play seem more interesting: musicians can directly be onstage, like in Ariane Mnouchkine's plays, which openly adopt an oriental model that has never seen the two arts of theatrical play and music as separated. Moreover, they give sound to the play's structure as well as to its key moments, while maintaining the effect of atmosphere and of positioning within dramatic time and space (historicisation, exoticism, culture shock, etc.). In this way, sounds structure the performance, particularly in fragmented plays, by creating auditory links. Similarly, the transmission or exaction of melodies, refrains and known airs aid the spectator's recognition of the fictional period or place. In addition to making the play dynamic, the use of music or sound, when it is repeated in a more or less identical way, can generate a leitmotif effect, which provides a sense of rhythmic, thematic or dramaturgical progression for the spectator, and guides her in her interpretation of the play. Moreover, using music and sound allows practitioners to create effects of rupture and of counterpoint (which is the way in which it is most often used in contemporary theatre). When, in Gilles Aillaud's

Le Masque de Robespierre [*The Mask of Robespierre*] (which he directed in 1996), Jean Jourdheuil interrupts the vicissitudes of the terror by the execution of a lengthy piano piece, he contrasts and creates a counterpoint between the political action and the musical interlude that implies the regulated, precise and sometimes passionate notation of a project – that of Mendelssohn. In this way, he commentates on the fictitious action, informs it and defines, through music, the attitudes and motivations of Robespierre, while creating a break vis-à-vis the spoken discourse of the play. As for counterpoint, it is easy to comprehend that its effect is based on burlesque play, where music ironically underscores a moment of the text or of the acting, as Brecht does with his songs using music by Kurt Weill.

In a different but equally experimental genre, American avant-garde theatre (that of Richard Foreman or Elizabeth LeConte's Wooster Group in particular) constructed plays with noises, gimmicks and pre-recorded sound effects, weaving them arbitrarily throughout the performance. Therefore, when Richard Foreman directed plays, he had with him a set of sounds with which he punctuated the acting onstage, based on his overall feelings or intentions. And when the Wooster Group played an adaptation of *Phèdre* (*To You, the Birdie!* 2002), the technicians recorded songs in real time, in order to underscore the scenic effects or the words pronounced or to make them appear unusual. The metallic sound of a step could come before or while the actor walked, in order to destabilise both the actor and the spectator. In Italy, Carmelo Bene has constantly played with sonorisation (or hypersonorisation) – that of collisions, belches, groaning from pleasure or from suffering. These sounds are live or pre-recorded; whereas Castellucci has, of late, brought in an entire orchestra only to choose not to have them play, while he himself played all sorts of discordant sounds (until the frustrated musicians left). Sounds thus becomes not only a raw material [*matériau*] but an aesthetic object [*matière*] for cutting, mounting and modelling, for working, for playing non-stop, for distorting, based on the techniques that have, in recent years, often been borrowed from musical practices such as *sampling*. Such a work can be extended also in certain cases through the use of standing microphones, but also HF microphones, and to the voice of the actor herself. Indeed, while the HF microphone can be used as a simple technical aid, its usage most often surpasses or exceeds this perfunctory employment, since it can provide for the actor other vocal registers and other possibilities of modulation, such as whispering and a more intimate kind of acting. Using the HF lends a slight effect of distance to the vocal presence of the actor, a sort of derealisation, whether this is for the whole of the performance or for a particular moment of it. It also allows the voice of the actor, through the use of technical sound effects, to gain the same importance, and this work can give rise to all sorts of modulations and deformations, plastic ones but also signifying ones, in which the voice of the actor can be fragmented, stretched, etc. The distortions that the voice of Laurent Poitrenaux underwent in *Le Colonel des Zouaves* hyperbolised the excesses of his discourse and of his acting, while manifesting, in parallel to the actor's use of his body, the mechanical alienation of his character (an overzealous domestic servant).

As we can see, stage music and even noises conceived for the stage and, more broadly, the craft of sound, are no longer to be considered as illustrations or mere accompaniment. They allow the practitioner to structure both time and spaces, by creating a dynamic tightly linking the auditory to the visible and that, through the creation of this rapport, changes both. The stage space, speech and movements of the actor thus give to sounds a particular deployment, while the experience of sound creates virtual worlds, mental landscapes and spaces of sensation that the practical space and the stage play of the actor cannot, by themselves, produce. Indeed, the craft of sound, when inscribed in a broad artistic intention and liberated from the traditional hierarchisation of a strictly dramatic representation, proves to be altogether particular, not only in that it produces specific emotions, but also in that it can affect and alter the primary categories of perception that are space and, even more, time. Through its usage, it contributes in a singular way to a different organicity of the stage, that which is part and parcel of a "musical" functioning in the broadest sense of the term: a matter of flows, of intensities and of many different kinds of affects potentially disjointed from the strict representation of actions, interpersonal conflicts and mimetic figuration. Creating issues of frequencies and modulations, sound is thus linked in a fundamental way to notions of time, rhythm and tempo, which we shall discuss in the next chapter.

Scenery, objects and stage props

There is no need to re-describe the technical elements that are at the disposal of the scenographer. We have already seen that the director was able to combine the use of ancient canvases with all sorts of inventions specific to the art of painting, lighting, sound and machines. By drawing on ancient instruments and techniques, as well as on new inventions and other arts, including painting, contemporary plastic arts (the principle of the installation), architecture (particularly ephemeral architecture that rests on the deployment in a given place of light and moveable installations), scenography and directing now have an even greater liberty of action. The fact that the theatre has opened out to other places has enabled the invention of apparatuses that break out of the stage frame or that stage the promenade of both actors and spectators. Moreover, the ability to transmit videos of fixed or moving images that were previously recorded and then shown throughout the performance, have added a whole other dimension and, above all, have allowed for other plays to surprise, inform and disturb the spectator to thus give them pleasure.

As we have already seen in traditional perspective, the scenery was tasked with the creation of an ideal, illusory and credible elsewhere, a dramatic space capable of containing a fiction so believable that the spectator could simultaneously project themselves into it while admiring the way it was technically produced. The technical apparatus thus served to foster an illusion on the one hand, and represent an authentic, mimetic world on the other. At the same time, it appeared ostensibly to be a virtual tour de force. But we have also seen that this illusionistic principle, already altered by the awareness of the fact that it existed only because it was produced by very capable craftsmen, could just as easily be parodied, distorted, denounced ("metatheatricalised"). It is in this area, particularly with certain explorations of Kantor (*happenings*) or those of Bob Wilson and his deployment of choreographic models, that *performance* theatre has managed to break absolutely with mimesis. However, it is difficult to impose a completely abstract approach in the space of Western theatre, in the sense of abstract painting or music, since the theatrical event is carried out by living and speaking bodies, with tangible scenery and concrete objects that are always witnessed by the spectator as the referential elements inscribed within a principle of representation. The abstract component of certain staging endeavours could thus include the exploration of more sensual categories of perception within the theatrical act: the sensual experience of time, space, the presence of the actor, which proves to be, paradoxically, both the most necessarily figural element of the representation and one that will always partially escape any single framework of reception. It can also include the creation of various sensations (visual, auditory, etc.), which are not solely reducible to an illustrative or expressive function with respect to a possible story. This abstract dimension of staging can affect certain components of the representation: namely, the scenery and, more fundamentally, the scenic image;[10] the world of sound and music; the choreographic formalisation of movements. Last but not least, it will also try to disarm what could appear to be a narrative thread (identifiable characters, signs of an action), substituting it with arrangements that can be reduced to the pure play of forms, energies, rhythms and sensations. But one must note that it is difficult to talk about actions that are *purely* abstract, not only because the habits of reception cause the spectator to fall back on certain reflexes, if only at times, but especially because all attempts at abstraction take on the appearance, primarily, of a *deconstruction* of the mimetic principle. This is why a *mise en scène* has most often been, and remains mainly, a critical approach to the enterprise of mimesis. In other words, a lively, concrete reflection, active and ephemeral in its relation between the figurable and the depicted, which leads to a deeper theoretical and critical examination of both.

Therefore, the scenic space has mainly been able to depict the image of something, which transcends the stage: an extra-scenic space. However, this space beyond the stage is only ever a partial or composite depiction – in that sense, it establishes a relationship and not an equation – of one or several referential worlds. The bare stage, that depicts or represents the theatre while, at the same time, *being* it, must also be considered as a referential or self-referential world. Antoine Vitez, who is adept at spatialising concepts and using scenery to explore the foundations of theatre while firmly basing his *mise en scène* on a text, demonstrated all of this in his production of *Faust* in 1981 at the Théâtre national de Chaillot. What is theatre? The play of an actor (who has emerged from a suitcase at the beginning of the spectacle) on a bare platform capable of being filled with objects and with machines. What is *Faust*? The journey of a man and of a soul moving through the world and within the moving parts of a machine that is meant to be the embodiment of hell. As such, Vitez divides up the platform into two spaces: the dramatic and naturalist space of the world (the earth, the land, the plantations, etc.) where the comrades are; and the bare space of acting (the principal domain of Faust). The *mise en scène* is thus doubly referenced by the historical and social space beyond the theatre, by its pictorial and symbolic depiction of hell, which can function like a fable and like a theatrical performance wholly conscious of its own art. The machines and the smoke are not only hell but also the traditional iconography of hell in the theatre.

And when the *mise en scène* seems to denounce any sort of referential relation, it never fails to mention a reference to the stage itself and therefore to the theatre. Thus, when Claude Régy staged *Variations sur la mort de Jon Fosse* [*Variations on the Death of Jon Fosse*] in 2003 at the Théâtre National de la Colline, with Daniel Jeanneteau as the scenographer, he completely bared the platform, opened the space and arranged for the intensity of the light to be minimal, slowed down the gait of the actors, their movements and their diction and inserted many silences. His attempt at rarefication conjured up a menacing and problematic void. Undoubtedly, he refused the classic rules of representation, forbade all discourse on uttered words and rejected the expression of a strictly referential world on the stage. However, he represented both what can be seen of death and what can be said and seen of the theatre that represents it. Death *in* the theatre and death *of* the theatre are brought to the very forefront of the spectator's mind, etched in the way they watch the performance, and made manifest onstage. The very spectacle of disappearance becomes an ultimate reference point, not simply in the theatre, but as part of the unrepresentability of death itself.

In these exercises, both scenery and objects play a central role, since they smooth the often problematic movement between the world of the theatre event, the places and world of the play, the theatrical spaces and their union with the real "world" beyond the theatre, from which the spectator comes and into which they will return after an evening at the theatre. So much so that the elements of place (the precinct) will always become signs for theatregoers used to theatrical conventions, whatever one does with the scenery. Therefore, the real objects can be central (as in Ionesco's *Les Chaises* [*The Chairs*]) and constitute a scenery, so that the whole performance draws on their existence in order to deploy meanings that are foregrounded. In the eponymous play by Chekhov, *The Seagull*, the bird is an object named by the text that we perceive concretely, but this in no way prevents us from seeing in it something other than a simple seagull, as is the case for Ionesco's chairs. And to take another example of what can be done to articulate objects, scenery and scenography within an ironic and critically distanced exploration of different periods, both in the aesthetic of the production and in the referential system of the fiction, one can cite *Ruy Blas*, directed by Brigitte Jaques-Wajeman at the Comédie-Française in 2002. The *mise en scène* takes the general scenographic system proposed by Victor Hugo into account, and depicts a room in a palace with several entrances, while nonetheless moving away from the dense, pictorial and "realist" scenography that generally goes with the representation of a Spanish palace of the seventeenth century (as one would imagine it in the nineteenth century). It does so to imagine wall hangings, traps and all sorts of openings for the platform that spatialise this Romantic scenery in an almost ironic way. As such, the platform, although in line with Romantic staging, is in fact encumbered with referential objects that depict Ruy Blas' Spain as an ironic portrayal of romanticism: making each of the openings onstage clearly visible throughout the play. Here it is not a matter of reconstituting the Romantic aesthetic, but rather commenting on it through a contemporary *mise en scène*.

Depicting one or several referential times and periods, the scenery and objects thereby represent a social positioning, a state, a profession, a function, a character, etc. Therefore, the simplest and most traditional way of making objects function onstage is to use them as simple accessories by relying on what the text implies (either via the internal stage directions or external ones). The real objects can simply reiterate the text and function in relation to other objects and in relation to the *mise en scène*, each being tasked with depicting the same general signification (the scenery, the objects, the props, *signify* that one is in a bourgeois mansion, in a royal court, etc.). In that sense, they are referential insofar as they relate to an external reality that the theatre represents and they are manipulated in such a way as to complement the action based on what the text indicates: if the character of the text pulls out a knife, the actor will do the same.

However, as we have seen, the professionals involved in staging, as well as the authors of texts, have long been aware that objects, while they have a perfunctory role with respect to the action and to the referential framework, could simultaneously give place to a metaphorical interpretation. Professionals have therefore developed the habit of envisaging such objects as distinct one from the other, or in signifying groups. For example, such an object will be used to depict, by itself or with others, a part of the referential world that it represents (this is the nature of synecdoche – the part for the whole – and, by extension, one speaks of metonymy, which is the inverse – the whole for the part). In this sense, a piece of seventeenth-century furniture can be used to depict all of the seventeenth century, such as the audience might imagine it. But it can also depict the image of a feeling or of a supposed feeling or attitude of a character: a streak of blood on a dark suit might indicate the bloody or truculent aspect of a hero (as in *Le Cid* directed by Declan Donellan in 1999 at the Théâtre des Bouffes du Nord); a particular bouquet of flowers can be a clue to the feelings of Ruy Blas, etc. One can then say that this inanimate element, on the one hand, is manipulated by the body of the actor and acts on them and, on the other hand, that it functions or intervenes in the dramatic space as a practical or signifying element in multiple senses.

As a point of reference for the spectator in the comprehension of the performance, the sword in *Phèdre* for example, so long as it is emphasised by the director, goes from hand to hand (Theseus, Phaedra, Hippolytus, but also Œnone, depending on the production) and, by moving, will displace meanings in a sort of metonymic, metaphorical and symbolic chain. It becomes an ancient weapon and a weapon of the seventeenth century, a cross, a phallus, a transitional object, a prop for a monologue, a way of directing attention to the centre of the stage. One could then say as much, and with more meaning, of that of Rodrigue in *Le Cid*: the father's metonymic sword of power, the sword that practically and symbolically falls to the ground during the duel, the sword bequeathed to the son for vengeance, the sword carried during the provocation scene, the bloody sword entering into the house of Chimène after the murder of Don Gomès, the sword ostensibly shown during the epic monologue narrating the feud between the Moors, the deceptive sword endowed with multiple meanings that Don Sanche brings back and the sword for which Rodrigue is tried and that is reattributed to him after the verdict. Accordingly we can see that from early on, authors, actors and all the practitioners of theatre have learned to play with the polysemy of objects and their multiple modes of functioning.

Another illustrative example is Pirandello's use of objects within the scenery that he uses for *Liolà*. First of all, Pirandello creates a referential universe: the dramatic space becomes the farm of the Croce Azzara mother in the region of Agrigente with its large house, hangar, barn, stable, olive press, benches, windows, doors, etc. There he places objects around which characters are grouped: almonds are being broken by women, for example. These almonds serve, therefore, to reinforce the pictorial, to mark time (the beginning of autumn) and the scenery of the place. But, eventually, these almonds that the women break with two stones on their lap, acquire a signifying status that goes beyond the pure spatial and geographical referentiality to say something about the function of these women: they open significations and reveal the heart of things (the body of objects), while singing. This is, in the true sense, an opening for the dramaturgical system and, at the same time, the representation of the major theme that the plot will seek to develop. This opening, in all senses of the term, will then be echoed at the beginning of the second act, where one sees Aunt Gesa peeling potatoes and asking three young boys to go and search for onions (which she will then have to peel), before eventually bidding other women to help her in the task. In other words, these women peel, skin, work and act, unveiling what is hidden behind the surface, because they know the internal nature of things. And logically, at the beginning of the third act, a bit later in the play's diegetic framework (during the season of grape harvest), Pirandello indicates that the young Tuzza, seated on the bench in Act 1, is pregnant. From raisins to almonds, from opening of exterior surfaces to gathering of grapes, it appears that feminine labour is central for all harvest. From that point onwards, the play begs the question of the role of men (of Liolà), of their aptitude to be joined with nature and their symbolic responsibility in the process of harvesting, of birth and in the feminine cycle that characterises them. We can see in this example that the object, moving from an initial pictorial and referential indication, has become the centre of the symbolic and semiotic system of the entire play.

Finally, we can adduce a third example. When in *Place des Héros* [*Heroes' Square*], Thomas Bernhard images the scene in which Madame Zittel irons the shirts of the dead professor, he weaves together the long soliloquy of the governess with her handling of objects. While expressing deep resentment of the need to comply with the orders of the professor, she folds his clothes; however, while she folds, she decides to embrace her lot and the pressing and folding of clothes becomes the outward image of her pliancy, as she puts away forever in a box the object that contains the dead man. Madame Zittel thus becomes the one who acts and buries because she knows how to observe orders scrupulously, to hate them and to take pleasure in them. In other words, she knows how to take power over the master who constrained her and of whom she frees herself by being compliant. In this respect, and thanks to the clothes and the iron, the character of Madame Zittel is extracted from realism to depict the attitude of the text and one of the outlooks that Bernhard describes with respect to the world: hating yet loving this hatred by reiterating and renewing the same actions and indignations, by forcing oneself to do it scrupulously, making it into an object of art and thus producing a craft of hatred.

In the three preceding examples, we have dealt only with what the text indicates with respect to objects. This is based on a notion that the *mise en scène* must conform to what the author stipulates: the sword, the almonds, the clothes and the iron are all indicated by the text and the author in the staging and dramatic space, so that those who stage the play are obliged to use them and are afforded only a little creative licence for how to integrate them into their own interpretive and representational apparatus. In reality, however, practitioners have full liberty – provided that no moral authorial right is invoked to control them, as with Beckett and his inheritors – not to respect the indications of the text or of disrupting, partly or entirely, the use of the objects that the author proposes. They thus have all power to replace an object inscribed into the text by another, an element of scenery with another, even if this sometimes involves doing away with the object or rendering the scenery more abstract. It is a fact that modern theatre plays quite patently with objects, moving away from a utilitarian approach, to explore the intersections of the objects' dual status as a real element in the scenic space of the stage and a symbolic one in the dramatic space. Consequently, while the theatre may be the perfect tool for unsettling and reconfiguring the visible aspects of reality, it also displays the fact that it is a perpetual game, a playful transformation of the most concrete world and a concrete transformation of the most playful world.

One can then oppose or diversify the meanings of theatrical objects through metonymic or metaphorical devices or through anachronisms that allow you to show that plot, for example, is located in antiquity, but that it is composed in the seventeenth century, and also that it has an impact for the spectators of the twenty-first century. That is a first step: to have concrete elements representing three periods (or more) coexist at the same time is both a risk and an advantage, when this does not affect coherence. We have already seen how Matthias Langhoff's *Gloucester Time: Matériau Shakespeare* (1997) brought together on a crowded platform medieval objects, Elizabethan ones, the Underwood typewriter of a modern war correspondent (Hemingway?), a barber's or dentist's chair-cum-throne, all placed into a bric-a-brac in which each object, each piece of clothing and each point of the scenery served the function of indicating that Shakespearian political cruelty and violence was a thing that has existed in all periods of time and history, and that the audience would do well to be on watch against it. The stage performance became, metaphorically, all the wars of and for power and shed light on the text in this sense, whether Richard was in amour, his henchmen in fatigues or whether the queens were dressed in black English velvet or in dressing gowns.

Following the same principle, one can take real objects to alter their ordinary function and give them another signification (a kitchen chair can be a throne but can also indicate that this throne is a lamentable one) or an aesthetic functioning (a cord can trace the boundaries of an imaginary space, a stack of suitcases can become a stage, etc.). When, for example, Peter Zadek staged *Hamlet*, he placed an iron container in the middle of the stage, out of which the staging material, the objects and therefore, in a sense, the theatre itself, emerged. And while he placed this acting machine at the centre of the stage, he depicted the fact that the reality of this worksite ate up the Shakespearian universe and, indeed, the myth of Hamlet in the theatre. It may also be added that German staging, particularly that of Frank Castorf, makes it a point of duty to contradict the orthodoxy of the bare stage floor and of the clean, unencumbered acting space, by filling the staging space with objects of all sorts. The aesthetics deployed by Castorf in *Meine Schneekönigin* [*My Snow Queen*] (Volksbühne, Berlin 2004) involved systematically leaving objects "scattered" all over the stage so as to reuse them afterwards. A basin filled with water would be used in an initial scene to represent a sort of magical baptism, and in a second scene occurring much later, to represent a body of water in which a prince drowns. In the meantime, between these two usages, as well as after the drowning, the object simply remains there, like a residue of the action, an obstacle in the pathway of the actors. Thus, as time passes onstage, the actors are increasingly forced to step over all sorts of obstacles and thus to move away from the traditional system of acting.

In this framework, the world of the platform is both oneiric (like Andersen's fables), quotidian (a contemporary apartment), concrete (the heap of objects) and fragmented (several places of acting, multivalent objects serving multiple purposes, polysemic). Consequently, the actors must carry out their stage play within a discontinuity that is practically constitutive of the *mise en scène* itself. This discontinuity forms part of a coherent interpretive lens of viewing/showing, that of the encumbrance of memory, images, references and the motley heap of dreams and fables that mirrors the discontinuity of the daily world in which the spectator participates. By not clearing the platform, Castorf calls out to the spectator by forcing them to piece together the pieces of a broken mirror, the myriad parts of text, moments of play, the accumulation of objects, the multiplicity of significations. Under the appearance of a dream sequence and of a narration evidently lacking in continuity, the actors and spectators produce in the present moment of the performance a drama of vision where the virtual and the materialisations of reality overlap. Additionally, the *mise en scène* can also conceive of non-real objects: those that have no utility beyond the stage; objects that represent specific shapes rather than having a figurative role;[11] and/or stylised objects; out-of-scale objects of enormous or minuscule proportions (such as the hand that constitutes the entire scenery of *Ubu roi* staged by Bernard Sobel at Gennevilliers in 1993, was both extremely large and "non-real", since it was inanimate and made out of a box). One can therefore, depending on the scenario, inscribe the object within a dramaturgy of scenic surplus or of sparseness, of an empty playing space, to consider it instrumental and utilitarian, but also to play with it, by making it, with other objects, a decorative or aesthetic environment. It is then inscribed within a mode of referential figuration by deploying its meanings within the spectacle and would then be metaphorical or symbolic, or even reversing the usage prescribed by the text, while making it an object of concrete manipulation by the actor.

Our previous discussion of Peter Brook's use of the stage floor and of the carpets that covered it is particularly pertinent here. We might also add that the objects that he uses have the same function. The bamboo poles, for example, are real bamboo poles and make the noise of bamboo, but they can also be spears, prison bars, trees or any other figural representation, without ceasing to be concrete exotic elements and ones necessary for supporting the actors' stage play and, as they remain the supporting elements of the *mise en scène*, are indicators of verticality, horizontality or obliqueness. Similarly, we might recall the staging of *Medea* by Deborah Warner in 2002, where the director placed the protagonist in the middle of a worksite made of slats of wood, iron bars, nails and tools. The stage was therefore both a construction and a trap for characters and actors. As a character, ripped to shreds by the plot, she rebuilds herself, takes hold of objects and assembles them. Medea utilises disjointed materials to construct an apparatus of vengeance: she pins her second son between the two doors that she has built, turns a wooden plank into a walkway and climbs the scaffold that she has constructed to contemplate the bloody result of her act. Climbing to the summit of the staging space, Medea disappears into the sky. Consequently, instead of making Medea an abused woman who reacts with violence, through the play of objects, Deborah Warner presents a considered, constructed, crafted operation of a heroine who, once her work is accomplished, can fly off into the batten.

In that way, the object is not simply an accessory (a second element of the *mise en scène* that can be manipulated by the actor, a tool) but subtends the interpretation, lending it concrete signification while infusing it with a plethora of other meanings. Since it is a part of the staging apparatus and not necessarily of its verbalisation, it has the privilege of being there without necessarily being indicated by the stage directions. Alternatively, the director can avoid adhering to what the stage directions indicate or suggest. Like the scenery, the object can reveal a psychic, political, social landscape, but can also condense meanings and unveil possible interpretations while allowing the actor to use it as an acting machine. Therefore, the object may be neither purely utilitarian nor simply referential nor symbolic. In this case, it functions like a thing that is part and parcel of the place and of the space, which allows the actor and the other professionals of staging to produce relationships between the actors and between characters.

Costumes

What we have said about objects or props can also be said in relation to costumes or, perhaps to a lesser extent, even make-up. While these concrete elements provide signs to be interpreted, they must not be over-interpreted as they are also simply tools for acting. Likewise, costume and make-up have a story that depends both on conventions and techniques.

The specificity of theatre costume resides primarily in the concrete reality of the object, which is then subjected to the material necessities of the representation. However, it is also an object that "plays" and whose status is transformed: it is both clothing, which is socially encoded (and therefore referential) and dramatic costume (and therefore integrated into the necessities of plot). Clothing, a social object investigated by sociology, is thus represented in the theatre by the "cloak of performance". Both in its pure materiality and in its integral role within a semiotic system, it is not alone and forms part of the coherence of the *mise en scène* without taking it over. By itself, it determines a particular sort of acting that conditions the *mise en scène* and produces a context-specific interpretation on the part of the spectator.

It is interesting to consider what Giorgio Strehler does when he envisages his actors' entrance onstage on the platform of the Piccolo Teatro (1994) and the Théâtre de l'Odéon (1995) to play Marivaux's *L'Ile des esclaves* [*The Island of Slaves*]. What Strehler does through his living tableau is something both simple and central to immediately establishing the problematics of theatre and of acting. The entrance onstage simultaneously represents the beginning of a plot and the beginning of a performance for any actor: the fact of getting dressed differently or of giving a staged specificity to one's appearance, whatever the clothing that is used. And here, all of this must coincide with the beginning of a dramatic (comic) convulsion arising from a storm. As such, before the characters who have escaped shipwreck appear in the dramatic space of the "slave island", the actors stand behind a tulle curtain to abandon their "normal" city clothes and don their stage costume. Some will play masters, the others slaves and they are distinguished through their costumes. Nothing else, but that already is an indication that the apparatus of play built on the plot will examine the issue of appearance and of dress in performance and the belief that one is supposed to have with respect to them. Therefore, the actor-characters carry out a performance, with music, lighting, play-acting, etc., while they engage in a reflection on dress, human behaviour and inter-human relations. From then on, the masters and slaves, in accordance with the orders of the fictitious, insular and utopian space in which they are found, exchange their theatre costumes in Scene 5 in such a way that this play-acting and thought process is carried out throughout the whole play. The crisis follows its natural course. Harlequin violently paints his mask on to the face of his master and Cléanthis tears off Euphrosine's dress, so that, despite resistance from the masters, the valets invert appearances and signs.

One notable fact is that the very first scene imagined by Strehler – the transition from clothing to costume, from the actor-citizen to the actor-character – has indicated to the spectator that what is happening is a theatre experimentation *and* an entertainment spectacle, a comedy *and* a utopia, a social and political problematisation and a representation of the nature of theatre and of representation itself. And once this reflection-representation has been fully accomplished, thanks to the interplay of costumes, acting and Marivaux's text, Strehler can go one step further than the author by proposing something unique or different. In the final scene, instead of changing costume again, the masters and slaves return to their original costumes, which signify their "true" status: clothes that do not distinguish them from one another. Thus, because at the end of the play both masters and slaves are dressed in the same way, the audience can readily believe that the utopia has allowed for a more human, a more just and non-hierarchical society to be born. And, simultaneously, we remember that these clothes are those of the very first framing scene, that in which one saw the actors undress behind a tulle curtain to play a role; thus, the character-actors change back to character-citizen, equal in principle, without a master/slave hierarchy.

Costumes thus become an actor's main tool, their indispensable instrument of work, since acting always begins with the need for self-transformation. The first page of Scarron's *Roman comique* [*Comic Novel*], which describes the arrival of a troop of actors in the town of Le Mans, all presents a scene in which despite the urging of an audience that wants to see them play, the actors declare that they are unable to go onstage, since they have not got the keys to the chests that contain their costumes. They then only need to be given a few rags belonging to spectators for them to agree to perform. The object has not materially changed – the old dress that is offered is still an old dress – but it now functions in a symbolic manner within a dramatic space. All that was necessary was to introduce a break, an otherness, for the object to attain the desired degree of difference, gain the status of acting costume and become the material upon which this transformation relies.

Consequently, in traditional theatre, when the actor puts on their costume, there is supposed to be something that blends with their own appearance. In this respect, they may be confined to play a character onstage that is similar to the life-like one that exists in the city itself: Harlequin can only be Harlequin; Jodelet Jodelet; and Tabarin Tabarin. One even forgets their proper name. The colour, form, mask and accessories of the costume form part of their very person, they refer emblematically to their origin and behaviour, and are intimately tied to the movement of the character, to his accent (or to the dialect in the case of the *commedia dell'arte*, and to his state and social condition). The Dottore is an old sage from Bologna that wears dark clothes with a white ruff. Pantalone is an old Venetian with a goatee, his garment is red (the jacket) and black (the trousers), in the colours of Venice. The Capitano and Matamore are Spanish and Neapolitan and wear military clothing that is usually exaggerated. The young lovers are Tuscan. Pulcinella, the Neapolitan valet, is dressed in white and wears a conical hat. Finally, the other valet-*zanni* are from Bergamo, whether they are crafty (Scapino with his cape) or oafish (Harlequin with his bat costume). The captain Matamore and the young people do not wear masks in principle, and the others all have a distinctive mask capable of depicting the essential signs of their character: Harlequin can thus be a monkey with a wart on his forehead that marks the sign of the devil. Given this duly codified fixed type (*tipo fisso* in Italian), few things can change since the spectator comes to see its reiteration in a new plot that is only an opportunity for the staged manifestation of *this* type. Consequently, after a long and constant reiteration of these generic markers and after its gradual erosion, the costumes, body language and general characteristics of these types change and adapt to other traditions and other forms of comedy so that Harlequin can eventually take on a personality of his own. What these types do keep for a long time, nonetheless, is their specific costume, that is sometimes modified but remains recognisable.

We also know that up until the nineteenth century, the actor was responsible for their theatrical costume. It was their job to procure it through means that would vary based on their wealth and fame: perhaps they would buy it at a second-hand clothes shop, have it made by a tailor or perhaps even receive it as a gift. Tailors quickly began to specialise in making theatre costumes, taking into account the technical and material conditions of the representation (e.g. the need to be seen in poorly lit auditoriums and the need for a demarcation between the actors and spectators seated onstage). Brightly coloured fabric that could easily be complemented by light was thus needed (e.g. the colour of "fire" or flamboyant purple, is often noted in inventories). Actors also preferred fabric that did not require much care: candle lighting produced a lot of smoke and would blacken costumes; moreover, the products used for cleaning were harsh. Therefore, theatre costumes were rich and costly and had to meet luxury criteria, which is not at all surprising if one examines the society and the aesthetics of appearance in which they were anchored. The more luxurious the costumes, the more they testified of the investment of the actor who has managed to find the most beautiful attire to play tragedy or domestic comedy (farce, as we have seen, and the *commedia dell'arte* operate differently, since they function primarily based on stock characters dressed in a codified costume). The costume is therefore a specific object, which forms part of a specific economy of production, purchasing, sales or exchange and an object of prestige that represents the value of the actor, as much as it inscribes itself (sometimes) into the plot.

First, during the seventeenth and eighteenth centuries, it distinguished the actor from the person, which was necessary when the audience was onstage. Additionally, it underscores the individuality of a particular actor, which thereby distinguished him from the social rank of the character who he incarnated in the play. But little by little, it came to define the character, and this function became essential and inscribed itself within the dramatic space. The code of verisimilitude supplanted the first two functions. Given the efforts of great actors of tragedy (Mademoiselle Clairon and Lekain in the eighteenth century), and authors (including Voltaire, who strived for the verisimilitude of bodily movement, and Beaumarchais, who was keen on the appearance of his characters, to the point where he himself indicated the costume that each should have), habits were transformed and the initial conventions were abandoned (for tragedy, a sort of compromise between the nobility of the contemporary costume and a few elements that depicted antiquity) in favour of a more markedly historicised representation, as actors began to imagine and stage it (in particular with Talma). If the actor continued to be an object of spectacle, the appearance of his character needed to be integrated increasingly into the idea that he meant to have of the "referents" of his role.

And Molière was perhaps one of the very first to play with all the functions of costume by representing the porosity between costume and place, between "lived experience" and the presumably fictitious or dramatic space. Therefore, during the first staging of *Tartuffe ou l'Imposteur* in 1664, "the imposter appeared, if not in a Jesuit robe, then at least in a cassock and a broad-brimmed hat",[12] according to Father La Chaise, a Jesuit and the king's military chaplain. He levied his first criticism towards the theatrical appearance of the character, and towards the fact that Molière used ecclesiastical clothing to represent a hypocrite. And when Molière sought authorisation to stage the play again (after it was censured), he had to make clear that he had modified Tartuffe's name and clothing. He remarked that "it was in vain that I depicted the character as a worldly man, even if I gave him a little hat, long hair, a large collar, a sword, and lace on all his clothing".[13] But, ultimately, as he later added, "none of it served any purpose" since no one ever forgot that it was the first Tartuffe. As a result, the new Panulphe became an even greater hypocrite: both a character who hides his true appearance under a new and less dangerous one and who, simultaneously, proves to be dressed in a way that is ostensibly contrary to the religious zealots of the time, who did wear large hats, whose hair was long and who had bands on their clothing. Therefore, Panulphe became an even greater force with which Molière had to reckon.

In another way, the *Le Bourgeois gentilhomme* [*The Bourgeois Gentleman*] (1670) marks a break with costume as a tool of distortion [*travestissement*] and turns costume into a revealer, an object of porosity and one that represents the dynamics of appearances. The entire play is indeed structured by a series of changes in Monsieur Jourdain's dress. He comes onstage dressed in an *indienne*; in other words, in a costly dressing gown that immediately identifies Monsieur Jourdain as one aware of the fashion of the wealthy, desirous of conforming to it and financially able to do so. He then dresses in gentlemen's clothing – which is given to him during a veritable investiture ceremony during which clothing plays the main role – and finally, in that of Mamamouchi. He thus takes on three successive appearances whose meanings are complex. Farce is transformed, first of all, into a veritable initiation rite during which Monsieur Jourdain becomes a king-buffoon, which announces the final masquerade that turns into a joyous madness. By changing clothes, he also wishes to unambiguously become the character whose appearances he wishes to take on during the performance itself. Moreover, the costume that Molière creates for him shows up the whole thing. Indeed, Anne Verdier's research[14] shows that Molière's inventory of costumes, the famous *indienne* was merely a scarf, and not a dress, which reinforces the blindness of the bourgeois and generates laughter. Similarly, the gentleman's clothing, such as that of Mamamouchi, has nothing really luxurious about it, but is, in every way, like that of a street actor (this might be the meaning of *Mamamouchi*), i.e. an unimpressive minstrel. And all these items of clothing also represent the fact that Jourdain ostentatiously and ridiculously bears all the hallmarks of cross-dressing without mastering them. They merely make him a "disguised" person, and a madman capable of transforming reality for himself. This bourgeois man is therefore naively deluded into thinking that he has become what he thinks he is, whereas he has remained, in the eyes of everybody else, what he actually is. The status of clothing has thus transformed from a social convention primed to reveal an identity to become a sign of exclusion, blindness, madness and gullibility. At the end of the play, he is no longer bourgeois, husband or father, but a degraded actor character who believes that he embodies his role.

Contemporary productions of this text, which sometimes lack the knowledge of these details, do not play or reveal all these meanings. Rather, they tend to limit themselves to the fact that the bourgeois man dresses *truly* like a gentleman, or like an Ottoman, and simply require of the actor a kind of movement and body language that ridicules the character. Sometimes they exaggerate the costumes to give a more material feel or notion of the ridiculous, or turn Jourdain into a clown, which ostensibly distinguishes him from other characters. At other times they attempt a reconstitution – with candles – and point the spectator to a notion of what a seventeenth-century musical performance might be, which resolves nothing and substitutes admiration for an actual understanding of Molière's intentions. But they always have to face or engage with the issue of costumes and their meanings, even if they minimise their polysemy or dynamism, since costume is at the centre of this ballet-theatre. Indeed, in Jérôme Savary's staging of the play (1999), it is Jourdain's obsession that condemns him to "fall into the underworld", engulfed by flames, like Dom Juan. We thus see that costume is closely tied to all the functions of the other elements used onstage. It takes on various forms: stock characters, referential representation, contrapuntal systems, the play of polysemy and openness, devices for playing or even the embodiment of figurative or non-realistic tableaux.

Moreover, in the twentieth century, Picasso, Marie Laurencin, Vuillard, Sonia Delaunay, José-Maria Sert and the decorators of the Russian ballet (Bakst, Larionov, Benois) turn costume into a scenery tableau in its own right, and even into scenery on the actual body of the actor. It is important to emphasise that costume, insofar as it envelops the body of the actor, provides a formal support to acting: by being the object of lighting, it focalises changes in luminous intensity and provides a medium for their significations. Moreover, by virtue of its texture, weight, heaviness, volume and forms, it constrains the body and therefore its mode of acting; it structures movement and determines its degree of articulation, suppleness and fluidity. In that respect, it inscribes itself into the theatrical precinct, into space, into the performative and dramatic action, by determining postures in harmony with them, or in opposition or counterpoint to them. A change of costume during a *mise en scène* will necessarily indicate a rupture or sudden change in the storyline, or in the regime or mode of representation. But whatever the theatrical dress is, aside from the fact that it "comments" on an entire scene or *mise en scène*, through harmony, distance or counterpoint, it also indicates links between different elements of costume, between the "role" and the actor, between the entire play and another in the repertoire.

As such, costume is a fundamental element of dramatic movement, since it is part and parcel of space, action and time. It is a visible link and is immediately seen as being simultaneous a part of the scenery and of the body. It ensures the transitions between the actor and the practitioner, insofar as it is worn by the former and conceived by the latter. It establishes a link between place (as an object) and space (as a sign thereof); between the private self of the actor (their real body) and the self they play (either their character or their performance); and also between the referential world (the exterior and/or historical) and the world (the place and space of the performance). In doing so, costumes are at the centre of play. They are at the risk of disturbing and unsettling precisely because they seem to embody the fictional identity of a character, who is over-theatricalised through the ostentation of appearance, the convulsive and ritual facticity of which can lead to an intense interrogation into the nature of the subject to whom it is supposed to refer. This is frequently the case in Genet's theatre, for example in the scenes where prostitutes at the height of their art (Warda in *The Screens*, Irma in *The Balcony*, or the pope in *Elle*), magnify their *appearance* through dress and make-up. Costumes also unsettle and disturb when they appear alone without bodies to inhabit them (in the work of Genet, for example, Leila's face is "always covered with a sort of dark balaclava with three holes in it", speaking to and playing with the symbolism of the empty standing trousers of Said, her absent husband).

This is what Peter Brook represented in 1999 when he transcribed for the stage a South African short story by Can Themba called *The Costume*. It was based on a situation inspired by Feydeau (the lover flees from Philemon, the husband, leaving his clothes). The crisis, and then the drama, give rise to a dramaturgy of vengeance. Mathilda, the wife, is punished by means of the lover's costume – an article of clothing that Philemon forces her to consider as a subject and no longer as a concrete object. The lover is no longer there but his costume stays and permanently signifies the inexpiable wrong. Then Philemon orders Mathilda to take care of the costume, to do *as if*, as at the theatre, to make permanently present the absent body of the lover under the guise of his clothing that he has abandoned. He orders her to keep and take care of the object-subject, which is imprisoned in a sordid room that she cannot leave. She becomes a recluse in the empty space – the theory of Brookian space imposes just such an obligation – which the storyteller has defined, her sole occupation being to give life to an object. The convention of theatre, because it is taken seriously, is no longer only a convention, and becomes a "fantasmatic reality" that takes Mathilda into its web. However, the woman, a good actor, knows how to play with the signs and foil the husband's order: she dances with the costume, places it delicately down on the chair, sits as if on the legs of a lover, puts her hand through one of sleeves and caresses her own breasts, all the while under the watchful eye of the husband, who does not dare to say anything. The conventions of theatre operate naturally through the themes and devices of the story: punishment, contrition, the deformation of both, the husband's acceptance, the effect of the fourth wall and of projection. And one begins to hope that the *as if* that is "realised", undermined and then abandoned, finally gives way to a pardon, a happy distance, to living together again, a double play and, finally, to another world of performance. On the corded floor mats at the Bouffes du Nord, the psychological drama or the dramatic theatre then give place to a musical show. Thanks to a celebration imagined by the husband, narrated by the storyteller and depicted in the dramatic space, the characters take leave of their fictional roles and return to being actors who sing together, for themselves and for the spectators, so much that one forgets the theatrical framework, the dramatic world, the vengeance, the sentence and all that the costume stood for. The vaudeville turned drama of vengeance; the suffering of being attached to a quasi-subject; the pathos and the emotion fed to the spectator; the *as if* taken literally: all the traps of illusion theatre are no longer in effect, but since it is the object of the dramaturgical problem and the driving force of the plot, the costume – real object, virtual character and objective fantasy – "resumes its rights" to make its presence felt. Philemon obliterates the spectacle and, to savour his vengeance, forces his wife to dance with it before the other actors, who turn into guests again. After playing on all the aspects of the object-costume and all its functions, after taking the *as if* to its limits and to the ultimate consequences of illusion, Brook can finish the story. Mathilda, lying on the bed beside the article of clothing, is dead, and the spectator is not sure what has killed her, besides the constant transformation of the costume of her lover.

Masks and make-up

While costume is a sort of scenery pasted on to the body of the actor, replete with all of the consequences that we have outlined above, there is another kind of scenery and costume that sits even closer to the body of the actor: make-up. This is placed directly on to an actor's skin, clothing both soul and body, to reveal signs that simultaneously express something about the character and/or the body, be they those of the actor or their character. Indeed, while make-up is mainly placed on the face, it can equally mark and mask visible parts of the actor's body.

Make-up is not to be confused with wearing a mask. Rather than sticking to the skin, masks inscribe an otherness on to the body of the actor. The mask is an artificially created plastic form, which replaces the trivial plastic traits of the face and their movement through a numinous, non-naturalistic quality. In doing so, like make-up and costume, it differentiates types, hides, reveals, represents, accentuates and symbolises. But, because it is systematically engaged in an enterprise of de-realisation, and because it is radically other, the mask exceeds both the mimetic and the symbolic to become a coded, material and plastic image that can convey metaphysical and transcendental other spaces of the human. It is in that respect that it offers to the theatre, of which it is the material objectification, a very open field of practices by depriving the actor of what is dearest and most comfortable in her stage play, i.e. the traits of her face.

Make-up comes initially from a necessity: from the moment when the actor is far away, blurred and darkened, it is legitimate to want to illuminate their essential features and their expression in every way possible. The lighting can then be focused on the body and face, but also on the brilliance of costumes and on the effectiveness of make-up. In close connection, therefore, with the art of lighting, the techniques capable of illuminating the face and the body are often used to stress what is true to life, grotesque, mimetic, spectacular. Expressive traits of the eyes, the gaze, the mouth and chin, the nose, forehead, etc. are emphasised. In order to highlight the bottom jaw and the mouth of Harlequin means foregrounding the bulimic characteristics of the valet, the origin of his voice, his rather satanic grimace and his laughter. To whiten Faust's forehead and thereby enlarge it, will orientate the spectator's gaze towards the soul and the site of mental contemplation. To redden the cheeks and accentuate the contours of the nose directs the spectators towards the actor's breath in order to depict the character's state of health, for example. But above all, great care is taken with the contours of the eyes, because they are essential to the comprehension of the emotions of the actor who speaks: as the "doorway to the soul", the eyes are also the locus of the relationship between the watcher and the watched.

Given the different spatial positioning of the spectators in the theatre, the effect of make-up will necessarily be subject to change and may even become inverted. Whereas from a certain distance, the effects of make-up can contribute to producing upon the spectator a desired impression (which may vary from the plausible to the illusion of an emotion or of the perception of the "true nature of the character"), at a very close distance, the spectator will see something entirely different. In particular, the very techniques of make-up itself and, perhaps even its imperfections become visible. As such, the spectator will observe the theatricalisation of make-up itself: the demystification that takes the place of illusion. In other words, the spectator in the first row, much more than any other, will know that they are watching a codification, the demystifying effect of which she may get past or choose to evaluate (placing herself on the side of the practitioners, even if this means giving up her illusion). That said, all spectators, near to or far from the stage, know well of the existence of the code of make-up, all the more since they know how its social rules are harnessed by theatre.

The underlying idea is therefore to produce an effect of the spectator based on an accentuation of facial traits, in order to support or supplement the scenographic apparatus as a whole (scenery, objects, costumes, etc.). It is in that regard that make-up results in excessive accentuation, by ostentatiously revealing the outward elements of the character that the actor (or the director) wish to make immediately visible, and on which they rely in order to foster a desired mode of acting. If the spectators share the general code of representation of emotions, virtues and vices of humans at a given period and within a given civilisation, this hypertrophy of codified and shared signs becomes naturally comprehensible. The main function of make-up is to underscore the specific traits of the character and to facilitate the decoding of the nature of his character.

But this function of unveiling and revealing, envisaged first and foremost in the spirit of plausibility and based on a mimetic principle, can be overturned so that make-up, instead of revealing the "truth" of the character, actually ends up hiding it. Make-up functions within the framework of "deformation". Man becomes woman, white becomes black, old young, the ugly beautiful and the virtuous evil. Consequently, make-up no longer functions as an exaggeration aiding the spectator to immediately understand the truth of a character or a type, but as an ostensible lie whose meaning one can attempt to re-establish; in other words, like a filter, a false appearance that engages the spectator in play. This second function that consists of deforming the face and the body is as conventional as the other, insofar as it only has an effect to the extent that the spectator knows the rules of the game.

For a long time, Black or Moorish characters were played by white actors who were "daubed" and for a long time women were played by men. Cross-dressing could pass for being purely conventional, and therefore entirely acceptable without any ambiguity. However, we also know that authors and actors played with the convention to represent the defects of mimetic representation and, indeed, to open breaches that would create ambiguity. Therefore, we may say that Greek, Roman and Japanese actors play feminine roles, without their audiences (who are accustomed to the convention) necessarily imagining a precise and deliberate play on the difference between sexes. However, one must understand that once the audience, for one reason or another, does not adhere totally to the convention, the question arises. Moreover, we know that instituting a convention also allows one to deploy the ambiguities that such a convention contains. And if a non-initiated Western audience of today cannot view the *onnagata* with indifference, the Japanese convention naturally considers the fact that these young men playing feminine roles depict a homosexual eroticism that is widely recognised. Similarly, from the moment the author or actor decides to add movement, body language or a discourse that questions the unproblematised adherence to a code, the play on ambiguity can be developed. As we often see in Elizabethan, Spanish or French theatre of the early seventeenth century, in which men often play feminine roles, authors sometimes slip some particularly interesting play into the discourse or request the depiction onstage of problematic kisses.

The third function of make-up is to embellish the face or body, to the point sometimes of forming a veritable autonomous system functioning within its own aesthetic. The face then becomes a tableau in its own right, without any rapport with a plausible or realistic representation being necessary. In this respect, make-up marks theatricality, an ostentatious facticity, the performance of an aesthetic code. This is the case for performance in the Far East, but also for avant-garde theatres, particularly for Meyerhold's grotesque use of make-up.

Therefore, the art of make-up can both underscore the traits that define the character, or the face of the performer; transform the actor so that he radically becomes "other", if one allows for the convention to embellish the body and allow it to function within an autonomous performative system; or take distance with all three functions, making the representations problematic. It is then that it shows and hides at the same time, that it unmasks and masks; in other words, it is then that it is emblematic of theatre itself, a fact that allows actors to give complexity to their stage play as well as to its effects on the spectator, who thereby, spends a part of her time determining, for her greater pleasure, what make-up shows or hides, by evaluating the efforts or craft necessary to arrive at the virtuosity of such a stage play. The organisation of this polysemy is once more essential. The polysemy of traits, whether these are traits of make-up or of character, or even figural traits connected to the scenography as a whole, must thus fit into the overall coherence of the *mise en scène*.

11
ON THE DANGER OF INTERPRETING EVERYTHING

Of all the elements that contribute to scenic space, the staging platform and the dramatic space, one must remember that they all exist in order to signify. Thus, they are arranged in a coherent manner, both through their physical organisation (which must correspond to a possible expectation of the social spectator who comes to the theatre for a social but also an aesthetic reason) and via the network of signs that form the staging and dramatic spaces. However, one should not necessarily attribute signification to all of the signs produced in isolation in every type of theatre. Therefore, in the most traditional theatre, one can observe a replication of signs (objects, apparatuses, lighting, ground, scenery, costumes, acting, etc.) so that they represent a perfectly unified world. The staging elements that produce the universe of a boulevard play form a whole so as to signify the same thing: a bourgeois space where grotesque stories take place, where women have lovers, men have mistresses, children rebel against their parents, etc. As such, in this world that is meant to function as a duplication of the text, objects are linked very strictly to the scenery, reinforced by the stage play of the actors, so that everything works in unison to depict a perfectly coded space in which a signifying element is only a replica or an equivalent of all the others. One must not expect a Broadway performance to do anything more than simply frame the representation of the fiction it recounts, since the theatrical place is often simply the backdrop for a musical. Nor should we necessarily imagine that one should see in this some meta-theatrical, deconstructive endeavour. The actor-singer-dancers are there to act, sing and dance in an absolutely conventional framework – by definition, one that is universally known by the audience – and all the elements of the performance signify only that we are *actually* in a Broadway theatre. The spectator can thus experience the pleasure of the *facsimile*, which consists in seeing a dramatic space that is identical to its referential model – this is a mimetic pleasure in the strictest sense – and give in to the joys of the performance, since she appreciates the richness of the scenery, the perfection of the rhythmic orchestration and the different acts of the actors, singers and dancers. It is then totally useless to wonder what a sequin dress or a bright staircase signify, and one can save time to enjoy the entertainment proposed, the richness and bedazzlement of the effects – which serve the purpose of telling us that we are in the consumption and sharing of excess – and the nature of the choreographic orchestration and quality of the actors (*just enjoy the show!*).

The illusionistic or "realistic" stages that seek to construct a unified dramatic space function in the same way. One can thus represent, for example, Synge's *The Playboy of the Western World* in 2004 in Dublin (the Gaiety Theatre), directed by Gary Hynes, by scrupulously depicting a poor Irish inn, with a shabby table, shabby benches, a window that overlooks an offstage space that allows one to imagine a street or a moor, with a door through which those who supposedly come from both places enter and exit, etc. In this way, we find ourselves in the lineage of naturalistic theatre practised when the play was created in 1907 and we find ourselves within a ceremonial repetition of the repertoire. As such, the issue for the director and for the spectator is not to introduce objects that are distinct and that signify in an isolated manner, but to accumulate them with the objective of representing this inn. Emphasis will then be placed on the virtuosity of the actors' stage play, on the pleasure of saying or of hearing a famous text, on the interpretation suggested and guided by the actors and *not* on the originality of the dramatic reading, the scenic innovation or the legitimacy of a new *mise en scène*. It thus becomes a matter of scenically repeating what others have previously achieved in the theatre, while seeking to foreground the original and brilliant interpretation of the actors. This kind of conventional theatre does not seek to justify the necessity of a new *mise en scène* of Synge for reasons other than the well-known strength of the text and the calibre of the actors to be discovered or appreciated.[1] This is how the staging of operas has behaved for a long time. And if the spectator derives pleasure in this way, why complain, and why insist that another type of theatre is possible in other places and fulfilling other demands?

Conversely, what the *mise en scène* and dramaturgy of the twentieth century have consciously brought to theatre is the awareness of a distinct, discrete (in the linguistic sense of what particularly signifies something) and coherent signification of elements of the spectacle, without any necessity from them to create a uniform, signifying whole.

For a long time, it has been well known that objects, costumes and the ground can have other significations than what they represent in a transparent manner. Molière, who had evidently not read the theorists of the twentieth century, knew very well that a table can signify something other than a table (for example in *Tartuffe*), and that it could be an altar where one consumed material flesh; that trapdoors could lead, not only to hell, but also to the underpart of the theatre (*Dom Juan*), that the colour of costumes and their material could suggest polysemic significations; in sum, he manipulated signs. But he did not do it in a systematised manner or based on the elaboration of a theory. While, throughout the history of theatre, there has always been a staging of a series of polysemic, referential and ambiguous signs, it has been necessary for theory to glean the theoretical underpinnings and critical consciousness behind these signs, so as to create a critical tool capable of accounting for them.

Be that as it may, in a staging that does not seek to be strictly illustrative, "realist" or mono-referential, the theatrical sign plays a key role: whether an object, the body of the actor, costume, lighting or any other element placed into the staging space, it both signifies in isolation, or even signifies plurally, and is also integrated into a general network of significations that organises space. And because this complex layering invites the spectator to resolve a problematic figuration, it both provides pleasure and demands effort.

The questions we might ask of a *mise en scène* should not rely on a case by case decoding (which could, moreover, give interpretations that are both varied and fanciful, given what one can read into signs removed from the coherence of their context), but rather they should be based on the general network, on the coherence of the totality of the signs arranged in the scenography. It is always necessary to observe and define the dramatic space, as well as the means utilised by practitioners to depict this space. Indeed, it is important to take note of elements that, placed alongside each other, make sense or form meanings based on a certain number of clues that are more or less ostensibly shown. It is therefore based on a series of signs that one can determine a principle of spatial organisation, and it is in relation to an organisation of space that directors arrange signs, consciously or unconsciously. As a result, the simplest form of semiotic organisation is to place within a staging area objects, costumes, parts of the scenery, which relate to a single world, and one then tends toward the "realist" illusion that we have discussed above. But very often, the interesting thing in *mise en scène* is to use ambiguous signs that evoke several meanings or referential worlds, or to arrange alongside each other several series of signs that guide the reader toward several interpretations and toward several modes of reception (given how much the principle of these signs is to connect and bring together a generally open semantic intention with a plastic presence that can create tension with the former and make the way in which it is interpreted or understood more complex). The problem thus becomes one of ensuring that these sets of signs are coherent in and of themselves and with respect to each other.

One can thus signify concurrently several periods or several referential places (for seventeenth-century tragedy, for example, one can blend costumes or antique objects from the seventeenth century or the twenty-first century), or place within a precise referential world (ancient China, for example, in Frisch's *La Grande Muraille* [*The Great Wall*]) objects, costumes, modern social behaviours, which allow for the introduction of an aspect of play in the *mise en scène*, but also for the unveiling of meanings through the very collision of periods. Brecht systematised this principle to insist, not on the accumulation of several different realities, but on the representation of a process that the staging of several levels of reference illustrates. And numerous modern directors have followed him in this vein by revisiting repertory theatre and creating a main process for each play (the analysis of war, the observation of Machiavellian politics, class struggle, etc.). We have seen that in staging Shakespeare's *Richard III* (*Gloucester Time: Matériau Shakespeare*), Matthias Langhoff explores the theme of political violence and points the spectator both to the dramatic space indicated by the fiction and to the time of the representation, or to the wars of the twentieth century, in sum, to the theatre that he produces. He therefore truly fills the platform with networks of signs, all of which function as series based on the Shakespearian fiction. This lengthy foray into spaces and into what they utilise and contain allows us to understand the diversity of modes of functioning of the theatrical space. Admittedly, theatre is first and foremost a place where something simultaneously the concrete and imaginary happens. Centred on movement, voice and the body of the actor, the scenic space is a proposition intended for the spectator, who, based on the modes of play and representation, takes into account this proposition and interprets it.

The theatre thus never ceases to stage the unique and iterative experience of different categories of space that we call "theatricality". The spectator, who used to be simply a passive viewer, now has a greater role within the spectacle: they are taken into the imaginary transformation of things and bodies that the *mise en scène* and the stage play impose upon them, to the point where they actually participate in the play.

The pleasure of the audience

Despite the efforts of an increasingly large team of practitioners who stage the show for their benefit, during any performance the spectators remain mute and lacking in agency. We are all familiar with the experience of being unable to speak or give one's opinion, of not being able to seem even slightly intelligent after being bombarded with signs. How difficult it is to have an opinion and, especially, to verbalise that opinion when leaving the theatre? Regardless of whether spectators have been captivated, bored, disturbed or confounded by what they have seen, so much so that they can't immediately have the necessary distance to coldly analyse the spectacle, when leaving the theatre, they are solicited by others and dragged back into the world outside the representation. The spectator, who one often considers to be an informed and enlightened connoisseur, is encouraged to express an opinion even before it is possible to do so. In general, they need to wait, to allow the experience that they have just had to percolate and, if need be, to be reconsidered while the time, the fiction and the performance are subjectively reorganised in the mind. This is where time and space are widened and take on their full potential; they etch a sort of permanence in the memory of the spectator, a longevity that is based on the ephemeral proposition of the initial performance. If the signs that were felt, confusedly or clearly deciphered, do end up being indelibly etched into the mind of the spectator, then they can easily return to what they have seen to better understand the effects of the performance. Therefore, theatre must be lived in the present moment of the session, but also lengthened, expanded beyond it into the memory, at the risk of losing its impact, its acuity and its relevance, if there is no expansion.

And even for that to happen the elements arranged and the effects generated for the spectator must have been intense, effective and coherent. Rather than expecting any analysis or deep understanding from an audience that is already slightly tense before and after the session (and even sometimes during it), it is better to simply accept their presence and their pleasure (for which they have paid). It seems essential to recognise that the spectator should simply be made aware of the signs that constitute the playful process of theatre, and to repudiate the idea that they should be obliged to carry out a scrupulous effort at erudite, technical or meticulous decoding. Instead, they should be considered as playing, consciously or unconsciously, with this act of deciphering, and being moved by it. Consider the spectator the *partner* of the practitioner, replete with the attitude that irreducibly makes them a spectator: an individual who has come to enjoy a specific play that consists of experiencing feigned passions, while deciphering and interpreting signs capable of obliquely revealing their status as an individual and as a citizen. As such, it seems rather off-putting to speak about a "school of spectators", only to end up eluding the fact that the practitioners have not been able to connect with those who have not "been to school".

There really is a symmetrical relationship between the construction of the performance and the way it is received. Part of the activity of the spectator and, indeed, of the analyst, is to read the signs whose structure and organisation have been elaborated through the work of repetition, and to engage with the aesthetic presented onstage through which the work of the practitioners emerges. But this is only a part of the spectator's activity, since they also tend to reappropriate the aesthetic object that is offered to them. Such symmetry can thus only be partial, displaced and unstable. It is part of the very nature of theatre that the intentions of the practitioners are not immutable and that the truth (if there is "truth") of the theatrical object is found in the relation that it establishes with its spectator, in a complex interplay with the elements shown and the way they are grasped through the perception of individual spectators. In order for the spectator to understand and decipher this network of signs, while deriving pleasure from them, these signs must bear a specific relation to the spectator. Of course, such signs can also surprise, but the spectator has to be able to interpret them, appropriate them, and thus engage in the play of the performance itself. The spectator has to be able to get their "bearings". The game of the practitioner is to orientate the gaze of the audience towards their actions, making the spectator attentive to their practice by placing them in the frame of mind or attitude of a partnership, of a player capable of concentrating momentarily on the game proposed. The game of the spectator consists in responding with spontaneous play to the question posed to her by these elements on the stage, and to take into account the signs and to rearrange them in a coherent manner, while relying on the supposed coherence of the *mise en scène*.

Like any witty remark, the functioning of theatrical representation thus relies on the element of surprise, but a surprise that is prepared and that leads to something beyond it, a surprise that can be interpreted. This is why places and conventions exist, but it is also why they are generally transgressed. On the one hand, the spectator is fully aware of being at the theatre, and thus they expect to see a number of canonical manifestations and experience the mimesis of theatre. But, theatre is no ritual, and the spectator is not always given what they expect. For the sake of play and of interest, the audience must take a position; in other words, they must be captivated either in the moment itself or during the whole session. They must attempt to align their expectations with what they literally see in front of them. It is in this way that the audience triumphs over any hesitation in order to take pleasure from the show, precisely because they have moved beyond the initial surprise, and this mechanism applies as much to the details of the performance (and in the micro-sequences) as to the performance as a whole.

Thus, the illustrative image, or the illusion that it can engender in the spectator, is not purely characteristic of the theatrical phenomenon: cinema, television, painting and all the other arts of visual representation are all equally arts of the illustrative image. However, by contrast, theatre is able to extract itself from the principle of illusion of the image. Rather than directing itself towards the external representation of a world of fiction and appearances in which one should believe, it affirms the theatrical space itself: a place that is present, concrete and abstract, yet always ephemeral, and a space that is playful, aesthetic and primed to always be meaningful.

Notes

Part III

1 Samuel Chappuzeau, *Le Théâtre français* [*The French Theatre*] (Brussels: Paul Lacroix, 1867), chap. LV.

Chapter 7

1 Numbers in parentheses throughout this chapter refer to Figure 0.1, the cross section of the Opéra Garnier, at the beginning of this book.

Chapter 8

1 An example was mentioned earlier of Engel's *Kafka: Théâtre complet* [*Kafka: Complete Theatre*], but we could also cite his 1976 *Baal* by Brecht in the National Stud Farm of Strasbourg, or his *Week-end à Yaick* [*Weekend in Yaick*] a year later, where the spectators, who arrive by coach, like tourists, walk about in a fake Soviet city reconstituted from scratch.
2 Richard Schechner and a large number of productions of the American avant-garde; in France, Jean Boilleau, Ariane Mnouchkine, Jean-Baptiste Sastre, Christian Esnay, etc.
3 Or actors who are not acting, and who take turns to act as if they were enthralled by the spectacle they are watching.

4 Jacques Schréhre, *Racine et/ou la cérémonie* [*Racine and/or the Ceremony*] (Paris: Les Éditions G. Crès et Cie., 1982).
5 Chéreau, for example, revisits the principle of his previous production *Dans la solitude des champs de coton* [*In the Solitude of the Cotton Fields*] by Koltès (1955) and has engaged in a larger enterprise over the last few years of moving away from his former mastery of the stage as an image box. We will come back to this later.

Chapter 9

1 One encounters the same effect, though with different ambitions, in the productions of Matthias Langhoff.
2 This device has also been ritually used each year for the last century at the Théâtre du Peuple de Bussang in the Vosges region of France, regardless of which play is shown.

Chapter 10

1 At the outset, it was literally floorboards; hence the expression "the boards", which is used as a synonym for the theatre.
2 Georges Banu. "Le lieu: Théâtre des Bouffes du Nord" ["Place: The Théâtre des Bouffes du Nord"], in *Les Voies de la création théâtrale* [*Approaches to Theatrical Creation*] (Paris: CNRS, 1982), n.p.
3 Ibid., p. 68.
4 This strangeness, as of a menacing and surreal void, can be sometimes felt in certain productions of Claude Régy, for example, or in the productions of the Polish director Krystian Lupa.
5 As his latest musical plays show: *The Black Rider* with Tom Waits (1990); *Time Rocker* (1996); and *Poetry*, after Edgar Allan Poe (2000) and in collaboration with Lou Reed; or even *Saints and Singing*, an operetta by Gertrude Stein (1997).
6 The United Colors of Benetton published the controversial "Pieta" in 1991, a photographic expose of the reality of AIDS. It features the Therese Frare's photo of AIDS activist David Kirby, which was taken in his room in the Ohio State University Hospital in May 1990, with his father, sister and niece at his bedside. The image of Kirby in this photograph was considered to be that of a dying Christ, as suggested by the title of the expose. The photograph was included in *LIFE* magazine in November 1990, and went on to win the 1991 World Press Photo Award.
7 In Heine Müller, *Fautes d'impression* [*Misprints*], ed. Jean Jourdheuil (Paris: L'Arche, 1991), pp. 72–73.
8 Examples include the violent flashes of light that made the spectators feel truly assaulted during the first part of *Genesi*, Romeo Castellucci's play performed at the Odéon in 2000. In those cases, lighting becomes a key device used for questioning the spectator's mode of viewing and what they see, as well as a key component of performance as an experience not only of showing, but of troubling and questioning what is seen.
9 Georges Didi-Huberman, *Ce que vous voyons, ce qui nous regarde* [*What We See, What Sees Us*] (Paris: Ed de Minuit, 1992), p. 51.

10 Bob Wilson's scenic tableaux, for example, are very often oriented towards a model of geometric abstraction and a plastic exploration of lines, forms and colours.
11 In *Phèdre*, staged by Anne Delbée at the Vieux-Colombier in 1992, the stage was overhung with a massive symbolic triangular object descending little by little over the characters and representing the force of destiny that would crush them.
12 Molière, Molière, *Œuvres de Molière* [*Molière's Works*],Vol. 4 (Paris: Hachette, 1878), p. 326.
13 Ibid., p. 392.
14 *L'habit de théâtre en France au 17ème siècle: Contribution à l'histoire de l'acteur* [*Theatre Costumes in 17th-Century France: A Contribution to the History of the Actor*] (Paris: Champion, 2006).

Chapter 11

1 One of the tendencies of Anglo-Saxon theatre is, or was, moreover, to foreground the stage play and the virtuosity of the actor.

Part IV

TIME, RHYTHM, TEMPO

Time in the theatre is, above all, the result of a contractual agreement: at a precise, regulated and previously announced moment, individuals consent to meet in a particular space. The time and date at which they meet is thus a social affair regulated by custom and often validated by an institution. From the creation of the first closed theatre spaces, groups responsible for spectacles (Les Confrères de la Passion) bitterly negotiated the days and times at which they could open their doors. We know that after the ban on mystery plays in 1548, there was a need to ensure that theatre plays were not held at the same time as the numerous religious offices, and this need determined its hours of operation. Consequently, it was much later that it became possible to hold theatre sessions during vespers. Other constraints followed, such as the need to not play late at night due to the risk of public disorder and to the safety of attendees, to the time of the last metro, and to hours negotiated by unions.

But while this is a rapid historical summary, we remain mindful of the fact that there is always a series of warnings with respect to time constraints in a performance (bells, announcements, trumpets, oral requests), which are designed to ensure that there is a call to order at a precise moment so that the performance can take place as it should. These different effects, at the beginning of traditional performances, tend to set in place the original, ceremonial time of the representation, the "T-zero": the transition to this "other" time to which one bids the spectator, the dramatic time. Significantly, the synchronisation of the spectators' movements, but also those of the actors and other practitioners (lighting technicians, machine operators, dressers, etc.), is essential to the proper functioning of the place and to the smooth conduct of the session. In modern theatres, the stage manager, who follows the orders stipulated in his rehearsal notebook or on his computer, also becomes the master of tempo and of rhythm, and therefore of the temporal unfolding of the performance. The theatre session is thus characterised by the precise ordering of a continuity, of a process and an unfolding, punctuated by a predetermined and pre-regulated series of key moments, which make for its coherence. And while we can agree that all performances do not necessarily function according to this strict chronology, it is clear that certain decisions regarding time at specific moments must be decided for all performances so that the process of the session can exist.

The time of the session

Therefore, if one considers the time of the theatrical session, the very first thing that one notices is its discontinuity within an overall process, since the real time of the spectator and the practitioners is broken down into several moments belonging to different orders. There is the waiting time required for buying tickets, which favours the notion of theatre being an event that is more or less desired, and that constitutes a preparation for the event; the moment of the entrance, which implies a particular social ceremony, or a different code depending on the institutions and the countries; the time of the performance, often interrupted by one or several intermissions; the moment of leaving the theatre, which can be prolonged by discussions or various commentaries, readings and *a posteriori* debates. Therefore, it is within a set of qualitatively different stations that mark a discontinuity that the theatrical session functions.

Finally, there is the matter of duration, which, as we have said, can be the result of a police order, a negotiation, a custom or of a unilateral decision of the practitioners (or of the audience, who can leave at any moment), but that can, nevertheless, be determined by technical constraints (the duration of an act in the seventeenth century was around thirty minutes, the time it took for a tallow candle to be trimmed). As such, given the habits of the groups that gather, and depending on all the variables and constraints mentioned above, one might have daytime and/or night-time sessions, performances in the morning or in the evening, in the open air or indoors, which, evidently, has consequences both for the aesthetics of the performance and for its reception. Accordingly, sessions in the seventeenth century lasted as long as it took two stage two plays (a tragedy and comedy, and therefore around two hours and thirty minutes per five-act play, inasmuch as these were played very quickly at the time). Eighteenth-century theatre shows were longer, and evening performances in the Romantic period lasted around five hours. Conventions later changed, since it became customary in the theatre to stage only one play with one intermission, and sessions became shorter. However, they could, depending on the intention of the director and the material possibilities at his disposal, be staged in an hour or in a day, so long as the audience, accustomed to the standard of around two or three hours, was informed in advance. Such was the case for the famous nights of the *Soulier de satin* [*The Satin Slipper*], directed by Vitez, or of the *Mahabharata* directed by Brook. Rules have always existed and still do, since there is always a sort of basic convention. But, if the material conditions come together, these rules can vary at any time and be adapted according to the desired effect.

While the meeting time is thus "decided on", fixed and regulated, by several parties, it is also characterised by a duration shared by the spectators and the practitioners. Both are brought together for a period of time: the practitioners to show something; the spectators to watch, all within an instant. This present time therefore unites individuals who have decided to be there, whoever they are, and, consequently, they share the same experience, in real time.

But if one reconsiders the session as a whole, one will notice that although the overarching time that they share together is exactly the same, the moment of contact between the spatial and temporal presence of actors and practitioners, and the presence of the spectators, is diffracted into a series of connections according to the specific activity of each person. This is because the point of contact during the performance centres around the time that the stage has been occupied, the relationship to time and to the activity is thus different, depending on whether there is a joint presence or not.

This is why the time that precedes the beginning of the play is marked, on the practitioners' side of things, by the memory of all the rehearsals that precede the performance, by their concentration, their corporeal and breathing exercises, or by their excitement or stage fright, and the necessary rapidity of actions needed to "be ready" to begin. On the audience's side, the time before a performance is marked by expectation, by a lack of awareness of the stage, by discussions of all kinds, socialising, etc. Both audience and practitioners who generally do not see each other, are present at the same time, but are not together (neither in the same place, nor in the same rhythm, nor in the same activity). This split is so complete, moreover, that before the beginning of the performance, it is the practitioners who can spy on the audience and not the other way around. Similarly, when the representation is over, the curtain call is an entirely particular moment, since, though it is a point of contact, all the actors are onstage doing nothing else but smiling and bowing, whereas the audience can finally come to life by applauding, whistling, booing and getting up.

The exchange is therefore realised in a temporal process of reciprocity. The practitioners respond to the audience's act of paying for a spectacle by playing for a certain amount of time; the audience, in turn, then validates (or not) the act by which the practitioners honour this contract of exchange. The money that pays for the spectacle, money relative to the time spent and the pleasure felt, is then measured against the audience's applause, which is meant to ratify the pleasure experienced and legitimate the sum spent. As a result, if the contract is fulfilled and its validation is sufficiently public, the theatrical enterprise can repeat the process and rent other seats for a given time.

The reader will permit for one quick digression to add a few words on what is called "celebrity theatre" in France, which one sees in private theatres but that one will also find in a number of state-sponsored theatres. To have the star actor or well-known actors all to oneself, in one's living room (which would be too expensive), the audience puts money together and rents a space and time (typically for an evening) to share a moment with a given celebrity actor. Each person rents their seat, as one would rent an apartment, in order to be in the infinitely desired presence of the actor and see him up close, in the flesh. In one way or another, the audience borrows the time of the celebrity actor for a few hours, to see them up close and share the same time and space for an evening. The idea is then to be as close as possible to them and to be able to rent, generally for a large sum of money, this fully private and pseudo-magical time. It is about possessing the time of the other because one cannot do it in private or at the cinema. The one who plays then sells themselves, because of their profession and their reputation; they rent their living body out for an evening, a matinée, merely to be seen "for real". As a result, the *mise en scene*, regardless of whether it is by Bernard Murat or whoever else for that matter, becomes absolutely secondary, since the time spent in the presence of the celebrity body becomes the major reason for the gathering. By renting this shared time, what the audience enters into is the other, their flesh, their body, their art of existing onstage and drawing crowds. We do not have the time here to venture into the long history of the relations between actors and prostitution, but certain parallels are clear, from the point of view of this shared experience of time purchased to be shared.

Finally, the time spent with actors will vary, depending on how much time is allowed to the actor onstage by the director of by the play.

So will the pre-eminence of the actor, both from the point of view of his prestige or authority and from the point of view of his importance as perceived by the spectator. The fact that all the actors of the group tg STAN are onstage the moment the audience arrives and remain there, whatever their role and whatever the play that is staged, tends to show quite ostentatiously that this is a close-knit group whose function is to share their time with the present audience throughout the entirety of the session. Hence a greater facility in winning over the audience, in instilling a relationship with them, but also in breaking with the convention of a dramatic time that would be on the same footing as the dramatic space, during the representation.

Stage time and dramatic time

Before examining the complex relationships between the lived time of the spectator and the time of the fiction or the plot, we should note that the first evidence that the spectator perceives, when the plot and the representation commence, lies in the temporal clues that situate the story in a historically dated elsewhere-place, or in an abstract elsewhere-place that seeks to exclude all historical reference. That applies as much for repertory theatre as it does for so-called "contemporary" theatre. Costumes, scenery, objects, discursive indications, the form of discourse (alexandrine, verse, prose, etc.), allow the spectator to situate the time of the fiction (and even that of the writing of the fiction), and also sometimes to understand its unfolding. Through these spatial and textual clues, one represents the movement into a dramatic space and into a fictional time, with all the possibilities of estrangement and intersections already described in our study of space. To depict the unfolding of action, the same clues can be used, and perhaps even reinforced by make-up: a given actor changes costume and gets a few wrinkles, or is located in different scenery when his character grows old. In this case, the stagecraft consists of depicting temporal manifestations through the use of spatial artifices. Moreover, the referential time employed by the *mise en scène* is not a real time, but a representation of the real that depicts an idea, an interpretation of the referential real. When Planchon tries to situate *Tartuffe* in the atmosphere of a bourgeois house from the seventeenth century, it is evidently not a strict reconstitution that he undertakes, but rather the representation of the *idea* that he wishes to give the spectator of this house (based on the codes with which they are familiar), based on his reading of Molière's text. When realist theatre seeks to represent "a slice of life", it is not some universal idea of a rundown that it attempts to reconstitute, but the scenic and ideological idea that it has of it, even if the authors have previously done all the on-the-ground research. The director thus chooses to foreground his historical reading, the reference to the historical present of the representation (by proposing, for example, clues that link that historical present to the current social and political situation), or a multiplicity of references that constitute a system and establish an interpretive coherence. Or, conversely, the director can seek to represent an abstract or universal time by limiting referential historical elements or by completely removing them, as we have already seen in our discussion of the use of space.

But what will be clearest to the spectator as the performance moves forward is that there exists a shared convention with which one can play, once you have recognised it. This convention, which belongs notably to dramatic theatre but is not entirely escaped by epic theatre, makes a distinction between the time shared by actors and spectators (the real time of play in the space of staging) and the dramatic time of the fiction (the virtual time represented in the dramatic space). It forces you to take into account the *scenic time* of the theatrical session and the time of the theatrical production, and, on the other hand, *dramatic time* or the time of the fiction. This observation analogises the distinction already made between places and space, the difference being that, unlike space, which organises a perception of the dramatic world as exterior to the perceiving subject, dramatic time is common to both parties insofar as it relies on the contact, or the concurrence, of their temporal experience founded on a present time. When an actor speaks and acts in a given time, the spectator thus sees him at the same time as he sees her. Therein lies the theoretical principle that constitutes theatrical representation and speech, which rely, therefore, on the strict concurrence of scenic time (the time of representation) and of dramatic time (the time of fiction). The real time of the presence of the spectators and of the practitioners should, in principle, contain exactly the overall time of the fiction played. For example, in a three-hour performance, there is meant to be, therefore, in Western theatre, the same three hours of fiction.

The plasticity of time

However, once again, this belief, this principle and this ideal prove to be entirely false when one observes the way in which the representation functions. Once again, it is within a relation of play between both categories that theatrical time appears and that it is perceived by the audience.

The spectator can always testify to the fact that the time that is played out during a performance, which seems as familiar to them as it does to the practitioners and to the "character", is not actually the same as their own time: it is deployed differently and sometimes, rarely, it comes together with theirs only to move away from it again.

But, why make a fuss about it? If someone comes to the theatre, it is surely not to see places, which they could see elsewhere, to exist in the same time as outside the theatre and to witness stories that they themselves could have experienced. Consequently, theatrical spaces, time and plots are organised differently than referential places, times and reality. It is this difference, which grabs hold of the spectator and allows them to think harder about the actual world in which they live. Where place is concerned, certain conventions are readily accepted by both spectators and practitioners to allow for virtual spaces to be set up and to bear a clear, analysable relationship to the spectator's world. Time, on the other hand, although shared identically by these same parties, acquires all sorts of plastic possibilities that differ from the real referential time of the spectator: temporal jumps are numerous, time is mobile, discontinuous, it can slow down, accelerate or disappear based on what authors, directors, actors and practitioners, decide, and the spectator will be bidden to a great game of decoding based on her acceptance (or non-acceptance) of the conventions.

Therefore, while it is true that at the theatre one only represents the present in the present, via utterances spoken in the present, it is also true that the time represented is not exactly the same temporality as the spectator's time. Instead, time at the theatre is appreciated as being in between the represented time (dramatic time) and real time (scenic time) of the performance. Consequently, the spectator recognises that the time they see onstage is not entirely superimposed on the present in which they actually exist, or on the utterances they hear at that moment. And although the principle of perception rests on a fiction of the concurrence of these two times, or an ideal superimposition of both (a character speaks at the same time as the actor and is heard within the spectator's time), there are, nevertheless, effects of distortion (accelerations, slowing down, ellipses) on which the theatre, once again, plays.

Insofar as the staging time is concerned, there is a temporal concurrence between the speaker and the receiver. Whereas for dramatic time, successive times are at odds with the continued presence of the spectator. Conventionally, one must first admit that the staging time represents a past time as if it were the present: Augustus is Roman, but he speaks in seventeenth-century alexandrines spoken by an actor in the twenty-first century. What the spectator hears and sees is therefore the result of this temporal layering. Conventionally, once again, one must also admit that the continuity of life of the characters is not altogether, or not at all, superimposed on the continuity of perception of the spectator. One therefore invents various techniques of cutting or different conventional effects that are able to minimise or go beyond the temporal volume of the spectator's perception (and therefore the fiction of temporal simultaneity in scenic time), which gives the representation a particular temporal depth and rhythm. The majority of theatrical plots therefore intersperse moments in which fictional and representational time are superimposed, and moments that involve a temporal rupture (often reinforced by a special one). In the context of an apparent continuity (or simultaneity) between scenic time and dramatic time, one is therefore faced with moments of discontinuity in which the time varies.

What does it mean to think? What does a person do while they think? And how long does the process of thinking last? This moment of rupture in the action, the moment of a monologue, is therefore, most often, an absolutely implausible time (one never speaks to oneself aloud, or one seldom does). In other words, it is a temporal sequence that slows the action down, or stops it, and that develops a discourse that should not, in principle, be heard and that should not take as much time to be spoken.

What is a fight, a death, a kiss, a declaration of love, a break-up? How much time do they take in real life and how much time does it require to represent them so that they are visible and audible onstage? In other words, so that they are admissible and plausible based on the conventions in place at the time in which one plays, and based on the genre that one plays? Surely, the answers may be different depending on the attitude of the author, of the audience, of the actors and other practitioners, but they necessarily take into account the rapport between the "real" duration of these actions and the "virtual" duration of their representation. A battle, in the theatre, cannot last an entire day. Shakespeare, in *Macbeth* or *Richard III*, must represent fragments of it, which are condensations. If Kleist in *Penthésilée* links fighting scenes mainly to the offstage space and to narrative accounts, the time of these accounts and this even while they are presented as simultaneous with the battle, live (as is the case of the account of Antiloque, in the second scene), represents, nonetheless, a condensed time. While a struggle is usually very long in real time, the majority of players and performances are hard-pressed to depict its entire "true" duration, in other words to depict it for more than a few minutes (unless this is the object of the play, as in Regnard's *Le Légataire universel* [*The Universal Beneficiary*], later adapted by David Ives as *The Heir Apparent*). A kiss that is too long becomes a scandal: for example in Hitchcock's cinema, when Ingrid Bergman and Cary Grant stage what contemporary adverts claimed to be "the longest kiss in cinema" in the film *Notorious*. Therefore, the kiss in the theatre is often brief, and therefore condensed, perhaps because a long time would incite the spectator to no longer perceive characters onstage but "real" actors, no longer the fiction, but the consciousness of the time of the representation. Confessions, from the point of view of the duration of representation, give rise to a veritable experience of deceleration or acceleration, or even of ellipsis, through silences or what is unspoken, because there are few conventions in that regard. Additionally, there are breaks that last for five acts, as in *Bérénice*.

For any theatre, convention states that the discourse spoken by the character, and even his stage action, should overlap both with real time (that of the spectators' hearing of his discourse, or of the action that he does such as it is perceived by the audience) and the variable time of fiction or of play that can be cut, stretched, condensed or elided. A monologue, therefore, often expresses an intimate set of thoughts while stretching the time "really" necessary for its realisation. Inversely, an effect of stichomythia (sequences of rapidly alternating lines) or an acceleration of actions carried out onstage, condense the plausible time of the plot: Antigone and Creon answer each other quickly, and Claudius does not suffer in death throes for a long time. Furthermore, stage play, body language, a machine, a change of lighting, can catalyse a temporal ellipsis: a sudden movement followed by the darkening of the stage can depict a temporal jump of a few years. These are merely examples, since the effects are multiple with respect to *mise en scène*. However, as one will notice, any theatre depicting a dramatic or virtual space and time or a fiction, will play with the representation of time, to the point where the referential time of the spectator will be constantly disrupted and will have to adapt to the gaps and leaps provoked by the effects realised in the performance – both via the discourse and the *mise en scene* – as the following examples should illustrate.

The simple presence of an actor at the forestage, while something in the plot happens at the back of the stage or behind the cyclorama, allows for a disjuncture between the real time of the discourse uttered in the proscenium and the fictitious, hidden time (the time "in the distance"), which can be slow or fast, caught in an ellipsis or subject to a distension. When Sosie, in Molière's *Amphitryon*, holds his candle at the forepart of the stage, at the doors of the palace where Jupiter and Alcmene frolic, the spectator is frustrated by the arrangement of space and place that prevents her from viewing the love scene and forces her to listen to the philosophical discourse of a foolish man. But this initial spatial scenographic play is followed by a play on time, insofar as, in the fiction, the night of the lovers lasts much longer than Sosie's speech. The night is therefore long and sweet for the couple, and condensed for the spectators in order for them to prolong it themselves in their imagination, due to their dual spatial and temporal frustration. The distended time of Sosie's monologue and the condensed time of the lovers' pleasure are therefore pitted against the referential time of the spectator, who enjoys the game that is proposed to her.

The recourse to pantomime, or to machine-aided stage effects, and therefore to conventions known to the spectator, is also very useful in depicting a journey or some other movement of time, simply in a few minutes, a period of several hours, or over several years. This can be observed in Japanese Noh as much as in Shakespeare's *Pericles, Prince of Tyre*. The slowing down of movement (difficulty of walking mimed by the actor), the animated canvases depicting a storm combined with the sound effects of thunder (which disrupt temporal perception and lead the spectator to imagine that the storm lasts longer than its representation), the circular journey of the actor-character depicting a distension of epic time, which one encounters repeatedly in the work of Brecht and that reminds us of the famous rotating platform of the Berliner Ensemble (itself borrowed from Piscatorian theatre of the 1920s), the hieratic posture of a character delivering a monologue, the silences that are also means of distending time through the suggestion of gaps and shifts.

Besides scenic effects and machines, music, silences and sound effects can also play a role in facilitating the perception of a transition from one time to another, the prolongation of a moment or its condensation. Since the invention of lyric theatre (and in particular since the invention of sixteenth-century Italian opera and of seventeenth-century French lyric tragedy), the spectator knows that sound and music allow for all sorts of effects of ellipsis, of distension or of the condensation of time, since, as far as these effects are concerned, the spectators are prepared to adhere to the conventions of the genre. It is known that a tune is the amplification of an instant (distension), that a piece of instrumental music represents several years (ellipsis), or that a single moment is the object of several distinct tunes sung by several characters (condensation). As such, in seventeenth-century French theatre, the violins that played for about ten minutes during the interval – the ten minutes needed to snuff out the candles amid the hubbub of conversations – did not only serve to entertain the spectator, but also gave them the impression that a certain lapse of time had passed, and that this time might well exceed the real time taken to execute the pieces. As a result, the entrance of music, which can depict an autonomous time and have its own rules of representation far more than discourse, provides an excellent means for playing with time within the *mise en scène*. Music, and more broadly sound, is the art of time par excellence, since it instills its own rhythms and temporalities that can complement and reinforce the other staging signs, or disturb or offset them. The different modes of dramatisation that it can give rise to – accelerations, augmentations, incongruous tones, modification of the textures of sound, effects of de-realisation, appeasing but also anxiety-provoking ones – play on the way in which the fictional time of the world displayed onstage is represented, but also on rhythm inasmuch as it *physically* influences the state of reception of the spectator. And if we grant that work of art can refashion the fundamental categories of perception of the frame in which it is inscribed, particularly space and time, in the case of theatre, music and the world of sound will prove to be more than just the rhythm specific to the stage play, but rather the privileged modes of the sensual construction of experience specific to the time fashioned *also* by the theatrical performance.

Thanks to the techniques of discontinuity internalised by avant-garde theatres, and to the ellipses of cinema, the spectator has grown accustomed to a certain degree of flexibility more recently. As a result, a contemporary author (Koltès in *Roberto Zucco*, for example) has no need to justify temporal ruptures, and the spectator, who views the sequence of places and times of the play, accepts, without difficulty of comprehension, the discontinuous arrangement of the plot. Conversely, contemporary theatre sometimes slows down the action and the discourse disproportionately, radically offsetting them from the habitual perception of the spectator, as in the theatre of Claude Régy, for example. Therefore, in the staging of Jon Fosse's *Variations sur la mort* [*Variations on Death*], the actors, in a languorous atmosphere accentuated by a dim light, slow down their gait, their speech, the movements of their bodies, in such a way that the audience witnesses the expression of another time, one other than theirs, a mental time that they must slowly adapt to, in order to experience it, and the time of the dead that the play seeks to represent. More broadly, such an effort at temporal distension is part and parcel of an attempt at denaturalising representation, the mode of viewing and effects of which vary, depending on the practitioners who resort to it. More than an attempt at aesthetic formalisation, the distension of time in the *mise en scene* arises for many other reasons. First, there is a desire to reorient the perception of the spectator and to break up movement into its smallest component parts. From the photographs of Etienne-Jules Marey and Eadweard Muybridge, at the end of the twentieth century, to Régy's theatre that distends time, there is a qualitative enlargement of perception. Another reason lies in the estrangement of certain kinds of violence in figurations that are soundless, enclosed in an image, and all the more poignant because of their static visibility. Such an estrangement effect can sometimes find itself reduced to a sort of "trash spectacle" in a purely naturalistic treatment. Yet, this is not the case for Daniel Jeanneteau in his treatment of Sarah Kane's *Blasted* in 2005. He allowed for the deployment of the human complexity set in motion in this play, whereas other, more strictly realist *mises en scène* had taken it in the direction of dramatic "grand-guignol" whose provocation might seem gratuitous. Another reason might be the desire to depict a temporal gap that produces a sensual effect of estrangement that provokes the idea of another, perhaps more mythical, time. The plays of Bruno Meyssat, such as the aptly titled *Grupetto: Impressions d'Œdipe* [*Grupetto: Oedipal Impressions*], which he presented in 1999, are particularly successful in this vein. Additionally, and perhaps more frequently, the distension of time serves to turn the space of representation into a mental, interior and oneiric world in which time is subjectively deformed. And, in a perhaps even more subtle and troubling way, this device allows you to constantly play with the effect of uncertainty while eliciting the dizzying sentiment of a permanent reversibility between the exteriority of an "objective" and realist representation, and the interiority of a subjective and hallucinatory vision. It is this very sensation that the plays of Polish director Krystian Lupa evoke in the spectator.

However, what is rarer and more difficult to achieve is the technique of the flashback. The cinema is an expert at manipulating this effect, first by fading certain scenes into one another and then once the audience is used to these temporal manipulations, by turning the entire scene black through a simple "cut". Whereas the common expectation at the theatre is that the narrative linearity, which is organised via a series of "pure" presentations, is simply a progression of "acts". However, the technique of the flashback no longer seems to be a problem today, even if it still surprises the theatre spectator, who must make an effort to accept this convention. Since Arthur Miller's *Death of a Salesman*, and Armand Salacrou's *L'Inconnue d'Arras* [*The Unknown of Arras*], this distortion of time forms part of the conventional artifices of theatre. But the most famous case is surely that of Brecht's *The Caucasian Chalk Circle*. In Brecht's dramaturgical arrangement, the first fable, that of the escape of Groucha with the governor's abandoned child, is suspended just before the episode of the trial that will give rise to the test of the "chalk circle" – giving way to the representation of the story of Judge Azdak. The story of Azdak thus begins around the same period as Groucha's, and will come together with it at this point, where it has just been interrupted – at the moment of the trial. To further endorse this narrative detour via the flashback, the singer who leads the representation announces directly to the spectator: "Listen now to the story of the judge". Thus, the device, once it can be understood by the spectator, gives rise to effects that are increasingly complex in modern theatre.

We may recall the case of Corneille here, who attempted this kind of exercise in his *L'Illusion comique* [*Comic Illusion*]. He nonetheless represented a conventional time and place concurrent with those of the spectator, and, on second stage internal to the first, a past (the story of Pridamant's son) that slowly unfolds and gradually becomes concurrent with Pridamant's present and with that of the spectator of 1635, who, thereby, is able to witness a new phenomenon of the theatre of his time. From a conventional present, to a flashback and then to a temporal unfolding that links the distant past and the plot's present, the different times are imbricated and lead to tragedy as it was practised then in theatres and, on the other hand, to a feigned, yet real and common reality of the actors who count their money, of the characters of the conventional present and of the audience to which, finally, the actors speak directly, extolling the virtues of the theatre in general and of this comedy in particular. For this, an exceptional staging arrangement was needed (stage, upper stage, sceneries, costumes), a series of external discursive indications (the author's stage directions) and of internal ones (what the wise man says), which, following each other, aided in scrambling the temporal perception of the spectator and in re-establishing it (according to previously discussed principles).

What can be seen in the examples and discussion above is that playing on different temporalities, and even on the plastic functions of time (which are taken to be relative to the audience's perception), are systematically explored by the theatre. Theatre enjoys playing with the plasticity of time to transgress the generally accepted idealised and fictitious code, which suggests that dramatic time is coterminous with scenic time. In order to place the spectator in a state of moving or travelling through time, or of going back into it by following what the plot proposes, directors and authors (in their conceptions of how a given play is staged) are generally keen to produce an effect of lighting, a scenographic break, a movement from the point of view towards a place different from the one where the present referential time is represented, so that the audience can be aware of the fictional time in which the action is being played. And thanks to these ostensible signs, the spectator will consider gaps, leaps, incongruities and become comfortable in admitting the distance between their own time and virtual time (even if they get caught in the trap of conventions, as in the case of *L'Illusion comique*). The texts of Heiner Müller play with divisions and frontiers so that the audience sees and hears, not the linearity of a plot accountable for the deployment of a fictional time, but the establishment of a process founded on a complex temporal layering. Through just such a collage effect, *Hamletmachine* superimposes scenic time on to historical time so that the time of the actors and that of the spectators, the time in which a kind of *Hamlet* is represented, the history of East Germany and more broadly that of Germany and the entire Eastern bloc, and all the possible temporal intervals between these times, are interwoven to form of poetic panorama that fuses, links and brings together *all* times, since *all of time* is ruined in death and in the tragedy of History. Müller's stage thus becomes a nexus of time, a place where disjointed times can loom up, collide and contrast with each other. A text such as *L'Enfant trouvé* [*The Child Found*] (the last in the cycle of plays known as *Volokolomsk Highway*, staged in France for the first time by Jean Jourdheuil and Jean-François Peyret under the title *La Route des Chars* [*The Road of Tanks*]) constantly interweaves the speaker's contemporary time (the time of memory), that of his visit to West Berlin (1973), of his arrest after his father gives him up during the Prague Spring of 1968 and the time when he himself gives his father up during the period of the construction of the Berlin Wall (1961), in addition to the numerous evocations of the German socialist past. He does this by recounting a memory and thus displaying the temporal complexity inherent therein, but Müller's stage is also a place where temporal determinations are placed in a state of flux: it presents itself most often as a space of spectres. And, in that respect, Müller mainly underscores what it is an age-old characteristic of the theatrical space: from the ghost of Darius in Aeschylus' *The Persians* to that of Claudius who appears at the opening of *Hamlet*, and to the theatre of death (a theatre of memory propounded by Tadeusz Kantor), the stage is a space of spectres par excellence, where one can represent their return and, through them, replay, reconfigure and re-confront what historical and human time makes unattainable. This is even the case in the most dramatic theatre: one need only recall the ceremonial fiction invented by Diderot for *Le Fils naturel* [*The Natural Son*], mentioned earlier in this study. We can clearly see that despite the dramatic utopia of a pure mimetic present of the stage, theatre has also been frequently utilised as a space where time can be subverted and its demarcations blurred and rendered porous, a space where it can be reconfigured and where different temporal strata may be interlaced.

Theatre practitioners, including authors, directors and scenographers, do not deprive themselves of playing with the temporal plasticity of the stage. Rather, they revel in juxtaposing elements belonging to different referential temporalities or by organising intricate and troubling shifts and movements so that one time may hide another! To return to more narrative configurations, it is mainly special effects (the movement from one place to other places, from one dramatic space to another virtual space) or discursive and auditory ones, which are used to carry out temporal breaks. It may be noted that in a very general sense, it is the stage directions (change of scenery, change of act, change of place), verbal remarks or the construction of narratives that allow the spectator to understand when there is a change in time. Furthermore, based on certain accepted conventions, one supposes that this audience will accept that the play covers the duration of an entire life in a few hours of representation.

The succession of sequences, the condensation of the 24-hour period and the transition to timelessness

Medieval mysteries, Elizabethan theatre, early seventeenth-century Spanish and French theatre, romantic theatre and contemporary theatre will often play on the effects of rupture, simultaneity, condensation or distention of the time of fiction to unbalance the harmony between the spectators' real time and the virtual time of character and plot. The spectator, who is sensitive to conventional discursive and staging clues, is then able to decode temporal transitions and breaks and thus becomes able to mentally construct a continuous relationship between staging time and dramatic time, so as to establish a temporal homogeneity based on this organisation of episodes and phases, which is based on the discontinuity within the performance.

Therefore, the arrangement of a performance is most often realised through scenes, stations, tableaux, "poignant" and "interesting" moments that allow actors and practitioners to shine and the spectator to be captivated or arrested, to enjoy their brilliance while constructing their own continuous interpretation of the story they watch unfold. Deriving pleasure from the practical execution of scenes, the spectator is also encouraged to reflect on the different intervals and on the play of time. This is because they are sometimes the only one that vouches for the temporal and spatial continuity of the representation, unlike the actors who come and go or the constantly changing scenery. The spectator is summoned, as it were, to oversee the homogeneity, the organic naturalness of the play, by constructing a linearity and a continuity from the sequences and fragments of time that they witness. In that respect, they can sometimes be aided by a character, or a games master figure, a sort of representative of the author or playwright, who helps them to recompose the narrative organisation from all the sequences. The performance itself can either help them in this project by organising signs or obscure any attempts at temporal and spatial consolidation by blurring the trail of signs and rendering the game of interaction more difficult. The problem then becomes one of knowing to what extent the spectacle can be fragmented before the spectator, overwhelmed by an excess of discontinuity, leaves the game. It is therefore a matter of dosage, convention and complicity, which depends on the habits of spectators and on the cultural and aesthetic prerequisites specific to the historical moment in which the play is staged and to the nature of the targeted audience. It all comes down to knowing what the spectator is willing to agree to in terms of the complexity of the intellectual game of reordering and reorganisation that practitioners propose.

If, for example, the audience is accustomed to playing with temporal discontinuity and knows fully well how to handle the code, as in the case of mystery plays, Elizabethan theatre, Golden Age Spanish theatre, French lyrical tragedy or opera, the plot can be represented in the form of episodes that give rise to brilliant acts (by actors or singers) and to technical and scenographic virtuosity that is entirely admitted by the spectator. The audience's game consists then in appreciating these acts in scenic time for what they are, in endorsing a part of the process of representation and in interpreting the intervals based on the homogeneity and the continuity that the representation proposes or that the spectator wishes to give to the performance. On the other hand, if the audience is not accustomed to "working" in this way – in other words, if it tends to consider that the layout of a representation must be homogeneous, linear and unified – then it will be more difficult, or transgressive, to propose stations. This is precisely the problem of romantic theatre such as *Hernani, Ruy Blas*, which, seeking to move away from classical continuity, prudently pauses time and invests the principle of the scenic image or tableau (which already feature in seventeenth- and eighteenth-century tragedy and in the drama of Diderot) to show disjointed sequences. It was therefore by accentuating a certain episodic or sequential nature that was already a feature of classical tragedy, albeit by presenting it as radically foreign to that form of theatre, that the Romantics managed to instill their own representation of time and to encourage a willing audience to decode it.

In the history of theatre, there is a constant desire to represent a stretch of time through a series of episodes, stations or images that themselves depict a pause or a slowing down of an action whose duration is, in principle, considered to be more or less equivalent to the lived time of the spectator. The spectator must understand the order of sequences and re-situate them within a linear and continuous deployment of the plot. Consequently, Brechtian fragmentation, the episodic functioning of epic theatre, is in no way revolutionary, except perhaps In Brecht's theoretical advocacy of the practice. That, moreover, is the reason why Brecht's episodic theatre has not caused too many difficulties to the audience that, for a long time, had been accustomed to appreciating sequences for themselves (as is the case for cabaret, popular theatre and in all the genres previously cited).

Thus, we can gather that theatre, even so-called "classical" theatre, does not exactly accomplish the superimposition of the time of the represented fiction on to the spectators' lived time. The dilation of time, based on the rules of classical theatre (which require an exact superimposition of the spectators' time, that of the actor and that of the character), takes place during the interval when the fiction most needs it, even if it must not last too long (this is the 24-hour rule). In this theatre, the spectator is thus thought to consider as plausible the sensation of an identical fit between the time it shares with the actors and the time that the characters "live". However, this rule, which is too often considered to be absolute, has never ceased to be adapted, displaced, undermined, refused or perverted by seventeenth-century authors. Corneille was the master of such subversions. That is why *Le Cid* is often considered to be "unclassical", as it dilates the time of the intermissions to insert into them actions that take well more than ten real minutes (the famous battle with the Moors, but also the duel between Rodrigue and Don Sanche), so much so that it appears implausible that the plot only covers 24 hours. And *Le Cid* is not unique in that respect, since we can see where many authors of the period contest this restrictive 24-hour principle and spend their time undermining it. Therefore, with regards to the temporal organisation of scenes, actions and discourse, seventeenth-century theatre, as with all other features of the theatre at that time, constantly slowed down, accelerated or elided the duration of time while also taking into account, not the spectator's real perception of time, but the nature of probability, of what the spectator was prepared to accept in relation to the plasticity of time.

On the other hand, when it suited them, authors would go as far as condensing the periods of intermission so that the performance would be governed by an implacable continuity, or so that duration of the fictional time would be shorter than the duration of the representation. For example, *Bérénice* is a play that represents only a brief instant – that of the separation of two lovers – but that amplifies and examines it, makes it controversial and delays its execution. This naturally results in the slowing down of the rhythm of the play: the intermissions involve no action, and much importance is given to lyrical ornamentation. As such, even in Racine's work, dramatic time does not totally overlap with the "real" time of the spectator, insofar as dilations and, above all, ellipses and decelerations are played out in the play's discourse. The effects of *Bérénice*'s ornamented commentary on passions, of the insertion of epic accounts or of exaggerated deliberations, is that, although they take place in the strict present tense shared by the spectator and the character, they slow it down through the use of a rhetorical amplification that makes time "stop for a moment", so that one can carry out an in-depth examination of the time proposed by the fiction. ("Let us stop for a moment" are indeed the first, emblematic words of the play.) This is why the famous 24-hour rule, which often becomes a merely superficial dogma, is meant to ensure that the dramatic principle is not unduly exceeded and that the relationship between staging time and dramatic time is plausible. In other words, that there is an agreed convention that is as close as possible to the audience's sensation of passing time, so long as in this context of a day transcribed into a few hours, the play on time remains feasible.

The conventional mechanisms of representation thus tend to establish a correlation between the continuity of the characters' lives and the limited real time of the participants in the performance (practitioners as well as the spectators). They imply a notion of superimposition of both times, and hence the need to begin the plot closest to its *dénouement* and to close it with a death that puts an end to the life of the character at the same time as it ends the life of the play. However, within this framework, as one eventually realises, time remains plastic: it could accelerate, slow down, or be elided; narratives allow for jumps into the past; oracles could embody a jump into the future. In other words, discourse allows the 24-hour principle to be exceeded. If this rule has ended up being respected, it is not because a law of constraint simply emerged out of the blue; rather, it was because it was convenient and entirely adapted to the politics and the habits of representation founded on a contract of plausibility admitted to by all parties. Inscribed into a politics of condensation, an economy of means, the concentration of emotions, this temporal plausibility was needed to better captivate the spectator, given her perception of time, and to make her attentive to the plot and story as much as to her own reactions, inasmuch as they were synchronised to those of the characters.

The realist theatre from the end of the twentieth century that sought to create the strict concurrence of staging time and fictional time in order to clearly represent a "slice of life", functioned on this same principle and sometimes ended up constructing a tableau of daily life that showed the spectator the fixed image they have of the world they are observing. In this regard, one can see that this effort at the strict concordance of time of staging and fictional time, which slows down the fiction and turns it into a tableau, has the effect of halting time, plot and action in a discursive exercise. It becomes interesting for contemporary actors, and in particular for Beckett, to go one step further and to imagine the presence of beings situated out of time, who express themselves directly to the spectators who are sharing this experience. The characters speak without being imprisoned in a temporal progression and are faced with a negative or cyclical time, without any other movement than that of a discourse that exerts itself theatrically. Faced with these shadows and these figures removed from habitual temporal categories, the spectator then perceives the aimless duration of their own present. The equivalence or *quasi* concurrence between real time and of speech without action or event induces the perception of a suspended, indistinct, eternal, cyclical, timeless and present time. This is, without doubt, the expression of an existential perception of the duration of human life, but also that of the performance to which this discourse points. From the opposite perspective, epic theatre productions, or those practices that give rise to them, depict a long, extended time by the use of episodes and stations, which correspond to a deployment of historical time and allows one to capture the world in its duration.

Therefore, the temporal illusion, as it is used by dramatic theatre, is largely framed by broader systems of depiction of time. Throughout the entire history of theatre, discontinuity, stations, temporal sequences separated by cuts, compete with or replace the more or less strict equivalence between fictional time and that of the representation: medieval mysteries or European tragedies at the beginning of the seventeenth century testify to this. Even before Brecht's formalisation of epic theatre, the model of "station drama" (*stationendrama*) developed by Strindberg, for example in *Road to Damascus* or *The Dream*, and that was to become the form most used by expressionist theatre, favoured the model of the journey to the contraction of dramatic time around an interpersonal action. In so doing, it threw into relief a character traversing the world, stage by stage, station by station (as if in stations of the cross), in a position that is both that of an initiation and that of a witness's gaze – in a time that is already rather extended and based on a dramaturgy of the succession or accumulation of episodes.

Play, rhythm, staging

Admittedly, it is much more difficult for the spectator to take a temporal step backwards rather than a spatial one, since, as we have previously observed, while the spectator is not in exactly the same space as the actor or character, they nonetheless share the same time as them. But if one can thus consider the fusion of staging time and fictional time as an idealised feature of a certain part and period of Western theatre, our examination above has shown that it functions equally as a principle to be transgressed in practice, so as to create a new dynamic and rhythm that plays with the spectator. And since fictional time constantly slows down, accelerates or is elided, the spectator is always able to mark the distinctions between the present onstage and in the dramatic space from his own, to consent to distortions proposed to her and that are actualised by discursive and staging effects. Therefore, there are always several levels of temporality with which the spectator must play.

However, this play has a rhythm, which depends on the succession of forms of temporal organisation, on elisions, accelerations, decelerations of actions, on discourse, on movement, but also on their place within the process of representation. Thanks to the alternation of effects, to their concentration at a given moment in the performance or thanks to their harmony, rhythm is perceived subjectively by the spectator based on these coded systems. Each representation of a fictional time and each performance therefore has its own rhythm, which is generally decided in advance by a more or less timed apparatus that seeks to control the effects and their impact on the spectator. Expectation, surprise, slowness, the brief violence of an appearance or of a convulsive moment, effects of discontinuity, of alternation – all of this is calculated and experienced from the moment when everyone agrees on the conventions of staging and when all are in sync and there is an overall coherence.

This coherence can be traditional: the conventions of the *commedia dell'arte*, for example, are such that the alternation of amorous scenes, *lazzi* and scenes where the action moves forward, are the result of an orchestration (the musical term is not used innocently) prescribed and accepted by all. Based on the skills of each actor, a combinatorial system is imposed on the entire cast according to the chosen theme and the audience is fully aware of this system. But rhythmic coherence can also be the result of dramaturgical craft and a scenographic execution that confers a certain objectivity both on the fictional time and the time of representation. This will lead to a sort of musical score that is rehearsed before the show, which sets the order in which events will unfold and that will be entrusted to the stage manager in the form of a rehearsal book. By dividing the sequences and assigning to each a specific duration and rhythm (in diction, gesture, light or scenic movements), and then organising them in terms of simultaneity, linearity, echoes, repetitions or breaks, one can then give a rhythmical form to the play (linear, broken, circular, *crescendo* or *decrescendo*, at random, etc.) which must correspond to the interpretive, dramaturgical project (exposition, rise of the action, climax, falling action, etc.). These coordinated, parallel, redundant or off-beat rhythms, whose visual or auditory signs appear throughout the entire staging, must therefore be consistent with the practitioners' reading of the spectacle. And it will be essential that rhythm be calculated according to the perception one wants the spectator to have of the performance, as the rhythmic dimension of a play proves to be fundamental for the way in which it is received. There is also the matter of rhythm, which captivates the spectator and assimilates her into a sense of sensual empathy. Thus, the role of the director and playwright will be to decide on the temporal or rhythmic potentialities of the text and then to orchestrate (or not) the mimetic, condensed, dilated or elided adaptation of the fictional time to the time of representation.

 This objective management of time, which can (or ought to) involve several modes of segmentation, the viewer will be able to be captivated by the sensual impact and the semiotic complexity of the rhythms. Provided that they are interested, the spectator will be able to recognise the presence of leitmotifs, experience the alternation of high and low moments and note the entanglements of the different segments or aspects of the plot. Because the "musical" dramatisation produces effects on viewing and sensual reception, through the syncopations and the volumes it induces, it instills within the spectator a rhythm, which makes it possible to induce both moments of expectation and of suspense, or moments of rapidity, rhythmic excess, precipitation triggering anguish, laughter, entertainment and, in the case of slowness, a time for contemplation, fascination, reverie or the reflection.

 However, this ideal of precision where nothing is left to chance appears only very rarely in certain modern productions, such as those of Bob Wilson. It is so rare because theatre is imbricated in the uncertainty of play, improvisation and sensitivity to circumstance beyond any regulated score. There is an altogether different problem where declamation is concerned, since the actor's tempo, while it can be the result of a staging process (especially in Claude Régy's productions), is at the same time relative to the cultural norm and filtered through the subjectivity of the interpreter. This tempo – which determines speech rate, rhythm changes, phrasing, pauses and silences, the means used to slow down or accelerate declamation – is supported by the gestures, movements and postures of the actor, can be pre-regulated during rehearsals, but remain his prerogative. Even when guided from near or from afar, the actors are the ones who appropriate the text and who, in their individual ways, situate their actions in the overall coherence of the *mise en scène* through their own temporal management of their speech. Thus, there is a system of order and principles in the theatre, a play on this order and these principles, but also on circumstances, which form a series of parameters that it is fortunately impossible to fix and that also make this art interesting. The spectator does not necessarily capture all the temporal signs, or may decide not to take them into account; external circumstances may prevent some from existing, or produce others; the actor may forget to mention them, or refuse to transmit them, etc. Moreover, because what happens onstage is situated on a temporal line that cannot go backwards and that has as its principal characteristic the ephemeral, there is always forgetting, the uncommunicated, the unseen, the unheard, if only because no spectator is attentive to everything for three hours. Hence the desire to see a show again sometimes, knowing that a new ephemeral duration and new relationships will then appear. Even if everything is planned so that the piece is performed "identically" from one staging to the next, it is well known that every night improvisation is inevitable.

Whether we are describing space or time, we see that the theatre is a matter of ideal conventions and principles, but also of broken contracts, of porosity and play. Continuous in theory, it constantly offers breaks that attest to its discontinuity. And it is in this respect that it maintains our interest, because it does not necessarily respect its contracts and because such transgression creates new interactions with the spectator who revels in them. Because this porosity, this practical and theoretical ambiguity are capable of perverting the most solid set-ups, the spectator can interrupt their natural distractedness to direct their gaze towards the game before them. A play of spaces, of temporalities, but also, and especially, a play of bodies.

Part V

THE BODY, THE ACTOR'S PLAY AND ILLUSION

We could have started here, like almost everyone else, by foregrounding the actor and saying that without them no live theatrical spectacle is possible. "Who's there?" That is how *Hamlet* begins. However, we have chosen the space and time in which the theatre is given ("there" rather than "who"), with the spectator witnessing it. Not because of ease, but because, having chosen to foreground theatrical reception, that is to say, by taking the viewer into account, we have chosen to see the theatre first from the outside, as though by this enterprise, we had entered the building, then into the auditorium and only then, at last, reached the stage. And now here we are in front of the bodies.

Where is the body?

We have already distinguished the concrete physical place in which the actors are "really" present in their relations with an audience who sees and hears them (the place of the stage or platform), and the transition from the stage space to an abstract entity of signs that form the representation, figurative or not, of an "other" world than the "real" and concrete world of actors and the audience: the dramatic space. In a delimited portion of space, the actor, a living man or woman, moves, touches objects or calls out to other actors and speaks: there is, on the stage, real material. But, because this space is double, the actor, the objects and all that is matter or reality in this portion of space, take on another or other senses. And the medium through which this distinction, this duplication is produced is the body of the actor accompanied, or not, by scenery, objects and costumes. It is through this body emitting verbal and non-verbal signs that stage play happens, between the concrete and the abstract: the dual body of the actor establishes the playful aspect of the theatre, that is to say its ambiguity, the transition from an apparently real world to another world that the game produces. The animated body of the actor is thus the site of a performance, a physical and material practice that provokes imagination on the theatrical stage and in the spectator's mind; in other words, a series of available meanings, which are not necessarily controlled by the actor himself or by the director.

Sometimes the show is meant to be "pure", grotesque, spectacular, without referent or reference, a physical and playful work in which sounds, body and the act of playing with objects, are essential. Therein lies one of the ideals of theatre: its "pure theatricality". This is one of the main concerns of twentieth-century theatre, from farce, circus, street theatre, to dance. The issue is not always one of denying the text, but of giving it another place, a less dominant one, of letting body and gesture take possession of space. Pure theatricality can thus move away from being simply a representation, towards becoming a performance of the body, or towards the image of a ceremony of the body in action. This is the path traced by Antonin Artaud, among others, in *The Theatre and Its Double*.[1] However, the more or less ambiguous transition from the concrete universe of reference (the human actor's body, the real objects that are in the scenic space, etc.) to the fictional universe (the body of the actor who "becomes" the character, the body that moves, speaks and represents), most often implies a sort of copy, or rather a replica of the real universe by the world of representation. The representation thus clings to "icons" intended to imitate the real, to give an illusion while indicating that it is indeed a relationship and not a strict match. Nowadays we would say that these are kinds of interfaces between the concrete world (the real one) and the abstract world (fiction).

But this body – this interface – has precisely a real and social body that is already formed. This is the problem: the actor is not interchangeable and will always be seen from the very outset as an individual, a silhouette, a voice, a gait or even a personal history endowed with distinctive features perfectly external to his role or performance. Boulevard theatre and, more broadly, private (non-state-sponsored) theatre in France are particularly significant in terms of the importance of acting and the actor's body for the viewer's perception. What is essential, both from the point of view of the producers of the event and for the audience that attends, is the fact that known actors are included in the cast. We see that it is sometimes the same in state-sponsored theatre when Isabelle Huppert, for example, plays in *Hedda Gabler* (Odéon, 2005) and the auditorium is packed. But who is really there to see Ibsen, and who is actually there to see Eric Lacascade's directorial work (even though his *Platonov* was one of the greatest successes at the Festival d'Avignon two years previously), or for Pascal Bongard, Norah Krief, Elisabetta Pogliani or Jean-Marie Winling (the other actors), besides the theatre connoisseurs who, for once, do not make up the large battalions of spectators? The theatre has always had well-known stars and virtuosos, and European continental theatre, unlike Anglo-American theatre, witnessed an innovation when the director was elevated to a kind of celebrity status, often to the detriment of the actors he directs. The issue that then arises is to understand the relationship between the actor's social body and the role he plays from his point of view, from the point of view of the director and from that of those who watch him (the spectators, of course, but also the other actors).

First and foremost, the actor must have a physique, a voice and a type (or types) of acting that then becomes characteristic of the way in which theatregoers recognise them. When the actor is not a complete novice, such characteristics will be doubled up by their experience onstage, or by their celebrity, which necessarily modifies the attitude the spectator has to their presence onstage. Their fame or reputation will enable them to get a role that is "tailor-made" for them or a "challenging role" that breaks away from the typical image one might have of them. And this referential history that is specific to the actor will predetermine the reaction of all the other participants (there will therefore be talk of change, surprise, disappointment, etc.). Moreover, since the theatre is marked by repeats and has its own history, one will compare their performance with those of other actors.

Thus a kind of transformation-transmutation will take place, without anyone, neither the director nor the spectator, forgetting the presence of this real, social, individual body that is external to the role. Naturally, tradition has built myths tending to give credence to the idea that the actor disappears behind his character, is absorbed by him, is even transformed by him to such an extent that this or that actor has become the other he played, with all the risks involved. And it is known that beliefs, when they are effective, have effects: Montfleury died thinking he was Orestes, Gerard Philipe "embodies" Rodrigue or the Prince of Homburg, Marlon Brando fancied that he was the young thug of *A Streetcar Named Desire* and Ruggero Raimondi never recovered from playing Don Giovanni. The identification of the actor with their character, which is at times theorised and favoured by the director, has its virtues: in particular, the fact of promoting the illusion and identification of the spectator with the character via the actor. However, in modern theatre, which most often questions the issue of illusion as well as the virtues of identification, the spectator observes that the actor constructs his character and chooses the signs of his role: either by seeking to efface his individual traits in order to compose a system or a model (which the director imposes on him); or by imposing his own signs by working on the relation between these signs and the imaginary figure that he has to play. Either choice has consequences for the verisimilitude upheld by the directions of the text: the principle of composition aims for an illustration of something, whereas the opposite will create an impression of disharmony and misalignment.

Generally, then, the Western actor usually composes a vocal and gestural score that combines all sorts of signs, which enable the spectator to decipher the clues that allow them to perceive the actor's body as someone else entirely. At the same time, the spectator, who becomes caught up in the game they have agreed to play, knows full well that all this is the product of craft and theatrical technique. Once again, we encounter the saying: "I know full well but still . . ." But here the interesting thing about this technique and craft is that they appear as both visible and hidden.

Ostensible presence, exhibited communication

As we have said in the analysis of space, an actor is first and foremost a professional man or a woman, an actor who enters or appears on the stage, takes up space there, then leaves. In other words, he is a body that displays its presence both on the boards and in front of those who watch him. Whether the actor has to take on a role or a character, or is there for a non-mimetic performance (no character and no role to take on), he is directly perceived as a living being, here and now, which makes manifest his presence and designates it as a thing offered to the gaze of others.

An actor's body is thus first *seen*. In other words, it is incorporated into a communication system, which is more than it *is*. An actor in action is not able to see themselves (a mirror or a control screen are not enough to take into account the process thus created). They produce their own gestures and sounds according to an image they have of themselves and that they must control to engage certain effects of meaning. They are transformed according to the perception they have of their own play, of their partners', of the audience and, during rehearsals, of the director whose main function is then to observe the movement and expressiveness of the bodies of those who are unable to see themselves and to verify the impact they produce. This body is capable of making physical and phonic movements, which must be checked at all times by the actor in order to ensure the effectiveness of their movements in the eyes of the audience. In order to do this, the actor's body must capture their gaze, follow a predefined strategy (conscious or not), produce meaningful forms and be able to take into account the reception they induce, even if it means modifying strategy, technique and the production of effects. The purpose of the director, or the one who takes his place, thus becomes one of preparing this production of signs and effects, and of giving the actor a (privileged) feedback on what is perceived throughout the performance. The director (and other practitioners) will therefore be the one who sees the body of the one who cannot see his body, to help him in the awareness of its likely impact on the spectators. During the performance, practitioners (both those who are behind the scenes and those on set) and the audience will be the ones who will give their own oblivious body an idea of the effects of its action (through their silence, their looks, etc.).

It is thus not without just cause that some actors prefer to forget that they *are seen* in order to imagine that they *are*. Some might demand a violent and frontal lighting in order to take full advantage of the fourth wall and not see the audience; to be in a position not to take full account of the fact that it is a play; to imagine that one is another and that one lives and acts as him/her; to consider that the other actors are no longer actors but fathers, wives, husbands, lovers, kings, valets; to want to think that one is in a room, a living room, on a moor or in a palace, despite the machinery, the wings and the apparatus hidden to the spectators. All this helps the actor to construct a personal fiction in the practice of Western acting. Surely by not wanting any sort of feedback, the actor is able to concentrate on their own character, in other words, to imagine being another person, so as to aim a realistic authenticity. From then on, the spectators, accepting their role as voyeurs, may be able to embark on the great adventure of illusion, of which we will speak later. However, while the will to fiction (which consists in wanting to be another person) is perfectly legitimate, identification can only be partial. For, as we shall also see, this exercise of blindness is necessarily limited in time and by the place in which it occurs, because the "blind" actor will always meet their voyeurs.

One might notice from the outset that the eyes, the expression and the face are some of the most important features of the actor. What constitutes his humanity, on the other hand, and that conditions his ability to communicate meaning to others, is his discourse: the words and phrases he uses, borne by the voice. Hence the importance of the mouth that projects both. Finally, because it must accompany gaze and discourse, comment on them, place them in communication situations, sometimes deny them or replace discourse with a non-verbal (or "extra-verbal") system, the importance of the rest of the body (including the whole face) and its movements becomes clear. Facial expressions, verbal discourse, gesture, body language and movements, when considered as an ensemble, all allow for the control of the transmission of messages and their projection towards one or more targets, to receivers who are in the staging space or to the audience – in any case, to someone who is able to respond, but who does not necessarily do so.

What an actor does first is make the signs, tools and artifice of communication visible. They become perceptible in a distinct way. In this regard, an actor takes into account the fact that the spectator sees the signs emitted through the lens of their own experience, through the lens of their own "normality", as one not engaged in the stage play. They evaluate this deviation in order to interpret the communication that the actor offers them. In this regard, too, the actor who reveals the conditions of his action, who denotes the codes and sometimes ostensibly distinguishes them, then plays with them and can, if necessary, propose unusual relations or demonstrations. For example, if the different emission sources are supposed to be homogeneous and concur to form a single meaning, they can desynchronise or dissociate the expression of the face from that of movement, in order to create more or less complex or paradoxical effects that change the function and meaning of the message.

The message is then organised differently: it becomes distinct from ordinary organisation, pronunciation and utterance and is based on exhibited conventions that allow it to be deciphered. The spectator then immediately sees and hears that the communication in question deviates from ordinary communication. Taking as its point of departure the classical function of discourse, which is to form a message through signs, and to make it perceptible in the clearest possible way, the actor is the one who knows the technique of forming these signs and of playing with them in order to explore the communication process. And because the function of the actor is to make such communication visible and audible, they can amplify, cancel or pervert it. This is why the depiction or representation of the message is generally amplified in volume (if only in terms of sound volume) so that it is perceptible and specific, even if it is only necessary to ensure its realism. For the theatre is above all a place of hyperbole. The common code of representation will therefore require that facial expressions, and therefore gestural communication and its effects, be visible and therefore denoted and supported, that the voice does not come out of the throat but of the abdomen so that it can be amplified, that diction is carefully crafted and that gestures and movements are visibly coherent with the totality of the staging.

The handling and history of codes

The first question, therefore, is not whether a particular actor is in his "character", or whether he mimics reality, but on the contrary: if he knows how to use the codes of theatrical representation and the techniques that produce it. And this even in the case of realistic play, where the problem will be whether the actor knows how to make manifest the code of banal communication, illustrating it by means of the codes of theatrical representation.

But codes have a history. Without taking into account non-Western performance or Western performance forms specific to the circus, the opera or street theatre, we must admit that there are many different types of codes, historically situated and based on different genres, forms of theatre, actors' training and and traditions. Likewise, there are several codes, states and historical stratifications of realistic acting that claim to be "natural". One therefore need only consult documents from different periods (and especially audio-visual documents from the twentieth century) to realise that different ways of conceiving the body exist, depending on the time and place, and that the different types of acting have evolved, though they were considered "natural" in their day. Sarah Bernhardt does not recite like Marie Bell and Marie Bell does not pronounce lines like Maria Casares. It is a matter of tradition, of convention and therefore of the relationship between the actress and the audience, even before it becomes the fruit of labours of a *mise en scène*. A tragic actor at the end of the seventeenth century, who adopts a style of recitation and gesture based on the rhetoric of the pulpit and the bar and who stands facing the audience without really addressing the other characters, will have a completely different stage play from an actor from the late eighteenth century who saw and heard English actors, who moved away from traditional rhetoric and adopted postures from bourgeois drama. Their audience, too, will not have the same prerequisites or requirements, even if they have chosen Racine's *Phèdre*. The "naturalness" one attributes to Montfleury is different from that of Molière, but both would appear to us to be incredibly un-natural.

All this is obvious, if one wants to learn about the near or distant past. Just as it is clear that an actor of comedy or *commedia dell'arte* has neither the same tone nor the same body language, nor the same expression as that of an actor of drama. Nowadays, we do not play boulevard theatre at the Théâtre du Palais-Royal as one might play Daniel Danis at the Théâtre de la Colline, or Shakespeare in Paris as one might play him in London. So, as we saw earlier, it is a matter of knowing where, who and what one is about to see, of deciding whether one is ready to adhere to the code of place and time or even of genre. It is also, in this context, a matter of being reinforced in one's choice or surprised by types of play that were not expected. And since our objective here is to do provide a history of the art of the actor that would take into account all historical parameters, traditions, the training of actors, reception habits and their intersections throughout time, it suffices to point out that the relation between the actor's acting and the degree of adherence to this acting by the audience relates to all of the above-mentioned criteria. In fact, it is absolutely necessary to have this awareness, in other words to see the theatre as a relative and changing art, which varies over time, and incorporates, rejects or forgets ways of speaking and of moving onstage, ways of addressing the audience and other actors and that sometimes reinvents them or recycles them by making them "modern".

And while there are several conceptions of play, diction and recitation, several ways of thinking about actors' gestures or movements, these are really just choices that have been made at some point in the history of theatre and that often break with previous or competing traditions or form a transition point between them. They are choices, which, because they are in no way definitive, can and are recycled, interwoven and mixed with others. It is this hybridity of forms and their perpetual displacement that makes the arts of representation, including theatre, interesting, but that also disturb zealots of the fixed and orderly.

The game of signs

The second question that concerns the spectator will be how to understand the clues that are manifested by the actor's body. It is not an arduous task, since, as we have just seen, codes are either generally known or are quickly accepted as soon as the viewer is attentive to the stage and takes the step to "buy into" what is proposed to them (while, at the same time, questioning the execution of the whole thing). On the other hand, it is extremely difficult, if not useless, to describe here all manifestations and all clues as they are so numerous and depend on the traditions and the personality of an actor. We will therefore only examine the frameworks of observation here.

Besides the general physical appearance of the actor, which can be interpreted based on the role or function they are given to perform onstage, we must also consider the eyes, mouth and the whole body as a signifying whole that one speaks and of which all the parts interact. The actor's performance cannot therefore be dissected, at the risk of losing sight of the whole of his play: a type of diction only makes sense in relation to a rhythm, a tone, a movement, a gesture and, more broadly, the whole of staging and scenography. The remarks that follow are therefore only a few axes based on the three sites of the body that appear immediately to the viewer.

Let's consider the actor's eyes. The expression they produce and the movement of the face that helps to support or amplify that gaze, are fundamental to the "intentionality" of the discourse and to the direction it takes. Combined with the rest of the body, eyes also provide a kind of centrepoint for the emotion produced by the actor, which will then be projected on to the spectators. Thus, when the spectator is too far away to clearly see the actor's facial expression, they are nonetheless aware of its contorsions, its direction and impact, even if they might feel frustrated at being in the position of a distant listener and voyeur rather than as a partner in direct communication with the actor. On the other hand, if the viewer is very close to the actor, they generally do not benefit from any direct address. Rather, if the actor's gaze is directed towards the audience, it tends to aim for the middle of the theatre unless there is another more specific intention. When up close, a spectator might connect with the actor either through an emotional proximity or by adopting a mental or technical distance, which consists in observing the body of the actor rather than focusing on what their acting is meant to depict.

From this point on, the actor can synchronise facial expressions, discourse and gesture, depending on the effects they hope to create, or aim for a realistic type of acting by directing their gaze at their partners and the scenery while never looking directly at the spectators. Conversely, an actor might turn to the audience through a frontal style of acting contrary to the principle of realism, addressing the spectators in an ostensible denial of a fictitious fourth wall. Finally, the gaze may try to avoid any speech communication (in other words, any vocal address to the audience or to an acting partner) by producing an abstract effect that does not involve looking at another, but that implies a sort of inner gaze upon the text being spoken and a greater authority of voice and discourse.

More often than not, the intention and direction of discourse is classically linked to the relations that the actors and/or characters seem to maintain among themselves, so that, even if the spectator does come into the actor's field of vision, they will not have the feeling of being seen by either actor or character. Despite there being an indefinite number of people in the audience, the spectator may also be made to be the ostensible target of an actor's gaze and gesture: any address to the spectator, in other words the way in which the show presents itself to its recipient, is a matter of *external address*. The actor will then fix their gaze on an indeterminate point within the audience without isolating a particular spectator, and this will function as a sign of the address to the whole audience and to each of the spectators. The illusion will then be avoided or broken and the principle of the role cannot be taken into account (either knowingly, or because actors emerge from their acting through a break in concentration or because of an unforeseen incident, as Marie-Madeleine Mervant-Roux notes in *L'Assise du théâtre: Pour une étude du spectateur*.[2] Sometimes, and all the more so if the audience is lit, the actor's expression can divide the audience by making the message appear to be specifically addressed to a particular spectator, which will make it possible to particularise the transmission of the speech, frustrating or amusing other viewers, either making the target feel uncomfortable or including them in the show for a short time.

It is via the mouth, and its many different impressions, that the main passions and interpretations of the play are constituted. Above all, it is a conduit for the breath, the voice, the sound that it projects, as well as the discourse that it produces. Each spectator is aware that there is a corporeality to the voice: a fleshly materiality that is found first in the breath, in the air expired by the actor and that ends up in the voice projected simultaneously in the spoken text and on to the spectator. This breath of the actor, which comes from the internal abdominal and intercostal muscles and involves real physical work (that of recitation) is quite audible and gives the voice its body and power. Consequently, the articulations of the text are observed, structured by sound and rendered first by the energy of the breath. That said, the relationship between breath and words, or between breath and the placement of words in speech, varies according to language. While in English, blocks of meaning seem to be more or less compatible with the rhythm of the breath, and while they may appear disjointed without jarring the structure of the language, in oral French, it is the breath that is paramount and imprinted as long and continuous, in such a way that units of words are unable to register against this principle.

In other words, unworked, demotic oral French functions according to the length of the breath, so that a persuasive or dominant discourse will have to play on the continuous and long production of a breath produced by the speaker. Conversely, written French produces words arranged on a page and linked by different operations of syntax, the whole is not necessarily meant to be pronounced, and therefore subjected to the physical exercise of the breath. Some authors will thus be able to link breath to words, even if it means breaking syntax to give their text an oral "feel" (Céline), others will incorporate orality into their syntax, thereby characterising their text as much by the use of breath as by the arrangement of words (Flaubert), and the majority of theatre authors are forced to take into account the physical capacities of actors, and thus the production of their breath, so that their words and phrases are performed with maximum efficiency. The problem of the actor, then, will be to take account of this matter of orality (which rests on the speaker's ability to have a continuous and long breath, but also to play on continuity by varying the flow of the breath produced or by interrupting it thanks to breathing effects that involve numerous audible silences), while taking into account a text that sometimes brings out the principles of the written word, principles that favour the arrangement of words. What is to be done when one is caught between the necessity of producing effects of breath and that of producing the effects of the words written by another? That is the question that every actor constantly thinks about, even if unconsciously. Similarly, the spectator, who shares with the actor the same practice of oral French, will hear and understand this breathing exercise directly, before grasping the words, and will be drawn into the flow of breath imposed on them by the speaker.

On the other hand, the reader has difficulty feeling these physical sensations, or in producing them, because any contact with the text is generally based on another type of device: that of words and syntax. However, we know that in their writing, authors often use diacritical marks and punctuation to "arrange" the effects of breath and seek to coordinate them with the words and meanings they intend to convey by their text. Racine's lines, or even more generally the majority of seventeenth-century theatrical texts, are punctuated according to the breath of the actors rather than as a function of the "general" sense of the written sentences, which is proof that at the time alexandrines were composed with staging in mind, or at least for oral use. And if this tendency of authors to play simultaneously with breath and words (including in the practice of the alexandrine) tended to weaken in the eighteenth century, it reappeared in the Romantic texts, based on new oral practices, then became a real area of experimentation for dramatists of the twentieth and the twenty-first centuries, from Claudel (the breath of Claudelian verse is famous for that very reason) to Valère Novarina (who plays on the held, elongated, impossible flow of the breath and on the possible breaks within the oral text).

By appropriating the text (and this text can take into account his physical fitness, or rely, in the case of foreign texts or repertory theatre, on a physical aptitude and on breathing habits different from his own), the actor thus decomposes its discourse into blocks (of projected breath) and into intervals (inhalations of breath), possibly following the author's suggested versification, punctuation or accentuation, or replacing them with their own. Thought and feelings are then translated through the use of the breath, which at the same time signals the extreme presence of the actor's body and its capacity to impose a particular meaning, the singularity of the interpretation specific to the actor-individual, and finally, the diction specific to the actors as directed by the director or as they belong (historically, by virtue of the troupe, or by training) to a certain type of recitation.

It is on the basis of this entanglement of codes and this effort at distinction or cohesion that the actor can vibrate their vocal cords to produce grave tones (from the chest), sharp or mixed ones (from the head or by falsetto), resonating (pharyngeal and nasal) ones and others in which the mouth itself is particularly important (jaws, tongue, palate, lips), fashioning them and articulating them. Hence, the voice will give rise to controlled sounds, which can be defined according to their frequency, intensity and timbre and will form a discourse. And according to the continuity or the discontinuity of the verbal flow, the caesurae and the pauses deployed, the speed of speech, the emphasis or effacement of the voice will be audible thanks to different effects. Whether conscious or not, the actor appropriates the text through their mastery of all these elements of a score; they organise and situates themselves onstage and in relation to their partners and spectators. The relationship between individual variations and cultural habits then allows these elements to fit into, or play with, theatrical codes and conventions.

Thus all diction that takes into account flow, pronunciation, intonation, accent and articulation, is first and foremost a matter of fashion, of tradition: a means of historically coding emotions. Thus, in seventeenth-century tragedy, it gave rise to the establishment of rules for recitation, which were themselves based on the theories and rhetorical practices of the pulpit and the bar. Except that these rules were adapted for the theatre, by actors who were sufficiently free to modify them for their use and sufficiently aware of their usefulness. Thus, they distinguished their articulated discourse from common speech, acquired a certain prestige by performing the code, while reserving the right to adapt it to their role and their own technique, finding there the means to make themselves (and/or their character) distinctive within a general code. From then on, and based on the innovations introduced by actors, sometimes even on the suggestions of authors (the image of Racine explaining the diction of his verses at the Champmeslé, the famous actress, is well known) and provided they are popular with the audience, recitation evolves, deviates more and more from traditional rhetoric and acquires a kind of autonomy. One aims for the "natural", even if, as has been said, the notion of naturalness is relative to its conception at a given period. The idea of the "public crier", already denounced by Shakespeare (*Hamlet*, III.ii), gives way to rhythmic melody, and then to techniques, which are supposed to resemble the flow and articulation of the common oral language. However, it is well known that the stage, while it can and does do away with a declamation deemed pompous, bombastic or archaic, requires a particular diction that differs from the phrasing of the spectators and that individualises the representation of the characters and actors. From this perspective, diction becomes one of the elements at the disposal of the actor in the creation of his role and participates in the construction of the character or the figure interpreted. Stanislavski, in *An Actor Prepares*, gave a preponderant place to the diction of the actor-character. Thus, the figure that is portrayed has its own diction: a testimony to the psychological or poetic work carried out by the actor from the text, from its meaning, from the character's words. Diction is thus configured around the creation of the character that will be interpreted onstage.

And when new theatricalities have come to question psychological realism and the notion of character, the tried and tested techniques of "natural" diction have had to evolve. A different, non-realistic approach to diction that worked through the study of language, as opposed to any copy of reality, could thus indicate its assonances and associations and the work to be carried out by the actor. Furthermore, when the text, or the dramatic poem, is not interpreted in the spirit of the artificial transparency of naturalism, or in the mechanical repetition of fetishised techniques, a new vocal dictionary aims at the "invention" of a distinctive oral language. The frequency of pauses and silences, the discontinuity of the verbal flow, then appear to convey the idea of hesitation, a quasi-musicality, an overstated orality or a feeling of strangeness. Breaking with melodic continuity, which relies on syntax to impose meaning and emotion, discontinuous diction thus separates words and possible senses into groups of breaths so as to create emotional breaks and paradoxes for interpretation. This radical displacement that rejects both the classical rules and the copy of a "natural" speech (of which one often forgets the extent to which it is socially constructed) makes it possible to underscore the irreducible character of diction, to no longer strive for the transmission of meaning, but, through music or rhythm, for the distortion (or for the "opening") of meaning: to speak is no longer necessarily to impose a meaning and a pre-established and closed intention. As such, dictions work to voluntarily violate the "natural" intelligibility of the text. The evolution of diction thus seems to be articulated around less historically marked terms, such as *utterances* or the invention of unknown languages arising from new spaces and temporalities, and is given as one of the poetic materials of representation, which it has always been, but that dogmatic uses tended to cover.

Thus the actor who, through his training, has learned a trade that consists of knowing the codes, the handling of signs and the expression of clues, is able to realise a sort of montage of the fragments of the physical actions he controls, and that the director asks him to set up in collaboration with his partners. Each action, sequence and image is manipulated accordingly and, in an interactive relationship with the other actors, is inserted into his acting as a whole as well as into the overall *mise en scène*. However, the acting of the actor only makes sense in relation to his verbal communication, and therefore in relation to the audience and in relation to the partners of the stage. According to the position and situation of the actor onstage, the spectator is able to interpret the way in which the actor's body fits into the configuration of a signifying and living whole, itself composed, among other things, of other bodies, so that we can note (what the spectator does automatically and without worrying about distinguishing them) different criteria in the presentation of the body.

The orientation and arrangement of the front of the body in relation to the stage location and the spectator's position (facing, sideways, back, etc.) has aesthetic, psychological and practical effects: a direct audience-facing position does not correspond to the play of realist illusion. Having one's back turned to the audience, a position long forbidden by tradition (but that may also appear in some cases as an affirmation of hyper-naturalism), forces the actor to raise his voice, causes problems for the audience who hears less well or does not see expressions of the face and gives the spectator the desire to see what she does not see (and hear and feel that intimacy that is hidden from her, being positioned sideways or obliquely is suitable for the illusion game, etc.).

Postures, in the physical sense of the term, determine how the body is inserted in the space of the stage and on the ground. Because it is the norm, a vertical posture is rarely significant, whereas oblique or horizontal postures indicate a specificity, which amounts to a deviation (in the case of oblique posture, the actor literally has difficulty standing, with all the effects that this implies). Attitudes, which are represented by somatic positions of flexion or segmentation, give rise to a significant rhetoric that points to a coded and visible expressivity and, more generally, a representation of the body's relations with its environment. Finally, movements and the dynamics of the occupation of the stage entail an entire craft of practical and symbolic representation.

From the choices around bodily orientation, postures, attitudes, movements – to which we might add facial expressions, the grammar of which is made manifest through signs and their permutations – the actor thus determines a kind of selection of clues to execute and effects, in contact with his acting partners, a preliminary montage that can vary during the stage representation based on circumstances and improvisations. And the person in charge of this montage is the actor when he is onstage, even if the rehearsals and the prior work with the director have determined specific scripted behaviours.

There is therefore nothing that is fixed; rather, there are microelements, pieces of code, which the representation organises in a vast system of combinatories and interactions that produce effects on the body of the spectator. All this will be called the actor's play, the way they act during the show in a verbal and non-verbal interactional communication. In addition, this assembly is itself produced through concrete or abstract psychological and behavioural constructions that the actor himself (along with other actors) formulates through prior research that obviously exceeds the question of mere mechanical montage and is articulated around mythical "presence". Thus, very often in Western theatre, this is the very way in which a "character" comes to life.

When one body hides another: the virtual body of the character

As we have already seen, while the *performer* acts in their own name alongside the execution of the show, neither playing nor "representing" another role, it is clear that in Western theatre, the actor is seen, first and foremost, as a simulator. Their body is always present on the stage, but it becomes quite different when entering the dramatic space or even when it contributes to its creation. He then appears as a shadow and a simulacrum.

THE BODY, THE ACTOR'S PLAY AND ILLUSION

This shadow is most often a character: a fictitious construction produced by the author, the actor, the playwright, the director and other practitioners, with the complicity of the spectator who completes this construction through the way in which they receive the character onstage. During preparations in rehearsal, the actor thus establishes their role based on a vocal and gestural score, and on the verbal and non-verbal behavioural indices that enable their body, voice and affects to become a specific figure. And the less visible these signs and constructions are, the closer one gets to the technique of the naturalist actor, which consists in making one believe that the actor is effaced by his "character"; the more the spectator gets drawn into a state that believes this character really exists, while all the signs of the theatre insist that this is not the case. By thus making the viewers "forget" any techniques, the actor relies on the spectator's codes of plausibility as well as on their own experience of the world, of emotions and common values, so that the audience can immerse themselves in the world represented by the actor. Once the show is over, if an amateur of naturalistic acting has been gripped, they will praise the technique of the actor by saying that the actor played well by *being* the character. However, if the actor stays *in character* and does not break the illusion, he presupposes a concentration on effects, a mastery of the chosen codifications and conventions exhibited, with a constant going back and forth between the character and the actor and, finally, on the part of the audience, sustained attention and an equally codified volition to enter into the illusion. If the actor persuades himself to become the very shadow that he will play onstage, he can then identify himself with his role and thus pretend to believe that this character is a totality and not a text. Conversely, the actor who plays on distance will pretend to pretend. By temporarily breaking out of character, he can prove that he is not caught in a trap in order to show the process of showing itself and to make a comment on the way in which he is representing this shadow.

In this sense, the character is a person, a *persona* in the legal sense and according to the traditional etymology that is given to this term. According to the classical meaning, the *persona* is first and foremost a theatrical mask designed to carry the voice, and is designed to represent a type to be staged: a condition of father, son, slave. The mask then has a dual function: that of hiding the face behind a stereotyped and frozen expression that indicates its role in the play without there being any manifestation of particular feelings by any mimicry; and that of making the voice resonate and "carry" so that it can be heard. Hence the person and the character are concrete constructions as well as abstract entities that function in the theatrical play in the case of the character, and within the social and legal representation, for the person. Neither of these are either autonomous psychological entities or Kantian subjects, but fictions and figures whose words carry and who assert their place: that of a recognised role in the city, or onstage. Neither of them have bodies in themselves, but both use a concrete body to act and speak. There is therefore no need, in principle, to confuse a person or a character with a man or a woman since they are fictions and are neither real nor corporeal, in contrast to the bodies of those who bear their qualities.

But if the distinction is clear in principle, we shall see that this is no longer the case when the masks come off and when a certain conception of imitation and a simplistic idea of mimesis take hold of the system. Indeed, while one reads clearly in Aristotle's *Poetics* that mimetic imitation in the theatre is based on a comparison of the model and the representation of that model, and not on a strict match (and therefore that it is organised around a play of dissonance with respect to reality, or around a rapport of plausibility), it eventually became a commonplace notion, particularly in the eighteenth and nineteenth centuries, that it was necessary to equate the true with the plausible, a fact that changes everything. For the idea is no longer to distinguish between the model and its representation, to recognise that there is an irreducible qualitative difference between the character and the body, which bears it, but to assume that both can be ideally identical. Similarly, the common meaning of the term no longer attributes to the "person" its fictional quality, but a reality that mixes body, soul, social role and the new psychology of the individual. Henceforth, the character and the person no longer appear as forms and fictions working in the world and on the stage thanks to a certain number of referential indices that allow them to be inserted in a relation with the real world, but as individuals supposed to be identical to those that the "real" world contains. The referential indices then become indices of resemblance, which favour illusion, capture the viewer who, because they see "people" who resemble them onstage, might consider identifying with their speech and their action. Imitation and mimesis have thus become synonymous. The outstanding actor is considered to be the one who plays the game and mobilises the affectivity and experience, which he shares with the spectator. The body of the actor can thus be deliberately confused with the virtual body of the character, which common belief turns into a "real" body.

At the end of the nineteenth century, the death knell was sounded for this deliberate confusion-illusion, and the contested status of the subject evidently played its role in this. Chekhov, Ibsen or even

Strindberg, to name but a few, caused the spectator to witness the diffraction of the subject they represented in the guise of a role. Thus, the simulacrum reappeared on the stage in all its splendour, since the so-called soul of the character was splintered, its unity fragmented by the manifestations of what would later be called its unconscious, while the actor and the director, faced with the diffraction of the subject, were constrained to depict the discrepancies highlighted in the discourse and the actions of the character, basing their work on the manifested stage reality of the double body of the actor. Nora, Hedda Gabler or Platonov were no longer unities, they could no longer appear as absolutely coherent entities. Consequently, actors, through their play, and staging, through its apparatuses, had to depict shifts, paradoxes and ambiguities, during performances. In other words, the theatre needed to maintain a certain distance and take into account the diffraction of the subject. In this sense, we can say that the person and the character are finally deconstructed and can thus regain their origin and their original rights.

But is it certain that confusion and illusion have, at any time, so clearly functioned in the theatre? Is it possible to postulate that the character was so easily and openly confused with the actor that mimesis completely became a matter of strict imitation? Rather, it seems that intentions, theories and ideals must again be distinguished from the real conditions of production and reception of the theatre, and that one must admit that two lines of force govern its history: that of authors and theorists (and sometimes actors) who seek to pull spectators into their virtual world by asking them to believe that it is exactly their world, and that of the real behaviour of the spectators who, at any moment in the theatre, see that it is a decoy, that any character is also an actor, that the fictional world is a constructed world and, finally, that the theatre is a network of signs.

However, it cannot be denied that a sort of contract has been made in the interests of all parties around the need to believe while knowing that it is an illusion. And as we are speaking here of the theatre, it is clear that an agreement has been reached on the necessity, or interest, or pleasure, of believing in the representation of a dramatic space in which pseudo-real characters may seem like a lure so seductive that one can fall in love to the point of fantasising that it is true.

The dual utterance of the two bodies of the actor

The placement of figures, and especially when such figures are conceived as characters, allows us to consider how the utterance of signs doubles up as it moves across dramatic space and time. The textual and discursive entities seem to speak to one another and interact in order to evolve in a virtual world. While actors continue to address the audience through the groups they form and through their performance, the technique of play causes other types of bodily address (looks, speech, gestures) to be directed towards each other: it allows onstage dialogue to take place; an exchange between the shadows to be set in motion; and virtual situations of utterance to form seemingly autonomous representations, or what might be called "pure drama". A twofold speech thus emerges: actors remain actors; they speak and act according to the audience who watches them, while the figures they have constructed enunciate a text that the spectators watch, which means that the characters talk as if they were living beings.

We know, however, that the characters are neither real souls, whatever one may believe, nor living beings. They are semantic entities produced by the elaboration of distinctive textual traits that function according to a predetermined and conventional structure. It is sad to say, but that's the way it is. This textual and abstract construction, which is elaborated according to a process (or according to a syntax) within a precise poetics, has the function of being concretely actualised by the bodies of the actors, in the present time onstage. So much so that the technical work of the actors helps to create a world of concrete and imaginary representations that constitute the virtual plot in which the spectator can invest. This transmutation presupposes, on the part of practitioners and spectators, an adherence to the conventional codes that bind the real to the virtual through the use of referential indices. And these indices, which are also coded, combine to form the unity of a specific world and the unity of individualised characters.

In this, the actor does not imitate something or someone who exists, because the basis of their character – the textual construction that forms a fiction – has nothing real or living about it. This is why the actor must first read and imagine the text in order to constitute the fiction of the role. Then, this imaginative reader concretises this fiction in the place and moment of the stage, using a litany of techniques and references that enables them to represent it in space and dramatic time. We have seen such techniques and know that these references depend on the dramaturgical project that has been set by the precedent of other practitioners. Among these references, there is also what is called "the memory of the role" in the case of repertory theatre: the way in which others have played Phèdre, Hamlet or Rodrigue; and the social, cultural, psychic, historical references that the actor has in common with the spectators. Thus, by presenting the distinctive features that the text as a whole proposes to them; by pronouncing the discourse that the text indicates under the name of the character; by updating the actions inscribed in the internal and external staging indications, an actor is able to concretise the constraints of the role while being able to modify, transgress or re-invent them.

What will produce the effects of reality, illusion, even identification, is the system of signs used by the actor, a system inscribed in the body and based on a frame of reference that is recognisable, fully or in part, by the spectator. But the recognisable frame of reference is not the real, the historical, nor the quotidian, but the common and individual image that the spectator and the practitioners have of it or the relationship they have with this reality. A soldier, a father or a traitor does not necessarily resemble the image of a soldier, a father or a traitor; a declaration of love does not necessarily resemble Chimène's; nor do real death throes necessarily resemble the deaths of the fifth acts of tragedies. It is therefore the contractual or implicitly accepted signs of the soldier, the confession, the agony that must be performed onstage, or at least that we must assume at the outset of the work of representation, to integrate them into this relationship between the real and the image to be produced. Falling into cliché would mean missing the illusion and falling into parody. What one will encounter, therefore, is something more than the referential standard, an individualisation that makes itself distinct from the model, the type or the traditional construction, but that must be recognised or that must coincide with the lived experience of the spectator: "I recognise myself, I recognise him, or I recognise the image that I have of me (identification) or of him (illusion) and of which I know well that it is at the same time false (imaginary) and conventional".

From space, time and body, to representation

From all this we can conclude that representation is a mediation, a deferred system (like any artistic system) that is both visible and evident, and that "art" often tends to hide. Hence the idea that for there to be a transformation, a transition or a conversion and therefore *representation*, means that there must be also be a technique (the passage through a semiotic code) and an agreement by the receiving parties that validates what is played onstage is indeed the (*ideal*) *representation* of a fiction. Consequently, the process is accompanied by references that appear in the form of clues, and that deal with events, feelings and social behaviours that the spectator recognises.

We see that the question of representation leads us to think of imitation, mimesis, verisimilitude, the codes that underlie them and the ways of actualising them on a stage. Thus, representation is always a technique, a trick consciously and skilfully orchestrated, and that may be more or less difficult to realise, given the circumstances and good will (or lack thereof) of the receivers, and admitted to by the spectators. It is an inverse figuration of reality, but also an artifice capable of producing emotion, thanks to a mobilisation of the passions. This is why, in both "classical" and "realist" illusionist aesthetics, the ideal viewer would be one who accepts being taken in by the recited text, being guided by an effective body language that expresses and decodes the passions of the characters and prescribes the interpretation that the spectator can carry out. At the same time, the spectator agrees to "recognise" and appropriate the proposed signs and thus to be "transported" into (and by) the represented fiction. They agree on being controlled by a principle of suggestion that is increasingly capable of keeping the spectator in their state of illusion (hence the units of time, place and action in classical theatre). This is how the recipient gains access to the fiction: by agreeing to these principles of representation and accepting their illusion, knowing that they are merely a simulation, but nonetheless revelling in the pleasure of this poetic discourse.

Roughly speaking, this would be the manifestation of a *perfect* or *absolute illusion* that could be applied as much to the reading of the theatre text as to the practical representation of it onstage. Since at least the seventeenth century and up to recently, all poets and writers have been searching for this complete illusion and hoped for the continued attention of the audience, but they also know that such ideas are impossible, and even dangerous, in most theatres. Therefore, as we read in the *Encyclopaedia*, in the middle of the eighteenth century, one might as well take the theatre for what it is and mourn the death of a utopia.

> In tragedy, it has been well observed that illusion is not complete: 1. It can not be; 2. It should not be. It cannot be, because it is impossible to fully disregard the real place of theatrical representation and its irregularities. As stimulated as the imagination might be, the eyes warn us that we are in Paris, while the scene is in Rome; and the proof that one never forgets the actor in the character whom he represents is, that at the very moment when one is most moved, one cries out: "Ah! That it is well played; we know that this is only a game."[3]

We might return here to the distinction between dramatic place and space, but highlighting even more fervently that the ideal scenario would be for the dramatic space to be separated from the concrete place of the session, that it should take place in a *theoretically* autonomous universe that is separate from the theatrical building. This abstract, fictional and dramatic secondary space-time is ensconced in an aspect of theatrical reading – what d'Aubignac calls "intimate reading", which he claims is the best place from which to appreciate a tragedy – from which the actors are able to produce the fiction we watch onstage. Such fiction is informed by the confluence of the actors' imagination as well as the characters, the plot and the spatio-temporal stage directions proposed by the author and mediated by the text. And it is thanks to the imposition of this ideal, to its practice *despite* the reality of the session and of the place, that the actors become characters and that spectators are able to believe that the place of the session can be co-opted into the space of fiction. What has been imagined by the author, and that is quietly imagined by the reader, could thus be transmitted in such a way as to form a theatrical illusion in which the gaze, the mind and the imagination of the spectators can project themselves. But, as we know, the imposition of this ideal of perfect, continuous theatrical illusion remains imaginary and utopian, even if it has become a kind of theoretical norm. We have thus returned to our point of departure: illusion is impossible, but it is postulated as indispensable. We must therefore investigate further.

According to Furetière's *Dictionnaire universel* (1690), illusion is defined as

> false appearance, artifice to make appear what is not, or, what is, other than it is in fact. Optics make a thousand delightful illusions appear through polyhedral lenses, or in the magic lantern [. . .] Men feed on chimeras, visions, illusions. "Illusion" is also said of the artifices of the Daemon that cause what is not to appear as though it were. The currencies of the Devil are oak leaves, which he makes golden by illusion [. . .] All apparitions of mind are illusions.[4]

We see, then, that illusion is quickly understood as a dangerous artifice. And in his book, *Le Lecteur Intime, de Balzac au journal*,[5] Jean Rousset revisits some testimonials of actors of the eighteenth century who were interrupted by spectators visibly caught in "a happy delirium" causing them to believe that the actors had totally taken on their characters. Except that these delirious interruptions are immediately punctuated by tears, laughter, a distance with respect to the stage and finally by an interruption of the play itself. So much so that the total immersion effect induced by identification is immediately followed by its opposite, the effect of absolute distance, returning to the spectacle as an ostentatious play and a kind of reckoning by the "ordinary spectators" who know how to distinguish the fiction from the stage. Spectators, and even actors, are thus in a position to go back and forth between illusion and distance, to play a game of Freudian *fort/da* that we now know well.

Jean Rousset concludes that the theatre has the possibility of concealing its own theatricality: a garden, for example, is no longer a setting but an actual garden, yet the spectator, lured into a conspiracy, lets themselves become complacent in order to experience "the sweetness of being deceived", according to the expression of the actress Clairon, from the middle of the eighteenth century. Citing d'Aubignac, "while they are deceived, the spectators' minds must not be aware of it",[6] and Du Bos, the theatre claims to "make us believe that instead of attending the representation, we are witnessing the event itself",[7] Rousset asserts that the theatre makes sure that everything is arranged so that the spectator takes the imitation of the event for the event itself. But, realising that he is yielding to a certain enthusiasm, even a frank animosity towards Brecht, Piscator and Pirandello, Rousset, because he is honest, also specifies that Du Bos "defines the illusion that he considered to be utopian very well" and wonders if this rather strange phenomenon ("we know Brecht's objections to this method considered to be alienating") was "achievable in the seventeenth and eighteenth centuries, with rooms, lighting, with spectators on the stage". Voltaire and Clairon appear to Rousset as saviours: "Nevertheless, in the name of this criterion, Voltaire or Clairon justified the reform of costume or decor, or suggested that the actors themselves judge their success".[8] Thus, in reading this work, we sense a sort of hesitation, a kind of a reiterated doubt due to the resistance of the conditions of representation, the modes of play and the form of the theatre. For Rousset himself, the scenographic apparatuses of theatres are

> in reality not very favourable to illusion: three to seven compartments simultaneously visible, spread out on all three sides of the stage; these places, often very distant in fiction, are contiguous on the stage; the actors move in the centre of the platform in a neutral space; one does not play *in* the scenery itself, all conventions of plausibility thus being excluded.[9]

Rousset's integrity, which allows him to give us all the elements that might contradict his argument, tells us that there is a problem here that affects theatre critique as a whole and our wonderful belief in illusion à la d'Aubignac.

For though he was at pains in his *Pratique du théâtre* [*The Practice of Theatre*] (1657) to say that one must play "as if there were no spectators", that actors should play "as if no one but those seated on the theatre benches saw and heard them", one had to wait for Diderot's *De la poésie dramatique* [*Dramatic Poetry*][10] to imagine a fourth wall with all its paradoxes. It would appear then that Diderot refined d'Aubignac's stipulations, which then gave rise to the modern theatre, which postulates an absolute, or at least continuous, illusion. However, we can see clearly that the curtain always rises, that d'Aubignac is only a theorist, that Diderot seemingly is his double on the issue of dramatic illusion, that this aesthetic, despite all their efforts, is in no way persistent during theatrical performances and finally that the rule, if one may call it a rule, is the reverse of all this. Thus, when Brecht, in *Dialogue aus dem Messingkauf* [*The Messingkauf dialogues*], declares "we want to cut down the fourth wall",[11] it is simply a wall constructed by theorists and reinforced by the dramatic theatre of the nineteenth century, or perhaps simply further endorsed by theoretical fiction. For no wall existed before, certainly not in practice in any case. Can we therefore, with regards to the practice of theatre, postulate the existence of an illusion, and how then does one account for the process of identification?

Illusion and identification

In the first chapter of *Racine et Shakespeare*, written in 1823, Stendhal answers with an anecdote:

> Last year (August 1822), the soldier who was on duty inside the theatre of Baltimore, seeing Othello who, in the fifth act of the tragedy of that name, was about kill Desdemona, exclaimed: "It shall never be said that in my presence a cursed Negro killed a white woman". At the same moment, the soldier fired a shot, and broke one of the arms of the actor who was playing Othello. Not a year goes by without newspapers reporting similar facts. Well! This soldier was under an *illusion*, [he] believed the action on the stage to be true. But an ordinary spectator, at the most intense moment of his pleasure, at the moment when he rapturously applauds

Talma-Manlius, saying to his friend: "Did you know this play?" [B]y the very fact that he applauds, is not under a complete illusion, for he applauds Talma, and not the Roman Manlius; Manlius does nothing worthy of applause, his action is very simple and entirely in his interest.[12]

Thus, as long the audience and the audience are caught up in noise, movement and a loss of critical distance, it is evident that brief moments of illusion and identification are possible. And it seems necessary to examine the definitions of this brief, mysterious moment.

First of all, and even if D'Aubignac concludes his *Pratique du Théâtre* by claiming that it is better to be a reader than a spectator to appreciate a tragedy, many spectators, authors and critics agree that text is nothing when it is not put onstage, especially for comedy. "Comedies are only meant to be played, and I recommend reading this only to people who have eyes to see, to discover, in the reading, all the play of the theatre" affirms Molière, in his preface to *L'Amour médicin* [*Doctor Cupid*].[13] And in his preface to *Les Précieuses ridicules*, the very same Molière justifies himself in his edition by declaring:

> But as a part of the virtues found therein depend on action, and the success they had in the performance so complete, I had resolved to show them only on the stage [. . .] I have been told of the necessity of being published, but this is a prospect that gives me no pleasure.[14]

To see an actor perform is therefore a pleasure, different and stronger to reading a text, in spite of the dispersion and the multiple demands on the individual's attention during the theatre session. As one can already see, it is a pleasure that can lead to moments of fascination, captivation and empathy, very different from a single "belief" or an illusion that consists in projecting oneself into a simple belief in the reality of the fictitious being and universe; a fascinated attention to a singular presence, as one might also experience in front of other sensual and plastic objects (visual elements, even sound or density of lights) of representation. But there is another pleasure, this time in terms of tragedy, which is closer to illusion: to experience the beauty of verses, and be charmed by the art of the acting.

> The narrative of the actors in tragedy is a kind of song, and you will admit to me that La Champmeslé would not please you so much if she had a less agreeable voice. But she knows

how to use it with great art, and she gives to it such natural inflections that it seems that she truly has in her heart a passion which is only that of declaiming.[15]

Here again one speaks of a sensual pleasure and not necessarily of a true "belief". This is, moreover, what constitutes one of the aesthetic advantages of *performed* theatre over theatre that is merely *read*. And this pleasure of seeing the passion in the body and the heart of the actor — even if one knows that it is simulated — then gives rise to a whole series of anecdotes that prove that passion overflows art/artifice to become truly felt. One almost feels that, for the actor to completely charm the spectators and communicate any passion for them he himself must come under a spell. Indeed, of the actor Mondory, is has been said that

> playing the character of Herod proved very costly for him; for, as he had a strong imagination, he almost believed, in the moment, that he *was* what he representing, and, in playing that role, there fell an apoplexy on his tongue which has prevented him from playing since.[16]

It is therefore through a technique relayed by the illusion of being "almost" the character, that the actor manages to shed tears and, especially, to command the full attention of the audience. And at the same time, it is well known that there is danger for the actor himself, or even for the viewer, in making this identification, and that it is necessary to stick to the illusory safety of "almost" that saves one from going mad.

There are, in fact, many examples in the history of theatre of such a contamination. In England, for example, in 1679 it was said that Dryden and Lee's *Oedipus*, because it had been written by an author on the verge of madness (Lee), always on the hunt for a "striking effect", and because it had been performed in Dublin by particularly expressive actors, had driven a musician in the production — who was therefore both practitioner and spectator — to the point of madness. This is why Mondory should have limited his effects and his involvement, and not literally let himself be *possessed* by the role of Herod by offering his voice, body and heart to the character. It was for the same reasons that Montfleury fell victim to identification, while playing Orestes in 1667. Subject to a mercurial temperament, of course, but above all, as legend would have it, entirely possessed by the delirious character he played, Montfleury turned this tragic role into a deadly one:

> And this death-lady,
> Watchman of the parricidal,
> Carried out many homicides
> And a great beautiful potpourri
> In assassinating Mondory,
> Who, in a manner unequalled,
> Played in the royal band,
> No roles tender and gentle,
> But of transport and wrath,
> And who has, in playing Orestes,
> Alas! Played to his death.
> O tragic and deadly role,
> How much you rob the Hotel
> In slaying this inimitable actor![17]

Certain performances can therefore succeed in dramatising and questioning the fears that are installed in the spectator by this *fiction* of identification. Such was the case in Redjep Mitrovitsa's staging in 1994 of the *Notebooks* (also known as *The Diary*) of the dancer Nijinski, written while the latter was sliding into schizophrenia and into a mystical madness (sensing God – but also evil – everywhere, entering into communication with him and sometimes even taking himself for God, or for his love). Sitting all dressed in white (half dreamer, half psychiatric patient) at a white school desk (there is no entrance, and there will be no curtain call at the end to break the pact of representation), Mitrovitsa seems to present the performance as a sort of reading: he has the text before him, but he will ultimately not rely, or only intermittently, on this safeguard of the notebooks that he has in his hands. On the contrary he seems to abandon it, sliding out of the framework, which is displayed – the reading apparatus. And, without the spectator ever knowing whether it is the case or not, the performance can then give the impression of spiralling out of control, in that, often in a hallucinatory manner (rhythmically, vocally and physically), Redjep Mitrovitsa seems to embody the writing of the *Notebooks*, through the movement of a spiralling, frenzied spirit, whose binary attempt at grasping the world (loving / not loving, good / bad, truth / lie, life / Death) becomes lost in madness and delirium. There is, of course, no identification or fusion on the part of the actor, but, on the contrary, the strictest mastery of acting (technique, concentration, body tension, investment of energy) and it is this mastery that, paradoxically (?), creates the most danger for him: the convulsions and speed of a person out of control, repetitions, jumps, flows and breaks in intensity; the voice that shakes and breaks, flowing sweat and snot. If the spectator is so disturbed by such physical and emotional convulsion, it is because, in the conjunction of this text and this body, Nijinsky's schizophrenia intensifies the one, which is also somewhat mythically the actor's own. It spills over on to it, as it were, but, in fact, the "actor's schizophrenia" also intensifies Nijinsky's. For the viewer then, there is the troubling feeling of viewing not only the performance, but in a certain way witnessing the very act of slipping from reason to madness. Where is the limit? Between the lucidity and the delirium of the character, but also between the distance of the actor and their imagined identification? A performance never ceases to play with the blurred lines of borders and landmarks. The representation of a fictitious slippage into schizophrenia and the fiction of a potential schizophrenic identification of the actor to his role are thus tied up to present the viewer with a game of deception and an experience that is dizzying and disturbing.

For there must be a certain distance between the actor and their role, under the penalty of death (as pointed out by the wizard Alcandre to the father Pridamant in Corneille's *L'Illusion comique*), lest the act of identifying with one's character endanger all the participants in the show. We might say that the actor should keep their role in their mouth, play it *as if* it were in their body and heart, while preserving the distinction that separates them from others. Illusion may be introduced into the actor's play for rather long moments, whatever the constraints and codes used, but an illusion must remain a one-off, isolated in time, lest one create havoc on the stage and in the auditorium:

> It is a mistake to think that the actor, onstage, lives reality in another form. If this were the case, the physical and spiritual organism would be incapable of standing up to the work imposed upon it. As you know, we live onstage with our emotional memories. These memories sometimes reach such a degree of illusion that they have the appearance of reality. Although it is possible to completely forget oneself and to believe firmly in what happens on the stage, this is quite a rarity. We know that there are independent moments of varying duration during which the actor is lost in the "subconscious domain", but the rest of the time, truth alternates with plausibility, conviction with probability.[18]

And earlier in the same text by Constantin Stanislavski, *An Actor Prepares*, we see Tortsov taking the example of a joke made by friends, which consisted in miming an operation of which he was the patient:

"This was, of course, not genuinely true, and I myself did not really believe in it," said Tortsov, recalling the impression he had had.

> One might almost say, however, to apply it to the theatre, that I really experienced these impressions. I constantly oscillated between faith and doubt, unable to distinguish between my real and imaginary sensations. As long as it lasted, I told myself that if I had to undergo an operation, I would feel exactly the same feelings.[19]

What Stanislavski expresses in *An Actor Prepares*, we have heard practitioners and spectators say in other words since the dawn of modern theatre. Corneille and Racine, who knew how to distinguish the mouth from the heart, the word from the body in the roles of the characters themselves, constantly insisted on this necessary distance and on the need to account for the dangers that an absence of distinction would create.

Continuity/discontinuity

Thus, not only is the continuous illusion a utopian ideal, but it would be a very dangerous thing if it actually existed. As such, it may as well remain utopian, or it may as well be controlled it so that it remains half-illusion, as Marmontel would say:

> What is this half-illusion, this continuous and constant error mingled with a critical reflection that belies it, this way of being deceived and while not being so? It is something so strange in appearance, and so subtle, in fact, that one is tempted to take it for a being of reason; and yet, nothing is more real.[20]

As the spectator is sensitive both to the reality that surrounds them (the session) and to that of the dramatic action, they can only move between one and the other by relying both on their passions and their reason, in the show and in fiction. We are dealing here first of all with a discontinuous process, but then we will also see it as a process of simultaneity.

What is it that appeals to us about a firework display? The lights projected into the air, the spectacle of fire, of course, but also the expectation, that black space that separates the eruption from the disjointed spectacular elements, elements that can be articulated within a linear motion, from its syntax (the disjunction ends in "the grand finale", which is a sort of acme at the edge of a dark chasm). However, what appears is the discontinuity of effects within a performance, the collection of brutal, expected, desired emotions that can give rise to pleasure or disappointment. What draws us to fairground attractions? It is the same thing that happens: the disjunction of boutiques and stands, each one offering its own theme and particular emotions for the one who decides to enter after having chosen and waited. And it seems that this discontinuity is one of the two major tendencies of the aesthetics of the spectacle, for fireworks and fairgrounds, as much as for opera or theatre. Often too caught up with the notion of the Aristotelian "beautiful animal", we sometimes neglect this fact: that theatre, the art of representation, is also an art of the spectacle, in other words a series of effects and bursts of emotion that do not belong to the "essence" of fiction, but to the fact that the show forms part of a session, of a gathering, and takes place in a moment and a place that are not exclusively tasked with representing a story or a fiction. We forget that if we love the Matamore of the *Illusion comique*, it is primarily because he performs a "number" and displays Corneille's art, that of the actor who (self-consciously) becomes a *performer* onstage.

Guided by the conventional and wise idea that attendants at a show should ideally be attentive, silent and focused, we also forget or repress the fact that even when the lights are off in the auditorium, even when the audience is silent, and even when the convention requires us to follow the performance all the way through, our attention wavers, our mind wanders, our eyes depart from the stage or the characters. The intense attention cannot be continuous, especially when one is being entertained. Playwrights know this well: they who highlight information, recall situations, stage isolated sequences and imagine entries onstage that can captivate the eyes and ears through a series of spectacular effects. So why should we doubt that the theatre, particularly during periods when there was no darkness over the audience, no public silence and no real possibility of concentrating on the actors' play alone, evolved, in practice, in the context of discontinuity? Why deny the fact that such an audience was even more inclined than we are to experience "eclipses of attention" and be able to concentrate on an object outside the storyline as well as to join its tears to those of the characters? Why then ignore that the playwrights themselves, because they want to be successful and because they are also spectators, take this fact into account in setting up their plots?

It is true that all this is a bit of a nuisance for advocates of the continuous, zealots of perfection, of perfect composition, of constant illusion and of the total and miraculous involvement of the spectator in the spectacle. And it must be confessed that this discontinuity is so essential and irritating that the body of theory has tended to contain it, to exclude it or evacuate it, or in a certain way to domesticate it in the service of a supposed linearity and an apparent and satisfyingly controllable continuity. Theoretically, it was necessary to abandon the aesthetics of discontinuity in order to represent a world, to tell a story, to compose a beautiful, smooth and well-liked animal, to compose a lesson and to capture the spectators in a process with its beginning, middle and ending. However, in spite of (or even alongside) this theoretical and dramaturgical effort, the spectacle, the session and their audiences, seemed to resist other expectations that were more aligned with the appreciation of a moment, a highlight, a show-stopper, a "number", a singular quasi-autonomous performance (and not necessarily the same for all spectators) in the face of the linearity of fictional representation. In contrast to the "beautiful animal", the monster of discontinuous moments has had a hard life. This is also what Stendhal, or Proust, exclaimed when speaking about opera, the arias of Berma, or the superb pieces of music for which one arrives at one's box in the second or third act, before returning to other interests, other thoughts, other theatres. This is what the novels of the eighteenth century narrate, when describing evenings split between the opera, the Opéra-Comique, the Comédie-Française and the upper-class theatres.

How, then, can we ignore this fact of practical reception, when we consider the spectacle of the theatre, observing not only the points of view of the audience, but also the aesthetics displayed in the plays? For opera, lyrical tragedy, musical art and dance are not the only ones concerned. It is evident that masks and anti-masks in England, the entry of ballets into France, are sometimes conceived on the pretext of linearity or of a vaguely developed theme, but above all they are a means of adding spectacular moments to a performance. *Les Fâcheux* [*The Bores*] is always quoted to show how much Molière knew how to weave together a rhapsody from disjointed entries and pieces, which become ways of delaying a conventional end. It is also known that monologues and tragic soliloquies are "highlights" that the spectators both desire and expect. They are appreciated for their isolation, the singular effect of the case and its broader stakes, the brilliance of the actor. It is also a well-known fact that readers want to read such "highlights", as if caught up in the beauty of the singular line, to learn them by heart. So much so that the theoretical and practical struggle of the zealots of the continuous, of a more or less demonstrative and in any case fictional linearity, must be vigorous against the discontinuous state of the spectacle and that it is ultimately this very struggle that produces the main dynamic of the evolution of the theatre.

Consecutivity, simultaneity: a necessary disillusion?

There is therefore a risk for the spectator in believing in the play. A danger in participating in the illusion, in forgetting that it is an artifice, in being fooled by the continuous or in respecting the illusionist theory of the authors. Rather than a continuous illusion, it would be necessary, in the theatre, to consider that some moments of illusion may come to be called moments of grace, infinitely problematic if they were to be extended, but impossible to extend, almost by nature. These are the rare moments when, in the midst of the crowd, the spectator, individually or not, listens fully and produces a particular silence, audible to the actors.

> Do you think that from time to time, for example, two or three times in an act, and each time for a second or two, the illusion is complete? [. . .] It seems that these moments of perfect illusion are more frequent than one generally believes, and, above all, that the truth of this is not admitted in literary discussions. But these moments last for such a short time, for example half a second, or a quarter of a second.[21]

Thus, around these desired moments and given the discontinuity that marks them, theatre can be organised according to the contradictions that define it: it is a place of sociability that contains a fiction claimed as such; it is a representation of the duration of a linear fiction, but it is also a discontinuous duration made up of spectacular numbers and separate moments; it is an event that involves critical distance and it is also an illusion machine. If magic, or artifice, operates and determines an illusion, illusion, artifice and magic must express their own limits through their inscription in the staging phenomenon.

Simultaneously and consecutively (before and after the representation of the fictions as well as during the intervals, but also during the representation of the fiction) several performances will thus be carried out in the theatre building: the performance that the city puts on for itself; the performance of exchanged glances; the performance of the fiction represented on the stage and impinged upon by the social performance. Thus, we see that the boundaries between what is represented (fable, fiction) and what one represents to oneself (the reception of the spectators) are far from being fixed and that the barriers are infinitely porous. And from the point of view of the isolated spectator (one of several), and whatever the social and technical presences that are visible onstage and in the room, a consecutive or simultaneous work of belief and non-belief will take place. This does not only function based on denial, but based on the production of a specific state, a kind of theatrical *fort/da* – a Freudian game of the wooden reel.

At times consecutive (I am gripped, I suspend my judgement, then I judge, I am taken by emotion, then I think, I see the actor, then I believe in the character, finally I project myself into him), this process can be simultaneous: to be gripped and to judge, to feel a certain emotion and to think, to see the staging place yet project itself into the dramatic space. That is the essential position of the spectator of Western theatre: to know that the place becomes space, to understand that the time of the session is at the same time the time of representation, to realise that the actor is also the character or the body of a performer and to be in this paradoxical state already noted in this work:

> I know well that I am witnessing a fiction, but nevertheless I believe in this fiction; I know that I participate by vision and hearing in this spectacle, and that, if need be, I can throw myself into it, but nevertheless, at the same time, I have all the latitude to think, to judge, to dream, to put myself at a distance and think about the process in which I am included, or in which I agree to include myself, and even to escape from it.

However, other forms, derived from this paradoxical state, on the margin, or even opposed to this process, have marked the history of the theatre and continue to manifest themselves today.

The blurring of the real and the virtual: delirium

This type of theatre relies on the possible adherence to an alterity to the point of being confused in it, on a belief that makes the virtual real. Of course, it is well known that the moment of illusion is discontinuous, isolated, that it exists for a split second and that it is always corroded by the consciousness of the theatrical place. Nevertheless a belief, or rather a decoy, has taken hold in which we believe. Consequently, each spectator, or each actor, while perfectly aware of the traps of illusion, can then, consciously or not, refuse to consider the contradictions, the balance or the essential distinction between reality and illusion and passionately fall into the trap. Because the spectator finds enjoyment in escaping reality and reason, in witnessing something that is madness, like the actor, they can then put themselves in such a position that they love the decoy and no longer consider them to be merely a theatrical trap, even in Brechtian theatre. So much so that the theatre can make one crazy, because "between life and the theatre, there is no longer any clear cut distinction".[22] Insofar as this art can spread, proliferate, contaminate, like the plague, as Artaud would always say, the spectator, transported by the principle of belief and caught by illusion thanks to the art brilliantly deployed by the playwright and the practitioners, can become dazzled by this artifice in which she knows however that she must not believe, but that she then believes for good. And this is one of the tendencies of theatrical art, which is to push the illusion (or the captivation, the empathetic projection) to its limits by involving the spectator and the actor to such an extent that they imagine taking the representation for reality and that they seem to no longer know, either simultaneously or consecutively, that there is life on the one hand, and theatre on the other. It is in this fashion that a part of the European theatre of the early seventeenth century in England, France and the Netherlands, or Jesuit theatre of the seventeenth century in Rome, in particular, is ordered. By bringing the bloody cruelty of punishment to life, this theatre sought to provoke a striking effect, which contributed to placing the spectator in a state of adhesion to the performance such that they were called upon to participate in the excess of the stage. Jesuit theatre, guided by an approach that was both pedagogical and militant, sought to go further, in using this "emotional connection" for the purpose of conversion. Thanks to this excessive poetics accompanied by a debauchery of technical effects that contributed to the development of a staged representation (also based on excess), this theatre could promote hatred for wicked, barbaric and execrable actions and the tyrants who carried them out. All this to the benefit of a confirmation of the spectators in religion and in virtue, even a conversion of the spectator to the values of reference. Counter-reformist pedagogy and religious proselytism were thus supposed to spread, by means of the spectacle. Preferred over Aristotelian purgation and compassion, exemplary horror, ostensibly visible and carefully represented, resulted, in principle, in the production of a horror of horrors and gave the spectator the courage to wholeheartedly embrace the faith. Dramatic excess, the sheer size and richness of the features of the stage, the terrifying physical presence of the actors, reinforcing the action and discourse of the characters, made this great integrated performance (music, singing, dance, machines, special effects) a way of gripping the viewer and persuading them that regeneration is possible, *through* the rejection of horrors and the identification with the suffering of the martyrs. The whole of this sacred device establishes a kind of ceremony that seeks to eliminate the boundaries between the real and the virtual, the conceptual distinction between the watcher and the watched, in the name of an adhesion to the process of belief. At the same time, it testifies to an unusual confidence in the efficacy of signs and in their ability to deliver a sole meaning, thanks to the impeccable mastery of the practitioners – who, serving God so well, end up replacing his almighty power.

It should be noted, however, that this "affect" that binds the viewer to the show is usually voluntarily or forcibly – and sometimes in spite of the intention of the authors or the practitioners – distanced by the fact that the viewers remain distinct from the watched and that the intervention of the viewers is, if not prohibited, at least not intended by the fiction. As if to suggest that confidence in the process of common and empathic belief, and in the ability of signs to produce pure excess of sentiments, was impossible. For while there is an attempt to contaminate the audience, to instil a sense of excess in the minds of the spectators – or to excite a hatred of barbarism through the representation of execrable actions, for the militant Jesuit theatre or even for militant theatre in general – the community participating in the show does not necessarily form a homogeneous bubble and therefore does not take its place in the sacred ceremony. Consequently, there is no longer communion, sacred ceremony or dramatic apologia, but just theatre and tragedy.

In order to envisage fusing the real and the virtual within a theatrical ceremony, it is necessary for certain practical and social conditions to be met and for the practitioners and spectators to adhere to the same belief system (which does not necessarily entail homogenous viewing and perception). It is necessary to break with representation as it is generally produced in the theatre and to establish a device, a system of play, a performance and a mode of viewing that make it possible to envisage the spectacle as a totality. For Artaud, during the modern period, the goal was to realise this totality in order to arrive at what in clinical terms we could call delirium. A delirium that gives the impression of living emotions, or passions, and that mixes the reality of things and their scenic figuration. So that by actively participating in a feigned emotion, the spectator is able to really experience false suffering, even false compassion, in front of simulacra, so that emotion, suffering and simulacra themselves, jump out of their virtuality. As a result, the art of theatre, which is essentially communicative, false and effective, then has the terrible quality of spreading, contaminating all those who attend the spectacle, to the point that all the spectators are literally "taken", captured by a delirious illusion that leads one out of reality, or rather confuses the real and the virtual in another state where a distinction no longer exists. To witness the spectacle of representation thus becomes the delicious danger of believing in what is artificial and false, of being moved by the pain of false representation, and of conceiving joy, interest or disgust, by experiencing, for example, a feigned suffering or an irrelevant compassion. By reversing the issue of illusion and giving a major positive value to its dangers, theorists like Antonin Artaud magnify the powers and effectiveness of the theatrical genre by giving it an almost magical impact, and insisting on the power of performance and ritual, make the contagion of spectacle the very goal of the art. It is therefore necessary, in their opinion, to indulge in the theatre, insofar as man must retain that part of delirium, madness and that specific connection with the mystery of illusion into which he must enter by right. And if this attitude leads him to evil, or to good or even to madness, it does not matter, since it is not a question of making it a useful tool for the city, but of accounting for the fact that, in the social order, a place must be given, via the theatre, to mysterious contagion. It is natural to do theatre, in the sense that it is natural to depart from the real – perceived as distinct from the virtual – and from our ability to judge, in other words from our conventional social behaviour, towards the common celebration of a ceremony of "metaphysical" reach that is beyond good and evil: the ceremony of belief, the confusion of lures with the real. The work of Grotowski, that of Eugenio Barba, the first performances of La Fura dels Baus, certain pieces by Carmelo Bene, Jan Fabre or even by Rodrigo García, underscore this idea, as we shall see in the next section.

Illusion and autistic performance

If the theatre has spent so much time putting distance between embodied experience and madness by setting up a critical distance between a real body in a real place and a virtual body in an imaginary space, it is of course, as Artaud has said, because there is a danger in confusing the real and the virtual. However, we have seen that while Western theatre is fully aware of the risk of confusing these two categories, it seems to strive to move past representation and the schema of mimesis towards direct figuration, towards the absolute sameness of the actor's body and the virtual body of the character: from feigned madness to real madness; from make-believe death and "feigned" blood to veritable death and true bloodshed. This volition to go beyond representation and mimesis in order to represent horror and make fury, suffering and blood exist unquestionably on the stage, means resorting to the extreme performance of bodies, creating actor demonstrations or freeing the performer from the character, so that the transparency and the confusion of words and things seize both the actor and the spectator within a dangerous experience of passions. Let's take a very recent example to illustrate this.

Dealing with the most famous play in Western theatre, from that tragedy of language in whose history a multiplicity of directors and actors have etched their mark – not to mention the different voices of critics from all walks of life – Romeo Castellucci sought to break with the historiographical tradition and go back to the original violence of *Hamlet*. To erase the character and turn his Hamlet into an autistic body: a body standing, vibrating with anger or lying in silent suffering. A body that does not know what a subject is and whose language has imploded. An actor's body whose strength lies in what it does not say, in the impossibility of saying, or of representing. The *Amleto: La veemente esteriorità della morte di un mollusco* ([*Hamlet: The Vehement Exteriority of the Death of a Mollusc*] 1994, replayed at the Odéon in 2004) places itself here in the line of Castelluci's performance work that forbids the spectator from observing only a moving and distant image, forcing them to witness a kind of revelation beyond any common language by a divided and exposed body that places the boundaries between the real and the virtual in suspension. For it is indeed a matter of dividing, of breaking down this monumental play by having a forbidden body appear onstage.

The scenographic device is crucial to achieve such division. The actor is alone on a strange platform, preserved from the energy of the city: around the board (front and sides, the back being a wall) are aligned non-identifiable machines that will come to life during the show, and on an inner row, truck batteries provide all the energy needed to illuminate the platform. The machines and batteries, which create a frame that orients the eye, power neon lights that are aligned in the centre and in front of the stage and hoisted on to metal structures in the shape of a cross. Alternately illuminated on the right or on the left, the structures project a weak and diffuse light, as in a mediocre hospital. The actor is, properly speaking, played and illuminated solely by the energy sources of the stage.

This is the place in which Hamlet will not act, where he will keep himself in play only through the energy of the turbines, which he himself renews with precise technical gestures, and this is where he will live out his suffering for an entire hour and a half. Rather than a character (a son, a prince, a hero), the actor is an anonymous body, isolated, fragmented, oscillating to the rhythm of the machines. The spectators, on the other hand, are seated on tiered seats: they are few in number, about two hundred at the beginning. Bombarded by violent noises and sudden shots, the audience is no longer a homogeneous entity, but becomes diffracted, reacting differently, either leaving or enduring the scene as they suffer individually from their own perception. The performance impacts so forcefully on it that it also breaks up into shards.

At the beginning of the show, Horatio-Amleto (Paolo Tonti, who never acted in anything other than this play in his life as an Italian teacher) wears a padlocked necklace that links him to the role of Horatio – that of the survivor of the disaster that compels him to recount and bodily perform the terrible story of the Prince of Denmark: he is therefore expected to speak. But the padlock bursts open, Horatio disappears and the narration will not take place, since Castellucci's theatre never ceases to say that it shouldn't exist. Rather than abandon his convictions, Hamlet will deny himself, for Hamlet/Amleto is either dead or not yet born in his tragedy: he is either a figure that exists before it, as in the Nordic sagas or in the childhood of Hamlet; or he is shown to exist after the story of the murder and the revenge, beneath or beyond the representation of the Shakespearean myth. As a foetus born in the rubble of Elsinore, and perpetually chained, Amleto reveals himself without the character of Hamlet. The actor is there, alone on the stage, on this strange and surprising place, with no other charge than that of being exposed, without the support of the myth of Hamlet. But without his own fable, Amleto can only be mad: he is a young autistic man who does not know, or no longer knows, how to separate words and things, who no longer knows words or his own name. There is thus no longer history or fiction, but a figurative presence that reveals the performance of a body struggling with childish eroticism, anality, without a possible mirror.

Surrounded by autonomous energy, and encircled by the electric batteries of a truck, which isolate him and isolate the spectators from the spectacle, Amleto tries in vain to construct himself within the space of representation. As an inchoate foetus, he appears on a stage, flounders in a place that could be the San Clemente psychiatric hospital and from the outset expresses the shame of being there, surrounded by the glances of other people, before writing on his chest that he is a son and that that is what defines him. "Shame" and "son" appear to be Hamlet's only two words. However, his gestures and sounds, his noises, destroy him as he goes round in circles, like a haggard reptile or a distraught baby. It is then time for the actor to erase the "n" from "son", as if he were already refusing to be a son, or a Hamlet, and were becoming a "so", a non-descript entity.

A madman, a rejected son, a clinical psychotic, he then plays with real revolvers and inadvertently fires shots: they seem to be discharged almost in spite of him, acting outside of his control. Then, the old, hackneyed allegory of the tragic son that has endlessly replayed in all the theatres of the world appears, relying on transitional objects to try to be something and become *somebody*: the curmudgeon towards the father; the speaking puppet (who cries "again, again") for Ophelia; the talking parrot (whose playful envelope contains a tape recorder) for himself; the female kangaroo for the mother. The partners he thoughtlessly manipulates are toy-objects, and it is with them, on them that he plays, without even knowing that he is playing. The madman is mad, it is his role, and one might not be surprised to see him in one more *Hamlet*, but this is not an actor-madman, some clown or a jester; he is a truly autistic person who expressly repeats insignificant gestures, or rather signs whose signifier and signified are split, non-articulated and unrelated, even arbitrary. Amleto stops as if by chance on sounds, objects and reproduces *ad nauseum* their functioning, noise and movement, in the midst of his delirium. The ball-pen slams, the spoon emits a sound under the mouth's breath, the revolver fires though scarcely touched and all this comes alive without the human who holds them seeming to suspect that he is at the source of the movements and the noises, without anything emerging but gestures and sounds separated from things. Amleto's drool runs down and makes bubbles, long and repetitively, automatically (like the revolver). The actor's body *performs*, without devoting itself to representation, without falling into the illusion of the character. Henceforth the body mercilessly executes the gesture of one who violently resists the crossing of the frontier of life and death, then, little by little, deliquesces, until it is nothing but soft flesh. Hamlet is no longer even a machine.

Thus, in this chaos of disjointed signifiers, literally disarticulated from possible signifieds, the autistic child will have to say at least something to those on the other side of the energy: he will have to articulate signs. This is why the child finds his feet (trying to separate himself from the mother to whom he is shackled) and seeks to name himself, brands his back with an iron "A", as the most guilty of humans or grazing animals, but without being able to speak, even when being brandished. Only the letters remain that make up words that are written in charcoal on the hospital wall: another "A", an "O", and then other letters that end up filling in the blanks, providing meaning: "L'mAtO" (the madman), "ArtO" (Artaud, the madman of the theatre, his double),

"AbortO" (stunted child), then "OfeliA", "phAntOm", "liability" (in English), as if suddenly, the immense story of Hamlet was inscribing itself on the wall through the hands of the silent body, as if memory was flowing out without a consciousness to solidify it. All the words overlap, referring to one another, simply because a certain number of letters are repeated to compose them. Writing, strictly speaking, is noted without the signs being signs, and if signifiers appear, it is again only perhaps by chance in this world of chaotic repetition, which is structured only because we want it to be (the audience is caught in its trap of always wanting to seek meaning) and that finally seems to lead to a beginning of discourse. We hope that one day Amleto will be able to express himself. But the energy of the machines and their mechanical noise, animated by batteries, then challenges the human existence of the body, and indeed its function of representation. The platform, doubly encircled by batteries and electrical machines, will therefore not allow the body to bear any aptitude for delivering an articulated meaning. The autistic child is condemned to its fate, its former state, as in the worst of all asylums. Amleto, in a way, falls into line and returns to the first stage that was known to him, when he was nestled in the position of a foetus in an iron cupboard at the back of the stage (the mother, who one comes out of, bruised).

There is thus a move backward, a regression and return to an anal literality: Ophélia, the doll, must be drowned in urine; then, after defecating in his baby chamberpot, Amleto traces with his shit, on the wall "so" (*I am so*, or *so it is*), the first two letters of a "son" whose "n" has disappeared. Two voices come, like a mechanical chorus, to comment on the story of this stunted mollusc of a child, and one realises very late that they are emitted by two hidden actors, embedded in an iron box that had been taken for a loudspeaker. And while we as spectators suffer from the violence of noises, gestures and images, we have also understood that the Shakespearian hero, after his death, returning to the origin of his myth, had all the time to recreate the path which, simultaneously, constitutes and destroys him. He rocked his father's bear, drowned his doll, listened to pens and spoons, fired a gun without a care and patiently, technically, burnt on his iron bed the symbolic image of his mother, under a stuffed kangaroo toy. Later, after a crisis of dementia, Amleto takes back his bottle and, refusing the electrical energy of the stage, lights a candle. He empties the bottle, blows out the candle, then collapses while taking aim at the maternal stuffed toy-object.

The voices in the box cry one last time ("father, I'm crying"). The play is over, the lights go out and all representation has been violently repudiated. Amleto could not take the place of the ghost-father (who he ended up putting away in the iron wardrobe) or that of his mother (even by milking his breasts in front of the kangaroo and by drinking long draughts of his own imaginary milk), nor his own place or name. He is merely a droned song, a melody that replaces his *self* before everything disappears. Amleto is, and is not: he has stayed there, on the set, without penetrating his enigma. He has danced on the iron bed without gaining access to his primal state; then, as an obsessive technician, he has only confronted a poor simulacrum of his mother. Everything else is silence.

Through this example, we can see that if performance replaced mimetic representation, and if it violated it so violently, it was not merely for the sake of doing so, but in order to demonstrate the power of non-saying and the subject's inability to constitute itself. Via the body of the actor seized by the power of the platform, it becomes possible to avoid the character, to renounce the hero and articulated discourse, to enable the spectator to see directly that the real and the virtual are confused during the ephemeral time in which she views the spectacle. This is not illusion as it has been described, or the shared belief of militant theatre, but the expression of a blurring of things, of words and real gestures that suspend the distinction between the real and the virtual, both for the actor and for the viewer. Summoning madness, autism, performing fantasies, producing discontinuous images, then amounts to setting up a true illusion, so to speak, trafficked through an infra-discourse and that, expressing itself, gains access to the universal. The problem is no longer whether Paulo Tonti resembles Horatio or Hamlet, or whether he plays the role of one or the other, or whether he can make the spectator believe that an archaic prince of Denmark, rewritten by Shakespeare, still speaks to her. The issue here is that what makes the myth of Hamlet, in other words its deep structures and its truly human mechanisms, should appear through the performance of the actor's body on this stage and that when they appear they are well recognised by the spectator in the depths of her psyche. In using the dual pretext of Hamlet and the autistic, what Paolo Tonti's body shows, with all the necessary strength and suffering, *for (or against) the spectator*, is the fear of not being able to tell the difference between the real and the virtual, and not being able to put in place the work of reason that separates them. And thus by exhibiting the body in action, the theatre has managed to bring the audience into an experiment, whether voluntarily or by force. And the fact that so many spectators judged this play to be unbearable suggests precisely that they had been seized and engaged by the inability of the stage to separate words, things, gestures, images and articulate them reasonably.

Theatrical illusion and cinematic illusion

If reality in the theatre is hard to feel, and if, on the other hand, it is ultimately the problem of the clear and distinct separation between reality and virtuality that the theatre best represents, it is an art that knows perfectly how to foster belief in a reality without even showing that this belief is difficult. For the cinema, the phenomenon of belief seems obvious.

And for the sake of clarity, and also because these two arts continually play with each other in our contemporary period, we shall address some differences in the phenomenon of belief between the theatre spectator and the spectator of the cinematographic screen.

In his article "A propos de l'impression de réalité au cinéma" ["On the Impression of Reality in Cinema"],[23] Christian Metz sums up the problem very well. What intrigues us about the cinema, is our astonishment at the impression of reality we feel. The spectator experiences a perceptual and affective process of participation:

> [The cinema] finds at first a kind of credibility – rarely total, obviously, but stronger than elsewhere, sometimes very intense overall – it finds the means of addressing us in terms of truth, in the convincing mode of "it is so". It easily yields to a kind of utterance, which the linguist would describe as assertive, and which, moreover, is more often than not taken seriously. There is a filmic mode of presence, which is largely credible. This "air of reality", this effortless grasp of perception, has the gift of drawing massive crowds, far more substantial than the ones who go to watch the latest play, or buy the latest novel.[24]

There is a *cinematic grip*, which is apparently more intense than the theatrical grip, whose foundations are psychological and that operates by directly feeling this credibility.

The issue is thus to determine what produces this sentiment and state. For Metz, the strong impression of reality in the cinema depends on the interaction between the perceived object and perception itself. Cinema, an indexical art, thus produces a strong resemblance to its real models recorded and stored on film, thanks to an accumulation of obviously recognisable indices of reality. Additionally, what distinguishes cinema from photography is movement: a feature that is entirely essential for creating another index of reality for the elements represented; an impression of the corporeality for the objects depicted;

and the perception of a present actuality. Furthermore, we know how the vision of the spectator is constructed at the cinema: by being physically placed between the projection source and the light of the screen, they are caught in a perceptual bubble, which includes them spatially in the system of projection. A sort of "real presence" emerges (exactly like what the Jesuits of the seventeenth century dreamed of in the theatre), even if it is well known that cinema always broadcasts past images.

Unlike the theatre, this movement on screen does not bring the viewer into an opposition or sort of resistance towards the cinematic bodies and objects. It may give an impression of corporeality and presence, conveying multiple indices of reality because it offers a projection of successive images, and thus an unreal presence of bodies, but none are *actually* real.

Unlike the theatregoer, a viewer of cinema is not obliged to adopt a position towards the real objects and bodies they see. They can forget the real bodies and real objects to imagine them and transfer them into a world of virtual reality, knowing that they are forever objects and "real" bodies. They do not have to negotiate the fleshly weight of actors, the materiality of objects, nor adhere to a sort of contract of conventional complicity with the practitioners, which says that one must abandon one's awareness of the stage in order to envisage the dramatic space or that one must put oneself in a paradoxical state, which is to consider both simultaneously. "It is because the theatre is too real that theatrical fictions give a weak impression of reality",[25] continues Christian Metz, and vice versa, according to Jean Leirens:

> [T]he film's impression of reality does not at all relate to a strong presence of the actor, but rather to the low degree of existence of these ghostly creatures who are moving on the screen and are incapable of resisting our constant temptation to invest them with a "reality" which is that of fiction (the notion of "diegesis"), a reality that comes only from us, projections and identifications that mingle with our perception of the film.[26]

The spectator's identification with the cinematographic spectacle is also based on the fact that there is a great deal of accumulated and depicted reality indices on the screen, that a captive perception works both through fascination of the screen and through the inclusion of the viewer in the projection bubble. It will be noted that when the cinematographic viewer is no longer in their "bubble" (when watching a film on DVD or on television, for example) the illusion tends to wane without disappearing since the other elements remain: the unreality of bodies, the index system, movement, succession of images, etc. This identification moves forward because of the way in which the spectator "yields" to the represented movement by plunging themselves into the cinema to fill a void. In other words, cinema gives an "impression of life" because it is totally virtual or "unreal", in contrast to the theatre, which, as we have seen, always remains in a world that interferes with fiction, in a real production from which the spectator and the practitioners can only leave by convention. For in the theatre, we have seen that fiction is never hermetically isolated from reality, so that there is always resistance to the participation of the spectators.

Similarly, the theatre spectator, even if caught by fiction, is not "encompassed" by the room and is thus more able than the cinema viewer to check that they are not the only one to be seeing and hearing. They are more likely to feel their own body (which, as a result, may well "resist" the fiction, consciously or not), whereas the cinema viewer will tend to forget both their body and their neighbours', to constitute (fantasise) the virtual body and the indices of reality that appear in the film, not as visual and auditory signs transmitted by light and sound but as tangible reality. Because there is no bond of flesh and no objects that ensure the passage from reality to fiction – except the screen that produces a kind of luminous hypnosis and that accompanies the viewer in this the process of captive perception – cinema can thus "disconnect" the viewer from the world while giving rise to an affective, perceptive and intellective activity that accomplishes a kind of transfer of reality.

It could therefore be said that theatre, as it is generally envisaged, is an art, which systematically works on the perception of reality and plays with it to the point of supposing that the spectator is witnessing actual events (play, presence, transformations of place) that allow her to assume that they are like fictional events. In this, the theatre is organised in a material whole that mimics the unreal, in other words a dramaturgical and scenographic construction, without ever being able to break completely with the materiality of the world of origin. We have seen that the fable on which the establishment of fiction rests, as well as the dramatic space that contains it, are indeed imaginary constructions. And it has been found that fiction, like dramatic space, can be actualised only by the intervention of concrete elements (scenery, objects, bodies, artifices, etc.). We thus go from the concrete, the real, to the abstract or to fiction, without being able to forget the concreteness of the scenic real.

Conversely, cinema is an art that systematically works from the unreal, from a diegetic construction of organised fiction, which aims to give the viewer the impression of a reality by means of the printing of images on a transparent film that the viewer can forget. This allows the spectator to conceive of another reality that seems more tangible and in which she can believe and can therefore take for reality. We go from the abstract or the unreal to the abstract, which becomes real, being able to forget the materiality of the film so as to believe that all this past construction exists in the present of vision. It is as though the spectator, not having to resist or oppose the real, is then able to invest unreality with a reality she builds as the images pass. So much so that the use of the moving image, articulated in a temporal succession and enriched by an indefinite sum of indices of reality, ends up allowing for more imagination and producing more illusion than a real and concrete production of a fiction on a theatrical stage. We might note that the cinema has enormous difficulties in making the spectator remember that there is a camera, a frame and artifices behind the reality in which they are engulfed, and thus there is a struggle to produce the sort of distance that is natural in the theatre. Consequently, it becomes necessary to invent ostensible signs and disturbance systems when one wishes to prevent the viewer from entering the image, as in Jean-Luc Godard's work, or particular narrative systems that question the viewer about their own activity, as with David Lynch.

The negative impact of theatre on the viewer and on the world

Having tried to differentiate the theatre spectator from the cinema viewer, we might now turn to more topical discourses on the impact of theatre on the spectator as an individual and as a social being. Having examined the principal aesthetic and philosophical theories of cinema, we were struck by the danger and the utility of this art. As both the history of the theatre and our current times show us, there is nothing innocent about making theatre in any given society. Taking a schematic approach, we will therefore consider some of the major positions, which characterise opinions on the theatre, of which at least two have been fixed since antiquity.

The first tends to exclude the theatre of the city, under the sheer pretext of its dangerousness. The principal readings that have been made of what Plato says in the Republic are that Plato condemns the theatre and rejects it from the ideal city on the grounds that it is not only useless but also harmful. In reality, the Republic attacks the theatre according to a very particular audience, which is that of the "guardians of the city". For Plato, "guardians" who mingle in theatre, or go there as spectators, cannot properly perform their duties. On the other hand, it is not necessary to deny access to philosophers or informed citizens who know how to be suspicious of illusions. However, what the Christian tradition has preserved from this Platonic position is the prohibition, not only for a specific group of individuals, but for everyone. The radical condemnation and exclusion of this art of representation, in the name of the dangers of illusion, is based on the fact that it is dangerous to enter into a kind of illusionist delirium that gives the impression of living emotions, or passions, and that distances from the reality of things. This moral and political position is then taken up over the centuries by all those who regard the art of representation as a lure that diverts men from the realities proper to their true action and function in the city. Saint Augustine takes up the Platonic arguments, adding that it is indeed a terrible entertainment, since it removes the spectators from the truth of God and from the only true suffering, which is that of Christ. To witness the spectacle of representation is to run the risk of believing what is artificial and false; it is to be moved to the pain of false representation and to imagine joy by experiencing feigned suffering and compassion out of context. Considering it from another perspective, Tertullian adds that if the theatre is not in itself dangerous, it is the assembly that is harmful since it groups all sorts of individuals who do not necessarily know how to read, how to interpret the signs, how to distinguish between good and evil or even how to be moved virtuously, to the point that some not only experience joy in the suffering of the characters but also take pleasure in their misfortunes, without any compassion. Finally, Rousseau, in the *Lettre à M. d'Alembert sur les spectacles* [*Letter to M. d'Alembert on the Shows*],[27] unites both of these positions in the same censure. The theatre is therefore dangerous not only because it takes men into the trap of their illusions, but also because it allows anyone to interpret its signs, posing difficult and dangerous questions to all its attendees that may threaten social cohesion.

By taking as its foundation the idea that the theatre has everything to do with plague and evil, the theatre of the twentieth century, and more particularly the theories of Antonin Artaud (*The Theatre and its Double*), reverse the argument. This position, which accepts the fact that Plato, Saint Augustine, Tertullian, Nicole, Bossuet and Rousseau are in a certain sense right to be concerned and, deep down, right about the dangerousness of the theatre, then valorises the phenomena of illusion, seduction and contagion noted by the detractors of the theatre by making them assets. Similarly, by legitimately doubting that catharsis does not necessarily have anything to do with virtue, or that the spectacle and the session cannot be seen as invariably contributing to the healthy and virtuous education of the spectators, this position takes a step away from the categories of teaching and instruction or from the narrowly pedagogical and political function of theatre. By revalorising illusion and making its dangers major qualities, theorists like Antonin Artaud magnify the powers and effectiveness of the theatrical genre by giving it an almost magical impact, insisting on the power of ritual, and making spectacular contagion the very goal of the art. It hardly matters whether this attitude incites spectators to evil or to good, since the issue is no longer to make the spectacle a useful tool, or to justify it through some notion of morality, but rather to turn it into the space that distances itself from the paths of social virtue to enter into the communal celebration of a ceremony that is beyond good and evil. Consequently, the integrative and social harmony of the representation is repudiated in the name of ritual that integrates man, not into the social structure, but into a nature that is not necessarily limited to the walls of the city.

Seduction and utility of theatre: the thorny issue of "catharsis"

The second position is marked by the need to wager on a moral theatre that is virtuous and useful to the city. This becomes a theatre of integration, and puts a moratorium on any sense of exclusion. Faced with the condemnation of the most radical theorists, and especially by those religious theorists who distrust representation from Saint Augustine to Rousseau to Nicole and Bossuet, the defenders of theatre take up an Aristotelian position (morally, politically and religiously speaking) that is then reviewed and corrected by Horacian, Thomist and Jesuit perspectives. Far from condemning theatre, it becomes necessary to accept representation, to master it, to theorise mimesis, to deepen catharsis, to domesticate and to regulate the spectacular effect. In sum, to make theatrical representation a weapon of formidable efficiency, assets for an art that must be inserted into the social world by giving it a function of utility. The attempt to rehabilitate or empower the theatre within the city is thus to ensure that the spectacle – which is known to be dangerous and can give rise to overflows in terms of illusion (believing in what is false) or in terms of reception (giving an audience the freedom to act in relation to the session offered to it) – is first controlled by a poetics whose aim is to make the spectator and the citizen more morally virtuous, and more politically integrated within the values of the city and, from the religious point of view, more able to respect the gods, or God. If the theatre is able to please, so must it instruct, as Horace declares.

By experiencing suffering when watching a performance, the spectator is somehow cured of the passions they are not supposed to act on either in the enclosure of the theatre or in the city. It is through terror and pity that this purgative function can take place. It is a therapeutic, medical, aesthetic and social wager, but also an interesting strategy to integrate an art that in any case exists in the world. By putting poetics on the front line, taking care of the composition of the text, limiting its action to catharsis for tragedy, relegating the *opsis*, the spectacle and the technique to a secondary position, filtering the audience or "training" it, it is possible to legitimise an art that is clearly accepted as useful, healthy and inclusive for all those who read and go to see it and that no longer turns authors, practitioners and spectators into outlaws. Henceforth, all the work of the various theatre professions, which we know are systematically threatened by the very radical Platonic and Augustinian positions, will be to ensure the legitimacy of their art by always claiming the utility, morality and pedagogy of their function. And the efficacy of this art, which, for Socrates, was "frightening", could be harmonised with the virtuous designs of those who insist on their social, moral or religious purpose, and who know that it is through an appropriate poetics that this goal will be achieved. And if, for the most part, authors and texts are foregrounded in this process, if the spectacle and the theatre session are most often considered suspicious, we can also suppose that the spectacle and the technique (the *opsis*) are directed towards a fixed purpose, that they capture the spectators' attention to entice them to do good, that the spectator is seduced in the name of virtue (this is the position of the Jesuit theatre). This presupposes, of course, that the audience is either selected, or so well educated that the unruliness and excesses condemned by Tertullian will not take place: it is then a matter of educating the audience prior to the event, or of policing them during the session. It is on the basis of this rare poetic and aesthetic device that the art of the theatre is able to assert its specific function without being systematically condemned and rejected, and by deepening this cathartic device at all levels (technical, poetic, ideological), by making it possible to convince those who read and see it of its usefulness, that it became an art in its own right, recognised and admitted as integrated into the city. Consequently, it is based on the theory of catharsis, which is so often evoked in discussions of theatre, that the poetic, aesthetic and even moral impact of the theatre on the spectator has been described.

One cannot at first understand how catharsis functions without relating it closely to the notion of mimetic imitation, which owes its central role in the critical tradition of theatre to Aristotle's *Poetics*. Imitation in fact translates the Greek term of mimesis. Plato already characterised artistic activity as an imitation of things, or rather an imitation of their appearance. Since things themselves offer only a degraded reflection of the idea, the work of art becomes an imitation in the second degree, an "imitation of imitation". In Book X of the Republic, he justifies his condemnation of poets on the grounds that "the art of imitation is far removed from truth".[28] If the most imitative literary form is tragedy, then it is all the most condemnable. He contrasts it with the dithyramb, a form of poetry that, according to him, is purely narrative and with the mixed genre (both narrative and imitative) of the epic. On the other hand, Aristotle exalts the characterisation of tragedy as mimesis: it produces less a copy of the real, as a story (*historia*) would do, than its re-creation in a sort of fiction (a *muthos*, i.e. a fable, but that implies the idea of a specific arrangement, of an organised configuration), which allows us to transmute emotions and thus to experience a particular pleasure in the spectacle of passions (terror and pity), which frees us from their grip.

There is thus no longer any basis for opposing narrative (*diegesis*) and mimesis: the Homeric epic also provides the example of a representation of action, certainly not by means of theatricalisation, but by those of narration. Thus, Aristotle pretends to base his poetics on a natural faculty (the instinct to imitate), which would account for artistic activity as a whole. It is thus almost a hundred years after the end of the epoch of high Greek tragedy (middle of the fourth century BC) that Aristotle expresses himself on the rules of tragedy in the *Poetics*. The "treatise" of the ancient philosopher has baffled many theorists and fostered many polemics, as soon as it was rediscovered during the Renaissance. In this treatise, the question that seems to have been most widely interpreted is that of *catharsis*[29]: Aristotle, in reference to the aims and consequences of tragedy, observes that by representing pity and fear, tragedy effects "the purification [catharsis] of such emotions"; but it can also be said that tragedy, "through the medium of pity and fear, accomplishes the purgation of emotions of this kind".[30] And in Racine's notes on Aristotle's *Poetics*, one reads that tragedy

> is not made by a narrative, but by a lively representation which, exciting pity and terror, purges and tempers these sorts of passions. That is to say, by exciting these passions, it deprives them of their excess and vice, and brings them back to a moderate state conformable to reason.[31]

Katharsis (or *catharsis*) is therefore a thorny issue. In Greek, it is a word in the medical vocabulary, which, in Aristotle's *Poetics*, has the status of a metaphor: to purify, one must purge and expel. And it is thus necessary to explain that fear or terror (*phobos*) and pity (*eleos*), which are disagreeable emotions, themselves allow for a purgation, a purification of these painful emotions, which implies an expulsion of these disturbances through the aesthetic experience of theatre. Emotions of suffering, such as fear and pity, are thus transformed into pleasure through the theatre, or else they are expelled in order to make room for pleasure. Thus, it can also be understood that this sort of identification with the spectacle corresponds to an emotional discharge that allows the spectator's sense of self to regenerate. We can see that the difficulties of translating Aristotle's ideas mean that aesthetics and ethics, or even morality, find themselves placed on the same ground. That is why we are able to appreciate the justification of the morality of the theatre (sixteenth to seventeenth centuries) in these few words: by showing the terrible consequences of terrible actions, tragedy allows us to experience the fear and pity that heals the spectator by "purging" them of all evil passions by watching this terrible spectacle. Another slightly different interpretation is that by making the spectator feel the positive passions of fear and pity, they are then led to reject the evil passions represented onstage. In the nineteenth century, we can still see the expression of a medical and moral functioning: by making us experience purified passions (which is the role of mimesis), tragedy guarantees us "full" passions, and the pleasure that is then freed up thus constitutes the relief provided by this operation. Thus, by representing crime, tragedy necessarily taught virtue. To conclude, in psychoanalytic terms, catharsis can become, in the theatre, a pleasure that one derives from one's own emotions at viewing the spectacle of the emotions of the other, emotions that can be those of a repressed or denied ego.

If we allow that catharsis consists in creating unbearable emotions and at the same time tempering them with art and clarity, we can say that tragic art attenuates emotions by favouring clarity of form and transforms them into pleasure. There is thus a paradox, since, in reality, one should die from the emotions that tragedy produces. But thanks to the art displayed onstage, the spectator does not die: terror and pity become pleasure (and "therapy"). Thus, in seventeenth-century French theatre, *mimesis* and *catharsis* are intimately linked. Mimesis allows us to see the representation of the horror and pitiful story of kings and heroes, which represents the human condition. But the spectator does not have to reproduce what the unfortunate heroes do; on the contrary,

THE BODY, THE ACTOR'S PLAY AND ILLUSION

he is able, through the functioning of mimesis, to experience emotions complementary to those of the heroes and to establish a relationship between them and him. The heroes "live" terrible and pitiful stories on the stage, commit notorious offenses, while the spectators experience the terror and pity induced by those passions they witness onstage. These must, however, be modified by an aesthetic: in this case, the art of tragedy; and more broadly, the art of theatre and representation. Tragic pleasure is thus another way to experience mimetic pleasure when looking at the images of things whose sight is painful in reality. In other words, pleasure in recognising sadness and mourning as well as a certain pleasure in discarding them while being caught up in the conversion of this vision into terror and pity. Recognition, the moment of revelation or *peripeteia*, thus has an emotional impact on the mind of the spectator, which proves to be very useful for morality. Indeed, since there is neither excessive anxiety nor unbearable horror (thanks to the seventeenth-century importance placed on plausibility and propriety), there can be reflection, understanding and conversion. Stylised and abstract aesthetics is a filter that attenuates the horror of representation and converts the pleasure of the viewer into reflection/reasonable emotion so that the goal of instruction is attained.

But the process does not end there, insofar as terror and pity, even when attenuated, do not refer to a complete and unambiguous moral lesson. The question we must pose is what is it that is added to terror and pity, so that a purgation or purification, in any case some sort of emotion, is induced? In sixteenth-century Italy, where the usefulness of catharsis was sometimes doubted, it was proposed that fear and pity be replaced (or supplemented) by horror and *meraviglia* (wonder, surprise, astonishment). France followed the practice of horror and wonder (late sixteenth to early seventeenth century), then revisited *catharsis* by adding admiration (Corneille) and compassion (Racine). Admiration for Corneille is thus a positive passion that allows the viewer to set up a modelling relationship: if the spectacle of tragedy allows the viewer to reflect on themselves, inciting them to "purge, moderate, rectify, and even uproot the passion that plunges the people [whom he pities] into misfortune",[32] the admiration of the hero's conduct results in an imitative response from the viewer. It is not exactly an identification, since there is distance and distancing, but it is a matter of the spectator imitating (in the sense of *imitatio* in rhetoric) the heroic categories proposed to them. Racine does not give a true positive horizon to most of his tragedies; rather, he incites the spectator to share the pain, anxiety, even the misfortune, of his heroes through their tears. In other words, Racine incites these emotions through the Christian version of pity – compassion. Yet, for him, there is nevertheless the risk inherent in any representation of these passions: they must fascinate the spectator to the point where they must sink into the acute pleasure of viewing evil. Thus, in the next century, the controversy continues. Rousseau, condemning the theatre, reproaches catharsis for being only a passing emotion that feeds on tears, has no positive consequences for the spectator and does not limit the dangers of the theatre. Diderot and Lessing try to prove that catharsis can transform the passions of the spectator into virtue through his emotional participation in the pathetic and the sublime. At the mid-point between pity and terror, the spectator, after having experienced the pathos of the spectacle, can find a happy medium (Lessing). In the twentieth century, Brecht sees in this emotional participation a device of ideological alienation that emphasises the apparently ahistorical values of the characters, which are, in reality, perfectly bourgeois. But we see that little by little reflection moves away from moral issues and refocuses on aesthetic problems. Goethe, in his *Proof of Aristotle's Poetics*, claims that catharsis can help reconciliation between opposing passions, but above all implies a formal perfection. Nietzsche, then, comes to a purely aesthetic definition of tragic emotion by making catharsis a means of forging "a form of superior art", by offering the viewer an aesthetic activity so that he can "reach [particular] states of aesthetic sensibility".[33]

If we take it as a given that catharsis is not ethical but aesthetic, it is clear that a more satisfactory answer can be found: when we compare this passage from Chapter VIII of Aristotle's *Politics*, in which the author affirms that the music proper to enthusiasm is very dangerous, we see that it can cause disturbance in the hearers, but that it contains in it the means of effacing these troubles, which allows the spectator to be relieved. Thus, one can conclude that tragedy makes it possible to take pleasure in images whose sight is actually painful, so that when faced with a frightening or pitiful story, the spectator experiences the same emotions, but through mimesis: by establishing an aesthetically purified, distanced relation, which allows them not to feel uneasiness but pleasure (or, under discomfort, to imagine pleasure). The distanced consciousness (the reflexive attitude) and the experienced emotion (identification) are then two simultaneous processes whose very unity is then, precisely, cathartic.

In doing so, the theatre will obviously have a function intended to celebrate common values, admitted or prescribed by dominant ideological devices, but through the same aesthetic, it will also be able to introduce poetic and spectacular means of critically reflecting on these values. And this is where utility changes its meaning: because the theatre has somehow won its legitimacy, it is now able to free itself from the primary function that made it legitimate in the first place, that of reinforcing dominant morality and virtue. On the one hand, the theatre can now turn against these basic underlying principles to occupy a supremely critical function, and, on the other hand, it can claim an aesthetic autonomy, which sets it free from the issues that threaten it. For a long time, it has been known that the theatre, which is sometimes keen on reinforcing attitudes of full integration with respect to the laws and values of the city, also questions them with the complicity of the audience, who comes expressly to play with values, make fun of them or defy them. In this context, the work of practitioners and authors consists in using the theatre to go against integrative rules, to challenge the outside by striking inside, in the centre, through the channels of representation and performance, through the most established virtues and the safest codes. And if it is necessary for the theatre to be considered by the defenders of the order as a social evil, why not admit it? Therefore, by renouncing false cathartic defences, utility and integration, the theatre proposes all possible experiments, provided they disturb and disrupt, provided that nothing solid is preserved and all questions are asked radically. This is not to suggest that it is necessary to take sides for evil, which would amount to recognising the idea of good and that of virtue, but that one must systematically resist the normative points of view on which the city rests.

It is from these great poles that we have schematically gone through here that the theatre plays with its various strategies, composes its actions, positions itself as a harmonious centre or disturbing margin or a human ceremony beyond the walls of society. It should be added, however, that the artisans of the theatre, and sometimes the authors, have no other object than to entertain and seduce by all possible means, and that the spectators have no other object than to take pleasure during the session. They admire what they are shown, compare their tastes with what the artisans of the show, including the author, propose, project themselves into the characters or make fun of them or sometimes do something quite different from watching what is shown to them. While being an art of supreme consciousness, the theatre is also pleasure without consciousness, an immediate, willingly inexplicable one.

Spectacle, reading and judgement

For the most part, Western theatre fully admits that the production of such intersecting spaces and different points of view during the time of the session, merely toys with the distinction between the real and the virtual, rather than confusing their properties. In this respect, it often endeavours to include ambiguities or porosity, without having to integrate them into any spectacular totality. Theatre is tied up with verbal and non-verbal discourse, and thus it often formulates different "cases" that carry many different points of view. It is therefore through an articulated discourse, structured as a fable represented by contradictory characters or figurations and forming a scene to be judged, that the theatre finds a centre and the spectators find a pretext for being there. The relevance of this discourse establishes the relevance of the spectacle itself: its capacity to enlarge space and its claim to express itself about this very enlargement.

Since the theatre (that is to say theatrical space, its fiction, its representation plus the actual place of the theatre) divides itself into qualitatively different spaces, and since it is invested with so many different points of view (in the fable, the contradictory characters, in the reception, instances with multiple judgements), theatre shows and realises the aesthetic, legal and social scene of the whole world, starting from a complex example. It is because it determines spatialised relations of judgement that it may be of interest, because it provides both examples of conduct (in the fable) and, for spectators, opportunities for exercising their point of view under the gaze of other points of view and in all consciousness. The centre of theatrical space is therefore truly discourse: not the discourse of the fable alone, but the sum of the discourses assembled together in the represented discourse of the fable. And if, because the code of representation requires it, a particular version or lesson is favoured by the text, the actors or a majority (or hierarchically superior) part of the audience, the configuration of places and spaces make it possible, and even necessary – authors and practitioners even foresee it – that other judgements, from other points of view, come about in full freedom from the case expected and based on the expectations of those who judge. Based on the discourse that arises from the voice and body of the actor, and based on the staging apparatus, the theatre session becomes a public stage, surpassing a mere illusory interpretative dimension and giving rise to a hermeneutic of intersecting solidarities.

The theatre would be hard-pressed to make the spectator either a receptacle of signs or a passive consumer of what is being addressed to them. The spectator actively plays a very specific role. But it also seems that the position of the spectator is not that of another actor just eager to enter the game of those she sees playing. For, sitting in reality, she is there to enjoy and to think from what is proposed to her; she is there to produce, alone among many, even alone with her fellows (the other spectators), a specific activity that is at the same time to feel, to reflect, to share, in the time of the session and beyond, the experience of being, or having been, a spectator. And she knows well that going onstage would be "something else", would imply a reversal of her function, since she would be looked at and would adapt her relationship to the theatre accordingly. There is therefore a co-presence, a physical presence between two communication partners, a close interaction, but this co-presence, this physical presence and this interaction are mediated by the construction of a spectacularity. The relationship between the actor and the spectator is thus neither a simple partnership allowing the inclusion of the spectator in the universe of the actor nor a tete-a-tete. In this respect, the spectator is a gaming partner in the whole of theatrical production, but not a full partner in the actors' game, since she receives the discourse and can only reciprocate with diffused signs of her own presence (silence, whistles, coughs, various interventions, applause, etc.), signs qualitatively different from the ones emitted by the actors. And even when the actors try to include her in their work (by direct address, by calling her onstage, or by sitting beside her), the spectator remains another, an alterity indispensable to any finalised theatrical production.

Furthermore, although the theatrical venue is a place of assembly, or session, its main pretext is the performance of a fiction that we can judge: aesthetically, we judge art; and axiologically, we judge developed ideas. Even if this fiction is followed with waivering attention, even if it is discontinuous, it deploys a series of difficult cases onstage, in front of different audiences, which give rise to rational judgements and sentiments that are animated by sensual passions and experiences. Without it even being necessary to believe in an illusion of reality, the spectator's duty to understand, to sense, to judge the quality of the actors and the spectacle, is all based on the scenarios they perceive and by believing in the space in which they find themselves.

During moments of distance and during the brief instants of illusion in which one gives in to emotion, the organisation and practice of the theatrical apparatus thus sets in place an art of judgement and of suspending judgement. Be it judgement on fiction, on the fictitious cases arranged, on the aesthetics of the stage play or on the art and artifices of practitioners, the theatre empowers the audience while it incites its passions and makes it feel, examine and express the propositions that practitioners convey to it. If this audience refrains from reacting, they do so knowingly. And in another way, those who read plays (who follow a different path, which is perhaps more intimately emotional and closer to the theoretical ideal because they do not have to consider the real conditions of representation and to take account of the achievable performance, its techniques and the social gazes of the theatre gathering) are also called upon to judge the theatre text through imagination, feelings and reason as another type of semiotic proposition. If the reader's position is more normative, because they can control the whole, it is nonetheless oriented towards judgement (whether it is one of taste, or a moral, aesthetic or political judgement). The two aspects of the theatre can thus be united under the banners of emotion and judgement: the performance, the place of viewing, the space of sociability; and the text, the site of reading.

This, then, is the main illusion provided by the theatre: the position of mastery in which both the receiver of the spectacle and the reader of the text find themselves; an *informed* and *implied* mastery that allows them to take the place of the "prince", the censor, the theoretician, the author and the actor, to form their judgements, in the midst of others, or alone, during their reading. A mastery of the interpretation of signs in the face of the mastery of the producers of signs, the mastery of the spectator in the face of the actors and what they depict, the reader's mastery of the text. Thus, everything that happens in the theatre session, including the fiction, can be a pretext for debate: open debates, since theatre is a place apart, deferred, intermediary between reality and fiction; debates on questions specific to the city, to domesticity, to intimacy, to perception, to the art that expresses them and the taste that appreciates them, but debates that can be feared when this intermediary world touches the real world too closely, or tolerated when it remains in its place.

Theatrical illusion? Isn't it more the fact that the theatre actually expresses a sort of worldly reality, that the art it develops and the judgements that take place within it exert an action outside the building? Is it not an illusion consented to by partners of an overall game, wherein the theatre provides the means of expressing a sort of power over the world? Illusory powers? Illusion of power? These questions will not be resolved here, if they can ever be resolved, but we will find that the only way to counteract the fact that the action of the theatre on the world is only an illusion, is in fact to set up a theatre that takes account of the spectators, the discontinuity, the necessity of spectacle and distance, which allows the exercise of reason, reflection, as well as feeling and sensation, in order to provide a certain space, through devices of aestheticism, for contradiction and contradictory expression.

This is perhaps the way to transform the illusion that art can act on the world as a representation of this very question. For if we do not know whether or not art has an aesthetic, social, political or ideological impact on the world, we can still contribute to representing it as such. One can contribute to asking questions of the world, even if one doesn't change it, and to disrupting its order by the implementation of another order, which is placed on the ground of aesthetics and in the social and political sphere. Thus, the fictional – case-shaped debate – can then come into contact, through its contradictory representation, and problematised on the stage, through the distanced representation of an action, through the discourse articulated in poetic form, with the real debates situated within the precincts of the theatrical space and in the social site that contains it. Thus, this representation – a pretext for the real debate – will alone be able to have an impact on the world, provided that it exceeds the space of the session. For it is the questions it raises, more than the mimetic illusion that theorists attribute to it, which will allow this overflow and extension of the field of debate.

Notes

1 Artaud, Antonin, *Le théâtre et son double* [*The Theatre and Its Double*] (Paris: Gallimard, 1938).
2 Marie-Madeleine Mervant-Roux, *The Foundation of the Theatre: Towards a Study of the Spectator* (Paris: CNRS, 1998).
3 Marmontel, "Illusion", in *Supplément à l' Encyclopédie*, vol. III (1776), n.p.
4 Furetière, *Dictionnaire universel* [*Universal Dictionary*] (Rotterdam: Leers, 1690), n.p.
5 Jean Rousset, *Le Lecteur Intime, de Balzac au journal* [*The Intimacy of the Reader: From Balzac to the Personal Diary*] (Paris: Corti, 1986).
6 "il ne faut pas, tandis qu'on les trompe [que l'esprit des spectateurs] le connaisse". F. H. D'Aubignac, *La Pratique du théâtre* [*The Practice of Theatre*] (Paris: Champion, 2001), p. 317 (original work published 1657), n.p.
7 "nous faire croire qu'au lieu d'assister à la représentation, nous assistons à l'événement même". Abbé Du Bos, *Réflexions critiques* [*Critical Reflections*], vol. I (Paris: École nationale supérieure des beaux-arts, 1993), pp. 453–454 (original work published 1719).
8 Rousset, *Le Lecteur Intime*, p. 99.
9 Ibid., p. 102.
10 Diderot, Denis, *Discours de la poésie dramatique* (Paris: Larousse, 1970) (original work published 1758).
11 Brecht, Bertolt, *The Messingkauf dialogues* [*The Messingkauf dialogues*] (London: Bloomsbury, 2002), n.p.
12 Stendhal, *Racine et Shakespeare* (Paris: Le Divan, 1928), p. 19.
13 Moliere, *L'Amour médecin* [*Doctor Cupid*] (2018) (original work published 1665). www.toutmoliere.net/l-amour-medecin.html (accessed 20 November 2018).
14 Molière, *Les Précieuses ridicules* [*The Pretentious Young Ladies*] (2018) (original work published 1659). www.lingq.com/lesson/preface-des-precieuses-ridicules-141315 (accessed 20 November 2018).
15 Anonymous, *Entretiens galants* (1681), n.p.

16 Tallemant des Réaux. *Historiettes*, vol. 2, ed. A. Adam and G. Delessault (Paris, 1960), pp. 775–776.
17 Robinet, *Lettres en vers à Madame* [*Letters in Verse to Madam*], 17 December (1667), vol. 242–255, n.p. My translation of the original: "Et cette madame la mort, / L'intendante des parricides, / Fit d'un grand nombre d'homicides / Et de tout un beau pot-pourri / En assassinant Mondory, / Qui, d'une façon sans égale, / Jouait dans la troupe royale, / Non les rôles tendres et doux, / Mais de transport et de courroux, / Et lequel a, jouant Oreste, / Hélas! joué de tout son reste. / Ô rôle tragique et mortel, / Combien tu fais perdre à l'Hôtel / En cet acteur inimitable!"
18 Constantin Stanislavski, *La Formation de l'acteur* [*An Actor Prepares*], trans. Élisabeth Janvier (Paris: Payot, 1995), p. 282.
19 Ibid., p. 281.
20 Jean-François Marmontel, *Éléments de Litérature* [*Elements of Literature*] (Paris: Firmin-Didot, 1879), n.p.
21 Stendhal, *Racine et Shakespeare*, chap. 1.
22 Artaud, *Le Theatre and Its Double*, p. 151.
23 Christian Metz, "A propos de l'impression de réalité au cinéma" ["On the Impression of Reality in Cinema"], *Cahiers du Cinéma* 166–167, May–June (1965), pp. 74–83. Reprinted in *Essais sur la signification au cinéma* [*Essays on the Significance of Cinema*] vol. I (Paris: Klincksieck, 1978).
24 Metz, "On the Impression of Reality", p. 76.
25 Ibid., p. 78.
26 Jean Leirens, "Theatre and Film", in Jean Giraudoux and Honoré de Balzac, *Le Film de la Duchesse de Langeais* [*The Film of the Duchess of Langeais*] (Paris: Grasset, 1942), n.p.
27 Rousseau, Jean-Jacques, *Lettre à M. d'Alembert sur les spectacles* [*Letter to M. d'Alembert on the Shows*] (Amsterdam: Marc-Michel Rey, 1758).
28 Plato, *The Republic of Plato*, Book X (Oxford: Oxford University Press, 1941), n.p.
29 Aristotle, *Poetics* (Oxford: Oxford University Press, 2013) chap.VI.
30 Ibid., p. 23.
31 Jean Racine, *Principes de la tragédie. En marge de la Poétiques d'Aristote* [*Principles of Tragedy: In the Margins of Aristotle's Poetics*] (Manchester and Paris: Manchester University Press/Librairie Nizet, 1959), p. 11.
32 Pierre Corneille, "Discours de la tragédie" ["Discourse on Tragedy"], in *Œuvres complètes* [*Complete Works*] (Paris: Le Seuil, 1963), p. 830 (original work published 1660).
33 F. Nietsche, *The Birth of Tragedy*, XXII, trans. F. Golffing (New York: Anchor Books, 1956), n.p. (Original work published 1870).

Part VI

THE READER OF THEATRE TEXTS

The theatre is thus an ephemeral, present event, shared by practitioners and watching spectators in a given place. A spectacle located in and carried by bodies, oral, gestural and scenographic performance, it is a specific act of aesthetic and social communication. Thanks to the historical and theoretical reflections above, we can understand how the spectacular event has been organised in certain places, at certain times, with certain bodies. We also see that from these places, from the present time of the social encounter and from the bodies of the actors, spaces, that virtual times and specific entities or identities (characters, allegories) could be created, emerging from concrete elements to engage spectators in grasping depictions or fictional representations. In the course of a social session, particular representations and depictions may be developed, which, when accepted by the spectator as conventions, allow for imaginary universes based on actions, discourses, the body and real and concrete scenery to exist virtually. The gathered spectators are then able to verify the reality of the scene, the reality of the stage, that of the actors and the sets, while at the same time considering with varying degrees of "belief" (according to the modes of representation that the practitioners employ) the virtual universe offered to them.

Consciously or not, any theatre spectator knows all this, first because they have made the move to go to the theatre and, second, because once they have entered it, they can then observe the mechanisms and processes of spectacularisation and having observed them, they can then classify, decode and reflect on their impact. Faced with those who actually perform, the spectator is the one who also engages in the activity of playing, but in a different way to them; in other words, the spectator grasps the conventions, accepts them so as to receive what they have waited for, but also transforms, perverts, moves or works on transgressing some of the expected conventions of the spectacle. What we have done so far has been merely to draw attention to the spectacle's mechanisms, to shine light on a few details, to glimpse its play and evolution and to consider them in relation to a spectator who, we suppose, is eager to understand their purpose in the theatre, and their reasons for attending. We hope to have thus contributed to the determination of some points of view, approaches and observation criteria, which may be of use both to the contemporary spectator in general, to the spectator who wishes to perform a sort of performance analysis and who seeks to explore what performances, practitioners and spectators were like in the past.

However, to limit oneself to the spectacle and to the ephemeral moment of the session is insufficient for taking into account the reception of theatre. For there is another posture, hitherto neglected in this book, which is that of the theatre reader. Here, we come to the text no longer in the position of the spectator watching the spectacle, but in the position of the reader handling the theatre book. We could not, however, begin with it, inasmuch as the theatre reader is supposed by the dramatic author to know what the scene is, to the point where it is often with this prerequisite knowledge that the author plays, in complicity with his reader. We shall now turn to this act of reading, since we have now described what the reader should know: that writing and reading serve the purpose of imagining an event, a place, a scene, a game. These are the essential prerequisites for the act of reading, so that the imagination operates based on the text that the author proposes. However, the theatrical representation cannot appear only to be the missing and long-awaited part of the theatrical fact, nor the text as a simple sketch for representation, which would be its only possible completion. And while there is often a complementarity between text and representation, reading and attendance at performances, it must be emphasised here that this supposed complementarity is in no way simple, nor even entirely necessary.

Having thus recognised that these prerequisites exist and that they compose the frames and images on which the reading is based, it is necessary to understand that these are not the only presuppositions of reading and that it is important to separate the spectator's operation from that of the reader. The reader, unlike the spectator, sees only the arrangement of words on a page (and perhaps some illustrations) and at best hears only their own voice. And if it is another voice who reads the text aloud, this becomes another sort of spectacle itself that is based on reading and representation, *a fortiori* for radio readings, which are quite particular auditory spectacles). Thus, in a time and place different from those of the spectator, the reader engages in a series of complex operations that imply a knowledge of several codes: that of the stage, as we have seen; that which governs the theatre text; and that which applies to any reading of a literary work.

The reader can take their time, organising their reading at will without having to adhere to the fixed time of speech or action at the theatre. They can also choose where to place their own body in relation to the text, rather than depending on the physical place assigned by a ticket. Finally, the reader can read what they want, and in particular a story, a fiction, the virtual event of an imaginary representation or words, the disposition of sentences, the organisation of the text. They can choose a coherence, a meaning or glimpse others, simultaneously, without being assigned to the elaboration of a staging and therefore to a transmission of their interpretations. And while following the fiction, on the one hand, and imagining the virtual theatrical event on the other, the reader gives themselves the task of ensuring that the practical and spectacular effects, which are "seen" in the mind's eye, are still moving or interesting. The reader thus belongs to all the imaginary places of the representation and the session. As an actor, scenographer, dramatist, actor, director or spectator, they intervene immediately after the act of writing and publishing, envisaging the transition from page to stage, from the place of their reading to the place of a possible stage. It is therefore on the basis of the text that virtual spaces and times are constructed, in whole or in part, efficiently or in a perfectly unrealisable way, as well as the actor's play, the conduct of the characters, costumes and clothes, the lighting of the plateau and the light that illuminates the events of the fiction. And all this does nothing to extricate the reader from a fourth operation, which appears right from the start: the manipulation of a book. Indeed, since they open an object that contains "literature" and that ostensibly has all the characteristics of a published "work" (author's name, title, volume, etc.), sentences, their literary character, their composition and the aesthetic, poetic, stylistic quality of this printed work all appear in front of the reader's eyes.

Consequently, if the reader is in charge of imagining a sort of transposition to a stage that may be either impossible or idealised, they also have an interest, as if they were reading another kind of text – a narrative, for example – in believing in the story that is proposed by the fable, to enter the writing of an adventure, and/or to evaluate, in parallel, the adventure of a piece of writing so that this readerly pleasure is complete. What the reader then discovers is that they are not reading a document, but a text; that the writing of a play obeys specific poetic and typographical rules that distinguish it from other genres, because the author also has had this double consciousness of the specificity of writing – the style, the way of composing the fable or the text, the subject, the ideological stakes of the text – as well as the transposition of this writing to the stage.

Just as there is not *one* single spectator, nor an essentialist view of the spectator, but rather many *spectators* of theatre, we can argue that there is no *one* single reader, no arch-reader, but rather a multiplicity of readers each equipped with their own specific outlook and each engaged in the various operations that have just been described. Some follow the fiction, others give themselves the right or the duty to imagine a possible or impossible staging, others enjoy writing, stylistic arrangement or constructions and dramaturgical effects and some also do all this consecutively or simultaneously, or at random, as the desire comes to them, or as determined by the particular circumstances of their reading. And the different outlooks, as well, can overlap. It should be noted, however, that the more frequently theatre texts are read, the more they take on an ordinary sort of spectatorship; the more the initial reflexes of the so-called "naïve" reader attached to the fiction, and even those of the "literary" reader attached to the text, to its own aesthetic and its particular style, are complemented by a sort of necessity to "see" the text read on an imaginary theatrical stage. In other words, by familiarising themselves with theatre, by reading and regularly attending staging as a spectator, the reader comes to adopt the attitude of a *quasi-practitioner*. This allows them to read the actual scenic indications of the text as interpretable elements in the name of a transposition to the stage. Thus, without ever renouncing his original posture, which is to follow the text as a text, fiction exposed as fiction, this same reader can play at being playwright, actor, director, scenographer, and can thus attend their own imaginary theatrical production. From then on, the reader assumes a new thrill, a *jouissance*, which is closer to that of the spectator: taking pleasure in the imaginary scenic representation that they construct for themselves with the constraints they decide to adopt. All this is obviously foreseen by the text itself, including in its typographical arrangement.

Thus, the reader opens a book and approaches a particular text. From a typographical distinctiveness (which may have changed over time and become more and more precise) that specifies the mode of reading, the reader engages in a laminated reading, follows the course of the text, imagines the author's proposals, produces, if need be, the imagination of a fiction, simultaneously stages a supposed representation and finally evaluates the literary quality of the written work according to taste and aesthetic choice.

The appearance of the book and its pages

A book is above all an object: its format, its paper, the quality of its ink, its binding are its first visible signs. One will not be indifferent, for example, that the folio format is more respectable than the quarto, the royal, the octavo or the demy, particularly when one makes sure to bind it in leather rather than printing it as a paperback. In the same way, the workmanship that produces the book will testify to its social position, to that of its author and its editor. We know how the first professional of theatrical literature, Pierre Corneille, was attentive to such things, even going so far as to visit his printer's very workplace to assess his work and to convince his bookseller of the format of his publications so as to have greater control over the impact of his works. In addition to its format, appearance and cost, a book has one or more pages that indicate the title of the play, the name of the publisher, possibly the name of the collection, its place of publication, most often (almost always now) the author's name and sometimes the genre of the play and the date of first performance. In addition, if necessary, a frontispiece (or an illustration that modern editions will also place on the cover) that already gives the reader indications about the plot, the author or the mode (traditional, distinctive, conventional) of representation of the text. The position of the words on the cover and on the first page is important and can change according to times and periods, traditions and publication intentions. Such elements inform not only how the reader chooses to read the contents of the book, but also how they begin to determine their expectations of it. But as it will be admitted here, there is no really specific difference between the general and material appearance of the theatre book and that of the novel, for example, if not from the point of view of illustration (unless one undertakes to trace the history of theatre books, which is not our purpose here), we will go directly to what distinguishes the theatre book from another book, i.e. to the presentation of its text.

What is striking in theatre texts are the spaces, the empty typographical gaps left for the eye to peruse while reading. These spaces on the page are therefore also signs that indicate the passing of time, changes of place, the possibility of an intervention on the part of the reader and the practitioners, and they simultaneously divide up the text. This division of the whole of the text into parts is indeed singular: whether it displays episodes, dialogues and choruses, as in ancient

Greece; acts as in Rome; tableaux as in the Middle Ages; circumscribed acts and scenes, as in classical dramaturgy; days, fragments, sequences, movements, pieces, parts; or whether it is given as continuous – all this according to the generations, periods of production, the aesthetic leanings of the author – the theatre text is divided according to the readerly and scenographic use that can be made of it. Opening the theatre book therefore means already engaging with a specific textual deployment indicated by the typography. The choice of the authors is then placed in reference to, or in rupture with, a tradition, but also in terms of a world of their own: they organise their writing, use typographic scansion as spatial and temporal markers, organise the entrances and exits of characters, or insert the system of discontinuity that suits them. In classical aesthetics, the decoupage ideally testifies to a sequence and a continuity barely broken by the intervals, as we have seen, and in the majority of other aesthetics (French, Spanish, English theatre of the beginning of the seventeenth century, Brechtian epic theatre, etc.), it arranges on the pages discontinuity, ellipses, an alternation that gives the reader "gaps", and therefore time, to organise their reading, since everything is not said about the chain of causes and effects, nor of the logic of intrigue, nor of the sense of history that the play records.

Moreover, the typographic presentation of the dramatic text proposes a main text, supposed to be pronounced by the actors, and a "second" text, the *stage directions*. It should be noted that tradition has made it a habit to prioritise these two texts by giving precedence to the text that is to be said out loud, while relegating how it is to be actualised onstage, according to the author, to second place. The articulated text is presented in the form of a dialogue or a monologue, endorsed in the imagination of the reader by the person who says it (for example the actor playing the character), which allows the reader to visualise the sources and to imagine how these sources are expressed. And it is on the basis of this imaginary visualisation that the reader can build, if they so wish, a particular fiction based on the textual proposition submitted to them by the playwright. The second text then allows, during the reading, an imaginary scenic update of the first. And, in general, the second text does not have a governing function since there is no theatre narrator in principle (and when there is one, the effect will be sensitive and it will be, textually, a kind of character). The scenic indications, the spatio-temporal *stage directions*, as well as the repetition of the names of the characters, the "gaps" left graphically between the utterances, the frames and notations proper to the poetic arrangement of the piece (notation of acts and scenes, for example) are, in principle, ignored by the spectator but read by the reader, which gives rise to a discrepancy between what the reader knows, what the practitioner must interpret by his *mise en scène* and what the spectators see and hear.

The so-called "first" text, the text that is spoken, will thus be the primary object for all that encounter it: practitioners, spectators and readers. And the text known as the "second", the "practical text", a scenic updating, will be that of the readers and the practitioners (the stage directions were initially intended for the interpreters). This hierarchy is quite understandable, given the history of the theatrical text, inasmuch as dramatists initially did their work (producing a text for practitioners) before selling it to others who, then, took charge of the staged realisation. There was no need, therefore, for the authors to assume functions that were not their own, and they confined themselves, alongside the composition of a recitable text, to the title, the list of "speakers" and the imaginary place of fiction. Very seldomly, discrete external stage directions would give the practitioners the procedures to follow in terms of representation (internal indications allowing one to imagine the space of fiction and the gesture of the actor are much more frequently used). The first concern of the authors was the constitution of a plot, the implementation of a poetics of the text, its stylistic realisation, while the "rest", as Aristotle said, the spectacle, was the business of those who had the function of taking care of the stage. Among the Greeks, this would be the "*skenopoïoi*", the decorators, and the "chorus-leaders", while at the beginning of the seventeenth century it would be the actors and decorators. For both aesthetic and economic reasons, the writers in charge of the text came to take a very direct interest in the representation of their texts onstage and wanted to somehow control the performance. Stage directions thus developed and in the published works one began to observe the claim of a greater authority of the author by an inflation of prefaces and circumstantial and theoretical paratexts. At the same time, theatres saw an increasingly constant presence of the authors, and finally, in the deals struck, an increasingly pressing economic demand on the part of these owner-authors of the text. As a result, artisan-actors became "actors" in the "service of the text", and all practitioners abandoned their autonomy, so that the totality of the theatrical process, from writing to staging, became controlled by the authors. The second text, reinforced by the paratexts, then began to function as an increasingly imperative injunction, and the reader themselves became influenced by this evolution during the reading. Conversely, it can be said that after a long mastery of the author, the contemporary staging of the texts of an author is no longer entirely envisaged as the actualisation of the writer's orders, but as an interpretation that can be made of the injunctions noted, an act in which the reader also participates. Thus, in view of these developments, it does not seem entirely right to speak of "first" and "second" texts, since their hierarchy varies, but rather, on the one hand, the text to be said, or pronounced, and, on the other hand, the text to be put (even imaginatively) onstage, in action and in fiction. In other words, the practical text or stage direction. A series of third texts could be added to these first two texts (the text to be spoken and the practical text): these would be composed by the dramatist, the director or even noted by the prompt in the nineteenth and twentieth centuries, by depicting the implementation and articulation of the text to be said and the practical text at a precise moment in the history of textual reading and performance. And since, as we know, writing proliferates from a publication, we must finally consider that another series of texts or para-theatrical discourses (including images) appear as soon as works are printed, at the point of contact or in parallel to what is generally considered to be the script to be played: warnings, dedications, prefaces, frontispieces and illustrations, notes, post-faces, press reviews, pedagogical texts and other plays in verse that support the author or boast of his work, which sometimes have their place in the printed work. However, the para-theatrical text also includes parodies, opinions, letters, articles and statements that analyse, defend or attack the author's work, critical texts, which will not appear in the edition (except, of course, in critical or pedagogical editions), but will nonetheless determine the reception of the text.

We will consider only the first two texts here, endeavouring to place ourselves on the side of the reader who deciphers words, typographical appearance, phrases, utterances, and who imagines the text they are reading while appreciating the literary arrangement that supports the whole.

The oral text and the act of reading

Whether we like it or not, it is evident that theatre, and very precisely Western theatre, is most often based on a literary text, which has been previously drafted and consecrated as such. Indeed, it is published before, after or independently of the performance in order to establish it as a literary monument. Consequently, if the reader decides and, *a fortiori*, if the author claims it, there is nothing to prevent the separation of the process of reading from that of the staged actualisation of the text, if only for hypothesis. It may even frequently happen that the author seeks to replace, or to complete, the traditional scenic actualisation by a personal and intimate actualisation located in the act of reading and based on a particular style and poetics. The dramatic text can then appear as an incomplete proposition, endowed with a dramaturgy in the process of becoming in which the reader must, through their own activity, intervene, one supposed to give rise to an exercise of imagination. This is not the imagination that we have already described, the practical imagination (the intimate and virtual realisation of the possibilities of staging the show in an ideal imaginary place). It is rather the use of an orality specific to the reading of the theatre text. Indeed, a book is first and foremost a particular object that one touches, that one sees, that one randomly feels, but that one does not hear. The great problem is therefore to know what voice can come out of the book, or rather how the book can bring forth something like voice, or an orality. Consequently, since in this instance, orality is a matter of a text that is inscribed on the page, it becomes necessary to disengage it both from a parasitic criticism that looks only at its authorial human origin (it is not necessarily the voice of the author) and from the way in which it would ideally be handled onstage by actors. Except in very rare circumstances, as we have seen with Diderot, the author does not intervene directly in the theatrical utterance and does not have a governing function as they would in a novel. Indeed, there is no reference to an individualised or humanised author in the act of reading a play, the author is not entitled to the "I", but simply a relation to the overarching text itself. It is important to note the marks, which constitute orality, on the basis of notions of style and tone, which refer to writing and reading that are apparently abstract and silent but ostensibly phonic, rhythmic and prosodic. One must also observe discourse markers and determine particular statements endorsed by entities, characters and/or a choral community.

Before we come to discourse markers, a few more observations should be made about the marks of orality (we refer here to Marion Chénetier-Alev's work, *L'Oralité dans le théâtre contemporain: Herbert Achtenbusch, Pierre Guyotat, Valère Novarina, Jon Fosse, Daniel Danis, Sarah Kane*.[1] The stylistic quest for orality does not limit itself to spoken language in its staged representation, but aims at the production of emotion in writing, beyond the act of reading aloud. In this sense, orality does not necessarily need real vocalisation, or any presence other than that of the reader, in order to exist, since silent reading is considered capable of giving the text all the resonances indicated by the text in its composition. It is then clear that this textual orality introduces, both formally and physically, an exchange between the textual apparatus and the body of the reader, which moves, if only by imagining or producing its own voice based on the text; so that the oralisation of the reading becomes a stage that allows the reader to appropriate the work. In the contemporary moment of the history of the theatrical text in which plot and character are effaced in favour of language – there is much talk nowadays of a "theatre of language" or "of speech" – theatricality mainly manifests itself through the oralised "language" of plays (those of Daniel Danis and Valère Novarina, for example, or of Pierre Guyotat before them), who practice the "elevation of discourse" [*l'exhaussement de l'adresse*] and the "exacerbation of the act of speech". The self-exhibition of speech, the use of oral forms, the play on rhythm, on sonorities, on the visual dimension of language and onstage directions bid the reader into an art of inner diction. According to this principle, the externalised verbal excess, cries and glossolalia of Artaud are thus replaced by the rarefying interiorisation of Beckett or Sarraute, which seeks to reinforce the intensity of verbal and nonverbal discourse through the practice of rarefaction itself. Thus, orality, as read by the reader, takes into account the fact that written speech aspires to go beyond dialogue, style, language, in a poetic and literary enterprise. A kind of use of speech, articulated around the play of sounds and rhythms and around the exploration of the poetic relationship between the signified and the signifier, would thus be manifest in the very act of reading and would give rise to a real intimate (auditory, articulatory, respiratory, temporal) practice, specific to the reception of dramatic writing. In presenting a particular text, which poetically explores the foundations of language and speech, the theatre manages to programme the effects of orality, placing them in the ear of the reader, in their silent voice and in their mind. *Speech, therefore, already takes place in reading*, even before its actualisation, since the reader is, in a sense, forced to articulate silently and to hear those silent voices, which are poetically inscribed in the text they read.

By approaching the act of reading as it is programmed by the text – in the same way and perhaps even more so than in the act of staging – one can go beyond the opposition between text-centrism and staging-centrism, since it is a matter of showing that the text invites the reader to be something other than a pseudo-practitioner. Thus, while we can observe that authors, through the textual effects they employ (orality, rhythm, style, prosody, didascaliae, etc.), enable the reader to imagine a proper staging, which is a first step, they do not just place them in the role of a future practitioner. One could cite Kleist, Claudel, Genet, Koltès as great practitioners of "invisible theatre": inventors of visionary theatrics that exceed and repudiate the staging habits of their time but who also craft, particularly, the literary marks of orality in the theatre text. What is more, these authors simultaneously refer the reader to the possibility of an individual and ideal setting *and to its impossibility*, by substituting a mode of reading for a mode of oral, visual, spatial and gestural expression that is always limited and qualitatively different. The twist achieved through writing, and that enshrines the gap, however imaginary, between the textual and oral orality of the stage, presupposes a shared enterprise between authorial and readerly functions. And, at the same time, it can evidently allow, as *another* possibility equal to the reading of the text, its staged actualisation.

This is why the reader's job is not just to imagine a staging or different stagings from the text proposed, but to physically and mentally work on reading the text according to its phonemic qualities, on rhythm, prosody and tone, to find a meaning or a series of meanings. In other words, the reader takes part in a figural interpretation of the words and the overall movement created by the text on the page. Orality, far from being only the compensation of the lack of a voice, a body and a space in writing, is also the production of another voice and another way for another performance of the text. This space is not the same as the space between text and stage performance; rather, it is the specific space and time of the reader's reading, and thus another apparatus that is both abstract and bodied. For the means deployed by textual orality are not only intended to realise the potential or habits of actors and practitioners, they also signal that a specific readerly reception is possible outside of performance, from an articulatory respiratory, temporal, audio-visual point of view, at least. Given the same rhythm, the same phonetic proposal, the same prosody, the same style, the practitioner (i.e. the spectator) and the reader are separable because the sonority of speech may give rise to various theatricalities: the theatricality of performance and the theatricality of reading.

It thus behoves us to also speak about this theatricality as not necessarily committed to a real performance, one that can overlap with or pre-empt performance, but that attempts to exclude it, at least hypothetically, during the time of reading. Now this theatricality does not necessarily refer to the imagination of an unlimited fictional space, as does the novel, nor only, as we said, to the practical imagination of an implementation on an imaginary stage. Another dual intention of the theatrical text thus appears: not only a staging intention (in which the text is always more or less the orphan of space, bodies, voices, performance and the audience) but also a readerly and linguistic intention, silently vocalised (or not, in the case of a reading out loud), and present (since the text becomes no longer a past fiction but a present textual performance).

By relying on the fact that reading has specificities that performance does not – stops, flashbacks, replays, acceleration, leafing, cursive reading, distraction, not to mention moments of interruption, comment or complete – the activity of the reader can thus be absolutely present. But it can also allow for a time dilation, and through stops and breaks, for moments of reflection (and self-reflexive moments) in which one examines one's own reception, during the time it takes for such a reflection to occur. Therefore, sounds, images and text offered to the reader may range widely depending on reading habits and the intentions specific to each reading. The text resonates while the reader, caught in this resonance, *reasons* based on the orality that is observed and *felt* in each reading. In this case, orality becomes the focal point of meeting from which a textual theatricality is possible. Consequently, through orality itself, reading no longer appears to be the only chance to imagine a perfectly proper staging and comply with aesthetic canons, as d'Aubignac would have it, but as an access point to aesthetic, mental and physical realisation, by the reader, of a theatricality that is an alternative to the theatricality of the stage. Note also that it even happens that practitioners (Stanislas Nordey, for example) aspire to preserve or integrate into their live versions – even if this means thwarting expectations of traditional theatricality – "something" of the fun of a first reading, the memory of a specific practice, which is that of the reader. Thus, as a space for nostalgia, the stage can also sometimes chase after this "orality" and after this relationship to the *text*.

Evidently, this theatricality is intimate, specific to each reader, perhaps mysterious and therefore difficult to observe or theorise. However, critics and the reader themselves can at least describe the access points, and all the more so when they are claimed or ostensibly prepared by the author. One should note here that these access points vary from author to author but that they are nevertheless linked to a period, i.e. they can be historicised based on the modes of expression, styles, tone, rhythm and prosody that they institute or to which they conform. It is as if that figural meaning, which is given as an overarching mode of production of meaning could be described based on the texts, according to their configuration and their historicised organisation. Thus, parallel to the history of theatre considered as the history of live performances, it is possible – abandoning the idea of a normative or essentialist reading of the theatre – to establish a history of the readings of theatre. For writing bears temporal markers, thanks to which it is subjected to lexical, phonemic features, to standards of punctuation and to other specific constraints. Consequently, we observe that Molière and Corneille share commonalities with respect to writing material, style, setting and the codified staging of the theatrical text, and some critics who are lexically myopic and naively scientific can therefore confuse them (by serving up old and worn material, or through hocus-pocus of the kind advanced by Pierre Louÿs, who claimed that Corneille wrote Molière's plays). Both are products of the same time, did similar studies, experienced the same type of theatre and included in their text the same orality and even the same theatricality. Except that the oral tradition of Molière is profoundly spatial, it is always in the play of the actor, while Corneille's functions in a close relationship with the reader, as distinct from the listener. One can still note the specificity of the lines of Racine and their punctuation, which, through natural phrasing, suggests a particular play to the player, or notice the phrasing of Claudel's verses, which are all signs of orality for reading, etc.

Finally, orality or, rather, points of orality recorded in the text, are also observable signs of the emergence of a speech in the subject of writing. Beyond the notion of character, or, in contemporary theatre, refusing the notion of character, speech is then expressed without the intermediary of fiction, as a second or interstitial, autonomous language, based on elaboration of a figural meaning that has its own codes, its specific operation and performative strategies. For without recourse to the fable and having eliminated the character, the dramatic text becomes a craft of communication, about the pragmatics of speech and language(s). Current events show that many of the theatrical texts that end up in the hands of readers are not written based on a traditional "dramatic" dramaturgy. So, we can distinguish what we can still call "plays", based on a "dramatic" design, from certain texts "written for the theatre" that function at the borderline of theatre. To take an example, we can say that Noëlle Renaude's *Ma Solange, comment t'écrire mon désastre, Alex Roux* [*My Solange, How Do I Write You my Disaster, Alex Roux?*], is part of the latter. This text is placed beyond the limits of what can be called a play, strictly speaking: a text that can certainly claim to be "theatre", but that is not based on an organisation of action or even actions.

In this sense, part of contemporary writing produces a kind of verbal laboratory that contributes to the constant search for the conditions of a drama in the making. We can thus observe the verbal creation proper to each writer through the emergence of language and the manifestation of his peculiar orality. The reader is faced directly with a language, which they should voice silently (or aloud), decrypt, then own, so as to consider, if they wish, its origin, the author-function inscribed in the title. Lexicon, rhythm, prosody, phonemics, specific language, must then be taken by the player and recorded in their body, so they can chew the sounds and words they read. Thus, we can say that Novarina assigns the reader a sort of mastication that is geared towards the lexical and phonetic origin of words that gush forth, which makes him recognisable on the one hand, and, on the other, will place the reader in a position of interacting with the text in a particular way, as a participant in the primordial magma. And we can understand that Guyotat causes the reader to prostitute themselves by selling out to the hyper-sexed words and sounds of the orality of *Éden, Éden, Éden*. Thus, by excavating spectacle in the interest of their dual relationship, the author and the reader communicate both physically and directly through the orality of the text. Finally, when Michel Vinaver in his *Écrits sur le théâtre* [*Writings on the Theatre*], in 1982, said, "I have begun to think that what I do is a theatre of listening rather than a show, a theatre that has not found a director interested in overturning hierarchies and foregrounding the auditory dimension",[2] one must believe and follow his work not only for the semantic, political and social effects it offers, but also for its sound effects. In this way, the reader is directly involved, both as a producer of possible sounds and as auditor of these sounds. Therefore, the reader can simultaneously see and hear *Les Huissiers* [*The Bailiffs*], *Iphigénie Hôtel* or *Les Voisins* [*The Neighbours*], while observing that they are reading the polyphony of writing (multiple writing that tries to take the whole world into account) and the sound or musical polyphony of words, lines or characters that also aims to exhaust all the sound resources that the world and language have to offer. It is therefore in reading that sounds and meaning are placed into contact.

> The first site of theatre is the blank page where the author, from top to bottom, aligns utterances by writing by hand or machine.
> [...]
> Throughout the writing of my plays, no event has undermined this certainty, i.e. the primacy and autonomy of the text with regard to representation, the absence of any difference in kind between a play and other literary forms – poem, novel, essay. What mattered to me above all was that my texts can be read.[3]

Doubtless, in these assertions by Vinaver, there is a kind of defence of theatrical reading and, at the same time, the realisation of an old dream of literary theatre, which, here, acquires absolute legitimacy. This theatre, which since Aristotle has always been wary of representation and of the audience, finally triumphs. This is why it seems first of all necessary to distinguish *mise en scène* from reading, because *mise en scène* — this is its function — removes or minimises the author (or text) as much as the consideration of a reader, always given as secondary, chronologically or hierarchically, with respect to the practitioner/audience relationship. Thus, the *opsis* and the spectacle, which routinely represent the orality of the text through their own orality, presence and action, are elsewhere. There is therefore no reason to speak of a supposed inadequacy of writing when emphasising orality or the performance, or conversely, to be indignant at a supposed dominance of the written over the oral when actors are meant to serve the text and theatre is treated as literature. On the contrary, it seems that one must distinguish the principle of reading from that of the staged work, as well as the role of the author and their impulse in either endeavour, so as ultimately to put reading and performance in a head-on opposition for reasons that range from the aesthetic to the Homeric struggle between authors and actors and the struggle between living spectacle and reading.

Literariness, utterance and dramatic reading

While it is necessary to consider that the first attitude that the presence of a text requires is reading, i.e., a way of relating to the page, to the written word and to the sequence of words, organised in a particular way and giving rise to an understanding and an overall interpretation on the part of the reader, we can also agree — but without absolute necessity, as we have seen — that this reading undertakes, in the case of the theatre text, to virtually actualise the text in a space, in time and according to the conventions that the reader already knows at the time of reading.

The fact remains that this work, which is, in principle, to be spoken, recited, made actual by a body with a voice, a breath, an expression, a natural rhythm, is also a literary work and often poetically written. The activity of the player, again, lies in-between in a constant game of back and forth between all the specific pleasures experienced in the reading of a literary text and the job that renders this text actual through bodies; between the observation and sensual evaluation of the poetic enterprise and its physical implementation, between the written words and their possible phrasing. It is therefore based on the particular form of the theatrical text, both typographically and generically conventional and individually practised by the author, that the reader will build up their reading. Thus, they will observe the conventions as they are performed by the text, enjoying the way the author individually appropriates the specific constraints of the theatre by means of their own style. Simultaneously, the reader will propose a series of interpretations and singular appropriations based on their reading, but also based on what they know or want from the theatrical experience.

By opening the theatre book, the reader is faced with a private statement of the practical conditions of enunciation. And as we have already we said, the reader must both imagine these special conditions by linking them to a possible session, all the while taking into account the conditions of reading itself. However, because they are able to observe a discursive whole present in the text, the reader is far more able than the spectator to observe that this whole is organised by an author (an author-function, not necessarily a particular author). Thus, initially, the reader reads a sum of orders written by an author ("I must say this, do that") that helps to activate the imagination and, of course, to indicate to future reader-practitioners what they should say and do.

But if the entire text (both the text to be said and the stage directions) functions as a long series of injunctions to the reader, the source of these injunctions is not indicated by the speech given, but is usually specified on the title page (where the author's name appears) or in the paratext. Even the stage directions, which can appear as mere authorial indications, are usually written in the impersonal mode or given as a kind of account of what the entity that speaks does, or should do, both in the staging space (the actor) and in the dramatic space (the character, for example): they are the imaginary conditions of registration of the speech onstage and the conditions of exercise of this discourse. The reader then sees immediately that this is not a text literally supported by an author, since the author does not intervene through their own name. And it is this diffraction, or elision, of the source of transmission of the message, this masking of ostensible authorial intention, which allows the speech registered on the page, and the commands contained therein, to be delegated to entities that operate multiple heterogeneous relays between author and reader. Such various, multiple entities are supposed to speak for the author, without the visible mediation of the latter (since they hide behind given orders). The reader therefore faces a block of text, a literary text with its own specific poetic totality, to which they may assign an individual style, a series of meanings, as with any literary text. But the reader also faces a text that is clearly fragmented and that shows, typographically and otherwise, that it is not individual or individualised, even when only one person writes it. And it is in this sense that the written speech digested by the reader supposes three levels of interpretation: simultaneously attributed to an issuer-author, an actor or a virtual entity that can be a character. We must therefore read the theatre while also becoming aware that the diffraction of emitters (or senders) also implies a diffraction of recipients. That is to say that the reader is essentially a diffracted subject. First, the speech of the author is addressed to the reader of a text that is taken to be a literary and fictional whole and to the future reader-practitioner who has the job of making it representable: in this, the author gives instructions so that both, united in a single "person" ("the" reader), create a fiction that is imagined to be directly represented by a series of characters (or virtual talking and moving entities). But, simultaneously or consecutively, the reader can see that it must be a fiction that encompasses the speech given to actors who, along with practitioners, have the charge of depicting the dramatic fiction and the interactions between characters (or virtual entities that speak).

In the same way that the author, when they write a play, is no longer the only emitter, the reader is not the only recipient, or rather becomes someone who is diffracted and occupies several places allocated to several different recipients (themselves, the practitioners and "an" imagined audience of spectators). Thus continuously throughout the activity of reading, the reader will be caught in this network of communication and play with the polyphonic score of the theatrical text.

However, for the convenience of analysis, we can distinguish two major speeches that, as we have seen, can intermingle. There will be the author's text, written as a series of orders for future reader-practitioners, which is to indicate what is to be said or done on the site of a stage. And once they grasp this first code, the reader may consider that the author's discourse no longer refers to a series of orders for staging, but to the discourse of fiction, to virtual situations acted out by virtual entities: to a fiction in which a group of characters, for example, take part, these characters being supposed to articulate an autonomous speech in an autonomous space (dramatic space). And this discursive group itself will diffract into a series of discourses autonomous with respect to each other and interacting with each other.

The author's text may therefore be called the discourse of the staging space, or the *scenic text* (stage directions), and the seemingly autonomous discourses articulated by talking entities, the discourse of the dramatic space or the *dramatic discourse*. Between the scenic text, which gives the author's orders for representation, and dramatic discourse, which proceeds *as if* there were no orders, since entities, time and spaces are presented as autonomous, one can glean the hidden presence of the "author". Because the author is a mandatory presence, it is they who produce the staged representation and the establishment of a fiction that presents itself as autonomous, but also because their presence is hidden, or simply proposed, the author also leaves a game for all those orders to be performed, in whole or in part, by the reader's imagination and of future reader-practitioners. The author's text thus functions like a series of orders with which one cannot entirely comply or, in any case, with which the reader, like all practitioners, can play.

Thus, when receiving the speech of the characters (or talking entities), both reader and spectator should not believe that one dramatic appearance or another has a psyche and a life of its own, but rather that it is a construction addressed to them, as well as at the same time to various other recipients, through different discourses: that of the author, the actor and practitioners, the imagination. The attentive reader should not be able to believe, in principle, that this construction of speaking entities, or characters, has an action that is independent from that of other discursive constructions, since this textual construction written by an author is geared towards determining a set of interactions, not between living individuals, but between written discourses within a controlled poetic structure. The nature of each type of discourse and of each of the speaking entities that articulate it, is thus only to fulfil a function that is specific to the information it must provide about what it represents in the fable, and to the action it is supposed to do and say relative to other entities or characters – thus, to the communicational situation in which it is placed and to the emotion it should give the reader. And, at the same time, this discourse still carries a general poetics of communication specific to the piece of writing itself, which is essentially connected to the author.

Yet even if this discourse written to be spoken is fundamentally heterogeneous in its function, its construction and its communicative intention, the transition to dramatic speech that occurs through the medium of characters in Western theatre is, as we have already seen, based on a denial of the heterogeneity that we have described, in favour of creating a fiction in which one is meant to believe that the character is a person, that they are autonomous, that they have a biography, a psyche and that they live before and after the discourse that the author wrote. In short, that they have a soul. It is often by relying on this belief that actors are able to analyse their role, develop their psyche and mine their own experiences to fully "get into character". So why should it be different for readers, if they so wish, since the idea of dramatic theatre, commonly practised by authors and practitioners, invites them to do so? We might conclude from this paradoxical development that the reader, like the spectator, albeit at different levels and different rates, are subject to the same processes: believing or not believing;

knowing that the play is originally a text or a series of theatrical techniques; and *yet* thinking that there is good reason to give oneself up to a virtual world that is not totally demarcated from the real.

The dramaturgical work of the reader may therefore confer a dynamic on to this textual body and pull together the major lines of interpretation capable of producing the individual pleasure of the simple reading of a literary work, the pleasure of supposing that the world of fiction that is read refers to a world of "virtual and real" people in which they can see themselves and the imaginary construction of a possible staging. But for this readerly work to operate, there needs to be a desire and an evaluation: a recognition of the text as potentially able to provide the main material of this business. Thus, in most cases, the reader will evaluate the text based on its "literary" quality – this often depends on taste, the aesthetic values in the text, as much as on the stylistic, individual work that the author has provided – as well as on what they make of the possible conditions of a practical staging of any kind. Because the reader is faced with a written art, they will conduct an assessment of the literary quality of the sentences, the rhetorical devices and their treatment according to the qualities they can attribute to the writing. These will differ according to various parameters ranging from taste to convention, from the pleasure of transgression to requirements of social utility, from assessment of an individual aesthetic to that of an ideological commitment, etc. The text will also be judged according to the way in which the reader can imagine the theatricality. So, the reader, who can obviously allow themselves to be guided by the fiction that is written on the page, or even by its poetic form and textual orality, is also able to imagine the simultaneity of the signifying chain of the words they read and the opportunity to put phrasing and words into action as part of a practical theatrical process. We must therefore take into account the fact that the theatrical text is read based on a series of aesthetic poetic and stylistic requirements, which derive from literary requirements, with regard to the necessity of imagining its actualisation in a place of staging as it may be conceived by the reader, and also with regard to its specific import in terms of writing, fiction or fable. For what seems most often to link these different approaches is the contact with the fiction proposed by text; a contact that the reader has chosen to appropriate from a given text.

Haphazard reading and the reading of a story

We have seen above that reading consists both in being captivated by fiction and in carrying out a dramaturgical reading based on the text, a spatial and chronological institution of, as Patrice Pavis was said to have put it, the events that form the backbone of the story represented. Through the filter of the dramatic text, the reader will assume that a narrative exists, or can exist, and that it depends on what the reader makes of it or on what they choose to read. And that's the whole point of reading. There is no absolute truth in dramaturgical reading, no more than there are true or false ones, but readings made based on spatial, temporal, event-oriented or logical signs that structure the story written by author.

Nevertheless, these signs do exist. Neglect is not only ridiculous, but inconsistent, since it is on them that dramaturgy should be based (even if it involves abandoning them or contradicting them). While there is no absolute truth, there is still the possibility of errors of reading, of being blinded or producing misinterpretations. However, after observing the objective elements arranged in the text (the signs of place and of time, the events and the logic of the text), the reader can perfectly cultivate the principle of error, blindness or misinterpretation, except that it is essential that they do so knowingly.

In addition, if one agrees that reading, once informed of all this, may wish to separate itself from the objective cognition of these elements, it must do so in such a coherent way that its interpretative choice can be considered sufficiently legitimate (though going against the instructions given by the text). This is why the first stage of reading is to make textual signs intelligible and place them in a narrative chain that mirrors the act of reading. The reader organises a decryption strategy by building a different kind of "text" using codes (implicit rules that control reading, representation and dramatic writing at a given moment), depending on the objective elements identified and on what is already known about the play (title, author, date, genre, etc.). Another reading can then be determined based on elements that the reader wishes to focus on, and/or based on the potentialities that they attribute to the text. And it is this set of facts, placed against the background of his different motivations and desires, which will lead to one or more personal interpretations.

For example, how does one read Molière's *Misanthrope*, or rather, what do we read when we read the text? Is it the story of a man who hates all mankind, and who passionately loves one who represents what he hates most about this humanity? Is it that of a moraliser who has no ability to manage himself? Is it that of a prude who ends up marrying the one she does not love, pitted against that of a coquette who marries no one? Is it that of a poet sufficiently convinced by the necessity of his art and by his ability to write to the point that he is ready to fight in court for the recognition of his true value? Is it that of a ridiculous and untalented poet who wrongly places poetry in the domain of justice? Is it that of a man being sued by a villain who never appears? Is it that of a society of young people without fathers, who do nothing but spend their time minding appearances? Is it that of a young man similar to his peers but who seeks to distinguish himself from them and who wants to *be* whereas everything in the world obliges him to *appear*? Is this a story that shows in five acts that it is better to tolerate the world instead of trying to make it perfect? Is it a moral comedy that stigmatises social vices, representing them in turn in the form of disjointed pictures? Is it a comedy about an honest and sincere man who is punished for being so because he is in a society that admits neither honesty nor sincerity? Is it a clinical analysis of passion, of the appetite for totality, of the mania of wholeness? Is it that of Molière who, through his comedy, transcribes his own life? Is it that of a young, rich and beautiful widow who seeks at all costs to remain in command of the small world she has been given and that she governs? Is it that of young courtiers who take revenge on this feminine authority by using its own power against it? Is the establishment of a relationship between those who want the widow to marry (men) and a womanly character that wishes to remain as it is? Is it the development of cross-relationships between types and characters that imitate each other? Is it the contrast between a dynamic of speed and movement, embodied in the male characters, and a desire (embodied by a female character) to simply last and remain onstage? Or is it the path taken by an actor who, in five acts and for a few hours, plays on the stage: who comes onstage saying he will only play if others leave, and, since they do not, leaves the stage at the end of the play? Or is it a story that we have already seen staged by Vitez with a distancing wig; by Engel, in a carousel with real horses; by Lassalle, in an intimist stage design; or by Braunschweig, with a bed and mirrors and that we would still like to imagine otherwise? These are only minimal questions that the reader may randomly ask themselves, and that it is absolutely necessary to reckon with if one wishes to establish some criteria of observation.

As we will have seen in this attempt at a general overarching reading, the first trend – which is perhaps not surprising – is to personalise the story, to divide it up character by character, without considering that the theatre is a system of interaction and the progressive development of a dramatic action. The second trend is to favour the plot, that is to say, to place oneself in the middle of the fiction, whereas it is imperative to take into account, first of all, the dramaturgical apparatus and the structure that produces it. The third trend is to mix everything, because a reader is perfectly free to do so. We shall confine ourselves here to categorising the issues based on possible reading criteria and to placing them into critical systems capable of making them work effectively. This merely reflects a concern for simplification and clarification of motives, but it is important nonetheless. We shall take as a point of departure what we have considered to be objectively observable criteria: spatial and temporal signs, ones relative to the event, discursive volume (the number and the importance of utterances) and the logic between them. Clearly, in principle, the text provides sufficient guidance to the reader so that they know where and when what is presented onstage takes place, what happens and with whom, according to what sequence of actions and speech: it suffices, after all, to follow the text and make the most precise observations possible. A second undertaking, and that is more complex, will be to determine how all of this is organised, according to which poetic and stylistic principles. Finally, and even more complex, there will be a point at which one considers why and for what purpose this whole was constructed, published and laid before the reader.

Places, spaces and the reader's time

The reader, by definition, has their place and time of reading, which are specific and that they organise as they wish, which gives a unique dimension to the theatrical: the private appropriation of places, spaces and times (scenic and dramatic) through the "real" time and place of reading. The time and place of reading may be single or plural, continuous or discontinuous, according to the will of the reader and the "accidents" of their own affairs. We deduce that this specific dimension implies an added distance, and an added play of appropriation, specific to personal reading, which obviously goes towards greater individuality. The reader is not "one of several" – even if they think they are by "being transported" by their imagination to a theatre or among actors or characters. No, they are alone before the book (unless they share the reading with others, which is already a *performance*). It is therefore crucial to analyse the reading process, not to describe all possible approaches, or all possible accidents, which would lead nowhere, but to see that there are many levels of places and times of reading. The first level is the "real" reading where the reader is alone with their text in one or more places that can sometimes change, depending on whether the time of reading is continuous (which is rare) or discontinuous (which is most often the case). It is an intimate process, individual, most commonly fragmented and subject to History. Indeed, to speak of the reader is not necessarily to speak about oneself or to speak about a contemporary reader, but about all the possible readers of a text from its first publication (and perhaps even before, if one follows what Borges says, but that is another matter). Just as one cannot speak of the spectator in general, but of spectators based on their individuality, on the place, the time, conventions and ideologies that they have at the time of the session, we must speak about the reader in the same way.

However, because it is important here to generalise the position of these individual readers based on the observation of this complex art that is theatre, we now come to the other levels of reading, which are more theoretical. As we have seen, while in their individual and historical places and times that can be analysed from the perspective of various practices, readers must deal with texts that contain a second level of interpretation, which is the fictional now, the place and the time of the stage, and a third level, which is the dramatic space and time. And here, the process is different from the process that defines the position of the spectator, since the reader envisages the work, sensually, via a page and a text, considering the reading of dramatic space and time, as recorded on the pages based on the fiction that is written there, and imagining, at the same time or consecutively, the second level, which is that of the performance place and time, or the place and time of a possible session.

We have already seen that, from the outset, the spectator faces a performance area, they are caught in the session time, and when the performance is set in motion, they are transported to a dramatic space and time through a series of techniques that help them believe in the illusion. So, while they enter the process offered by the theatre, they simultaneously see actors, machinery, spectators at their side, hear the text and, also, as one among others, they see and hear the characters, and "enter" into a virtual world. On the other hand, the reader, when they open the theatre book, cannot initially imagine the *mise en scène*, because they are alone, because they are not in a place of theatre and because they are primarily dealing with an author's literary, poetic and dramatic construction: with fiction or the written matter of the text. The reader is therefore dealing with another Freudian *fort/da* effect, since they are participating in the fiction and in a staged actualisation through reading, and simultaneously, clearly all they are reading is a page with printed letters. The reader is fully aware that these are typographic signs, yet they can "believe in them", not because others develop before them a technique, but because they themselves create, through a mental technique, the means by which to believe in the fiction proposed. And, simultaneously, they will have a perception of the text that is "felt" and appreciated, of the fiction imagined and conceived, and finally, of the possible *mise en scène* that they can envisage in a practically imaged time and place. Then the reader may also, if they want, "dream" or build a practical technique capable of transforming the spectator and practitioner, with all the tricks they desire. Thus, guided by external indications (stage directions) and internal ones (in the speech of the characters) provided by the author, the reader is able to get a sense of dramatic space and times in which the author registers the deployment of text, action and speech distributed into blocks of characters, or into talking or moving entities. And while imagining dramatic space and times, the reader remains invested in this moment of reading (i.e. in their real position, which is that of observing printed words on paper). But still, even through rudimentary concepts of the habitual conventions of theatrical staged performance theatre, the reader can produce, individually and for personal pleasure, a link between the imaginary space and the performance space – imagined at another level of imagination which may be termed "practical imagination" – of a possible representation. The reader will then be between the time and space offered by the dramatic fiction (such as they are to be imagined), the imaginary place and time of performance that they *practically* play at reconstituting or anticipating, and the "real" time and place, in which they find themselves before an open book and a literary text. Once this process has been described, we can deal more quickly with the material appearances of places, spaces and times in the text, since these have already been mentioned.

The indexical reading of places, spaces and times

We have shown that space and time are essential elements of the theatrical event itself. But they are also crucial elements for organising and informing the reading of the theatrical text. Accompanied by action and speech – that situate the movement of the body and voice in space – space must thus be voiced and read, which is not a simple matter. Space and action, in texts, cannot always be ostensibly indicated by the author: staging indications are few in number compared to the plethora of descriptions in a novel. Every stage direction, which works as a call to the reader's imagination, will have an impact and will allow for an immediate personal representation. It also facilitates the possibility of representation for practitioners. It bears noting as well that the events that happen offstage are featured in the text through long narrative accounts, stories, descriptions and signs bodied forth by the characters.

The markers of space and of staged and dramatic action can thus be spotted in the spoken text itself (spatialisation through dialogue, through internal stage directions, as in the line, "Take a seat, Cinna"), and in the stage directions – the external stage directions that, in principle, are not spoken onstage, but that one may sometimes hear or see through projections or signs in some stagings. These provide more or less precise stage directions: rare and imprecise in the classical theatre, more voluminous and close to the genre of the in bourgeois or romantic dramas, designed to be interpreted and adapted in other texts, highly accurate and long in the work of Beckett (even constituting the whole work, with no spoken text in *Acts Without Words*). They comment on the actions and allow us to imagine the way place and space are filled, such as "pacing", for example. From the first stage directions ("*the scene takes place in* . . ." is the minimal element, which, naturally, can be significantly expanded), the reader has to imagine a dramatic space from the external stage directions, the internal indications and from the conventions that they know (type of location, type of theatre type of show, genre, etc.). The inscription of external stage directions, most often in italics, allows for the reader to make an immediate distinction between the text that is spoken and the accompanying text: *exit* indicates the movement that the actor should have; just as *furiously* or *drawing his sword* do as well. That is the conventional rule of which we can conclude that the stage directions are both intended for the reader considered to be a future practitioner (they relate to the place, the stage time and the type of acting to be adopted), but also to the reader of fiction (they concern the dramatic space and time and the action of the characters).

But other indications, closer to novelistic markers, such as "*this is a villain who speaks*" in *Tartuffe*, are more equivocal and presuppose an interpretation, which is sometimes different, on the part of the reader, actor or director. Similarly, while in principle the indices cannot describe intimate thoughts, render an interior monologue or reveal feelings, we will often initially find indications of the physical manifestations of these situations (*thoughtful*), or sometimes a kind of novelistic inserted passage (such as in Diderot's plays), which helps the reader, but makes the actor appear thoughtful. Finally, based on tradition, the internal directions contained in the spoken text ask the reader to imagine (and the player to act out) a particular action when the text is spoken ("Are you crying, Madame?"), but can sometimes operate by recurrence or prolepsis: a line can thus describe, in a subsequent scene, the attitude or gestures that a character ought to have played before (this is recurrence); and, conversely, we can read, thanks to a line, what a particular character will or will not do, or what he or she will have to do (prolepsis). The line "You are crying, it seems?" addressed to Sganarelle by Molière's Dom Juan indicates such a bias towards a specific, and also problematic, action to be adopted by the valet-actor before the line is said. And while we see, especially in the theatre of the eighteenth century, with Diderot, and the twentieth century, with Beckett or Genet, how stage directions become extended and sometimes take on a veritable poetic dimension, we can agree on the fact that they are also there to control and direct the actor's play and the spectator's reading. All this seems to suggest that the writers, recording this information, seek to retain control of their text onstage – a text that is no longer theirs – or to limit the interventions of the reader's imagination and that of the practitioners. Genet, for example, continued to rewrite his dramatic texts by developing this kind of second text, by building on Blin's *mise en scène*, but complementing or contradicting them, through these interventions. Conversely, an abundance of stage directions, particularly when they become ambiguous, impossible to "see", or problematic to play, render reading more complex and require the reader's active interpretation. That said, the stage directions are only guidelines, proposals, often simple and sometimes ambiguous ones, made by the author of the text and addressed to a reader with whom he has a relationship (which can, for example, in the case of Beckett or Genet, be ironic), and do not necessarily require (particularly in contemporary staging) the actor to play in a specific way, nor necessarily the reader to follow the author if he takes the position of a quasi-practitioner. This is where so-called "naive" reader, who follows the text word for word, applying in his imagination the indications produced by the author, is different from the reader-practitioner who establishes a countervailing power and who challenges the text within the context of a staged, albeit imaginary, production. In this, these features we have just mentioned complicate the reading, create critical distance between the reader and the textual object, and require interpretation on the part of both readers and practitioners. And contemporary *mise en scène*, except when it is legally prevented from do so by a living author (Beckett went as far as forbidding certain productions), tends to move away from authorial stage directions, or to contradict them, according to the directors' wishes. So, the reader, who is even freer than they are – and perhaps also influenced by this desire for freedom – builds an independent reading away from what are thought to be mere proposals.

However, even if it leads to personalisation or to conflicting interpretations, the space that the text contains is necessary, primary to the reader's imagination, even when no stage direction is noted, in the sense that the reader, if they follow the conventions of the theatrical text, can only envision the text in a theatre (unlike the novel). It may be argued, in response, that the reader is free, as was have said above, and can therefore read the text as a novel that "happens" wherever and whenever they so desire, and not necessarily on a theatre stage, whatever its kind. Similarly, an author may very well write a text without necessarily thinking of a possible staging, thus giving himself greater freedom of imagination. However, all will agree that the theatre text, including in its formal aspects, is specifically assumed to be linked to the undertaking of a staging of some kind. And when the author does not respect this agreement, which is both a formal (in the typographical arrangement, for example) and an aesthetic one (by ignoring or wishing to ignore that their text is constructed to be staged), and when the reader, likewise, reads a text, which they know to be "theatre", while refusing to envisage any possible staged production and transfer of the text to the bodies of actors, they are, of course, perfectly free to do so and can obviously find particular enjoyment, but they knowingly violate the code and thus distinguish themselves, knowingly, from the convention and the norms that imply that a theatrical text is given as essentially a pretext (in both senses of the term) for a theatrical production.

Consequently, it is in the dialogue and in the blank spaces that separate the different utterances that the reader will need to work to bring their reading to life, just as they will have to imaginatively depict and envisage a set design, bodies, voices, costumes and an audience to see and hear them. Despite being written and printed, the theatrical text "comes to life" during reading in the framework of the theatrical codes to which the reader has agreed. Herein lies perhaps one of the reasons why the printed text has, as we mentioned at the beginning of this chapter, blanks and gapes in the most real sense and takes up space on the page. Because it leaves voids to be filled, work to do and an open text. The theatrical text is located both in a book and in an imaginary space or a potential place inhabited by imaginary bodies, all of which are available to the player, the actor, the playwright, the director and all those who care to mobilise sentences by "bringing them to life" (in imagination or in reality).

The typographical indications of performance space and theatrical thus imply, for any reader (theatre practitioner or simple reader), the dual referent of the theatre text; first, because it is a performance space to build and imagine, a concrete space for the practice of a representation; and second, because based on the stage directions, the reader should, by following them or rejecting them, imagine and construct a space of fiction proper to the fable they read. Therefore, again, but this time in the reader's imagination, two spaces are set up: the space of the place, the theatre or type of platform used, the stage (which may be plural, depending on the choice(s) of the reader) and the "fictional" theatrical space, that determined by the text. Also, as mentioned, by representing to themselves fiction and stagecraft, the reader is invited to observe the impact of their imagination on themselves, to the point where one can then speak of a kind of duplication: I imagine a dramatic space based on a material space that must, for the technique I develop, carry me into the space where I will live out my illusion and in which I can be moved.

Suffice to say that the internal and external stage directions, as well as indications of events that take place off the stage in the stories and dialogue (which themselves serve in principle to imagine the fiction, unless the reader decides that they should also be represented in the staging produced by their practical imagination) are easily discernible, if not precisely interpretable. The same goes for time, which is often precisely registered in the two kinds of text, or, conversely, completely ignored.

Thus, the inscription of places and times in the text (stage directions and spoken text), as we have seen, does not necessarily mean that they are easy to use, since authors so frequently like to use the conventions merely to pervert or break them. Spatial and temporal cues may be perfectly conventional and clear, but they may also, and very often, lead to the active involvement of the reader who will engage with their ambiguity, or practical impossibility, and interpret them. There is no absolute regime of spatial directions, since princely palaces, other palaces, cherry orchards, even Russian ones, crossroads, mornings, springs, nights, are there as proposals and agreements that invite one to imagine a malleable world. It could also be said that, according to the era and its poetics, locations can be single or multiple, while time can either be in harmony with the performance time – the clock time of the staged representation – (sometimes even less in the case of *Bérénice*), an entire lifetime or even centuries. If the orthodoxy of verisimilitude has, for a long time in France, represented a kind of ideal beauty, one knows that the fictions of Western theatre are mostly played in multiple places and cover a period of time much greater than the performance time. And we also saw that even in this classical theatre, as it is called, time leaps, ellipses, the effects of slowdown or acceleration or flashbacks, but also of disjunctions of place, were also frequent.

Lastly, because the reader reads a text that was written, designed and made by an author, they may linger on the stylistic and metaphorical details that would enable them to lend a series of meanings to time and space. The reader will then endeavour, by means of stylistic and literary analysis, to consider how the author inscribes something of place and time through adverbs and adverbial phrases, verbs, the sequence of phrases and utterances and punctuation that produces the rhythm of sentences and reflects on the pace of play. Space and time, then, make sense. In the speech of the characters, one can thus read the way they are conceived by virtue of their own grasp of time and space, which gives them an identity and a depth (some are in the past, others in the present, some seek to escape the present, wait, project themselves into the future or, indeed, are learning about the passing time, etc.; some are given as being in another space, others mark dramatic place and space by their willingness to be present or are in an undefined elsewhere, etc.). This analysis and retrieval of metaphorical spatial and temporal occurrences aids in the construction of networks of meaning, which, through what characters say about time and place, resonate throughout the fabric of the text. This can thus give the impression of a nostalgia for a past time or a place that we cannot represent, that of a projection into an undetermined mental time and space, or that of a timeless, space-less universality.

But above all, assuming that one could answer more or less answer the complex question of where and when reading, dramatic fiction and imaginary *mise en scène* take place, the reader will necessarily rely on the information they read to determine a succession of times and places in fiction by linking them with actions often produced by a discourse spoken by entities or by characters. Because once the reader becomes aware of the time and space in which they are located, compared to the dramatic time and space about which they are reading, as well as to the time and place in which the imaginary staging is taking place, the reader will naturally desire to tell a kind of story built from these successive spatial and temporal indices.

From reading time and space to the reading of a fable

What's it about? Who did what, with whom? These issues can be clarified from the observations that the reader makes from the indices in the reading: from episodes framed in times and places and organised by the author based on a series. Like the spectator, the reader can obviously decide not to make such observations, and of course not to produce them upon first reading. However, these appear without them necessarily being aware, since these elements are there to precisely produce effects, passions, a state of mind that can create an impression and facilitate a general interpretation of the text they are reading. But since we chose here to deepen our observations about what the reader reads, and to uncover the processes through which they pass, we shall consider these indices crucial to the analysis of the text and therefore for the (even unconscious) activity of reading. What we do, as with the description of the position of the spectator in the experience of the session, is to exhibit the elements that are constructed in advance – in this case, by the author – and thus provide the possibility of grasping them. And if, during our analysis of the position of the spectator, we named and classified the different resources available, and if we thus elaborated a theory of the spectacle, we might now proceed in the same way with the reader: deepening our examination of the resources available to them so as to implement the principles of a dramaturgical analysis of the theatre text.

This series of events, which is ordered based on the indexation of textual signs and on a principle of chronological deployment, may well end up distorting chronology and not be linear. If, in the logic of the beautiful Aristotelian animal, there is a beginning, a middle and an end in the *fabula*, all of which are moored to a linear chronological succession (the beginning is at time zero of the story, and the ending at the final point that closes the representation), it is undeniable that the sequential systems produced by authors, both ancient and modern, do not always follow the tranquil movement of the hands of a clock and that places themselves are not necessarily given in a diegetic succession. As the text can be written by having several places function at the same time (this from as far back as the mysteries), time can break, be elided or reversed. Finally, there may be no indication of time and place and thus a succession without apparent logic and any possible timeline.

The way the text notates the sequence of events and actions gives the reader (as much as the spectator) the job of deciphering and re-establishing a thread according to the standards of chronology. So that while the reader recovers (or tries to establish) a chronology by reclassifying the parts into a comprehensible linearity, what happens when they are faced with a non-linear operation of the fable, is that they wonder why they have been proposed in this way. What effect has the author sought to disturb the perception of time and space? If there is then a gap between the temporal and spatial logic of the play, and the temporal and spatial logic of the text proposed by the author, the reader is then surprised: they give themselves the job of erasing the gap by restoring a common standard, but will also be summoned to experience and interpret what appears to them to be a break with the code.

The impact of spatial and temporal interference will thus be comparable to the operation of witticism as described by Freud: at first, the reader comes with their conventional code of reading that consists in following an action based on the linear succession of times and facts, but sometimes the text offers them something else, a transgression in the linear arrangement, which surprises them, puts them in the state of a work of logic, then obliges them to restore meaning and linearity. If there is sufficient evidence in the text for them to succeed at this task, they will triumph and will be pleased to have figured out the meaning (this is the moment of laughter in the joke), then, possibly wonder why this task has been imposed in the first place. If the reader cannot establish meaning, because there is not enough evidence to reinstate a linear common logic, they will experience a sense of disappointment, wonder why they have failed, naturally wonder why such a task has been inflicted and, in that too, will interpret both their own failure and the author's desire for them to fail. This second operation causes a second type of pleasure, which is the disappointment of meaning. In the first case, the reader will find (easily if the proposed work is easy, or immediately if the exposure of the story is linear) what the story is about. In the second instance (if the resolution or re-establishment of chronological order is impossible) they will have to abandon the search for such legibility and address what this intractable deployment of the story seeks to show. In other words, how this failure of meaning, or this disappointment, calls the reader out and forces them to question their entire function. Consequently, there are texts that recount in a non-surprising conventional chronology, in entirely imaginable spaces; fables that the reader follows without difficulty; and there are other texts that play with the conventions while allowing the player to redistribute the fable according to their common sense of space and time. These first two devices engage the reader in participating with the author to build a readable and understandable history. However, there is also text that cannot be redistributed according to common logic and then refer the reader to themselves, via their disappointment, and to what this disappointing experience tells them about themselves and the world in which they are found. Finally, as the reader has more time than the spectator, and since they can, when they want, slow down reading, and stop for a moment to meditate, or to question, they will be more sensitive to these effects and all the more able to observe the way in which the author assigns them to examine their own thinking activities.

We see that the indexing of events, like the logic that structures them, can be complex, but that, nevertheless, it also instils and a game of decryption for the reader based on their observation. It is because they carry out (consciously or not) indexing and appraisal that the reader can construct their own reading or story, and can establish a plot and build a system of interactions based on the coherence that they deduce from this whole. And, besides the notation of occurrences of temporal and spatial indications, they must also take into account the specific discursive system of the text.

Reading discourse and the constitution of characters

Thus, it is crucial to address the modes of discourse and their articulation, since the theatrical text also features stretches of interactive utterances. Jouvet was made to say that theatre is easy: "I speak to you, you answer me". Granted. But who speaks? For how long (in verses, or prose)? At what point (where in the room, scene by scene, act by act, vignette by vignette)? To whom (by interweaving moments, the quantitative weight of discourses, the appearance of characters to make a kind of tableau of interactions and therefore of moments dialogue; or, if the utterance is delivered by a single character onstage, moments of monologue)? How (via long tirades that are rhetorically constructed, versified lines delivered in staccato fashion, by asides, by silences, by parallel dialogues without exchange, through a chorus and, if appropriate, with what specific characterisations are they able to individualise the speaker)? Here are the key questions to be answered precisely if we are to understand the "pre-construction" of the text, and one will then frequently see a different picture emerging from what could be assumed upon a first reading. Taking notice of the "discursive weight" of each character, their importance in terms of stage presence and finally their discursive position (the value of their speech scene by scene and throughout the text, when related to what they are, for example) will correct a first reading that is often impressionistic and oriented toward the plain, obvious meaning, and will allow for a better observation of the dynamics and deep power relations throughout the story. Noting in detail the speakers' presence onstage, the number and importance of their lines and their monologues, the type of sequence of lines, the intersections or dialogues – in other words, the modes of discursive interaction between speakers – in addition to the transitions to external communication (the audience, the gods or other presences supposed and not shown), will lead to some objective conclusions that might guide one's interpretation otherwise and deepen the idea that one can have of the work of the authors and of the impact they desire to have on readers and spectators.

We will take a few canonical examples to illustrate the relevance of this process. The first example will be famous, to the point that one consistently offers it as an illustration of the *agon*, in other words the clash of discourses in the theatre. In *Antigone*, Sophocles causes Antigone and Creon to meet in a major episode after the transgression of the royal edict, and if we take note of the discourse that opposes them at this point, one will notice that they each have the same number of verses to say, that the dialogue is accelerated to arrive at the form of the *stichomythia* (dialogue in which two characters speak alternate lines of verse) and finally, after this battle of utterances, this *agon*, Creon makes his decision. Both speakers have therefore had the same discursive weight, both have opposed each other frontally as in a trial, both had equal time to present their arguments, and both were right, each according to his/her order (the order of the law of the city for Creon, the order of divine law for Antigone). Taking account of utterances based on their interaction in scenes and their structural importance in plays also aids in better understanding the poetic dynamics of the texts.

Going back to the example of Molière's *The Misanthrope*, we might note that Alceste has a considerable stage presence, except in the third act, which is that of Célimène. Alceste, as we have seen, wants to leave the stage or have all those who encumber it removed (he says so himself at the beginning of the play, appears without Célimène throughout the first act, and uses 247 verses to lay out his point of view and most of his discourse – 747 verses, amounting to 40 per cent of the text – confirms this attitude); and the other, Célimène, during the third act (117 verses compared to Alceste's 43) constantly seeks to occupy the stage (or living room) with these characters who Alceste wishes to get rid of. One character, for 17 scenes, is in a dynamic of urgency; the other for 15 scenes (but she has only 279 verses, or 15 per cent of the text, to speak), clings to a state that she intends to make last. Alceste wants to marry or leave, Célimène wants to remain a widow, young, rich and free, without resolving to be alienated: both dynamics clash and eventually lead to failure. This time, the moment of *agon* will be when, after repeated and unsuccessful efforts, Alceste can talk to Célimène on a one-to-one basis, when we are already two-thirds of way into the play (Act 4, Scene 3), but at this point it is too late for a decision or for an effect of harmony to be produced. It is ultimately the sum of the other discourses (45 per cent of the text) that triumphs over their two contradictory discourses, however developed, which amount to no effect. The last scene thus shows clearly that Célimène cannot stand up to all the discourses that condemn her (she has only 20 verses to say in a scene that has 139, in addition to the reading of letters), and that Alceste concludes the play (57 verses) accomplishing what he himself had announced: he flees to the "desert". Consequently, as we can see, the precise analysis of speech, made first in terms of discursive weight and the determination of the presence of characters onstage (how long and when?), serves to underscore the profound dynamics of a work, to reveal its general movement and also to propose a dramaturgical line of interpretation of the text that can help readers (and the future practitioner) to represent it onstage.

The test of the title

In this light, we can note that the reader first reads the title of a work, and, if the title emphasises one character or another, then they will, in fact, consider that they must build their own version of the fable around this eponymous character. This will be the initial instinct. But by noting the discourse markers as we have just proposed, we notice that the title, which can refer to an eponymous character, does not necessarily refer to the character that appears the most or who speaks the most, or that the subtitle nuances the title and strikes a balance between the title character and the character who appears, structurally and quantitatively, as the "main character". Corneille's *Cinna ou la Clémence d'Auguste* [*Cinna, or the Clemency of Caesar Augustus*] is a good illustration of this system: Cinna appears in the tragedy much less frequently than Augustus, but is foregrounded in the title of the play. We can then read the tragedy not as a kind of diegetic tracking of the itinerary of a tyrannical ruler turned legitimate thanks to the practice of clemency, or as the story of a conspirator, but as a play of opposition-contradiction between two ways of relating to politics, to the private and the public (the opposition between Augustus and Cinna), which are complex in themselves (Cinna and Augustus are both caught in the contradictions that their text confers on them). Thus, in order to have a closer and clearer view of each play, it becomes necessary to absolutely take note of previously set elements in order to understand what informs our reading and interpretation of the text and thus what pierces through the obvious.

All this is ultimately very simple, and may take time. But it is extremely effective to capture how the effects are designed by the author and are actualised in the composition of the dramatic system (lines, monologues, choral passages) or the system of the text itself. A particular scene, for example, bringing together the main characters that provide the dynamics of the plot, will be all the more important when it is central (e.g. in the middle of Act 3 for "classical" tragedies), or placed at the end, etc. Finally, the way an author forces the reader to wait, for example, by not initially giving the eponymous character the importance that one would expect, can be important: one has to wait until the second scene of the third act to see and hear Tartuffe, whereas the whole of the cast has already described what they think of the eponymous hero. The reader (or spectator), who obviously knows the title of the piece, and keeps hearing judgements about the literally hidden hypocrite, thus becomes caught in a dynamic of waiting and in the desire to see (or "read") that character, constantly frustrated until the wait is over. By waiting, the reader will have mostly seen and read the character of Orgon, and have been led to focus their attention on the painful and ridiculous adventure of this family man seduced by a man who, decidedly, does not appear. And when Tartuffe comes down the stairs, making his entrance, he surprises while at the same time fulfilling expectations, but he is thus placed in opposition, in the reader's view, to this Orgon, whose story the reader has been following from the beginning. The impact of this is initially to marginalise Tartuffe, at least to put him on the outside of this family that he seeks to enter, and to place the spectator or the reader in solidarity with this family that is already torn apart by the narrated actions of him who has just appeared. And until the end of the text, the discursive weight of Tartuffe remains minor compared to the discursive weight of Orgon, until, finally, the hypocrite is, in all respects, rejected and silenced by a singular, but absolute, utterance: that of the king.

Another example is more complex, and once again, comes from Corneille. *Rodogune* has as its title the name of one of the two heroines of the tragedy, but if we take into account the "weight of speech" and the number of occurrences of the characters onstage without forgetting the strategic and theatrical organisation of these appearances (monologues, openings and closures of acts, etc.), it is Cleopatra who triumphs. So why was the Queen Regent not chosen as title character? Why hide this evil queen that figures so prominently from the title? Why, moreover, make sure that the name of Cleopatra is never spoken when it is naturally noted in the stage directions? Corneille explains this in his preface by saying he did not want the "listener" (the spectator) to confuse her with the famous Queen of Egypt who he had previously staged in *La Mort de Pompée* [*The Death of Pompey*], whereas the reader who has the leisure of thinking, can read the name of the wicked queen every time she speaks, and at the beginning of each scene. So the reader will go a step further by asking if there is no other reason for this name to be hidden and may, if they so wish, ruminate on the truly *unspeakable* character of the ambitious and cruel Machiavellian Queen Regent.

The relationship between the words of the title, particularly when they contain the name of a character, and the deployment of these words in the dramatic text, must be precisely observed, evaluated, interpreted during reading. Given the title of Synge's play, *The Playboy of the Western World*, and observing that the term is used in the text initially with an ironic connotation, then in the mouth of Pegeen in the last line of the play and after the departure of the hero in a nostalgic way, the reader is led to observe specifically the fact that the play is not the adventures of a "playboy", but the transformation of the character of Christy Mahon. How a pitiful and pathetic young man who has committed "nasty deed" (murdering his father by driving a pitch fork into his head), becomes a playboy: a smooth talker and seducer, but also the entertainer of a community. By focusing specifically on the distribution, the length, magnitude and catalogue of the lines of the character in the play, especially through the different versions the story, the reader will see how Christy Mahon, first frightened, plaintive and taciturn, discovers lyricism. A lyricism that he practices initially under the effect of amorous desire for Pegeen Mike and in his dialogues with her and that grows in confidence until the playboy is finally transformed. But the reader will also find that it is always when pressed and encouraged by the questions of the other characters that Christy is led, from version to version, to embellish his story. We can then question the centrality of this playboy, the ambiguity or the multiple meanings of the term, the function performed by the character in the rural community into which he makes a sudden appearance and on the mechanisms of staged presence and words, which the play builds around him. We find that the play opens on to the scene of Michael Flaherty's pub, a pit stop and the meeting place where this small community gathers – this community that is shown to be committed to stability and tradition but also worried by the external word, anticipating trouble, disorder, misfortunes. This playboy is the one who does introduce the disturbance, the gambling, the theatrical play. Christy – the theatrical hero – therefore irrupts into this place of community, and until the end of the second act, the principle of the play will be to leave it permanently on the stage: occupying space, he is in the centre. The "playboy" is a veritable centre of attraction since everyone comes to see him to make him tell his story, but also to take ownership of him and take him home (the widow Quin) or carry him far away (Shawn), while he, the wanderer, decides to stay and settle there (by marrying Pegeen the boss' daughter). And in this central – and theatrical – position of the one around whom all others take their place, and that he must justify through his speech and the reiteration of his story, Christy appears above all as the pale figure on to which the community projects its fantasies and desires for myths and heroes, one who brings to it a disturbance unconsciously expected – and by which it is revealed to itself, in a kind of carnivalesque moment. Until in the last act they carry him offstage to enthrone him in the village games, in which he himself appears transformed (he is an all-round winner), and has really become a potential hero and "smooth talker". That is, until the father who is thought to be dead returns, and Christy repeats his act in front of everyone (this time it seems that Old Mahon really is dead). The myth collapses, and the community in a lynching scene destroy its idol and expel the disruptive intruder, completing a traditional comic schema (stability/introduction of a disruptive and revelatory element/return to order through its expulsion). Therefore, the reader will note that the play tells the story of this community just as much as the story of Christy Mahon, and that an exchange is thus produced: the community reveals itself (and is revealed to itself), is then disturbed and transformed around this alien character and entertainer while the latter, in turn, is transformed by the experience, truly becomes the confident "smooth talker", having discovered the powers of language, imagination and poetry. Moreover, what this play can depict, via the name of the playboy and via the evolution of the name, of the character and of his speech throughout the text, is theatre itself, which entertains, disturbs and worries, so that the community of men sometimes then rejects what it has so loved.

What is at stake here?

It seems that the key question that a reader may ask of an author's text, considering both the entire play and every scene and line by itself, even before asking "what is being acted out?" is "but what is the actor playing?" What does the actor experience, what do they produce that is so remarkable and that is not to be found elsewhere, what do they write that is so unique, what puts them in a position to be an artist, a virtuoso, a good craftsman worthy of being read because they elicit interest and are surprising, because they take into account what the reader knows and play with what the reader knows for their greatest pleasure? And this is valid as much with respect to the staging perspective of the play as to the overall operation of reading. When Molière surprises his reader, suddenly reminding him, in *Dom Juan* (it is the "You are crying, it seems?" of which we have already spoken), when

Sganarelle exists whereas he has not been given any line for a long time, he is forcing his partner-reader to re-read the scene, to interpret the existence of a forgotten silent role forgotten for a moment and to enjoy his own imagination by taking into account, retrospectively, the play of the actor and its impact on the audience – the audience to which the "you are crying", indirectly and ironically, is also addressed. At the same time, it enables the reader to contrast the "you" with the "I", "crying" with "thinking" and to reflect on the fact that the servant falls into emotion while the libertine master never ceases to think of Elvire's lines, her tears, her attitude of conversion. In that, Molière plays his game, takes risks, surprises as much in writing as onstage and differs from all the *Dom Juan*'s past and future.

To take a contemporary example, the reader of Bernard-Marie Koltès' *Quai Ouest* [*Quay West*] can take advantage of this analytical approach to overcome the traditional dramatic appearances of the play and penetrate further into its complexity. It will be noted first that the piece opens with a character, Koch, and appears to pose as a typical main challenge the action of achieving the goal that the character has set himself: so we read that Koch has decided to go to the docks – on the fringes of the city, where the play is set – to commit suicide by jumping into the river. But it appears very quickly that the reading must refocus on another character, who Koch must face upon his arrival: Charles, whose presence and interests then manifest themselves as the true centre of the first half of the play. The aim of the action is thus displaced on to him, his operations and his stated objective: by taking advantage of the arrival of Koch, to leave the docks to go start a new life on the other side of the river in town. This is the first *decentring* (we borrow the term from François Regnault) of the action and the dramatic focus that the play offers to the reader. But we are also led, simultaneously, to take note of the uniqueness of a third character, that of the Noir Abad, a mysterious entity who is given no lines – Abad does not deliver a word in the play – but seems nonetheless to occupy a special role. While the textual portion allotted to this figure is zero, the reader should, nevertheless, imagine the vital importance of his mute stage presence, which is posed as the inverse of the logorrhoea and rhetorical devices that characterise some of the other protagonists. Therefore, the reader should examine what revelatory function Abad may represent. When other characters such as Charles, in particular, speak to him in long tirades, which he does not answer, the reader is able to take into account this deafening silence. By extending this approach to the rest of the play, we can see that even the central importance of Charles becomes nuanced and that his stage presence becomes more intermittent in the second half of the text. Playing on such focusing effects, the representation is diffracted as the other characters enter into play: each pursuing their own interests. Charles' mother, Cécile, who appears rather late (end of the second part), is just one example of this. Consequently, the hierarchy between a possible main plot and subplots is blurred, the various threads become intertwined in such a complex fashion that the reader, just like the characters, seems likely to get lost in them, as the only scene bringing them all together (at the beginning of the fifth part) seems to attest. And we can also see that the character – Rodolfe, Charles' father – who has the least stage presence in the text, and who appears only after the middle of the play, is nevertheless the one who helps to resolve the knotty and complex plot (by giving Abad the Kalashnikov that he has been carrying hidden for years). In the meantime, since the portion of speech allotted to Charles has been reduced, the reader is led to consider this collapse of speech and place it in connection with Charles' apparent acceptance of death in the last scene of the play, just before being shot by Abad. He will thus wonder about Charles' giving up on life, and the retrospective consequences that can be drawn for his reading of the entire play. From decentring to decentring, the reader thus sees that the principle of the *deal* and a complex play of focalisations constitute the structure of the play, and that the play rests on a principle of variations in points of view – which can also be seen in the spatial apparatus developed by the author. Finally, as a reader and unlike the spectator of a performance of the play, one wonders about the most suitable way of integrating into the reading the novelistic "interior monologues" of three characters (Abad, Rodolfe, Fak) that Koltès has inserted into his printed text, while being mindful that they are not intended to be played.

In a reading of this kind, it is necessary to look very specifically on forms of dialogue, on the modalities of internal speech, and to seek to determine, beyond appearances, who speaks to whom and how. Thus, in this play, by observing the balances and imbalances that may characterise the exchange of lines, the reader may also find that the dialogue is imbued with the "monological". Many parts of the dialogue resemble soliloquies, intersecting or plain soliloquies, addressed to a perpetually silent character (Abad). It is therefore the principle of exchange and dialogued conflict that is thereby subverted, turned on its head – and, with it, the understanding that the reader may have of the characters. This same precise observation will allow us to see that, very often, these dialogues appear ambiguous or "indirect", since they do not address clearly the issues and objects of the conflict.

They then progress by means of innuendo and even misunderstandings: the text presupposes an object or desire (like sex) without naming them explicitly. Moreover, this situation of diverted dialogue makes the reader unable to work out motivations, goals and a fixed identity for the characters. Each of them is indeed presented as being in an awkward position, and any affirmation of identity is in this very particular dialogued framework and under the essential influence of the relation to the interlocutor. Readers are led to conclude that the presence of a speaker (who is usually mute) decentres the character or furthermore, reveals a fundamental decentring of identity. The reader is thus unable to construct characters, doubting their identity and questioning the communication they apparently maintain, by noting that under the guise of traditional conversational, it is simply a representation of self that is being played out between characters. This version of a self is proper to the principle of the *deal*, to the need to give a seductive or impressive *image* of oneself, but also that which rejects the gaze, real or perceived, of the Other. Behind their assertions of radical singularity *and* otherness, which are always produced under the influence of the theatre and determined by the presence of the Other, the reader notices the game of mirrors in which the characters themselves are lost. From the observation of this process of dialogue, monologues and soliloquies, we can conclude that in *Quai Ouest*, the characters are lacunar subjects. They are marked by an uncertainty of identity that is sensitive only to the lack of affirmation of these profoundly *reactive* images. The reader can then read this extract of Charles' soliloquy before Abad with a fresh perspective:

> Besides, you never understand what I say, and I have no understanding of what you think; you always do as I think that you think that you don't want to do, and afterwards, you correct; that's why I think you function; but you can't always correct, nigger. To be honest, I really have never understood you. So don't try to understand, just stay there, stay calm.[4]

Thus, trying to determine through analysis of the forms of dialogic relationship, the identity of a particular character, the reader has encountered the fact that Koltès' writing reveals the character and reveals itself as much as it hides and is hidden. The words of Abad's "interior monologue" are also therefore addressed to the reader: "But the more I say, the more I hide [. . .], don't ask me anymore who I am".[5] Alternating between defence and accumulation of identity traits, between overdetermination and gaps, between self-affirmation and faults, Koltèsian dialogue presents the character in an unresolved dialectic between the suggestion of a complex identity and the opacity of pure superficiality. For, when all is said and done, it is with the reader's desire that Koltès plays, by offering him the lure of a secret, of a complexity and depth of the character, while denying it, i.e. by leaving it to his imagination. In so doing, Koltès manifests, in the character and in the reader, a perpetually shifting, relative subjectivity, whereby the *intersubjective* foundations that preside over traditional drama are destroyed. The reader will thus be able to better understand the tragedy of the famous Koltèsian incommunicability: not a thematic pattern, nor a psychological given, but a structural principle, rooted in the lines of the play and foundational to the construction of relationships.

As we can see, by conducting a careful analysis of the dialogical system, by simply examining the issue of who speaks to whom and how, by diligently seeking to construct classic characters and failing, and once he approaches each dialogue with the specificity it deserves and with a concern for an overall view of the play, once the reader questions their own reading and function in relation to the text, they are perfectly able to realise (with objective arguments and thanks to their own observations) that Koltès patiently builds a dramaturgy that foregrounds the principle of relativity. And by observing the dialogues and the materiality of the text, and by noting how the identification of the "subject-character" is blurred, by observing the extent to which the author blurs notions and feelings of will (that conventionally impel dramatic action), the reader gains the keys that will simultaneously determine aesthetic judgment and the attitude of reception that must be adopted to get into the game that the text proposes.

Besides the benefit, in terms of dramaturgical analysis and interpretation of the text that one can derive from taking note of the communicational protocols in the theatrical text, one also comes to understand that none of the discursive constructions and speaking entities are able to fully bear the author's intentional discourse. This is one of the advantages of theatre: breaking up speech and spreading it across different entities that carry it and that, in fact, are usually contradictory. Conversely, non-fragmentation will have a special meaning, as it does sometimes in the case of the choir that can produce a feeling of unison or of political, sensual, moral or religious harmony. Except that even choral arrangements, from the chorus in Claudel's *Le Livre de Christophe Colomb* [*The Book of Christopher Columbus*] to all the most contemporary dramaturgies of chorality, very often integrate features of diffraction and contradiction. Through fragmentation, the elision of the place of authorial transmission of the message and the effect of contradiction, the authorial "I" cannot, by definition, appear as homogeneous. The rhapsode is in no way unitary, continuous, homogeneous or harmonious, since his time and speech are dedicated to diffracting his own exercise. The author, through the mode of speech specific to the theatre, must first speak to themselves before engaging in a dialogue with the reader and practitioners, which allows him to never directly take on the appearance of a particular character, to never exactly take on (even if he has the "intention") of a particular speech, and therefore to preserve him, but also to give the reader the opportunity to choose the speech to which he will adhere. Thus, this multiple dialogue is never fully established, nor made precise. Instead, it plays on ambiguity and remains infinitely porous. If one knows more or less which entity is talking to which on set, one also knows that all discourse has at least one addressee but can have multiple meanings, and one does not quite know the truth or the main meaning (if there is one) that the entire text carries: one just reads that entities or bodies speak to other bodies and that the different forms of dialogue are intertwined.

Because of such fragmentation, there is still room for interpretation and for play within this dual communication [*double énonciation*] and this opposition effect of dialogue. As we have said, it is not that the author sometimes does not choose their cause or truth, but that, because the author writes theatre and must interest the reader (and the audience when the play is staged), they must give almost as much strength and weight to the character they are supposed not to support as much as to the character they promote. And it is in this play of balance, of balancing of functions, that the reader can deviate from what is assumed to be the judgment of the author, or even from the restoration of a conventional pacified order, which often occurs at the very end (in Shakespeare or in Corneille, for example).

From general reading to reading of plot

From these observations, the reader appreciates that theatre is first an exchange of lines proposed by an author, a text interspersed with gaps that depict silences or varying lengths. In other words, a score. From the inscription of these lines in discursive entities in interaction, from which the reader can *imagine* characters capable of depicting entities that are autonomous, animate and endowed with a psyche, the reader is able to work with the text (and/or with the author) to build, according to this succession of imaginary words uttered onstage, a fantasy action in a virtual time and a space. The text thus proposes a composition and formal clues for *imagining* the enactment of a story, and the reader will complement them. It is through this specific space of dislocation, located between words and speech conventionally inscribed on paper, on the one hand, and their *imaginary* actualisation in a convenient place of verbalisation and in a fictional space and time, on the other hand, that we can say that in theatre, "to speak is to do". Reading thus becomes imagined speech, and speaking amounts to putting in place a fiction that one can build based on the discursive interactions proposed.

Admittedly, much has been said about *imaginary* and *imagination* in this last paragraph, in contrast to the formalism in which we previously engaged. The thing is that the reader's activity entails precisely this: producing a fictitious enactment, in a fictional world and/or on a fictitious stage; or more precisely, determining what the play is about depending on the way in which this fiction is presented in the text itself. Further, since the reader spends time reading and appropriating this reading, they must dedicate themselves to another activity than that of a pure receiver. Consequently, their activity consists in organising, for themselves, a discursive, conversational or tangible event-based composition of actions, i.e. one or more *fabulae*. The *fabula* can thus be defined, not only as the sum of actions performed (the Aristotelian sense of the term), but as the sum of actions accomplished *and* of discourses articulated that, as manifested in the text and in the reader's imagination, can be made into stories.

What the reader imagines, can then be stories about themselves (for example, what does that tell me about me?), or fables about these discursive simulacra whose fictitious actualisation they have imagined. The succession of lines, places, times, speech events and actions noted in the text will cause them to produce a number of imaginary stories about these simulacra often turned characters. This is the first of their activities: to offer themselves the reading of a story (or of several stories) thanks to a text whose purpose is to produce meaning. And for that, the reader will naturally use the references they have: their body, the society in which they live, the idea they have of people and of the world and finally the information they have about the referential system given by the text. Their imagination will therefore carry out an ordering of times, places, events and an arrangement of speech, to facilitate the cognitive gap we mentioned above. It will also engage in an ownership of the entire material they read and of the meanings they find that can bring them pleasure. And even if some texts (often contemporary ones) want to escape the development of a "story" and offer disjointed, fragmentary, pictorial sequences without a denotative link, the reader will nevertheless have the possibility of constructing one or several stories [*fables*] based on their perception of the text and what is read. They do so by associating the fragments and oppositions that still structure the dynamics of the text and its temporal deployment. Therefore, to constitute this story, or these stories, and to implement the logical and chronological development of the play, each reader builds a kind of narrative that is not necessarily linear or anecdotal. To do this, they have at their disposal some conventional formal tools, especially when it comes to repertory theatre. The model of the plot with its exposition, conflicts, *peripeteia*, its Aristotelian *anagnorisis*, among other canonical terms, allow them (with all the poetic theories that we will not develop here as they have been treated in other more specific studies) to build this narrative, or these narratives, in close relation to the dramaturgical layout of the text. Depending on the established conventions as observed by the text, the reader will therefore appreciate how the author reacts to these canons or conventions to produce their own work, and derive a bit more fun from having an aesthetic and poetic perspective on the text itself.

And to better understand how the reader can develop a tale from a precise observation of the plot, here we take the example of so-called "classic" tragedy: the emblematic form of seventeenth-century French theatre. Through analysis of the *dispositio*, which is a form of organisation of a work based on the unity of action and the rhetorical development that one is meant to follow, the reader of a tragedy may determine a logical and functional thread that forms the whole subject of the play and that includes "a beginning, a middle and an end", as Aristotle says. The subplot, when it exists, consequently has to contribute to the resolution of the main plot in order to fit within the rhetorical model of demonstration. Reading, then, is based on a number of prerequisites driven by criticism and poetic tradition. Before they read the first lines, the reader-connoisseur will know that a "classical" tragedy normally begins *in medias res* (in the middle of the course of the story): that at dawn (beginning of the 24-hour period), in a given place (in the hall, the courtyard of a palace, etc.) a hero, usually, and a confidant speak about the situation and recall what happened earlier, which immediately orients the tragedy toward a crisis, the essential point. They know that this scene of exposition focuses the subject and that the following scenes continue to present the action while introducing the main characters (delaying their arrival is thus an effect) and complicating the plot. They then notice that obstacles, judiciously placed, deepen the crisis as the main characters arrive, and that this chain also follows the thread of logical order, so that all obstacles, misunderstandings and *peripeteia* seem necessary for the progression of action toward its end, without the intervention of chance. They note with pleasure that, formally speaking, the scenes are linked to each other (within an act, the stage must not be empty, hence the usefulness of linking scenes to announce the arrival of a character or justify the start of another), and that dangers are also linked (one jumps from one danger to another, or one danger arises from the previous one). They realise that obstacles hinder the intentions of the characters and form the crux of the play – they are said to be *external* if the will of the hero clashes with that of other characters, *internal* if they arise from within the hero's own passions. The reader-connoisseur is also aware, given their knowledge of canonical tradition, that the author may also utilise the archetype of tragic misunderstanding – often found in oracles, for example (*Iphigenia*) – or *peripeteia*, which is an unexpected event that creates a reversal in the situation of the hero. *Peripeteia*, while often used by Corneille, is rejected by Racine because it is outside of the plot and is a reversal of the action, not just an unforeseen development. Finally, as they get to the fifth act, the same reader will take pleasure in noting that the author has made sure that the ending happens as late as possible. This is so that they can enjoy for as long as possible the disorder of the world that precedes its ultimate rectification or, alternatively, the startling catastrophe to which it leads. For the reader, the denouement will therefore be the final event, which cuts the thread of the action by the cessation of dangers and obstacles – misfortune is consumed in a poignant event. But they will also know that the denouement of a tragedy is not always tragic (a tragedy can have a happy ending, like *Cinna* or *Horace*), or, though tragic, is intensified by a second end providing a "way out" (like the declaration of an external or innocent character who "saves" the plot from absolute disaster, as in *Phèdre*). Thus, the reader is able to compare the play with a system, to understand additions, differences and transgressions proper to the play in order to then see its specificity. In *Bérénice*, for example, Racine can be seen as the author who is closest to the canon, while Hardy, Rotrou, Pierre Corneille in *Le Cid* (a tragicomedy that has become tragedy) and Thomas Corneille, in *Timocrate*, can be seen as those who veer away from it. Admittedly, all these authors, though they are from the same century (seventeenth), are not writing in the same period. Hardy and Rotrou, for example, come before the rules become generally accepted, Pierre Corneille resists some of them, while Racine performs them well – in *Bérénice*, precisely, an absolutely exceptional work, an experimental one even, for its time. It must be said, however, that Racine performs these rules in his own interests and for the benefit of his own dramaturgy.

Admittedly, this whole theoretical and normative way of reading a tragedy allows one to compare a work to a code, which simultaneously helps to determine a canonical principle of evaluation and produce in the reader's imagination a well-standardised narrative. However, it can lead to a dangerous and annoying scholastic decoding accompanied by a value judgement that is based on no other reality than that of an ideal and ideological critique. What is generally agreed on is the following: that the system of so-called "classical" tragedy, which we have described here very schematically, is generally accepted by the critical tradition; that it is based, in part, on a reading of Aristotle's *Poetics* and confirmed by the main "learned figures" of the classical period (including by d'Aubignac's *La Pratique du theatre*); that it is considered and taught as a system by prestigious academic critics and used by equally prestigious directors of modern and contemporary theatre. Nevertheless, it is a *theoretical* system, often adapted or contradicted by "classical" authors themselves, and is even unrepresentative of seventeenth-century tragedy taken as a whole, as it was represented then. Many tragedies of that era do not perform the said code, the foremost among them being the most frequently performed play of the seventeenth century, Thomas Corneille's *Timocrate*, a considerable success that could properly be regarded as the canonical standard of the time. This is why it is very important to take a step back from the canon and, above all, to not turn it into an analytical framework by which to determine what the elements of a great tragedy must be. In other words, it seems reasonable to expect and accept that a canonical system exists, but that it was built in part by the scholars of the seventeenth century, and especially by all the periods of criticism that followed and that often established this code as an unsurpassable theoretical ideal moment in French theatre. The idea is not to measure a work according to a code that has the force of law, but to know that a kind of law was enacted by the reading traditions and by successive critical postures generally concerned with grounding the notion of a national classicism. The result was a way of seeing the tragedy of the seventeenth century, which today, fortunately, often gives rise to debates, especially during its staged representations. However, it does not seem appropriate or fair to deny the fact that some tragedies of the seventeenth century, which have been retained by tradition and repertoire, conform to the system described specifically because, dialectically, they perform it even as they shape it. Tragedy is thus conceived as an Aristotelian "beautiful animal": it has a beginning, a middle and an end; it is generally consistent with the rules, or attempts to be; it tends to unify the plot, etc. In a certain way, it is inscribed in our memories as a system. It is necessary to know the rules, even while observing their relativity, and one must also be able to put them in historical perspective or, frankly, in question.

While the contemporary theatrical text stands out, unlike "classic" drama, because of the fact that there is no conventional standard but a multiplicity of codes or existing, manipulable models, it remains important to register the referential standards in relation to which a writer positions themselves – standards that they revisit, to which they adhere and with which they play. An author may well use a complex structure in their dramaturgical construction, mounting several different conventions, thereby offering a particularly open reading, producing shifts that the reader should identify, and with which they will in turn play to replenish their own fiction, establish the statuses of characters, consider the represented action and build one or more tales and interpretations.

Thus Sarah Kane, for her first play *Blasted* (1995)[6] begins by posing in the first part the framework of a realistic representation. In a simple dialogue form, she juxtaposes a mature man, Ian, of a clearly determined identity with a girl, Cate, who we are told is 21 and lower-middle class. A southerner with a south London accent. Ian is 45, Welsh but has a Leeds accent, is a reporter for the local press, divorced, has a son that he no longer sees, is always drinking gin and smoking cigarettes. Cate is specified as having a mentally retarded brother and a kind mother, she is vegetarian, religious and likes soccer. The setting of the play is a "very luxurious hotel room in Leeds" – however "the kind of room so expensive it could be anywhere in the world". So we are in a "generic place". While some details of the relationship are clearly presented here, as "characters" can appear blurred at times, the action is conspicuously presented through the lens of interpersonal conflict and realist dialogue. They were lovers but had not seen each other for a long time (Ian has not called back for a while; Cate now has a boyfriend); Ian wants to make love to Cate, who refuses. Ian rapes her (it seems) that night; he dares her to kill him; she tries but cannot, etc. We are thus faced with extreme domestic violence and cruelty in the context of a sexual relationship. Ian does not have much longer to live (he has cancer), and is afraid of dying. Nervous, he draws his weapon and is worried as soon as someone knocks at his door (it is only a bellhop who brings the sandwiches Ian has requested, but the figure is still invisible). Or he drops to the ground when he hears the small explosion of a tyre that has burst outside. Then there are elements of another virtual plot and of another literary genre: he claims to be secret agent and believes there is an attempt to assassinate him. The reader is therefore dealing with a realist representation in a tight dramatic framework – as in an Ibsen play. Cate even stutters at times, a fact that seems to shed light on the character and her psychology ("*a stutter when under stress*"), and in the same vein but more troubling, she loses consciousness on several occasions – moments when, according to her, "the world don't exist [...] / Looks the same but / Time slows down. A dream I get stuck in."

But at the end of the second scene and a little after the play's half-point, Cate announces that she is going home, then leaves the stage for the first time, disappearing into the bathroom, which allows us to leave the strict framework of interpersonal conflict. Ian is alone onstage, and so the aesthetics change: there is a knock on the door, a soldier enters, disarms Ian, and for a long time is face to face with him, holding him at gunpoint. As the soldier is hungry, he eats both breakfasts, looking for the "woman" who he "senses" in the bathroom and discovers that she has disappeared. He then announces that the place is filled with "a lot of bastard soldiers out there" like him and takes over the space, declaring, "Our town now". There is "a blinding light, then a huge explosion" before the lights are dimmed. *Blackout*. The reader finds the two men (Ian and the unidentified soldier) lying in the ruins of the room that has been bombed. Ian sneers about the soldier: "Worse than me". They converse, or rather the soldier questions Ian and tells him of the atrocities that he and his fellow fighters commit in the place they have come from (a war with massacre of civilians and even ethnic cleansing reminiscent of Bosnia). He asks Ian if, as a journalist, he knows and bears witness to this, and tells him how his own girlfriend was raped and tortured before being killed. He asks Ian if he himself has ever killed someone, and what he would do if he had to – "Imagine", the soldier adds, in an imperative that the reader can also receive for themselves. Finally, he rapes Ian, before sticking the gun into his anus, as his torturers did to his girlfriend, asking him, "What's it like?" He makes clear to Ian that his personal situation does not count over all that he has seen and done. And when Ian asks if he is going to kill him, he sucks his eyes out and eats them. Lights down, *blackout*, lights back up: the soldier is dead ("He has blown his own brains out"). Cate returns with a baby who turns out to be already dead. She opens the scene with the words "You're a nightmare" addressed to Ian. Ian wants to die but, being blind, can do nothing, while Cate refuses to help him kill himself. A few short vignettes follow, depicting Ian's long purgatory, as he suffers alone, awaiting death. Cate finally returns from the outside with meat and gin and shares it with Ian, whose "thank you" closes the play.

If we stick to the idea of a realistic reading, the second half of the play thus marks an extreme development in the representation of violence.

But with the entry of the new character that is the soldier, one alien to the relationship between the two protagonists, and with him, of an external world whose evocation was previously very limited, it seems that a major deviation from the action of the play has occurred. This deviation shifts the referential universe, revealing underneath the realistic theatrical setting that Sarah Kane has described as an "odd theatrical form, part war zone, part dreamscape",[7] an ambiguous universe that opens the possibility for other codes of representation, other models of reading, to be at work.

The play thus presents itself to us in three parts, whose coherence the reader must examine: the Ian–Cate relationship; the arrival of the soldier up to the moment of the explosion; the time after the explosion. The reader may of course receive and perceive all the scenes depicted as being of the same style and the same degree of fiction, and think that they should all be read as a uniform whole. They make even take the war that arises as something absolutely realistic. They might, of course, be incited to do so by virtue of the fact that there is spoken language throughout, a continuity of violence, and dialogue, for the most part. But they might also be incited to wonder whether the confrontation with the soldier, the explosion, and Ian's death throes (about which Kane evokes Beckett, after suggesting a Brechtian influence for the confrontation between Ian and the soldier) must be placed on the same plane and read according to the same representational framework as the previous scenes with Ian and Cate. They may also wonder whether the entrance of the soldier and the blinding explosion do not also mark a change in the overall protocol of representation, moving it into a spectral space (that of a character, for example Ian, alone and faced with the flip side of his own violence and his own fear of dying, or one created by the author-function). Indeed, they may begin to wonder if the first scenes that are seemingly realistic and interpersonal should not be read retrospectively in the light of the latter scenes, and also be considered as a mental projection, delirium or a fantasy (on the part of Ian, of Cate the victim or of the author), or even as a metaphor for the conflicts of war, broadly speaking. In any case, the reader is led to wonder how personal violence and the violence of war, how the private and the political, can be articulated through the image of a wall that is blasted apart and through these shifting references: "what could possibly be the connection between a common rape in a Leeds hotel room and what's happening in Bosnia"?[8] They will ask themselves what relationship they can establish between the two to inform or shed light on each other. They may also call upon literary archetypes, which they seem to recognise (Cornwall gouging out Gloucester's eye in Shakespeare's *King Lear*, blind Oedipus, for example). They will do all this, not necessarily to establish a closed angle of representation, or to re-establish a single prism of reading that would be *the* truth of the text, but rather to play on the different possible angles, the different dimensions, the different possible modes of representation and, through them, on the echoes, openings and the dynamics of meaning that are fostered. The real problem that the reader faces, then, is how to draw on the habits and conventions that they must know in order to experience optimal pleasure, while posing the questions that the text asks of them, transcending their first legitimate impressions to seek out underlying meanings.

Additionally, because they may already know one of Sarah Kane's later plays, *Cleansed* (1998),[9] or may be curious to read it so as to acquire personal knowledge of how this author plays with the codes of realism, the reader can bring similar questions to the new text. Again, they may well decide to take the fiction at face value, and thus only see in it a realistic depiction of a university transformed by a frustrated pervert (Tinker) into a kind of "concentrationary" world. If they follow this impulse, they will imagine a world of sadistic torture and experiments in which a heroine (Grace), a modern Antigone, lives; in which Grace's brother (Graham) has died of an overdose. They will be surprised to see the ghost of Graham appear and passionately throw themselves into the world of the marvellous. Of course, they will be obliged to consider how they can integrate into their reading stage directions such as "*Grace is being beaten by an unseen group of men whose voices we hear*" or "*Grace is being raped by one of the voices*". And that is perhaps when they will change their mode of reading, and wonder if the tri-partite structure of *Blasted* is not spread over the whole of the representation of *Cleansed*, and if the two codes of representation (realism/fantasy; "objective"/subjective), rather than operating successively, are not twinned in this play. This is the benefit of contextualisation: that one reading may be enhanced by others. Consequently, the reader will consider the disturbing similarities between Kane's world and the world of psychiatry, and will be intrigued by this heroine character driven by a desire for amorous fusion with her dead brother. They will also wonder about the fact that she wears Graham's clothes from the third of the play's twenty scenes; they will see how this desire for absolute love, this tension between desire for otherness and recognition, marks the other couples in the play and lies beneath the work's representation of horror. They will be led to wonder about the comparisons that can be made between the proposed representation and the model of hallucinatory, paranoid or schizophrenic perceptions. They will also question the Mephistophelian figure of Tinker who burns corpses and who claims to be "a dealer not a doctor" or, vice versa, to be able to satisfy "everything [you] want". They will wonder about this voyeur who is sometimes lost in a reverie ("Tinker is thinking"). Taking into account all these signs – or these symptoms one might say – the reader will be able to see that Sarah Kane uses the concentration camp model as a metaphor for alienation and the loss of love as much as she uses the field of love to shed light on the unrepresentable world of the concentrationary camp, on politics, on the (non-)human. And in the play's economy, there will be no need for establishing a hierarchy of these fields; rather, the reader will see that it is their reversibility that activates the senses. It becomes possible to construct a reading, or readings, based on the possible levels of interwoven interpretations available to the reader. These interpretations require a decryption game, and the reader, through this game, derives pleasure from their reading.

Thus, it is by knowing the conventional prerequisites – however debatable they are – that the reader can establish a series of variables (as opposed to a judgement) in relation to the ideal canonical vision of the play's plot, or in relation to the levels of interpretation that tradition has generated. And it is precisely this consideration of the history of readings that allows each reader to simultaneously build their own interpretation and their own story. That is why we have seen that, to produce a kind of narrative of what they read, the reader has to place themselves at the heart of fiction, to imagine the author's process of composition and therefore reconstitute its parts. They must also consider the history of "canonical" traditions within which the author must position himself. They must take into account the theoretical and dramaturgical points of view that have preceded the work of the author, insofar as the play becomes a sum of readings and interpretations derived from critical and theatrical traditions. And it is only after this has been done that they can finally go against the implicit models and finally arrive at a mental construction of the progression of an action. In doing so, the reader is able to account for the history of the principal conflict between entities or characters, to establish a narrative and consider a series of relationships between the major causes and essential effects suggested by the dramatic fiction.

One final example will be mentioned very briefly, to demonstrate that the same questions also arise for so-called "non-dramatic" texts: narrative texts that, though theatrical, do not display the traditional signs of the theatrical text. The status of a "material" such as *Bildbeschreibung* (*Explosion of a Memory* in English, *Paysage sous surveillance*, in French) written in 1982 by Heiner Müller, is a complex case in point.[10] The text is advertised as a description – the original title means "image description" – of a drawing that could represent the murder ("perhaps a daily one") of a woman by a man, while a bird watches in a tree. It is a description that flows through the subjective filter of the one who describes it and, as indicated by the French title, a "landscape". "The text describes a landscape beyond death. The action goes any way you like, since the consequences are past, explosion of memory in an extinct dramatic structure", says the author in a note following the text. And this is how it truly appears in the first eight and a half pages of a set that contains nine in the French version. The narrator, detached from the object they describe, is manifested only through phrases like "maybe" or "impossible to know", but nothing through an "I" that could potentially be involved. With the last lines of the text, however, everything is reversed. The speaker's "I" comes fully into the picture, switching the perspective around:

> the knife is the wound, the neck the axe, is the fallible supervision part of a plan, to which device is the lens fastened, which sucks the colour from the gaze, across which eye-socket is the retina stretched, who OR WHAT asks about the picture, LIVING IN THE MIRROR [*Spiegel*],[11] is the man with the dance-step I [ICH: capitalised in original], his face my grave, I [ICH] the woman with the neck wound, right and left in the hands the divided bird, blood in the mouth, I [ICH] the bird, which shows the murderer the way into the night with the writing of its beak, I [ICH] the frozen storm.

The description becomes a drama of the self, and the condensed and suspended image becomes a potential dramatic context (it contains virtually all the elements: scenery, characters, action, albeit frozen), The "I" of the writer appears as such and projects itself: in a reversal, the description becomes like a glove turned inside out, a monologue. The speech is in the first person, revealing the "explosion of a memory" in the psyche (*Explosion of a Memory* was the English title of the play). The reader is then led to reconsider their relationship to the speaker's voice. The fact that this "I" is projected in all the figures of the image complicates the reception of the text, the whole description becoming the *mirror* of the authorial "I". This authorial "I" is both diffracted and condensed in the scene described, through a dizzying layering of masks which the reader must rearrange to build their own fiction(s).

From the plot to actantial narrative schema

We agree that in some cases, the complex pleasure that we have been discussing presupposes that the reader is a "curious connoisseur", knowledgeable about poetic conventions and the historical conditions that govern their production and can also disregard them. But we still affirm that through the observation of the plot and the historically coded identification of dramatic forms that they carry out in their reading, they may get locked in a speculative description of a superficial model that seeks to understand how individual characters within a particular aesthetic function. It is thus possible for the reader to fail to grasp the dynamic forces that govern the plot – in other words, to fail to take account of actual theatrical action in the true sense of the term.

Produced from theories of narrative that seek to provide a tool for describing the action of any narrative outside of historically dated aesthetic categories, actantial analysis, a macro-structural model rather than the analysis of plot, may be a helpful tool. Anne Ubersfeld in *Lire le théâtre* [*Reading Theatre*] (1977), adapts the theoretical model of Greimas for the stage, in order to "discover a small number of relations between terms that are much more general than character, terms that we will call actants".[12] According to Ubersfeld, this can help to describe the deep structures of the work as they appear in the theatrical text. The advantage of the system lies in the fact that one can dispense with both the psychological analysis of character and the analysis of a specific aesthetic, since its primary purpose is to identify some element of the work that sometimes escapes the reader, who is habitually more focused on the psychology of characters and on the dramaturgy of the theatrical text than on the emergence of abstract forces and their syntactic arrangement. The second advantage of this tool is that it works, in a very general way, on the whole of the play, and in a specific way, at each movement of the dynamic of the action, scene by scene, or even sequence by sequence. Finally, the main usefulness is that this model is an excellent way to ask questions and to find several answers. Put differently, this model is not a key that would establish *a* "truth" about the text but a simple hermeneutical apparatus for establishing and clarifying the choices of the reader and director with respect to the dynamics of dramaturgy and the creation of meaning.

The first movement is thus to determine *actants*, not necessarily characters. The actant, which may or may not be present on the stage (it can appear only in the discourse of one or more characters), is a collective character (the chorus, a group of soldiers, etc.), abstraction (the society, freedom, love, God, etc.), a group of characters or a character.

It is a subject in the grammatical sense of the term, i.e. an element that is in the text and that has an object – a purpose or a goal that determines action – that does or seeks something (or someone). To do this, it is helped by other elements or, on the contrary, other elements oppose the pursuit of this object. The *subject* wants and seeks an *object*, assisted by *helpers* and opposed by *opponents*. This is the basic summary of the narrative and dramatic actantial system. Consequently, we can ask in what name and for what reason this subject seeks its object, what abstract force drives them forward. We then assume an addresser, and will also wonder what the subject is moving toward, what abstract thing it seeks and thus also assume that there is an addressee. Thus, driven by a force, an addresser, the subject seeks its object to go toward an abstract destination, an addressee.

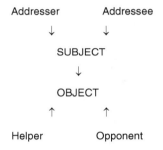

The actantial model does not propose one single right answer, or any certainty that ticks all the right boxes, but only a proposed schema for reflection that encompasses the entire structure of the text or a particular moment in the story. The structure is conceived as *a machine for reflection* rather than as a system to which the play could be reduced. This actantial schema is therefore a tool – sometimes helpful, at other times less so – a way of building views on the action, of asking questions, to which there will not necessarily be single answers. On the contrary, the answers will be the ones that the reader makes depending on what they observe in the discourse expressed by the text. The schema serves simply as a procedure by which to think, by which to ask the deep questions that govern the structure of the play. By asking those questions, it also allows the reader to put aside, at least during this process of reflection, their natural tendency to imagine that the characters are living men and women, for example, and to remember that they are textual constructs. In addition, because they set up a network of meaning governed by syntax, this scheme necessarily engages the reader to think of the actant, not as a subjective unit, but as a discursive entity caught up in a network of relations with other non-subjective discursive units. As such, an actant may have as object another actant, and it can be helped by actants that are also helpers, or countered by actants that are also opponents. An actant, a role or a character can thus no longer be seen independently, but according to mobile, evolving relations with other actants, roles, characters that are contained in discourse.

Since we have spoken of a "questioning machine" (or hermeneutical machine), let us ask a few of our own in order to deepen our demonstration of how the actantial model can be applied to the reading of theatre. Based on a schema developed by Anne Ubersfeld in a slightly modified form, it can be said that in *Oedipus Rex*, Oedipus is an actant (an animated actant) and that he is a subject. To the question "What is he looking for?" or "What does he want?" we can answer that his object is "a culprit", that is to say "himself" or, more simply, "Oedipus". It is not insignificant to note this and to note that at the moment when the culprit is named by the play, the objet will be unknown, plural and ambiguous, the replica of the subject himself. Similarly, while it appears that Oedipus' helper was Creon, or the Chorus or the city, and that his opponents were Jocasta and Tiresias, one will see that all may well change camp as the scenes (or rather episodes with the different protagonists in conflict, and the *stasima* of the Chorus) and the action progresses. Jocasta will slow the progress of recognition in her own interest and in the interest of Oedipus; Tiresias tells the truth in what he considers to be the interest of the subject and his quest for the object, and the Chorus also moves from one position to another. As for the addresser, by asking the question "what makes the subject act?" or "what is the force that drives the subject to act?" or "on account of what does the subject act?" we can answer "society", or "the gods" or "destiny". In posing the same question with respect to the addressee, the answers may be the same, but may also be "the self" or "identity". The issue is therefore not one of finding a right response to questions that are, by definition, open and ambiguous, but to reflect on the functioning of the play through a sort of sentence, a kind of syntax that allows for the development of several responses and for the setting up a narrative structure that takes account of this. The narrative structure operates both on a macro-systemic level (in relation to the play as a whole) and on a micro-systemic one (in relation to a single moment).

Again, this actantial schema, which some have turned into a panacea, is only meant to help describe a play without having to appeal to the notion of plot and by trying to avoid the trap of character psychology – nothing else. The actions and speculations of the reader are as follows: (1) to use the syntactic structure of a typical sentence such as "because of X, and with the objective of Y, a subject has a goal, and for this they are aided by Y and opposed by Z"; (2) to fill in as many parts of this hypothesis as they can (or to fail to do so, which can also be helpful) while thinking about this based on the discourse observed in the text; and (3) to understand the reasons (which they must find in the text) why they fill in their hypothesis in such a way. And this is how they can, with a bit more purpose and objectivity, build a series of abstract tales that can account for what they read.

From dramaturgical reading to dramaturgy

With each reading, the text becomes an object of appropriation. It carries within it the potential for the elaboration of the reader's own fiction, for a virtual or real representation, for play and even for the opinions that one might have on a given theatrical text. Therefore, thinking about what happens as a result of reading is really a case of actualising this potential. It is a way of appropriating and exploiting reading: the need to read, interpret or actualise such a given text onstage; to render the operation of reading a text, or this particular text, legitimate. If we consider what comes before reading, we must account for the development of objective criteria governing this reading: What are the indicators of space and time? How do we establish a dramatic structure or logic based on a reading?

Thus, once the reader has noted (mentally and more or less systematically) indications of space, time and events, the number of lines and how they are distributed, and the principle by which they are linked, they will be able to rebuild, build or tell several stories from the dramatic sequence they have determined. The big question will be to know which one they choose, or if they choose several. But nothing prevents the reader from assuming several narrative threads and multiple perspectives at once, from the very moment they have found evidence for them in their reading, not being bound to represent the story in a theatre. However, as we have seen, when the reader who becomes a practitioner comes into contact with other practitioners, they must at some point in the rehearsals adopt a common view on the narrative that will provide the general line that the process of representation will follow. This is so that information, impulses and the overall composition of the show and the audience's pleasure can be shaped around a common axis. We should note, however, that theatre practitioners themselves can, if they wish, make their staging complex, adopt several points of view and "tell" several stories. First, during rehearsals, since one needs to consider various pathways before choosing, then also during the staging, to make several interpretative lines available to the spectator. And, of course, the effect on the audience will not be the same for a staging that seeks to bring across a single narrative line as for one that plays with the polysemy of the dramatic apparatus. Finally, in many contemporary texts, narrative, action and the concept of plot are questioned, deconstructed, weakened or erased. Consequently, the consolidation of *mise en scène* around a tale, or a few major tales, is no longer possible. Accordingly, Koltès creates a system of complex relations and exchanges that relate to a series of micro-stories that challenge the notion of a main narrative point of view. Instead of knowing what the story is saying, the reader must try to figure out, in each sequence, what this fragment is telling them. They must try to determine the complex relations that exist between a given fragment and all the rest or, alternatively, to establish what it does not say and what the reader or spectator must themselves elaborate upon coming into dialogue with the text and with the practitioners.

Now, according to the biases of the reader and/or the author of the dramatic work, the text can be used in very different ways: it can be cut, modified or rewritten for the theatre. One can also represent it in all its literalness (the text, the whole text and nothing but the text). So, we agree that reading is just like an ordinary stage in the staging process as it too produces a dramatic interpretation. And when preparing the transition to the stage (for example, during "table work"), the dramaturg (in his function as reader) will make their choice from different networks of meaning and different forms of staging, after giving full consideration to all and at the risk of circumscribing the performance. For the dramaturg, a coherent "reading" of the text is important, one that can foster coherence in staging. The first way to avoid the pitfall of a closed reading is then to observe the initial results on the platform. This affords another view of the text. The second way is to avoid working at a table, "to do everything straight away", as Vitez would say. One then puts the text into play, without any prior thinking, linking it to the work of the actor. When the jointly composed readings around a table (involving director, dramaturg and production team) are dispensed with, a different, more spontaneous kind of energy can emerge, which unleashes the imagination of the actors. One also avoids the dogmatism of the prompt book that is carefully composed by the director and dramaturg with the production team based on a series of readings. But this process can also be a sham, in the sense that the director often has not "done everything straight away" and ends up controlling his practitioners even more, insofar as these practitioners have not been presented with the main choices available to them, the director having made *their* choice. And the skill and honesty of a Vitez are needed so that this approach does not end up being a false democracy under the guise of the "let's just do it" concept. Indeed, an overall incoherence is another danger.

A third way has been devised by the group known as tg STAN. It involves doing away with the director. The actors take some time (at least a month) to discuss among themselves the way to read, interpret and play the text, and the overall use of the stage (set design, general movements of the actors). Afterwards, the actors "stage" the play directly before an audience. The actors must therefore always be on the set, watching each other play, even when they do not have to intervene. As can be expected, the energy is at a maximum and coherence must be worked out on the spot, as the practitioners (the actors) interact and as the audience observes this entire process. However, this very modern invention is also a recycling of past behaviours of the actor, in a knowing, self-conscious way. What remains particular to this practice is the immediate implementation of the play without a director, or with a director who has not analysed the text, or who has not sufficiently worked on it, and who, on the grounds of preserving a high level of energy, often sacrifices coherence and depth. That is where we frequently observe the drawbacks (but also, sometimes, the risky pleasures) of pure stage dramaturgy based on the immediacy of sensation. Even so, a dramatic reading, or staging, achieved through table work or directly on the stage, or through a balance of both, implies choices. Indeed, it implies a series of possible readings that are abandoned in the interest of coherence, which itself must also be readable and visible. Thus, even without a dramaturg, the *mise en scène* still creates a dramaturgy.

In his *Écrits sur le théâtre* (1982), Michel Vinaver quotes Vitez as saying, "I believe in the merits of an unfinished text, one that presents challenges to directors and actors. An unsolvable text."[13] The text, according to Vitez (quoted in Vinaver) consists in words addressed "to the reader, the actor and the director, for them to imagine a play".[14] And those to whom the text is addressed must construct their own world of representation, whether the author proposes transitions between states, does away with punctuation, decides to add layers of complexity to their text or make it polyphonic, or writes with the unhindered "flow of words". The dramaturg, the reader tasked with formulating *a* reading of the staged actualisation of the text, after giving an interpretation, fades away to just leave the director.

Building on the work of Joseph Danan and Yannic Mancel, we can therefore outline a kind of possible operation of the dramaturgical function as it is conceived at present in France, from the act of reading to the act of staging. In the course of reading at the stage known as "table work", the dramaturg and the director, along with actors, costume designers, set designers, lighting designers, musicians, sound engineers, stagehands, platform managers or technical directors, first read the text line by line, focus on difficulties, discuss the meanings and order of words, syntax, connotations, sonorities. At this stage, the dramaturg must remain discreet: encouraging questions; not imposing any definitive answers; carefully cultivating queries, indecision, hypotheses, if only to give others the freedom to think and create play and meaning. Far from hammering home meaning and truth, the function of the dramaturg is to take inventory of, and deconstruct, the features of the text, so as to effectively reassemble them afterwards on the stage, during rehearsal, and under the watchful authority of the director.

What is necessary then is to use, materially, concretely and objectively, what the text says about characters, space, time, movements and circumstances, to constitute a narrative structure, or some sort of "fable" (which is not necessarily a linear one) based on articulations, images, elements specific to a staged arrangement. In addition to this textual analysis, crafted beforehand but in a group, the dramaturg is responsible for "feeding the imagination" of the other practitioners by giving documents linked to text to staged. Another aspect of their work is to aid in the analysis of words, phrases, fragments and scenes, by providing all sorts of historical, literary, critical, artistic and cinematographic material that can shed light on these. This is so that the different partners can approach the text through the lens of a given referential system, which each must then appropriate. The dramaturg is an analyst, researcher, translator, a curator of references and a "raider of concepts" [*cambrioleur de concepts*], and is above all a mediator who must be able to transmit what he has gathered. They must also be able to listen to those who have not done the work that they have, but who come with their instruments (techniques and physical capacities) to elaborate, with them, a specific space and time of play based on the text. The dramaturg communicates and transmits, but does not impose, and does not decide, contrary to the director. Sometimes, they suggest. And when they return to the theatre to watch the first run-throughs, they see the work through a lens that is both old and new, and can then "post-rationalise" as Jacques Lassalle has said, all that the unexpected, the un-planned-for, the random and the accidental have imposed on the empirical and artistic process of *mise en scène*. They are the spectator par excellence. They can give some advice, but without breaking what has been done, so as to open up new meaning, from and in what had been considered closed.

At the end of this journey, which has taken us from the position of the spectator to that of the reader, and from that of the reader to that of the dramaturg, we now find ourselves back on the stage, in the event, at the point where it all starts. However, we hope not to have gone around in circles, but to have carefully described operations that are at the heart of the two fundamental relationships specific to the reception of theatre. To describe breaking down dynamics allows us to show that the theatre beckons its spectators and readers to a witness a series of specific activities rather than simply passive reception: this is what we hope to have shown. We have laid bare the foundations and principles of the theatrical spectacle, and of the theatrical text, while always foregrounding those to whom both media are addressed. By so doing, we hope to have provided, if not theoretical tools to describe, understand and think of these relational and communicational dynamics, then at least some deeper insights. At the end of this journey, the reader of this work should be in a position to ask some critical questions, and even to venture their own analysis of theatrical performance, of dramaturgy and, above all, of their own behaviour. By constant recourse to the history of forms of representation, play, reception and writing, we have, to a significant extent, we hope, framed this complex and paradoxical art of theatre. What remains necessary, at this stage, is to consider its current state – in other words, what the different forms of theatre have offered, in recent years, to spectators and readers. This will now be our objective, as we use the prism of this question to examine the self-conscious practice that is contemporary *mise en scène*.

Notes

1 Marion Chénetier-Alev's *L'Oralité dans le théâtre contemporain: Herbert Achtenbusch, Pierre Guyotat, Valère Novarina, Jon Fosse, Daniel Danis, Sarah Kane* [*Orality in Contemporary Theatre: Herbert Achtenbusch, Pierre Guyotat, Valère Novarina, Jon Fosse, Daniel Danis, Sarah Kane*] (Sarrebrück: Éditions universitaires européennes, 2010).
2 Michel Vinaver, *Écrits sur le théâtre* [*Writings on the Theatre*] vols I and II (Paris: L'Arche, 1982), n.p.
3 Vinaver, *Écrits sur le théâtre*, n.p.
4 Bernard-Marie Koltès, *Quai Quest* [*Quay West*] (Paris: De Minuit, 1985), p. 60.
5 "Mais plus je le dis, plus je le cache [. . .], ne me demande plus qui je suis." Ibid., p. 20.
6 Sarah Kane, *Blasted* (London: Bloomsbury, 2003).

7 Sarah Kane interview, in Natasha Langbridge and Heidi Stephenson, *Rage and Reason: Women Playwrights on Playwriting* (London: Methuen, 1997), p. 131.
8 Sarah Kane quoted in Michael Billington, "Picking Up the Pieces: 1990–1997", in *State of the Nation: British Theatre Since 1945* (London: Faber & Faber, 2007), pp. 352–353.
9 Sarah Kane, *Cleansed* (London: Bloomsbury, 2003) (original work published 1998).
10 Heiner Müller, *Explosion of a Memory* (New York: PAJ Books, 2001).
11 Literally mirror, but also the name of the leading German magazine.
12 From the translation by Frank Collins, *Reading Theatre* (Toronto, ON: University of Toronto Press, 1999), p. 33.
13 Vinaver, *Écrits sur le théâtre*, n.p.
14 Ibid.

Part VII

STAGING
Traditions, concerns

How can we describe the current theatre scene(s)? What benchmarks can we establish, given the diversity that characterises theatrical practices at the beginning of the twenty-first century? It is difficult to orient oneself in the contemporary theatrical landscape as it seems fragmented, marked by the coexistence of multiple and singular practices. It is all the more difficult because it appears that the early 2000s is a very peculiar period, perhaps one of transition, caught between the aesthetics of great historical figures who appeared in the 1960s and 1970s and the new positions of an already different time that seems to be defined in reaction to them. It will be additionally challenging for the Anglo-Saxon reader to have the same exhaustive knowledge of French scholarship that we referred to in the original French edition of this book. Of course, we do make a few references to the current British and American theatre scene, but the majority of our reference points tend towards continental Europe.

The last decades have been a unique kind of age, a "golden age" according to Antoine Vitez, of the relatively recent phenomenon of *mise en scène*, which has been enshrined, often institutionalised and manifested itself in striking, brilliant and historical ways. But we have also seen the advent of a period of mutation that marks both the passage from one generation to another and an undeniable change in context (political, aesthetic, ideological) leading to a profound questioning of the art of theatre. Between the shadow cast by the author-directors of the generation of 1968 and the stakes involved in new practices, the frameworks and principles allowing for an understanding of the art of staging are more polymorphic today than they have ever been.

It is in this space of uncertainty that all the aspects of staging and dramaturgy are played out today: in the space between what must surely be considered as an essential inheritance, and the necessary recognition of a new situation. The affirmation that characterised the second half of the twentieth century has thus given way to interrogation. The certainties of the powers of the stage and of a triumphant theatricality have been displaced by doubts and attempts at reinvention, with all the complexities and paradoxes that the term "reinvention" conveys – nothing is ever truly invented; every "new" thing is, in fact, a thing rediscovered. "Reinvention" floats between a desire for novelty and the quest for an original essence, and involves a tension between tradition and the search for singular affirmations. After fifty years of affirmation and exhibition of its legitimacy and its powers, staging practice seems to be trying to redefine itself, as much out of a sometimes narcissistic quest of an irretrievable "essence" of theatricality, as out of a desire to recast its links with reality. And at the heart of these approaches, whatever may be said sometimes, it is the art of staging that remains the primary object of these questions. Under the sometimes overwhelming shadow of the great figures and the great explorations of the 1960s and 1980s, the issue of staging, not as dogma, but as a bringing together of the interplay of the different parts and stakes of the theatrical work, thus returns to an exploration of its fundamental principles.

Should we always exalt the nostalgia of an historic golden age or embrace the supposed external signs of "modernity"? In this period of change, a number of official or unofficial commentaries, declarations and proclamations testify to the consternation that such diversity elicits. The most varying and reductive discourses, coming from institutional circles or from certain critical ones, not to mention from the practitioners themselves, most often reflect a search for magical solutions, whether it be the invocation of old or foreign models, or the permanent redefinition of a new "nature" of the theatre. The apparent thinking among such circles is that it is necessary to renew the outward appearance of theatre, conferring on it a new calibrated identity or, conversely, to save it from a supposed decline by returning to values of craftsmanship deemed to be eternal and established.

Thus, we will have encountered recurrent discourses claiming that theatre is an outdated art form, and that its only viable future resides in the incorporation of "new media": video and other visual arts, technological devices, interactivity, etc. Discourses of renewal also focus on the necessary process of hybridisation that characterises many other contemporary practices, to create an "interdisciplinarity" that intersects with other arts. French performance practices, in particular, have been criticised for becoming too lax and lacking in sufficiently rigorous training. Then we heard that only a handful of "masters", predominantly hailing from Eastern Europe, have retained the *tradition* of the actor and eschewed the presumption of decadence now associated with it. We also heard that the salvation of the actor could be inspired by the German pattern: from the permanent *troupes* that made their mark in Germany, most notably the great theatre houses in Berlin led by headline directors (Thomas Ostermeier, Frank Castorf, etc.), not to mention the artistic quality of smaller, less well-known theatres in other *lander* (Cottbus, Augsbourg, etc.). The same goes for *mise en scène*, a source of perennial debate, redefinition and interrogation along the lines of whether we should display stage creation as a *supposedly* non-hierarchical, "collective" enterprise, or whether to use it as a form of self-affirmation by practitioners and institutional induction, blending aesthetic concerns with different ways of doing theatre? These different *modi operandi* are like waves that constantly return but in new (redefined) ways, that call on different visions of the artistic, societal and political present and on various filiations, real or imagined.

It is even more telling that the discipline of theatre has recently invested in specific *mise en scène* courses within the most prestigious theatre schools, an endeavour that has only ever been tried once before when Vitez was at Chaillot. Whether it be an *ab initio* course at the National Theatre School of Strasbourg (TNS), a modular course that runs alongside other core aspects of the degree at the National Conservatory of Dramatic Arts (CNSAD), a master's degree in "*mise en scène* and dramaturgy" at Paris-Nanterre University or any of the other permutations that are starting to appear at different universities and theatre schools, these new training programmes are of great political importance. They testify to a new, if slightly ambiguous, governmental drive to aid "burgeoning" *mise en scène*, poised somewhere between a historic legacy that must be passed on and a practice that needs reviving. The question is, of course, exactly on which principles and paradigms are such ideas based. Perhaps one of the most gratifying aspects of this pedagogical surge is that the first directors to graduate will undoubtedly experiment with unique and heterogeneous aesthetics that are anathema to any dominant model. Indeed, in 2004, the first public performances of two students graduating from the National Theatre School of Strasbourg testify to the importance of a personal rather than standardised approach: their work was highly accomplished, yet radically different. And so were the productions of some of the former interns of the former Unité Nomade. No less pleasing is the fact that many more women are being encouraged to become directors (for example, Aurélia Guillet with *Penthésilée-paysage*, inspired by Kleist and H. Müller, 2004/2005; Irène Bonnaud with *Tracteur*, by

H. Müller, 2003; *Lenz*, by Büchner, 2004; Célie Pauthe with *Quartett*, by H. Müller, 2003).

Would the solution to the crisis of *mise en scène* require us to articulate its various inheritances, whether of the "great masters" of the 1970s–1980s or to indulge in more recent practices? All this points to a thread uniting memory and contemporaneity, and suggests that around it distinctive aesthetics are emerging, just as much as a movement is being prolonged.

Writing for the theatre today

In the pages that follow, our aim will be to draw up a kind of landscape of some of the issues that have underpinned *the art* of staging for about half a century, issues that determine the understanding one can have of the contemporary stage. Having presented some elements in the previous chapter of how to approach the reading and analysis of the theatre text, and given that numerous publications have, of late, made it possible to take stock of the intense activity of writing and publishing the theatre text, we shall return to it only in terms of staging. Michel Azama's interesting anthology in three volumes[1] should, nonetheless, be mentioned here as it guides the reader through the vast maze of editions of theatrical texts in French. As does a recent issue of the journal *Critique* (Editions de Minuit, no. 699–700, September, 2005), and *Théâtre/Public* (no. 223, January–March, 2017) on new writings in Europe. These will enable to reader to set up some interpretative tools in the way of theatre critique.

The relatively little importance given to the publication of theatrical texts (especially those of contemporary authors), both in the press and by the major publishing houses, hardly reflects the large volume of publications among less powerful publishers (les Solitaires intempestifs, les éditions Théâtrales, Théâtre ouvert, Actes Sud-papiers, for example), or the increasing number of translations of plays initially written in German, English, Spanish, Catalan, Italian and many other languages. Furthermore, the profusion of manuscripts, deposited with the SACD and sent to the editorial boards of the theatres, testifies to the enormous vitality of theatrical writing. It would take too long to list all the French-speaking authors (since the Francophone theatres of Africa, the West Indies and Quebec are extremely profuse, lively and creative) and all the foreign authors newly translated (thanks in particular to the efforts of the Maison Antoine Vitez – International Centre for Theatre Translation [*Centre international de la traduction théâtrale*]) that have marked the theatrical landscape of recent years without even having experienced the honours of the stage. The construction sites of contemporary writing are vast, diverse and very encouraging, even though they are rarely cited by the mainstream media. Initiatives such as the "Mousson d'été" and the "Mousson d'hiver" in Pont-à-Mousson, among other major events, funding for dramatic writing and writing residencies (Chartreuse de Villeneuve-lez-Avignon, for example) also allow the emergence and diffusion of talents, texts and writings. And we will never be able to account for all the work of the young troupes and what are wrongly called "small theatres", which keep looking for new works that can be represented when the "big theatres" confine themselves to the well known, the tried and tested. (Of course, we exclude the Theatre de la Colline from this category, and also, in another sense, the Théâtre du Rond-Point, whose vocation is precisely to stage contemporary plays. The Théâtre Ouvert, like the Théâtre du Rond-Point, has for many years also been indulging in the superb task of discovering and bringing new talent to the stage.) Yet in recent years, in the United Kingdom, Germany and France, it seems that a larger audience of readers and a lot of the more famous theatres are becoming more interested in the contemporary, opening up to the current trends in dramatic writing. And in London, the Royal Court is a brilliant example. It is high time.

However, just like for contemporary music, the general public seems timid, lost, unsettled at times by forms it does not know, and especially that it does not recognise. Theatrical writing, since the days of Anouilh, Giraudoux or even Sartre, has changed, like all artistic forms. It has become "freer", and no longer truly respects genres, categories, conventional layout, character, plot, Aristotelian action, psychology or the "dramatic" point of view. It focuses on language, on "the speaking" ["*le dire*"] of the text, as we have seen when discussing the text's "orality". It works to

> accentuate the play that speech performs with itself, but also rhythmic activities, formal variations, the changing arrangements of affects, verbal overflows of any kind. It places diversity elsewhere than in individuation and mere psychological artifice: in degrees of communication for example, or the differentials of intensity.[2]

It explores the anxiety of being, the complexity of the ego, the search for the intimate, as, for example, the work of Jean-Luc Lagarce, and especially his latest texts *Le Pays lointain* [*The Distant Country*], has been able to do through its distinctive poetry. It questions the world and its catastrophes and suffering, but also, always, its social and political issues. But it does so in another way, without resorting necessarily to fable and characters. It seeks to produce other ways of speaking, figuring and recording the theatre through the exhibition of sounds and words, the recording of gestures in writing, and the sequencing of these in sentences, whether fragmentary or otherwise. Aware that the theatre is space, time, body and also writing, authors apply themselves to forging links between their poetics, their poetry, their style and their way of writing, with this space, time and these bodies that they imagine for the construction of their texts. All of this in a world that is also in search of itself, experiencing one of the most radical and detrimental crises in history, where the meanings that seemed to have been found in history have now been destroyed. Filled with all kinds of doubts, caught up in a radical catastrophe, vacillating in the ruins of great ideologies, contemporary authors continue to write nonetheless, chiselling form, reordering and *dis*ordering language. What language should one make theatre speak, what should one make it say, when the issue is no longer necessarily one of *telling*? Few things, but precious ones nonetheless: play, speech, breath, rhythm, questionings and doubts, construction in the making – in short a broken, fragmented or sometimes lyrical, discontinuous discourse. The texts thus play on what is exactly at the heart of contemporary human behaviour: a verbal exchange that is uncertain and perpetually being questioned.

> Writing for the theatre today is a question of writing about catastrophes and the world, considering what they offer us and allowing us to work primarily on forms. If humanity speaks, it is because something has happened to people: a precise event that forces them to take a stand and speak about it, and thus to give voice to sites of humanity that have not yet found their form.[3]

It is from this necessity to recount the disasters of the present time that contemporary writing, the text in motion, is born, so that the power of what demands representation, writing and thinking (the power of seismic shocks) is expressed. It is also in this respect that the theatre is a constant political operation, even if it wishes to deviate from politics, because the desire to eventually bring individuals together in one place presupposes that writers and practitioners speak to audiences and to themselves under the blows of the catastrophes of history, whether they like it or not. And catastrophe is what the twentieth century has most succeeded in, and the twenty-first century seems to be following hard in its footsteps. The question then arises as to how the theatre takes account of it, or, on the contrary, how to open new possibilities within it.

Memory and forgetting

In order to establish itself, Western theatre, unlike, for example, Far Eastern theatre, has been obliged to abandon pre-existing forms: to break with them in order to invent others. At the same time, although these inventions and ruptures are not absolutely new, their intentions have already been realised, consciously or not, from the memory of other forms already inscribed in the history of Western theatre, or those existing in the reality of other non-European forms of representation or ritual practices. Through recycling and appropriation, novelty is then developed from elements borrowed from other historical or geographical spaces.

And these three phenomena can be perfectly simultaneous: a phenomenon of forgetting and abandoning forms of representation that have become inadequate, and that are, at certain moments in history, overshadowed by forms that are deemed more modern and adapted to fit into a particular aesthetic and social function; a phenomenon of invention, of the formation of seemingly or truly new forms, which may appear as ruptures in relation to old, abandoned ones – in other words as an aesthetic progress in line with modernity as it is conceived or perceived at a given point in history; and finally, a phenomenon of memory, re-reading and rediscovery of old forms that are recycled within these modernities to give them historical legitimacy, and thus greater authority, even if it means disguising them or adapting them to the apparent ruptures.

But there is no place, here, to speak of an immanence of forms. For while it is clear that Western art likes to repeat generic forms to the point of exhausting them, it also has a tradition of opposing pre-existing forms, of eclipsing them, of "forgetting" them. It recycles forgotten forms and revisits ones "ignored" and foreign to its operation, so as to invent other aesthetics of representation. In addition to the phenomena of masking, recycling and hybridisation that can be observed in every period of the history of the theatre (and the history of all the artistic genres, for that matter), it is as a result of this dialectic that radically new forms appear that are neither past forms belonging to another layer of historical practices and aesthetics nor exogenous forms directly imported. Similarly, practitioners, or the public, are not to be blamed for not necessarily knowing the forgotten forms on which the ruptures that are displayed are constructed. These choices, or evolutions, will simply be explained here by looking at the way in which the novelty of formal experiments, whether apparent or not, has taken root.

In addition, we know that "representation", which we have defined in aesthetic terms, presupposes that there must be a memory in order to be clearly situated. To speak, to act, to intervene in a discursive and social relationship is to know the place from which signs are emitted. Without consciousness of this place, there is indeed no condition of transmission of the message, therefore neither interaction nor communication. And to determine this place, it takes a memory. In other words, via an awareness of location, of the time in which the communicative relationship is situated, and *through* consideration of those who are being addressed, one must take into account the referential system that frames this situation. To represent something, or to *perform* an action and speech, is first to situate oneself and to represent oneself, to imagine place, time and the other from a memory that, somehow, allows the present message to simply exist. I cannot be there, and I cannot act and speak except in reference to pre-existing statements and actions, and in relation to the referential systems that inform and produce my own presence and define the relationship I have with others. These are self-evident facts and even banalities that are not worth extending, however, because theatre is primarily a communication situation. Thus, we must consider that the relation to the past, via the memory one has of it, is always essential, regardless of the form that is used. And even when theatre challenges the notion of communication, questions the relationship to place, time and others, or forgets or attempts to forget the past lives of certain generic or aesthetic forms of communication, it underscores their history by virtue of this very rupture. It "represents itself" otherwise, but in an attitude of rupture with the past, thanks to the polemical or schematic memory of it that it has. This chain of memory – which also includes its reverse, forgetting – concerns both practitioners – authors, actors, directors, scenographers, etc. – and spectators, since the theatrical event overall rests on the history that precedes it.

Thus, within an "area of play" in the sense in which Erwing Goffmann understands it, in a pragmatic and sociological framework specific to any one communication scenario, the theatre aims to present an original, deferred, aesthetic mass of communication. To do this, it can "unframe" the system so as to highlight or disrupt readability, or to play on levels of readability while ensuring the possibility of decoding based on the references known to all the partners of the communication process. Thanks to the recognition of elements that are fixed or presented as such, whether they are traditionally arranged, shifted or otherwise distributed, the theatre simultaneously relies on the memory of past communication situations and can, depending on the situation, repeat, transgress or abandon them. It can also create new ones (which themselves will be repeated if their use is well received by audiences). Consequently, recognition, which presupposes memory, and surprise, which disturbs repetition, together foster the play of theatre.

Forgetting, renovating, transgressing, repeating, recycling, inventing, breaking with traditions, recalling the past, surprising... but to what end? The aesthetic and political urgency resulting from the bloodbath of the Second World War sealed the erosion of dramatic forms. And we wondered whether it was still possible to write, or imagine another world possible for the theatre when radical doubt had set in. But we have written, despite all the doubts about this tattered world. The theatre has been instrumental as a space for writing that sought to imitate the breakdown and breaking apart of words and values. Perhaps there was nothing more to be done than to perform the catastrophe of meaning, of history and of the theatre itself, but we have always written regardless. Faced with this historical, political and aesthetic failure, which denies any possibility of action, on the stage as in the world, it was possible to exorcise the obsession with death, catastrophe and doubt, through the sheer number of words, through the screams of those who drew up the catalogue of horrors, with no other syntax than that of accumulation or fragmentation. After indignation, pity, horror, derision, the denunciation of crimes against humanity, whatever they may be, and the stigmatisation of mankind's violent inhumanity, the theatre could yet reveal the human and political foundation that lay beneath all these misfortunes and that it was urgent to identify and combat through the use of the theatre itself. To doubt the world, to account for its explosion, is thus also to propose an organisation of words, phrases, discourse and theatrical devices that corresponds to the radicalness of the project. Guyotat, with *Eden, Eden, Eden*, or *Tomb for 500,000 Soldiers*, Genet with *The Screens*, Gatti overall and with *Public Song Before Two Electric Chairs* in particular, Heiner Müller in Germany, Edward Bond and Howard Barker in England, have thus played, each in their own way, on this multiple stylistic, dramaturgical and ideological explosion/stylistic diffraction that bears witness to an after-apocalypse, a post-catastrophe situated in and beyond the struggles, actualised through a dialogue with the dead and through the death of all things. In doing so, they drag the spectators into a crisis from which they can no longer return. The question "Why do you kill?" posed by Congolese writer Sony Lab'ou Tansi in *Parentheses of Blood*,[4] does not require an obvious answer and does not assume an easy moral resolution. That is not the purpose of theatre. Engaging with this question implies, for all theatre practitioners, including the author, an effort at complexification, at putting things in opposition, an exploration of words, sentences and performance spaces so that no spectator is tempted to answer simply. In this way, the great and perpetual scavenger-wrecker that is theatre will say *something* about the shipwrecks of the world.

It is thus clear that our role today is to avoid being timid by responding to the violence of a world in ruins with the violence of performance and text. The project would thus be to replace traditional dialogue with an absolutely brutal dialogue of body and scenographic space, as Rodrigo García has proposed, without always rising to the challenge:

> Theatre is a place for dialogue. But I do not want to talk peacefully. I want to establish another dialogue, perhaps more brutal, in any case more surprising and more uncomfortable. As in all my plays, people are the central theme here. People I know and for whom I work, actors who aspire to represent all the faces that we do not want to see, all the tears that we prefer to swallow, all the muscles that we dare not move, all the hopes that are buried. As in all my plays, bodies are the central theme. Bodies that are most beleaguered by problems, not those that we see in advertisements on television or in *Vogue*. As in all my plays, there is no shadow of shame or a truce for shyness. To live timidly is the cowardice that the governments we elect, and our trials, expect from us.[5]

This is why we do not oppose text and staging, dramatic literature and performance, in that some people's drama in the making sometimes has everything to do with the *work in progress* of others. But since our task in this work, as we have said, is not to take stock of contemporary writings, but rather of staging events, let us just say that events, *mises en scène* and performances obviously espouse the authors' concerns, if only because they often make them the material of their staging action. In the following panorama, we will encounter the questions that have been posed by authors, and will see how, with what tools and perhaps also why they manifest themselves here and now on the stage.

Finally, our approach is not intended to be exhaustive (because it cannot be so in our framework here). Instead, we intend to make a number of essential observations based on the position we have taken here of Western culture, and more particularly Europe and France. We wish to follow developments and to identify trends, but do not attempt to exhaust the field of individual practices, or to foster belief in the existence of any teleology. We also insist that the examples chosen are in no way a sort of prize list (there are ceremonies for that). If we are led to dwell on this or that spectacle, or on such and such a director, rather than on others, as we have done in the preceding chapters, it is because they prove to be significant: they illustrate trends or seem to concretely explore aesthetic questions specific to the practice of staging and its status. Thus, our ambition is to provide a number of benchmarks from which the reader, from the distinctive position of *current* spectatorship, can ask their own questions.

12
THE AGE OF ALL POWERS

The century of *Mise en scène*: this is how we can characterise the twentieth century in the history of the theatre – it is even more specifically the case of its second half. More than any other, it is the figure of the director that recent history has placed at the centre of the edifice of theatrical representation, in terms of aesthetics and public recognition, the institution and the production system. Jean Vilar, in the 1950s–1960s, still used the simple title of "stage manager": the specificity of his style resided, moreover, in a fundamental and classical desire to efface himself, giving pride of place to the work of the actors, the text and the tale that was told. His conception of a popular theatre was based primarily on the notion of texts to be played for all, ones capable of forming a common *repertory*. However, recent decades have established the director as the real *author* of the show, and with it a whole conception of stagecraft as a singular work of aesthetic and semantic creation, but also as a specific reading of a textual material. During the same period, from the 1960s to the 1980s, a generation emerged, in France as in most European countries, which embodied the advent of this central figure of the director who, in Vitez's words, was a "manufacturer of unique works, sand castles made of delicately assembled signs".[1] They were the director-artists, regardless of how they formulated the nature of their art. Planchon, Chéreau, Vitez, Vincent, Sobel, Mnouchkine, Régy, Brook, Strehler, Bob Wilson, Grüber, Stein, Langhoff and Fomenko are all signatures that bear the aesthetic identity of representation. Thus, as different as their aesthetics might be – and, more significantly: *in that* their aesthetics are diverse, distinctive – these are the names that appear at the forefront of the theatrical machine.

As Roger Planchon put it, "the contemporary era has revealed a new attitude towards the theatre: it establishes the difference between a dramatic writing that is called text and a scenic writing, called staging".

And, as a true historian of the performing arts, he adds: "of course, these two writings have always existed, but for centuries we did not realise it".[2] The assumption of staging as the centre of the theatrical event – as confirmed in the second half of the twentieth century – represents the empowerment and consciousness of the stage organisation in relation to the primacy of a text that remains the principle of representation, but whose concrete realisation is no longer supposed to be entirely and naturally contained within itself. The textual material is no longer self-sufficient, and the whole purpose of the art of *mise en scène* is to complement it, to embody it and make it actual (in the primary sense of the term), twinning it with another writing, that of bodies and voices in the space and time of representation. The director becomes a conductor, the centralising agent of the activities of the whole team of practitioners engaged in the show and the great director of the theatre. This is the great idea that has asserted itself in recent decades, and has suggested a recognition of a genuine act of creation, rather than a natural gesture of implementation. The director's work, insofar as it enacts the concrete signs of the stage based on the words of the text, amounts to a second act of "writing".

This movement of consciousness of stagecraft as autonomous creation is certainly not new. As we had occasion to mention at the beginning of this book, it takes its sources in the claim of the total Wagnerian theatrical work, and begins, from the beginning of the twentieth century and even the end of the previous century, with the naturalism of Antoine or the symbolism of Lugné-Poe, with the art of the actor of Stanislavski's and Danchenko's Moscow Art Theatre, with Craig and Appia. It developed through the staging aesthetics of artists like Dullin, Pitoëff, Baty and Jouvet. It has also been shaped by the methods of the Russian Meyerhold – and others. The generation of the 1960s and 1980s is therefore not the first generation of the art of staging, and is established on the foundations laid by a previous wave. A wave whose main concern was, in the words of Bernard Dort,

> to elevate representation to the dignity of the text, to make it the equal and the reflection of the literary text [. . .] And we have begun talking about scenic writing, the latter being considered the other side of dramatic writing. As its double and its accomplishment.[3]

This new generation is thus second, at least, but it is the one that concretises and boldly embraces the autonomisation of representation, the global displacement of the conception of theatre. It makes complete the movement that Dort has called a "Copernican reversal", which sees the centre of gravity of representation moving from the text to the stage, from dramatic writing to the art of staging. It consecrates the (now commonly recognised) advent of the director to the status of a veritable creator and master artist of the construction of signs that is the theatrical spectacle.

The meaning mill

The Brechtian model has been essential for most practitioners and critics of this generation. In this respect, June 1954 is a watershed moment in France: it is the date of the *Berliner* Ensemble's tour of Paris, with the staging of *Mother Courage and Her Children*. Other representations would follow, with as much impact, and it is known that thanks to its success in France and, more broadly, thanks to his success throughout Western Europe, Brecht was able to resist the accusations of "formalism" from the proponents of socialist realism, which made his situation very precarious in East Germany. It was therefore true for many a "revolution" and especially for members of the magazine *Théâtre populaire* (created in the wake of Jean Vilar's theatre), who decided to dedicate themselves to the dissemination of Brechtian aesthetics in France.

It was indeed a "sudden illumination". "This illumination was for me a fire", declared Roland Barthes a few years later,

> there is nothing from French theatre that is left before my eyes; between the *Berliner Ensemble* and other theatres, I have been made aware, not of a difference of degree, but of nature and almost of history [. . .] For me, Brecht made the taste of every imperfect theatre easier to swallow.[4]

It is not that he was completely unknown in France at the time: some articles had been devoted to him, some published translations had been published, and Vilar himself had staged *Mother Courage* at the TNP in 1951. It was the *performances* of the Berliner Ensemble that were historic, not the mere influence of Brecht the writer or even Brecht the theorist, but an overall practice of theatre, a practice of *staging* above all, which would represent a model for nearly a generation, in France and in Europe.

What then did people like Barthes or Dort discover in the Berliner Ensemble's performance at the Theatre des Nations that could fulfil their theatrical expectations? An exemplary practice, whose nature seemed to them to solve the contradictions to which the theatre falls prey and to reconcile the multiple aspirations that were then being articulated around the art of staging. Aspirations that Vilar's model of popular theatre had partly borne, but not fulfilled, and that Brechtian theatre would surpass. Here, finally, was a theatre that, to use Barthes' formulations, was "intelligent, political and of ascetic sumptuousness", "without hysteria", but also "pleasant", "refined while being popular", "an art at once accessible and difficult", "a theatre at once revolutionary, meaningful and seductive, what could be better?" "Where there was a desire for a popular Marxist theatre and a need for an art that rigorously monitored its signs", Barthes writes, Brechtian theatre was called upon. Based on the very plasticity of the scenic event, on the concreteness and the pleasure essential to it, Brecht thus offered the long-desired model of a "dramaturgy that fashioned a mode of thinking that was both political and 'semantic'".[5]

It is therefore the combination of the material and the symbolic, of the entertaining and the political, of pleasure and reflection, which was at the heart of the admiration for the Brecht's *critical* theatre. It offered practitioners the opportunity to reinvest the idea of popular theatre by reclaiming in light of the political stakes that shaped the ideological landscape of the 1950s and 1960s. Brecht's theatre was associated with "progressive" thought in general, and, specifically, of a Marxist kind. Brecht has thus allowed theatre to go beyond the sober legibility of the Vilarian stage (where the scenic elements are effaced by the text and its interpreters) toward a legibility of the *spectacle*, based on a self-conscious dramatic reading of the fable, a self-exhibiting arrangement of its material *signs*. The model of the Brechtian theatre thus intersected with another aspect of the intellectual landscape of those years, namely the development of semiology. Consequently, the stage, just as much as the text, becomes the site of the production of discourse by means of signs. The theatre is no longer placed in a position of authority, or granted the power to fascinate its receiver, but is conferred with the responsibility of placing its spectator in the critical posture of "distance", that of a reader of signs, one aware of the theatre's function. Furthermore, the idea of playing for a few was now a thing of the past. In other words, the theatre was no longer to be geared towards elite "connoisseurs" of theatre. It now had to orient its critical posture to a popular audience that would overcome its own self-alienation *thanks* to critical thinking. Without losing any of its materiality and theatrical efficiency – on the contrary, it would rely on these – the theatre stage thus fully became a site of production of signs and, therefore, a meaning mill: a total *writing*, a *comprehensive* creation, of which the artist-director becomes the guarantor, the primary producer, the new author.

The business of staging no longer claimed to reveal an allegedly eternal and universal nature, and would no longer hide its mechanisms in order to create an "illusion" that required the concealment of the theatricality inherent in it. Rather, it affirmed and displayed it, so that it could be *read* in the true sense of the term. It became an intervention, a commentary, a self-conscious performance of the textual material. It became discourse, a text superimposed on to the dramatic text, one constructed from it. The system of concrete signs that it implemented reflected a *critical* perspective on it, proposed a product, which was necessarily also a *reading*. It no longer claimed to be innocent, it not only became a *work*, aesthetically speaking, but it became *meaning*. The meaning no longer lay entirely in the words of the text, since the latter must be reactivated by the specific means of the stage within a global, coherent, conscious and semiotised interpretation.

While the first part of the twentieth century saw the advent of staging as a singular creative practice (from Stanislavsky to Jouvet) commonly referred to as "art theatre", the second half of the century confirmed this practice by basing it on the model of "critical theatre". With the Brechtian model, it was the political effectiveness of the theatre that was thus asserted. However, it should not be forgotten that it was around contemporary concerns that the "Brechtian revolution" came to take form. So much so that the Brechtian model in France came to surpass and replace the quest for a popular theatre as Romain Rolland had conceived of it at the beginning of the century and as it was embodied by Vilar (or others, like Jean Dasté at the Comédie de Saint-Etienne). In the intellectual and political context, particularly in the Marxist context, between the 1950s and 1960s and, in a different way, in the post-1968 period, the Brechtian conception of the theatre fulfilled the legitimacy of staging practice in its relation to reality. It was thus an aesthetic and semantic practice, an instrument of public awakening and the manifestation of the necessity of a discourse on the world, and finally, an essential political and social tool, with obvious political significance.

The keystone of this critical thrust, and of this autonomy of scenography elaborated from textual material, is thus the notion – also a Brechtian one – of "dramaturgy", which then becomes the heart of stagecraft. Dramaturgy is no longer understood in the sense of rules of writing and construction of the dramatic text, but rather its domain becomes that of scenic writing, and specifically, that of the transition of textual material to the construction of representation. While the logic contained in the text previously implied the forms of its representation, the advent of the director as author, and of *mise en scène* as a work in its own right, necessitates the reconstruction of the internal logic of the performance, which is no longer conceived as mere transposition or natural realisation of a play, but as a reading, and, more broadly, as a re-creation. There will be no longer just one *Tartuffe*, but that of Planchon after that of Jouvet; no longer one *Bérénice*, but the *Bérénice* of Planchon, which is quite distinct from that of Vitez that of Grüber; no longer one *Hamlet*, whatever the proposed staged version, but Chéreau's and Vitez's and that of Grüber, for example. So many different works, constructing their own interpretations and thus their own semantic discourses, but also their own aesthetic universes from the same textual material. The coherence of these different works must thus be reconstructed in the staged reality of the performance. Each one must establish a particular *point of view* that is ideologically based, which implies that the transition from written text to a specific system of signs (i.e. representation) must be clearly thought out.

Re-reading the "classics": the issue of interpretation

This sort of "re-creation", as we have deemed it, is most observable in the case of so-called "classic" texts, since the historical distance that separates the moment of writing from that of its representation doubles up and exhibits the hiatus that already exists between the text and its staged representation. Far more than for contemporary pieces, this historical and critical distance requires a specific point of view with respect to staging and to the "interpretation" of the work. In that regard, the dramaturgical and scenic interpretation of the play ostentatiously manifests a contemporary engagement with its material. It is this sense that Planchon has in mind when he remarks that, unlike contemporary plays, "the staging choices of a 'classic' are more clearly seen: we can measure the originality of the work".[6] Conversely, such a work of critical "re-reading" of the classics is only possible when the practice of *mise en scène* becomes *aware* of its singularity and of the autonomy of its writing. It is therefore not surprising that it is the staging of classics that has crystallised much of the most important debates of the day, that these staged classics have become historical examples and that they have testified most obviously to the critical dimension of *mise en scène* with its overall dramaturgical re-readings. To put it a little schematically, dramaturgy in the 1960s and 1970s set up, in all good conscience, reading grids that conditioned how a performance would be implemented, and proposed an interpretation that sometimes tended towards the univocal, in giving the theatrical act the responsibility of existing within these grids. With this temptation, by nature semiological and political, representation was then strongly oriented toward the spectator, who was supposed to find in the show what their "authors" had wanted to put in it. The spectator was thus offered, in this way, a pre-interpreted text and was happy when they correctly decoded the message, the understanding being that its dramaturgical approaches conveyed an ideology that was wider and more encompassing than that of director. Significantly, in nuancing his notion of the director as distinctive creator, Planchon, as he was supposed to have said, would point out that "it is not I who read *Tartuffe* but an era that reads it through me", as other periods read it through Coquelin or Jouvet. The era, thus, read its classics, appropriated them in the name of an overall sense of the times and represented them through the interpretative filter of psychoanalysis and Marxism. However, this semanticism often had the good fortune of being proposed by intelligent artisans, who themselves maintained a critical distance. They were, by and large, artists of the theatrical act, and not illustrators besotted by ideological machinery.

The *Tartuffe* cited above, directed by Planchon in a first version in 1962, then in another in 1974,[7] thus remained as the historical example of such a critical approach to the classics by means of the scene. Already, his 1958 interpretation of Molière's *George Dandin* had proposed a significant approach, which consisted in rejecting the presumed psychological and mythical timelessness of the classical work, in order to historicise it by delving back into its socio-historical context. In lieu of the traditional "romantic tears" by which Dandin was portrayed as an unfortunate cuckold, Planchon substituted a reading that highlighted a specific historical, social and political context of discourse. The cuckold Dandin proved, above all, to be torn between two worlds, and was the image of the bourgeois who had betrayed his class, fascinated by a feudal nobility to which he wanted to belong through marriage and that does not cease to frustrate him. The realisation of the fable was thus conditioned to a specific social environment and its interpretation guided, directed towards an essentially political and social meaning. The contextualisation was aided by the scenery that René Allio designed for the show (which represented the courtyard located between the house of the new Monsieur de la Dandinière and the farmhouse that brought Dandin his fortune), and Planchon's staging was characterised by the abundance of concrete signs that reflected on the platform the difference between the two worlds: the movement and daily activities of farm employees on the one hand, and the social rituals of the aristocracy on the other. In a typically Brechtian approach, the play was not driven by the psychology of the character but by their *situation* which imprinted itself on the fable. Its implementation on the stage involved the deployment of concrete signs contributing to the establishment of a certain realism, one that could provide an anchorage for a critical (and historicised) point of view. This sought to confirm the principle that "the goal of theatre is to translate the idea through concrete action" and that "the actor and the director must stage situations that they begin by describing and end up judging".[8] Contemporary critics saw in this *Dandin* a pathway to a "new use" of our classics",

> here was a Dandin that was not rehabilitated but understandable: neither cuckold, nor Hamlet, a little of both perhaps, but indeed a conflicted man, divided, split, bearing witness to his error, to the error of a whole class that has betrayed itself.[9]

This *mise en scène* was thus considered to be a contradictory case to make it readable, by a social contextualisation that drew on Marxist categories to account for "a conception of the work of Molière [. . .] through its inscription in the performance space, through its *material* re-creation".[10]

These are the same principles that govern the production of *Tartuffe*. Allio's scenery for the first version reimagined Orgon's house as an opulent one whose parquet floor and paintings reflected the bourgeois taste for private comfort that Tartuffe disturbs. However, its many pious paintings also testified to an imaginary sensual piety that revealed the religious ideology of the 1960s. Within this scenery a certain naturalism was displayed, but this space functioned mainly as a "playing machine" accompanying the movement of the fable, a decoy mechanism that analogised the structure of the play: with every passing act, panels rose up revealing a new part of Orgon's house and enlarging the performance area, until the arrival of the king's officer. In this surprise twist appearance at the end, an example of the plot device of the *deus ex machina*, the officer is haloed in a dazzling light streaming from a large backdrop door. He appears in a darkened space where the wheels of a giant mechanism are shown (and are then replaced by the equestrian statue of the king in the second staging, in 1974). As such, between material signs that fostered the reconstitution of a historical-ideological framework and more symbolic ones reflecting a dramaturgical-structural reading of Molière's play, the staging apparatus revealed a strong analytical approach, and translated a critical point of view which the stage was to transmit in a concrete and living way.

Therefore, in Planchon's *mise en scène*, an analytical and didactic clarity was intersected with a modern naturalism. The reaction from critic Gilles Sandier was enthusiastic: "No more mythological Tartuffes [...] Here at last is the clear, evident reality. Life in its romantic depth and with its social dimension: History and desires."[11] Indeed, this sociological-historical contextualisation, amounting ultimately to Marxist reading of the classics, considered desires in their carnal manifestation but also in their psychoanalytic depth, in that Planchon sought to show the ambiguity of Orgon's fascination with Tartuffe. "This staging is full of genius from start to finish: it explains, illuminates, analyses, illuminates, giving rise, alternately, to laughter, smiles, curiosity, anxiety [...] But this magnificent stir still serves the purpose of demonstration and of life",[12] declared Sandier, summarising what was expected of the new powers of the stage. The art of staging, an illustration of which Sandier finds in the work of Planchon, is thus to provoke a broad spectrum of feelings in the spectator, to account for a density which is none other than the density of reality, to construct in the most seductive and vivid way possible an intention that is readable and analysable, articulating the magnitude of a historical and ideological point of view and the sensitive complexity of private desires – "the history of desires". The second version of *Tartuffe* (1974) pursued even more manifestly such an articulation of the private and political, the subjective and the ideological, as Planchon saw in the play, "in an exemplary way, the 'tensions' between feelings and ideology", and considering in the character of Orgon,

> a man who supports the King's policy and at the same time maintains friendly contacts with the opposition, without being in conflict with himself. As if to suggest that politics should stop at the threshold of the personal. What does it mean that the sphere of the personal is thus enlarged?[13]

History and desires, far from being confined to the work of Planchon, can be found in many of the staged production of those years. Certainly, one finds it in the first productions of Patrice Chéreau. Examples include his representations of Marivaux (*L'Héritier de village* [*The Heir from the Village*] in 1965, at the Festival of the Théâtre Universitaire de Nancy; or *La Dispute* [*The Dispute*] in 1973, one of his first productions as co-director, with Planchon, at the TNP in Villeurbanne, and one of his most famous); his production of Jakob Michael Reinhold Lenz's *Die Soldaten* [*The Soldiers*], which he first staged in 1967; his staging of Molière's *Dom Juan* (1969); or even his interpretation of Shakespeare's *Richard II* (1970). Chéreau's creations emerge from the Brechtian and Marxist foundations that characterise an entire era, while being characterised by the expressivity of bodies and by a questioning of the most instinctive aspects of human desires. These were to be his "trademarks" throughout his career. Sandier finds in these productions, and particularly in *Die Soldaten*, an illustration of "how a staging space built to be an 'acting machine', a particular society at a given moment in its history, and the demons that lie deep within us, can function together, and how their workings act on each other".[14] To the critical engagement with the "underside" of reality is added a troubled eroticism: Freud, Sade and Marx are brought together and "Brecht's student becomes a libertine".[15] The Dom Juan that Chéreau presents is thus at the same time a cynical quasi-Sadian libertine and a progressive but individualist intellectual, who betrays his aristocratic class but who nonetheless is incapable of actually leaving (and is, in the end, put to death by his own). In this staging, Dom Juan is also unable to leave the stage of the masters, which turns thanks to the enslavement of those who, below, activate the wheels – literally, in the play's scenography, as the trestle table on which the action was represented, a sort of Brechtian turntable, was supported by a machine operated by workers dressed in rags. As for the pleasure-seeking and hedonistic Richard II, played by Chéreau himself, whose excessive white make-up paints the picture of a fanciful, precious and effeminate character, he is the victim of a brutal and savage feudal law, embodied in Bolingbroke's armed henchmen clad in fur-trimmed coats (as Elvire's brothers were, in his staging of *Dom Juan*), from whom he cannot escape. The space, moreover, is designed as a sandpit, that the characters can enter only by means of drawbridges that, once used, are immediately raised. The choice of *La Dispute*, in the early 1970s, would prove emblematic of Chéreau's theatre aesthetic: the very principle of the play is to combine an analytical mechanism (the science of inquiry and observation, in the prologue: the inquiring, hidden gaze of the aristocratic voyeurs) with a natural, instinctive, primal desire (the discovery of love and narcissism by the "wild" teenagers who had hitherto been prevented from entering the social world, and who are the guinea pigs of the experiment). In Chéreau's theatrical machine, French *marivaudage* is supplanted by a Sadian corporeality and darkness. The staging caused a scandal among the most conservative supporters of the national tradition: it was an approach that allowed Chéreau "through the fusion of bodies, to examine games of power as well as romantic relationships".[16] And *La Dispute* was also an opportunity for Chereau to make an imprint in theatrical history: the play is still remembered today as one of the most exemplary illustrations of pictorial aesthetics from a director. The high walls and the pool designed by Richard Peduzzi and the chiaroscuro lighting by André Diot testify to a mastery of plastic composition, which was already one of Chéreau's strengths.

Following the Brechtian heritage, staging became the site of all possibilities, and especially the site of a critical examination of the theatrical work and, through it, of an effective discourse on society and on the subject. From Gabriel Garran to the Compagnie Vincent-Jourdheuil, via Bernard Sobel's "orthodox" Brechtism at Gennevilliers (from the Gennevilliers Theatre Ensemble that he created in 1963 to the CDN, which he still directs on the same premises), numerous Brechtian (and "post-Brechtian" approaches) have placed dramaturgy and (Marxist) political engagement at the centre of their preoccupations. But the influence of this model of a critical theatre is even wider: the theatrical stage became a site in which signs were arranged in view of their readability – it became a meaning mill.

The classics as a symptom: a prospective overview

It may be useful here to focus for a moment on the staging of classics in France, as it is symptomatic of conceptions of the art of staging, more broadly speaking. Briefly broadening the temporal spectrum of our approach will provide an overall understanding of the way in which the most emblematic authors of the repertoire are treated, but it can also provide us with a prospective overview of some of the major trends and developments in *mise en scène* from the 1960s to the present day. We will return then to a more contextualised approach of staging, but this diversion, it seems, will provide us with an excellent opportunity to engage with certain questions that will be encountered again in this chapter.

One result of this search for meaning *through* the interpretative process of staging, was that Corneille, one of the major playwrights of seventeenth-century France – the Baroque Corneille, the political Corneille, the master craftsman of theatre and of the art of contradictions – emerged victorious from this period (from Vilar to the late 1970s). Because there was a search for meaning, especially possible political meaning, his theatre became, at last, an object of *thought*. In other words, it was finally being approached as theatre and play, as a system in action, and not as a heavy, monolithic and didactic work. At the same time, his Alexandrines were also re-evaluated, and he was taken again for a poet who plays on words, for one who is passionate about curious names and who is capable of double meaning and of flashes of wit. Thus, thanks to the new sensibility of audiences and directors for what was called the "baroque" (illustrated remarkably well by Jean-Marie Villégier), and that fostered other debates grounded in a political sense of dramaturgy appropriate to Corneille's work, Corneille's theatre became alive again. Through Corneille, but also Marivaux and Molière, the period we are talking about challenged a certain idea of classicism in the theatre and in literary criticism that was based on the authority of ancient figures, on the nation or on a scholastic conception of the superiority of the seventeenth century. The "century of Louis XIV", which simply became the seventeenth century, was enriched, diffracted, revisited and suddenly became more useful to all through this new thinking. Instead of setting standards, it was now regarded as providing ways of thinking about the world, about history and about the role of theatre in its irreducible complexity. And that is how the critical reflections on this period were brought in line with what theatre truly was: an art of critical distance and contradiction; a way of not leaving a performance with the same ideas one had on entering; a mode of questioning more than a set of answers.

In this reinterpretation of classicism, there was also the case of Racine. Since the work of Jean-Louis Barrault in 1942, Racinian theatre was represented by all as a mixture of strength, poetry and musicality of language; of historicisation; and of eroticisation and the cruelty of desire. During the twenty-five years that followed Barrault's *Phèdre*, there were very few notable stagings of Racine: since Jean Vilar, who preferred Corneille, had decreed that Racine was no longer relevant to the times and not many persons had bothered to contradict him. However, the representations of Racine in the late 1960s insisted on cruelty, political subversion and the emergence of sexuality. People began to find in Racine's fables energies and material that would allow them to transcend the "Racinian music" that Proust famously praised and to consider the force of desire by playing on the plasticity of bodies, cries and incantations. There was also critical thought about how to deliver Racine's verses without sacrificing anything in the way of meaning.

It was between 1971 and 1981, under the impetus of Antoine Vitez and in the wake of the academic quarrel between the proponents of New Criticism (Barthes in particular) and scholars such as Raymond Picard, that there was a renewed interest, within staging practice, in a certain idea of classicism and in the most emblematic authors of this era. The *mises en scène* of Vitez were not, or not only, formal *mises en scène*: they aimed to say something about the represented world, to show how an era, a society (the seventeenth century and, to a certain extent, the twentieth century) used myth or history to tell their stories. *Phèdre*, for example, represents, for Vitez, a social body that becomes devoid of vitality because power has made it impotent – so impotent that the only weapon available to the privileged yet castrated body expressing itself onstage is its language, its only horizon infinite despair. Politics, fable and tragic language were thus deeply intertwined and Vitez was able, through Racine, to pose questions about convention and tradition and to examine the issue of desire as portrayed in the theatre. For him, the theatre of Racine is "our French Noh" as it exacerbates the form of speech and its poetry to give that curious impression of strangeness that surprises and interpellates the spectator, while at the same time reveals the terrible impotence of the characters. Actors speak, sing, proclaim, declaim, superimpose a gestural rhetoric on to prosody to create, by a constant effect of surprise, a formal distance necessary for thought. Antoine Vitez thus sought to revisit the Racinian text in order to represent, in a polyphonic and coherent fashion, not only the past, but a theatrical and poetic form and a series of philosophical questions, including that of the limitless nature of desire. For, as he himself says, desire is the "autonomous character of tragedy" and represents dissatisfaction, which is its law.

Vitez's practice was emblematic of an evolution in theatre, whereby classicism came to be considered as a bodily and vocal expressivity, the manifestation of a poetics, an art in service of the text, and at the same time a way of recounting a fable with multiple meanings, including political ones. Theatrical staging in Vitez's era thus combined the need to tell stories with the requirements of poetic declamation and the necessity of embodied performance. It foregrounded personalities over schools and laboratories, as the times required. One aim was to "spatialise" writing, as it were – "the scratching of Racine's pen on the paper" – and its musicality – as can be noticed in the indications that Grüber gave his actors during rehearsals for *Bérénice* in 1984. Simultaneously, one also aimed to account for a history whose relevance was undiminished. Some, like Jacques Lassalle, were intimidated by the halo of myth that surrounded Racine's language and placed emphasis on narrative; one of their qualms being that Racine devoted little attention to the soul and to the workings of the psyche. Others, like Anne Delbée, unfailingly chose to emphasise narrative and the quest for meaning, and as if freeing themselves from the burden of language, represented desire in action and in all its (supposedly modern) violence. Otherwise, they sought to portray a vague idea of a hidden God by indicating, through their scenography, that a kind of threat was hanging over the stage. Moriaki Watanabe, in Japan and France, used Noh and Kabuki techniques to "inject an estrangement effect" into the text, as Brecht and Vitez advocated – to show how the act of making conventions ostensible served the expressivity of the text itself and allowed for an unexpected deciphering of the fable. As for Eugène Green (director of *Mithridate* at the Chapelle de la Sorbonne in 1999), he followed a very different path, relying on baroque diction, *actio* and gestures, which he reconstructed – though he contests the term – in an effort at conferring on the entire corpus of seventeenth-century theatre a "period" appearance, in which phrasing, declamation and postures were meant to function according to the transcription of a precise and rather restrictive code. The result was, here again, a strangeness that was sometimes fascinating but that often masked the meaning of the verse for a contemporary spectator, by virtue of the impressive melody or lyricism in which it was couched. Thus, Racine has become a continent that one approaches with apprehension, which one can read, but that one dreads to play to the point that one wonders if it is necessary to do it, but one confronts anyway. Finally, Daniel Mesguich has approached Racine as an exploration of desire, mixing genres, playing on drama, melodrama, cinema and parody, to show how much Racinian writing can be diffracted and recomposed, in new ways. For many, and especially for Mesguich, it was therefore urgent, from the 1970s onwards, to work on diction, on words, on the Alexandrine, but also on the experience of the body and on violence and tears, to hear the vibrations of text and voice, in the now – vibrations that worry, reveal and demand a constant deciphering of the world, without a notion that one will encounter a single, unitary, satisfying meaning.

Contemporary reinterpretations and appropriations of classical texts have thus allowed both for critical thinking and the historicisation of narratives, as well as their actualisation (in an effort to make them relevant, even contemporary). They have also harnessed the materiality of the text and of play, and for critical reflections on the theatrical performance itself.

And throughout all this time Molière has been staged and restaged everywhere, in every way and theatre audiences do not seem to tire of it. Perhaps for comfort, or pedagogy, but whatever the reason, Molière still makes the cut. Molière has therefore been constantly re-read, revisited from the time of Vilar, Planchon and Vitez onwards. Each season brings its share of "Molières", without it being possible to determine a unifying tendency, or even tradition. Approaches vary according to the director: Molière-*commedia dell'arte* (Dario Fo); farcical Molière (Savary, J. Deschamps, Footsbarn); serious Molière (Lassalle, Vincent); Molière the philosopher (Jaques-Wajeman); musical

Baroque Molière (Villégier -Christie); political Molière (Planchon, Vincent, Mnouchkine, Villégier), etc. It is not our aim to review all these Molières, all of which are interesting and often successful, but rather to note a few major trends. First of all, Molière represents the image of contemporary theatre, in its complexity and fragmentation, with two poles: that of "pure" theatricality and performance (the farcical and the gestural) and that of the quest for meaning (philosophical significance, historicity, political impact). But in fact, many *mises en scène* show that it is possible – and even necessary – to link these two poles in any given practice. Although few directors today mean to stage gratuitous, over-the-top farce in the way that Savary does, the majority of directors are fully aware that Molière, like Shakespeare, incites us to go beyond the idea of pure theatricality or entertainment to search for a multiplicity of meaning. It then becomes a case of whether it is relevant to consider all interpretations at once or appreciate them consecutively.

The 1998–1999 theatre season in France, offers one example of how Molière can be used for radically different lessons. First there was *The Misanthrope*, staged by Jacques Lassalle in a manner highly reminiscent of Ibsen or Strindberg and in which Célimène is tortured by his impossible love. There was *Dom Juan*, in a decidedly comic and grotesque staging by the Footsbarn Theatre in a style bordering on collective creation and inspired by a farcical production by Caubère, but that nevertheless managed to foreground the provocative aspect of Molière's erudite libertinism. Then there was *Tartuffe* directed by Villégier in Versailles, in costumes from the 1940s. This production raised the issue of the relationship to power and of resistance to hypocrisy, in general – one that concerns not only the seventeenth century but any period in which society is subjected to absolute power. Another production of *Tartuffe* was that directed by Jean-Pierre Vincent, which oscillated between abstraction and historicisation and aimed mainly to give a contemporary political lesson, since Vincent attempted to give an abstract depiction of hypocrisy and of an intra-family power struggle moored in a certain type of social violence. The production aimed at condemning all political hypocrisy, whether past or present, even if, at times, this took on slightly moralising overtones. A final example is the fully philosophical and theatrical *Dom Juan* produced by Brigitte Jaques-Wajeman in Geneva (1999–2000), which clearly posed questions about the value of materialism and the relations between art and commodity.

It is therefore clear that Molière contains meaning – a range of meanings – but meaning that is always connected to modern issues, such as materialism, realism in politics and the role that theatrical entertainment plays in society. The possibility of creating both associations and distance, in order to provide the spectator with the means of interpretation; of historicising plot lines while making them current, while all the while providing pleasure; of underscoring all the contradictions and ironies represented in the work, without side-lining either farce or drama – such are the urgencies that current directors perceive in relation to the staging of the great Poquelin.

Thus, like the society that it represents, theatre cannot escape repetition. To survive, it must use its inherited framework and its history, making them the subject of debate. This is perhaps the whole challenge of our contemporary era: to go beyond stasis and towards a self-justification of the theatre and a liberation of meaning. The survival of the theatre, in the 2000s, is linked much more to its official status than to the events it produces, and this behoves the theatre to represent itself as a survival, to place this issue at the centre of debate with each production. The desire for interpretation, the ever-present risks of the ephemeral, the ideal of the real, has thus been supplanted by the practical necessity of simply being there, with its classic status, occupying a place of its own in the city and in its suburbs. And this has to be emphasised, not only in the interest of securing financing for the building itself and its activities, but also in the interest of debate and reflection. The theatre of the 1960s, led by Roger Planchon, had, as we have seen, been used to re-reading the "classics" in an effort at rescuing them, from normative interpretations etched in stone, and taking into account the contradictions of the text, placing emphasis on the heterogeneous character of the classic text itself. In so doing, it allowed the texts of the classic repertory to have an impact in the present society, without letting go of the multiple meanings that they were supposed to deliver in their time. The theatre of the 1980s–1990s foregrounded such "theatricality": the play of theatre, the issue of language, the discipline of the spectacle. Thus, it ran the risk of eliding the impact of the contradictions contained in the texts that were being re-read, to the point where the productions became artistic and cultural ones that excelled by their practical, technical and individual virtuosity, reinforcing the idea of a unitary, cohesive idea of theatre, despite thematic disparities.

As we mentioned briefly above, while the dramaturgy of the 1960s and 1970s had a tendency to set up reading grids that proposed somewhat singular interpretations – despite encouraging a dual emphasis on theatrical play and the theatrical art itself – in recent years, we have seen a real reversal of this approach. Representation no longer seems strongly oriented *towards* the spectator, who was supposed to find in the show what their authors had wanted to put in it, but postulates instead that meaning must be created, freely and *ultimately, in the mind* of each spectator. Nowadays, we think that we must ideally leave this lone spectator to interpret the played text that they are watching. This laudable and theoretically justified requirement of freedom of thought with respect to the theatrical act tends to give rise to directors and playwrights who refuse to play a didactic role, seeking instead to evoke many different meanings within the audience. They dread creating more signification than intended and feel guilt at pre-interpreting a little more than they ideally should. Of course, this creates a contradiction. The guilt, however, is considered inevitable insofar as the theatrical work, if it is to avoid being wishy-washy, must provide solidly articulated concepts. As such, there must be a dramaturgical thought manifested in form, so that the spectator can create their own thought at the moment of reception. Otherwise, as the playwright Joseph Danan has remarked,[17] vagueness will only lead to more vagueness. Thus, the staging of repertory theatre, nowadays, must simultaneously move away from didacticism, foster the diffracted reading of the text (while, at the same time, guiding the spectator towards interpretations), speak about the theatre itself, justify its presence, put on a show, make fun of itself and of course question itself. One might say that, rather than play on a specific interpretation of the text, contemporary *mise en scène* has come to question the very fact of representation, to pose the question of what it means to stage a work. Consequently, the issue at stake is no longer the quest for and the implementation of a meaning, but the quest for meaning through staging, with the text – often a classical one, as we have said – as a pretext and as material.

Consequently, since ideological interpretation has been given less priority, or has been diffracted, to allow some freedom for the spectator to develop it themselves and perhaps to reunify it, the consequence is generally that the field of representation is shrinking and becoming "re-classicised", and that the scenic experiments are dwindling, since everything is played within the limits of traditional theatrical convention. The directors are reclaiming, as it were, their own place, which is the frontal space. The theatre, then, bravely displays its emblems: it embraces the curtain, the pit, the frame and the frontal view, as essences. But by using these constraints that are as permanent as they are obsolete, it can still play, disrupt, divert and shift meanings, while remaining in its space of memory. Scenery and costumes highlight this state of affairs by being simultaneously true and false: true sand and false shore, false beach and real wave, as we have seen in Luc Bondy's *mise en scène* (*Phèdre*) or that of K. M. Grüber (*Iphigenie auf Tauris*). Theatrical memory, depiction of reality and the representation of scenes are imbricated within *mise en scène* so that the space of the theatre becomes one of indefinite hesitation, accounting above all for the ambiguity of all that it represents. In doing so, the theatre moves but seems indefinitely trapped inside a convention area. It is analogised by the first scene of the *Marriage of Figaro*, in which the exposition of a story runs parallel to the exact calculation of the space of play. The theatre represents itself while calculating itself. In that respect, it displays itself, by obstinately exploring the definitions of its exercise and identity. Therefore, it seems natural that theatres should stage repertory texts and that they should repeat the same plays infinitely in order to regularly explore the meanings and ambiguities that directors give themselves the task of depicting. The confrontations between the defenders of contemporary texts and those who favour tradition seems to be a thing of the past, and debates around the virtues and limitations of collective representations have now faded. Everything in the theatre seems consensual, at least in terms of the discourse around the role of the theatre itself. Accordingly, all the technical responses become acceptable. Everything else becomes a matter of individual choice. As such, the main question today is no longer why and in the name of whom or what the theatre is producing; but rather, how can a production be realised successfully with good techniques and with a coherent aesthetic approach.

This is why the attention devoted to the actor's acting and to the actual practice of the theatrical art becomes central to the point where everyone in the theatre agrees on *praxis*, even if this implies a seemingly self-evident ideological conformity embraced without qualms. The representation of *Elvire Jouvet 40*, directed by Brigitte Jaques-Wajeman in 1986 at the Théâtre de l'Athénée is, in this respect, significant and brilliantly heralds this trend. From the notes and texts of Jouvet, the play shows how the actor bases his identity on the play he has with his character (Elvire) and his "director", or rather his pedagogue (Jouvet), on the other. Language, diction, the body, the execution – in a word, practice – become the major questions, more than their role in the city, since it seems obvious that we all agree on this role.

After the long struggle of its directors for legitimation, the theatre has now become autonomous and constitutes a field of its own, with its own territory, its own stakes and its recognised teaching. Rather than a philosophical or political conduit, it is a self-conscious discipline that reflects on itself. One caveat, however, is that Brigitte Jaques-Wajeman – the title of the play and the mention of a specific date, 1940, bear witness to this – is well aware that the theatre is not only a dramatic performance within a discipline, and that playing Elvire in the cold, during the winter of 1940, can be important for the body, for diction and for the interpretation of Molière's *Dom Juan*. The same Brigitte Jaques-Wajeman, who in 1986 represented Jouvet as the holder of a forgotten tradition and Elvire as an apprentice of her language, her body and herself, took the risk in 1999–2000 of philosophical and political interrogation in the theatre. After staging *Angels in America* by Tony Kushner and *Le Passage* [*The Passage*] by Véronique Olmi, two contemporary plays, one on the body of a man suffering from AIDS in a society that rejects him, the other on a Russian poet – Marina Tsvetaieva – who chooses to escape reality in an attempt at accessing art, Brigitte Jaques-Wajeman turned to Molière's *Dom Juan* (Théâtre de Genève, 1999; Théâtre de l'Odéon, 2000). *Dom Juan* portrays the risk of philosophy, of a consciousness of matter that displaces God – in a word, libertinage of the flesh, of the soul, of art. Jaques-Wajeman, aided by François Regnault and Jacqueline Lichenstein, investigates theatre's potential as a means, rather than as an end, as a vector of philosophical, material inquiry into matter. Accordingly, he assigns to it a social role: that of materially portraying the world by elevating the world to the level of art, through material representation in the form of play and machines. As we can see, this demanding brand of theatre, which uses both contemporary texts and traditional ones, is gaining ground, as it seeks to go beyond the palimpsest and the enclosure in which the theatre seems to be locked. There are other examples, and that is a good sign.

Behind the apparent consensus on the political role of theatre and the critical inquiry on its technique, lately we have been witnessing, nonetheless, the hint or the emergence of some philosophical, political and social urgencies. However, we do not know, at present, what role repertory theatre intends to play, now that it has lost its political and even militant vein and is more clearly interested in representing contradictions than in giving political lessons, now that it has taken on an autonomous quality of legitimacy, as a respectable field and as a discipline in its own right. Is there a way? Can repertory theatre finally imagine talking about something other than itself? One consequence of the apparent defeat of the staging of meaning is that each director must foreground their own research and aesthetic. Some may say this approach is too personal and sidesteps the issue of why one stages the classics, focusing instead on the practical realisation of staging and on the hermeneutics brought to bear on it. Though one may understandably think that those in charge of production seasons are playing it safe when they often programme the same play, we can also agree that directors, when they accept the idea of producing repertory theatre (or when they advocate it or programme it themselves), are extremely demanding and seek to take the plays' history of production into account, even if this means facing their contradictions. There is very little radical invention as a result, some will object, but is this a time for radicalness and must we, or can we, nowadays, necessarily be radical in order to understand detail and nuance in signification? We shall not broach these questions here.

Admittedly, the theatre reads itself, re-plays itself, contradicts itself and proposes other meanings within its own field. This is one of its characteristics. Nevertheless, it is regrettable that it so often adheres to form and to a rather limited repertoire. Suffice it to say that this repertoire, despite a few rediscoveries, is still rather limited and is even shrinking. However, for almost thirty years, the Baroque period (the early seventeenth century, or the entire seventeenth considered overall as the "Baroque period") has been the focus of renewed interest. It has even become central on the operatic stage. While stage music (ballets, operas, lyric tragedies) is now better known, thanks to the work of Villégier (*Atys*, *Médée*, *Le Malade imaginaire* [*The Imaginary Invalid*]), William Christie and the Arts Florissants, and while musicians and instrumentalists themselves have begun to call themselves *les baroqueux*, French theatre must realise that a different repertoire can emerge. One involving the comedies of Corneille, the English Elizabethan theatre (Shakespeare, Marlowe, but also Ben Jonson and John Ford), Spanish golden age theatre (Lope de Vega, Tirso de Molina, Calderón) and even sometimes French theatre writers that have been forgotten, such as Rotrou, Desmarets de Saint-Sorlin or Mairet. Saint-Sorlin's *Les Visionnaires* [*The Visionaries*], for example, is being produced at the Théâtre de Reims thanks to Christian Schiaretti. *Les Galanteries du duc d'Ossonne* [*The Galanteries of the Duke of Ossonne*], by Jean-Marie Villégier, but also Tristan l'Hermite's *La Mort de Sénèque* [*The Death of Seneca*] at the Comédie-Française and Larivery's *Le Fidelle* [*The Faithful*] staged at Chaillot and at the Théâtre de la Monnaie in Brussels, are some of the lesser-known works of the seventeenth century currently being staged. To these examples, we can add readings of Garnier and other sixteenth-century texts in the auditorium of the Louvre, the staging of works by Rotrou and Corneille at the Athénée, etc. The Comédie-Francaise itself has recently staged Rotrou's *Saint-Genest* and Corneille's tragi-comedy *Clitandre*. The theatre, through these re-readings and stagings, has developed a sense of control over its history and over history itself. It must therefore continue the movement initiated by the advent of the "Baroque", resume the experiences of Villégier and follow the examples of Schiaretti (Calderón's *autos sacramentales* at the Comédie-Française in 2002), and Didier Bezace who, at Aubervilliers, in 1999, made the most of Jean-Jacques Rousseau's *Narcisse*. We would like to see theatrical directors propose, in addition to a few plays by Corneille, Racine, Molière, Marivaux, Goldoni or Beaumarchais, bloody tragedies from the beginning of the seventeenth century, tragedies by Rotrou, even by Thomas Corneille or comedies that have seldom, if ever, been played within the last two or three centuries – astonishing ones, some of which have now published in modern editions. Can nothing be done with Hardy, Cyrano de Bergerac, Beys, Mareschal, Scarron, Lesage, Dancourt, Regnard and the 350 comedies written between 1680 and 1730? Is there no potential in Voltaire's or Diderot's theatre? Let us get rid of this old idea that they are minor. If we want the repertoire to be interesting and offer up new meanings, one not only needs to re-read it, but also to flesh it out, to rediscover it, in order to stage it.

Thus, it seems that as we go through the evolution of the staging of repertory theatre between the middle of the twentieth century and the beginning of the twenty-first century, something is lost both in terms of appetite and of discovery – perhaps because of the demands of production, and perhaps this will also lead to an opening up to other repertoires. It also seems, above all, that the need to convey an interpretation, or rather a line of interpretative thinking, has decreased. The febrile exploration of theatre, of its form, its self-representation, the image, the body and the language these convey, now seems to take precedence over the use of the classics as a way of thinking through contemporary issues. This obviously raises the question of the usefulness of the repertoire and, indeed, of its necessity. In this specific matter, and specifically in France, focus has shifted away from the importance of history and of its interpretation. It is a sign of the times. Similarly, in another sign of the times, the responsibility of the director and playwright, which, in the past, had been asserted and even advocated, seems to have moved away from an ideological point of view and be concerned instead with form, or with an enquiry into the theatrical object itself. Yet another sign of the times is the fact that the director's responsibility, which, before, had been ostensibly displayed, is now portrayed as being more discreet, and sometimes even appears to be delegated to the spectator. It is now up to the spectator to play, and to seek the pleasure, the luxury perhaps (and certainly the interest), of constantly rediscovering the whole theatrical repertoire. We will continue this overview to determine whether we are dealing here with particular trends in the staging of "classics" or if theatre as a whole is following the same path.

The image factory

As we have seen particularly for Planchon and Chéreau, the construction of meaning was of paramount importance in the theatre of the 1960s–1980s, though this meaning was not generally intended to be abstract discourse, nor display the mere predominance of the signified. The pre-eminence of concrete signs and of pictorial mastery during this period attests to this: if the work of the artist director signified and made sense, it also did so *by means of the image*, insofar as scenography dually articulated the semantics of the performance space and the plasticity of the creative act of staging. The director, author of the staged work, was also the creator of a distinctive visual (and sonic) world. Beginning at the golden age of *mise en scène*, the "meaning mill" has taken shape around a search for the image and a critical reflection on the body and on language, to such an extent that image, the body and language sometimes become autonomous aesthetic and signifying objects.

In that sense, another symbolic date in theatre should be highlighted, one that had the effect of an explosion on the theatrical landscape (crystallising already latent aspirations). This is 1971, the year when American visual artist and director Robert Wilson staged his play *Deafman Glance* at the Festival de Nancy (and later in Paris). It was a long silent play that produced the effect of a distension in time. It was the work of an artist who did not belong to the European tradition of text-based theatre and dramaturgy, but rather to that of contemporary dance, visual art and performance. Developed around the Bob Wilson's work with an autistic child, *Deafman Glance* abandoned the traditional benchmarks of Western theatre: it presented neither a mimetic dramatic representation of reality, nor an epic narration, but a series of tableaux, images, a mental and dreamlike universe. It mixed incongruous fantasy (a banquet presided over by a giant frog; an ox that swallows the sun, starts to shine and loses its head; a polar bear next to shirtless dancers) and traumatic hallucinations (a woman who stabs a child in extreme slow motion) in a dilated time-scape and without any given referent and hermeneutics.

To get an idea of the effect that this work produced in France, one only need read what Louis Aragon wrote in an "Open Letter to André Breton on *Deafman Glance*", which he published in *Lettres françaises*: Aragon speaks of a "miracle", of "the experience of a science that is yet without a name", of a "new beauty, of which, without a doubt, the play that I am speaking about is the first dawn".[18] In further praise, Aragon states,

I have never seen anything more beautiful in this world since I was born, never has any play equalled the brilliance of this one, because it is simultaneously waking life and life with the eyes closed, a convergence zone of the everyday world and the world of each night, reality mixed with dream, the inexplicable of everything in the eyes of the deaf.[19]

For Aragon, *Deafman Glance* was not a surrealist play, but "we, from whom Surrealism was born, dreamed would come after us and go beyond us".[20] An inner world, or "image theatre" as it would later be called. We can clearly see how this is in no way a critical theatre, that the particularity of the theatrical work does not lie in the reading of a text (there is none) or in the development of a network of meanings; nor does it arise from a political will. There is no constructed discourse. Instead, the play's world is of an absolutely aesthetic nature and imaginary order – between dream and a purely visual construction. Born from the drawings of Raymond Andrews, the autistic child who appears onstage, the world of *Deafman Glance* escapes not only semantic or semiological logic, but even language and rationality and becomes a waking dream and a subversion of conventional modes of perception. Subsequently, after further work around the autistic experience (*A Letter to Queen Victoria*, 1974), Bob Wilson's performances continued to produce a succession of visual tableaux and singular soundscapes that would become increasingly characterised by extreme formal rigor, geometric abstraction and minimal precision, "abandoning the profusion of bric-a-brac in favour of a visual essentialism reduced to its elementary components: pure lines, clean forms, rigorous volumes".[21] Wilson's visual and sound universe would be characterised by his play on minute variations within a repetition-based time (he would collaborate on many occasions with composer Philip Glass, the emblematic practitioner of repetitive music). Also key to his aesthetic was the distention of time: one of the most famous sequences of *Einstein on the Beach* (1976) is where a gigantic rectangle of neon light moves, for about a quarter of an hour, between a horizontal and a vertical position. The actor is merely one element among others, in the same way as light, sound or objects, within a purely plastic universe, even when it comes to staging texts, theatrical or otherwise. The Wilsonian stage thus rejects the dramatic principle (based on action) as well as the epic principle (based on narration), for an aesthetic that we might characterise (following Gertrude Stein's landscape plays) as a "landscape aesthetic": a revealing term that refers both to the immanence of a visual spectacle and to the idea of a mental universe (an "interior landscape"). It is thus one of the most striking examples of the notion of "postdramatic theatre", a concept defined by the German critic Hans-Thies Lehmann in the late 1990s and to which we shall return later.

But what Wilson's example testifies to in particular is an additional step towards the consecration of the autonomy of the stage – freed from the text. A "total" work of art, entirely determined by the creative act of the director, it is a completely aesthetic creation, and an ostensibly subjective one. Above all, it represents the apotheosis of the scenic *image*. In this, it permanently marks the directors of the world – including the French ones, even the most Brechtian among them. Legend has it that after seeing the staging of Marlowe's *The Massacre at Paris* by Chéreau in 1972, Roger Blin, as the legend says, maliciously remarked: "The *Deafman Glance* did not fall on the ear of a blind man".[22] Wilson's work would be decisive, including for Planchon, because it represented the second pole of scenic writing in all its omnipotence – that of the *image*. "Outside of Brecht's work, the work that I find perhaps the most impressive is that of Bob Wilson", Planchon declared. For him, Wilson's innovations

> prove that one can carry out scenic writing that is completely independent of the text. It is a revolution in the theatre. It proves that one can make images that are not ridiculous in relation to painting, for example. For a long time, everyone thought that an image in the theatre would always be weaker, more ridiculous than in cinema or in a painting. Wilson proves the opposite.[23]

And many a director emerging in the 1970s would come "under Wilson's influence" – for example, Georges Lavaudant and his *Palazzo mentale* [*Mental Palace*] (after Pierre Bourgeade) of 1976.

This was "image theatre", strictly speaking, or critical theatre that gives pride of place to the image, in a fusion that in itself was in no way contradictory. It became clear, and even more so after the shock wave of Wilson's example, that the empowerment and the powers of scenic writing could also assert themselves in the field of plastic creation. However, many debates would emerge from this in the 1970s, since, because of their excessive taste for the beautiful scenic image, supporters of both a critical and popular theatre and of the theatre that emerged after 1968 gave in to aesthetic complacency and narcissism and withdrew – which was the case of certain directors like Patrice Chéreau – into a gratuitous formalism. Critics then began talking about "a drift in the theatre towards the spectator". The irony of history would be that in the 1980s–1990s, a new generation would embrace this same shift by opposing those who had denounced it ten years earlier.

The use of space is part and parcel of this conception of the image factory that was *mise en scène*: as the term "stage manager" (which now applies to one who manages the technical aspects of the show) became replaced more and more often with that of "director", the term "decorator" faded away and was replaced by "scenographer". It was no longer a matter of "decorating", but of conceiving a *space* that, for each performance, conditioned the overall framework of the staged interpretation of the work and that itself would also constitute an image and contain meaning. With the Brechtian model, the scenery became a "playing machine" that could also highlight the structural movement of the work and the critical discourse of the staging. As we have seen, the space designed by René Allio for Planchon's *Tartuffe* is a revealing example. Such a setting must participate in the construction of meaning as much as it must be functional, and reveal the theatre as a "machine for seeing and showing".[24] As such, scenography is not a creation independent of the rest of the staging enterprise, nor is it totally subject to it. Rather, it asserts itself as an integral and essential element of what we have been referring to as "scenic writing", by supporting its plastic aspect in a fundamental way. The 1960s and 1970s thus saw the emergence of great scenographer-director duos: Planchon and Allio, but also Strehler and Lucio Damiani or Strehler and Ezio Frigerio at the Piccolo Teatro in Milan, Stein and Herrmann, Chéreau and Richard Peduzzi and also Vitez and Yannis Kokkos. Whether its references are more pictorial or rather architectural, the scenography imposes itself on the viewer's eye, and organises the theatricality of a "magnified stage".[25] It also "narrates" and contributes to meaning, while organising the way the actor is visually displayed. It conditions the imaginary world of the performance, accompanies its form and tones, displays its particular aesthetic, supported by the use of light: the flat two-dimensional impression reinforced by Baroni's lighting in Damiani's scenographies highlights the play of Strehler's actors by giving them a plastic relief thanks to an attenuated depth of field. The high walls of *La Dispute* (Marivaux) or the inundated space designed by Peduzzi for *The Massacre at Paris* (Marlowe), enhanced by the lights of André Diot, set the scene conducive to Chéreau's dark, torn and nervous romanticism. For Vitez's *Faust* at Chaillot, Yannis Kokkos created a contrast between the naked platform in the foreground and the disturbing profusion of the fantastic imagination of the second stage in the background, and developed an "enchanted realism" (the expression is Vitez's) that accompanied the aesthetics of the second "phase" of Vitez's career. For *Hamlet* in 1983, Kokkos would create a minimalist scenography made of large blocks whose abstraction, or rather whose extreme geometric stylisation and bright whiteness, would highlight the formal work of Vitez, the clarity of the narrative and the play of the actors, whose shadows and flesh the lights of Patrice Trottier emphasised by highlighting this whiteness or colouring it.

But scenography has also been used in counterpoint to the *mise en scène*, as a visual response to the text, in a way that resists a centralised organisation of the stage. For Peter Zadek's *mises en scène*, the German scenographer Wilfried Minks, influenced by pop art, created a contrast between a space left empty for play and flooded with spotlights and a peculiar plastic presence – an enlarged photo of a young English actress for Wedekind's (1965) *Spring Awakening*. For Zadek's production of Schiller's *The Robbers* (1966), Minks installed a gigantic cyclorama bearing a painting by Roy Lichtenstein of a man shooting a rifle, surrounded (in keeping with Lichtenstein's own style) with smoke and with detonating sounds. In a case such as this, the dynamics posed by the scenography are autonomous and inescapable and the director must decide how to *respond to it* in the way he directs the actors (and Zadek is experienced in this matter). The work of Klaus-Michael Grüber in Germany or Jean Jourdheuil (or Bernard Sobel) in France is also characterised by a conscious choice of not reducing the scenographic presence to a functionality or to a meaning, and of not submitting it to the overall mastery of the *mise en scène*, but, on the contrary, of making it resist such a reduction thanks to its own plasticity. Grüber, Jourdheuil and Sobel are directors who collaborate with painters such as Gilles Aillaud, Titina Maselli, Lucio Fanti and Edouardo Arroyo. By collaborating with painters and making them co-creators of the production in a 1970s reaction to the Brechtian "playing machine", these directors established a polyphonic stage, making the platform a space for art and its aura. For them, it became a matter of foiling the system of *the analysable image* through a "work of art as an ontological document which cannot be measured by the yardstick of a (general) truth external to it: rationality or politics",[26] as Jourdheuil writes about Aillaud. They thus played on the materiality and plasticity of the staged work or apparatus and its ability to provide a counterpoint to discourse, resisting a reduction to/of meaning, so that a play is established between the elements that make up representation. Additionally – and we have given examples of this in the previous chapters – the directors and their scenographers (Grüber, Recalcati,

Aillaud, Engel, Rieti) can also choose performance spaces other than traditional stages, non-theatrical spaces that the scenography is forced to utilise based on their own identity, and not the creation of a framed, traditional theatrical space: a *site*, i.e.

> a place limited in space, marked by history, and having the weight and the materiality of objects that occupy a very precise function in human activity. A site is incapable of lying [. . .] is not transformable into images. On the contrary, it will always stand in opposition to them.[27]

The overall dramaturgical project and all the constituents of the performance are thus made to coexist with this site, and this "monster will live if all the elements establish mutual, contradictory and obvious relationships of dependence between themselves".[28]

The actor as a collective body

And what about the actor in all this? Are they abandoned, do they become a mere puppet in the hands of an all-powerful director, like many discourses and expressions (such as the announced "return of the actor") seem to imply? The centralisation of powers and recognition in the hands of the author-director might lead one to believe this. But, looking at it more closely, this is far from being the case. Because such valorisation of the staging practice *necessarily* relies on the actor, they remain de facto the ultimate manipulator of concrete and living signs and their consciousness and responsibility are committed to such a process of constructing of meaning. The 1960s and 1970s saw various utopias built around actors and their practice and they remained the undisputed centre of these utopias.

The first political utopia of the actor is that of the collective, which became particularly significant in the years following 1968. The example of the Théâtre du Soleil is typical, and it is particularly emblematic of the possible reconciliation between the figure of the director and the primordial place of the actor in the act of creation and in a global collective approach to staging. A troupe leader, trainer and stage director, Ariane Mnouchkine is the central figure of the Théâtre du Soleil, and undeniably recognised as such, just as much within the team as outside. She became one of the main artistic figures of French *mise en scène* in the last third of the twentieth century. Nevertheless, the whole identity of the Soleil was built around the notion of collective creation, and, more broadly, around the idea of a living community, of work, commitment, the equal sharing of tasks, on the theatrical model of the troupe and on the social-political model of the cooperative. Moreover, this community ethic is based on ideological foundations, but also on a conception of the very nature of the theatre. Theatre is created together, relies almost exclusively on the actor's practice and on their perpetual learning. It is thus essential that the collective of the Soleil be a framework for theatrical production but also a place of permanent training, and all the forms of theatricality to which its aesthetics resorts (*commedia dell'arte, theatre de la foire*, oriental traditions) belong to the great universal traditions of the actor. These are traditions that are transmitted within the framework of the family or the united group and whose mastery is the result of long training and a high degree of personal accomplishment. From *Clowns* to *Dernier caravansérail* [*The Last Caravanserai*] and *Une chambre en Inde* [*A Room in India*], through *1789* or *L'Âge d'or* [*The Golden Age*] along the way, the actor is doubly central to the work of the Théâtre du Soleil and is bound up within two inextricably linked utopias: at the heart of the collective creative enterprise, and the very object of the art that is transmitted and constructed within it.

Another collective model, of Brechtian tradition, which marks the 1970s, was created at the Schaubühne in Berlin, around Peter Stein, and would later be imported to France at the Théâtre National de Strasbourg under the direction of Jean-Pierre Vincent, from 1975 to 1983. In this model, the sharing of decisions is collective (the Schaubühne was created in 1971 as a cooperative production), and the key word is dramaturgy. These two enterprises are clearly inscribed within the lineage of a critical and political theatre. Stein's shows have remained famous for the enormous amount of table work devoted to their dramaturgical elaboration, historical research and hermeneutics. Vincent, after having worked for several years within the collective framework of the Théâtre de l'Espérance, in partnership with the playwright Jean Jourdheuil, led, in Strasbourg, what Bernard Dort was to define as "the critical moment of the theatre of the 1970's [...] reanimating all the various questions of the post-1968 period"[29] about the potentialities of theatre in society. He surrounded himself with a collective that brought together actors, intellectuals, authors, painters and all sorts of practitioners gathered around an overall dramaturgical research not limited to the interpretative field, but integrating all the aesthetic questions of theatrical practice. In addition to political questions, of course, the collective would focus on analysing the relationship between theatre and reality, as with a "documentary" production like *Le Palais de Justice*. This play was created from real court hearings in Strasbourg, which the actors took turns attending for six months, and that were directly transposed to the theatre stage. The Théâtre National de Strasbourg under Vincent devoted much attention to the role of the spectator, to the limits of representation and, for the actor, to those of the situation of "play" (especially in the productions by Engel that we have already had discussed). As at the Schaubühne, the dramaturgical would be collective and enormous (six months for *Germinal*, an adaptation of Zola's novel, and five months for *Le Misanthrope*, both staged by Vincent). And as at the Schaubühne, where, beside the work of Stein, that of Grüber developed outside the walls, in non-theatrical places; Vincent's *mises en scène* happened alongside those of Engel (*Baal*, *Kafka-théâtre complet*, *Weekend à Yaïk*, already mentioned); but also the productions of Michel Deutsch and Michelle Foucher.

While the actor is not the only centre of the theatre, and while the importance given to the many official playwrights may at first seem to relegate the actor to a role of simple performer, they remain, nonetheless, essential, since they are involved in all the decisions of the theatre, taken collectively. They are essential also since they are integrally involved in the construction and dramaturgical choices of plays, and since, in the end, they become actor-dramatists, responsible for their practice and fully aware of the signs they display and of their techniques for displaying them.

Another example of the relationship between the actor and the collective is the unique experiment that the TNS represents, at least in France. This is a structure characterised by its brilliance but also its crises, doubts and its permanent attempts at pushing the limits of the theatre, but also its constant search for the balance that could guarantee the life of such a collective and establish its continuity from project to project, while always constructing the company around the central role of the actor and their play. As such, at the moment when the TNS began to operate, ideology was not the centre of everything. The centre was indeed the actor, tasked with becoming the producer of meaning for the audience and the citizen. The experience, over the eight years of its existence, has thus taught everyone.

> The directors: that beyond the programs, the dramaturgical approaches, there is the simple urgency of attending to the actor: the physical element that is a *sine qua non* for the representation. The actors: that they can become their own playwrights. "I allow myself to be permeated by the theoretical idea of the playwright," says Evelyne Didi: "I *invent him*. I rewrite the texts ten, fifteen times to remember them, says Lapalus. It's like becoming the producer".[30]

The actor is therefore a concrete and conscious producer of meaning, and, within the framework of such a permanent collective, becomes the bearer of the continuity and the coherence of the overall project of the theatre. The latest productions from the TNS, be it *Le Palais de Justice* or the very choral *Dernières nouvelles de la Peste* [*The Latest News on the Plague*] (written by Bernard Chartreux), testify particularly, onstage but also in their conception, of this collective *approach* where dramaturgy is given not only as a means but as a project in itself, and where "the *theatre* becomes the meeting place for people working on a theme, a form; the meeting place of contradictory and varied points of view, rather than one of synthesis".[31] It is also significant that many of the major players who have influenced and still influence French theatre come out of this adventure or were trained at the TNS school during this period: the late Philippe Clévenot, Evelyne Didi, André Wilms, François Chattot, to name a few.

The actor as an individual body

But it is not only the collective approaches that take shape around the work of the actor. If the advent of the director does not in any way relegate the actor to a secondary role, it is because, even before being the creator of signs, meaning and images, the director remains, above all, a midwife of sorts, one who facilitates the emergence of actors. Going hand in hand with the powers of the director, the empowerment of the stage and the celebration of the theatre's powers are also, in a way, a celebration of the omnipotence of the actor, the one whose body and poetry can accomplish anything. All of Peter Brook's work, for example, translates that: with Brook, the stripping down of theatricality to the bodies of the actors and, as we have seen, to some minimal accessories (fabrics, sticks, etc.) that they use and transform, allows the creation of an "immediate theatre". Brook produces a theatre of presence and living, combining the simplicity of the story with that of play: a theatre of craftsmanship, "the art of the empty space". This theatre of elementary signs and evidence based on "the joy of *doing* theatre", exalts the powers of the stage, but a stage that exists only by the mere presence and play of the actor. The stage director is thus a trainer and accompanist of the actors in their approach to the text, and his production is not then of the nature of "*the image*, produced by the director-king and his actor-jester, but of *the event*, produced by a group oriented by a guide".[32] A guide, a pedagogue – a "master", as they are often called in Eastern traditions – the director reveals the actor (to themselves as well as to the audience) and places them at the centre of the theatrical fact – even as a single element.

The utopia of the actor can also be one of self-discipline and individual mastery, which can even dispense with all the other elements of representation and be reduced to exploring and learning the infinite capabilities of the body – the rediscovery of Artaud in the 1960s is fundamental in this regard. The work of the body or, rather, a work on the body, would give form, politically speaking, to the idea of personal liberation or the hedonistic rediscovery of the body, an idea that was often a reaction against social conventions, in the counter-culture currents of the 1960s. For example, the trances of the Living Theatre, an American troupe led by Julian Beck and Judith Malina, such as in *Paradise Now* that caused an uproar in Avignon in 1968. However, critical and/or aesthetic reflection around the body and how to use it in the theatrical space can also lead to the development of a more mystical and ascetic approach, which goes so far as to abandon the very notion of representation and reduce the scenic writing to the figure of the actor, as was the case in the work of the Polish director Jerzy Grotowski. The theatricality that Grotowski constructs within the Laboratory Theatre that he created in Poland in 1959 (first in Opole and then in 1965 in Wroclaw) is based solely on the exhibition of the actor, who gives entirely the gift of his body in the theatrical play: an actor-saint, one "who reveals themselves and sacrifices the most intimate part of themselves",[33] peels off the masks of the everyday and builds their own language by going deep into their organic, physical and vocal impulses. One who utilises all the physical-bodily powers of the actor, which emerge from the depth of their being and their instinct, springing into a sort of "translumination". He does not learn techniques per se. Instead, "everything is focused on the 'maturing' of the actor, who reveals themselves through a tension pushed to the extreme, through a complete stripping, through the exposure of their innermost self" – all this without egotism or delectation. "The actor makes a total gift of himself", writes Grotowski in his collection *Towards a Poor Theatre* (1968).[34] And the theatre as a whole is reduced to the offering of the corporeality of the actor (that of their muscles, their sweat, their deepest impulses) in one "total", ritual and transgressive act, in an "art in which the living organism strives for higher motives".

The signs deployed by the stage can then only be "organic signs", and the "poor theatre" that Grotowski claims is opposed to "rich theatre" or "synthetic theatre", which would associate the aesthetics of scenery, costumes, lighting, etc., with the living actor – whose arrangement, in a word, would represent the work of the director. On the contrary,

Grotowski's work strips off all these elements and is reduced to the actor as sole creator. One of his most famous theatre performances, and one of his last, Slowacki's *The Constant Prince* (1966) based on a drama by Calderón, exposed the body of the actors, and, more particularly, the sacrificial body of the title role played by Richard Cieslak, inside a small bare rectangle surrounded by a wooden enclosure. From the top of this enclosure, a very small number of spectators watched a representation below, which resembled a kind of mythical ceremony or scientific experiment that would get caught by surprise. His approach was a metaphysics of the body of the actor, as well as a search for a ritual, one that would lead him into cross-cultural ethnotheatrological research. It was an unlimited exploration that sought to enable the actor to surpass their physical capabilities and to find the roots of their physical actions in the depths of their psychic being. It was an ascetic and absolute enterprise: it was inevitable that Grotowski's research would lead him to reject the very notion of representation. He stopped presenting theatrical plays in the early 1970s, after a final production of *Apocalypsis cum figuris* (from biblical motifs, and that, in France, was played at the Sainte-Chapelle), to focus on the *training* of the actor, in the unique (and almost monastic) framework of the laboratory. The director thus reduced himself to the function of guide and trainer, of "master". His approach was to devote himself solely to research into the psycho-physical faculties of the actor, which would also give rise to, among others, the work of Eugenio Barba's Odin Teatret as well as post-Stanislavskian experiments on the physical actions of the Russian director and pedagogue Anatoly Vassiliev.

As we can see, the affirmation of the singularity and autonomy of the scenic creation is not incompatible with an emphasis on the actor and their role. The advent of the central figure of the director as keystone of the theatrical creation does not involve an instrumentalisation of the actor, since the commitment and presence of the latter is at the heart of the affirmation of the powers of the stage, and their practice is the object of assertions and the most radical research. We have seen this illustrated in the approaches just mentioned and that, significantly, are built around distinctive and exemplary directorial figures. As such, in the collective utopias in which the actor is involved at all levels of the theatrical enterprise, participating fully in the awareness of their art, in the utopias of singular presence in which the actor alone plays – in which the actor is *the* whole theatre – and even within the critical practices where they become, by their play, the manufacturer of signs par excellence, the actor remains at the centre of the staged event.

Between tradition and invention: the play of forms

The actor is at the heart of the dialectic between tradition and creation, memory and invention, which characterised several major moments in the theatre in the 1970s. This actor is an explorer as much as a re-inventor of an ancestral art that must constantly, through them, reaffirm its actuality and its efficiency. The actor – and the director with them – is thus the one who examines forms, plays with them and with their conventionality, perpetuates them but also reinvents them. They are a creator of signs, but even more so, a creator of their own language, which they can feed into other traditions (both European and non-European), but it is always a matter of making use of a current subject. After the critical theatre in which the means of the theatrical space converse directly and on the same level with the real world, the theatre of the 1970s questioned itself, its own grammar and its own conventions. This theatre then participated in one or several traditions, considered itself as a play of forms, without abandoning an engagement with its time or renouncing the political. On the contrary, this detour, as it were, through forms and self-conscious reflection on theatrical memory is in itself political.

Let us take the example of the Théâtre du Soleil. Arguably, no theatre troupe has embodied the alliance of political commentary on its time and the appropriation of the most codified traditional forms of the theatre so well. Théâtre du Soleil's work is characterised, at its foundations, by improvisation and *commedia dell'arte*. Allied with these are the great forms of Oriental theatre – Chinese, Japanese, Indian, Balinese. And it is always through these forms and codes, not utilised exactly in their original ways, but reinvested and reappropriated, that Ariane Mnouchkine's troupe endeavours to create performances that are not "archaeological" but anchored in the present time. Admittedly, *1789* (1970) stages history through a popular, epic and festive theatricality, using acrobats, jugglers and other such figures, but the overall purpose of the performance was to question the notion of revolution in the wake of May 1968. *L'Âge d'or* (1975) inscribed this mixture of temporalities within its overall project (the society of the 1970s seen from the 2000s and passed through the filter of eighteenth-century Italian theatre) and the Italian mask designates the immigrant worker Abdallah/Harlequin, exploited by the boss Marcel Pantalon. Later, when Théâtre du Soleil abandons collective writing and starts to stage works of the theatrical repertoire or texts specially written by Hélène Cixous (which began from improvisations), three of Shakespeare's plays are staged through the lens of a dream-like kabuki theatre (*Richard II*, *Twelfth Night* and *Henry IV*, from 1981–1984). Then came, among others, *L'Histoire terrible mais inachevée de Norodom Sihanouk roi du Cambodge* [*The Terrible But Unfinished Story of Norodom Sihanouk King of Cambodia*] (1985), *L'Indiade ou l'Inde de leurs rêves* [*The Indiad or India of Their Dreams*] (1987), Aeschylus' *Oresteia* and a Greek tragedy also reminiscent of an Eastern ceremony around the case of contaminated blood (*La Ville Parjure* [*The Perjurous City*], by Hélène Cixous, 1993), and recently a production of *Dernier caravansérail*, which seems to operate as a kind of cumulative experimentation, a sort of recycling of certain major forms used by Théâtre du Soleil. This production saw the construction of scenes on the basis of collective improvisations, the use of bunraku already used in *Tambours sur la digue* [*Still on the Dyke*], the previous play. Throughout its adventure, the Théâtre du Soleil has thus endeavoured to be a voice of its time, but by the means of ostensible theatricality, centred on the art of the actor, a theatricality self-consciously aware of the traditions and the conventions out of which it arises. To make theatre, for Mnouchkine, is to put oneself "in the school" of great forms, to try to understand how one can use them to engage with one's time. In such a practice, the actor, around whom the gesture of staging is constructed (if only for Mnouchkine, by the generative material of their improvisations), is then the essential point where tradition and innovation are articulated. The theatre is therefore a manipulator of signs, certainly, but also, simultaneously, a preserver and inventor of forms.

Following a completely different mode, the artistic approach of Antoine Vitez, which deeply impacted French theatre during the 1970s–1980s, is also one of play between tradition and reappropriation. It approaches theatricality as play – the actor's play, the play on forms and on the memory and the intrinsic convention of theatre. For Vitez, theatricality is, above all, the art of the actor. The actor is an inventor of forms, but is aware of this invention and conscious of being part of a history, of manipulating codes, of exploring and reinventing even as they invent. Vitez's actor is "a non-naturalistic actor, a master of the game of lures he produces".[35] In this respect, Vitez's activity as a trainer and pedagogue is fundamental in his approach to the theatre. Consequently, at the source of Vitez's directorial practice is the principle of *exercise* that nourishes his whole creative practice. His theatre is characterised by the space of playful but self-conscious freedom. For Vitez, schooling is foundational. Moreover, it is through this principle that his heritage has been spread: at the Conservatoire, in the workshop-laboratories that he created in Ivry in the 1970s, at the Théâtre National de Chaillot when he directed it in the 1980s. A whole generation of actors has been trained by Vitez: Aurélien Recoing, Richard Fontana, Redjep Mitrovitsa, Nada Strancar, Evelyne Istria, Jany Gastaldi, to name just a few. The work and aesthetics of Vitez are therefore part of a fully formal approach, which is based first of all on the example of the great Russian formal directors of the inter-war period, and in particular Meyerhold. A theatre that was originally radically anti-realist and anti-Stanislavskian, based on the belief that one can "show reality through non-naturalist play": "a theatre that shows the world through metaphor, through the radical reworking of forms, instead of representing it by showing people at home, with a haystack",[36] Vitez would claim, in ostensible reaction to the aesthetics of Planchon – who, himself, did not miss any opportunity to position himself in relation to Vitez.

Vitezian formalism was about "showing the world": it was in no way meant to be a gratuitous aestheticism, and does not in any way contradict the deep political commitment that characterised the man Vitez (who was private secretary to Aragon, a long-standing member of the Communist Party who would continue to relate his critical inquiry into art to an overall reflection on the world). On the contrary, formalism was, for him, a moral and political claim, summed up in the expression "elite for all" that Vitez would use at Chaillot. This communicated shared, artistic demands that resisted the norms of bourgeois, reactionary realism that Stalinism, as Vitez would often recall, heralded as the dogma (and in whose name he disposed of Meyerhold, charging him with a "formalistic drift"). There is thus a politics of form and of forms in the work of Vitez. His productions truly elevate the pleasures of theatricality and he brings back life to the notion of "art theatre" that re-emerged at the start of the century. However, this is always based on the belief that "the theatre is force field, a very small one, in which the whole history of society is played out", a "laboratory of human behaviour, a conservatory of gestures and voices, a site of experience for new gestures, new modes of expression – as Meyerhold dreamed – so that ordinary man can change", as he wrote in 1985 in his editorial of the first issue of the journal *L'Art du théâtre*.[37] It is a fact that Vitez has always refused the German conception of dramaturgy, and was a believer in the idea of "everything right now", as we have already mentioned. But at the same time, he has always upheld his desire for an articulation of form and meaning. In sum, he never ceased to be a great *thinker* of history and of the theatre, in his dialogue with the propositions of theatrical play.

Vitez's work was therefore both a laboratory and a conservatory, especially with respect to language, all the more since he was part of a French tradition of formalisation of diction and of delivery, and therefore of a need to "make the text heard". This French tradition, another of whose representatives was Vilar, resisted any moves that would make the text prosaic on the grounds of orality in the theatre, and opted instead to emphasise the distinctive poetic and lyrical flair of an author (be it Racine, Claudel, Hugo or even a contemporary writer like Guyotat). However, in a much broader sense, Vitez's practice was one of invention and reappropriation of traditions, codes and forms, of bodily and verbal signs (where these two could be dissociated). The actor would develop their movement, posture and voice, and invent their own grammar and scenic language. While they could, of course, develop these *ex nihilo*, they would also delve into the *memory* of the theatre, i.e. the forms handed down to them by history. Vitez's plays would therefore often draw on various traditions to explore them. These included circus, puppetry and even the silent film for Maïakovski's *Les Bains* [*The Bathhouse*] (1967), the oral tale for Evgueni Schwartz's *Le Dragon* [*The Dragon*] (1967), the *commedia dell'arte*, the théâtre de la foire, the theatre de boulevard, opera (e.g. for Marivaux's *Le Prince travesti* [*The Prince in Disguise*] (1983)), and even realism (Jarry's *Ubu roi* [*King Ubu*], 1985).

Let us take the example of the "classics" (as we have done already when discussing Planchon) to give an illustration of Vitezian aesthetics. His production of *Andromaque* in 1971 did not adhere to the critical and "concrete" reading characteristic of Planchon's Brechtian work: a bare platform, lit by a steady bright light, having only a ladder, a few chairs and a table, which would become acting props, signs and images. Everything relied on the actors who arrived dressed in everyday clothes and with brochures in hand. They would share roles and stage play, and their stage play made identification with the characters difficult. Vitez's *Andromaque* was a production based on exercise and editing, but above all on the text, and more specifically, on Racine's writing and the Alexandrine, which was respected, exhibited and displayed as a form. On a shiny stage and in seventeenth-century costumes, this production of *Phèdre*, which took place in 1975, was made to exhibit the Alexandrine and the conventional poetic quality of Racine's language. There was an extremely rigorous work on prosody, on the musical qualities of the language: a spinet and a viola were placed onstage and certain passages were set to music by Georges Aperghis. The production exhibited a formalism that took it far away from everyday language and traditional diction. It made no claim to any historical reality, but exhibited all its strangeness (so, for instance, all the mute "e"s were pronounced, even at the end of verses).

Vitez's aim was not to "revive" the classics, which would imply that the object that had laid dormant was intact. For him, "the object itself has fundamentally changed, even if the text is perfectly intact. We cannot read it like the ones for whom it was written": it has been deformed. "Texts are therefore traces whose memory has often been altered, modified. [...] We must not seek to reconstruct them as they were. We must instead strive to make imaginary reconstructions".[38] As such, the director's job is not to update the text or naturalise it, but rather to show the "fractures of time", to preserve and even to reinforce the effect of strangeness that accompanies them:

> [O]ne of the essential needs for me in staging is for the theatrical act to appear as an enigma [...] that demands to be solved. It is interesting when work is not transparent, when it does not give away all its clues. It must be perceived as a monster from the depths of history, from an elsewhere place in whose corridors one can perambulate. [...] Enigmatic is the nature of what will strike the imagination, of what will remain in the spectator's memory.[39]

Strangeness, formalisation and metaphorisation are, therefore, key staging concepts for Vitez. It is because the codes of an ancient work have been lost that they can be reappropriated by the actor, as material for play and invention: "We bring different aspects of the works back to light, without ever reconstituting them, because in any case the use is lost. Instead, we use these different aspects to make new things".[40]

Vitézian staging thus produces imaginary reconstructions, fashioning a kind of theatre conceived as an "art of variation". The fact that throughout his career, Vitez staged Sophocles' *Electra* three times, each time differently – in 1966, 1971 and 1986 – and each time with Evelyne Istria in the title role, is an illustration of this. Ultimately, a similar principle underpins his famous declaration that it is possible to "make theatre from anything", with which he justifies his work on what he calls the "theatre-narrative" based on Aragon's novel *Les Clôches de Bâle* [*The Bells of the Basel*]. This production, named *Catherine* (1975) saw the actors sitting around a table while having a meal. Passing the book back and forth between each other, they read passages, miming them a little sometimes.

Language and verse are at the centre of Vitez's work, as conventions and as poetry: Racine's alexandrine but also Molière's (e.g. Molière's *Tartuffe*, *L'École des femmes*, *Le Misanthrope* and *Dom Juan* played in a tetralogy by the same team of actors and in the same space in 1978) or

Hugo's (*Hernani*, 1985). He staged Claudel's verse (from *Partage de midi* [*Break of Noon*] in 1976 to *The Soulier de Satin* [*The Satin Slipper*] of 1987), but also that of contemporary poets Aragon, Ritsos or Haitian poet Jean Metellus. Vitez was therefore also a translator and revealer of lesser-known voices. Admittedly, at Chaillot in the 1980s, Vitez's work reconnected with a certain brand of realism, becoming more figurative and at times rather Stanislavkyan (another use of convention). He even abandoned the bare performance space in favour of plastic scenographies and Yannis Kokkos' "enchanted realism". Nevertheless, it was the same principles that underpinned the play of forms in this glorified theatricality, which was always to be half way "between enthusiasm and convention".[41]

Triumphant theatricality

The debates that marked the theatrical world during the 1960s and 1970s were numerous (Vitez versus Planchon, as we have seen; political discourse or the metaphysical quest of the actor; the "quarrel over images", etc.). What we can clearly see, nevertheless, is that these oppositions all question the hierarchy and the merits of the various powers of the theatre, and, ultimately, rest on an unshakable trust in them. They do not question the fundamental belief in their effectiveness. The various stakes included making sense, making images, political performance, the importance of the actor's personal quest and the inexhaustible laboratory of forms, as we have seen. While individual approaches mobilised various stakes differently, the profession of *mise en scène* not only conquered its autonomy, but also seems now not to have to doubt its legitimacy, or even its capacity to account for reality and to intervene in the world. As we have seen for certain examples, all these facets appear linked, intertwined in a triumphant theatricality that the theatre stage is then frequently used to emphasise. Meaning and the image, tradition and revolution, formalism and popular appeal, personal fulfilment and collective stakes seem to unite for an overall glorification of the art of the theatre.

Everything seems to appear as if, behind the aesthetics and the particular claims, there was no *absolute* contradiction between the different approaches to theatrical creation – if only as it relates to the distinctions between critical theatre and art theatre. Accordingly, the great Italian director Giorgio Strehler, in the last lecture he gave at the Vieux-Colombier on 28 November 1997,[42] summoned the great founding figures of various conceptions of the theatre as pillars of one global enterprise spanning the twentieth century: the great and singular adventure of "art theatre". For this he uses a text published by François Regnault in 1986, *Le Conte des trois cités* [*Tale of Three Cities*]: "The first expected everything of the theatre; for the second theatre was nothing but theatre; the theatre for the third was the theatre and also something else".[43] Regnault was describing Copeau, Jouvet and Brecht with this sentence, as "three different, opposing understandings of the role of theatre in society". Strehler adds to them a fourth city, a founding one, represented by the Moscow Art Theatre of Stanislavsky and Danchenko. "Four cities of art theatre", where art theatre in the strictest sense and Brechtian critical theatre could cohabit, where the issues and goals pursued could merge or at least intertwine into a single global thought that is nothing other than theatre in the absolute. Theatre as art, as an autonomous practice (as "profession") and as a political and social intervention, is realised, simultaneously, in its mode of communication and in its inscription in the world (its effectiveness in relation to reality): "art theatre, public theatre – the questions seem different, and yet they are close. One must connect them",[44] says Strehler in the introduction to his remarks. Four different enterprises, but that in fact merely represent the various paths of the same quest, four poles whose tension and ideal fusion would constitute the quadrature of the circle of a fully justified and consecrated theatricality.

Strehler himself could in some ways be seen as the symbol of this "multipolarity" par excellence. His work at the Piccolo Teatro in Milan spanned fifty years (from the founding of this theatre in 1948 to his death in 1998), and involved more than two hundred productions, and demonstration of all the powers of theatricality. Partly trained alongside Jouvet, but constantly focusing his practice on the Brechtian demand for theatre in the present world, Strehler is at the crossroads of issues raised in these four cities. He is at the same time master of the image and an "actor's director", a builder of a repertoire destined to combine theatrical tradition and social and political questions. If one looks at the most famous and exemplary productions of his vast output, the range of theatrical traditions appear extremely numerous. Strehler has staged, for example, *Arlecchino servitore di due padroni* [*Harlequin, Servant of Two Masters*], a play symbolic of a very Italian art of theatre, appropriation of the tradition of the *commedia dell'arte*, production that would be constantly revisited over the space of forty years and one whose demanding roles were constantly reworked over time by two emblematic actors (Marcello Moretti and Ferruccio Soleri). Besides this single play, Strehler has had a lifelong interest in the work of Goldoni, the founder of modern Italian and European theatre, whose works he staged in a carnival fairground style (*Le baruffe chiozzotte*, which he staged in 1964; *La trilogia della villeggiatura*, stated in 1954, then in 1974 and 1978; and *Il Campiello* in 1979). Strehler has also staged some of the finest *mises en abyme* in theatre, such as Shakespeare's *The Tempest* (1978) or, in Paris (at the Odeon Theatre of Europe of which he was the first director), Corneille's *L'Illusion comique* (1984), in which Alcandre the wizard, in the first act, appears in the darkness of the stage, from underneath the platform. In this staging of *L'Illusion comique*, the adventures of Clindor are played on a stage framed by rocks (Alcandre's cave), on a black marble floor in which the scenery and the actors' silhouettes are reflected. The staged is flooded with warm and cold (changing) lights and its pictorial *contre-jour* effect evoked an atmosphere of mystery and the magic of theatrical illusion.

Strehler was also one of the greatest opera directors – especially of Mozart – of the second half of the twentieth century. We do not have the time or the space here to list all of the productions that have remained in the minds of spectators as period-defining events in the short history of *mise en scène*, as well as exemplary illustrations of the aesthetic powers of the theatre stage. Many of these productions have provided images that have become part of a collective memory: examples include Chekhov's *The Cherry Orchard* (1974), with its white platform and costumes ("Strehler's white" became an emblematic reference), the veil of tulle sprinkled with cherry leaves that overhung the stage, Lyubov's umbrella, the small childish train that silently crossed the stage. With his sensuality and aesthetics, the pictorial beauty of Lucio Damiani's and Ezio Frigerio's sets and the emotional quality of the acting, Strehler became the emblem of an absolute mastery of the art of staging. But Strehler also had a constant political engagement, the desire to testify to social realities, with historical *mises en scène* of Gorki's *The Lower Depths* (1947) or Bertolazzi's *El Nost Milan* (1955 and 1974). (The latter provided the material for Althusser's "Notes on a materialist theatre".) He is, above all, one of the greatest European Brechtian directors. His productions of Brecht include the *Fourpenny Opera* (1955), *The Life of Galileo* (1963), *Schweik in the Second World War* (1956), *The Good Soul of Szechuan* (1958, 1980, 1996) and *Saint Joan of the Stockyards* (1970). He was a director who devoted his masterful skills to an "otherwise ambitious enterprise: that of "bringing together the Theatre and the World", as Bernard Dort wrote in his preface to Strehler's collection of texts *Per un teatro umano*.[45] This "theatre" is one that, as Strehler remarks in his staging notes for *La Cerisaie* (Chekhov's *The Cherry Orchard*, which he staged in France), would articulate three levels:

"true" sensibility that corresponds to the characters and the story that the fiction presents; "History that moves", and "life: the great sphere of human adventure".[46] And, more broadly, it is one that relies on a full awareness of its own activity – its craft – not to restrict itself to it but, on the contrary, to constantly remember that it only holds its legitimacy by the relation it must constantly recreate with reality. To remember that, as Strehler writes in a "Letter to a young director",

> these forms, these gestures, these acts that make the theatre serve some purpose, cannot really exist without "content". Without this content, there remains [. . .] "nothing" but a gesture of theatre, nothing but a [. . .] work (as if the work, in itself, was worth something) [. . .] behind the greatest performance in the world, behind the greatest poetic adventure, there is only death, if we do not know for whom and for what we are acting".[47]

As such, Strehler's theatre always begins by "affirming the theatre"; however, it does not do so in a gesture of complacency. If it deploys all the powers of the theatre, it is to make them disappear, since "for Strehler, the onus is not – or at least, not only – to make beautiful productions. Instead, he aspires to a transparent theatricality".[48]

"A relative totality"

Such is the paradox of Strehler's theatre: that this theatre that seems to unite the different poles of theatricality (the four "cities"), that seems to reconcile "art theatre" with the political demands of a popular Brechtian critical theatre, that is recognised equally for the plasticity of its images, its musicality, the performances of its actors and its dramaturgical construction of meaning – in sum, this aesthetic that seems to represent a fusion of the theatrical ambitions of the second half of the twentieth century – is a theatre that is based, as Dort writes, on an absolute refusal of "all total theatre, i.e. theatre which is fully self-sufficient and autonomous".[49] Strehler's theatre masterfully deploys *all* the powers of the theatre, but without a totalising ambition and without ever turning in on itself – the stage does not claim to be a substitute for the world, nor to produce a discourse that would fully account for it and exhaust its complexity. And the director, as surprising as it may seem for the one who appears as the very epitome of the *maestro*, is not an author claiming absolute control of the creative act. As he says in an interview,

> Autonomous creator, never! That has never been my approach or the nature of my work. [. . .] I have freed myself of the demonic need of many of my fellow directors who want to be the authors *themselves*, not just of the performance, but of the actual text.[50]

Thus, the director is a creator, but their art is a fragile balance, one based on the full awareness of its precariousness and even more of its *relativity*. This relativity is of the stage itself in relation to the world in which it fits; relativity also in that the creator cannot wall themselves off in a production that is finished, self-contained and self-sufficient. Indeed, for Strehler, the work takes shape by virtue of a constant *tension*, a dynamic that Strehler describes, in the conclusion of his last lecture, by using the German term *"streben"*: "a movement towards that which is not there". If Strehler's performances represent exemplary demonstrations of the multiple powers of the theatre, a clear image of the triumphant theatricality of which the second half of the twentieth century constitutes a remarkable illustration, this example also reminds us that the totality to which the act of staging – and theatre in general – aspires is one that can only be a *relative totality*. It is therefore the opposite of an all-encompassing, rigid, *narcissistic* theatricality lost in the contemplation of its own powers, since the *fusion* of all the poles and all the powers of the theatre is, without a doubt, impossible.

Therein lie the limits of creation, authorship and even scenic writing that claim to be self-sufficient and closed systems. Yet, this seems to be the danger and the potential stalemate of the drive to make the stage autonomous and the director creator: that a relationship to the real is lost, that staging turns in on itself in a semantic and aesthetic autarchy, that it loses the tensions that unpin it. These tensions are both what is proper to the interaction of the different objects onstage and what naturally results from their confrontation and from the heterogeneous nature of the spectators. It is around these issues that new and significant questions about the means and functions of theatre, and about the functions of staging, would develop from the 1980s onwards.

13

THE EXPERIENCE OF RELATIVITY

As such, a potential setback that *mise en scène* has brought with it, from its heyday in the 1960s to the 1980s, is closure and narcissism. The *mise en scène* movement, at its apogee (in the 1980s), achieved institutionalisation in the French theatre. By placing theatre directors at the head of numerous well-endowed theatrical institutions, Jack Lang, then minister of culture, endorsed and elevated the great figures of this generation. It was under Lang that Vitez was appointed director of Chaillot, that Chéreau became head of the Théâtre des Amandiers in Nanterre (which was completely renovated for him) and that Bernard Sobel saw the Gennevilliers Theatre Ensemble, which he led for nearly thirty years, become a Centre Dramatique National [National Dramatic Centre] (CDN). Additionally, many directors found themselves at the head of the new National Dramatic Centres created in the provinces in a new wave of decentralisation. It was a decade of institutional enshrinement, one that also witnessed, as the late 1970s had already begun to do, a number of ambitious productions, adventures involving significant risks and that sought to embody the unique aesthetics of this or that director: Wagner's *Der Ring* [*The Ring*] staged by Chéreau in Bayreuth, beginning in 1976, was certainly one. His *Hamlet* in the courtyard of the Palais des Papes in Avignon (1988) was another, but in another mode, bare and restrained (we will come back to this). Also in the courtyard at Avignon, Claudel's full-length *Le soulier de satin* was a fusion of poetic form and language, at once a precarious and refined theatre, which appeared to many to be Vitez's last masterpiece (1987). It was a night in which the theatre shone in all its nobility. But Vitez's production, while embodying theatre in all its greatness, was also an illustration of theatricality in its simplest apparatus, in a twelve-hour production, from dusk till dawn. Two years earlier, for an entire night (twelve hours), Peter Brook had invited the audience at Avignon on another journey with

The Mahabharata (1985), a sprawling Indian epic that, in the natural space of the Boulbon Quarry, seemed an exemplar of Brook's theatre, with its emphasis on the oral tale, on play, on the actor and objects, on natural simplicity and the mixture of cultures. In the Parisian staging at the Bouffes du Nord, it also produced a similar effect.

The second generation of directors, mentioned by Dort, "foregrounded the practice of staging". This movement, which culminates in the 1980s, is one that celebrates the "glory of theatricality" (as fragile as it may be) that was, without a doubt, "the utopia of a theatre [...] that would reconcile opposites: the text and the performance, the individual and the audience, perhaps also the West and the East, in the fullness of a big play".[1] If these large totalities and institutional enshrinement mark a climax, like all climaxes, they also announce the moment when certainties waver and the inevitable coming of that "third generation" of directors, who would question this triumph of theatricality, "confronting the theatre itself, revoking or suspending its illusion". With this third generation, the theatre would be made to "question itself and its own play"[2] – and, primarily, the place and function of *mise en scène* itself.

As such, it is at its highest moment of celebration that the art of *mise en scène* begins to be questioned, to the point of having to be defended. The editorial that Vitez writes for the first issue (spring 1985) of the magazine revealingly titled *L'Art du theatre* [*The Art of Theatre*], which he created at Chaillot, is, in this case, quite symptomatic. Instead of claiming and affirming the autonomy of scenic creation, this issue proposed a retrospection, an interrogation and a defence of the practice. Vitez characterises the previous "thirty or forty years" as a "golden age", a time of "profusion of the theatre itself". "Rarely have we seen so many experiments, and so many ideas about what the stage should be, and about its capabilities", writes Vitez.[3] He inscribes his thoughts on theatre and on *mise en scène* within a historical framework that includes Craig, to which the title refers, but also Jouvet, who he consideres as an exemplar and as the "last *metteur en scène* of the old era, and first of the new". While he affirms the freedom of the stage, Vitez no longer does so on the basis of a limitless number possible choices, noting that choices of interpretation were "not as infinite as we might have thought up to recently, and that [...] the choices of staging also are limited to a few essential types". He also defines the theatre and its mission in opposition to the images spread by the medium that has now become the new mass vehicle of representations – television. And he finishes his text by defining as the founding task of the magazine the defence of this art of staging, a historical achievement that, as he lays out, was now the subject of various attacks, both from "conservative common sense" and "populist demagoguery":

> Finally, we will defend the function and the very existence of *mise en scène*, which today again are being challenged in principle. We will not be locked into the ineffable relationship of the actor to the text and to the audience. We will not allow theatre to be stripped of its historic accomplishment, the founding of what has been called art theatre.[4]

The art of staging was therefore ostensibly located within a history, and above all, it is now something to be defended. Significantly, two years later, the sixth delivery of the same magazine is dedicated to this enterprise, under the title of "Deffence et illustration de la mise en scène" ["Defence and illustration of *mise en scène*"]. And this defence is simultaneously a gesture of revisiting and of interrogating anew: "to defend it is to reformulate its vocation and, thereby, to find anew its raison d'être", Vitez remarks in the opening pages.[5] It seems that something needed to be reassessed, at a time when various discourses criticised the centrality of *mise en scène* and the notion of scenic writing to claim anew the primacy of the actor or of the text. And reassessment undoubtedly involved finding the balance, the play and the organicity of the elements of the stage *mise en scène* organises, insofar as there was some risk that it was too directive and suffocating, that it was withdrawing into self-indulgence or complacency.

The round table discussion that opens the issue entitled *L'Art du Théâtre* (and that brought together the editorial board of the journal: G. Banu, J.-M. Deprats, R. Durand, M. Millon and D. Sallenave) notes that there was a diffuse rejection of the importance of *mise en scène*: a rejection mostly implicit, however, except that it equated the director to a master of thought, and a role that was too directive. More broadly, the issue that arose was that of *mise en scène*'s visibility, and the validity of this visibility. This visibility was conceived as a spectre between "competing scenario and erasure". In other words, if what was at stake was the freedom of the actor, this was expressed primarily in relation to the text, which *mise en scène* was accused of masking in order to exhibit itself, whereas its nature was intended to be a *responsible mediation*. There were therefore attempts at revisiting the definition of *mise en scène*: was it a visible equivalent to the text (a visual translation of its opacity), or was it the manifestation of a concept or a visible production of meaning? As such, the main points around which the questions of the 1990s would crystallise were already emerging in the mid-1980s (the reaffirmation of the primacy of the text, the calling into question of ideological biases, the issue of whether scenic writing could be a discourse on the same footing as that of the text, the desire for effacement behind the text).

Thus, in some cases, there was an attempt to strip *mise en scène* of its powers in order to rediscover its foundations. The example of Chéreau's artistic evolution during the 1980s is particularly problematic in this respect. Chéreau, the prodigy and virtuoso of the French theatre, had emerged, after his Brechtian beginnings, as the aesthetic director par excellence. After the failure of his militant adventure in Sartrouville, and in reaction to the positions of his colleagues following May 1968 (especially during the Villeurbanne Conference), his text "Une mort exemplaire" ["An exemplary death"], published in 1969 in the journal *Partisan*,[6] pointed out the contradictions and the "naiveté" of popular theatre and "cultural militancy". It distinguished a truly proletarian and revolutionary theatre from the work of an artist with its "*ambiguous*, indirect speech" and preoccupation with forms – a distinction that foreshadowed his repositioning on the artistic side of theatre practice. His productions from the 1970s in Villeurbanne, from *La Dispute* to *Peer Gynt* (1981), to Wagner's *Der Ring* (1976), which he had staged in Bayreuth, had seemed to display a strong and personal dramaturgical reading and demonstrate an incomparable virtuosity in the creation of pictorial images, which were to become trademarks of his "allegorical theatre". But it was, paradoxically, when he took over the Amandiers of Nanterre (with its sizeable auditorium and large platform) and, therefore, an apparatus custom-made for the deployment of his artistic mastery, that there was an about-turn in his aesthetic. Indeed, Chéreau's aesthetic became more and more pared-down. As if he was trying to give up the pomp and power of the theatricality he had forged, he "seemed to renounce in one go the dream power of the Italian box theatre" that had brought him glory – as Anne-Françoise Benhamou has shown, portraying him as Prospero breaking his wand and undoing his magic at the end of *The Tempest*, "placing his art through a trial by ordeal".[7]

A major illustration of this point is that moment when the great auditorium of the Amandiers was transformed into a cinema for Genet's *Les Paravents* [*The Screens*] (1983), which was played mainly among the spectators, and where the stage, reduced to a narrow band, was used only to represent the world of the dead. It was a production that seems to have as its objective "the undoing of the image", to quote an unpublished review of the play by François Regnault. There is also the example of *Lucio Silla*, an opera by Mozart (1984), in which the high walls of Peduzzi are no longer in the background but set at the front of the stage, in a tragic rejection of scenic depth. Heiner Müller's (1985) *Quartett* was also staged in front of the same scenery (the high walls at the front of the stage), where Roland Bertin and Michelle Marquais wandered between the edge of the stage, a fragile bridge placed over an empty orchestra pit, and the room itself. There would also be Chéreau's *Hamlet* (1988), in which the high walls of Peduzzi would be made to lie flat, becoming an archaeological ground filled with holes and on which Gerard Desarthe (who played Hamlet) would wander. Finally, there is the example of the bifrontal device initiated with Bernard-Marie Koltès' *Combat de nègre et de chiens* [*Fight of the Negro and the Dog*] (1983) and that Chéreau uses again a decade later, after leaving the Amandiers, for *Dans la solitude des champs de coton* [*In the Solitude of Cotton Fields*] by the same Koltès (1996) and then for Racine's *Phèdre* (2004). In these productions, the performance space amounts to large spans of concrete: there are the actors and a few spotlights to enlighten them — it is a minimal theatricality that abandons sensual seductiveness and is condensed in the tormented bodies of the actors beneath the gaze of the audience overlooking them. At the Amandiers in the 1980s, and this can be extend to the rest of his production, Anne-Françoise Benhamou sees Chéreau's work as

> a constant attempt at exorcising [. . .] the temptation of perfect mastery, the temptation of a theatre where the art of the theatre is forever celebrated, of a theatre where the world would refract easily in the pure language of the stage, of a theatre that would develop comfortably thanks to the now acquired partitioning — 1968 is now far behind us — of the theatrical world and the real world.[8]

Indeed, it is this "perfect mastery" — the separation of the stage and its disconnection from the real, a narcissistic self-celebration — which forms the boundaries of triumphant theatricality. The demon of self-sufficiency undoubtedly caused many directors to give in to the temptation of totalism, which as we have seen with Strehler, could never be anything but relative. Consequently, the director, who had become organiser of meaning, an overall master who aspired to put into play in the staged work all — or almost all — the existing or possible readings of a text, as Daniel Mesguich tried to do, realised that, by dint of wanting to embrace all, everything diffracted or faded.

While, for a quarter of a century, theatrical creation had been centralised in the hands of a director concerting the various constituents of the theatrical act under his law and his conception of the unity of the theatre, the 1980s mark the beginning of a reversal: that of a greater diffraction, of a new autonomisation of the various elements and constituents of a theatricality that would give up part of its claim to unification. This theatricality, contrary to the ideal of a fusion of the arts and of an organic meaning, would consider as essentially important the *play* of these elements, and would consequently turn more attention to the spectator, who would become a builder of meaning.

The "emancipation of representation"

Once again, the critical reflections of Bernard Dort prove essential here in their singular lucidity. It is indeed toward the end of the 1980s that he began to elaborate, as an attentive witness, the notion of "emancipated representation" (which would be the title of his 1988 collection of essays)[9] This is an important notion, not only in that it highlights the issues important to this decade, but in that it anticipates the movement that would very strongly characterise a good part of the theatrical practices of the 1990s. What Dort finds is that the "Copernican revolution", represented by the new primacy of representation over text and by the advent of the theatre director, was being eclipsed by an "Einsteinian revolution", which, rather than annulling the first, was extending it. This transformation can be formulated in a few sentences, as we read in his posthumous collection *Le Spectateur en dialogue* [*The Spectator into Dialogue*][10]:

> the supplanting of the harmony between text and stage in favour of an overall relativity of the factors of theatrical representation in their relationship one with another. We come to renounce the idea of an organic unity, fixed in principle, and even the notion of an essence of the theatrical fact (a mysterious theatricality), and give way to a signifying polyphony, oriented toward the spectator.

The "organic unity, fixed in principle" is, of course, the one built by the director, as it *structures* the representation and organises the various elements of the stage (dramaturgy, actor's play, scenography, treatment of time, objects and accessories) as a unified construction, a "static assembly of signs or a meta-text", in the formulation of a given meaning. Behind this desire for unification and of aesthetic and semantic coherence, there is in fact the dream, which goes back to Wagner and Craig, of a global (i.e. organic) theatricality, which would represent the fusion of the various arts that constitute it in one unique art and totalising art. "It may be time", says Dort, "to rethink [this design], not to deny the importance of the director and their role in the theatrical act, but to valorise the roles of the different components of the theatre"; not to question the fundamental awareness "of the signifying power of the elements of representation" but to emphasise their shared responsibility, and to substitute for a closed and established assemblage the theatre's own *play* as "a dynamic process that takes place in time and is actually produced by the actor".[11] The construction of meaning is, indeed, *process*. It is in motion throughout the theatre session, rather than something fixed. As such, the various constituents of the stage *free themselves* from a centralising logic in an "agonistic" conception of the stage, which involves "a struggle (albeit a peaceful one) for meaning – a struggle in which the spectator is, ultimately, judge. This agonistic conception of the stage should be replaced by "a non-unified representation whose various elements would enter into collaboration, even rivalry, rather than contribute, by erasing their differences, to the construction of a common meaning". Dort invites the reader – and signals, in this sense, an emerging desire in the theatre – to view theatricality through the lens of a polyphony whose relative explosion would reactivate the place of the spectator: "Then, the spectator could choose, fill the gaps or erase the overflows of such a polyphony in which there would no longer be any dominant component. They are the ones who would be the keystone of the representation".[12]

We see that in spite of appearances, it was not in a deep questioning of the achievements of critical Brechtian theatre that Dort was relentlessly engaged in the 1950s–1960s. On the contrary, his call was for a return to the "true" roots of Brechtism, which places the thought process and activity of the spectator at its centre, as well as a reassessment of its stakes, when placed against the background of a new historical-aesthetic situation. Dort was not putting meaning on trial, either. Instead, he was fully aware of a profoundly Brechtian gesture (and one that is linked, more broadly, to the very nature of the theatre, as we continue to show in this volume), i.e. that the stage must be, above all, a site of contradiction, and that "the very vocation of the theatre is to be a critique of meaning. This is how *play* takes on its full power. As much as it is construction, theatricality is predominantly the interrogation of meaning".[13]

Consequently, "if staging is placing in signs, playing is moving the signs, instituting the movement and the sliding of these signs, in a space and a definite time".[14] This reorientation of how we conceive of scenic signs and, therefore, of theatrical discourse, revalorises the two most characteristic elements of the metamorphosis and polysemy that the staging platform produces: the temporality and the play of the actor. In the same collection for example, Dort dedicates a very beautiful text to Jean-Louis Hourdin's (1980) staging of Büchner's *Woyzeck*,[15] and especially to the actor François Chattot, who plays the character of the Showman, a kind of presenter and conductor, a bridge between the fable and the audience, who provides an attentive external perspective on the fiction but who plays certain roles in it. This "Showman with undecided functions" is, for Dort, the very incarnation of a permanent mutability, of this game of construction and deconstruction of unstable signs that are perpetually reorganised in the service of an active and open meaning; not an actor's work that would accumulate, throughout the representation, the converging signs of a singular "thickness of signs" (the expression comes from Barthes). It is a meaning factory, of course, but a factory in motion – a complex and contradictory metamorphosis. Because "the stage is not a place of certainty or truth [...] the multiple and varied signs displayed there never constitute a closed system of meanings. They put each other in play and at risk".[16] The theatrical act is thus reactivated as a process and not as a self-sufficient and fixed work, as tension and sharing of the responsibilities of its different elements, under the aegis of a director who no longer builds a discourse or a unified aesthetic object, but who implements a theatricality based on the dynamic play of meaning, of which the spectator is the active receiver, the true constructor and interrogator. "Theatricality, then, [...] is also the displacement of these signs, their impossible conjunction, their confrontation under the gaze of the spectator of this *emancipated* representation".[17]

Let us be clear: "emancipated representation" is a notion, and more specifically, an emphasis on the spectator's observation, and not a theory or a real aesthetic program. Nor can it be taken for a justification for making the staging go in any direction (i.e., nowhere). On the contrary, the sense in which it is particularly interesting and extremely significant is that it observes and translates an important mutation of the landscape of *mise en* scène, which, as we have said, becomes crucial during this turning point of the 1980s. Except for its belief in signification, as we shall see, it would fit many aspects of the work of the generation of directors that would follow the one we have been discussing in this chapter. It would also be used to characterise, at least in part, certain approaches that, while bearing the mark of the foremost directors and their most recognisable "techniques", and while appearing absolutely unique in their aesthetics, call into question the closure of the work and the unification of its elements, integrating within the heart of them the impossibility of a fixed meaning and an essentially polyphonic theatricality, naturally open on the reception of the spectator.

Excess/void: Matthias Langhoff/ Klaus-Michael Grüber

In the light of the above, we shall consider two directors who are radically different, save from the fact that they are both German and both readily welcomed in France. They represent two inverse (and therefore symmetrical) experiences of such a transcendence of the framework of scenic autonomy and semantic closure of the discourse of staging. They represent two experiments in the testing of limits, so to speak, one through excess, the other through restraint: they are Matthias Langhoff and Klaus-Michael Grüber, two directors who we have already mentioned several times and whose general approaches it will be necessary to consider more closely.

Matthias Langhoff's work clearly inherits a Brechtian lineage. Born during the war in a German exiled family closely connected to the theatre and to anti-fascist intellectuals, he entered the Berliner Ensemble in 1961. It was there that he met Manfred Karge, with whom he staged his first productions (*Mahagonny-Songspiel*, then Brecht's *Le Commerce de pain* [*The Trade in Bread*] at the Berliner) and with whom he would collaborate for twenty years – until the beginning of the 1980s, when Langhoff chose to remain and work in Switzerland and France. Langhoff has consistently rejected dramaturgy of identification – a result of his own Brechtian heritage – embracing instead an aesthetic strongly marked by contradiction and by a construction based on montage. He also places a major emphasis on the concreteness of the stage ("The truth is concrete. I do not know how to play an idea",[18] he states), the concreteness of the body and of the actor's play, the concreteness of the situations presented on the stage, the concreteness of the staging techniques (scenography, lights, etc.) that Langhoff places at the centre of his aesthetic. As the actor François Chattot attests,

> all the different fields of activity are like "objects"; out of the collage of these "objects" the representation appears. Langhoff thus turns his back on the psychological linearity of characters, situations, or spaces. We observe a montage of real, dreamlike, burlesque and tragic elements, whereby all sentimental

behaviours, along with their share of nostalgia, are evacuated. Through montage, Langhoff points rejects the illusion of a continuity of feelings fostered by chronology.[19]

In a word, Langhoff's dramaturgy is one marked by discontinuity (as would be Peter Zadek's productions of the 1960s) and of the contradictory montage of objects.

Nonetheless, Langhoff's theatre seems to have slipped away from its Brechtian foundations – perhaps a sign of the times? While Brechtian montage used to be organised in order to clarify the real, around a belief in knowledge and in human reason, Langhoff's use of montage seems to make much more of chaos, and, through the profusion that characterises it, to escape from a rational grasp of reality: the elements remain isolated in their meanings and no globalising knowledge seems able to emerge. On the contrary, Langhoff – marked by war, exile and the wounds of history – seems to stage shifts in reason in the face of the real, entangling heterogeneous referential strata whose accumulation escapes any globalising grasp and exceeds any unifying reading. Such a move opens meaning and testifies to the clash of reason in the face of the real. In a certain way, it is a baroque aesthetic, which, moreover, regularly draws on the Elizabethan repertoire (*King Lear* (1986), *Macbeth* (1990), *Gloucester Time: Matériau Shakespeare* after *Richard III* (1995), Webster's *The Duchess of Malfi* (1991), his use of haemoglobin and coffins, etc.). As such, Langhoff's is an aesthetic of profusion, accumulation and the assembly of heterogeneous elements. The Langhovian stage (as we have already seen with the example of *Gloucester Time: Matériau Shakespeare*) embraces referential anachronism as one of its founding processes: to signify the discovery of King Duncan's murder upon waking up, the guards in *Macbeth* have their morning cornflakes; and to enter the fortress of the king in this period of medieval Christmas, Duncan's assassins will dress up as Santa Claus. The mayor's bathroom in his production of Gogol's *The Government Inspector* (1998) had the kitsch luxury of those of any nouveau riche in present-day Russia, and the timid false inspector of the beginning returned in the finale dressed as a young modern Western businessman. As for the fairy tale Italy in which Büchner's Princess Lena and Prince Leonce escape (Georg Büchner's *Leonce and Lena*, staged by Langhoff in 2002), it resembled a Parisian metro station, and the romantic disillusioned wandering of the heroes thereby became a concrete way of "bumming around". These examples should not, however, suggest that Langhoff's preoccupation is with "updating" the fables he stages. His *mises en scène* demands that various historical strata collide, as well as different dramatic registers (the tragic and the grotesque, the burlesque and the farcical, etc.). Langhoff's aesthetic is an aesthetics of the heterogeneous, and also of excess: it displays such an abundance of various signs that they cannot form a system, or even a linear and closed discourse – they resist singularly and face off with each other constantly. It is therefore excess that supplants, in Langhoff's *mises en scène*, the closure of meaning, to bring it back to the materiality of the various elements of the theatre session: for a long time, the spectators of the first ranks at *The Government Inspector* will be able to recall the smell of fish that the mayor's servant, without apparent motivation but in an actual gesture of work, prepared in front of them. Meaning is also brought back to contradiction, to activate the spectator's agency and also portray a world whose chaos no discourse can resolve.

His scenographies, profuse to excess but always held in precarious balance, provide striking illustration. The one he designed for Heiner Müller's *Philoctète* in 1995 represented a rocky island-dump, two-thirds of which was occupied by the remains of a house with crumbling columns and walls, with a half-collapsed roof and the tiling destroyed. In his 1997 production of Euripedes' eponymous play, the *Trojan Women*, the women remained in a Greek ruin as they waited to be chosen as slaves by the Greeks. In *The Government Inspector*, Langhoff produced a series of spaces using the movements of an immense helical turntable, which occupied almost the whole stage and depicted an infernal machine always on the verge of collapse. These scenographies portray a shaken world, where history has left scars. The ground of the stage is very often uneven and its uncomfortable irregularity influences the actor's game, preventing any abstract stylisation. The set often makes pictorial references to painters, like Goya or Bosch, who propose a grotesque distortion of reality. Here, Langhoff's theatre attempts to represent and question the chaos of a world beyond rationality (*The Government Inspector*) or that of a world of absurd super-rationality (*The Island of Salvation*, following Kafka's *The Penal Colony*, in 1996), and the atrocities of history. His staging of Chekhov's *Three Sisters* (1993) featured a whole century of Russian history, from the dawn of the revolution to the dislocation of the Soviet empire, not in a global and direct demonstration, but by different allusions (painted canvases or projections between the acts, aspects of the scenery, with the neoclassical appearance of a Soviet state hotel during the first two acts, costume elements or accessories), and most of his productions of the 1990s would turn a critical gaze on the catastrophes of the wars, which at that time haunted Europe as well as the East.

With its imposing scenography, the multiplicity of scenic elements proposed by its accumulative aesthetics, but also by the performances it requires of the actors, Langhoff's theatre is certainly spectacular. But, as we can clearly see, it in no way seeks to become a "monument": it is above all materialist. Behind its depiction of the chaos of the world, the fragmentation and accumulation characteristic of the stage serve only to provoke reflection on the issue of the human. *Lenz, Léonce et Léna chez Georg Büchner* [*Lenz, Léonce and Léna at the Home of Georg Büchner*], at the Comédie-Française (2002), demonstrated this. Langhoff resorted again to the use of montage: the representation of *Léonce and Léna* is interspersed with the text of *Lenz* performed in a choral way (the one after the other in turn or, on a few occasions, in unison) by the actors. The combined effect of the montage of the two texts and of this choral performance of Büchner's novella is a vertiginous spreading of one text over the other. Thanks to the choral treatment applied to *Lenz*, and to Langhoff's use of profusion and accumulation on the stage, the play brings the Büchnerian theme of madness into relief. *Leonce und Lena* is stripped of all appearances of light comedy and produces a sense of disillusion. Dialogical situations are undermined by a lack of communication and the incongruence of the dialogue produced becomes tragic. The play is entirely pervaded by Lenz's madness and by all the deep questions it provokes: what is the soul, where does it dwell (the performance began with an excerpt from Buchner's medical thesis)? What is the void filled by the human mechanism? "Am I this? or that? or that?" as a line by the jester Valério (played by Jean-Yves Dubois) asks. Carried by the actors in their costumes of *Léonce and Léna*, the text of *Lenz* is diffracted and rubs off on the action of the comedy. Against the background of this madness, and the progressive disconnection from Lenz's world (because of its violence), the play became a critical thought space on the ultimate point of the human and Langhoff's fragmentation as a whole became grounded in this central issue. The performance, which opened with video images filmed by Langhoff on the trail of Lenz's journey in the Vosges, and at the end of which the Struthoff concentration camp appears, came to an end (disappeared, one might say) in new video images, like an unfathomable vanishing point, while the mountains painted on the bottom cyclorama remained slightly lit. These video images showed tracks in the sand, a small boat of African fishermen on the sea, a beach, a child, the beach again, a crab advancing on the sand; rudimentary African tombs – with pickets and, sometimes, a wooden plaque to represent a stele – and finally, a tree bent by the wind in the sand floor. In this vanishing point of the final film we experience what *Lenz*'s chorus had evoked throughout the performance and infused into *Leonce und Lena*: the search for refuge and the irreducible quest for life, the concrete and pathetic loneliness of death; the ultimate – and common – limits of the human.

Through it uses impressive scenic means, the Langhovian theatre is a theatre of fragmentation, of diffraction and of contradiction; it is a theatre that does not refuse provocation and that even endorses the Brechtian conception of a theatre that divides. But it is also a theatre that refuses to "shed light", deeply resistant to "ever belittl[ing] the audience, to ever imagine that it knows something better than it".[20] It multiplies signs but does not attempt to reduce them to a discourse, or to a coherence of interpretation. On the contrary, the different elements come into tension, not to create a unilateral meaning but rather an association of referents that makes it possible to clash various interpretive layers and leave them at the disposal of the spectator, who interprets them in light of the complexity of reality.

The theatre of Klaus-Michael Grüber also refuses to embrace a *discourse* of staging, but in a reverse process: not through excess and the proliferation of signs, but on the contrary, through their rarefaction. Not through fullness, but through void: it is a stark theatre of evidence and simplicity, a minimal theatricality devoid of the theatre's masks (or at least the belief in their false illusion).

In the first place, it is at the level of actor directing that Grüber's work manifests its specificity. All this consists of stripping the actor to their barest essentials, to get them to go deep into their inner selves by shedding the artifices of their craft, of the "trappings" of expressive technique: making them lose their usual bearings in order to bring forth the truth of an emotion, though not in histrionic ostentation and the artificial production of pathos. German actress Angela Winckler explains that, "Grüber 'deflates' his actors, he strips them. In rehearsal, very cautiously, he begins to pull the mat from under their feet until they know nothing".[21] And there is an entire lexicon of Grüberian expressions revealing the same gesture of making bare: do not "call" (that is, do not announce beforehand a theatrical effect that is to come), "do not bolster speech and gesture", "cry on the inside and not on the outside", "do not emphasise while talking".[22]

> The actors must give up a lot of things, be very weak. It's easy to win, we have to learn how to lose, to not settle. Do not send direct so much attention on to yourself, be attentive, be simple, almost nothing! [. . .] Do not become established![23]

His whole conception of the stage presence is based on restraint and on a fundamental refusal of effects and overacting, romantic effusions and sentimentalism ("E=MC2 is not sentimental", he would hammer home during the rehearsals of *Iphigenie auf Tauris*[24]). He rejected the artificial expressiveness of the actor. "Warm heart, cold speech", as he instructed Ludmilla Mikaël in the role of Bérénice. In a certain way, his attempt was to "de-theatricalise" the theatre (which is the same as recognising it for what it is), to remove the superfluity and the flourishes, to find, rather than a manifest expressiveness, the truth of an intimate and concrete human emotion, through letting go and through absolute sincerity. Grüber's is a theatre of calm and restraint, of silence and whispers, one endlessly engaged in the search for "an emotional simplicity".

"Grüber is not a director who explains", says the actor Udo Samel.[25] And what works for the actor's direction is also valid for the relationship between the *mise en scène* and the spectator. Grüber's theatre is a theatre of presence, of being-there and not of seduction and affirmation. It seeks to have a concrete sensuality and not to display artificial and didactic signs on the stage. It is the non-demonstrative theatre par excellence, both semantically and emotionally speaking. "It is below or beyond hysteria", as Bernard Dort writes, and its identity "is not defined by expression – Grüber does not seek to have his work say this or that – nor the impact of spectacle – it is defined by the gaze, by attention and affect.[26] This theatricality of restraint, an example of which we find in Grüber's production of *Bérénice*, mentioned above, this "oblique movement" (B.Dort) or this "pared-back" (B. Pautrat) theatre, seems engaged in a permanent move of shifting and decentring. In the 1970s, Grüber had distinguished himself with performances outside the theatre walls, such as *Winterreise* (1977), after Hölderlin's *Hyperion*, which he had created in the huge Olympic stadium in Berlin, laden with its sinister memory. Going outside the theatre building in this fashion was a means of playing the resistance of the real and singular identity of the place (stadium, and Nazi monument) against the artificial fusion of the elements of the stage. Similarly, in 1975, *Faust-Salpêtrière*, created in the chapel of the former Charcot hospital, imposed the memory and madness of the place on to the representation of Goethe's text, while allowing Grüber to build the performance around the spatial fragmentation and movement of the spectators. But this fragmentation was, however, underpinned by the suspended time of the sand that, for an hour, slowly fell from a bag occupying the centre of the space that had been cut at the beginning of the representation, and by the enigmatic presence of a turtle on the stage.

While in the 1980s, Grüber returned to the interior of strictly theatrical buildings, it was to define within them the same approach, to re-examine theatricality from the inside and use the platform as a *frame* ("You must never cry without a frame", he remarks about Racine's formal rigor[27]), which provides a form and favours attention, but that would not be that of a fusion or aesthetic unity. In fact, Grüber often harnesses the void of this framework of the stage to isolate actors or certain elements – to highlight them in the peaceful and material evidence of their solitudes.

While Grüber's theatre might appear like a theatre of the intimate, this intimacy is in no way revealed or exhibited. Rather, its understated nature, restraint and materiality make it a theatre of enigma and opacity. It is the same opacity – the same silence, we could say – the same resistance to a given meaning that characterises many of the objects found in his *mises en scène*: be it the big stone that occupied the centre of the platform in *Bérénice*, the turtles of *Faust-Salpêtrière* or the sand of *Iphigenie au Tauris*. The visual texture of the colours that scenographer Gilles Aillaud usually uses matters most: it is their materiality that is important, because it resists pinning them down to a static meaning and function, and works against a reduction to an image or interpretation that would subsume them. It is therefore not surprising that, far from any desire for unity or univocity and any aspiration to completion in a work, Grüber's theatre derives its density and continuity of emotion from the fundamental principles of de-dramatisation, essential precariousness and fragility. In this sense, his staging of *Sur la grand route* [*On the Road*] (1984) has rightly been considered exemplary. First, Chekhov's short play deals with the expectation of a dramatic event that only arises *in extremis* to vanish soon afterwards. It is the simple description of the expectation of characters whose solitudes are united for one short night in a secluded inn, which they will leave in the morning. Chekhov's text is presented as "dramatic sketch", in the precarious and suspended style of Grüber that brings together simplicity, fragility and density of emotion. Concerning his relations with the actors, Grüber has made this confession, which says much about the nature of his theatre: "I'm lucky to be such a weak man. Because of that, they know I'm not cheating."[28]

It is, indeed, a very special game that takes place in Grüber's theatre: it is a theatre of withdrawal but of an emotion not mediated by the play of expressive signs, an intimate theatre that opens itself up to the spectator but that is based on opaque and non-demonstrative presences. Grüber seems to constantly test the limits of theatricality by means of stripping and restraint, thus paradoxically rearranging its poles and recognised principles. "We must not forget Brecht because he was right. But at the same time, we must get to the emotion",[29] Grüber declares to Jean-Pierre Thibaudat when *Bérénice* was being staged. In Grüber's theatre, materialism, the separation of the elements and a fundamental sense of distance, prove to be the paradoxical vectors of emotion and empathy.

From the ascendant and then triumphant authority of the director, through Strehler's concept of relative totality and Dort's reflection on emancipated representation, we have thus reached a less global and less totalising conception of staging. Previously, we had observed, where the representation of the repertoire was concerned, that, in the 1980s, the principle of interpretation depicted by the performance, which sometimes gave rise to an unequivocal lesson, had given way to a reflection on form, images and language, but also, *through* an openness of meaning ensured by representation, to a sort of delegation of interpretation to the spectator. As we have just seen, this trend does not only concern classical repertoire, but the whole theatre. The excess of Langhoff or the restraint of Grüber testifies to the extent that both, as good materialists, take into account in their very aesthetics the resistance that the real poses to all hermeneutics and all harmonising interpretations. Both invite the spectator to fill the silence and emptiness, or to give unity to the appearance of the disjointed through risk-taking and a specific hermeneutical activity. However, it was also understood that the mythical moment of triumphant theatricality had not been as totalising, totalitarian or didactic as one might have thought: while the theatre's mandate had been to revisit works through a didactically political and ideological lens, its artists were conscious of their art and gave to the theatrical act, to the image, to the body and to language, the emphasis, and indeed the autonomy, they deserved. The emphasis on polysemy and the plastic and aesthetic concern with space and body are therefore not to be seen as salutary reactions to a kind of didactical Stalinism, but as a coming into awareness, perhaps in a more rigorous and more ostentatious fashion, of elements, which, strategically, had not been ostensibly claimed.

On the other hand, the decade of the 1980s clearly represents a turning point with respect to the awareness of the limits of the director and perhaps also the end of an obsession with power. As we have seen, the 1980s brought with it a general realisation of the limits of the director's power and function. Moreover, in a certain way, realising the vanity of any claim to totality, the majority of directors, having acquired legitimacy and status, returned to what some had never given up: to uncertainty, to the necessity of collective thought and, it must be said, to a certain humility. *Mise en scène* could then be carried out increasingly in the spirit of sharing: with the dramaturg, but also with the painter, the scenographer, the actors and the audience; with the text, its language and its author too. In addition, this European theatre, which had just produced the great epic and lyrical adventure of the conductor-director, was then able to return to what should be called performance, get closer to the events of the visual arts, to encourage choreographic experiments and to experience hybridity. Sharing, performance, an emphasis on the event, hybridity and multi-culuralism were new concepts with which directors were working, and these directors, it must be said, were rediscovering an aspect of theatricality that, in reality, had not disappeared.

Collage, montage, hybridisation, performance

We must not forget this other side of theatrical production, with its extreme vitality. Because *happening* and *performance* are not only about running their course. While tradition has too often tended to consider them as marginal and parallel to the evolution of staging as it is understood canonically, it is clear that they have had an impact on the art of staging in institutional theatre. In the same way, the logic of montage, of collage, of artistic "interdisciplinarity" and of the crossing of genres have constantly energised the performing arts. Beyond the fact that the theatre has often combined dance, music and declamation without using the label of "pluridisciplinarity", it is undeniable that hybridisation has been a constant in the history of theatre and that recent history is no exception.

While we praise the "newness" and "innovation" of performance (e.g. at the recent festival in Avignon, 2005), we should go back further in time – as far back as the "invention" of *mise en scène*, strictly speaking, at the turn of the nineteenth and twentieth centuries – to understand that it is part of a continuity, rather than being entirely new. We know how much *Ubu Roi*, in 1896, shocked the public not only with his expressly vulgar burlesque nature, but especially with its anti-realist aesthetic: Jarry, wishing to free the imagination of the spectators, abandons psychology, draws on puppets and Grand Guignol, and refuses the local flair and linear chronology. In 1917, with *Les Mamelles de Tirésias* [*The Breasts of Tiresas*], a "sur-realist drama", Apollinaire experiments with simultaneity in action and refuses to provide a narrative thread. In 1913 (Marinetti's first manifesto is from 1909), the Futurists compose a manifesto on the Théâtre des Variétés, and praise the importance of variety and therefore of discontinuity, as such. By claiming that acrobatics, songs, dances, cinematographic screenings, clowning and drama should systematically and even simultaneously appear onstage, in the orchestra and in the boxes, the Futurists resisted the traditional distribution of genres and, above all, the value judgements that ranked these from the most popular to the least (and therefore from the most to the least respectable). Marinetti in Paris, London and Italy, thus invented futuristic performances, dynamic and synoptic declamations and all kinds of "installations" *avant la lettre*, where exhibitions of paintings and monosyllabic declamations bordering on sound effects, and where the use of heterogeneous objects found in the street was the rule. One may note, for example, the performance at the Galerie Doré in London in 1914, where Marinetti, surrounded by all this, sketched schematic diagrams on the blackboard, and, phoning the painter Nevinson, who was in another room, gave him the order to beat on two drums. The respectable press spoke of provocation, but in the minds of the Futurists it was essentially a question of mixing music, noises, the visual arts, play, theoretical reading, poetry and drawing. Following the Italians, the Russian Futurists and Constructivists proposed multiple collaborations between poets, visual artists, musicians, dancers and actors. The Manifesto of the Synthetic Futurist Theatre (1915) proposed the compression in a few minutes, a few words and a few gestures, of situations, ideas, sensations, facts and symbols by simultaneously using sets, costumes and diction. According to Alexander Tairov, the music hall was then the only place where spectators participated in the performance and, as such, it was necessary to utilise it. As a result, Moscow became, just before the Revolution of 1917 and until the 1920s, a place where theatrical academism was shattered. Circus, variety theatre, music hall, Japanese theatre, puppets, dance, cinema and theatre were intertwined in these productions, before Stalinism quashed them. At the same time, with Dada in Zurich, with Tzara, Hugo Ball, Rubinstein, Arp and Kandinsky, with Satie, Picasso, Cocteau, Picabia, in Paris, then, after the war, with other Dadaist and Surrealist productions, we saw circus, music hall, typewriters, dressing gowns, umbrellas, interacting on dissection tables with magicians and finally, little by little, we heard infiltrating jazz. In Germany, the Bauhaus called for the "unification of the arts"[30] and in the early 1920s made puppets, mechanical figures, masks, geometric costumes and pantomimes the central elements of his performances, while Gropius introduced the students of the school to metaphysical dance, variety theatre, Japanese theatre, Javanese puppetry, circus arts, Russian Constructivist productions, among other arts. And in Berlin in 1922 (*RUR*, a play by Kerel Capeck staged by Friedrich Kiesler) cinematographic projections made their entry into performances.

As such, from the beautiful unified dramatic object (considered then an unsurpassable goal), theatre had transitioned to the practice of collage, juxtaposition and montage, conceived as fundamental structures for the performance. Artists used plastic collages, for decorations, juxtaposed genres and forms in the composition of plays, but also, with regard to the text itself, fragmentated and atomised sounds or syllables. Gertrude Stein involved the spectator's perception in the theatrical process, starting from Cézanne's cubism and harnessing the work of Braque, Picasso and Matisse. Extrapolating from their belief in the necessity of perceiving a painting in its totality, of finding the configurative parameters of the work, Stein actively involved the spectator in the elaboration of their vision of the work. At the same time, because she chose to deal with the individual's unconscious rather than confining the character in complex psychological situations, the author rejected linearity, fragments time, uses words as sound elements and/or manipulable signifiers, so that the Aristotelian control of meaning and the mimetic effect could no longer work. This forced spectators to focus on the style of the writing, the sound of the words and the unconscious of the human representations that one hesitates to call characters. Claiming that a play is what the author decides to call a play, and nothing else, she rejects images, metaphors, figurative language techniques and, of course, the classical idea of representation, while placing a narrator (whether male or female) in control of the text for performance. This narrator comments, digresses, freely associates disjointed remarks, accumulates words and fragments conventional configurations. The repetition of words and gestures then takes on its full importance as the character takes shape in cyclical movements. To the spectator this repetition gives impressions of an arbitrary unfolding of sound, gesture and meaning in that these impressions depend on what they see and hear. This is what Stein calls landscape drama: the spectator sees and hears images and ideas in a direct experience that they must themselves control and to which they must give meaning.

Though Gertrud Stein, who came to Paris in 1903, died there in 1946 without ever living again in her country of origin, her texts were well known on that side of the Atlantic, as were those of many German, Viennese and French artists, before, during and after the Second World War. Such artists ranged from Josef and Anni Albers, teachers at the Bauhaus before its closure by the Nazis, to Marcel Duchamp, who caused a scandal in 1913 at the Armory Show with his *Nude Descending a Staircase*. While Europe was mainly interested in the brilliance of dramatic theatre and in Brechtian epic theatre, there emerged on the American continent forms based on an aesthetic of collage, non-linearity, montage and hybridisation, in direct connection with the movements we have just described.

Indeed, the American avant-garde theatre after 1945, and especially that of the 1970s–1980s, systematically revisited these forms, each time going a step further in terms of experimentation. Performance art and *happenings* have brought together musicians, visual artists, actors, singers and dancers, transcending any notion of hierarchy within the arts or of their impermeability or self-containment with respect to each another. As early as 1952, at the Black Mountain College in North Carolina, musician John Cage and dancer-choreographer Merce Cunningham, who were regularly invited for classes and experiments, performed the first "events", juxtaposing, in the campus refectory, lectures, exhibition-installations of paintings (by Robert Rauschenberg mostly), poetry readings, recitals (David Tudor on piano), concrete musical performances, choreography, theatre, among other things. Allan Karpow, in 1959, performed *18 Happenings in 6 Parts* at Reuben Gallery in New York based on the same principles. In the United States, therefore, the interaction games and European performances of the beginning of the century were being continued but in a radical fashion, while artists took advantage of new technologies in image and sound. And to round it all out and conform to a political ideal of democratisation, these performance art forms incorporated, in a playful way, references to mass culture – or "pop culture" from England transposed into American "pop art" – whether from song, radio, image, advertising or television. The belief was that any human production could be incorporated into the artistic phenomenon as material: Oldenburg's *happenings* in the 1960s were evidence of this. The spectators participate, intervene, flow into the performance. In the space of these open shows, they are infinitely present. There is no longer a closed system, neither in body language and voice or in dramaturgy, or in the use of genres and media, and one even comes to doubt the term "theatre", since everything is mixed in what was then called performance. It was as if, after a long journey from East to West, we had come to the conclusion that it was no longer useful to fight over the definition of the theatre, let alone exhaust ourselves in a search for its essence. It was as if the word "performance" was itself limited too, so that the term "*performance art*" was invented, in order to break with the old classifications that European artists of the beginning of the twentieth century had already denounced. Julian Beck's Living Theatre, which we have already mentioned above, had no difficulty in inserting music (jazz in particular), or the masks and dances of Japanese theatre in its shows. Robert Wilson, as we have seen, exercised full liberty in borrowing from the visual arts and from the ideas of John Cage on chance and indeterminacy the essential components of his aesthetics. Richard Foreman was able to take advantage of the mixture of forms by juxtaposing grotesque dance, slapstick comedy, jazz from the 1930s, television, radio and advertising. Fragmenting text, image, sound and stage, Foreman divided the platform, forced the spectator to make visual, auditory, interpretative choices, drew axes in space using strings, placed accessories at intersections, captured and divided the audience's gaze, prevented any identification, refused a unifying overall vision and accumulated materials. Texts, gimmicks, wallpapers, paintings, disparate objects, glued ribbons, discarded rugs share the space with the actors while snatches of narration and moments of burlesque humour, half-political, sometimes sexual, fit into the discontinuous sequence of the performance. Thus, something like theatre continues, in the form of experimental theatre, mainly in the south of Manhattan and in the universities, while the cinema continues to cultivate illusion and the big productions of Broadway, founded on special effects, magazines, variety and the sumptuousness of means, preserve their part.

It was thus in the 1970s that a small number of experimental intercultural theatre companies made their debut in the United States and elsewhere. Within this prolific realm of activity, as Richard Schechner asserts in 1981,

> we are confronted with profound aesthetic questions in an unprecedented way. What is theatre? On what sites should it be played? Are these sites "sacred" or particular? Is it legitimate to speak of "secular ritual"? If so, does it define the theatre? What kinds of performers does the theatre need? Why? What is the centre of the theatrical enterprise? Is the text (still) the primary thing? Do theatre practitioners have to "serve" the writer by giving their "version" of the play? If the text is not the essential element, to which element should one give priority? As for the theatrical event (one no longer talks about play, performance, or drama, but about "event"), must it follow a linear progression, and if not, how does one secure its cohesion? Does it need cohesion? What is cohesion? [. . .] What is the relationship between theatre, dance, popular entertainment, religious rituals, therapy, games, sports, child's play, the characters played by politicians and other public figures? Can we develop a "universal theory of performance" in order to account for all these "performative genres"? Does this theory as such matter to theatre practice?

How does the audience participate in the performance, if it is decided to participate in it: as a spectator, speaker, witness, integral participant, as in Grotowski's paratheatrical work from 1967 onwards? Should the audience stay aside from and just watch? [. . .] What training should performers undergo? If Stanislavski's system is no longer valid – if it has ever been – with what should it be replaced? Are Asian training methods, derived from Kathakali, Yoga, Tai Chi, Noh, Kabuki, Chinese Opera, adapted to our Western theatre? Will their adoption lead to the emergence of a new kind of American performer? Once they have completed their training, what means of expression do the performers have at their disposal? Are they still subject to the author, the director, the set designers? Are performers required to wear a character mask? Should they expect the greatest benefit from the temporary distancing recommended by Brecht (who himself then controls, as a writer-director, the commentary of the actor on his character)? Many interpreters wanted to tear off the mask of the character, a construction by which an author would literally put words into the mouths of actors; then these words, and the very bodies of the actors, were again modified by the director during the composition of the performance, imposing on the actor an additional mask. The authority of the author first, then that of the director, were questioned and reversed. Many questions remained unanswered.[31]

Thus, in the space of a few years, performers, directors, choreographers, composers (understood in a broader sense rather than a strictly musical one), authors and set designers, working sometimes in collaboration, sometimes in competition, sometimes in mutual ignorance, thus operated individually as "primary creators" in their contact with audiences. The audiences closely associated the productions they saw with these "primary creators" and envisaged them through "participatory" lenses. And the many unexpected and spontaneous exchanges between visual artists, actors, choreographers, musicians, dancers, social activists, scientists, directors, writers, ritualists and ordinary spectators who rose from their seats (when they had one) to participate in the representation fostered the belief that, together, it would be possible to change the art of performance and, simultaneously, the world. Alongside the rise of the Brechtian and post-Brechtian director in continental Europe, the performer or rather the author (collective or otherwise) of *performing arts* took hold, in the United States particularly. Before turning into a mainly formal experimentation, and then creating more and more room for performance artists and actors, the goal of this landscape-altering movement with its very diverse form of experimentation was not only to create a seismic shift in the landscape of theatre and the arts, but also in the world. Of all this, there remains today a memory, a nostalgia, only an idea of revolution. Bob Wilson, having created the iconic *Einstein on the Beach* (1976) with Philip Glass, has now moved on to large-scale international production. Einstein the scientist and Einstein the dreamer have both disappeared. The repetitive images, the dramaturgical structures fashioned by mathematics, the fragmentation of reality and of the image, the isolation of gestures and actions, the play of lights, have become essentially formal. We have spoken before of *The Temptation of St. Anthony* (which has been adapted several times by avant-garde theatre, including the Wooster Group in 1987) and of the fact that it has now become a chic exportable Gospel revue instead of a work of *performing arts*. However, Richard Foreman, an exemplar of an author and director who creates work based on non-linearity, continues his Ontological-Hysterical Theatre at St Mark's Church, and the Wooster Group does sometimes come out of the Performing Garage for long international tours while continuing to produce impressive works (e.g. *House/Lights*, from Gertrude Stein's *Doctor Faustus Lights the Lights*, in 1999 and 2005; and *To You Birdie!* an adaptation of *Phèdre*, in 2002). Despite the economic difficulties faced by theatre on the other side of the Atlantic, other companies such as Radiohole, the Builders Association or Elevator Repair Service follow their elders by blithely mixing cultures and forms. The world, in the meantime, has not changed, and these groups continue to experience a difficulty of transforming their collage/improvisation into a kind of theatre that is relevant to the world of politics. And in this respect, experimental theatre is not unique.

In recent times, and in light of Hans-Thies Lehmann's work, which we will have the opportunity to explore later, it has been appropriate to speak about the "postdramatic" in reference to performance theatre and to point out how the theatrical event creates a space for hybridisation and includes the audience within a participatory system. However, it is necessary to recall not only that non-dramatic theatre has always flourished, as far back as one can look in the history of theatre. Our present period, albeit called postdramatic, has not emerged from nothing, but feeds directly on the models offered by previous avant-garde tendencies.

Kantor as an emblem

Here the theatre of Tadeusz Kantor is exemplary. The absolutely unique and subjective model of "total theatre" has never departed from the spirit of the visual arts and *happenings* at the very foundation of Kantor's work. Kantor is a painter inspired by Dadaism, surrealism and constructivism – the European avant-garde. The "Cricot 2" Theatre, which he founded in 1955, would go on to produce as much, if not more, happenings than staged works (*mises en scène*) strictly speaking, at least insofar as any of the works he produces could correspond to the appellation of "*mise en scène*". Take the example of *The Madman and the Nun*, in which actors play beside and around a stack of chairs in precarious balance, or *The Country House*, where the actors play in the tight space of a wardrobe. His happenings ("cricotages") include the 1967 *Panoramic Sea Happening*, or *Rembrandt's Anatomy Lesson* (1968–1971), where an actor wearing cut-up clothing lies down on the stage in a position resembling that of the corpse in Rembrandt's famous painting.

His fame as an "absolute creator" seems to be illustrated by Kantor's own presence on the stage: he is an author who is the first spectator of his shows, who accompanies them, correcting a gesture or the position of an object, marking rhythm, directing them like a conductor or rather projecting on them the eyes of the creator on his world. Because it is *his* world that he brings to the stage, a lost world but one that the stage can revive through this "theatre of death". And, from *The Dead Class* (1977) to *Wielopole, Wielopole* (1980), *Let the Artists Die* (1985) and *I Shall Never Return* (1988), Kantor would continue to strengthen the autonomy of his creation. His productions from the 1960s and the early 1970s were based on texts by Witkiewicz (*The Country House*, 1961; *The Madman and the Nun*, 1963; *The Water Hen*, 1971; *The Beautiful and the Ugly*, 1973), and this was again the case with *The Dead Class*, which included extracts from the play *The Cervical Tumor*. But Kantor's aim, to use his own expression, was not to "play Witkiewicz, but to [play] with him".[32] The text is then only one element among all those that make up the show, and from *Wielopole, Wielopole*, the text is also the work of Kantor himself. A director-author par excellence, Kantor would later, with *I Shall Never Return*, not only assume the first person in the very title of the show (since his death in 1990 would prevent him from completing the staging of a last show entitled *Today Is My Birthday*), but revisit and bring back his own creative world on the stage. Characters from his previous productions would come back and he himself would not only be present as an onlooker but would integrate his own character.

In 1944, when he was doing clandestine theatre in Krakow during the German occupation, Kantor produced *The Return of Ulysses* – he represented Ulysses as a soldier returning from Stalingrad, and in the "real" space (not a theatre stage) of a poor room ruined by war. This figure of Ulysses returning, a living dead, would become both the emblem and the matrix of all his theatre, and especially his "theatre of death", whose preoccupation is a return to the scene of his own memory. The theatre of death is a ritual theatre that summons the ghosts of a scene where figures of his past and, through them, Polish history, meet each other. These are animated paintings of an imaginary to which the stage brings back life. The old men, in black suits and waxy, grim faces, sitting on the school benches in *The Dead Class*, bring back the ghostly doubles of their childhood and end up mired in repetitive gestures: the little old man at the WC, the little old man on the bike; but also the school monitor, the sleepwalking prostitute, not to mention the Sweeper who is also Death. These are the characters from the world of childhood in his home village, Wielopole: the priest or the rabbi, the father going to the front, the mother, the deported man and his violin. There is also a gallery of more generic figures: the bride, the cabaret prostitute, the soldiers. And the mannequins that are mixed with the living actors. Because just like the mannequin, and contaminated by its inert presence, the actor has nothing left alive. He is, like the mannequin, inanimate and a figure; the unnameable thing, death that haunts memory. Kantor's theatre is thus a singular, personal and organic universe in which the artist fuses with his work and the work fuses with the artist in a large network of self-citation that never ceases to search for memory. The stage is, as a result, a site on which "the childhood room" is projected (*Wielopole, Wielopole*), or more generally a memory chamber, and in this biographical memory an imaginary is crystallised that exceeds the personal memory, becoming that of Poland, of a certain Europe and, more broadly, of the century.

Kantor's theatre is also a world closed on itself: the "theatre of death" thus claims to be an "autonomous theatre", a "work of art [which] has its own laws".[33] But this autonomous theatricality, born in the cellar of the Krzysztofory Gallery in Krakow (and that prefers the corners of performance rooms to traditional stages), is not a globalising theatricality. Because it is a theatre of death, of ghosts and because it is, indeed, the staging of memory: a past that can never be reconstituted as a totality and as an assured presence, but only, in the end, by bits and pieces, in the midst of a heterogeneous maelstrom, in images that resemble photographic shots. Kantor talks about "snapshots of memory": indeed,

Wielopole, Wielopole was based on a photograph showing a group of soldiers, among them Kantor's father, preparing to leave for the front during the Great War. The same production also offers a sequence where a camera turns into a machine gun. While Kantor's theatre produces images that are perfectly constructed in the pictorial sense, these are fragmentary images. What is also striking about Kantor's shows is the sense of organised disorder that emerges from them, their rhythm shifting from chaotic excitement to appeasement, from burlesque and grotesque to the most poignant emotion: how they seem to move between construction and demolition, and thus play up an overall tension. Heir to the practices of the artistic avant-garde, Kantor uses the logic of approximations specific to montage and collage, rather than the construction of a narrative and hermeneutical hierarchy. The images, the sequences of the show, the different elements of the stage (games, objects, music, etc.) and its signs circulate and transform themselves, without conventional linearity: a young man in black on a cross creates a Christ-like image, before coming down and leaving; thus, the cross, through constantly present through the show, will change its meaning over time (*Wielopole, Wielopole*); crates become a barricade (*Let the Artists Die*).

And above all, there are the objects: benches, school desks, crates, crosses (on wheels), bathtubs, bicycles, gallows, trolleys, rocking bed and, of course, the mannequins. Objects, not accessories or decorative elements: made of wood and scrap iron, miserable, they seem like abandoned and recovered pieces that vaguely take on a new purpose in their new site, rather than signifiers in a theatrical space and time. These material objects are uncertain, cumbersome but irreducibly present. They fall under this "reality of the lowest rank" that was as dear to Kantor as to Bruno Schulz:

> THE REALITY OF THE LOWEST RANK / In the "Autonomous Theatre" Manifesto/ (Year 1963) / I have defined the objects / which / have / lost their utility / in everyday life / "at the threshold of garbage" / as perfect and unique materials / to create / a work of art. / The notion of / POVERTY / permeated my Theatre / from the beginning / since the time of the underground Theatre.[34]

These objects fill the lives of his characters, like prosthetic limbs, and even become one with them (the woman behind the window, the woman in the mechanical cradle or the little old man on the bike of *The Dead Class*), and they have neither more nor less scenic value than the characters. All the elements of Kantor's theatre actually work the same way:

> when I take an object, or a character from real life, I deprive this reality of the past and of the future. I take, for example, an action which is useful in life, and I deprive this action of its cause, its motive, as well as its purpose, its efficacy. That's what I call "raw reality", the one I can manipulate.[35]

These objects are remains, traces, just like the figures of memory that make up his performances:

> They are clumsy, they stammer. These are the *remains* of the actions that, in their lifetime, were reasonable, but these remains do not mean anything. These are traces. Traces, for me, are more important than reality. Remains of costumes, actions, dialogues, but without beginning or end. I do not know where they lead.[36]

If the art of the "theatre of death" brings the figures of memory back to a kind of spectacular life, then this is achieved through the use of a "raw reality" and "of the lowest rank" that are emptied of meaning and functionality and that aim at an essential poverty. These then allow for the reactivation of meaning, which encourages the spectator to project their own imaginary on to it, as without this imaginary, there is nothing. The "triumphant and funereal PARADE" of *The Dead Class* is an "empty parade" and a "celebration that leads nowhere". Kantor's theatricality thus produces striking images, fosters a shareable imagination through a singular memory and claims the heritage of happening and the plastic avant-gardes of the century, but does not propose the model of a "great" theatricality: his model is rather that of the "court of miracles", in his own words. It is open and closed, and only open because it is autonomous. It is a dream-like theatricality whose art "must be enigmatic. Closed to the point of being inaccessible",[37] but the tools with which it accomplishes this are discontinuity, the grotesque, humor and the "poverty" of essential "raw reality". If Kantor has appeared to be the absolute artist, it is ultimately because he is, as Georges Banu puts it, "a genius who is neither entirely on the side of the theatre, nor entirely on the side of the visual arts" and because his "theatre of death" is on the scale of a testament, a "carnival testament".[38] Its totality is not of the order of homogeneity and purity, but in the image, often invoked by Kantor, of "poor shanty [. . .] The *real Theatre of Emotion*".[39]

We can thus better understand why Kantor is an emblem for the theatre of our contemporary moment as for that of the immediate post-war period. Because if it is autonomous and profoundly unique, it also makes the link between the experimental movements of the avant-garde and the theatre of disaster after Auschwitz and after Hiroshima. Plastic force, scenographic power, philosophical complexity, abandonment of plot, of the character, rejection of continuity, perpetual questioning of itself, all these questions are major preoccupations of its time as well as ours. Thus, like an ironic, burlesque and sensitive Ulysses, Kantor keeps coming back to himself in an afterworld, in the midst of the dead and the inanimate, with no other hope than to make this return absolutely present, precisely inscribed in the moment when the memory is realised and in the place where the conductor (in far more than a musical sense, as we have said) has chosen to make it visible.

Armand Gatti, another emblem[40]

Armand Gatti is another emblem of avant-garde theatre and one that has too often been ignored and marginalised. It would be wrong to say that Gatti, who died in 2017 at the age of 93, is at the fringes of theatre – he is simply elsewhere. An "elsewhere" that has its source in the "battles of the century" and that is therefore irreducible to the aesthetic sphere. His artistic influences – Piscator, Mao Zedong, etc. – testify to Gatti's disconnect from the fashions and canons that hold sway at any given time in the history of theatre. Although his work never feeds on his own life, his biography makes it easier to grasp the coherence of his research. In Gatti's film *l'Enclos* [*Enclosure*] – Gatti is also a filmmaker – the German communist resistor, Karl, maintains: "it's not the man that counts, it's his struggle". One and the other are inseparable for Gatti. Son of Italian immigrants, Dante Sauveur Gatti, called Armand, was in no way predestined to become one of the most important playwrights of his time. His theatre would never be at odds with this background: Gatti was the son of Auguste, an anarchist garbage collector, and of Laetitia, a housekeeper. Upon the death of his father, Gatti joined the French resistance movement in Berbeyrolle, Corrèze, and this was to be a pivotal experience in his life: there he found trees, his most beautiful spectators as he would later say, to whom he read Gramsci and Michaux. Arrested by the French gendarmerie, he stated bravely, "I came to make God fall in time". To his cellmate, Ruben Muichkine, who asked him why he wrote, he answered: "To change the past".[41] That encapsulates everything. Sentenced to death, pardoned *in extremis*, he was deported to the Baltic. He discovered the theatre in the form of three statements chanted by three rabbis: *Ich bin, ich war, ich Verde sein* [*I Am, I Was, I Will Be*]. This discovery was essential: in a few words, it was the victory over the unspeakable (the camp), and in this act of resistance, as derisory as it was pivotal, the poetic quest of Gatti took shape. When he escaped, he joined the Allied armies as a parachutist, took part in the Liberation and then became a journalist in Guatemala. While there, he met an Argentine doctor, Ernesto Guevara and a young translator, Felipe, who was murdered before his very eyes. However, he came to sense a limit to what a reporter could do, which left him frustrated.

So he began to write again. A friend sent one of his plays, *Le Crapaud-buffle*, to Jean Vilar, who staged it in 1959 at the Théâtre National Populaire (Théâtre Récamier). The critics were scathing. Vilar advised him to persist. And persist he did: in a decade, Gatti wrote more than a dozen plays (including *La Seconde existence du camp de Tatenberg, Le Voyage du grand T'Chou* and *Les Treize soleils de la rue saint-Blaise* [*The Second Existence of the Tatenberg Camp, The Voyage of the Great T'Chou* and *The Thirteen Suns of Saint-Blaise Street*]), staged five (including *Chroniques d'une planète provisoire, Le Poisson noir*, and *L'Homme seul* [*Chronicles of a Planet in Suspension, Dark Passion* and *Man by Himself*]), and made two films (*L'Enclos* and *El otro Cristobal* [*The Other Christopher*]). His theatre examines the struggles of his century and, to do this, tries to get out of what dramatic writing and theatrical laws seem to impose – and hinder. The staging platform would always be too narrow for one who wanted to embrace "the only acceptable measure of man: excess".[42] Each theme calls for a singular dramatic treatment. The set embraces the gigantism of Erwin Piscator's staging, expanding it to the multiple dimensions and layers of the world in its contradictions, discordant temporalities and antagonistic movements. "A theatre of possibilities", wrote Dort.[43] And, indeed, the platform embraces a variety of possibilities, entangling places, actions and time. Besides, the platform is certainly one of the most important actors of his theatre: the time of the struggles, which precedes us; the present, which calls our attention; and the future, bearer of hopes or nightmares. Far from being absorbed by the present, Gatti's theatre, without ever evading it, invents an unprecedented temporality that aligns disparate times into a single contemporaneity. *La Vie de l'éboueur Auguste G.* [*The Life of Garbage Collector Auguste G.*] was a homage to his father and to struggle itself, and it explores the possibility of Auguste at seven different stages of his life. The play summons all of these issues onstage. *Chant public devant deux chaises électriques* [*Public Song In Front of Two*

Electric Chairs] dedicated to Sacco and Vanzetti does not reduce itself to a historical pageant. The play challenges the responsibility of the spectators: will they let the crime happen again? Gatti installs them onstage. For now, they are still played by actors. But if he is enthusiastic about fights for emancipation, he does not take refuge in a blissful optimism. His theatre is a memory of the horror of genocide, and of the camps. He is still looking for some flashes of hope, struggles, memories of those who have defied the logic of the executioners.

In 1968, the play *La Passion du Général Franco* [*The Passion of General Franco*] (renamed diplomatically, but this was actually in vain, as *La Passion en violet, jaune et rouge* still remains) was removed from the TNP's programme. The resistance of the theatrical milieu, which supported the play against a government that then included Malraux as Minister of Culture, would be short-lived. Gatti headed to Germany in search of Rosa Luxembourg. These were years of insurrections, anarchist and leftist communities and of manhunts too: Gatti meets a young journalist, Ulrike Meinhof, who would soon become a clandestine Red Army Fraction activist. Arrested and tortured, Gatti would dedicate a play to her, *La Moitié du ciel et nous* [*Half of Heaven in Us*]. The urgent question that Gatti must face is that of knowing how one can invent a dramatic act in absolute solidarity with the present and the event that justifies it. First, by doing without canonical theatrical characters, since history shows that "theatre characters have died in the street" as one of Gatti's poem-manifestos affirms. Already mistreated in the previous plays, the characters disappear, and there are only situations played by activists, acts, the signs of a performance space used to address, through the spectators, the real recipients of the theatre. Gradually, Gatti moves away from professional actors. This progressive break was begun during his tour with *V comme Vietnam* [*V for Vietnam*], in 1967, where actors assumed roles that were contrary to their political opinions. Then in Germany, Gatti meets "actors who are at the same time full-fledged characters in Street Theatre, of which Berlin is a daily the stage". Actors who agree to put their identity into play as a starting point for writing: *"moi Inga, moi Ralf, moi Dieter"* [*"I Ingo, I Ralf, I Dieter"*].[44] At the same time, he, along with some Belgian students, carried out "collective creation experiments", without using the Épinal images traditionally associated with this type of work. Gatti becomes the public writer of a struggle that is invented and defined in the very process of work. To avoid reifying ancestral battles or turning them into a museum, one had to find the form and the words to pursue them in the present.

But the long walk was not over. Gatti returned to France in 1975 with *La Tribu des carcana en guerre contre quoi?* [*The Carcana Tribe in War*

Against What?] Carcana is the pseudonym of the Spanish revolutionary anarchist Buenaventura Durrutti. As always, Gatti avoids the pitfall of historical reconstitution: "We must destroy the narrative of him (that of the revolutionary militant) to get to the heart of his approach".[45] We then see that, definitively, Gatti turned his back on what, in the theatre, obstructed the possibility of entering into struggle: he removed the actors, the spectators – those who always remain outside the fight – but "the essence remains". A painful collective experiment in Saint-Nazaire devoted to Soviet dissidents, Le Canard sauvage qui vole contre le vent [*The Wild Duck that Flies Against the Wind*], marked the end of "the era of leftist words", though Gatti does not for all that turn his back on his previous affinities. He remains faithful to the combatants, resistors or revolutionaries, to those who have not ceased to make "man bigger than man": Blanqui, Rosa Luxemburg, Jean Cavaillès, Che Guevara, etc. But being faithful to them does not mean mummifying their struggles. On the contrary, it is necessary – and in this Gatti is very Benjaminian – to pursue them in the uncertainty and novelties of the present.

Starting in 1984, with *L'Émission de Pierre Meynard* [*Pierre Meynard's Programme*], Gatti began his companionship with those who he would later call his "*loulous*" ["hoodlums"] – the "excluded" according to society. Misunderstandings accumulated: removed from theatrical spaces, Gatti's work rapidly became associated with social activism. He took this characterisation to good use: "The decisive weapon of the guerrilla is the word" affirmed the Guatemalan guerrilla fighter Ion Sosa, and Gatti has long since endorsed this certainty.[46] Words – but also letters – became the real characters of his theatre, freeing themselves from all psychologism. At the theatre: "who is speaking to whom?" Mao Zedong's remark to Gatti in the 1950s became the bedrock of each new experiment. One must answer: "who am I?" and "to whom am I speaking?" and thereby take note that the participants are not interchangeable but come laden (sometimes burdened) with their past, and that it is within them, in the encounter with the poet's obsessions, that the possibility of a "poetic event" lies. Thus, far from engaging in performances for which the "theatre spectator" would be the natural recipient, Gatti demanded a re-definition, each time, for him and for each *loulou*, of the function and value of speech communication, which went well beyond the cramped dimensions of any theatre. Again and again, Gatti sought to create resistance camps whose fragile weapons could only be words.

In the decade of the 1990s, Gatti became concerned with languages. His theatre, if his experimental and political quest can be so called, entered a new phase. After having explored speech communication through the lens of the word, his theatre began to question each language (be it philosophical, scientific, mathematical, dramatic, etc.), showing how each was fragmentary and approximative, and how, in the long run, each revealed its powerlessness to tell the truth. Deepening this conception of truth as a fragmentary field using fragmented words, his work would later be influenced by the concept of the quantum in physics, and by the concept of "possibilism", which would significantly modify Gatti's writing without affecting his quest. It would allow him to bring together his different preoccupations and experiments in an absolutely new form. By this experimentation with the word, without characters, actors or spectators (just a few witnesses), Gatti revived the research of other poets – V. Khlebnikov, for example. In Geneva and in Besançon, for presentations of two or three evenings, like a hiatus in an ongoing research, the *loulous* explored the *Incertitudes de Weiner Heisenberg. Feuilles de brouillon pour recueillir les larmes des cathédrales dans la tempête et dire Jean Cavaillès sur une aire de jeu* [*The Uncertainties of Weiner Heisenberg. Rough Draft for a Narrative of the Tears of the Cathedrals in the Storm and of Jean Cavaillès on a Playground*]. This performance piece was devoid of realism and had no characters – there remained only the words that filled the space, which created movement (the hexagrams and trigrams of the Yi-king) and that strove to bring the "right words" of a desired liberation into the unique present.

As we can see, the avant-garde is not necessarily where we would have believed it to be, and is not only played in postdrama or performance installation. It can also be an unremitting, demanding quest that is always in touch with the world and its struggles and that refrains from adopting a disillusioned outlook on political issues. Even if it means exploring scientific theories and quantum physics in unconventional places, in front of a few witnesses and using marginal characters as participants, the important thing is to persist and to attempt to open up new ways of envisioning the future. The stage, the *mise en scène*, the theatre itself, may all be radically altered, and even shattered, when, in the same vein as Gatti's work, one attempts to uncover the spectre that is the "possible".

14

THEATRICALITY QUESTIONED
A theatre without illusion?

Mise en scène is now an artistic practice in its own right. A crucible for the making of meaning, a space for depicting the powers of the image, a moment that emphasises the liberation and elation of the actor, it has sometimes been conceived as the site of all possibilities. However, as we have seen, the art of representation is always caught between the temptation of a total work, whose mastery it could show, and the assumed heterogeneity or play of that which is represented, whereby a role is given to the spectator whose status is openly acknowledged in the present-ness of the theatrical session. These questions are not new; they have been posed throughout the history of theatre and, more particularly, the history of *mise en scène* itself since the end of the last century. Indeed, this oscillation animates all the questions around the theatre's identity. It is therefore not surprising that after the emergence of the figure of the director and the enthusiasm around "triumphant theatricality", the theatre has returned to an examination of the different conceptions of representation, since it is now inscribed in a different ideological and aesthetic context. Recent years have been marked by practices and positions that, in some respects, are opposed to those of previous decades. We have discussed, above, Bernard Dort's observations of the signs of these changes during the 1980s: a greater autonomy of the objects in the performance space, the revocation or suspension of illusion, an attempt at giving an active role to the spectator as true constructor of meaning, etc. The latest changes in *mise en scène* have confirmed Dort's analyses.

Contestations

In this regard, the transition from the 1980s to the 1990s clearly marks a turning point in the French theatrical landscape in particular, and often in the rest of Europe. It is part of a change of political, ideological and even institutional context (with respect to theatre), which is fundamental. But we are also dealing with a generational turning point: the generation of directors of the 1960s and 1970s, who had achieved fame in the 1980s, was now being gradually succeeded by a new generation, which often asserted itself by taking opposite positions to those of its predecessors. In France, there are certain symbolic dates: in 1990, Patrice Chéreau resigns as head of the Amandiers de Nanterre and chooses to move away from theatrical *mise en scène* to a career as a film director; Antoine Vitez, who left Chaillot in 1988 to become director general of the Comédie-Française, died suddenly in April 1990. They are two of the most exemplary figures of the French stage, who either abandoned *mise en scène* or died. Other French historical figures continue their artistic career, of course: Jean-Pierre Vincent, Georges Lavaudant, Bernard Sobel, Jacques Lassalle, Alain Ollivier; and abroad Peter Stein and Luca Ronconi, among others. But they are focused on *continuing* their practice, rather than on creating and inventing novel practices, regardless of the natural attempts at renewal manifested by their different performances. Moreover, many of them find themselves confronted with what is, in a way, a new challenge: the power and constraints of the institution.

Indeed, if Jack Lang's cultural policy (as the culture minister from 1981–1986 and then 1988–1993) in France set the groundwork for bolstering the theatre's self-affirmation over the last third of the twentieth century, by fitting it into numerous structures and by placing predominantly artists at the head of these new or existing institutional structures, this policy also had its setbacks – those common to any effort at institutionalisation. Indeed, large structures are cumbersome to manage and, as a result of their production budgets, they wield considerable influence in the power stakes. Placed at the centre of the production system, the artist must also become a manager amidst a network of theatrical sites torn between different stakes: issues of artistic development, on the one hand, and, on the other, those that relate to the idea of a popular theatre, capable of filling large auditoriums (in sum, the budgetary stakes attached to massive audiences), in a society where other media (primarily television) keep growing in importance. This point is important, because the challenge of "institutionalisation", or some of its consequences, will form the basis of a number of disputes that mark the decade of the 1990s and the early 2000s. These disputes emerged between those who, on the one hand, decried the theatre's renunciation of artistic and those at the other end of the spectrum who accused theatre institutions of refusing to embrace change. Thus, the use of headliners and crowd-drawers in theatre roles (Gérard Depardieu in Lassalle's *Tartuffe*, or Jane Birkin in Chéreau's *La Fausse suivante* [*The Double-Crosser's Comeuppance*], for example), a heightened level of sumptuousness and magnificence in the theatre and the transformation of communitarian impulses into assumptions of mass consensus, provoked controversies around which certain political and aesthetic aspirations would take shape.

This turning point in the 1980s–1990s saw the emergence of a new generation of practitioners, who challenge the established position of their elders. In the early 1990s, new directors (and with them new actors and new scenographers) emerge on the theatrical landscape, thirty-somethings who, typically, had begun to produce in the 1980s and would be defined in relation to the generation of great founding figures who were now generally in their fifties. And "in relation to" generally meant "against", not necessarily in an all-out rejection of their heritage (as practitioners or as spectators, they were partly trained by these same elders), but in a conflictual dynamic that in many ways resembled a father–son opposition. In this schema, it is hardly surprising that the sons claimed their share in an institution whose fathers then occupied all the spaces. In the name of aesthetic modernity and the evolution of society, we would see the sons relegate their elders to a past time, and the thirty-somethings accuse the fifty-somethings of having abandoned the ideals that had given rise to the commitments and boldness of their youth.

It would, of course, be wrong to limit the recent changes in the theatrical landscape to this, and it is necessary to see on what broader issues new aesthetic claims rest, what conceptions of the theatre underlie such criticisms. A large number of the directors who appeared in France in the 1990s affirmed their will to reject, or at least circumvent, the games of institutionalisation, merchandising and crowd appeal within theatrical creation. It is true that the younger figures primarily associated the compromises of their more senior counterparts with political resignation, the loss of a fundamental connection to the real world, a submission to ultraliberal mindsets and the cult of entertainment and the consensus, and with narcissistic temptation (the shameful complacency of the director-author). However, they also did so as a means of underscoring the need for a theatre that remains a space of artistic resistance, a site that is simultaneously open to the social space, to the demands of aesthetics and to a more precarious art.

A text by author and director Didier-Georges Gabily, "Cadavres, si on veut", written for a series published in 1994 in *Libération* under the generic title "Où va le théâtre?" ("Where Is the Theatre Going?"), appears particularly symptomatic of many such positions. The language is sharp:

> This society only adheres to the *spectacle* which it names by abuse of power "theatre", only adheres to the reiteration of the same in its most trivial forms: naturalism and identification as ersatz *jouissance*, the imposition of dominant (?) artistic models under the guise of a diversity of *subjects* and – this is major – all-round and constant pressure around the notion of "audience" as the totality of its tastes, its supposed desires, its disgusts, its (obviously) limited abilities.[1]

The theatrical institution is seen in this text as a "beleaguered citadel, recluse and reduced to barely hatched, yet already faded, principles",

> money still prevails, and has even spawned children – but for how long? We can see what is left of ideas. Between the temptation of egotism (being one's own text, one's own theatre) and the pandering to a media-crazed world [. . .], the 1980s have left the theatre void of what has *always* been its essential substance: today's word for today; [. . .] the poem of the world placed in its centre, major and dominant, though fractured, though hesitant.[2]

And it is not only as a writer that Gabily claims a primacy of the text, and of today's text, over the performance and the art of *mise en scène*. But also as a well-known director with a strong and personal aesthetic, who questions what seems now to be an unshakable historical achievement:

> what we call, by abuse of language and abuse of power, "scenic writing", which belongs, as we know, to the director. There are no "scenic writers". There is only, there should only be, artists, "conveyors" [*des "passeurs"*] – to use Claude Régy's expression – actors and directors, servants of the stage, at school, as it were, listening to these texts that are trying to portray the world as it is happening.[3]

This refusal of the notion of a "scenic writer" may seem like a radical negation of thirty years of theatre history. But, for Gabily, it is not a question of denying the powers of the stage, or even the work of the director as a purely artistic activity. Rather, it is a rejection of the notion that the director's work should stifle the other elements of the stage, by substituting his discourse for that of the text. Practitioners who emerge in the 1990s have absolutely no intention of questioning the artistic nature of the act of staging. What they are trying to redistribute is, in a way, the play that is established between this gesture and the text that it must "serve" – instead of making it disappear under the monument of the director's work. And even beyond the issue of the text, and of today's writing, it is the ability of the theatre to speak about the real and about the current world that matters. This new generation thus emphasises the conjunction of these two requirements: the need for the theatre to inscribe itself in the social real, and a link with an audience that is not limited to a cultural elite, but (without giving in to demagogy or to politically correct consensus) that strongly affirms its artistic nature. In a word, this generation aspires to a theatre that is art theatre *and* public theatre. "An island of formidable resistance of thought, a necessary place where people face each other, some to tell and others to watch and listen to stories written by poets": this is the claim formulated by Stanislas Nordey and his team when he was appointed head of the Theatre Gerard Philipe of Saint-Denis in 1998. Significantly, Nordey also mentioned his desire to "position his theatre as a pioneer, with all its lucidity and its madness. And if the path is steep, we will climb it happily and with the insolence of our thirty years".[4]

The insolence of thirty years would ultimately be to re-examine the theatrical practice as it was bequeathed by a social, ideological and aesthetic horizon that had changed, and against the risk of fossilisation. In the end, it was to be about *building theatrical practice anew*. The word "rebuild" may seem grandiloquent, even naïve, and the actual results were very diverse; but that is what it was about. Because, while behind the posturing, one can always recognise the well-known game of intergenerational conflict, we must not underestimate the real ideological and aesthetic stakes that arise at the end of the 1980s, marked as much by the advent of the media age as by the crisis of ideologies. How does one maintain the relation of art to politics when the great revolutionary ideologies have collapsed? How does one maintain the art of community in an exploded, diffracted society? How does one foster an art of connection in an era of "globalisation"? How does the theatre maintain its efficiency as an art of fictional representation and depiction when film and television screens reach an infinitely larger number of people, and with dramatically superior means? How does it remain a site of discourse, or at least of points of view on the world, when the media peddle so many perspectives and when our era is marked by an overabundance of discourses and the questioning of all discourses, by relativism? At the beginning of the 1990s, it turned out that most of the evidence on which the theatre of the 1960s–1970s was built (political evidence, hermeneutic evidence, public "popular" evidence, etc.) have collapsed, and that, moreover, the theatre had to rethink its place among the other arts or processes of representation – which also led to an attempt at redefining the *specificity* of the theatrical medium. That is why the renewal of practices initially became a kind of redefinition of minimal identity: a sort of search for "fundamentals" and, through them, of a singularity – as well as an ethic (in so far as this was connected to the theatre's distinctiveness). In a way, we could largely reduce the extremely diverse approaches that are then asserted to a simple underlying question: what remains, specifically, of the theatre, in the era of media?

Other aspirations, other practices

These practitioners would then claim theatrical singularity and ethics in several forms. The first will undoubtedly be the notion of proximity, the affirmation of the theatre as an opportunity to create social bonds. This happens first of all by registering many companies in their local environment, especially through workshops in schools or with amateurs. This is the case with many practices that multiply and that the state encourages, sometimes at the risk of transforming companies into community organisers. But, more broadly, it is the question of audience, which is at the centre of concerns: how can one expand it to make a real "theatre for all" and how does one take its diversity into account? Because while there is more or less a consensus around the need for a theatre of "public service", the notion of "popular theatre" no longer has good press. The term "citizens' theatre" will be preferred instead (particularly by Stanislas Nordey). And if the spectator was placed at the heart of their concerns, it is precisely because these practitioners spoke about "spectators" and no longer about "audience", strictly speaking: the big difference is that the audience is no longer given as "massive". These directors, who are often suspicious of large auditoriums and their grandiosity (and of the fact that they presuppose a fusional identity of the spectators), prefer small spaces to gigantic stages and try to bring together distinctive human beings rather than search for an "organic" audience. The theatre is no longer addressed to the masses, to a collective united by a minimum of ideological, social or cultural *commonality*, as Vilar, or Mnouchkine in her festivals, might have desired. It becomes a matter of always questioning and seeking to create a "theatrical assembly" and the link it can create, but now this ambition is based on an essential investigation of the role of *the* spectator. Moreover, the issue of a minimal community that is supposedly formed around the theatrical performance is undoubtedly at the heart of many current debates: the philosopher Jean-Luc Nancy speaks of a community that is now "idle", one that is no longer underpinned by the existence of pre-existing communitarian ideologies or myths, which no longer constitutes a "work" or a "communion" but that has given way to a simple co-presence; "a being-together without assembly".[5] With a thought process that is not as specific as Nancy's, but that is nevertheless concerned with the same sort of inquiry, these practitioners are obliged to constantly revisit the foundational question of the theatre, which is that of "being together". They are caught in a dialectic between the demands of social cohesion and the refusal of the mass, the recognition of singularities as well as the necessity of a differential *communication* with the audience: the search for a sensual relationship; a presence in the social that goes beyond the trappings of the spectacular; the desire for more intimate, or at least more "human", frameworks of representation; but also, in a more aesthetic register, the desire to reduce the separation between the stage and the auditorium – particularly as it relates to the "frontality" mode. We will come back to this issue a bit later.

While the issue of "being-together" is particularly emphasised through different explorations of the role of the spectators, it is also affirmed among production teams (the theatre practitioners themselves) and their renewed fascination with the notion of the collective, and all that it implies. If the director figure remains central, a number of approaches are foregrounding again (and this harks back to certain values and practices of the 1970s) the importance of the group, if not the troupe. The 1990s witnessed the appearance of new "crews" ["*bandes*"], to use Jean-Pierre Thibaudat's expression, involving a long and (more or less) constant "companionship". This embrace of the collective has not led to a rejection of the figure of the director; it is rather the Mnouchkinian model that one encounters, that of a group welded around a central figure, the director or "trainer". The case of the Théâtre du Radeau, headquartered at the Fonderie du Mans, around the director François Tanguy, is a good example, but the example of Didier-Georges Gabily's group T'chan'G is even more illustrative. Indeed, Gabily's (1955–1996) work in the early 1980s was as a trainer of actors, the facilitator of a workshop (a workshop, not a school; and a group, not a troop, he insisted) whose activities were underground, not linked to an institution or even to a fixed structure and not to the production of theatre performances. The *mises en scène* that came about, first that of Claudel's *L'Échange* (1986), and then, in 1989 only, the "official" creation of the group T'chan'G around actors from these workshops (who had also had careers elsewhere), were on the primary foundation of Gabily's collective excavation methods carried out previously. The group then engaged in the production of plays, without closing the workshop or reducing its requirements, and in the staging of texts written by Gabily himself (but not exclusively: there was also, among others, in 1992, *Les Cercueils de zinc* [*The Coffins of Zinc*], based on the work of the Russian journalist Svetlana Alexievitch on the families of the disappeared soldiers in Afghanistan), such as *Violences* (1991), *Enfonçures* (1993) and *Gibier du temps* [*Target of Time*] (1995) – written texts for the actors of the group, based on rehearsal work. While, strictly speaking, Gabily may seem close to the traditional position of a "master" ("the boss", as many called him), trainer, writer and director all at once, he is so only based on the primary nature of the group: "the subject of work, the subject that works is the group – and not a succession of individuals",[6] on the basis of a relationship of exchange and of fundamental trust, and in the framework of the permanent *worksite* that this group constitutes.

The example of the group T'chan'G is doubly exemplary of the aspirations of this generation. The desideratum of the collective is linked to another claim: that of working time and experimentation, as opposed to the mere time of staging – the rendering to an audience – of the performance. And this desire also appears in the public manifestations of the practices concerned (far more presentations of "small forms", readings, sketches and intermediate states of a work), even in the aesthetics of staging. The rejection of the theatre as a spectacular and cultural object of consumption thus takes the form of a reaffirmed claim of the stage as a place of research and experimentation (and thus of presentation to the public of this work), just as much, if not more, than the presentation of closed and finished "works". It is no coincidence that the term, originally Vitezian, of "proposal" became popular in the 1990s among many directors to characterise the scenic result of their work. This obviously does not imply that they do not intend to carry out their staging, or suggest that their work is unfinished: however, it is an attempt at de-emphasising, all things considered, the director's position of *authority*, the posture of truth that could be attached to the proposed representation. To describe a performance as a "proposal", as many do, is thus to present the chosen form as relative and not as a work that is absolute, to display its biases as such, and emphasise that the performance is not a closed discourse or definitive interpretation. It is also to present the scenic object not as something imposed by the director on to the audience, but as something designed to be reassessed by the latter: as the result of a work in process and not as a self-sufficient object. The platform thus becomes the place where the state of a work is shown, rather than the result of a single interpretation – although it is obvious that the proposals are intended to be strong and coherent. In rehearsals, but sometimes also in the traces that remain in the representation, there is a dimension of precariousness and the experimentation, a practice of *mise en scène* that is not like a finished "reading" of a text, or like a "discourse" proposed by the scenic writing over the textual writing, but rather as a relative approach, as an attempt to submit the text to a form that could resonate with it or make it resonate, without pretending to subsume it or to make it absolutely explicit: the theatre as a workshop, as a laboratory. Thus, for example, the actual representation of the text of Hervé Guibert's *Vole My Dragon*, in the staging done by Stanislas Nordey in 1994 at the Festival d'Avignon, took up only one hour in a performance that lasted nearly seven, filled as it was with the experiments of rehearsal work, and especially with an extremely rich encounter with deaf-mute actors who had finally become the main subject of the show.

These practical claims (of a less distant relationship to the audience, of a relationship that moves away from consumption; a more collective, but also more hazardous and experimental framework) are underpinned, as we have already seen with Gabily's text, by a distrust of the primacy of stage writing and the figure of the director, insofar as they would consist in the imposition of an aesthetic unity and in the construction of meaning. The spectator is then considered as a partner as much as a pure receiver, and the theatrical work is defined as a process as well as a construction of a result: the framework of the construction site and of the sharing of the creative experience is based on a conception of theatre that aspires to testify to an approach rather than to constitute a perfectly accomplished object.

Crisis of representation, crisis of meaning

This attitude becomes strikingly obvious at the level of signification, rather than on a strictly aesthetic level (since gestures remain distinctive and strongly marked). Where in previous decades, the director had been turned into a dramaturg-interpreter, a "reader" of the text and a constructor of signs, interpreter and one who holds a point of view on the story – and, more broadly, on the world – which they would then reveal to the audience, numerous directors of the 1990s patently reject such a position. While for them, the director is the one who takes a specific *look* on a play, this look is no longer a "reading" that would impose a meaning or construct an interpretation by means of the arrangement of the signs of the performance space. On the contrary, the key words of this generation would be "the opening of meaning", the expansion of the signifier's fields against the reign of the signified, the interpretive disengagement of the director and the primacy of the formal work over the temptation to elaborate a meaning: the spectator is, therefore, left the sole constructor, the only "interpreter". It was not really a refusal of meaning, but an approach to *mise en scène* that would be of the nature of commentary or explanation, pedagogy or demonstration. It was beyond simple neutrality – which would not awaken any kind of meaning – but less than a construction of an interpretative discourse – in the words of the director Alain Françon, speaking about the staging of Greek myths, it was a matter of "provoking meaning without signifying",[7] of fostering an openness of meaning.

Such a questioning of the principles of the art of staging, as they had been constituted in previous decades must be related to the time in which it was taking place, and to the ideological mutations that mark the transition from one generation to another. Indeed, we must bear in mind that these changes were occurring in the context of a global ideological-aesthetic shift, a change of eras. The generation of Planchon, Sobel, Chéreau, Vitez and others, born in the context of the ideological engagement of the 1960s, had experienced 1968, and had, for the most part, a strong political conception (a Marxist one, for most of them) of representation. More broadly, they were convinced that theatrical performance could and should create meaning and talk about the world of which they were a part. However, the approaches of the directors who appeared in the 1980s and 1990s were inscribed in a quite a different ideological and aesthetic worldview. We could dwell on the disaffection of politics and more broadly the crisis of meaning that marked the 1980s: a crisis of ideologies, dilution of the socialist alternative in the exercise of power, the fall of the Berlin wall, the collapse of communism and more largely of communist utopias, the ascendancy of individualist liberal ideology, "globalisation" and the numerous proclamations of "the end of history", the advent of the mass media era, etc. A whole range of values, which united dramaturgy, even in its various forms, around the idea of the political necessity of theatre and the belief in the stage as a site of explanation of the world, became problematic and an entire conception of representation lost its self-evidence and began to be questioned.

Changed from a place of readability and interpretation of reality, the theatre stage now became the mirror and the *laboratory* of the opacity of the world and reality. From a meaning factory, it was turned into a framework for exploring its own resistance to meaning and to easily formulated discourses, a site of polysemy and the plurality of receptions, and of inquiry into what may remain as a minimal constituent element of the theatrical assembly in its shared dimension. Theatre, in that respect, was merely following a more general inflection, which was also at work in the other arts (visual arts, in particular): the time was one of "openness of meaning", of the critique of imposed monolithic interpretations, of a return to a raw "presentation" of materials. This was underpinned by a fear of imposing a discourse on to a spectator or viewer now left as the only interpreter of what the work shows, which often implies that no presupposed common (ideological, political or cultural) base could be found that would unite the spectators with the stage and the spectators to each other. In fact, with these new approaches, it was the very foundations of the great theatrical philosophies of the second half of the century that were being shaken, and that some practices would try, with more or less success, to revisit. Beyond the issue of the author-director-interpreter and (sometimes pedagogical) builder of signs, the matter of the relation of the stage to its audience was now the object of urgent questions, particularly as it related to the dream of a popular theatre: was it one that was still relevant? It is therefore not surprising that the main points common to the multiple approaches that appeared in those years concerned the interrogation and activation of the spectator's role, the questioning of the process of signification constructed by the staging through a move away from interpretation and through the emphasis on polysemy, the presentation of a "raw" textual material, the diffraction of meaning and the primacy of formal work. All this contributes to a global questioning of the issue of receptivity, if only through the crisis of realistic mimetic representation (a domain in which theatre cannot compete with cinema and television), and to the transformation of the theatre stage from self-evident site of discourse on the world into a place of experimentation and questioning of perception.

Showing writing: another relationship with the text

The question of the relation to the text can thus be a significant example of the return to the "fundamentals" of which we have been speaking. These characterise a significant part of theatrical approaches that appear in the 1990s and 2000s. The discourse of many practitioners in this period gives back centrality of place to authors, to the "poets", as many like to call them, and therefore places the director in a position of humility compared to the written text. The theatrical text is consequently revalorised, paradoxically, in its literary dimension, even if this dimension is oralised and vehicled through the bodies of the actors. It is, above all, for the practitioners, a matter of making the text heard – in fact, for some, it is only this that matters – without claiming to illustrate it or build from it a privileged hermeneutical point of view, but in its formal singularity and in the multiplicity of its meanings, to give it voice. The stage, at a minimum, is thus designated as the primordial place of an offering [*profération*]. The term offering (which means to bring a text in front of an audience) is found, for example, at the heart of the discourse of Didier-Georges Gabily and Stanislas Nordey.

This primacy of the written text (by the poet, whether he is a dramatic poet or not) and the spoken text (voiced by the actors), also indicates a refusal of the image – at least of the illustrative and spectacular image – that often accompanies it. There is the notion that the image taints the spectator's reception and needs to disappear from in front of it. Its dominance in the media, and especially on television, makes the image an element of suspicion in the reconfiguration of the elements of the stage. It is suspected of too much "grab" or of exerting too much impact on the spectator, of misleading and deceptively overpowering feeling or interpretation – like anything that could create too much spectacularity – that *opsis* marginalised by Aristotle and neglected by classical dramaturgy. We see here that we are coming back to very old debates. Consequently, what directors like Gabily and Nordey reject is both a theatre that uses abundant images and one based on the "dramatic" model: they distrust both the dramatic principle and its naturalistic mimesis. If the text is primarily addressed as a poem, it is largely in a lyrical sense that it is carried by the actor who embodies its flow, musicality and pace while explaining its meaning, illustrating any conflict or showing the underlying psychology of the characters. Indeed, for a majority of directors of the 1990s, naturalism was the aesthetic to reject, and the theatre could no longer be the site par excellence of realistic mimesis – since cinema or television execute it with technical means much more apt to make a story credible and to provoke empathic identification. What remains then (in a manner comparable to the theatre of the symbolists in the early twentieth century) is the presence of the actor, the sensual experience of the direct encounter (mediated neither by a screen nor in time) between a performance and assembled receivers, and the stage space, precarious but open to all possible and (almost) all forms.

It is therefore not surprising that the text (and the relation of bodies to this text) is then approached in a rather formal way, in a demonstration of writing, language and the word. The stage is no longer used as much to transmit a text through image and the representation of actions: it is no longer a matter of realising what the text can only say in words but what mimetic bodies and space can fulfil by performing them (since they can only do so in an illustrative and, what is more, derisory way). On the contrary, the aim was to now make these words be heard, to give back to them what print obliterates: to emphasise that these words are meaning and discourse, but also sound, rhythm, potential intensities, *orality*, a vocal presence – the bringing to life of a text-material before assembled spectators. The relation to the text would therefore be underscored, in certain practices, through the idea of an *offering*, which may involve the introduction of codes of diction and an insistence on the musicality of language. For the function of the theatre thus conceived is that of communicating the text through voice, and this would take precedence over the issue of the virtual or of interpersonal actions. Abandoning the primacy of the character, psychology, the fable, mimesis and the illustrative and spectacular image, these practices focus on the body and voice that deliver poem, speech and text. The staging then highlights the materiality of the writing and attempts to take an interpretative distance that would leave open the virtuality of all possible meanings, preserving polysemy.

In a word, then, the director and the actor's play are *seemingly* relegated to secondary importance, the text is presented as text and orality is exhibited. Such a conception explains the frequent recourse in many practices to a frontal staging arrangement where actors are face to face with the audience. The aesthetics of Stanislas Nordey, particularly in the first half of the 1990s when he staged Pasolini (*Bête de style* [*Beast of Style*], 1991; *Calderon*, 1993; *Pylade*, 1994), was, accordingly, built around the face-to-face relationship of the actor and the audience and the notion of a frontal communication with the spectator. The notion of a "theatre of language" and a "poet's theatre", in which the *mise en scène* would constitute a journey through language, took shape. What was desired was that the "discourse" would be bodied forth collectively by all its interpreters before being diffracted into the traditional constituent parts of theatrical fiction. It was a "discourse" in that it was public, civic, pronounced in front of a community; it was a "language" inasmuch as it was the distinctive experience of the thought and writing of an author. Nordey is a symbolic case of such a reduction of the definition of theatre to its simplest expression. Sometimes it is the relation to the text: "I have trouble talking about theatre, I would rather talk about poetry. The theatre is poetry [...] Poetry voiced by the bodies which incarnate it [...] Theatre is poetry in the form of dialogue", he remarks in *Passions civiles*, a collection of interviews.[8] At other times, it is the very issue of the stage. For him, *mise en scène* is thus essentially, if not almost exclusively, the place where the text (this language, this discourse) is transmitted, the place where words are uttered and resonate, as they are "carried" by interpreters. This takes place in a frontal framework and in an actor's work that does not rely on any identification but on the author's thought (to which the director must take a back seat) and on the rhythm of the language (his staging of Jean-Luc Lagarce's *J'étais dans ma maison et j'attendais que la pluie vienne* [*I Was in My House and I Waited For the Rain to Come*], in 1997, thus takes on the feel of an "oratorio").

The director desires a process of unveiling and starkness that refuses to pin an interpretation or a presupposed imaginary on to the text. It seeks instead to be part of a process of deciphering: Nordey often refers to the first pleasure of reading, and his *mises en scène* do not claim to explain the text but lay it bare, and cause its distinctiveness to be heard:

> When you read something you do not know, you do not have any preconceived ideas. There is something virginal that offers you a simpler access to its essence. And often in the theatre, the director tends to do the opposite: he adds layers, making the thought and language opaque. Because he wants to safeguard his thought, his language.[9]

Conversely, Nordey defines his theatrical practice as an approach aimed at "enlightening, unveiling, revealing. It's like someone clearing away the dust and patina from a stone of hieroglyphs, little by little, just to reveal them and make them readable; that is all".[10] In this context, the actor does not have to build a character and situations, to put on a series of masks. On the contrary, Nordey assigns them the same task of laying bare the world of the play, so that the actor is erased. It is no coincidence that nudity is relatively frequent in his *mises en scène*. The work of staging must make real human lives (and not fictional characters) appear on the stage, carrying a text and revealing the poetic language (diction, rhythmic scansion) of an author. And significantly, Nordey confesses that his dream is "to one day make an opera in which the actors and singers are naked, just so that we can see the functioning of voice, breath and rhythm".[11]

Nordey's theatre thus seeks to give voice, literally, to the poem's literary quality, to valorise the lyrical over the dramatic, but also to display a language that is distinctive insofar as it is not only as non-naturalistic but also something other than a mere tool of communication or a vector of information: consciously or implicitly, it is Vitez's heritage that partly makes a return in Nordey's theatre, insofar as the formal work on the text exhibits the conventions and play that are proper to it (rhythm and prosody, versification, codes and registers of language, inflections and accents, materiality of phrasing, etc.). The use of the term "interpreter" by a number of practitioners referring to the actor also comes from Vitez: the actor-performer is the actor who is responsible for meaning – by taking some of the burden off the director – but, even more importantly, this term is used by them to evoke the idea of a musician performing a score.

It is thus not surprising that music frequently becomes a determining or characterising gesture of staging. This is the case with Frédéric Fisbach in his staging of Claudel's *L'Annonce faite à Marie* [*The Annunciation*] in 1997. Not only did he reinstate the score written by Darius Milhaud for the play, but he based his approach on the definition given by the author of this text – a "speech opera" – and took Claudel's verse for what it was: not a unity of meaning but a unit of breath (and emotion). The staging was thus governed by the ostensible application of, or play on, prosodic and poetic codes (diaeresis, pronunciation of mute "e"s, absence of liasons and antirhythmic breaks), and by the search for a musicality of language taking the form of a score. Claudel's verse was thereby marked by counterpoints that paradoxically underscored its structure and lyricism, while avoiding declamatory pathos. Almost motionless, the actors stood on a table without touching each other for most of the play, only making a few gestures regulated by the text score (they put their fingers on their mouths at each *silence* that the didascaliae indicated, as if an ineffable secret inhabited them): they were interpreters who looked like performers or reciters, and played in a way that, while being extremely sensitive, was ostensibly distinct from a naturalistic mode of acting. The story of the young Violaine became a naive and terrible tale addressed to the audience by a chorus. Consequently, the production of emotion did not arise from situations, but through other means: by the overall movement fostered by this form and the particular way in which the interpreters let the writing resonate in them and "offered" it to the audience, delicately and intimately. A few discreet presences were felt throughout the performance: the "interpreter" of Pierre de Craon, the builder of cathedrals, painted throughout the whole performance on a plastic tarpaulin in a corner of the stage and the singer who played the score of Milhaud brought, like a stage servant, the few accessories used. The staging thus served both the narrative and its relativisation, introducing a rhythmic and emotional movement through its formalism while creating effects of distance. Thus, throughout all of Act 4, while the resolution of the play is taking shape behind a tarpaulin, the singer looks at the audience, book in hand and with a smile on her lips, as if to indicate that the religious reconciliation that was being played then was impossible. Represented exclusively in non-theatrical spaces, often collective social spaces (medical centres, disused factories, etc.), the staging blurs distinctions between the fictional Middle Ages imagined by Claudel and the humdrum of daily life. The reception of the spectator is thus built on an initial strangeness, with which they gradually become familiar, in a process of discovery (they gradually return to a common language, to the rules of the game thus established, recognising and sharing them little by little). They enter into the emotive movement created by this musicality. The distance produced by the assumed artificiality of these codes shifts the reception of the fable, to create a non-mimetic emotional intensity, that of a musicality of writing that rests on the sensitive presence of the performers. As a demonstration of the text by its form, the musical approach builds another emotional entry into the play. It also constitutes a kind of a detour, a point to which we will return later.

The musical model becomes fundamental in this approach to theatre that emphasises textual material, turning it into a discourse and a formal score. It would therefore be frequently used. The theatre of "text" thus employs musical motifs that condition the relationship to writing but also structure the space-time representation. These motifs also mobilise the text and play with it, rather than simply accompanying or illustrating it. The friction between text and musicality can then be manifested as the hybridity of two forms, of two writings of similar status. It also reinforces the lyrical dimension of the textual material, whether this material is dramatic or not. The stage thereby becomes, above all, a place for *discourse*, and the text a material whose incarnation (inasmuch as it is the body that carries it) is, first and foremost, an object of voice and rhythm. The theatre thereby becomes a site, not only of the image, but of the poetic *word*. It is this that the actor is responsible for carrying, with a slight distancing effect – not necessarily a Brechtian *Verfremdung* (the actor as demonstrator), but the distance of the performer, the interpreter, who reveals this *word* as a sensitive work on language, on its intensities and forms.

We see that dramatic action and the character thus fade into the background behind the display of the text as writing and as material. The actor must therefore no longer aim for a strict identification, a fusion with the character they embody, since they now represent a much broader relationship to the very fact of speech: a relation that

Olivier Py describes in his lecture *Epître aux jeunes acteurs pour que soit rendue la Parole à la Parole* [*Epistle to Young Actors Or "How to Give Back Power to the Word"*] as the need to "make visible the miracle of the Word", and "to be become one with its speech, with the desire to say and to speak, which is the only thing performed by speech [...] . Incantation is but one letter away from incarnation".[12] Although all of Py's colleagues do not share the same mystical background, like him, many of them see the theatrical text as an overall gesture of writing, rather than in its diffraction in lines and characters. It provides the space of an orality that must be foregrounded as its most important manifestation, before assembled spectators; an orality of which one must not forget the sensual and playful pleasure, an essential quality that attaches itself naturally to all "setting in discourse". The textual and scenic creations of Valère Novarina are a particularly enjoyable example of such a play on phonemes and signifiers.

The actor exposed

As such, in a certain number of practices, the playing field of the actor-performer and the modalities of their appearance – of their *display* – are defined in other terms, which are, broadly speaking, those of theatricality. As an actor-interpreter, the actor can thus permanently blur the line between appropriation of the character and the neutrality of a "disappropriation", between fictional embodiment and the demonstration of their own presence and their role as performer (and not of their belief in their identification with their role). The relationship to the text that we have discussed above leads to a complex negotiation of the eternal question of the presence of the actor. In the first place, such a conception of the interpreter is translated into a discernible split between our perception of the performer they are then and the imaginary figure they embody. Their body and voice are thus displayed in a certain withdrawal with respect to the expressiveness expected from the point of view of a mimetic construction of fiction. But this "alienation" is not merely meant to provoke a critical denunciation of illusion: it is intended to produce a specific emotion. As a result, because of this relative withdrawal in the embodying of their fictional identity, the actor's play becomes the object of a dual reception, based on a kind of ambiguity of the exposed intimacy of the fictional embodiment (since even when it is played in a minor mode, embodiment implies intimacy).

Fictitious intimacy thus has superimposed on it the intimacy of the actor-individual, which the spectator either recognises or catches by surprise. And, it is in this gap, or this complex knot, that a good part of the theatrical emotion resides: it can certainly be the appreciation of a technical display, alternating with the appreciation of an actor-*performer* or builder of fiction, but it can also entail making the "human" dimension noticeable, as we have already seen with the example of Nordey. Behind the mask of the character, this gap reveals the person, the bearer of the writing, who grapples with it and who, rather than hiding behind a role, is affected by the text to which they give voice. In this way, one is dealing with theatre and its ambiguous, fragile and problematic presence, via the actor *and* the text, not via a fable or character. The singular presence of the interpreter-individual, then glimpsed alongside the fictional identity that he bears, is not meant to produce a sense of mastery or the actor's virtuosity, but to present the risk of an *exposure*. Fiction is no longer merely dramatic fiction, but a fiction that feeds on the present and on the actor's exposure within it, which highlights the stage and with it the theatrical relationship, as the visual display of a fragile humanity, which is always in danger. We see in this an illustration of the desire to find the specificity of the theatre compared to the other modes of representation: as a *living* spectacle whose presence is unmediated, its role is then not so much one of affirmation of appearances and of the reproduction of fictitious identities, but of a site where the audience can have a particular sensual experience, with face-to-face contact – the experience of a living presence in its bareness, which acts without mediation, on what is beneath (or beyond) individuality, whether fictional or real.

Sometimes this play and this gap described above are underpinned by an attempt to arrive at a more universal expression. By moving away from traditional expressivity and displaying the actor behind the character, the actor's play would become more neutral in the way Blanchot may have suggested, insofar as the sensual, universal and irreducible experience of intimacy and humanity can be acted out in its simplest and most irreducible expression. What is thus played is, contrary to the expressiveness expected of the actor, a *raw* emotion, born through a breakdown of the subject's masterful control of the character: in this sense, theatrical exhibition presents in a sensitive way the issue of the human, in opposition to the cult of appearances and the control that characterise social life and mediate representations.

It is with this notion in mind that director Marc François (1960–2006) defines the stage as a space where inner freedom is reborn. For François, "the actor does not have to contain things; his role is to be affected by them. He does not seek to possess, as one does in life, and is therefore delivered from this perpetual insatisfaction".

Abandonment of control thus allows the actor to lay themselves bare in a way that would "liberate [them] from [their] appearance, from [their] social existence", "rid [them] of the codes of everyday life" even as it rids them of their actor's appearance.[13] The stage becomes the place where all *appearances* and representations of self are thwarted. Thus, François uses cross-dressing in his staging of Shakespeare's *As You Like It* (1992), in which all the roles are played by male characters, no longer as the addition of a mask, but as a paradoxical exposure. The stage becomes the site of an ontological quest – similar to that of Claude Régy, for whom Marc François has been an actor on several occasions. But, for François, this quest is based on the experience of the fall (social fall, falling in love, etc.), on pain, mutilation and humiliation: on a foundational experience of loss or of incompleteness, of an *absence* that leads to the collapse of appearances, to a reversal of alienation and to a reconnection with the world. This experience is one that seemingly attempts to represent borderline "states of being", such as Johannes' in François' adaption of Hamsun's *Victoria, la lettre* (1998), where Johannes is on the verge of madness and the heroine, Victoria, is on the verge of death. "Dear Johannes, when you read these lines, I'll be dead": this is how Johannes' monologue begins. It occupied almost the entire show, establishing a peculiar status of time and communication: it produced the sensation of a *threshold*, one fostered by the scenography – a narrow space as of a hallway whose white lights produced a menacing aura – and the play of the actress (Margaret Zenou), sitting on the edge of her chair, in attitudes alternating between stretching, tension, the dislocation of the body due to pain, calm, abandon and self-effacement – as of one who, already, is no longer there. The titles of some of Marc François' shows are also revelatory: *Les Mutilés* [*The Mutilated*] (H. Ungar, 1990), *Esclaves de l'amour* [*Slaves of Love*] (K. Hamsun, 1993), *Les Aveugles* [*The Blind*] (Maeterlinck, 1994). From Ungar to Maeterlinck, François seems to chart a path between expressionism and symbolism – two aesthetic reactions to the advent of industrial modernity. This is in no way surprising, as his is a theatrical approach that also seeks to consider the place left for the human in modern society. And when Marc François stages Corneille (*La Mort de Pompée* [*Death of Pompey*] followed by *Cinna*, 1994), the work is "like a space of disaster". Against the background of an astonishing chaos, the *mise en scène* as like a physical illustration of his conception of theatre as "a place that is essentially in fallow", one whose disorder and even violence allow a human speech to emerge and, with it, a de-alienated relationship to reality, a renewal of movement.[14]

It is in this context that Marc François declares:

> [T]he theatre − mine in any case − absolutely has this function: to be a place of reunification post mutilation. These two things are imbricated: we cannot get back in touch with reality if we did not experience failure. Wherever the man is mutilated, wherever he gets to a place of loss, a place where he is not whole, there he is likely to become finally whole again.[15]

And, in a certain way, it would be around this common failure, around the exposure of the actor(s), that the theatre community would be built. And here François draws on figures such as Lacan, Genet, Bataille, Blanchot and Robert Antelme, when he affirms that: "We cannot attain wholeness if we do not experience mutilation and lack [. . .] What connects us is this law of *"the human species"* which dictates that there is always something missing in man".[16] In sum, his theatre is neither a spectacular construction, nor pure withdrawal, but an intimate experience proposed to the spectator who will *recognise himself* in it and experience its destabilisation − as an individual and as part of a whole.

Overall, this type of theatre thus bases itself on the unsettling, if not total collapse, of the actor's mask, on exposure. And its work is thus devoted to the experience or the search for a "humanity" that the social world, just like media representations, stifle, but that the space of the stage is able to make visible. Neutrality or effacement no longer seeks to be a tautological process of affirmation (show the actor as an actor, manifest the text as text), but the search for what is underneath (or beyond) the actor's play and individuality. The theatrical relationship is then played as intimate to intimate (stage to spectator) with the aim of placing actors and spectators into contact and awakening recognition, actualising in a certain way this injunction that we find in Derrida: "We call you to share in what is not shared: loneliness".[17] This relationship undertakes, as Anne-Françoise Benhamou writes, to make the spectator

> he to whom all singularity, all solitude is addressed. [For] these *mises en scène* do not want to make the spectator a voyeur, let alone as an arbiter: they seek to put him in touch with his own distress, the one he plays hide-and-seek with, in order to survive. This collapse of the mask and loss of control are also those of the actor, turned towards us, the smuggler of a text that says more of him than he can ever say of it, the mirror of our powerlessness beyond the stage ramp.[18]

While it is obvious that such an exposure does not necessarily take on a neutral appearance, and that it also takes risks, the general idea is the same: that the intimate involvement of the spectator can only respond significantly to such abandon and risk-taking by the actor, that the theatrical experience can only be shared if it is engaged in from the perspective of uncertainty and a constant questioning of the idea of virtuosity and mastery. The stage is thus not a space of assertion, or of demonstration, but one of doubt. It is a space of fragile presence and the suspension of certainties, where the resistance of life is experienced in common. Added to the actor's exposure, there is also the exposure of the community of actors to the community of the audience, as we will see later when we address the issue of chorality.

With Gabily, Nordey, François, the actor is exposed in their singularity. Their presence does not construct a critical reading of the present, but results in the spectator being given a poetic energy that cannot be exhausted by normative discourse. The theatre works against normative frameworks, refuses the construction of an assigned interpretation, abandons the idea of a single meaning: the stage is open to the intimate and shared test of confronting an untraceable reality.

From the legibility of crisis to the questioning of perception

However, it cannot be said that theatre broadly rejects the idea of readability, interpretation and the ostensible construction of meaning. A director like Stéphane Braunschweig, to name but one example, is clearly inspired by the staging traditions of previous decades (including the work of Vitez, his teacher at Chaillot, but also that of Sobel or Chéreau). Furthermore, it is significant that his theatre is based primarily on the pillars of both dramaturgy and scenography. Braunschweig conceptualises his own staging apparatuses. These are generally large and function as real "playing machines"; they are of major importance in his work. For him, *mise en scène* is an unapologetic affirmation of a point of view, which makes no claim to withdrawal or erasure. It consists of

> providing a point of view on a play that allows the spectators to enter into an imaginary dialogue with this play and its author. The role of the director is to prepare for the arrival of the spectators, to hollow out a space for them in advance.[19]

It is all about "mastering the signs that produce meaning", and the director is "an active reader and an interpreter" who provides a hermeneutic orientation to, and a critical point of view on, the work. Therefore, Braunschweig rejects what he calls "generalized 'polysemy'", on the basis of an active choice that he considers necessary for the way in which the work is received: "there must be some sort of bearing that allows the spectator to choose [. . .] the production must affirm something"[20]; they must be able to "enter the complexity of the work with a sense of clarity".[21]

Braunschweig's theatre is therefore one that fosters readability and has been so since his first productions in the early 1990s. It is oriented by an act of *mise en scène* that is based on an ostensible dramaturgical reading: the stage is an exhibition space, in a quasi-*graphic* sense (since this "exhibition" purports to be a kind of inscription that showing itself as such). Bodies, positions, movements and play are visible signs that make power relations and strategic and/or ideological positions explicit, and that clarify, and even comment on, the points of view of the characters for the spectator who "can then look at them 'from above'".[22] In other words, the spectator can see their denials, their Freudian slips, their possible blindness. Significantly, Braunschweig has also used the inclined platform as the basis of his scenography on several occasions in the 1990s (for example, with Shakespeare's *Winter's Tale*, 1993). The use of the inclined stage is part of his technique of highlighting the "artificial" aspect of the staged action, but is also part of his attempt at amplifying the meaning and readability of each stage element. With such a technique, he explains,

> no gesture is natural anymore; nothing is anecdotal. Our perception of each change of scenery is magnified; everything signifies in an almost graphic way: the bodies become [. . .] a bit like letters on a page [. . .] The readability that this provides allows us to take a step back, to have a clear perception of the point of view of each character. We are no longer lost among them, drowned in their confusion. All power relations are laid bare.[23]

This was the case, for example, during the trial scene of the Shakespeare's *Merchant of Venice*, which he staged on a sloping platform in 1998. Thanks to the spatial relations that were displayed more vividly through the use of the inclined platform, there was a clearer depiction of the power relations during this judicial segment of the play. The sloping platform also allowed Braunschweig to play with the imbalance and complexity of the actors' bodies (especially Philippe Clévenot's, who played Shylock).

Space is thus used in a way that brings clarity and affirms visibility (though, as a result, this visibility becomes the object of questions) and a specific point of view. Indeed, spatialisation becomes an essential tool within Braunschweig's dramaturgical approach. It forms part of a "scenic writing" that arranges signs in such a way that the spectator "knows more than the characters".[24] It is clear then that in Braunschweig's conception of the theatre, *mise en scène* is the production of legibility (a fact that made him very successful as an opera director). However, his is not exactly a "critical theatre" in the vein of the 1960s: the very conception of the readability allowed by the performance space is quite difference, and, more broadly, the relationship between the stage and the outside world has changed. Indeed, Braunschweig noted in 1994: "theatre is no longer, it seems to me, a 'critical' institution, even if it remains essentially 'political' by virtue of being 'poetic' – a space of vigilance and discourse".[25] Braunschweig's type of clarification does not then claim to produce a meaning that could be affirmative or illuminating in itself; rather, it is a process of revealing symptoms and masks, especially the dimension of fantasy at work in any representation of the real. It is no coincidence that Braunschweig has been visiting the theme of madness in Shakespeare's works and in figures such as Molière's *Le Misanthrope* (2004) or Ibsen's *Brand* (2005) for several years, and that, through this theme, he has been critiquing and deconstructing idealism and ethical radicalness. The stage, for him, does not claim to be a place of truth; instead, he uses it to demystify and sharpen perception. Like psychoanalysis, which is very important in his overall theatre vision, Braunschweig's aesthetics of readability allow us to read, distinguish and interpret the symptoms and complexities of the real. Simultaneously, it accepts that *mise en scène* will always stumble on this complexity of reality without being able to erase it. Lived reality remains an "ungraspable reality", since life itself defeats any attempt to give it a coherent meaning (as Braunschweig says about *The Cherry Orchard* and the *The Winter's Tale*[26]). The issue, for him, is therefore how one should approach reality *after* leaving the theatre. In a word, this theatre is constructed on the ground of "discourse's inability to capture reality, to interpret it and give it meaning" and endeavours to "bring out in language the way reality resists every effort at representation".[27] Thus, even a practice as dramaturgical as Stéphane Braunschweig's testifies to a shift in the stakes of critical theatre. The relations to representation, to meaning and to reality, are no longer the same.

With practitioners such as Braunschweig, theatre becomes a space of resistance, which is no longer exactly the critical space of theatre as it had been previously conceived. Indeed, this sort of theatre highlights the difficulties of encapsulating reality in discourses and ideologies: even on a stage that is conceived as a space of demonstration or readability, the crisis of meaning and, more broadly, the crisis of representation that affect the theatre are emphasised. The theatre's political effectiveness is no longer taken as a matter of course. Of course, this does not mean that the theatre (and here we are speaking particularly of European theatre) ceases to be political – it is so by nature, and practitioners remain convinced that its political identity is essential. But these ideological-aesthetic mutations of which we have been speaking, in reference to Braunschweig, also affect the confidence one might have in the idea of the theatre's (in-built) political character. In other words, while the fundamentally political dimension of the theatrical act itself still remains self-evident (insofar as it is an aesthetic act produced in front of an audience), its ability to hold a political *discourse* may be seen as more problematic.

To pass the buck a little, we could say that one needs the commitment of an atypical American artist such as Peter Sellars to perceive the frontal staging mechanism as a means of questioning reality and engaging directly with current societal issues. We think of Sellars' minimalistic production of Euripides' play *The Children of Heracles* (at MC 93, Bobigny, 2002), which addresses the issue of refugees, exile, immigration and the right to asylum in the world. In this production, Heracles' children were played by teenagers from Bobigny, and the chorus of Athenian citizens by non-actors sitting at a table. Sellars took the model of Greek tragedy as a space of democratic debate before the assembled city whose citizens gather to deal with concrete political cases at face value here. Sellars' use of a social-political model of theatre is based on this confidence in myths and in the theatrical assembly as domains where political responsibility is highlighted, and around which citizens assemble like the Athenians did "to talk about the most distressing things in a society, to talk about it with dance and poetry" and "raise the level of [...] discussion in order to have a true democracy"[28] – in a word, to talk about the world and to imagine that it can change.

It was in that same spirit that Sellars staged Aeschylus' *The Persians* in 1993 with direct reference to the first Gulf War, seen from the point of view of the defeated (Xerxes = Saddam Hussein) and in response to its television coverage. The same worldview underpinned his representation of Pericles (1983) in Shakespeare's eponymous play as a homeless person in Reagan's America, his transposing of Ramuz's and Stravinsky's *The Soldier's Tale* into the suburbs of Los Angeles (1998).

Finally, it was what motivated his notable production of Shakespeare's *Merchant of Venice* (1994), which he set in contemporary American society, moving the action of Venice (Italy) to Venice (Los Angeles, California), having black actors play the Jewish roles, Latinos play the Venetians, Asian Americans play Portia and her friends and representing the final trial as an American trial filmed and broadcast on television. This transposition principle is also found in the many operas he has staged: from John Adams' *Nixon in China* (1987) to Handel's *Giulio Cesare in Egitto* likened to the political conflicts of the Middle East (1985) and *Don Giovanni* likened to the underworld of poverty and drug addicts in Harlem. Moreover, integrating both new technologies and popular cultures in its aesthetics, Sellars' theatre seeks to refer directly to the social and political reality that surrounds it, without innocence but with the belief in a necessary effectiveness. Despite this emphasis on social and political utility, Sellars' creations display an extreme rigor and attention to visual and plastic details (a fact that was beautifully demonstrated in his staging of *Tristan et Iseult* in 2005 to the Opera Bastille, in association with videographer Bill Viola).

It is clear that such an unqualified belief in the social and political reach of the theatre is now quite rare. However, theatre that is avowedly political continues to exist and we have seen, in recent years, productions that directly engage with current affairs. One specific example of this is *Rwanda 94* presented by Jacques Delcuvellerie's GROUPOV (Centre for Experimental Active Culture) in 2000. This production was a documentary-style investigation that was over six hours long and mixed political critique and satire in dealing with the media's and the international community's neglect of the Rwandan genocide. Opening with the testimony of a survivor, it also included a historical analysis of the problem (using the format of a conference) and extracts of poetry (the "Cantate de Bisesero" that ended the show). In a word, it used a hybrid and composite form, which thus harnesses reality as a raw material to build a performance. As we will also see, some productions use political texts as their material, for example to examine the legacy of Marxism in the contemporary moment (*La Conversation interrompue*, 2000, or *Le Bonheur d'être rouge*, 2003, staged by Benoît Lambert) or even the political engagement of the 1970s (*Foucault 71*, a collective project[29] of 2005). But it is indeed a matter of *examining*. It is not surprising that in reflection of the crisis of ideologies characteristic of the last decades, the political is no longer affirmed in analytical or demonstrative terms on the stage, but is posed, left in suspension for all to see – a suspension that reflects the perplexity of our time.

And when the theatre is ostensibly political and subversive, it does so by focusing on the deconstruction of dominant representations, consumer society and media models, often in a parodic and even satirical way. *Blackland*, by István Tasnádi (directed by Arpád Schilling, 2005) is an example of this move. It is a grotesque revue that subverts the canonical images of the history and national identity of a Hungary emerging from communism and entering into liberal Europe. Rodrigo García denounces the obscenity of liberal consumer society and the alienation of the human being that results from it, for example in *Compra una pala in Ikea para cavar mi tumba* or *Jardineria humana* (2003). His work features parody competitions for the "biggest son of a bitch in history" and human bodies covered up to their most intimate parts in food. Other forms of theatre subvert the form and dialogues of Brazilian *telenovelas*, insert in them economic terms or entire sentences borrowed from anti-globalisation speeches. One example is René Pollesh's *Telefavela* (2005). In a way, theatre becomes political and polemical through satire and the subversion of representations and mass ideology, especially as they are peddled by television or the cultural industry. Because they are, in fact, "the enemy", and it is with respect to them that that the theatre has to re-affirm itself. As such, political exigency consists of placing oneself in clear opposition to media modes of representation, or of circumventing them in order to denounce and subvert them. It is in relation to them that the theatre currently positions itself, as a space of "resistance" to their omnipresence and ideology.

Consequently, the theatre asserts itself as a space where the unformatted, unmediated "human" can be encountered, as a place where dominant discourse and media images can be abolished. We then understand why the stage is defined more radically as a space where one can escape discourses, as well as a certain hypermediated conception of the image, a place where one no longer seeks to impose meaning or to captivate the eye, but where one opens the gaze and unsettles and shifts the issue of everyday perception. We also understand better why directors turn away frankly from the naturalistic or "realist" representation, which has become the prerogative of television and commercial cinema. For a majority of stage practitioners, the political identity of the theatre is then defined in radical opposition to the media model and the consumerist relationship to the image it induces. The theatre is thus presented as the site of an experience, a place of *exhibition* and presence and thus one of rediscovery, of displacement of the gaze, where the spectators are able to *test* and question, in their freedom and their singularities, another relation to meaning and perception.

The troubled perception

The disruption of the gaze is no longer carried out solely thanks to the readability and analytical clarity of the staging language, nor solely thanks to a pedagogy of the signified. It is now linked, rather, to a questioning of perception, to the experience of the presences in the performance space and the extension of the fields of the signifier. In this respect, one could consider that recent years mark a transition, for many conceptions of the stage, *from semiology to phenomenology*. Is it a fear of meaning? Perhaps. But behind this, we must see more than just a negative reaction, because it is also a re-examination of the relationship between theatre and reality, the search for the principles that can reactivate a particular approach to the theatre, and in a certain way a return to theatrical "fundamentals", those that make it essentially a "performing art": whether it is the relation to the text, the space, the presence of the actor or the relationship that can be established with the spectator.

It is significant that "the veteran", the figure that many young French directors look to as a model – if not master or fictitious father – is Claude Régy. While he already has a third of a century of practice to his credit and has staged numerous contemporary texts (he was the main introducer of authors including Marguerite Duras, Nathalie Sarraute, Harold Pinter, Botho Strauss and Peter Handke), it is paradoxically the 1990s that brought him to the peak of recognition. His career and his aesthetic, which have hitherto remained markedly different from those of his contemporaries, have become an aesthetic and ethical reference point. Having never sought to be the director of a theatre, and having devoted most of his work (his company is called, significantly, "les Ateliers contemporains" ["Contemporary Workshops"]) to the staging of contemporary authors, like Gregory Motton or Jon Fosse in recent years, Régy can rightly claim to be the uncompromised elder, one who has distinguished himself from institutionalised directors accused of careerism and of chasing after power. More generally, Régy is recognised as a discoverer of authors, a director who has never claimed the status of "scenic writer", but who has always sought to be a "ferryman" (as Gabily has remarked) and to make the stage a space in which the text and the voice of the author – and not his own *mise en scène* – are highlighted (which does not in any way prevent his aesthetic universe from being very distinctive and recognisable). It is in this respect that Régy becomes, for many, a model, as he can rightly stake a claim to a theatre – and an experience – of "non-representation".

Theatre of presence and theatre of non-representation

The term "non-representation" may seem paradoxical; it nonetheless reflects a questioning of the very foundations on which *mise en scène* was constructed, whether it be the mimetic faculty of the theatrical performance or the exaltation of an exhibited theatricality making staging and the performance of the actor the essential object of aesthetic judgment. There is a specific nature in Régy's work that places it strictly on the *boundaries* of theatre – in other words, outside of a traditional theatricality, but focusing on the essence of theatre, or at least on its essential constituents, on their very tangibleness. The result is a disconcerting aesthetic, making the stage a mental and/or metaphysical space, creating a very special space-time that is in no way naturalistic or conventional – based on deceleration, and on the modification (dilation, primarily) of the spectator's categories of perception. In this context, the actor should not endeavour to "embody" a character ("There is an insulting aspect to embodiment in that actors impose themselves as the finished object of what must remain *unfinished*, in the sense of being infinite", writes Régy in *Espaces perdus* [*Lost Spaces*]). They must be the carrier [*passeur*] of the text, not in a Brechtian sense of *Verfremdung*, but by laying it bare in such a way that one "can find what underpins the writing".[30] In other words, the actor becomes a carrier of more than what the text says explicitly. They are ultimately the bearer of an *imaginary* that they transmit to the spectator, who, in turn, must try to grasp it. The theatre thus acquires the function of transmitting without imposing, of transmitting not as a discourse constituted of readable signs, but as an experience through the simple effects of presence and sensation.

Régy thus works on silence, immobility, slow motion and the intensities created by low light. For example, he has produced several "performances" using non-dramatic texts and a single and almost motionless actor. Examples include Charles Reznikoff's *Holocaust* (staged by Régy in 1998), which we have already mentioned in a previous chapter – a text whose very title indicates how much it could not give rise to "spectacularisation" – and *Paroles du sage* [*Words of the Sage*], an adaptation of the *Book of Ecclesiastes*, in 1995. The way he describes the beginning of this performance, which was radical and revealing in more ways than one, gives a good idea of the stakes involved in his scenic work:

> The audience is silent and focused while the auditorium goes dark very slowly. The auditorium is held in darkness for quite a long time, and then the light rises slowly, even more slowly

than when the house was being darkened. Then moments are created where the actor is at the limit of perception. Then he comes into the light and this presence is amazingly bright. This entrance takes ten minutes, but as we are at the limit of visual perception, we also lose any sense of time.[31]

Here, the creation of a static atmosphere serves to focus the spectator's attention and open it up to other categories of perception, in which their most hidden imagination lies hidden. As Régy remarks about the actor Martial di Fonzo Bo in *Paroles du sage*:

> This actor occupies a space and does not leave it, but at the same time, one realises that there is no immobility, that the face is a landscape that's always changing, that the body acts, moves and emits, and the fusion of speech and body is visible [. . .] His body radiated. His face, by virtue of its fixity, produced hallucinations [. . .] The light was fixed. We thought it was moving. So, vision is transformed into imagination.[32]

Thus, the real issues of Régy's artistic quest are to be found in phenomenology, psychoanalysis and the unconscious. His theatre also has a potentially mystical, metaphysical and ontological dimension, in that it seems to depict presences impacted by forces greater than the theatre itself and that exceed it. His aesthetic is ultimately moored in a symbolist worldview, and it is not coincidental that his most famous production of the 1990s is his staging of Maeterlinck's *La Mort de Tintagiles* [*The Death of Tintagiles*] (in 1997, twelve years after his staging of another play by the same author: *Intérieur* [*Interior*]). In any case, it is a theatre that is out of step with dramatic and spectacular standards: a theatre that is meant to be a place of experience and not of "re-presentation", a theatre of perception, of being and of the unconscious.

Is Régy's theatre an "abstract" one that dissolves the real and that is anti-theatrical and "spiritual"? Certainly, if we take as norms the usual canons. But, the very nature of this work suggests the reversal of categories. Indeed, it is an experiment that revisits with the fundamental principles of the theatre. "There is probably a relationship of silence, slowness and space. Perhaps they are all of the same matter", he writes in *L'Ordre des morts* [*The Order of the Dead*].[33] The bareness and exposure that are at the heart of his approach reflect a permanent exploration of the very notion of presence, an embrace of the values of concentration and density that he applies to the very principles of the theatrical act: space, time, speech and writing are all being bound in a great "nudity". It is perhaps "abstract" theatre, but in way than an abstract painter works on the basic categories of painting (colour, line, form, pictorial matter and so on). The scenographies created in the 1990s by Daniel Jeanneteau for Régy are extremely refined, but also conceived as global spaces (the proportions of the stage and the room, and therefore the conditions of reception of the spectator, are reconfigured especially for each show, and this down to finest detail). Dominique Bruguière's usually very weak lights accentuate the experience of emptiness that these spaces often put in play, and physically bring the viewer's eye to other thresholds of perception. The slowness of movements, or the micro-variations of body gestures that become the object of the spectators' gaze when the actor is still, alter the barometer of theatre reception. The slowing down and spacing of the diction of the text alter the flow of discourse and break it down. The denaturalisation of representation thus has the effect of making the play's elements more present. Realist representation is subverted and "opened" to give way to something else, to allow the spectator to feel the texture of space, time, silence and also to make these more resonant in order for the them to "work"[34] on the material that they receive in their own imagination.

Ultimately, it is the spectator who is the last "author" of what is presented onstage. Through its unsettling of representation and its essential experiments on thresholds of perception and their movement, this aesthetic aspires to a new vision or attitude of perception, reactivating the senses and the imagination in different ways to reach the hidden depths of writing, the imagination and the unconscious: "seeing outside of us what is in us" is one of Régy's definitions of his theatrical approach. His particular kind of theatre is, consequently, at a paradoxical crossroads between the oneiric, the spiritual (it is a staging of aura, of void, of the mystery of the presence of being and resonance – in other words, of a certain kind of sacredness) and the material (a materialism specific to the phenomenological experiments on perception, but also one that is linked to quantum physics, for example, which fascinates Régy). Therefore, the act of staging does not manifest itself as discourse, let alone as "reading", or as a closed construction of signs or even as an attempt at elucidation.[35] On the contrary, it reconfigures the frames of reception of a text – and, more broadly, of writing and of the "voice" that is supposedly that of the author – in order to break them open. While it is underpinned by an extremely unique and recognisable aesthetic approach, it is based on a gesture of openness, where the theatre spectator is recognised as part of the theatrical act. Only their imagination can reconfigure what the stage gives to them to perceive and experience. Based on this principle of "non-representation", Régy's experimental and plastic approach thus deepens the basic categories of theatricality, deviates from all spectacular and rational production, embraces an aesthetics of perception and not of meaning and fosters the opening of the spectator's imagination.

We understand better then why Régy is held up as a model by so many of the directors who emerged in the 1990s: it is because his approach, while chronologically contemporaneous with those of the great figures of the 1960s to the 1980s, is in absolute counterpoint to them. Some of the attitudes of which we have spoken can thus be found in Régy's work, in its uncompromising radicalism, in its commitment to contemporary authors and more broadly in its desire to present the text to the spectator without the mediation of a constructed reading imposed by staging. Régy's staging aesthetic, added to certain ethical positions of the man himself in relation to institutional theatre, thus represents the opposite of traditional theatrical practices and conceptions and becomes a point of reference. By appropriating Regy's work and its emphasis on the phenomenological dimensions of the foundations (rather than the manifestations) of theatricality and of the spectator's perception, some new directors find in it an alternative to semiotic construction and a possible re-orientation of the construction of meaning that is then considered to be the role of the spectator themselves. They find in his use of the stage as a sensual sounding box and a mental space, a negation of a naturalism that they themselves reject. By exposing the actor, and more broadly the theatrical stage, they also reject the spectacular and, very often, pathos and embodiment.

More broadly, Régy's work is thus exemplary of a shift in the domain of staging aesthetics over the last two decades: a transition from semiology to phenomenology, as we mentioned earlier, and, more broadly, a transition from the conception of theatre as a place of enlightenment and explanation to a space that examines the issue of perception. In this transition, theatre becomes a practice that explores the depths and strangeness of mental space, which seeks to lead the spectator into an experience involving their imagination and the most troubled areas of their unconscious. It seeks this in the heart of writing and its underlying "depths" and through the unique presence of the actor.

It is important to note, however, that such experiments do not necessarily resemble Claude Régy's "non-representation". Certain French practices do embrace such "abstraction", while placing emphasis on an exposition of the text (in its literariness) and on a certain level of formalisation. But the work on ambiguity and the unsettling of perception can also be found in other dramaturgies that seek to produce "increased perception" through effects of denaturalisation, disturbance or disturbing strangeness within fictions that question the complexity of our grasp of the "real". These other dramaturgies are situated in the space between objectivity and imagination (as in the creations of the author-director Joel Pommerat), or play on the sliding boundaries between reality and fantasy (already allowed for in the plays of Kleist and Heiner Müller, for example *Penthésilée-Paysage*, an adaptation of Heinrich von Kleist's *Penthesilea*, directed by Aurélia Guillet in 2004 and 2006) or Sarah Kane (*Blasted*, directed by Daniel Jeanneteau, 2005).

There are also other traditions, and, of course, other very different and distinctive practices, which raise similar issues (subversion of realism, disruption of space-time, sensual experience of mental spaces and the unconscious) by others means. The unsettling of perception can be used as a tool to "contaminate" works that are otherwise "realist", producing a disturbance, and even a reversibility, between mimetic representation and interior spaces, to create a kind of troubled realism, which, it should be said, is based on the work of the actor and the density of their presence, on an exploration of the roots of writing and on the transcendence of psychology.

The work of Polish director Krystian Lupa offers an example of this sort of troubled realism. His productions in France are exemplars of such an ambiguity or such reversibility. At first glance, Lupa's theatre might seem rather to be part of a certain tradition, the one that Western Europe generally associates with the great figures of *mise en scène* from the East (like the Russian Piotr Fomenko,[36] to name only the most famous in France): a theatre founded above all on actors with extreme technical virtuosity and whose in-depth approach to the character is based on a Stanislavskian or post-Stanislavskian approach of unmatched quality. The direction of actors is indeed the essential constituent of Lupa's theatre. But while he may give the impression of espousing a certain kind of psychological realism, this impression is very quickly nuanced by the pregnant feeling of strangeness that his *mises en scène* produce, and the mental images that they arouse. That the two "masters" that Lupa claims are Kantor and the filmmaker Tarkovsky is revelatory of his theatre's displacement with respect to the realist model: simultaneously concrete and mental, figurative and unreal, this theatre is always in an intrinsic tension.

Lupa's aesthetic is fundamentally linked to the very nature of the experiences he intends to explore through the theatre. It is indeed a specific time that his performances bring to the stage, a time of crisis and trouble, where certainties are broken. His theatre presents the individual crises of characters. But these are always symptomatic of broader identity crises, and in the end, of the spiritual condition of modern man. The textual material he chooses for his performances, be they dramatic plays or adaptations of great novels (*The Brothers Karamazov*, 1990 and 2000; Broch's *The Sleepwalkers*, 1998; works by Musil or Bulgakov; or ones by Thomas Bernhard, such as *La Plâtrière* [*The Lime Works*], 1992, *Extinction*, 2001, *Ritter, Dene, Voss*, 1996) is revealing of what he intends to bring to the stage: times of disruption and decomposition of identity and ethical values, and consequently shifts of perception, manifestations of the dark areas of consciousness and the limits of rationality, leading to the unspeakable, the unconscious, the unknowable.

As a result, it is *disturbing strangeness* that fills this offbeat, troubled, realist stage and manifests itself through the hues of the imaginary and the unconscious. Lupa himself speaks of "magical realism, deepened by psychology"[37]; but it should be pointed out that psychoanalysis (especially Jungian) is fundamental in its work. Through density, the concrete materiality of the elements present on the stage, and the echoes they keep on creating, through the deeply material nature of the seemingly realist sets and of the stage play and the disturbing dreamlike quality of a stage that resonates like a mental space, Lupa's theatre never ceases to create the disorder of a permanent ambiguity between the real and the imagined. The particular texture of Lupa's shows thus relies on the creation of an extremely singular space-time, supported by a disturbing sound environment (heavy layers or strident noises, insistent music that underlies the actor's play), the work of light (sometimes weak and floating ones, or lights that create a particular space for characters in the middle of the general twilight), by various optical and rhythmic processes, especially the "heady, poisonous, dilated" time (J.-P. Thibaudat) that permeates his performances: not strictly speaking the result of a slowdown, but a natural duration marked by gravity of concentration and the inner charge of the actor-characters, whose organic rhythmicity often turns the representation into "a dream devoid of any point of reference, a dream that is only a becoming-fluid".[38] There is a permanent ambiguity in Lupa's performance spaces, a blurring of frontiers and a constant interplay between absence and void and between external perception and inner space. The simplicity of scenery (a few pieces of worn-down walls, a few dusty windows, a few pieces of furniture – tables and wooden sideboard, metal beds) creates fragile islands, as it were, in the middle of the void, and Lupa's scenographies also frequently play on the coexistence of several visual planes that fluctuate in their relationship with each other (sliding between realistic topography and dreamlike visions).

Take the example of *Extinction*, Lupa's adaptation of Thomas Bernhard's last novel. In the first part of the performance, there is a double bottom space, in that the platform space itself was lined all around with windows (including a bay window). Through their reflections, they created doubles of the otherwise realist space of the Roman apartment of Murau, the narrator, who monologues for more than an hour. At times, however, and depending on the light, one can see characters behind this jumble of windows. They appear like mental images from Murau's memory and speech, and sometimes they enter the actor's space of play. The scenography, and the entire spectacle, therefore create a realism that is deconstructed surreptitiously, oscillating between the "objective" representation of a character delivering a monologue and the "subjective" mental space, mingling the narrator's present situation in Rome, where he is lost in his logorrhoea, and the outcrop of image fragments from his past in Austria, in Wolfsegg's family estate. This same ambiguity is also driven by the performance of the actor Piotr Skiba, as well as by the discreet presence of an interlocutor (Gambetti, pupil of Murau), who constantly navigates the viewer between the adoption of the subjective point of view of character and the moments when this point of view is defused. The interlocutor proposes a more distant and ironic point of view on Murau's morbid flow of speech. In this regard, the *mise en scène* accounts, in an exemplary way, for the complexity of the narrator's voice in any of Bernhard's.

In the second part, the setting is no longer Rome but Wolfsegg and we leave monologue and enter into a dialogue-based representation, since Murau has returned to the family property following the death of his parents. Surprisingly, he is not very talkative when he sees his sisters and other family relations. The double and congested space of the first part has given way to restricted spaces, occupying the front of the stage, and always seemingly realistic (partitions, furniture and so on) but slowly becoming more and more bare: the kitchen of the family home, the dining room, and so forth. However, at the end of the performance and after such scenographic restraint, the "children's room" is revealed. It is immense, with depth space; it is also empty and filled with a sense of repressed family memories: indeed, the parents had hidden Nazis on the run. With this impressive depth, memory returns in all its force, even as this space emptied of all its furniture and objects refers materially to the emptiness and dispossession of which the whole performance has represented something of an initiation experience.

Lupa's scenographies, which are emblematic of his typical approach to *mise en scène* in its entirety, thus present ambiguous spaces, with shifting status. They are also often full of stairs leading nowhere, or of high windows that only exist to create a sense of the vertical and of the unknown. They are full of doors opening on to corridors or transfer passages that themselves lead to another door (*Brothers Karamazov*, *The Master and Margarita*), of wall surfaces and door jambs placed in the middle of a void. More broadly, it seems that Lupa's stage functions, especially in the case of his adaptations of novels, are in many ways based on principles similar to those of the dreamscape, not only in that they combine the force of association and the feeling of unreality and of strangeness, but also in that they like to play on condensation, on over-determination and on juxtaposition, to subvert the logical laws of dramatic mimesis and perception. For example, Lupa inserts hallucinated "visions" of his characters into his shows: all the figures of Murau's childhood coming on to the stage for a brief tableau in the first part of *Extinction*; all the characters of *Sleepwalkers* briefly invading the platform in a movement of panic; or those of the *Master and Margarita*, in which Muscovites of the 1920s, as well as Pontius Pilate and Jesus, gathered in eternity on the scaffolding at the back of the stage for the last image of the show.

The various shifts and gaps through which Lupa disrupts the realistic appearance of his theatre place the spectator in an in-between space, as on a threshold. The exploration of the dark zones places perception against a mystery, an elusive strangeness that is not objectified through a clarifying or elucidating gaze. Inner and outer life interpenetrate, borders are porous, the spectator never knows which side of the mirror they are on. So much so that we could compare the strangeness with which Lupa confronts the spectator with what he says about Esch, a character from *The Sleepwalkers*. According to Lupa, he is

> a man who apparently stands firm on his legs, but unconsciously plunges into the dark and troubled regions of a very peculiar spiritual experience. The reality, which he grasped and accepted based on clear and invariable criteria, escapes him little by little until he becomes incomprehensible: Esch now feels like he is on an island that is constantly shrinking – the island of the verifiable and measurable, that is surrounded by the ocean of the amorphous [. . .] New thoughts assail him.[39]

Lupa further states that "all this is not lived in the inner world of his imagination, but in the circle of events and real people, suddenly discovered from a new and surprising angle".[40] The theatre, for Lupa, therefore seeks to explore what we do not know and what we can't name. It is the place where beings (and things) are perceived as strange(rs), and at the same time close, in that they relate to the deepest inner spaces, to the most troubling aspects of the unconscious. This theatre is thus close to the strangeness of a dreamlike model, if one wants to characterise

> the work of the dream [as] moved by a paradoxical visuality which simultaneously imposes itself on us, disturbs us, insists and pursues us – to the very extent that *we do not know* what in us is troubling us, what trouble it is.[41]

Indeed, inspired by psychoanalysis, Lupa's theatre does not seek to give lessons, or to create the sense of an objective gaze. Instead, it plunges into the complexity peculiar to its object. Despite its rigour and the strength of its images, there is nothing aesthetic in this theatre: on the contrary, chaos swarms, in a subterranean disorder that is only allowed by the extreme density of the presences of the actors – since it is on this that Lupa's aesthetic relies. Whether restless or weighed down to the ground, the characters always seem overwhelmed by the energy of their own dreams.

Indeed, the flow of energy is of prime importance, since the whole play and presence of the actor in Lupa's work seems to emerge, in a way, from a seismic force that extends from an epicentre. The density of this power can freeze the character, anchor them to the ground, where they are crushed by the loss of rational bearings and plunged into the depths of their thoughts (Jan Fricz, in *The Sleepwalkers* or Pontius Pilate in *The Master and Margarita*). Conversely, this power can be a *dis-quiet*, the troubled situation on which a dizzying neurosis is based (Piotr Skiba, especially in the role of Murau in *Extinction*). The epicentre is the "interior monologue" that is the basis of the work of Lupa's actor. It is not a question of an explicit subtext, but of the search for a movement, a complex flow, a point of impulse for the opening of a sensitive interior *landscape*. The work seeks to free the imagination so that it can concretely take charge of the body (the "*dreambody*", as Lupa refers to it). It also seeks to "amplify" the presence of the actor, to make movement the source of his play. This actor draws upon a subterranean dynamic that charges the body, which becomes only the visible portion of this overflow. Lupa's theatre is thus in no way "psychological": ethical references are scrambled, characters dissolved, motivations and objectives of characters become obscure or hidden. Consciousness has become opaque, inaccessible. This is a theatre of zones, in which psychology is destabilised and troubled. It is a theatre of the unconscious, since it is a theatre where there are no reasons that can be grasped, outside the complex evidence of an organic irreducibility. In its troubled realism, Lupa's theatre unsettles perception and enters into dangerous zones. It to go ever deeper into the unconscious, destabilising from within the reassuring frameworks of dramatic representation.

As we can see, from the example of Régy and Lupa, the forms and nature of the proposed theatricalities are extremely different. But whether it is through a primal refusal of realism and the idea of mimetic representation or through a radical subversion of realism and mimesis carried out from within, what is striking is how much in both these cases the stage is used to pull the spectator into the darkest areas of their psyche, and how much representation is used to divert the model of illusionist fiction to create a disturbance through *sensual* means. There is no critical dimension, strictly speaking, in these forms of theatre: *mise en scène* is conceived as the implementation of a sensual experience involving the intimate adherence of the spectator and representation is denaturalised in such a way that the spectator comes into contact with a kind of strangeness that displaces normative frames of reception. Moreover, while there are certain recurring processes of staging (dilation of time, a heavy reliance on lighting effects, and so on), this work is above all a work on the actor, on the presence, which is born of his imagination and his inner work. Finally, displacing the primacy of the dramatic representation of characters and of action, these various practices seek to return to the deeper stratum of writing and of the imagination that is its lifeblood – put differently, to an origin that would underlie the stage's organicity.

Experiencing the theatrical relationship and the present-ness of the stage: theatricality unveiled

The major issues of contemporary theatre can be summed up as follows: displaying living presences without constructing a discourse that defines them absolutely; troubling the spectator and their perception; exposing flaws; and questioning the notion of readability through the materiality of the set via the body of the actor. But the desire to embody a text and to create a strong organicity of the stage can, however, take on appearances that are radically different to the ones that we have already analysed. They can also be based on energy, playfulness and an ostensible theatricality. Indeed, contemporary theatre is also play, performance, exuberance, tautological over-affirmation.

The theatre, in a word, is given as a theatre, as a practice, in its tangibleness, and engages the spectator through the energy that it creates and through its status as an event.

Therefore, to so ostensibly display theatricality is a means of showing the troupe, revealing the performance as a place of work and of narrative enterprise. Consequently, actors are frequently shown at the edges of the stage, even when their fictional character is not in play. It is also common in contemporary theatre for actors to play multiple roles or to exchanges roles. Moreover, simple signs are often considered sufficient to show such metamorphoses and to exhibit all the processes of a visible theatricality; in other words, to openly display the skill of the actors as well as the theatre itself in its simplest sense – as play. What emerges, then, is a theatricality of odds and ends, self-consciously sharing with the spectator, not only a closer relationship (in the visible mode of the story that one group tells another group), but the same playful impulse; sharing with them the pleasure of a game that they witness in the process of production as it takes shape before their eyes. In a word, we are speaking about the pleasure of seeing actors appropriate a fiction, making from it *their* story and a material theatrical exercise. It is thus the energy of the stage, the playfulness and the game of the actor, which are displayed.

Showing the actors in their practice is also to base the life of the theatre on the energy of the collective, in other words, the life of the "pack", to re-use a term employed by Stanislas Nordey, whose first productions, especially his compelling stagings of Pasolini's plays, were marked by an energy directly perceptible by the spectator. These productions were based on the strength of a collective management of the stage. Their energy also arose out of a determination not only to experiment with theatrical norms, but especially to preserve in the public spectacle something of the workshop or of the laboratory – in other words, the innocence and spontaneity of rehearsal work.

In a completely different aesthetic sense, the collective energy of the seven actors who assumed all the roles of Brecht's *Caucasian Chalk Circle* in Ludovic Lagarde's *mise en scène* (1999) ensured not only the theatrical effectiveness of their own presence as actors, but also succeeded, by relying only on a few precarious accessories, in displaying the breath of this great Brechtian parable. Lagarde's theatricality not only emphasised the principle of representation announced in the prologue of the play (which is usually cut from productions) – the story of Groucha and Azdak is played by members of the Rosa Luxemburg collective for those of the Galinsk collective – but also utilised the model of *Lehrstücke* ("didactic plays"), and, therefore, the experimental model and the "great pedagogy" of the young Brecht. Lagarde thus abandoned the traditional Brechtian aesthetic (that became the hallmark of the *Berliner Ensemble* after the death of its founder), utilising instead an epic narrative emptied of all monumentalism, having achieved a profoundly Brechtian fusion of playfulness and the discontinuity characteristic of a heterogeneous mode of theatre that displays its complex network of contradictions.

Here, the operation is really about "carrying" stories — otherwise such moves would be reduced to the solipsism of a tautological and narcissistic theatre, to a virtuosity or a vain display, to the self-referentiality of theatre actors only addressing other actors or a small circle of "people of the profession" or connoisseurs. But most importantly, collective energy and the display of theatricality are a way of building a particular mode of *communication*, of involving the spectator in the very act of representation, of coming face to face with them and carrying them along with the energy. But also of presenting the representation to them, not as a result, but as a thing that is inventing itself, in the present. This may even involve a super-theatricalisation that functions as a kind of magnification, a passage through the extreme, intended to invite the spectator into the flow of the fiction, but also as an intensification of the present-ness of the stage. Showing process, and the "factory" that is the theatre, does not merely function as a distancing device, but as a way of intensifying the spectator's relationship to the theatrical act by reinforcing the present-ness of their reception.

The rare, but strong performances of the company La nuit surprise par le jour [Night Surprised By Day], mainly made up of actors from Gabily's workshop — some were also from Vitez's Chaillot school — and directed by Yann-Joël Collin, present this singular immediacy. An example is Brecht's *Man Equals Man*, which they staged for the first time in 1993: not only did the playfulness of the performance embody the very foundation of Brecht's play (the transformation of Galy Gay, created and dismounted "like an automobile") and its distinctive dramaturgy, but it ensured that this playfulness did not seem merely like a reproduction and demonstration of actors' talent. Instead, it invited the spectator into the movement of permanent invention that became an embodiment of the fable. So, for example, at one point in the show, where soldiers were seen trying to convince the main character, Galy Gay, to help them with one of their plans, one of them puts his hand in front of a projector, briefly cutting off the light. He does this inadvertently, it seems; however, the soldiers became intrigued and reiterated the operation, repeatedly waving their hands in front of the same projector. Thinking of a bike that had been previously abandoned in a corner of the stage, they pick it up, turn it over to place the wheel in front of the light beam, erect a board as the substitute for a screen, position Galy Gay as a spectator and finally place themselves between the projector and Galy and begin to mimic a few scenes, while one of them quickly turns the wheel. Thus, from a few concrete and elementary accessories, a mock projection and snippet of silent cinema was created. This was a concrete illustration of the propaganda carried out by the soldiers in the story (a dramaturgical sign invented in the present-ness of the stage). We see then that if the intention is to make the spectator "witness the making of the performance during the performance itself", it is not simply to exhibit the fact as such, in a self-referential way and for the sake of doing so, but to confirm the concreteness of what is told on the stage and to ensure movement; to inscribe the spectator into the present-ness of the stage,

> the present-ness of the act. We work like that, not to show the "theatre within the theatre" or play on distance. Instead, we want to show that everything happens here, now, with the objects that are before us [. . .] The actors set the text in motion even as they set the stage in motion.[42]

The staging of Shakespeare's *Henry IV*, presented by the same company in 1999, is a telling example of such a theatricality, whose overall energy reflects, throughout the seven hours of the performance, a cohesive narrative intention. The playful dynamics of a representation based, in principle, on the empiricism of the stage and on an accentuated theatricality, allowed not only a reappropriation of the stage, but also became a dramaturgical point of view. Between the comic grotesque – that of the glutton Falstaff – and historical tragedy – the dilemma of Prince Harry hesitating between royal inheritance and the temptation of social transgression – the very nature of Shakespeare's play also offered Yann-Joël Collin and his team a privileged material. Pushing the alternation of registers to the extreme, this most prolific staging deliberately played on contrasts, between excessive and limitless Benny Hill style comedy and a finesse of interpretation of the political situation. It thus displayed, strictly speaking, the principles of the grotesque as Meyerhold, for example, has defined it: "a theatrical style that plays with sharp contradictions and produces a constant shift in the planes of perception".[43]

All means were then acceptable to represent the epic fresco: puppets, video, mask, clown nose and so on. The battle scenes or political plots became long clownish numbers, so much so that their comedic value eventually wore out. But it is precisely this exhaustion of the comic that made something deeper in the room appear, behind the farce and the use of carnival. Ultimately, the objective was not so much to obtain a strong visual performance as to achieve a scenic excess, peculiar to the character of Falstaff, and thus to tap into a certain madness of Elizabethan theatricality. This staging went beyond the mere desire to play with the text (which often characterises the use of the clownesque), proposing through its theatrical profusion a distinctive approach to the piece, particularly as it related to the issue of intergenerational transmission. While Planchon (in his 1957 staging) had approached Falstaff from a popular point of view, Mnouchkine (1984), in the form of a contemporary Kabuki, had treated this tragedy with all the poetic distance of a myth, with the company La nuit surprise par le jour, the history of succession to the throne of England became linked with a meditation on the contemporary and deeply generational problem of inheritance (both in a political and aesthetic sense), in all the complexity that the play allowed.

The seven hours of performance, added to a style of play in which actors internalised some of the real stakes of the play, put in motion the contradictions peculiar to Shakespearean dramaturgy. Thus, the way in which Jean-François Sivadier, who played Harry, passed from comic to tragic made the character's breakdown more poignant, for example during the famous scene where Falstaff makes the prince repeat the conversation that he will have with his father about Falstaff's bad company: Sivadier (Harry) and Christian Esnay (Falstaff) imitated themselves *as actors*, until they burst out laughing. But when Harry reversed the roles and began to play that of his father, accusing Falstaff, Sivadier broke with the comic by strikingly passing from imitation to the expression of a real resentment. On the verge of tears, Sivadier, in the game of this make-believe conversation, banished Falstaff, thus announcing the real tragic end of the play as a painful but necessary mourning. As for the character of the king (Bolingbroke), the actor Nicolas Bouchaud broke with the traditional notion of a stiff, sectarian character without humanity (Planchon, in fact, had portrayed Bolingbroke as an up-and-coming social climber), building a character for whom the exercise of royal power appeared problematic, if not painful. The traditional image of the political usurper was thus replaced by that of a being eaten away by remorse, estrangement from his son, illness and the imminence of death.

Thus, while Yann-Joël Collin and his actors approached the play as a farce, and as a caricature of heroic values (those of court and of war), whose excess playfulness and theatricality were the measure of

Falstaff's character, they relied on this very excess to unearth the contradictions and the stakes of the play, in particular that of power and the inter-generational transition embodied in the subjective problematic of Prince Harry, torn between his two fathers – the marginal one and the king. In the performance, the lack of age difference between the three actors reinforced the emotional burden of their confrontations by placing them on an equal footing. The shifting of registers was felt all the more, and the carnivalesque, over-theatricalisation of the play turned the comedic excess on its head, casting light on its tragic underside. This was mirrored in the treatment of the character Falstaff, whose belly swelled gradually throughout the performance (tyre tubes were placed under Christian Esnay's costumes), to the point where he occupied a significant portion of the stage in the second part of the play. Here, his gluttony was being comically embodied, but so was his untenable immoderation, which became a sign of the impossibility of any permanent transgression. And when Falstaff disappeared at the end of the play, the set was bared of its contents, symbolising Harry's conscious mourning: thus, the scenography rejected the classic portrayal of a reestablishment of the kingdom.

As we can see in this staging of *Henri IV*, playfulness, collective effort (the to-and-froing of actors embodying several characters also revealed these actors' own stories) and the display of extreme theatricality were obvious without settling for self-sufficiency (or being gratuitous) – they endeavoured to bring to the present the scale and complexities of Shakespearian writing. But we also see, if only with the example of the two actors imitating each other to build the conflict that they wish to represent between their characters, that if the test of the stage's present-ness is its energy, it can, with Collin, also be based on a unique connection between fictional time and space and the time and space of the performance. We will consider another example. When Collin staged *La Cerisaie* [*The Cherry Orchard*] in 2005, as part of a workshop with the students of the Conservatory, during the entire Act 3 (that of the party during which the purchase of property by Lopakhine is announced), spectators are seated at tables where they are served by the actors playing servants and guests. But the important thing is not so much this participative conviviality, a partial process of inclusion of spectators in the show, as the effect built from it to concretely represent the last act, that of Lyubov's and his family's departure. Indeed, after the party and Lopakhin's speech, the lights come back on, the tables are cleared, some actors come back into the room as if they were no longer playing roles. They seem to be occupied only with disassembling the decor and putting away their props.

The performance appears to stop, as if the troupe had chosen not to represent this last act: the applause begins to die down. This produces a moment of hesitation, embarrassment and frustration. Collin's *mise en scène* thus makes the dramatic ending of *La Cerisaie* coincide with the (false) end of the performance, and it is out of this embarrassment, this sensation of incompleteness and of the in-between, that Act 4 is built, depicting a time after the event, and its sensation of loss. The moment of hesitancy and uncertainty was a test for the spectator, one that involved the present-ness of the stage. The effect of "realness" is what underpins it, making it concrete and deeply dramaturgical, allowing the spectator to enter significantly into the distinctive tone of this last act – *another* moment, in which the spectator experiences the common present and their relation to the theatre – and, indeed, the relationship of the theatre's different parts.

A similar principle of trust in the investment of the actors and in the seduction of the playfulness of a theatre built from minimal elements can be found in Jean-François Sivadier's *mises en scène*. His is a theatre that continues to be an art of carrying a story from scratch, in modular scenographies made from wooden planks and scrap metal, and built (by Christian Tirolle) from recycled materials. This theatre seems to constantly affirm the desire not to take itself seriously through its "schoolboy" or "prankster" quality, through the spectacular nature of the of actors' numbers and the demonstration of numerous finds: for instance, a play like *Italienne avec orchestre* [*Cue to Cue Rehearsal, with Orchestra*] (1996, restaged in 2004 with the title *Italienne, scène*, then *Italienne, scène et orchestre* [*Cue to Cue Rehearsal with the Stage and the Orchestra*] in 2018) invited members of the audience to take part directly (as chorists) in the performance, by going behind the scenes of an opera rehearsal where all possible mishaps and gags occur. This is revealing of the spirit that governs the work of Sivadier and his team, as are the festive and explosive playfulness that characterised *La Folle journée ou Le Mariage de Figaro* [*The Crazy Day, or the Marriage of Figaro*], his rendering of Beaumarchais' famous work. But equally significant is the fact that when he stages Brecht, he chooses *The Life of Galileo*, in other words, the play in which science, politics and theatre are indissolubly linked in the same experimental exercise – of doubt and the destabilisation of perception. As such, the playfulness is not gratuitous: it is an essential means of thwarting the clarity (and supposed readability) of the stage, of putting the relationship between stage and audience to the test and of establishing a risk and an attitude of uncertainty, as in childhood. It is to dispossess the actor of too great a mastery, to preserve the living matter of a theatrical act experienced in common and in the present, on a precarious knife edge. This allows a sensitive management of the narrative and its stakes, an adventure in which ostensible sensuousness and visuality build complexity. It also allows the practitioners to build connection and trust from which the viewer can be bidden into a journey of great sensitivity and real dramaturgical acuity, as Sivadier's beautiful 2005 staging of Büchner's *La Mort de Danton* [*The Death of Danton*] (2005) proved.

Such a theatre is neither a sumptuous object nor a pared down aesthetic à la Peter Brook, but is made of odds and ends. It is made from tinkering, is self-consciously out of joint and precarious, existing only by virtue of the childish pleasure of its act and by the collective energy of the actors who take hold of a story and its writing and bring them to the spectators, exploring the sharing experience constitutive of this act. Indeed, such a theatre is a theatre of actors, whose mode of address lies in this double game of complicit desacralisation and exposure. Such an exaltation of a fundamentally precarious theatricality can also take on more baroque appearances, sumptuously displaying subterfuge – and kitsch – and constructing great scenic epics on modest platforms and arousing the breath of a lyrical language on an improvised stage. One of the most exemplary cases at the moment is undoubtedly that of Olivier Py's theatre, whose stage productions ultimately work on the same principle as his dramatic writing. These consist of great initiatory narratives that last several hours and are based on the elementary structure of the oral tale. Py amplifies the simple narrative model of the initiatory quest and juxtaposes the oral quality of the tale, which, as we have already mentioned, is generally characterised by a religious dimension and vulgar or grotesque situations (rare are the productions that Py has created where an actor does not show his ass). Py's theatre thus constantly plays on the association of the material and the spiritual, of triviality and poetic speech. His stage is also a space where props can be magnified in an ostensibly artificial way: a flood of bright red light on a wall of wooden planks (*L'Apocalypse joyeuse* [*The Joyous Apocalypse*], 2000), a few minimal props that are painted in gold (Claudel's *Le Soulier de satin* [*The Satin Slipper*], 2004). With Py, theatricality is omnipresent, and amplified ("beyond all figures and all ideas, the only one that is adored is that of the theatre", he declares[44]), in all its forms: cabaret or grand-guignol, *mise en abyme* and a strong taste for cross-dressing. All this is in the mode of a theatre of pure *jouissance*, which is, nonetheless, based on a conscious precariousness. In other words, on a belief in the ability of the theatre to depict the world in great cycles (in particular *La Servante* [*The Servant*], a cycle of five plays, the entirety of which was shown for 24 hours a day at the

Festival d'Avignon in 1995) and to be the site of a lyrical and spiritual poetic "discourse". For Py, an author-director who defines himself as Catholic, homosexual and a man of theatre, the stage is a space for deploying a baroque theatricality: one that is ostentatious, overflowing and grand in scale, but that is, at the same time, based on consciousness, simultaneously exhibited; and that has its own artificiality – its own vanity.

Considered from a different angle, Py's theatre is about deploying writing and the imagination against the background of what is derisory. It thus exalts the powers of stage play in their fragility and elemental force. It sometimes even involves reducing the theatre's tools to their barest, most fundamental states, so that the theatre is based, all the more, on a simple act shared by actor and spectator, between play and the imaginary. This theatre thus presents itself as a childish pleasure. It is improvised but also underpinned by the energetic investment of the actors. In a certain way, one could take as an illustration the way in which distortion plays on notions of the false and the true, a feature we often find in Py's work, but also in work by Jean-Michel Rabeux or the Theatre des Lucioles: its ability for solidifying the spectator's relationship to the staged work is not based on its penchant for illusion, but on the ostensible fact that what presents itself to the spectator is the concrete presence of the interpreter who bodies a fiction that is obviously unreal, in other words, made-up, but that they nevertheless fully and enjoyably embrace. The spectator must be seized by a power of conviction, by the power of a writing transmitted by a collective body, which calls for the reciprocation of their (the spectator's) affective and imaginary adhesion, in other words, the projection of their imagination.

This is why taking account of the spectator's rapport with the work of staging is considered, from the point of view of a practitioner such as Py, to be a fundamental part of the theatrical experience: this is nothing new in itself, but it is what this theatre works on, what it strives to interrogate and amplify, by testing the theatre's connection with its audience, through the playful energy of its actors. Sivadier defines the audience as a group that "expects that everything that will happen, knowing that this is not true".[45] As such, the theatre must make the spectator *play* in the present-ness of the framework that connects the audience with the stage.

It should be noted, however, that such an amplification and demonstration of play have become, following the practices we have mentioned, a very common practice, at the risk of losing its revivifying aspects and turning into cliché, by virtue of constant imitation.

We might also add to that the risk it runs of turning into self-indulgence and a folding in of the theatre on itself. It can sometimes give the impression that the act of *mise en scène* should have as its main task, through demonstration and exhibition – and even the excess of such a playful theatricality – to permanently maintain the relationship of the stage to the audience. Put differently, the emphasis on play might suggest a desire to constantly maintain communication (and play) by all the possible means available to the theatre (to put it in linguistic terms: it is as though this sort of theatre had taken on a phatic function). This sort of understanding of theatre is dominated by the desire for sensuousness and visual appeal (through effort and skill), and one might say that its only stake is the production of a desire for the theatre, and for itself – regardless of what the theatre, in general, might have to say about the world. This happens thanks to the cultivation of an ironic attitude towards the play, a sort of collusion or theatrical pact (we can all derive pleasure from the play since we know it *is* a game). This irony thus creates a link, a distance that, paradoxically, creates a consensus and a shared elation among all who are involved in the theatrical act. Thus, what one might be tempted to consider, in Brechtian terms, as an attempt to distance oneself (to show theatricality at all times) is not so much an attempt at fostering a critical theatre as it is a communion in the enjoyment of theatricality: a paradoxical *playful illusion*, which seeks to foster connection and the immediacy of festive sharing by means of a shared ironic distance – at the risk sometimes of a kind of tautological confinement.

Choral aspirations

The desire to establish a particular *address* (i.e. a *protocol of communication*) that simultaneously foregrounds the spectator's relationship to the theatrical work and instills a collective management of the stage thus characterises many of the approaches in contemporary theatre. It is a desire linked, as we have said, to a volition to reintegrate the spectator into the spectacle, beyond the simple passive role of consumption, and more broadly to rediscover in theatre – the stage but also the relationship between the stage and the audience, the site of a living community.

It is therefore not surprising, especially given some of the practices and aspirations we have already evoked (collective renewal, frontality, text considered as a language embodied by all actors, musical model, attempts at returning to the fundamentals of the theatrical assembly, etc.), that the last fifteen years have seen a very obvious return of the choral model. The first half of the decade saw a number of performances that have been illustrative of this rediscovery or renewed desire for chorality. The arrival of Lev Dodine's *Gaudeamus* at the MC 93 (Bobigny) in 1992, and two years later, of *Claustrophobia*, made the headlines. These two performances, staged with a group of young actors who had just come out of the Moscow Conservatory, had a significant impact on the audience, both through the collective, jubilant energy of the work and through its critical, subversive deconstruction of the chorus through the "soviet" model of the collective (the army in *Gaudeamus*). The work also testified of the distress in Russian society after 1989. The two parts of the play *Lumières*, staged in 1995 by Georges Lavaudant were also landmark events: in this work, chorality was associated with the fragmentation of forms, and more broadly to a questioning of the ability of the dramatic form to grasp and render reality. The choral principle was a basis for gathering the pieces of an increasingly fragmented world. The "exploded chorus" of *Lumières* manifested the desire to rework the theatrical form to account for history.[46] Jean-Christophe Bailly (co-author of the performance, with Lavaudant, Michel Deutsch and choreographer Jean-François Duroure) thus saw in this form, underpinned by the myth of Noah's ark,

> the possibility – or necessity – for theatre to move towards a new form that would be that of a chorus without heroes: a theatre of pure chorality, a theatre that would be an exploded chorus, exploded into different figures, who are almost anonymous.[47]

The ark created

> a situation in which what is to be saved are voices and stories – the preservation of a memory of the world to take to another world. Noah will not be Noah, not an old man, he will be a group of men and women.[48]

The myth of Noah's ark therefore represented a gathering of ruins – "Under the ruins" was the title of the first part of the show – lights, fragments, and voices, all of this based on a principle of discontinuity. Bailly, Lavaudant and all the others had thus opted for principle of exploded chorality "to stop acting as if History were only a succession of arias and [. . .] and to listen, instead, to its tangled, lost, solitary and true song".[49] To account for reality was thus to acknowledge a crumbling of our world, to renounce heroes and the centralisation on the protagonist, to foreground a choral form that is not the carrier of a totalising discourse but of a diffracted memory, of the circulation of interlocking solitary voices.

As we can see, then, the chorality that appears on the contemporary stage is an exploded, diffracted one. Because while the issue that underlies the use of chorality is that of the community, an essential stake for contemporary theatre, as we have seen, community is an extremely problematic notion and its aim is fragile, uncertain. To pose the issue of chirality is thus to enter into all the contemporary complexity of the issue of "the social body". For if the reference to citizenship, which is naturally linked to the model of the chorus, is implicated in this issue, then there is also the awareness that this model is now proving insufficient.

As such, the choral model in contemporary theatre is built on a dialectical movement between the collective and the singular: indeed, if there is one thing that these new moves of chirality reject, it is the monolithic chorus. And when "mass" chorality is resorted to, it is with an ostensibly political and subversive intention, as in the plays of the German Einar Schleef. Schleef has repeatedly provoked shock in Germany through his subversive use of the chorus. In *Mères* (1986), he represented a mass of about fifty women screaming their lamentation. In Strindberg's *Mademoiselle Julie* (1976), he had sixty young people onstage dancing to rock music during the central love scene. He has transformed *Wessis in Weimar* (1993), Rolf Hochhuth's satirical piece about reunification, into a military chorus of naked men, dressed only in boots with which they stomped on the ground with deafening noise. For his staging of Brecht's *Mr Puntila and his Man Matti* (1995), he had several actors play the role of the valet Matti and invented a chorus of women in red. Similar provocative uses of the chorus include his staging of Elfriede Jelinek's *Sportstück* (1998), that involved dozens of nude gymnasts running, jumping and performing, and a martial chorus that moved like a wave from the back of the platform to the edge of the stage. These uses of chorality are not an attempt at glorifying the image, or even at rediscovering an ancient ritual. It was not only to work on the rhythmic and phonic material of the text (repeated, dislocated, accelerated or stretched, alternately whispered or screamed collectively, sometimes while the footsteps of the chorus on the ground hammered the floor), but also because the theatre, from Greek tragedy to modern drama, seemed to him to have the almost unique object of representing the process of individuation, the founding stage in which a protagonist is excluded from the chorus and becomes an individual:

the end of his *Miss Julie*, which saw the heroine leave the stage by the auditorium, walking on the backs of the seats and over the heads of the spectators to the back door, was a blatant illustration of this move.[50] Even in the provocative way in which it is embodied in Schleef's work, the representation of the chorus is never a glorification of a totalising and fantasised wholeness, rather, it is concerned with articulating the collective and the singular.

Everything is therefore played out in this dialectic, an unresolved and perpetual tension in the conception of the relationship between the theatre and community. Chorality, as such, depicts a *community in becoming*, and it is this mirror that it holds up to the spectator. It is endlessly formed and unformed in the present space of representation, even as it constantly shapes and un-shapes the role that it assigns to the spectator. In chorality, then, the compulsion of undoing and re-doing (a kind of "fort/da" game) defines the relation between openness and distance, between the problematic temptation of unification of two spaces (the stage and the audience) and the simple *exhibition* of the one in front of the other.

To illustrate this point, we will consider the example of Christoph Marthaler, whose performances are an illustration of the kind of chorality that involves music, favours discontinuity, gives the feel of a variety show, proclaims its own eclectic theatricality and emphasises the relationship between movement and song. In this theatre, chorality is, above all, musical, and it mobilises a principle of collage, hybridisation and performance. It is a theatre in which performers sing, alone or together – from Brahms to *boogie*, popular songs or *lieder*. More profoundly, it is a theatre structured as a musical *composition* that replaces[51] or displaces[52] the dramatic construction. Marthaler, an oboist by training, who, in the 1970s, belonged to a trio that sang comical and political songs in the breweries of Basel,[53] entered theatre through the pathway of music and, more precisely, through musical *happenings*. His first shows were musical evenings: in 1980, *Indeed* brought together in a factory a string quartet, a harpsichordist and three actors gathered around a collage of Dada texts (by Kurt Schwitters, among others) mixed with non-poetic texts found in trains (leaflets, advertisements, etc.). Another musical performance conceived by Marthaler in Zurich took place in a pharmacy open day and night and with numerous customers present: a pianist played Eric Satie's *Vexations* 840 times in a row. At the end of the 1980s, *Arrivée Gare de Bade* was an evening created in the precincts of this station of Basel, an entry point through which many Jews fleeing the Nazis during the Second World War had been sent back to Germany by the Swiss authorities.

During the performance, actors and musicians mingled with the travellers and passing spectators, in a confusion such that the contours of the representation disappeared almost entirely. Klezmer[54] music was played every ten minutes, giving rhythm and structure to the performance, regularly interrupting the noise of the crowd that accompanied it and drowned it in equal measure – and, above all, bringing back into the present the memory of this place. For Marthaler, musical form is not an addition to theatrical representation: it pre-exists and underpins it – it is, on the contrary, theatricality that has come to inject itself into a primary musical nature – fundamentally linked to montage and performance. And the two models of revue and musical chorality form the basis of his performance, montages but also rhythmic constructions and real scores with several voices.

Marthaler's stage does not dramatise a journey or evoke a conflict. It is a place where one *is*, waiting, in suspended time (at the back of the stage in *Murx* appeared the inscription "So that time does not stop"; the badly fixed letters slowly came loose and were falling during the show). Characters are brought together, as if by chance, in vast enclosed, composite spaces, which always seem like waiting areas: the scenography of *Les Spécialistes* [*The Specialists*] represented the interior of a huge plane, with portholes and luggage lockers, but the interior was emptied of its seats. A row of bus handles hung from the ceiling on either side. Most importantly, a back room brasserie, as one finds everywhere in the south of Germany, was reconstituted at the back of the stage for a group of guests. For *La Nuit des rois* [*Twelfth Night*], Anna Viebrock, its scenographer, did not represent the Illyria, where shipwrecked sailors landed, but condensed it into the image of the interior of a boat, designed on two levels in such a way that it also mirrored the structure of the Italian-style rooms in which the show was played – the second floor's guardrail thus doubled that of the first balcony of the public space. Boat, airplane in flight, but also seafarers' bars (*Siemannslieder*, 2005) or hostel rooms. As we can see, these are transit spaces and in them we find gathered characters bound by no conflict, nor by any similarity, except perhaps their solitude. They represent communities of fortune, of chance and this reverses the relationship of crisis proper to dramatic action. "His characters are trying to escape. They do not even want to be on the stage. As soon as they are dragged into some action, they are embarrassed and try to slip away".[55] But, in this apparently suspended time, they also seem to have been there forever: the spectator finds themselves looking at a community that seems to have preceded it – in Marthaler's work, then, it is the spectators who enter, not the characters. They are already there, they wait, they hope, they repeat the same actions in a sort of idleness, punctured by moments of acceleration, for example when they respond, in Pavlovian bursts of activity, to anonymous instructions or signals, as in *Murx* where the members of a socially owned enterprise rise as one individual to the call of a siren, as they are summoned to wash their hands and quietly find their place at the table, re-entering their suspended time. The structure of the scenic events is built much on repetitiveness, the return of accelerations, ruptures or burlesque gags. So, one by one, in *Groundings*, corporate executives watch the chair on which they are sitting cross the stage on rails and pierce the partition wall – which workers are forced to replace. The chair then falls off the stage and the executives are fired from the company. Marthaler makes ample use of the burlesque in his productions, and this burlesque is intensified by the indifference of his characters, who are hard-pressed on every side but remain seemingly undefeated. Marthaler thus has a fascination with falls. The fall unites characters even as it differentiates them: each one has their way of falling, but under the effect of an external incident.[56] It is common for all the characters on the stage, at once, to fall together. More broadly, these are real spectacular numbers that pierce the time bubble; so it is also with the acrobatics, moments of dance, skits, small burlesque shows, or singing – discontinuous and spectacular numbers, which require the vocal and physical skill of all actors, but that never give rise to climaxes and to a specific focalisation. Instead, somehow, these shows can resemble failed musicals, given how much they are undermined by gaffes, failures, excesses. The gags and overall humour are based on the ridiculous and the principle of failure, but this is carried to such a point of excess and repetition, and conditions the show so continuously that, by an effect of reversal, they are turned into emotion and melancholy. In other words, the rhythm created by repetitiveness and slowness fuse comedy *and* sadness. They also allow a harmony of the whole, though each part (each punctuating number, or each character going about its occupations), taken in isolation, seems nevertheless detuned, like an autistic bubble cut off from the rest.

It is therefore musical rhythm that invents a physical, plastic, pre-discursive language shared by a community, by these choruses united by a suspended time, punctuated by jolts and momentary shocks.

> By his rhythms, [Marthaler] testifies to a collective state of mind that takes the form of a neurotic nightmare [. . .] The characters wait, for life, for something that never happens to them. They always repeat the same actions, as if subject to a

common neurotic agreement. Sometimes dramaturgic disturbances occur following the fall of a flowerpot or a glass; then everyone falls back into the same devoted state of mind.[57]

The musical structure of his shows fashions a dramaturgy of the state of mind rather than one of action; it creates an atmosphere, a feel, a *mood*. These idle choruses represent communities that have survived, knitted together in spite of themselves – as if abandoned on the vestiges of an old order (the rites of the collectivised, socially owned enterprises of the GDR in *Murx*, the dining room of the bourgeois family in the second part of *Der Eindringling*) or by the chance meeting of a ship and a shipwreck (*The Night of the Kings, The Stor*). Marthaler's characters always seem to be in an "afterlife", or at least in an in-between space: as if with the loss of collective identity structures, as in *Murx*, or, more broadly speaking, after a disaster, there were only vestiges that one could grasp while trying to remain on one's feet. So the characters exist after disaster, but in a surprising lightness of being. It is true that fatigue and dejection – other burlesque motifs – haunt most of Marthaler's productions and all of his characters, and carry this theatre to the edge of sleep. However, in this transitional state in which we get a host of staggering hypnagogic images, an unsuspected vitality is born: we witness moments of performance by individuals or a stupefied collective, we hear a song whose performers seem absent. But the song emerges from the murmur, rises and is embodied, as a sign of human resistance. Moreover, we can sense the latent images that lie beneath the music: a moment of oversight, of self-forgetfulness, is enough to cause the vestiges of the past and of history to emerge.

In Marthaler's work, we see that chorality thus lends its own weapons – repetition, unison, absence, hiccups – to memory and to the emotion of a precarious humanity, between melancholy and exuberance, permanent failure and moments of unsuspected vitality. The chorality that characterises it is thus of a comic, melancholic and musical nature, but it is also that of an "in-between" community, of a break with history, from which, however, the repressed can spring up at any moment. Finally, what this theatre cultivates simultaneously, being inspired by the revue and the social context of bars, is the notion of the event, of performance and of discontinuity: the curious fact of people gathering in the same place to see others fall, whether this place is a theatre, a café or the world, and also to experience what connects these other people to them.

However, it is important to note, particularly with respect to the French stage, that the use of chorality does not strictly speaking take the form of a chorus, such as those that the German examples of Schleef and Marthaler bring to the stage. Many works take an underlying, internalised form that resurfaces partially while still re-working the model. While one finds choruses that are made up and displayed as in certain works by Gabily (for example, the chorus of the mothers of Russian soldiers disappeared in Afghanistan in *Des cercueils de zinc* [*Zinc Coffins*], a work by S. Alexievitch) or by Nordey (Pasolini's *Pylade*), chorality is, nonetheless, felt at the roots of work, rather than as a major constituent part of it. In such cases, the claim to "chirality" is a general organising mechanism of the whole stage (in its internal functioning, the expression of the collectivity of the actors and the relation it establishes with the community spectators). It thus constitutes a field of consciousness rather than an established model, a set of questions rather than a process, a tension and a protean aspiration rather than a given form. To be together, to represent the community, to depict difference in identity just as much as the group, and the permanent dialectic between the two, to open the representation towards the spectator and to be the vehicle of it: these are the many points of tension, characteristics of the time that are underscored by the use of a choral principle that never ceases to intermingle the awareness of fragility with the complexity of such issues.

Chorality can thus be embodied in multiple forms, whether they privilege the collective energy of the actors, the musicality of the text or its lyrical dimension, or whether they display a recognition of the spectator as receiver or exhibit formal codes and common rules of play posited as principles that govern the stage: here, we recognise points that we have already treated, and that we will not go over again. All these forms, in one way or another, presuppose in their principles a chorality that is intended above all to be a foundation, a base: the logic is to start from the set to build the play on the platform – and not to reinstate some unity after the fact on a hierarchical and split platform. The collective is paramount and its destiny is to be diffracted – it feeds on this diffraction. Once again, there is absolutely no question of reinstating a regimental model or a "mass" chirality – the objective of the use of the chorus is to explore the issue of what the community has in common, but this exploration is anchored in (and not against) singularity. The attempt to speak of the whole is thus grounded in the recognition of its inalienable singularities: those of the stage, but also those of the audience.

Once again, the relation to the spectator is at the heart of such questions. And in a way similar to what we have seen above when discussing the display of theatricality, chorality also arises out of a desire to embrace, or to create, a degree of presence that is in addition to the text and to the fiction, to reactivate the present-ness of the text to the viewer. In other words, it is an attempt to play on the dual status of representation, on the constant paradox inherent in embodying a fiction. Gone is the belief in a fusion of the interpreter and the character, or in a direct, face-value reception of the fiction by the spectator, based on an enclosed, illusion-producing stage. The theatre practitioner must make the spectator experience the singularity of the theatrical experience as a form of sharing that connects stage and audience, as an exchange *in the present*. Here again, representation focuses on telling, simultaneously with the fable, its own process: it is a kind of framing device, but, beyond that, a necessary means of reactivating the idea of theatre as *relationship*: the idea that a time and a space common to stage and audience can be created.

And on a strictly aesthetic level, it is also the influence of cognate artistic forms, in particular music and dance, which then provide models of chirality in theatre. Under the combined influences of these external models and the questions that the theatre poses about its own art and its relation to the world, the return of the chorus is thus the sign of a search for polyphony and for a plasticity of form. It is a principle that underpins staging, which cements a unity that then diffracts within representation, it is a principle of work as much as a form that is part and parcel of the construction of meaning. Chorality, in the ways in which it is now being revisited, becomes then the engine of a "de-centred" representation. Put differently, it is an underlying factor of unity but at the same time, by virtue of its polyphonic and polymorphic character, it becomes a "plastic" medium of work, allowing play to slide between forms, to constantly build and rebuild on the (moving) foundations of collective body – providing, in a word, the necessary basis for a desired explosion.

Decentring representation, diffracting reception: form as medium

In this search for polyphony and diffraction of reception, there is an attempt at shifting the play of affects and subverting the traditional hierarchical logic that governs the stage. Consequently, what is proposed is a de-centred representation: decentred in that it seeks to divert the representation from the primacy of character and dramatic action, not to deny them, but to disrupt the gaze that can be focused on them and to propose other focal points or points of attachment to the imagination and the emotion of the spectator.

This is the case in the work of Frédéric Fisbach, in which, as we have said before, the chorality of the performers is posed as the primary framework and cementing element of the *mise en scène*. Moored in very precise rules that render unstable the conventional fusion of interpreter and character, the work allows Fisbach to play on the gaps and slips that create resonances of the absent and virtual, places of emotion in which the spectator can invest their imagination, their emotion and can re-think their relation to the world. The chorality of the interpreters is, consequently, the natural base on which a formal work is built, by means of which the representation multiplies the reading surfaces for the spectator, if only in the first place, by giving them an opportunity to circulate between the place of representation and the space of fiction, between real presences and imaginary ones. But it is also to organise another relationship to the text, because this formal approach (the form of the text, the form of representation) represents a *detour*. An *indirect* textual approach, if we want to hear it, not in the sense that it would become unmoored from the fiction or from the meaning carried by it, but inasmuch as form is a revealer and proposes an entry point and a journey into the otherness of the work.

It is in this sense that one must understand the "formalism" that characterises many current practices: on the basis of the refusal, which we have already mentioned, of naturalism and of a conception of meaning as explicitly constructed by the stage. The mediation that is form becomes a means of opening, for the spectator, one or two other ways of grasping the text and the sensations organised on the stage. This is a means, not only of decentring and dismantling hierarchy, but also of maintaining an essential polyphony and polysemy, that which the spectator must inhabit. Fisbach thus notes:

> I am not working on form for the sake of form: form, for me, is like a tint that one applies to the text to better reveal it – form is a revealer, as in photography [. . .] In essence, I always work from the periphery; I always approach the text from the outside, from the point of view of form. I try to approach it in a way that destabilises the understanding that one may have of it. I create a different rhythm, in other words, a form that reveals.[58]

It is a process of displacement, a shift of point of view, in which the role of the spectator is questioned. By othering the work, one can, paradoxically, establish a more intimate relationship.

Let us return to the example of Fisbach's staging of Claudel's *L'Annonce faite à Marie* (1996). We have spoken about the representation and how it departed from the mimetic norm. The demonstration of the text itself was moored in the chorality of the interpreters, who shared the same rules of play and diction. However, the choral form (breath, voice, etc.) shifts and diffracts meaning, offering it differently to the spectator, through a detour that creates distance from the fable, the characters, etc. But this form is also given as rules of the game that the spectator gradually learns to share, to recognise and through which they can enter the movement of writing and so, finally, the narrative. Form is a way of accompanying and, even more, of building an emotional progression for reception. It causes what is said to be heard in a different way. In a certain way, it relativises what is said, making it a layer of reception, but on which the representation is not centred. Theatricality is not then in mimetic figuration, but, *first and foremost*, in the emotional movement developed by form and its evolution, a movement *through which* the spectator nevertheless reaches the emotion of fiction, but *indirectly*. As such, the formalisation of the musicality of writing constitutes a detour, which establishes in the first place a distance compared to the norms and traditional expectations of dramatic illusion, and this distance of the form, if it can have a critical function, especially establishes another relationship sensitive to the text: it is therefore an emotional distance, based on a paradoxical expression. And between the emotion of fiction, the emotion of form and the emotion proper to the sensitive presence of the performers, the spectator is made to navigate, as these autonomous layers necessarily play with each other.

The *mise en scène* of Racine's *Bérénice*, which Fisbach created in 1999 in collaboration with the choreographer Bernardo Montet, may offer an even more complex example. The work on language was complemented by choreographic work on the body, which created unusual affects and networks of emotions. Moreover, the very construction of the performance was based on successive transformations of forms and codes of representation. The show began on the principle of a dissociation of bodies and voices: the actor-dancers came on to the stage from the first row, and danced their characters, or more precisely an idea of their characters (since the spectator could not distinguish who was playing who). Meanwhile, from a boom box placed in the auditorium, a set of voices started speaking the text, and only then did individual voices gradually begin to be distinguished. It was only at the beginning of Act 2 that the text came on to the stage (in other words, started being spoken by the individual bodies of the performers). Initially, the text was a less than fully "embodied" discourse; it was a formalised and almost citational Racinean alexandrine: separated from the audience by a transparent plastic curtain, Titus and Paulin stood face to face and static around a suspended microphone of the kind that one might find in radio studios. Gradually, on the basis of the text's form and the performer's presence, something like the character appeared, the fiction took shape. A stage space consisting of movable glass panels, through which the bodies could be seen and in which they were reflected, was created in Act 3. Essentially, this sliding apparatus configured and reconfigured spaces. The diction and play became more "embodied", more expressive of the passions and tragedy of *Bérénice*, even if the staging apparatus continued to subdue their effects, until the culminating moment in Act 4, Scene 5 – the great confrontation of Titus and Bérénice. But this scene was followed by a new shift in the mode of theatricality: the performance moved into the auditorium, and the actors/performers began to play on a simple table among the spectators. They began to play at being masters and, what is more, some of them reversed sexes (Paulin becoming Bérénice, Phénice becoming Titus). After this carnival reversal, the tragedy ended with a return to the stage. The three main protagonists (Titus, Bérénice, Antiochus) could then be seen in the dim light, appearing and disappearing under a thin stream of infra-red light, their voices made distant by the use of HF microphones. They were now dressed in mythical toga: it was as if the representation was fading and the figures were now being enshrined in the collective imagination.

In this *mise en scène* of Bérénice, we find some the principles already encountered in *L'Annonce faite à Marie*: the formalism, the play of oscillation between the concrete presences of the performers and the fictitious presences of the characters, a decentring of the representation, reinforced in *Bérénice* by the fact that the performers stay on the edge of the stage and move the glass panels throughout the central part of representation. And the use of dance intensified all these principles. Thus, the whole representation was played out in an in-between space, between the presence of the actors and dancers as performers and that of the characters of the fiction in the spectator's imagination, but also between formal plastic space and fictional virtual space. We also see how the performance produced a shifting of forms; how, formally, it became protean; and how play was thereby shown from different points of view, as if the spectator were able to move around it. This sliding of forms was a carefully crafted aspect of the performance: its function was to produce a sensation of progression. Bodies and voices are dissociated at the start, then gradually become associated. However, the connection between body and voice remains relative until the big Titus and Bérénice scene. Following this scene, we then return to a disconnect between character and actor/performer, and then to *figures* charged with all the imaginary of the performance up to that point –figures displayed in a half-light. The show then ends with a sense of the imagination proper to collective memory. As such, the *mise en scène* was a trajectory through the different possible relationships to the work, which is, depending on the viewpoint, a story of bodies (warriors and lovers – forced and desiring), an elegiac poem, an oratorio in Alexandrines, a dramatic fiction or a classic text whose figures belong to collective memory and the imagination. Fisbach and Montet thus presented a *Bérénice* in perpetual motion, a representation diffracting and slowly multiplying the points of view on the text, like the glass panels whose mobility configured the space. And the spectator was thus invited to see various declensions of the tragic and its relation to a "classical" work, which then became simultaneously distant and foreign, close and familiar. Not only were they following the fable and the performers, but they were also witnessing the appearance and the erasure of the fiction, a metamorphosis of forms that instilled an emotional progression through the various relationships that one can have with this play, with its characters and its memory. Here again, strata are intertwined and the weaving thus created leads to a de-centred representation. In their weaving and in the spaces they construct, the spectator establishes their path, implements their own imaginary *play* between the text and the scenic image, body and voice, the present of the stage and the past of the work. *De-centring* the representation is thus to create for the spectator strata of reception that go beyond mere fictional mimesis; it is to play on the modalities of their reception by proposing several layers of reading, rather than build a single mimetic system; it is about working on the theatre's own play by creating "gaps between things: the distance that separates an actor from a character, an actor from the fiction [...] At the centre of the theatre is the spectator: they can only rely on themselves, the centre is no longer a given".[59]

Other distances, other presences

So we come back, again, to the matter of polyphony and the activation of the spectator, which we know to be inherent in all theatricality, but whose specific organisation and intensification arguably constitute, as we have seen, the most widely shared aesthetic aspiration among contemporary practitioners. We also come back to the conception of the stage as a specific space in which perception is questioned, explored and unsettled – we have already mentioned this above, especially in our discussion of Claude Régy's work. For the most part, current practices turn their backs on both naturalism and the construction of a demonstrative network of signs, preferring instead what can be considered as the "estrangement effect" [*étrangéification*] of representation. They are clearly based on a refusal of dramatic illusion. And this "estrangement effect" is a mechanism of "alienation". And in point of fact, the German term *Verfremdung*, used by Brecht, captures both notions (even if the term "alienation effect" has traditionally been used by translators[60]). It must be recognised, however, that such practices are not exactly based on a Brechtian theatre aesthetic and that the "work" (to use Regy's term) demanded of the spectator of such representations is not the same as that implied by the *critical* distance of "epic" theatre. The latter is supposed to allow a more analytical and detached reception of the represented fiction. However, while they do not in any way reject the use of reason, these representations seek, first and foremost, to activate the imagination and rely on a certain form, not of illusion but of *presence*, of empathy: an empathy that comes from the emotion produced by form, by the embodied presence of the performers or of the various visual elements. And while a certain binary opposition had been established, particularly post-Brecht, between empathy, the projective involvement [*capitation*] of the spectator produced by dramatic mimesis and the critical distance of the Brechtian epic, contemporary theatre is now re-theorising the spectator–theatre relationship, by complicating this binary opposition. Presence, distance, empathy and strangeness are being redistributed.

While many contemporary theatrical practices reject mimetic illusionism and do not seek to engage the spectator solely through fictional credibility, they nevertheless produce other distances and other "presences", which come from a desire to captivate the spectator. But this "captivation" is of a specific kind, it is a non-illusionist captivation that exerts itself on the spectator's physical faculties of perception, attaches itself to the various modes of presence and intensity at play on the stage, relates to the sensuous categories of perception and is based on the ontological and phenomenological experience of space, void, light, sound, material or the physical presence of the actor. As such, the issue is no longer to engage the spectator through fiction in its progress and actions, its mimicry and its suspense – in other words, in its *dramatic* essence. Indeed, captivation can, and does (in contemporary theatre), function in the absence of the theatrical text, or by complicating its reception. Such a *phenomenological distance* thus thwarts the traditional dramatic logic of theatre, but *also* the epic logic that highlights the very act of narration and privileges the reflective powers of the spectator.

It thus plays on the presence of the objects of the stage, transcending the primacy of the representation of narrative and of characters or in a potential disjunction from them. This distance is also a "plastic" one, fostering contemplation and aesthetic fascination.

What we have discussed above represents quite a change in how theatrical *emotion* is conceived, since this shift, or decentring, takes the form of a "disjunction of the affect of representation", to use the words of Georges Didi-Huberman.[61] We could also, more simply, speak of a shift of emotion. For that is what it is, in line with contemporary issues that arise in the theatre as we have seen previously. Given recent moves that question the powers of theatricality, that reject the spectacular effect and the "hysteria" of an over-representation of passions, and given attempts to open the theatrical act to the freedom and imagination of its receiver, there is now a focus on how the theatre can elicit affect without succumbing to the pitfalls of illustration or overacting. The stage can then be considered a poetic place without being a place of spectacle, it can produce emotions and sensibility without duplicating textual fiction in an illustrative way, it can be a site of artistic experience, rather than of consumption and consensus of feeling. Phenomenological distancing is not, therefore, a question of denying or defusing emotion, but of unframing it, in various ways, to reconfigure and reactivate its circulations – to remove all hierarchies within its operation and production.

Given the hermeneutical withdrawal that we have described above – but without necessarily giving up the dimension of the text or its status as a site of fiction – it is not surprising that contemporary theatre borrows from other artistic references such as dance, music or installation. It is not surprising either that it is conceived as an art of form, an art of materiality, an art of presence or that it works on *non-demonstrative presences*, on their "being-there". This brings us back to what we were saying above, with respect to Klaus-Michael Grüber's theatre, as well as Gilles Aillaud's sets, for example, about which Jean Jourdheuil recalls that they "restore the *aura* of the work of art",[62] that they attach themselves to a physical individuality and its material density, and not to their place in a semiological system of communication. We also notice some evolutions in scenography, whether in the use that is made of certain materials (wood, glass or plastic, for instance) and the way they are enhanced by the lighting specialists. And finally, it will be recalled that certain scenographers, like Daniel Jeanneteau, for example, try to produce, from figurative or non-figurative spaces, a phenomenological and sensitive experience of space, far beyond the mere functionality of scenery.

As objects of a phenomenological and aesthetic experience, these non-demonstrative presences thus participate in the decentring and diffraction of reception, not presupposing a community of meaning and common references or participating in a communication process. These presences initially escape the grasp of the spectator, who is consequently incited to rediscover and re-appropriate the theatre's unique and specific communication protocols, all this in the common space of the present time of the representation.

Deconstructing/reconstructing theatricality

If the illusionistic theatricality is to be shifted, deviated, decentred, diffracted, it must also be deconstructed, assembled and disassembled. Its conventions must be played with, as must its presuppositions. Just as the concrete reality of performance is sometimes unsettled, so theatricality becomes itself a material that can be exhibited to better denounce and exalt both its artificiality. Thus, in numerous theatrical works, theatricality itself becomes the object of the performance: Its spectacularity and its deceptiveness are played with (whether through irony or for sheer enjoyment). The pure freedom of the actor is sometimes displayed in all its subversiveness. The mechanics of staging are shown, so they can be criticised, reinforced or questioned.

To question the theatre, and particularly its dramatic heritage, is also to play on montage and on the association of disparate materials. This happens at the level of the textual material, first of all, insofar as non-dramatic but also non-fictional texts are brought to the stage and integrated into a dramaturgical structure without the works then being considered "theatrical adaptations" or dramatisations. Such staged works reject a canonical theatricality and the labels that go along with it. What is emphasised is their specificity and the particular ways in which they engage with space or with other objects. Underlying such moves is a desire to escape the mimetic model and to transform the stage into a site of experience and tension, not in a random way but by reconstructing new *dramaturgies*. This is what Jean Jourdheuil and Jean-François Peyret dedicated themselves to, in exemplary fashion, in the 1980s, when they brought to the stage passages from Montaigne *Essais* (*Le Rocher, la lande, la librairie* [*The Rock, the Moor, the Bookshop*], 1982) in a space (designed by Gilles Aillaud) filled with cartons that the actors moved throughout the performance. Jourdheuil and Peyret also staged Shakespeare's *Sonnets* within a scenery that was a reproduction (also designed by Gilles Aillaud) of Holbein's painting *The Ambassadors*, and also Lucretia's *De Rerum*

Natura in a scenery created by painter-scenographer Titina Maselli in the auditorium of the MC 93 (rather than on the stage). The last two shows also featured the music of Philippe Hersant, which offered a counterpoint to the work's text, play and space. And it should be noted that, at the same time, Jourdheuil and Peyret were also working on a staging of Heiner Müller's texts in France. These are therefore texts written for the theatre, but subverting or abandoning the framework of dramatic theatre. They are based themselves on a principle of montage, and imply on the stage a similar principle of autonomisation, juxtaposition and contrast of objects. Building other dramaturgies from non-dramatic materials is what Jourdheuil and Peyret continue to do, by turning the stage into a site of epistemological investigations. An example is Jourdheuil's staging of Foucault's writings in a space-installation by Mark Lammert (*Michel Foucault, choses dites choses vues* [*Michel Foucault, Things Said, Things Seen*], 2004).[63]

Diffracting the traditional categories of representation (text, play, space, music) is not only to allow to each a margin of play in the arrangement constructed by staging, but to truly de-hierarchise their relations in order to emphasise their coexistence and tensions in scenic forms that transcend generic distinctions. These trans-generic moves underscore hybridisation, without subscribing to the principle of a "total" theatre, since, rather than a desire for simple convergence, they are principles of friction, interaction and even shock that are thus established between different "arts" or the different constituents of the stage. Text and theatricality, strictly speaking, are brought into relationship with the plastic arts, video, dance, music, and so on. One example of such interaction (an *interplay* in the truest sense) is the creations of composer-director Heiner Goebbels, that fluctuate between musical shows and stage concerts: *Où bien le débarquement désastreux* [*Or the Hopeless Landing*] (1998) brings together electro-acoustic music, texts by Müller, Conrad and Ponge voiced by André Wilms, and a plastic space designed by Klaus Grünberg (*Eraritjaritjaka, musée des phrases* [*Eraritjaritjaka, Museum of Sentences*] 2004), which articulated aphorisms by Elias Canetti voiced by the same André Wilms. This production also included the presence of the Mondrian quartet onstage, performing musical excerpts from classical and contemporary repertoires, associating them with a dramaturgy of space and light and with the use of the video medium.

Indeed, the deconstruction of hierarchical relations between different elements of *mises en scène* and the diffraction of the spectator's perception have been affected, for some time, by the use of what are generally referred to as "new technologies". These allow for a plastic shaping, in real time, of the signs produced by the stage. This is how sounds can be mixed, distorted, duplicated or modulated by simultaneous (or slightly delayed) technical processes when they are carried out on the staging platform, as we have seen in the passage we devoted earlier to that phenomenon. We see this in Ludovic Lagarde's staging of texts by Olivier Cadiot (themselves what Cadiot refers to as a hybrid "novel-theatre-poetry") such as *Le Colonel des zouaves* [*The Colonel of the Zouaves*] in 2001 or *Retour définitif et durable de l'être aimé* [*Definitive and Lasting Return of the Loved One*] in 2002. This is how directors can also integrate notions of interactivity and virtuality proper to new media, for example by producing on the stage, from an interface enabled by sensors fixed on the bodies of actors, virtual organisms governed by artificial intelligence (Pasolini's *Orgia*, directed by Jean Lambert-Wild in 2001). This is how screens can invade the stage.

The integration of new technologies into the theatre is most clearly observable in the use of video. The two-dimensional image is integrated into the three-dimensional stage, the virtuality and mechanical reproduction of the cinematic medium form surprising interplays with the theatre's real and unmediated presence and the frame of the stage with that of the screen. This allows for oscillations and shifts in points of view and scales, and for a fragmentation – or a focusing – of perception. The use of video to enlarge the staging space (creating "real" documentary spaces or imaginary spaces) in *mise en scene* is not new: from the experiments of Giorgio Barberio Corsetti's experiments, such as *La Camera Astratta* [*The Abstract Room*] (1987), to the productions of the Canadian Robert Lepage (*Elsineur*, 1996; *Les Sept branches de la rivière Ota* [*The Seven Branches of the River Ota*], 1996–1998), video has long been a means of extending the possibilities of representation on the stage, of amplifying or diffracting the imagination of the spectator by appealing to images of the "world" outside or to the imagination of "inner" spaces. Moreover, the latest musical and choreographic performances of José Montalvo (Rameau's *Les Paladins* at Châtelet in 2004, *On danSe* at Chaillot in 2005) attest to the impact of previously filmed video introduced organically into the performance as an element of illusion that disrupts the spectator's perception of time.

But another unique quality of video, unlike the cinematographic image that always represents the past, is its ability to film and broadcast live. It is thus coterminous with the stage time itself, becoming a mirror of it, since it not only introduces another medium, but its presence creates a tension within the theatrical act. We will cite two recent examples, where the use of video, besides critically evoking television culture, produces a certain deconstruction of theatricality.

A usual process in Frank Castorf's latest shows is to add to his partially live images (broadcast on the stage) the presence of cameramen on the set. Additionally, actions performed offstage are filmed live behind the scenery, thereby extending the stage space. The actors can thus leave the set and continue to be followed by the spectators, through the mediation of the video image. Castorf's use of video thus ironic evokes the principles of reality TV, critiques the spectacularisation of reality and intimacy and satirises the global television aesthetic of soap opera. In addition, this use of video also puts the stage into crisis: there are frequent moments in Castorf's *mises en scène* when the vast, congested stage remains empty for a long time while the spectator watches an action taking place offstage – but just behind the scenery. Castorf's camera does not offer the marvels and illusions of cinema: his video images are of very poor quality. And even when he uses the screens to parody American cinema, he emphasises the artificiality of the effects of trashy images. Notwithstanding, the video is a way of capturing the actor up close, of showing and tracking them more intimately, especially through the use of close-ups and the framing and montage that usually accompany them. It forces the spectator to take stock of what is being shown to them as well as what is being hidden. Consequently, as a device that opens up other forms of representation and parodies media images, Castorf's use of video ruptures the illusion of theatre as much as its own, in a postmodern deconstruction of representation. A deconstruction that can be found at all levels of Castorf's work: as we have already seen with his production of *My Snow Queen*, this deconstruction is effected through the often exaggerated play of the actors, by a principle of montage, by accumulation at the level of scenography as well as of text and by the parody of cultural references.[64]

In a less parodic way, and with heightened ambiguity, *Eraritjaritjaka, musée des phrases*, Heiner Goebbels' production (2004), which we mentioned earlier, also replaced the presence of the actor onstage with their video image. In the middle of the performance, the lone actor, André Wilms, leaves the room, followed by a cameraman. Through video images, the audience sees him leaving the theatre and getting into a taxi that drops him in front of the door of a building, which he enters, climbing the stairs and finally opening a door that leads into an apartment: the apartment of his "character": Wilms explores the rooms while continuing to recite his aphorisms. He works at the desk, reads the newspaper of the day, cooks eggs in the kitchen, goes upstairs. All this was projected, on the stage, on the house facade that formed the backdrop. It was not until the end of the show, when the windows of the facade were opened, that the viewer perceived, or had confirmation (if they had already suspected it), that the actor had never left the theatre: the entire sequence of the apartment was actually filmed live, but behind the stage, where the apartment was fully reconstituted. The video had thus served to represent a journey and to create in the audience a perception of intimacy, albeit played out in an artificially duplicated space. But the video was not only there to produce an effect and an illusion: while the space of the house metaphorised the intimate space of Canetti's notebooks – which constituted the textual material – and, more broadly, the appropriation of the world by the individual – a theme that the performance explored – the video reinforced the feeling of wandering (first in the city, in a taxi, then in a private space), and established, in the very ambiguity of its status within the scenic representation, the idea a motionless journey, a blurring of the demarcations of interior and exterior space. Ultimately, the performance created an image of a mental space. All of this was made to work with the music and the presence onstage of the Mondrian Quartets, who continued to play in the space left empty by the actor.

It is possible for video projection to completely replace the real presence of the actor, as in Denis Marleau's staging of Maeterlinck's *Les Aveugles* in 2002, a "technological phanstasmagoria", in his words, that activated the strangest potentialities of virtual presence. The twelve characters of Maeterlinck's "static drama" were performed by only two actors (Céline Bonnier and Paul Savoie), but, even more, they were not present on the stage, nor even played simultaneously during the performance. It was on the moulded masks of their faces, multiplied and illuminated in an otherwise obscure space, that the images of their faces were projected, silent or whispering the text, depending on the moment. They became animated effigies, spectral presence-absences. Only a limited number of spectators could enter the room at a time. They knew in advance that there was a technological aspect to the performance. Nevertheless, in most cases, they could not refrain from searching for the two living "source" presences (corresponding to the two names on the programme) among the twelve video-animated faces. In fact, they continued to do so until a projector lit up the device at the end of the show, illuminating the twelve inanimate masks and revealing the complete absence of the actors. The video projection thus completely replaced the very principle of theatricality (the actor's living presence in front of the spectators), but not to substitute for it its own, two-dimensional image. Instead, by giving "life" to the masks, it created a different kind of illusion, whereby the spectator was faced with the virtual presence of the actor, with a kind of *double* of the theatre.

Contemporary *mise en scène* has thus questioned, rejected or deconstructed dramatic illusion. It has diffracted the ways in which performances can be "read" by the spectator and made this spectator question their own status and perception. It has experimented with performance space and has deconstructed the realism of space. It has questioned the aptitude of the theatrical precinct itself to constitute a space of representation. Finally, it has problematised the body, the voice and the utterance of the text, turning them into mouldable materials. And now it seems to have arrived at a general deconstruction, of an overarching character: it seems to be concerned with the temporal parameter of theatricality. This is why, in these major deconstructionist moves, it has not ceased, in recent times, to disturb the spatio-temporal order, through the use of the video image. Because the moving image has a greater degree of credibility than the mere presence of a body on a stage, cinematic projection could potentially threaten staging, or overshadow it. However, as we have said, when this image is simply filmed, it must give up the present-ness of its effect. This is why video is crucial, because it attributes to the image a present time that film cannot claim, and in this, it disrupts and impacts, with even more power, the real movement of the bodies that move and speak on the stage. Thus, the all-powerful moving image challenges head-on the world of real bodies. The spectators, witnesses to this violent confrontation, know how much the theatrical stage has already been deconstructed in various ways. Consequently, they doubt everything while clinging to the false reality of a mediocre image, the one they see every day on TV and of which they know the fascinating inauthenticity. All they have left to do is to enjoy the ruins of representation, to laugh or cry at the futility of meaning, images and forms, and to consider that the moment in which they watch the spectacle is nothing but the uncertain moment of a performance. What they do know, however, or what they still believe they know, is that they are there bound together by the transaction to which they have consented, and in which they are included. Through their own free will, they partake in a social de-sacralised, self-conscious ritual, which is being eroded even as it critiques and defines itself. So, what this assembly sees, hears and verifies by its very presence is: matter that is, objects, bodies, movements and their sounds.

The "postdramatic"

As we can see, a considerable part of contemporary theatre sets out to shift the principles of mimetic representation and drama. Such an enterprise is not new in itself: from Bob Wilson to avant-garde theatres to performance, the critique of this model is old, as we have seen earlier. Significantly, however, it is spread over a broad set of practices and generates larger questions about the very nature of a practice – the theatre – that seeks to reaffirm its specificity in relation to the other modes of representation that dominate the contemporary world. The questioning of perception, the decentring of representation and the diffracted play of its constituents, the experience of the presentness of the stage and the real presences that constitute it, the obvious involvement of the spectator in the construction of meaning and the organisation of the "fiction" presented to them, are admittedly "natural" properties of *mise en scène*. Nevertheless, current practices strikingly testify to a desire to accentuate and redouble their effects, in a specific mutation of theatrical forms. Thus, the German critic Hans-Thies Lehmann defines this evolution as a "postdramatic" theatre, the establishment of an aesthetic of which we can establish a certain number of common properties.

What Lehmann means by the term "postdramatic" is the disappearance of the "patterns which, conventionally speaking, made action the mainstay of theatre", chief of which is the "narrative, storytelling description of the world by means of mimesis":[65] in a word, this involves the disappearance of the traditional dramatic model. But, more broadly, the postdramatic deconstructs the whole hierarchy on which the canonical logic of representation relies: it is above all, a theatre that "dethrones synthesis", one in which the theatrical signs are presented to the spectators outside of any unified and visibly coherent regime of representation. For the experience of meaning constructed by the stage, the postdramatic substitutes a decentralised, disoriented, perception: "a postdramatic theatre manifestly embodies the exigency of an open, fragmented perception, rather than a unifying and cohesive approach". As such, Lehmann adds, "Theatre articulates through the mode of its semiosis an implicit thesis concerning perception",[66] and "Synthesis is sacrificed in order to gain, in its place, the density of intense moments".[67]

Consequently, here again, Lehmann describes the urge to transform the spectator into an enabled partner, and to achieve, as much as possible, a theatre that is lived as an experience in and of the *present*, in opposition to the mediated system of *re*presentation. In other words, the stakes Lehmann has identified are the urge to transform the audience from a passive consumer of culture and the affirmation of the specificity of the theatrical relationship as "a slice of past life lived in a community by actors and spectators in the atmosphere of a *shared* space where theatrical play encounters the receptive act of the spectator".[68] Thus, the postulate of the postdramatic is that the show has no *raison d'être* without the participative presence of a spectator turned co-producer, co-author, through their personal mental arrangement of signifiers that the stage puts into circulation. The spectator, in a word, is a builder of a meaning that is "deferred", since it is not constructed independently of experience.

This participative presence thus leads the spectator to record sensory impressions in erratic, indeterminate ways, unstructured by a commonly shared semiotic and representational framework. Since, as we have seen, the presupposition of a constituted theatrical community is in crisis, this theatre, according to Lehmann, finds "points of convergence beyond the individual" only in "the theatrical realisation of freedom – freedom from hierarchies, freedom from the imperative of completion, freedom from the requirement of coherence". And, forced to stand out in a mediatised civilisation, the theatre abandons the mimetic and illusionist logic of drama, which is the mainstay of the dominant media, to reaffirm its specificity of act and experience, to emphasise its qualities: its irreducible present-ness and the virtuality that underpins its relationality. In this respect, it cultivates its performative nature, its desire "more for presence than for representation, more for shared experience than for transmission, more for process than for result, manifestation more than meaning, impulse of energy rather than information".[69]

In light of the above, Lehmann has established what he considers to be the main characteristics of the postdramatic, stylistic traits emblematic of such practices. In the first place, *parataxis* or non-hierarchy and *simultaneity*, both of which lead to a "fragmentation of perception", which in turn implies a "postponement of meaning". Such postponement is not a lack but a liberating potential of imagining and recombining objects. To this is logically added a "play with the density of signs"[70] (since it is the whole traditional semiotic organisation that is modified), one that is based on economy and "deprivation" (such as in the work of Claude Régy or that of Klaus Michael Grüber, to use examples we have already mentioned) or, on the contrary, on plethora (the chaotic accumulation that often characterises Frank Castorf's performances, or even Matthias Langhoff's, both discussed earlier). Diverted from an assigned function within an all-encompassing and determining structure, the theatrical sign offers itself to the spectator in a resistance or an over-determination that partly empowers them. More broadly, they are global semiotic networks that become autonomous in relation to the overall scenic construction: Lehmann thus distinguishes *musicalisation* from the visual dimension of the work (the visual *dramaturgy*) (we discussed this distinction earlier on). He also insists on *corporeality*, and more precisely, on the idea of a "self-sufficient corporeality", identifying by this expression a foregrounding of bodily presence "not as a carrier of meaning, but in its physical substance and gestural potential", its non-explicit tensions and intensities. Finally, in discussing the *irruption of the real*, Lehmann emphasises postdramatic theatre's delight in ambiguity and in the indeterminacy of the boundaries between fiction and reality, and of the sign's resistance to one or the other of these two spaces. Reality is then the object of a self-reflexive aesthetic and therefore brings the postdramatic theatre, in many cases, closer to performance and to the happening, whereby a final characteristic trait can be observed: the *situation/event*.

The term "postdramatic theatre" does not stand for a particular genre or *form* of theatre: it covers the various practices that we have discussed in this chapter, and consist of approaches that have recently appeared, but also of others that are already very old. The fact that Lehmann cites Kantor, Grüber and Wilson as leading figures in the genealogy of the postdramatic is telling. The postdramatic is a spectrum more than a genre or a type of theatre. It is, in our opinion, an umbrella concept that testifies to a mutation in certain forms of theatricality: it does not represent a model, but a general tendency towards the construction of another conception of the stage, itself underpinned by a reconsideration of the theatrical relationship, of the specificities that constitute it, and of the role of the spectator. In a word, it encapsulates a trend that we have already seen at work in the previous pages. More than a specific structure, and beyond the different modes of scenic rearrangement that it describes, it represents a general displacement of the regimes of the theatrical sign, and a reshaping of the categories of perception. The "postdramatic" describes moves in the theatre that allow the spectator to encounter other distances and other presences (to use our expression from above), based on a theatrical relationship of differing degrees of intensity, on personal "labyrinthine associations". The signs of postdramatic theatre are the "'mute' immediacy of bodies, materials and shapes". By putting mimesis and its own fiction into crisis, postdramatic theatre probably finds the centre of its problematic in what Lehmann calls a "theatre of perceptibility", which "underlines the incompletion and incompletion of perception".[71]

Depending on the particular extent to which theatrical signs are refashioned, the spectator can note the ways in which staged productions shift and transgress the most traditional practices that they know. They can also observe theatrical forms that not only radically reject the dramatic model, but also the idea of narration. They will also be confronted with dramatic texts and/or performances that break entirely with conventional notions of fiction and with performance spaces that produce multiple layers of affects and sensations and rearranges perceptions and senses. They will then have to approach these *mises en scène* by abandoning the prerequisites that they usually have.

The spectrum of the postdramatic is broad, and so are its various forms. Indeed, Lehmann speaks of an entire "galaxy". There is no point, therefore, of transforming it into a category into which a performance or production fits or does not fit, and all the more since the characteristics of postdramaticity can be recognised in works that still subscribe to the representation of a fiction. Instead, one should see how these issues are worked out in a performance, how they work together and what shifts they imply with respect to traditional expectations. In sum, the notion of "*mise en* scène" must also be approached differently.

To illustrate this, we will focus on an example from France that manifests such a radical shift and in which we will find many of the characteristics just mentioned: the work of François Tanguy and the Théâtre du Radeau. This theatre began with the representation of dramatic texts (*Dom Juan*, 1982; *A Midsummer Night's Dream*, 1985). However, Tanguy's productions have quickly moved away from the traditional staging model and have become more personal creations, which, though based on a dramatic repertoire, overturn the codes of narrativity (*Woyzeck: Fragments Forains* [*Woyzeck: Fairground Fragments*], 1989), before completely freeing themselves from this model. The shows arrange fragments of literature not necessarily written for theatre. Some are borrowed from Kafka (*Choral*, 1994; *The Battle of Tagliamento*, 1996, which derives its title from a dream recounted in the diary of the Prague author), or the poetry of Hölderlin, Dante, Walser, Nietzsche, Péguy, Artaud, Gadda, among others. Tanguy creates soundtracks (vocal or orchestral works, Bach, Schubert, Verdi, Shostakovich or Luigi Nono, among others), not as a decorative element but as an essential constituent of his theatrical world, that feeds its dynamics and its emotion. Significantly, since *Orphéon* (1997), Tanguy's use of speech has moved far away from the dramatic model. Indeed, the words uttered by his performers are from different kinds of texts – theatrical, narrative, lyrical – of various origins brought together through a principle of montage. These texts are uttered or whispered, sometimes moreover in their (original) foreign languages. Therefore, the textual material is therefore never delivered according to traditional expressivity and audibility, nor attributed to figures that acquire the status of characters. Moreover, they are never tasked with building a fable. Instead, they are texts that exist on a par with the other elements of the show, the music in particular, with which they form different interplays, sometimes being carried, at other times being submerged, by it. In short, Tanguy's Théâtre du Radeau has changed a lot from its beginnings – *Les Cantates* [*The Cantatas*] (2001) or *Coda* (2005) are proof of it – and will continue to do so.

Tanguy's theatre is thus, in the first instance, a non-dramatic theatre (one does not really distinguish characters or roles, it does not represent conflict) or even narrative (he does not tell a linear story or build a network of cohesive meaning). It is exemplary of Lehman's "galaxy" of postdramatic theatre. Built on the montage principle, associating texts of various origins, theatrical or extra-theatrical (extracts of Greek or Shakespearean tragedies, fragments of Kafka or Artaud, poems of Hölderlin, fragments of Nietzsche and so on) that it constellates without weaving them into the thread of a story, it is a fragmentary theatre by nature. But these fragments are neither organised in the hierarchy of a continuous semantic construction, nor, for all that, abandoned to their fragmentation and to a simple succession of isolated tableaux. The play of the sequences that make up the show and, in the same way, the relations between the different elements simultaneously present on the stage within the same sequence, rest on their contiguity and on the tension between them. David Lescot, in analysing *Orphéon*, thus speaks of a "dreamlike syntax"[72] that characterises the configuration of the Théâtre du Radeau's performances. They are marked by discontinuity, juxtaposition, heterogeneity, as well as overlap, superposition and reciprocal disruption of the constituents, and thus establish a general shift in the spectator's categories of perception in regard to what the stage presents to them. The sequences that are linked in these shows form a very strong organicity. However, it is neither causal, thematic or semantic, but one of movement and permanent transformation, of sliding rather than the constitution of a determined, completed whole. This organicity is, moreover, always essentially marked by precariousness and manifested by the whole stage: thus, the scenic spaces are created, in permanent reconfigurations, around a few white panels that are sometimes lined with wallpaper, a few tables and chairs. And this space is not only moving but is not, strictly speaking, centred: even when the stage is deep, the stage play is rarely carried out in the middle of the platform. Instead, it favours the extreme forestage or the extreme downstage, when it is not playing simultaneously in these two different planes.

What goes for time, that is for the progression of the successive sequences, also goes for the simultaneity of the different elements (light, image, voice, soundtrack, body, text) and therefore for the sensory perceptions that the stage allows. These elements interplay but do not converge or merge: the platform functions based on rules of superimposition and disjunction. For example, at the beginning of the *Cantates*, an actor stands in the centre of the stage but against the light. He is like a shadow, uttering with tragic urgency and rhythmic intensity a text in Italian, with a cantata playing in the background and partly covering his voice. Later, another actor murmurs a soliloquy from Shakespeare in English. Later still, a sound loop carries a text by Plutarch spoken by a barely audible actress. Another example: in *Orphéon*, an actor seems to fervently recite Priam's great soliloquy in *Hamlet*, but we then realise that the excessive voice is somebody else's, broadcast by the soundtrack. Additionally, Tanguy frequently has two images, or two simultaneous "scenes", coexist on the stage: thus, in the *Cantates*, a male figure gently says an elegiac text, while at the back of the stage a female figure is getting dressed. The spectator can't decide whether they should search for a fictional link between these two figures or if there are two absolutely distinct scenes juxtaposed on the set.

As such, the elements *co-exist*, without being organised in explicit or even established relationships. Elegiac texts can be accompanied by pathetic music and conversely, and even the voices that are heard do not necessarily come out of the body that seems to carry them. This disjunction therefore affects the unstable and ever-changing relationships between the sensory objects and perceptions that the stage exhibits. These relationships are not organised based on hierarchy, but on disturbance, openness and *co-presence*. The interplay and organic unity of this stage is created by permanent movement – in other words, by an active co-presence. So that, in this deeply dynamic theatre, everything circulates, everything moves and everything is permanently transformed. There are no interruptions that would allow fixed images to be established. There are, for example, no blackouts in Tanguy's shows, and we have seen that scenes and movements of panels, but also entrances and exits of actors, overlap constantly, in plain sight. The theatre seeks to evoke images and a sense of their emergence, before they stabilise in a form that would reduce or freeze them immediately.

Accordingly, movement is fundamental in the sensory experience of the stage. Everything becomes a matter of flux, but also of intensities, of indeterminate affects, such as might arise from music, whether vocal or orchestral. Put differently, his theatre is grounded in a decidedly Deleuzian conception of the sign, in which circulation and instability are essential to any attempt at producing meaning and sensoriality. Therefore, as Jean-Paul Manganaro writes, the actor of the Théâtre du Radeau does not play a situation or in a situation; instead, they are caught in flows, and these flows imply and coordinate movements, leaps, organised interruptions according to dynamics that are opposed to dialectical, historical or psychological functions.[73]

In this sense, we could thus say that movement in Tanguy's theatre functions in a "musical" way. By saying this, we are not assimilating its workings to, say, the quality of a soundtrack. Instead, we are emphasising the fact that it is thought in terms of rhythms, time, tempos, frequencies, modulations and progression of intensities, and expression of non-narrative and non-illustrative affects. We could use the term "musical" also in the sense that the recognition of these affects is not dependent on an external referent of which this theatre would be a mirror in the mimetic sense. The movement of this theatre seems to be one of perpetual self-begetting. All the changes are done on sight, all the sources of sound and light diffusion are on the set, the stage seems directed towards the spectator but it seems to feed only off itself. And the material of Tanguy's work is theatricality itself, or, more precisely, its vestiges, since this theatricality is not a self-satisfied one, but the form of ostensibly obsolete traces. It uses the fragments of a mythical theatrical imagination: dated costumes, a cardboard crown that is enough to indicate the image of fallen Shakespearian kings, paper hats more or less evocative of derisory Harlequins; or Kantorian mannequins, angels with paper wings (choral), fragments of ancient Greek costume, black suits and turn-of-the-century top hats or Kafkaesque-Chaplinesque bowler hats; faces overpainted in white; burlesque sequences, monologues that seek to plumb the deepest intimacies, grand declamations and utterances.

In describing the work of Tanguy, critics often use the word "archaeological": it does indeed evoke the idea of a search, a search for memory, both collective and mythical, one buried in an imaginary that the movement of the stage reactivates and revivifies, unsettles and places into circulation. Fragmentation, juxtaposition and the play of affects and intensities serve this purpose: they are "the sole means of locating the images that populate the depths of our solitudes, of reviving them in our present, of repeating them, and endowing them with a vitality they had lost".[74]

Shared memory can only be approached by means of the interstice; in other words, through tension, thresholds and not on the basis of a pre-established common and presupposed vision. This is why the Théâtre du Radeau's stage exposes, in the words of Tanguy (in the programme of *Cantates*), "a raw material, grounded in splinters, fragmentations, ellipses, spirals of movements, and not in figuration". Lights, sounds, bodies, words are "affects, carving out mnemonic traces, material resonances, sensory mutations, from the spaces". Their capture is not subject to the identification of the object of a representation since the implementation of these materials is not linked to any desire for demonstration. It is therefore in pure immanence that affective and sensory associations occur on the set. This theatre is therefore

> an invitation to re-arrange the perceptions of sites of speech, of intelligibility, of listening, to reshape them based on a sensitivity to movement and imagination, to free them from certain "rules of genre", since we do not view them through the lens of convention and identity – we recognise that this process bids us into another adventure of the senses and perceptions.[75]

Tanguy's theatre is an exchange, a sharing, "an absolutely singular experience and necessarily a shared one" and binds audience and performance.[76] Admittedly, the stage feeds on itself, the scenic factory works autonomously, as we have said above. However, it simultaneously forces a certain mode of empathic co-presence. Not only because it does not give rise to any critical analysis, or because the permanent movement that characterises it is opposed to any principle of interruption, but because it constantly displays affects, whether in the arranged sound of the music, in the vigour of the utterance or in the intimacy suggested by the whisper. In a non-dramatic form, it involves an absolutely emotional and sensory material, and in the greatest semantic opacity, it activates the deepest imaginary of the spectator. Shifting the emotions and configurations of theatrical constituents, this decentralised stage confounds the two dialectical poles of distance and projection, near and far.

The whole paradox of this type of "postdramatic" theatre is that the activation of the spectator's imagination and the shared experience are fostered by a stage, certainly absolutely offered to the spectator's reception, but simultaneously closed on itself, in the sense of being autonomous and self-referential. The Théâtre du Radeau is not part of a mediated communication based on pre-established codes, but it emits and diffuses affects and produces strong perceptions. What Lehmann has identified as a "penchant for solipsism"[77] is also the condition for an experience in the present, and for the stage to defy a logic of re-presentation to regain the acting dimension of its nature. Beyond simulation, a sensuous, sensory reality can thus be born, where the objective is no longer one of producing images strictly speaking, but the act and experience of their emergence.

Such a paradox and ambition are issues that occupy, or have occupied, in a different way, many other practices. We know that in the 1960s, the Italian Carmelo Bene had already carried such deconstruction to the extreme, in a radical subversion of staging that became a "testimony of the impossibility of and the refusal to embody the theatre, or rather the conventions of the theatre", a theatre "with constant breaks and interruptions, and which is always built on the failure of the theatre".[78] Bene thus established a theatre of aphasia and physical failure: actors wandering onstage, stammering bits of inaudible texts, sometimes even just eating onstage before leaving without any performance – at least, the one expected – taking place (*Gregorio, cabaret dell'800*, 1961), voice oscillating from cry to whisper, from acute to severe, breaks and accelerations of rhythm, repetitions of text or gestures, stammering, stuttering, deformed diction, excessively stiff or, alternatively, "slouchy" gestures, accessories impeding movement, actors dressed in seamless costumes that would constantly slip off, hampering their movement and preventing their play (*Salome* by Wilde, 1964). For *Nostra signora dei Turchi* [*Notre-Dame of the Turks*], in 1966, the stage was separated from the audience by a glass wall containing a single French window that was closed most of the time (the scenes were therefore inaudible) and through which at other times objects were thrown into the room. The recorded text was broadcast over the actors' voices. For *Romeo e Giulietta secondo Carmelo Bene* [*Romeo and Juliet according to Carmelo Bene*], in 1976, the set was made up of giant objects and the actors had to act out, as in play-back mode, certain recorded passages. *SADE* (1977) contained an orchestra playing *La Traviata* directed by a leader dressed in a bathing suit, while on the stage the naked body of women represented objects (scenery, table, ashtray, among others). But, above all, these shows were based on Bene himself, the central object, showing himself playing this or that role, in an over-theatricalisation rendered more obvious by his diction inspired by futuristic declamations: whether he was seated on a throne, played two parts in the same scene by putting on or taking off a false beard, whether he refused to die when the character he plays (Mercutio, in *Romeo e Giulietta*) is killed or whether he ends up speaking over the microphone the text of all the other characters in the play. If Bene's exuberant deconstruction of the theatre was a criticism of the facticity of representation, it was also a baroque *way* of bringing it back entirely to the actor and to revitalise the theatrical act as the source of futuristic performance, as a place of subversion but also of intensities, energies and sensations:

those that his declamation and singular voice brought to the stage, founding an aesthetic of "continuous variation" that Deleuze would recognise in this theatre: "There is no subject, only emotions; no form, only speed".[79]

Perched on the shoulders of Bene, by his own admission, but following a different path and another imaginary, is Romeo Castellucci. He also works (with his sister and his wife, so we will refer to the Castelluccis) on presences beneath or beyond representation, and puts the bodily function of the actor directly into play. A prime example is *Amleto, the veemente esteriorità della morte di mollusco* [*Hamlet: The Vehement Exteriority of the Death of a Mollus*] by the Societas Raffaello Sanzio (directed by Romeo Castellucci), which we analysed earlier in this book, when speaking about "autistic performance". On a heavily mechanised, "autonomous" stage (machines and truck batteries power the neon lights, which the actor reactivates himself), the actor is neither Horatio nor Hamlet, not a character. He does not construct the expected fiction but only shows the non-occurrence of it. He is an anonymous and isolated body, faced with the energy and noise of the machines that surround him, and with the materiality of his body (drooling, urine, etc.). He is an autistic person trying to build and articulate signs but who fails to build meaning. This is a "less-than" *Hamlet*, to quote Carmelo Bene, the drama of *Hamlet* that will not take place. This also is a "postdramatic" stage, since all representation is rejected and Amleto, as we have said, is, and is not: he stayed there, on the set, without penetrating his enigma. He is an exposed autistic body, placing its reality up against the expected myth. The aesthetics are therefore extremely different from Tanguy's, but the questions that drive them are more or less the same, as we can see.

In the other works by the Societas Raffaello Sanzio, the preoccupation with the body becomes intertwined with questions around the image. Indeed, Castellucci's work is often referred to as "image theatre". However, the images they produce are of another type of plasticity and involve another kind of relation to sensation than, say, those of Bob Wilson. Their aesthetic embodies a strong tension between "*tableau* [...] and the *body*".[80] Romeo Castellucci claims to have chosen the name Raphaël for his company in reference to

> the opposition and conflict between the eurhythmic order, the perfection of forms, and the geometric beauty Raphaël's canvases on the one hand, and, on the other hand, the breaking of this order by unexpected flashes that disrupt vision by propelling it towards unsuspected, nocturnal zones.[81]

Castelluci's thus sees his work as an attempt to analogise the paintings of Raphaël that are "perfect and tense on the outside, but convulsive in their detail".[82] From their beginnings, the Castellucci have placed at the heart of their work the notion of *iconoclasm* and a Platonic suspicion of the image. They write in a 1985 manifesto:

> Theatre-goer, you will be disappointed, there are no images here [...] This is the theatre that rejects representation [...] This is the iconoclastic theatre: it breaks down each image to adhere only to the fundamental reality, the anti-cosmic Unreal, the unthought [...] the involvement must be total [...] The whole body must feel moved and convinced by everything around it.[83]

If there is visual power in the theatre of the Societas Raffaello Sanzio, the images must disrupt their own status as objects of contemplation. Far from being objects to be appreciated, they must assail, impact and disturb the spectator.

To take the example of *Genesi, from the Museum of Sleep* (2000), this can be achieved through the aggression of sound and light (shrill noises and flashes) as in the first part (where Lucifer is discovered in Marie Curie's laboratory, experimenting with radium energy); but it can also come from children dressed in white, and for some dressed in animal costumes, strolling, imitating adults (standing at attention, playing with a train) in the calm of a vast space that is also white, for a second part entitled "Auschwitz", about which Romeo Castellucci explains in the program:

> I absolutely must find a double current, a double sensation, a double emotion for this second act. You, spectator, you do not have to know what to think or what to say [...] I have to hide the horror with the sweetness of the lamb. Only so can it enter your home.[84]

The image must never become fixed in an object that can be grasped, or that is legible and aesthetically pleasing, but should always unsettle. It should also aim for a kind of violence and a sensory and mental force. It should create a scandal: here again, the artist is attempting to thwart the frames of re-presentation, and to provoke shock. It is not surprising that the Castelluccis constantly cite Antonin Artaud, or that they are deeply interested in ancient tragedy, its ritualism, its relation to sacrifice and chaos (from their 1995 *Oresteia* to the recent cycle *Tragedia endogonidia*, staged in ten European cities from early 2002 to late 2004).

It is logical, then, for the Castelluccis to try to produce a real sense of the theatre's physical power and presence, by foregrounding the body. Their *Giulio Cesare* (from Shakespeare's *Julius Caesar*, 1997) was treated as a work on rhetoric (and consequently on theatricality as a "corruptor of meaning")[85] It explored the most physical properties of voice, the "hyphen between word and body".[86] The show opened with the projection of the images of an endoscopy that an actor performed directly on himself, showing the inside of the throat and the action of the actor-speaker's vocal cords. Later, another actor gave a speech while inhaling helium and his voice was moved to the higher frequencies, while another actor seemed to have an obstruction in the glottis and larynx. The aim was to deconstruct the artificiality of discourse and representation; to explore the realness of the voice, the flesh and muscles; to also show non-common bodies (obese or deformed ones, for example). After the intermission, in a second part devoid of rhetoric, the actors playing Brutus and Cassius were replaced by two anorexic actresses: the stage was drawing attention to the distinctiveness of their bodies. On a stage, there can be *real* bodies, bodies in their actuality. This is what is seemingly suggested by a sign lowered on to the naked body of one of the actresses spread out on the ground: "this is not an actor". Aspiring to find the power of the event, of the act, so close to the performance and to thwart its natural artificiality, the theatre aims to produce the truth and irreducible reality of the body.

In the statement "this is not an actor", reminiscent of Magritte, however, things are a little more complex than a mere belief in the fact that showing scandalous reality on the stage would help to give it life and a palpable power and "truth". For Romeo Castellucci, the procedure has a self-contained paradox:

> [Magritte] affirms the pipe through a drawing and a calligraphy the better to deny it, and so that the negation itself becomes an affirmation. But the negated pipe, or dead Caesar's body, or the body of an anorexic actress, are not only not negated, they return in a kind of apotheosis. The idea of the actor becomes total.[87]

According to him, Magritte's genius is, "in the most radical way possible, to do away with representation *in* representation". Therefore, he continues, in writing "*this is not an* actor", I did not want to present a naked body in its obvious pain. I wanted to emphasize that it was an actor, and an anorexic body is symbolically, in this case, twice so. The theatre is not diluted, because it is the representation that makes way for itself.[88]

Castelluccian iconoclasm, therefore, is not only to introduce the body affirmed as real on the stage, nor simply to go over to the performance side and refuse "the theatre", it is to fight it from the inside, to work "against the figure *in* the figure"; to "register the 'as if' of the theatre, its status as fiction, in an ambivalent or amphibological dimension. To put the mirror [. . .] in front of the mirror".[89]

The relations are therefore complex between theatrical representation and the "reality" of a body whose function is to place it in crisis. The theatrical real is redoubled; but redoubled *in* the theatre. And this is the barometer against which one should question theatre's increasing challenge to the norms of dramatic fiction, its search for the immediacy of the body, for the irruption of the "real", and its attempt to get closer to performance. In the hybrid aesthetics that have been particularly obvious in the theatre in recent years, where theatre mixes with performance, dance or circus, it is also necessary to see how these crossings go in both directions, and how, therefore, performance, dance or circus, are theatricalised.

The example is particularly striking for circus arts, since, while theatre directors are incorporating into their projects non-signifying physical presences and the real danger of acrobatic performances, the recent evolution of the circus suggests a unification of its own discontinuity, through the creation of a unified poetic universe, and even the establishment of a fiction. A show like *Le Tas* [*The Heap*], by Pierre Meunier (2003), presents, through its philosophical and burlesque exploration the notion of "heap", two actors who are also, simultaneously, clowns and *performers* faced with the real danger of the heavy stones that they throw or of the gravel that sweeps over the stage. Similarly, in a movement that is less recent (which goes back at least to Pina Bausch's "dance theatre" of in the 1970s), dance is attempting to develop "characters" and to integrate speech, even while theatre seeks in the choreography a model of formal abstraction and a transcendence of text and meaning,

Nevertheless, the contemporary stage is working more and more on such hybridisations, endeavouring to create distinctive scenic forms that blur traditional boundaries: dance, theatre, performance. And it is the body that seems to be the central object of these scenic experiences. "Normal" bodies, and not the canon of beauty, "bodies that most often contain their fair share of problems, and not those seen in TV or *Vogue* commercials", as Rodrigo García, the former adman, states[90] – non-standardised bodies such as those of the spectators that García invites to come and remove their clothes on the stage (*After Sun*, 2003). And bodies attacked by the norms of a globalised consumerist society and that, in one of García's performances, coverf themselves with food and stuff all their orifices with it (*Compré una pala en Ikea para cavar mi tumba*, 2003).

It is the body in all its states and also in all its repressed naturalness that the Flemish plastician-choreographer-director Jan Fabre places at the centre of his transgressive search for "beauty". Fabre explores the animality of the human body, whether by placing it among actors dressed in huge animal costumes (frog, canary, etc.), or real animals (including spiders and dogs), or by creating choreographies with naked actors having bird feet or heads covered with rabbit masks. His modern-kitsch equivalents of the hybrid chimera created by Jérôme Bosch include a sequence in which chickens hanging from butcher's hooks file by in the background while the sound system plays "If I Could Be Like an Animal" by Sammy Davies Jr (*Parrots and Guinea Pigs*, 2002). Fabre also focuses on all the secretions and fluids that this body produces: sweat, urine, blood (*I'm Blood*, 2003), tears (*The Crying Body*, 2004; *The History of Tears*, 2005). More generally, it is the body's resistance to social and moral domestication, the "barbarity" inherent to it, its excess and multiple possibilities, which are the objects of his experiments on the stage. Fabre, in his choreographic theatre, stages moments and evocative fragments that mark the duration of a manipulated and "densified" time. And just as this stage conductor ostensibly manipulates time through the elaboration of consecutive units of varying length, he also manipulates the body. His stage space is first made of bodies, those of his "warriors of beauty", which are the objects of construction and the fragments of the general space. "The actors, dancers, warriors of beauty are also 'islands in themselves', having a reality within the created universe that is representation. They are islands that float to meet each other, come into contact, then move away again."[91] This means that musical, corporeal and sequential fragments are not articulated in a narrative or dramatic coherence. They generate meaning in their own right, and thus obtain more density. They are articulated in the spectator's gaze from images, movements and the repetition of gestures, words considered as forms. However, most of Fabre's shows, unlike other postdramatic performances, hammer home meaning and meanings, in all their forms:

> [A]ll the characters I create with the actors live in a world that is their own and embody ideas, metaphors and symbols. My theatre is not a theatre of identification, nor is it emotion reduced to the psychological. Emotions and relationships arise from physical and mental complicity within the agreed universe of representation. Like gangsters who attack a bank, beauty warriors are athletes of sensation. They see every drop of sweat and every glance. The relation, the conflict and/or the emotion are perpetuated in the tension field of the intermediate space. Or are present in detail. The world of my performances is hidden in the detail. The devil and the angel are in the detail.[92]

While these performances may often appear as moving rites, the spectator who is interpellated by the density of extremely focused, disciplined and manipulated actors, must themselves articulate their own meanings of what the stage offers them in the form of fragments, which all rigorously adorn the initial theme, each time repeated, each time presented as an athletic, bodily, musical, choreographic and mental performance. And if, with Fabre, the bodies are islands of representation, they are there to repeat, at each moment of temporal and physical density, that below the Mannerist, ritualistic appearance, there is a vulnerable internal space, which is poured out ostensibly on the stage. The body is not liberated, but on the contrary, constrained, subjected to the gesture of the visual artist, so that it produces and shows what is most intimate, most fragile and most vulnerable in man.

The body is also what Belgian choreographer Alain Platel shows on the stage, in a transgression that is much less ostensible but equally real (we have already mentioned Platel's *Bernadetje* of 1997). Professional dancers mingle with non-professionals, teenagers, children: "pure dance does not interest me. I want to deal with individuals who have unique ways of moving",[93] he explains, and it is from these individuals and their movements that he constructs his shows. These shows produce, from seemingly insignificant movements and activities, an astonishing vivacity, an explosive vitality and an interweaving of fragmented and motley actions, in a "happy mess" regulated like a fugue. *Iets op Bach* (1986) brings together a dancer with a crutch, fairground acrobats, a flamboyant transvestite and teens full of energy, while nine musicians played Bach and Purcell, in a setting that represented the roof of building with chimneys, antennas and air-conditioning systems. Recently, at the Opéra de Paris, *Wolf* (2005), built around Mozart's music, but also Celine Dion's variety songs, was imaginatively set in a commercial centre on two levels, where managers, homeless people, dealers, hip-hop singers, fashion victims, crossdressers, two deaf actors and a dozen dogs all formed the images, as the choreographies alternated between classical and contemporary repertoire, hip-hop and African dances. And in *All Indians* (in collaboration with Arne Sierens, 2000), the scenography consisted of facades of two mundane terraced houses, in front of which and/or behind the windows of which various characters, who were variously connected (a divorced fire-fighter and his sister, boisterous children, a charismatic teenager, a Kosovar refugee), moved in a tense dynamic between rapid images of bodies, fragmented words, social abandonment and exuberance. About this show, Platel remarked:

> When we started, in 1984, we made shows without words, precisely because we were tired of the theatre; but we were not dancers, for that matter... So we were looking for a form between theatre and dance, and I find it very beautiful that sixteen years later, with this last show, I have arrived at a rather theatrical play.[94]

The boundaries have therefore moved and have often become indistinct in staged works where the body is paramount, but where its presence and movement mingle with other elements in the desire to create a scenic event not limited by genre. The "Flemish" school is an emblem of this (we could also have mentioned Jan Lauwers, Luk Perceval and many others). The performances of the Catalan group La Furia dels Baus are another example. It is a hybridisation phenomenon, in a sense, an opening up of the respective fields: as we have said, the movement works in both (or multiple) directions. While many theatrical practices have an eye for choreographic forms, a part of current dance practice is to bring together figures, situations and the presence of text, whatever the form, creating a sort of theatrical whole. It bespeaks an attempt to produce a *fiction*. This is also something that can be done more experimentally and quite differently by a choreographer like the Portuguese João Fiadeiro with his method of "real-time composition" (and his RE.AL company), through which he presents to the audiences performances under the generic title of *Existencia*. Theatre, dance, *performance*: this third term is now in vogue again, in a strong way, and describes scenic practices that seek, by various means, to bring back the theatrical act to the present and concrete time and space of its realisation, to mix the artistic forms and mediums used (theatre, installations, video, interactive media, DJing and so on), to disrupt the scenic creation of a fiction while inviting the spectator to build theirs, to knowingly play on the boundaries between the fictional and the real event. But whether one plays on all this in the context of the stage, and theatricality, whether one deconstructs them or even "challenges" the spectator, it is still *representation* that is in question.

To finish this overview, we will take one last example. The English collective Forced Entertainment and their performance-show emblematically titled *Bloody Mess* (2005), an "epic tale for ten performers", a "postdramatic" theatre piece par excellence: characters, actions and stories collide, are never pursued and completed, are disconnected from each other and sink into chaos. At the beginning of the performance, the actors sit in a line, facing the audience, on chairs: addressing the spectators, they introduce themselves and explain the way they would like to be perceived during the performance. Already, during this presentation, disagreements and cacophony threaten, driven by a notion of "realness" that is obviously fictitious: derogatory comments from partners, disputes within the troupe, various incidents. The illusion will not take place, the creation of a narrative and an imaginary commonly shared by all the actors in the eyes of the spectators will not hold, fragmentation will reign. The show continues then, and to quote from the presentation that the company made of this performance:

> A strobe light flickers, pointed at the ground. A pair of clowns in smeared make-up start an ugly fight that threatens to take over the stage. A delinquent cheerleader dances and yells. A woman weeps in a fit of operatic grief then stops, changes costume and starts again. The strains of Deep Purple or maybe Black Sabbath blast from the PA only to be replaced by the Bach Cello Suites. A bloke starts to tell the history of the world from the Big Bang onwards but is quickly interrupted. A sound check. An interview. A seductive monologue. Rock-gig roadies creep across the stage – bringing disco lights, new speakers and a microphone that no one really wants. A woman in a gorilla suit chucks popcorn at anything that moves like a demented refugee from pantomime. A dance is performed by two men sporting only homemade tin foil stars. A beautiful silence is staged.[95]

Scenic fragments, show numbers constantly interrupted, *cheap* and ridiculous spectacle caught in the whirlwind and deceptive excess of this generalised "confusion": as its title ostensibly announces, it is a spectacle of discontinuity and dispersion that is presented in this "performance" displayed as "uncompromising political pop art", an "ironic and physically demanding trashy show", a "visual show that seeks to describe the contemporary world in all its beauty, horror and complexity". It is also, above all, the impossibility of constructing a dramatic fiction, or even a unified and coherent proposition, of imposing on the stage all that is of the order of dramatic, or even simply traditional, theatricality, which is *represented* here. There remains only ironic humour and the project of deconstruction, the spectacle of discontinuous performances and the permanent play on an aborted narrativity, playful observation and an interrogation of the relation – of the *play* – which may then, nevertheless, be established with the spectators. In fact, and as is the case in the other shows of this collective that constantly works on fragmentation (*Jessica in the Room of Lights*, 1984), failure, botching and disappointment (*Showtime*, 1996; *First Night*, 2001), or temporal expansion (*And on the Thousandth Night*, 2000), there is always an attempt at exploring the living relationship between a story, its narrators/actors, its listeners/spectators and the infinitely chaotic outside world.

In this chapter, we have therefore considered a contemporary theatre that explores the modalities of the construction of a fiction in front of an audience, the resistance of the real of the stage and the capacity of spectacular performance to produce surprise, pleasure and imagination. Despite being deconstructed and at times ironic, it is always about the same act, and its contradictions. In the present theatre assembly, one tells stories and produces an event and a fiction that simultaneously displays the inanity of the theatre as well as the world that contains it.

Notes

Part VII

1 Michael Azama, *De Zucco à Godot, anthologie des auteurs dramatiques de langue française, 1950–2000* [*From Zucco to Godot, Anthology of French-Language Drama Writers, 1950–2000*] (Paris: éditions Théâtrales, 2003–2004).
2 Joris Lacoste, "L'événement de la parole" ["The Moment of Speech"], in "Place aux écritures" ["Make Way for Writing"] [special issue], *Mouvement* 14 (Suppl.) Summer (2001), pp. 13–14.
3 Christophe Huysman, "Philippe Minyana, un artiste 'dans' le théâtre" [Phillippe Minyana, an Artist 'in' the Theatre"], in *Philippe Minyana, ou la Parole visible*, ed. Michel Corvin (Paris: Éditions Théâtrales, 2000), pp. 98–99.
4 Sony Lab'ou Tansi, *Parentheses of Blood* (Paris: Hatier, 1981).
5 Rodrigo Garcia, "Paroles d'artiste" ["Artist Lyrics"], in "Press File" ["*Dossier*"] for his first plays performed at the Théâtre de la Cité Universitaire, Paris (2003), n.p.

Chapter 12

1 Antoine Vitez, éditorial of the first issue of *L'Art du théâtre* (Arles: Actes Sud/Théâtre National de Chaillot, Spring, 1985), p. 3.
2 Roger Planchon, interview with J.-F. Halté and C. Tordjman, "Lecture des classiques" ["Reading the Classics"], *Pratiques* 15–16 (July 1977), p. 54.
3 Bernard Dort cited in *Itinéraire de Roger Planchon* [*Roger Planchon's Itinerary*] (collection of articles from the magazine *Théâtre populaire*) (Paris: L'Arche, 1970), p. 57.
4 Roland Barthes, *Écrits sur le théâtre* [*Writings on the Theatre*] (Paris: Points-Seuil, 2002), quoted in "J'ai toujours beaucoup aimé le théâtre..." ["I've Always Loved the Theatre..."] [review] *Esprit* (May 1965) and "L'éblouissement" ["Wonder"], *Le Monde* (11 March 1971).
5 Ibid.
6 Alain Girault, Bernard Sobel, Roger Planchon, Antoine Vitez, André Petitjean and Charles Tordjman "Entretiens avec Alain Girault, Bernard Sobel, Roger Planchon and Antoine Vitez" ["Interviews with Alain Girault, Bernard Sobel, Roger Planchon and Antoine Vitex"], *Pratiques: linguistique, littérature, didactique*, 15–16 (1977), p. 53.
7 See Catherine Naugrette, Béatrice Picon-Vallin and Marie-Christine Autant-Matthieu, *L'ère de la mise en scène* [*The Era of mise en scène*], Théâtre aujourd'hui [Theatre Today], no. 10 (Paris: CNDP, 2005), ch. 3.
8 Roger Planchon, interview with J.-F. Halté and C. Tordjman, "Reading the Classics", *Pratiques* 15–16, Metz (July 1977), p. 59.
9 Dort, *Itinéraire de Roger Planchon*, p. 63.
10 Ibid., p. 10.
11 Gilles Sandier, *Théâtre et combat: Regards sur le théâtre actuel* [*Theatre and Combat: A Look at the Current Theatre*] (Paris: Stock, 1970), p. 153.
12 Ibid., p. 154.
13 Roger Planchon, in the accompanying brochure to the 1974 staging, quoted by T. Kowsan in *Les Voies de la création théâtrale* [*Approaches to Theatrical Creation*], vol. VI (Paris: CNRS, 1978), p. 339.
14 Sandier, *Théâtre et combat*, pp. 158–159.
15 Ibid.
16 Anne-Françoise Benhamou, "La vraie vie est ailleurs" ["Real Life Is Elsewhere"], *Revue d'esthétique* 26 ("Jeune théâtre") (1994), p. 211.
17 Joseph Danan, "Entretien avec Christian Biet: le dramaturge, ce spectre qui hante le theatre" [Interview with Christian Biet: The Dramaturg, that Spectre that Haunts the Theatre"], *Critique* 61, no. 699–700 (2005), n.p.
18 Louis Aragon, "Lettre ouverte à André Breton sur *Le Regard du sourd*, la science et la liberté" ["An Open Letter to André Breton on *Deafman Glance*, Science and Freedom", in *Les Lettres françaises* (2 June 1971), pp. 3–15.
19 Ibid.
20 Ibid.
21 Frédéric Maurin, "Au péril de la beauté: la chair du visuel et le cristal de la forme chez Robert Wilson" ["At the Risk of Beauty: The Flesh of the Visual and the Crystal of Form in Robert Wilson"], in *La scène et les images* [*The Scene and the Images*] (Paris: CNRS éditions, 2004), p. 58.
22 "*Le Regard du sourd* n'est pas tombé dans l'oreille d'un aveugle."

23 Interview with J. Mambrino, *Etudes* (1977), cited in F. Maurin in *La Scène et les images* (Paris: CNRS éditions, 2004), p. 50.
24 René Allio, "Comment construire des théâtres" ["How to Build Theatres"], *Théâtre populaire* 35 (1959), n.p.
25 Giovanni Lista, *Encyclopédie mondiale des arts du spectacle dans la seconde moitié du XXe siècle* [*World Encyclopedia of the Performing Arts in the Second Half of the Twentieth Century*] (Arles: Carré/Actes Sud, 1997).
26 Jean Jourdheuil, *Un Théâtre du regard: Gilles Aillaud – le refus du pathos* (Paris: Bourgois, 2002), p. 28.
27 Nicky Rieti, "Scénographie" ["Scenography"], *Alternatives théâtrales* 12 (June 1982), p. 49.
28 Ibid.
29 Bernard Dort, "L'âge de la représentation" ["The Age of Representation"], in J. de Jomaron (ed.), *Le Théâtre en France* [*Theatre in France*] (Paris: Armand Colin, 1992), réed. Le Livre de poche ("Pochothèque"), p. 1021.
30 André Gunthert, *Le Voyage du TNS* (Paris: Solin, 1983), p. 48.
31 Ibid.
32 Georges Banu, *Peter Brook: De Timon d'Athènes à Hamlet* [*Peter Brook: Timon from Athens to Hamlet*] (Paris: Flammarion, 2001), p. 155.
33 Jerzy Grotowski, *Towards a Poor Theatre* (New York: Routledge, 2002), p. 35.
34 Ibid., pp. 13–24.
35 Antoine Vitez, interview with J. Kraemer and A. Petitjean, "Lecture des classiques" ["Reading the Classics"], *Pratiques* 15–16 (July 1977), p. 52.
36 Girault et al., "Interviews", p. 51.
37 Antoine Vitez, "Éditorial", *L'Art du théâtre* [*The Art of Theatre*], 1 (1985), p. 4.
38 Girault et al., "Interviews", p. 45.
39 Ibid.
40 Ibid., p. 45.
41 *Antoine Vitez, journal intime de théâtre* [*Antoine Vitez, Diary of Theatre*], a film by F. Pascaud and D. Gros, 1988 (la sept/vidéo, 1994).
42 Giorgio Strehler, "Les Quatre Cités du théâtre d'art" ["The Four Cities of Art Theatre"], in *Les Cités du théâtre d'Art: De Stanislavski à Strehler* [*The Cities of the Art Theatre: Stanislavski to Strehler*], ed. Georges Banu (Paris: éditions Théâtrales/Académie Expérimentale des Théâtres, 2000), pp. 9–16.
43 François Regnault, "Conte des trois cités: le Vieux-Colombier, l'Athénée, le Berliner ensemble" ["Tale of the Three Cities: The Vieux-Colombier, the Athénée and the Berliner"], *Théâtre en Europe* 9 (1986), p. 33.
44 Strehler, "Les Quatre Cités", p. 10.
45 Bernard Dort, "Preface", in G. Streheler, *Un théâtre pour la vie: réflexions, entretiens, notes de travail* [*A Theatre for Life: Reflections, Interviews, Working Notes*] (Paris: Fayard, 1980), n.p.
46 Streheler, *Un théâtre pour la vie: réflexions, entretiens, notes de travail* [*A Theatre for Life: Reflections, Interviews, Working Notes*] (Paris: Fayard, 1980), pp. 144–147.
47 Ibid.
48 Dort, "Preface", n.p.
49 Ibid.
50 Strehler, "Les Quatre Cités", p. 129.

Chapter 13

1. Bernard Dort, "Deux metteurs en scène de la troisième génération: Castri et Gosch" ["Two Directors of the Third Generation: Castri and Gosch"], *L'Art du théâtre* 2–3 (autumn 1985–winter 1986), p. 58.
2. Ibid., pp. 58 and 60.
3. Antoine Vitez, "L'art du théâtre: editorial" ["The Art of Theatre: Editorial"], *L'Art du théâtre* 1 (1985), p. 9.
4. Ibid.
5. Antoine Vitez, "L'art du théâtre: editorial", *L'Art du théâtre* 6 (1987), n.p.
6. Patrice Chéreau, "Une mort exemplaire" ["An exemplary death"], *Partisan* 47 (April–May 1969), pp. 64–68.
7. Anne-Françoise Benhamou, "Portrait de l'artiste en Prospero. Patrice Chéreau à Nanterre", in *Alternatives théâtrales* 37 (May 1991), p. 37.
8. Anne-Françoise Benhamou, "Patrice Chéreau: utilité et futilité" ["Patrice Chéreau: Usefulness and Futility"], in *Les Cités du théâtre d'Art: De Stanislavski à Strehler* [*The Cities of the Art Theatre: From Stanislavski to Strehler*], ed. Georges Banu (Paris: éditions Théâtrales/Académie Expérimentale des Théâtres, 2000), p. 303.
9. Bernard Dort, *La Représentation émancipée* [*The Emanciapted Representation*] (Arles: Actes sud, 1988), pp. 171–184.
10. Bernard Dort, "Le texte et la scène: pour une nouvelle alliance" ["The Text and the Scene: For a New Alliance"], in *Le spectateur en dialogue (le jeu du théâtre)* [*The Spectator in Dialogue (the Play of the Theatre)*] (Paris: POL, 1995), p. 270.
11. Dort, *La Représentation émancipée*, p. 734.
12. Ibid.
13. Ibid., p. 735.
14. Ibid.
15. Dort, "Le jeu et les signes", in *La Représentation émancipée*, pp. 161–165.
16. Ibid.
17. Ibid.
18. Quoted by Odette Aslan in *Langhoff, Les Voies de la création théâtrale* [*Langhoff, the Ways of Theatrical Creation*], vol. 19 (Paris: CNRS, 1994), p. 39.
19. François Chattot, "Le Danjeu", *La Gazette de Lausanne* (25 August 1990).
20. Matthias Langoff, *Le Rapport Langhoff* [*The Langhoff Report*] (Geneva: Zoé), p. 121.
21. Angela Winckler, "Être simple et fière", in G. Banu and M. Blezinger (eds.) *Klaus-Michael Grüber... Il faut que le théâtre passe à travers les larmes* (Paris: éditions du Regard/Académie Expérimentale des Théâtres/Festival d'automne, 1993), p. 93. The staging notes quoted in this paragraph are also taken from this work.
22. Rehearsal notes for *Bérénice*.
23. Ibid.
24. *Klaus Michael Grüber, l'homme de passage* [*The Man of Passage*], documentary by Ch. Rüter, Arte, 1999.
25. Udo Samuel cited in "*Klaus Mikaell Grüber... il faut que le théâtre passe à travers les larmes*", Portrait proposé par Georges Banu et Mark Blezinger (Paris: Éditions du Regard, Académie expérimentale des théâtres, Festival d'automne, 1993), p. 78.

26 Bernard Dort, "Le geste latéral de Klaus Michael Grüber", in Banu and Blezinger, *Klaus-Michael Grüber* pp. 21–27, quoted in Dort, *Le Spectateur*, pp. 205–216.
27 Interview with J.-P. Thibaudat, *Libération*, 6 December 1984, quoted in Banu and Blezinger, *Klaus-Michael Grüber*, p. 12.
28 Ibid., p. 64.
29 Jean-Pierre Thibaudat, "Kaus Mikael Grüber, Interview", *Libération* (6 December 1984), n.p.
30 Walter Gropius, *Bauhaus Manifesto and Program*, Weimar (1919). For further information, see www.widewalls.ch/bauhaus-manifesto-key-points.
31 Richard Schechner, "The Decline and Fall of the (American) Avant-Garde: Why It Happened and What We Can Do about It", *Performing Arts Journal* 5, no. 2 (1981), pp. 48–63.
32 Quoted in Denis Bablet, *Tadeuz Kantor, Le Théâtre et la mort* (Lausanne, éditions L'Âge d'homme, 1977), p. 20.
33 Tadeusz Kantor, "Le théâtre de la mort" ["The Theatre of Death"], texts collected and presented by Bablet, *Tadeux Kantor*, n.p. All other quotes from Kantor are from this work, unless otherwise indicated.
34 Tadeusz Kantor, "1955–1975", in *Les Voies de la création théâtrale*, vol. 11 ("T. Kantor, 1") (Paris: CNRS éditions, 1983), n.p.
35 Tadeusz Kantor, interview with Guy Scarpetta, *Art Press*, special issue "Le théâtre, art du passé, art du présent" ["Theatre: Art of the Past, Art of the Future"] (autumn 1989), n.p.
36 Ibid.
37 Quoted by D. Bablet, in *Les Voies*, vol. 11, p. 47.
38 Georges Banu, "L'homme du coin et ses fantômes" ["The Local Man and His Ghosts"], *Alternatives théâtrales* 50 (1995), n.p.
39 Quoted by Bablet, in *Les Voies*, vol. 11, p. 53 (emphasis in original).
40 We want to thank Olivier Neveux for his great help in this chapter about Gatti.
41 Quoted in Didier Méreuze, "Armand Gatti, le combatant", *La Croix* (7 April 2017).
42 "Donner aux hommes / et à leurs images / leur seule dimension habitable / la demesure". A. Gatti, "contre opéra", quoted in S. Gatti and M. Séonnet, *Gatti: Journal illustré d'une écriture*, published on the occasion of the exhibition "50 ans de théâtre vus par les trois chats d'Armand Gatti" (Montreuil: Artefact – C.A.C. Montreuil et Parole errante, 1987), p. 202.
43 Bernard Dort, *Théâtre réel: Essais de critique 1967–1970* [*Real Theatre: Critical essays 1967–1970*] (Paris: Editions du Seuil, 1971), pp. 223–226.
44 H. Chatelain quoted in A. Gatti, "Les Personnages de théâtre meurent dans la rue", *Axolotl – revue nomade* 1 (1996), p. 8.
45 Armand Gatti, "Preface", in *La Tribu des carcana en guerre contre quoi?* [*The Tribe of Carcana at War Against What?*] (Paris: Le Seuil, 1975), n.p.
46 Armand Gatti, *La Parole errante* [*The Wandering Word*] (Paris: Éditions Verdier, 1998), chap. 5.

Chapter 14

1 D. G. Gabily, "Cadavres, si on veut" [Corpses, If You Wish"], in *À tout va* (Arles: Actes Sud, 2002), p. 46.
2 Ibid.

3 Ibid.
4 Programme Manifeste du Théâtre Gérard Philipe (January 1998), n.p.
5 See, on this score, Jean-Luc Nancy, *La Communauté désœuvrée* [*The Idle Community*] (Paris: Bourgois, 1999) (original work published 1986).
6 Bruno Tackels, "L'atelier Gabily: former des 'servants de plateau'", in *Alternatives théâtrales* 70–71 ("Les Penseurs de l'enseignement", co-edited by Académie Expérimentale des Théâtres/Odéon-Théâtre de l'Europe) (December 2001), pp. 113–118.
7 Alain Françon, *La représentation* [*The Representation*] (Paris: éditions de l'Amandier, 2004), p. 52.
8 Quoted in Stanislas Nordey and Valérie Lang, *"Passions civiles"*: *Interviews with Y. Ciret and F. Laroze* (Vénissieux: La Passe du vent, 2000), p. 78.
9 Ibid., p. 96.
10 Ibid., p. 99.
11 Ibid., p. 105.
12 Olivier Py, *Epître aux jeunes acteurs pour que soit rendue la Parole à la Parole* (Paris: Actes Sud, 2000), p. 23.
13 Interview with A.-F. Benhamou, *Maillon, le journal* (December 1993).
14 Marc François, "L'impropriété, le fugitif" ["The Impropriety, the Fugitive"], in Jean-Pierre Thibaudat (ed.), *Où va le théâtre?* (Paris: Joëbeke, 1998), p. 48.
15 Remarks on *Esclaves de l'amour*, an interview with Anne-Françoise Benhamou, *Maillon, le journal* (December–February 1993–1994).
16 François, "L'impropriété, le fugitif", n.p.
17 J. Derrida, *Politiques de l'amitié* (Paris: Galilée, 1994), p. 329.
18 Anne-François Benhamou, "Qui parle à qui quand je (tu, il) parle(s) tout seul" ["Who Speaks to Whom When I (You, He) Speak Alone"], *Alternatives théâtrales* 45 (1994), p. 26.
19 *Mises en scène du monde* (Rennes, Brittany: Théâtre National de Bretagne, 2004). Text published for their conference organised in November 2004, n.p.
20 Ibid.
21 *La mise en scène: un art de l'interprétation* [*Mise en scène: An Art of Interpretation*]. Théâtre aujourd'hui no. 10 (Paris: CNDP, 2005), p. 191.
22 "Le réel retrouvé", interview with Anne-Françoise Benhamou, *Théâtre/Public* 115 (1994), p. 57.
23 Ibid., p. 90.
24 "La mise en scène: un art de l'interprétation", n.p.
25 "Le réel retrouvé", p. 58.
26 Ibid., p. 90.
27 Ibid., pp. 57–58.
28 Peter Sellars, *Conférence* (Arles: Actes sud-papiers), 1994, p. 20.
29 By Sabrina Baldassarra, Stéphanie Farison, Emmanuelle Lafon, Sara Louis and Lucie Nicolas.
30 Claude Régy, *Espaces perdus* [*Lost Spaces*] (Besançon: Les Solitaires Intempestifs, 1998), p. 97.
31 Claude Régy, *L'Ordre des morts* [*The Order of the Dead*] (Besançon: Les solitaires intempestifs, 1999), p. 44.
32 Ibid., pp. 44 and 48.
33 Ibid., p. 71.

34 Régy frequently uses this term to characterise the activity of the spectator, thus indicating that they are participants in the theatrical act.
35 Régy's exploration of the unconscious naturally implies a certain dimension of chaos, the unthought and the obscure.
36 Through his staging (2002) of *War and Piece*, adapted from Tolstoy's novel or Chekhov's *The Three Sisters* (2004).
37 "[*Cont.*]... cutting the umbilical cord with the theatre I practiced up to then, namely this "magical realism" deepened by psychology and which has become a sort of mania" (work diary for *Extinction*, 18-05-2000, 23.50 h 15, in the programme for *Extinction*, Odéon-Théâtre de l'Europe).
38 K. Lupa, programme of *Somnambules* [*Sleepwalkers*] at the Odéon-Théâtre de l'Europe. Here Lupa comments on the perception of existence within the "new man" described by Broch, one invaded by the irrational.
39 K. Lupa, programme of *Somnambules*.
40 Ibid.
41 Georges Didi-Huberman, *Devant l'image* [*In Front of the Image*] (Paris: Minuit, 1990), p. 180 (emphasis in original).
42 Y.-J. Collin, interview with P. Collin, in programme booklet of *Henri IV* for the performances at the TGP-Saint-Denis.
43 Gladkov, Aleksandr Konstantinovich, *Meyerhold Speaks, Meyerhold Rehearses* (Reading: Harwood Academic, 1997), p. 142.
44 "So, is this mainstream theatre? Yes, because it is so grandiose, so long, so philosophical, so metaphysical, so poetic, and because beyond all of the theatrical symbols and ideas, the only thing that is ever really desired at the theatre is the very notion of theatre." Olivier Py, interview with G. Costaz, about *L'Apocalypse joyeuse*, the Avignon theatre festival press pack (2000).
45 "Comme le doute dans la science" ["Like Doubt in Science"] [interview], *Alternatives théâtrales* 85 (2005), p. 98.
46 This was in line with Lavaudant's overall fascination with fragmentary theatre.
47 Georges Lavaudant and Jean-Christophe Bailly, *Bailly-Lavaudant: Théâtre et histoire contemporains III*, CNSAD, MC 93, collection "Apprendre", 5 (Arles: Actes Sud-Papiers, 1996), p. 50.
48 Ibid., pp. 32–33.
49 Ibid., pp. 32–33.
50 For a deeper investigation into Schleef's important work, see the section concerning him in no. 76–77 of *Alternatives théâtrales* ("Choralités"), as well as, in German, *Arbeitsbuch*, which dedicated the magazine *Theatre der Zeit* to him in 2001, and his book *Faust Droge Parsifal* (Frankfurt am Main: Suhrkamp, 1997).
51 In the performances written by Marthaler and his playwrights, especially Stefanie Carp: *Murx den europeär, murx ihn, murx ihn!* [*Screw the European!*] (1992), *Die Spezialisten* (1999), *Groundings* (2004), *Papperlapapp* in the Cour d'honneur of the Festival d'Avignon (2010) and so on.
52 In his mises en scène of existing plays (*Casimir et Caroline* [*Casimir and Caroline*], d'Horvath, 1996; *La Nuit des rois* [*The Night of Kings*], 2001; *La Mort de Danton* [*The Death of Danton*], 2004), as in his staging of operas.
53 The noisy brouhaha and the regular personalities of these breweries are the source of many of the figures and the polyphonic chorality of Marthaler's productions.
54 Musical tradition of the Ashkenazi Jews of Eastern Europe.

55 Stefanie Carp, "La vie lente est longue: le théâtre de Christoph Marthaler" ["The Slow Life Is Long: Christoph Marthatler's Theatre"], *Theatreschrift* 12 (December 1997), n.p.
56 For example, through the pitching of the ship (*La nuit des rois*) or a suction effect (*Les Spécialistes*).
57 Carp, "La vie lente est longue" ["Slow Life Is Long"], n.p.
58 "Être ensemble en restant singulier" ["To Be Together While Remaining Singular"] (interview), *Alternatives théâtrales* 76–77 (2003), pp. 84–87.
59 Ibid., p. 89.
60 Recent translators have opted, however, for the original term *Verfremdung* in their English translations. See the editor's introduction to the third edition of *Brecht on Theatre* (London: Bloomsbury-Methuen, 2014).
61 Georges Didi-Huberman, *Ce que nous voyons, ce qui nous regarde* [*What We See, What Sees Us*] (Paris: Editions de Minuit, 1992), p. 170.
62 Jean Jourdheuil, *Un théâtre du regard: Gilles Aillaud – le refus du pathos* [*A Theatre of Spectating: The Refusal of Pathos*] (Paris: Bourgois, 2002), p. 28.
63 For an in-depth commentary on this, see the recent issue of *Théâtre/Public* edited by Jean Jourdheuil: "Travaux d'atelier: Foucault Mozart Müller", *Théâtre/Public* 176 (2005), n.p.
64 Hence the insertion of dialogue from *Apocalypse Now* into *Forever Young*, his 2003 adaptation of Tennessee Williams' *Sweet Bird of Youth*, but also his parodies of American series or Hollywood movies, or his mixture of registers (melodrama and serial gags).
65 Hans-Thies Lehmann, *Postdramatic Theatre*, trans. Karen Jürs-Munby (London and New York: Routledge, 2006), p. 69.
66 Ibid., p. 82.
67 Ibid., p. 83.
68 Ibid.
69 Ibid.
70 Ibid., p. 89.
71 Ibid.
72 David Lescot, "Une syntaxe onirique (sur le Théâtre du Radeau)" ["A Dreamlike Syntax (on the Raft Theatre"], *Ritm* 4 (special issue: "Rêves: cinéma/théâtre"), (2001).
73 Jean-Paul Manganaro, "Retable pour *Cantates*", *Frictions* 5 (2002); reprinted in J.-P. Manganaro, *François Tanguy et Le Radeau* (Paris: POL, 2008), pp. 67–86.
74 J.-P. Manganaro cited in Lehmann, *Postdramatic Theatre*, p. 900.
75 *Les Cantates*, programme, Théâtre du Radeau, Le Mans (2001), n.p.
76 Ibid.
77 Lehmann, *Postdramatic Theatre*, p. 129.
78 Giovanni Lista, *La Scène moderne* [*The Modern Scene*] (Arles: Carré/Actes Sud, 1996), pp. 185–187.
79 Gilles Deleuze, "Un *Hamlet* de moins" ["A *Hamlet* of Less"], in C. Bene and G. Deleuze, *Superpositions* (Paris: Minuit, 1979), p. 114.
80 Romeo Castellucci, "Romeo Castellucci, entre tableau et scène du corps" ["Romeo Castellucci, Between Painting and Body Scene"], *Etudes théâtrales* 30 ("Arts de la scène, scène des arts", vol. III) (2004), n.p.
81 Romeo Castellucci, "Remonter aux sources inhumaines du théâtre" ["Go Back to the Inhuman Sources of Theatre"], *Europe* 873–874 (January–February 2002), p. 176.

82 Claudia Castellucci and Romeo Castellucci, *Les Pèlerins de la matière: Théorie et praxis du théâtre* [*The Pilgrims of Matter: Theatre Theory and Praxis*], translated from the Italian by K. Espinosa (Besançon: Les solitaires intempestifs, 2001), p. 35.
83 Ibid., pp. 15–17.
84 Genesi, from the programme for *Museum of Sleep.*
85 Castellucci and Castellucci, *Les Pèlerins de la matière*, p. 93.
86 Ibid., p. 84.
87 Ibid., p. 96.
88 Ibid., p. 97.
89 Ibid., p. 101.
90 Rodrigo Garcia, "Paroles d'artiste", in "Press File" ["*Dossier*"] for his first plays performed at the Théâtre de la Cité Universitaire, Paris: 2003.
91 Jan Fabre, "Le Guerrier de la beauté": Interviews with Hugo de Greef and Jan Hoet (Paris: L'Arche, 1993), pp. 90–91.
92 Ibid.
93 Alain Platel at www.lesballetscdela.be.
94 "Documentaristes de notre temps" ["Documentarty Artists of Our Time"], interview: Alain Platel and Arne Sierens with Jean-Marc Adolphe, *Mouvement* 8 (April–June 2000), p. 97.
95 Forced Entertainment, presentation of *Bloody Mess*. www.forcedentertainment.com/projects/bloody-mess.

CONCLUSION

In the end, dramatic illusion seems to have lost the battle against media illusion. Media images offer audiences such instant and immediate satisfaction that they have stolen most of the theatre's spectators. Faced with a dwindling audience in recent years, the theatre has thus had to find ways of winning them back. But how does one win spectators back over to an art increasingly perceived as archaic? Brecht has already asked this question, but contemporary theatre has reframed the terms of the debate. Rather than peddling the myth of theatrical illusion, contemporary theatrical performance plays on the co-presence of actors and audiences. In other words, theatre is increasingly played in the present tense, emphasising the present-ness of all its components. This opens up all sorts of potentialities and possibilities hitherto untapped. Rather than try to captivate the audience, contemporary theatre practice seeks to emancipate it (to borrow the terms of Jacques Rancière[1]) from its passive position as a consumer of cultural goods. The audience becomes a critical subject and co-creator of the performance. As such, the dominance and ubiquity of screens has led today to an *unframing* of the theatre.

Since it was no longer able to be the best possible source of "absolute drama", theatrical performance has had to become the ostensible manifestation of a collective event once more. In other words, it has had to go back to being, fundamentally, a group of assembled people (artists and audience). Consequently, we have witnessed a tendency in recent years to represent the specific tensions that inherently exist between theatre's spectators and its actors or performers, as well as the movement of signifiers between performance, the performance space and the audience in its entirety. It has become possible, in this way, to return to a fundamental curiosity towards the theatrical object. Practitioners propose potential realities and spectators increasingly want to participate (either via their gaze and/or their active involvement) in the elaboration of what is performed. So much so that contemporary theatre has offered the possibility of creating, or recreating, an illusion that is no longer *dramatic*, but *participative*, doing away with the opposition between the act of making theatre and the act of watching or consuming it. Through a succession of stages (self-reflection, decomposition and separation of the elements of dramatic theatre and so on), contemporary practice often places all the objects of theatre at the same level as the text and even thinks of them without the text. The author – if, in fact, there still is one – the director, the scenographer and especially the spectator, now witness the creation of (postdramatic) writing and stage work. The theatre has been renewed thanks to an attempt at presenting "the collectively spent and used up lifetime in the collectively breathed air of that space in which the performing *and* the spectating take place", as Hans-Thies Lehmann writes.[2]

In order to transcend illusion, practitioners now attempt to include the spectator in the theatrical performance and to emphasise the idea of a virtual here and now shared and composed by all. The experience they propose, or the fable that sometimes underlies it, thus knows neither before nor after, but only a personal memory. Consequently, through the plasticity of form, and by proposing to all the partners of the theatrical play (the spectator included) the production of a present and virtual moment (a performance), by inciting everyone to question the performance and the virtuality of this shared experience, this theatre, as theorised by Hans-Thies Lehmann, leads to a sort of communal ceremony. The limit of all this is that the "session effect" (in other words, the time spent sharing different tasks and inviting the spectator to be part of the practitioners' activity) rarely generates any other object of debate than the theatre itself, its communication protocols, its effect, its form. Part of what defines contemporary theatre is its rejection of theatrical illusion through an exploration of the very *form* of theatre: interested in the theatricality of the performance space and the text, and presenting them as the only subjects worthy of debate during the time and space of the show. By questioning the form of performance at the same time as that very form is being acted out in the here and now of the stage, contemporary theatre has allowed spectators to reconsider four fields of perception: the text, time, space and the body. Nevertheless, form is not everything, and to explore it constantly is to tire the very audience that one hopes to win over. The effect of surprise is soon followed by the terrible threat of solipsism.

The text, which hitherto was considered the sacred object that representation was meant to "serve", is one major element that practitioners return to, but is now often considered a mouldable material like any other. Alternatively, it is the basis for a staged performance, or is even sometimes altogether absent. The anteriority of text has been displaced by a more critical praxis in which text is *constituted* by performance, and in which textual materiality is regarded as a historical, aesthetic and social semiological entity: in other words, as an artistic event. As a result, spectators, conferred with a creative and artistic role – which in reality they had never totally lost – are now often considered by critics as being closely associated with the theatrical production. Significantly, however, the spectators' "participation" is in no way harmonious or perfectly ritualised. It is based on more or less accepted conventions, oppositions, multiple affective reactions, social behaviours of all kinds, which help to make the performance, not a fervent ceremony, but a field of aesthetic and social forces, in short, a theatre *session*. The recognised, affirmed presence of the audience induces a major relationship between actor, director, practitioners, the "author" and the spectator. It produces a tension that requires from all and at all levels: strategies, calculations, tactics for capturing and maintaining interest, circumvention, confrontation. And while recent times have brought with them, unfortunately, a growing homogeneity of audiences and practitioners (theatre is, after all, oriented towards those who practice it or towards connoisseurs), the fact still remains that the theatre's vocation is to address everyone, which implies a heterogeneous, and thus conflicting, audience.

In recent years, critics have finally recognised that instead of being ideally linear, continuous and illusionist, theatre could also be nonlinear, discontinuous and that there could be a porosity between spectators and actors/performers. These same critics have watched productions that openly affirm the death of the beautiful Aristotelian animal, and the implosion of the dramatic genre was obvious. In considering the practical conditions of this implosion, or crisis, and in seeking to establish a relationship of cause and effect, critical theory initially associated it with the crisis of modernity that emerged, more or less, at the turn of the twentieth century. Admittedly, there are many reasons to think that at this precise moment in the history of forms, something happened that could be considered a crisis. At the same time, however, one must admit that while this "crisis" was first openly identified and theorised in the late nineteenth/early twentieth century, its origins are much farther back in the past.

It therefore seems necessary to go back in time again; not to look for another modernity, or for the objective and tangible "roots" of such a crisis, but to realise and appreciate that it does not, in fact, have the radical or transgressive character attributed to it, but that it is rather a threshold, or seen from a different standpoint, that it is consubstantial with the history of theatre. There is no doubt that the notions of absolute illusion, the fourth wall and "dramatic theatre" did appear in the seventeenth and eighteenth centuries, with d'Aubignac, Marmontel and Diderot, and were more clearly theorised at the end of the nineteenth century. However, we also know that they are mentioned much earlier in the history of the theatre, if only in the work of Aristotle or in the sixteenth century, in Italy, where there was a practical desire to represent fictions by acting *as if* the actors were playing in front of an empty room, addressing each other without looking at the audience, to better embody their characters.

Even so, while such illusionist, "dramatic" forms were being sought after, "non-dramatic" theatre, based on principles of porosity, decomposition, separation, self-reflection and accompanied by paratactic, simultaneous, transgeneric and corporeal forms rather than textual ones, has always existed in theatrical productions. It thus does not constitute a break in the history of the theatre, but a part of what the theatre has always been: a social and aesthetic performance composed by several parties, bringing spectators and actors into interaction thanks to a series of plastic, musical, textual and corporeal actions.

This awareness of the session, the porosity of places and spaces and the questioning of illusion, are therefore nothing new in theatrical practice. If contemporary theatre presents itself as an art of *feeling* together and of *thinking* together, in a conflictual, heterogeneous and contradictory manner, this is in no way original. What the success of Lehmann's work indicates is not necessarily, or only, the discovery of a new trend in contemporary theatrical practice, but rather a social and aesthetic practice that has always existed in the history of theatre, even if during the long period of "dramatic theatre" (from the eighteenth to the twentieth centuries) this practice was largely underestimated by critics hungry for illusion and for a "literary" theatre. Despite the dominance of drama and illusionism in the media and the fact that spectators' expectations are still conditioned towards illusion, the current success of performance as an approach to theatrical production has allowed, not only for the reading of the present in the light of performance, but also for the rereading of the whole history of the theatre, thanks to this new practical and theoretical tool.

In the first chapters of this work, we have seen that both parallel to, and even before, what we refer to as "dramatic theatre" (broadly speaking), other forms of theatre and entertainment have always existed. Overall, it seems as if the separation between stage and audience, the effect of the fourth wall, the notion of illusion and that of absolute drama, were of little interest to audiences and practitioners, whereas they truly obsessed the great theorists of theatre, from Aristotle to Szondi. It also seems that in a host of traditions and experiments throughout history, no postulate has ever existed of a necessary and continuous break between dramatic space and theatrical place, or between the time of the fiction represented and the time of the staging. On the contrary, it does seems that, despite the apparently consensual idea that theatre is mainly "dramatic" and that it is essentially based on mimesis and illusion, audiences and practitioners have been, and still remain, conscious of the fact that the sessions, these moments spent in a theatre or any other place of performance, are, at their core, unique slices of life experienced communally by actors and spectators.

Therefore, in our opinion, the "postdramatic" category as Lehmann theorises it should be placed into an historical perspective. In other words, instead of a naive notion of modernity based on a rejection of the dramatic – as whether non-dramatic or postdramatic, it is still the dramatic that is being considered essential – it would be better to see in the "postdramatic" a constant feature in the entire history of theatre. Without doubt, theatre, either in its entirety or in part, has been "postdramatic" even before the theorisation of drama. As such, there is no longer any need to see the "postdramatic" as "post-", as there is no longer any need to link it necessarily, or essentially, to "drama". In this sense, a whole section of the history of the theatre awaits to be named. And what should we call it? Do we need to invent a new concept? Should we talk about epic or the spectacular? Should we name this concept based on the notion of performance, event or session? Or should we not come back to the *play*, in other words, to the fact that theatre necessarily introduces spatial, temporal, plastic, corporeal, textual and political "play" between the parts of the session, aesthetically producing open spaces, so that a playful interaction, one both entertaining and (politically, aesthetically, and philosophically) impactful, can captivate and engage its various partners?

The theatrical event, in this sense, has the function of producing a multiple playful interaction that summons, through its internal and external functioning, all (or part of) the elements of reality to make them interact within the context of the theatre's bifurcated real and virtual existence. As such, this play, this event-driven experience, this unstable, spatial, temporal, corporeal and textual approach to the relationship between the real and the virtual, can also affectively engage both the individuals who make the show (the actors and characters, the performers and practitioners) and all of those watching it – who thereby become producers (even if seated and silent). Because it has a social function, this play may orientate the spectator's gaze towards the space outside the theatre precinct, while rendering this exterior space concrete in the session and the show itself. In so doing, it produces a simulacrum of movement that is neither totally real nor absolutely virtual, and thus offers to those individuals assembled a projective, meditative or illusory interaction that is both entertaining and disturbing; a present, emotional, plastic interaction, entirely devoted to the celebration of play and the deepening of the relationship between the real and the virtual. The theatre could thus be defined as a performance figuration, a game event or a space of aesthetic and social interaction: a play of figuration, whose function and individual and collective operation consist in depicting a (critical) performance space in the context of a present event.

As a social, aesthetic, critical, figural and interactive play, the theatre exists in the empty space that society has carved out for it. The "play" it produces – both the theatrical play itself, but also the play, or slack, in the mechanism of the social machine – enables society to function, since without these "plays", in which the theatre may or may not actively indulge, all movement becomes impossible. This play of figuration is therefore essential to the proper functioning of society, on the condition that the theatre is still granted its intrinsic freedom. While the theatre does not always appear as obviously essential to the life of the social body, being located in the interstice of its social structures and forms of behaviour, it will always remain, in every respect, absolutely necessary.

Notes

1 See Jacques Rancière, *Le Spectateur émancipé* (Paris: La Fabrique, 2008) and Jacques Rancière, *The Emancipated Spectator* (London-New York: Verso, 2009).
2 Hans-Ties Lehmann, *Postdramatic Theatre*, trans. Karen Jürs-Munby (London-New York: Routledge, 2006), p. 17.

INDEX

Page numbers followed by 'n' refer to notes.

18 Happenings in 6 Parts (Karpow) 476
1789 (dir. Mnouchkine) 57, 73, 442, 447
1793 (dir. Mnouchkine) 73–74

The Abstract Room [*La Camera Astratta*] (Corsetti) 551
acoustics 92–93, 94, 162, 206
actantial analysis 393–396
acting space 51, 52, 57–60
An Actor Prepares (Stanislavski) 310–311
actors: art of staging the classics 432; audibility of 206, 558, 560, 563; celebrity and reputation 7, 264, 284–285; and characters 68, 112, 116, 135, 285–286, 287, 297–300, 306–311, 341, 505; collectives of *see* collectives; contemporary theatre 284, 286, 309–310, 444–446, 469–470, 505–509, 510, 514, 526, 557, 563, 564, 566–570; in the definition of performance 45; and the director in *mise en scène* 163; freedom and *mise en scène* 459; Gatti's move from using professional actors 486; Greek skênographia 89; Grüber's theatricality of restraint 469, 470; illusion of creating illusion 84–85; Langhoff's aesthetic of the concrete 465, 467; lighting effects 217–219, 233, 271; Lupa's troubled realism 520, 521, 522, 524, 525; in Molière's oral tradition 353; opening night 23, 24–25, 30–32; play of forms 447, 448, 449; and props 240; and readers 343, 377; seventeenth and eighteenth century theatre 141–142, 143, 144; shown in their practice 9, 202, 526; as a site of meaning 114, 140, 173, 178, 255, 290–297, 463, 464, 510; sound and silence 221, 224, 231; and spectators 52, 138, 183–184, 203, 208, 264–265, 336–337, 571; stage directions 365, 366; "theatre of language" 501; theatrical codes 289–290; training 67, 101, 144–145, 294, 296, 404, 442, 444, 446, 448–449, 495; watched players 44; *see also* body (of actor)
Acts Without Words (Beckett) 365
The Adventures of the Good Soldier Schwejk (Piscator) 166
Aeschylus 90, 92, 274, 448, 512
After Sun (dir. García) 213, 568
L'Âge d'or [*The Golden Age*] (dir. Mnouchkine) 442, 447
Aillaud, Gilles 229–230, 440, 441, 471, 548, 549
Albers, Anni 475
Albers, Josef 475
Alexievitch, Svetlana 496, 541
All Indians (dir. Platel) 570
Allio, René 421, 422, 439

amateur theatre 96–103, 148
Amleto: La veemente esteriorità della morte di un mollusco [*Hamlet: The Vehement Exteriority of the Death of a Mollusc*] (dir. Castellucci) 319–323, 564
Amphitryon (Moliére) 269–270
Andrews, Raymond 437
Andromaque (Racine) 202–203, 210, 450
Angels in America (dir. Jaques-Wajeman) 433
L'Annonce faite à Marie [*The Annunciation*] (dir. Fisbach) 503–504, 544, 545
Antigone (Sophocles) 373
Antoine, André 156, 158–159, 200, 416
Aperghis, Georges 229, 450
L'Apocalypse joyeuse [*The Joyous Apocalypse*] (dir. Py) 532
Apocalypsis cum figuris (Grotowski) 446
Apollinaire: Guillaume 473
apparatus *see* machinery
Appia, Adolphe 160, 200, 416
applause 227–228, 264, 306–307
Aragon, Louis 436–437, 449, 451, 452
architecture 70, 77, 80–85, 94, 103, 123, 162, 189, 231
Aristotle: catharsis 331, 332, 334; classic tragedy 331, 384, 386; dramatic mimesis 152–153, 299, 584; *opsis* and text 91–92, 93, 94, 347, 500
Arlecchino servitore di due padroni [*Harlequin, Servant of Two Masters*] (dir. Strehler) 202, 453
Arrivée Gare de Bade (dir. Marthaler) 537–538
Arroyo, Edouardo 440
Artaud, Antonin 284, 316, 317, 318, 328, 329, 350, 445, 565
L'Art du théâtre [*The Art of Theatre*] (magazine) 458, 459
As You Like It (dir. François, Marc) 507
Atelier Berthier *see* Odéon-Berthier
L'Athénée, Théâtre de 78, 214, 432, 434
d'Aubignac, abbé Hédelin 124, 146, 215, 304, 352, 584; *La Pratique du théâtre* [*The Practice of Theatre*] 33, 142–144, 146, 306, 307, 386

audience 494; *see also* spectators
Augustine (Saint) 328
autos sacramentales 64, 95, 98, 122
avant-garde theatre: and contemporary non-dramatic aesthetic 47, 479, 555; and Gatti 484, 487–488; and Kantor 232, 480, 482, 483, 484; make-up 251; Marthaler 537; montage and hybridisation 474, 475, 476, 477, 479; sound effects 230; temporal discontinuity 271; *see also* Schechner, Richard; Wilson, Robert (Bob)
Les Aveugles [*The Blind*] (Maeterlinck) 155, 507, 553
Avignon *see* Palais des Papes (Avignon)
Azama, Michael 406

Bailly, Jean-Christophe 535
Les Bains [*The Bathhouse*] (Maïakovski) 450
ballet 107, 108, 182, 228, 246, 313, 434
Le Bal [*The Ball*] (dir. Penchenat) 228, 229
Le Ballet de la paille ou la fille mal gardée [*The Ballet of Straw, or the Wayward Daughter*] (Dauberval) 182
Banu, Georges 203, 212, 459, 483
Baratto, Mario 21
Barker, Howard 411
Barker, Robert 150
Baroni, Guido 439
Baroque aesthetic 425–426, 434, 466, 532, 533
Barrault, Jean-Louis 201, 426
Barthes, Roland 417, 418, 426, 464
Le baruffe chiozzotte (dir. Strehler) 454
The Bathhouse [*Les Bains*] (Maïakovski) 450
Bauhaus 474, 475
Bavarian Passion plays 98–99
Beaumarchais, Pierre 58, 122, 136, 153, 190, 244, 435, 531
Beck, Julian 445, 476
Beckett, Samuel 55, 122, 237, 279, 350, 365, 366
The Beggar's Opera (Gay) 71, 228–229
Bell, Marie 181, 289

INDEX

The Bells of the Basel [*Les Cloches de Bâle*] (Aragon) 451
benches *see* stage benches
Bene, Carmelo 230, 318, 563–564
Benetton, United Colors of 218
Benhamou, Anne-Françoise 460, 461, 508
Bérénice (Racine): and classic French tragedy 385; director as author 420; dramatic time 269, 278, 368; Fisbach 544–546; floor covering 210; Grüber 223–224, 420, 427, 470, 471; stage space 190
Berger extravagant (Corneille, Thomas) 183–184
Bergman, Ingrid 269
Berliner Ensemble 216, 270, 417–418, 465, 527
Bernadetje (dir. Platel) 228, 229, 569
Bernhard, Thomas 237, 521, 522
Bernhardt, Sarah 181, 289
Bertin, Roland 461
Bertolazzi, Carlo 454
bifrontal staging 202–204, 209, 218, 219, 461
Bildbeschreibung [*Explosion of a Memory/Paysage sous surveillance*] (Müller) 391–392
Birkin, Jane 491
Blackland (dir. Schilling) 514
Blasted (Kane) 170, 272, 387–391, 520
Blin, Roger 226, 366, 438
The Blind [*Les Aveugles*] (Maeterlinck) 155, 507, 553
Bloody Mess (Forced Entertainment) 571–572
Bobnigy *see* MC 93 (Bobigny)
body (of actor): autistic performance 318–323; breathing 93, 292–294, 295, 408, 502; Brook's theatre of presence 444; coordinates of the stage 205, 214; costume and make-up 246–247, 248–251; duality 283–284, 300–302, 318; eyes/gaze 291–292; facial expressions 250, 288, 289, 291, 297; naturalist drama 159, 160; non-dramatic theatre's foregrounding of the body 284, 444–446, 514, 557, 563, 564,
566–570; orientation of 296–297, 510; perspective 116, 128–129, 135; and props 189, 235; the realism of the *mise en scène* 159, 160; sensors and video technology 551; sites and spaces 51, 52, 53, 56, 57–60, 113, 122; slowing movement down 233, 270, 271, 436, 516; voice and mouth 206–207, 288–289, 291, 292–296, 505, 566
Bond, Edward 411
Bondy, Luc 79, 181, 210, 431
Le Bonheur d'être rouge (dir. Lambert) 513
Bonnaud, Irène 165, 405
Bonnier, Céline 553
The Book of Christopher Columbus [*Le Livre de Christophe Colomb*] (Claudel) 381
The Bores [*Les Fâcheux*] (Molière) 313
Bosch, Jérôme 568
Bouchaud, Nicolas 529
Boudaut, Yann 227
Bouffes du Nord, Théâtre des 162, 212, 235, 458
Boulevard du Crime 71–72
boulevard theatre 71–72, 80, 172, 177, 207, 252, 284, 290, 450
Le Bourgeois gentilhomme [*The Bourgeois Gentleman*] (Molière) 245–246
Brand (Ibsen) 511
Brando, Marlon 285
Braunschweig, Stéphane 361, 509–512
Bread and Puppet Theater 65–66, 183
Break of Noon [*Partage de midi*] (dir. Vitez) 452
The Breasts of Tiresas [*Les Mamelles de Tirésias*] (dir. Apollinaire) 473
Brecht, Bertolt: alienation/distance (*Verfremdungseffekt*) 166, 418, 428, 478, 504, 516, 534, 547; Berliner Ensemble 216, 270, 417–418, 465, 527; on catharsis 334; *The Caucasian Chalk Circle* 167, 272–273, 526; Chéreau 460; collective models 442; Dort on 463; epic theatre 157, 165, 166, 167, 168, 270, 277, 346, 475, 527, 547; on the fourth wall 306; and Langhoff 465, 466,

INDEX

469; levels of reference 255; *The Life of Galileo* (Brecht) 454, 531; lighting 216; *Man Equals Man* (Brecht) 167, 527–528; and the meaning mill 417–418, 419, 425; *Mr Puntila and his Man Matti* (dir. Schleef) 536; Planchon 438, 450; and Rousset 305; scenography 418, 424, 425, 428, 439, 440; Strehler's productions 453, 454, 455; use of song 167, 228–229, 230
Breyzig, Johann Adam 150
Broadway 167, 217, 252, 477
Brook, Peter: Bouffes du Nord theatre 162, 212; *The Costume* 247–248; *The Mahabharata* 44, 162, 263, 457–458; rise of director-artists 415; and the Tazieh 99; use of space 172, 207, 212, 239–240, 247–248, 444
Brothers Karamazov (dir. Lupa) 521, 523
Bruguière, Dominique 518
buildings and sites: architecture 70, 80–85, 103; classic French theatre 106–110; contemporary theatre 76–79, 162–163, 201, 457–458, 504, 537–538; definitions 51, 52; Elizabethan theatre 70, 105–106; "going to the theatre" 43–44; Greek skênographia 89–92, 112; location 70–74; London (seventeenth-eighteenth century) 70–71; Middle Ages 94–95, 96, 98, 104; opening night point of view (spectator) 10; recycling and re-appropriating 72–76; relation to society 87; Roman scaena 92–94; shift from open to closed space 69, 70, 103–104; théâtre du Jeu de paume 75, 80, 110, 123; *see also* open spaces; proscenium (Italian-style) theatres

Cadiot, Oliver *see* Le Colonel des zouaves [*The Colonel of the Zouaves*] (Cadiot)
Cage, John 476, 477
Calderon de la Barca, Pedro 171, 434, 446, 501
La Camera Astratta [*The Abstract Room*] (Corsetti) 551

Il Campiello (dir. Strehler) 454
Le Canard sauvage qui vole contre le vent [*The Wild Duck that Flies Against the Wind*] (Gatti) 487
Canetti, Elias *see* Eraritjaritjaka, Museum of Sentences [*Eraritjaritjaka, musée des phrases*] (Goebbels)
Les Cantates [*The Cantatas*] (Tanguy) 559, 560, 562
Le Cantique des Cantiques [*The Song of Songs*] (dir. Fort) 182
Capeck, Kerel 474
The Carcana Tribe in War Against What? [*La Tribu des carcana en guerre contre quoi?*] (Gatti) 487–488
Cartoucherie in Vincennes 72–74, 77, 162
Castellucci, Romeo 226, 230, 259n8, 319, 320, 564–567
Castorf, Frank 184, 213, 238–239, 405, 552, 556
catharsis 329–335
Catherine d'après Les Cloches de Bâle (dir. Vitez) 451
Caubère, Philippe 429
The Caucasian Chalk Circle (Brecht) 167, 272–273, 526–527
Cavaillès, Jean 487
celebrity theatre 264, 284–285, 491
Les Cercueils de zinc [*The Coffins of Zinc*] (T'chan'G) 496, 541
La Cerisaie [*The Cherry Orchard*] (Chekhov) 156, 185, 454, 511, 530–531
Cézanne, Paul 457
Chaillot, Théâtre national de 226, 233, 405, 434, 439, 449, 452, 457, 458, 490, 509, 527
Les Chaises [*The Chairs*] (Ionesco) 189, 234
Une Chambre en Inde [*A Room in India*] (dir. Mnouchkine) 213, 442
Chant public devant deux chaises éléctriques [*Public Song In Front of Two Electric Chairs*] (Gatti) 411, 485–486
characters: and actors 68, 112, 116, 135, 285–286, 287, 297–300, 306–311, 341, 505; archetypes 58, 242–243, 389–390; dramatic discourse 357–359; eponymous

INDEX

374, 375, 376; Gatti's rejection of 486; psychology 393, 395–396, 422, 524–525; readers of theatre texts 372–374; Régy's theatre of non-representation 516; as semantic entities 301; and spectators 61, 243, 285–286, 298, 299, 300, 302, 304, 306–311, 315, 511; virtual body of 297–300

Chartreux, Bernard, *Dernières nouvelles de la Peste* [*The Latest News on the Plague*] 444

Chattot, François 444, 464, 465–466

Chénetier-Alev, Marion 349

Chéreau, Patrice: and Braunschweig 509; *Dans la solitude des champs de coton* [*In the Solitude of Cotton Fields*] (dir. Chéreau) 218, 461; *La Dispute* [*The Dispute*] 211, 423, 424–425, 439, 460; *Dom Juan* 423, 424; *La Fausse suivante* 491; formalism of 438; *Hamlet* 457, 461; lighting effects 218; *The Massacre at Paris* 438, 439; and the *mise en scène* movement 460–461; pared down aesthetics 457, 460–461; *Phèdre* 181, 202, 203, 204, 218, 461; resignation from the Amandiers 490; *Richard II* 424; *Der Ring* [*The Ring*] 457, 460; rise of director-artists 415, 420, 436, 457, 460; staging the classics 181, 202–204, 218, 423–425, 438, 439, 457, 461

The Cherry Orchard (Chekhov) 156, 185, 454, 511, 530–531

The Children of Heracles (dir. Sellars) 512

chorality: actantial analysis 393, 395; *Amleto: La veemente esteriorità della morte di un mollusco* [*Hamlet: The Vehement Exteriority of the Death of a Mollusc*] (dir. Castellucci) 322; author's voice 381–382; *The Caucasian Chalk Circle* (Brecht) 167; contemporary aspirations 534–542, 543, 544; *Gaudeamus* (dir. Dodine) 535; Greek tragedy 89, 90, 165, 395, 512; *Lenz* (Büchner) 469; *Phèdre* (dir. Chéreau) 203; printed texts 345

Christie, William 434

Cicéri, Pierre 151

Le Cid (Corneille) 109, 235, 236, 277, 385

Cieslak, Richard 446

cinema: Brechtian revolution in theatre 166; Gatti 484, 485; illusion 168, 258, 324–327, 477, 493, 499, 500, 514, 554; *Notorious* (dir. Hitchcock) 269; scenography 163; spectators 7, 8, 48, 62, 215, 324–326, 327; temporal ruptures 271, 272; theatrical hybridity 460, 474, 551, 552

Cinna ou la Clémence d'Auguste [*Cinna, or the Clemency of Caesar Augustus*] (Corneille) 172, 174n12, 374, 385, 507

circuses: circular stages 198, 200, 201; hybrid aesthetics 567; lighting of 218; pure theatricality 284; Russian theatre 474; scenography 163; surrealism 474; tradition drawn on by Vitez 450

citizens' theatre 494

Cixous, Hélène 447, 448

La Clairon 244, 305

Claudel, Paul: *L'Annonce faite à Marie* [*The Annunciation*] (dir. Fisbach) 503–504, 544, 545; *L'Échange* (T'chan'G) 495; invisible theatre of 350; *Le Livre de Christophe Colomb* [*The Book of Christopher Columbus*] 381; orality 294, 353, 450, 503; *Le Soulier de satin* [*The Satin Slipper*] (Claudel) 263, 452, 457, 532

Claustrophobia (dir. Dodine) 535

Cleansed (Kane) 390–391

Clévenot, Philippe 444, 510

cliché 302

Clitandre (Corneille) 434

Les Cloches de Bâle [*The Bells of the Basel*] (Aragon) 451

closure effect 152–154, 208, 457; *see also* fourth wall

CNSAD *see* National Conservatory of Dramatic Arts (CNSAD)

The Coffins of Zinc [*Les Cercueils de zinc*] (T'chan'G) 496, 541

collectives 441–444, 472–473, 495–496, 513, 526–530, 571; *see also* tg STAN; Théâtre du Soleil

591

INDEX

Collin, Yann-Joël 528, 529, 530
La Colline, Théâtre National de 233, 290, 407
Le Colonel des zouaves [*The Colonel of the Zouaves*] (Cadiot) 231, 551
Combat de nègre et de chiens [*Fight of the Negro and the Dog*] (dir. Chéreau) 461
Comédie-Française 17, 77, 80, 190, 206, 223, 234, 313, 434–435, 468, 490
comedy 90, 93, 109, 153, 307, 435, 468, 528, 539
The Comic Illusion [*L'Illusion comique*] (Corneille) 39n12, 131–134, 138, 171, 196, 273, 274, 310, 312, 454
commedia dell'arte 58, 161, 243, 244, 280–281, 290, 442, 447
Le Commerce de pain [*The Trade in Bread*] (dir. Langhoff) 465
community outreach activities 15, 494
Compré una pala in Ikea para cavar mi tumba (dir. García) 514, 568
confessions 269
Confrères de la Passion 70, 98, 261
The Constant Prince (Slowacki) 446
contemporary theatre: actors 284, 286, 309–310, 444–446, 469–470, 505–509, 510, 514, 526, 557, 563, 564, 566–570; alienation effect 164, 168, 546–547; amateur theatre 96–103, 148; ancient staging mechanisms 198–199; bi-frontal staging 202–204, 218, 219, 461; Braunschweig's aesthetics of readability 509–511; celebrity theatre 264, 284–285, 491; chorality 322, 469, 534–542, 535, 543, 544; and cinematic illusion 168, 258, 324–327, 477, 499, 500, 514; classics as symptom 425, 426–435; collectives 441–444, 495–496, 513, 526–530, 571; community, notions of 494–495; costumes 247; the curtain 9, 193–194, 309; curtain calls 227–228; cyclorama 196; on the danger of over-interpretation 253; *Deafman Glance* (Wilson) 436–437, 438; directors, new generation of 491–493; dramatic time 265, 271; emancipated representation 456, 458, 460, 461–465, 497–499; Fisbach's decentred representation 543–546; forms, play of 447–452; Gatti, emblem of 487–488; generational turning point 490–491; Grüber's theatricality of restraint 469–472; illusion and autistic performance 319–323; image factory, rise of 436–441; Kantor, emblem of 480–484; Koltès 218, 220, 271, 350, 378–381, 397, 461; lighting 208, 212, 215, 217, 218, 219, 220, 221; locations 76–78, 457–458, 470, 494, 538, 553; memory and repetition 78–79, 104–105, 183, 404, 430, 473, 584–585; and *mise en scène* 415–416, 458–460, 554, 555, 558; montage 207, 465, 466, 468, 476–479, 513, 549–550, 552, 558–559, 571; multimediality 163, 232, 404, 468, 528, 550–553, 570; non-illusionist captivation 547–549, 581–582; notions of performance 44, 45, 46–47; objects and props 238–239, 240, 466, 470, 471, 489, 548; oral text and act of reading 349–350, 353–354; perception, troubled and fragmented 515–525, 525, 528, 531, 542, 546–547, 550–551, 554, 555, 556–557, 560, 569; political dimension 408, 433, 486–487, 498, 511–514, 537–538; as "proposal" 496–497; scenography 114, 439–441, 461, 467–469, 509, 510; semiotic functioning of the stage space 178, 180; smell, taste and touch 183–184, 185, 467; social spaces 81–82; sounds and silence 221–222, 227–228, 229–231, 558–559, 565; stage floor 211–213, 233–234, 239–240; staging concerns 403–415; survival of 78, 493–494, 581; and the text 45, 492–493, 499–505; theatricality unveiled 195, 525–534, 549, 582; transitions and multiplicity of discourses 403–406; video 62, 232, 404, 468, 528, 550,

551–553, 554, 570; writing for the theatre today 406–409; *see also* postdramatic theatre
La Conversation interrompue (dir. Lambert) 513
Copeau, Jacques 162, 453
Copernicus, Nicolaus 119
Corneille, Pierre: "auditors" 186; catharsis 333; *Le Cid* 109, 235, 236, 277, 385; *Cinna ou la Clémence d'Auguste* [*Cinna, or the Clemency of Caesar Augustus*] 172, 174n12, 374, 385, 507; distance between actors and roles 310, 311; eponymous characters 375; format of the printed text 345; *L'Illusion comique* [*The Comic Illusion*] 39n12, 131–134, 138, 171, 196, 273, 274, 310, 312, 454; lexical features 352–353; *peripeteia* 385; standard theatrical repertoire 7, 434, 435; theatrical rules and systems 124, 277, 385; twentieth century interpretation 425, 426
Corneille, Thomas 435; *Le Berger extravagant* 183–184; *Timocrate* 385, 386
corrales 69, 162
Corsetti, Giorgio Barberio 551
The Costume (dir. Brook) 247–248
costumes 23, 24, 219, 240–248, 254, 265, 561, 563, 565
The Country House (Kantor) 480
court side 191–192
court theatre 64, 65, 106, 107–108, 117–119, 124, 199
Craig, Edward Gordon 160–161, 200, 416, 458, 462
The Crazy Day, or the Marriage of Figaro [*La Folle journée ou Le Mariage de Figaro*] (Sivadier) 531
critical theatre: actors 442, 445, 446; and art theatre 452–453, 455; and Braunschweig's *Merchant of Venice* 511; classic plays reinterpreted 420–425, 430, 450; and Dort's emancipated representation 463; and dramaturgy 419–420; emergence 418–419; and formalism 447, 449; ideological-aesthetic mutations 511–512; and the image factory 438, 439; Marxist context 419; and theatre of non-representation 525, 534, 547
Critique (journal) 406
La Critique de l'École des femmes [*A Criticism of the School for Wives*] (Molière) 138, 226, 451
cross-dressing 250–251
The Crying Body (dir. Fabre) 185, 568
Cue to Cue Rehearsal, with Orchestra [*Italienne avec orchestre*] (dir. Sivadier) 531
Cunningham, Merce 476
curtain call 108, 222, 226, 227, 263–264, 309
curtains: contemporary theatre 9, 193–194, 309; Elizabethan theatre 105; framing effect and the frontal staging 194, 431; marking session time 193, 222, 226, 227, 309; piquing the audience's curiosity 69; Roman theatre 93; separating the audience from the fiction 111, 149, 192–193, 545
cyclorama 194, 196, 206, 209, 216, 269, 440, 468

Dadaism 474, 480, 537
Daguerre, Louis 150
Damiani, Lucio 439, 454
Danan, Joseph 399, 431; opening night point of view 14–19
Danchenko, Vladimir 162, 416, 453
Danis, Daniel 290, 350
Dans la solitude des champs de coton [*In the Solitude of Cotton Fields*] (dir. Chéreau) 218, 461
Dauberval, Jean 182
The Dead Class (Kantor) 480, 481, 482, 483
Deafman Glance (Wilson) 436–437, 438
De Architectura (Vitruvius) 94
The Death of Danton [*La Mort de Danton*] (Büchner) 209, 532
The Death of Pompey [*La Mort de Pompée*] (Corneille) 375–376, 507
The Death of Seneca [*La Mort de Sénèque*] (Tristan L'Hermite) 434

The Death of Tintagiles [*La Mort de Tintagiles*] (dir. Régy) 517
De Filippo, Eduardo *see* Sabato, domenica e lunedì (De Filippo)
Definitive and Lasting Return of the Loved One [*Retour définitif et durable de l'être aimé*] (dir. Lagarde) 551
Delbée, Anne 260n11, 427
Delcuvellerie, Jacques 513
Deliers, Jean-Michel 204
delirium 304–305, 309, 310, 317–318, 321, 328, 389
Delpeyrat, Scali, opening night point of view 30–32
Depardieu, Gérard 491
Déprats, Jean-Michel 459
Le Dernier caravansérail [*The Last Caravan Stop*] (dir. Mnouchkine) 213, 442, 448
Dernières nouvelles de la Peste [*The Latest News on the Plague*] (Chartreux) 444
Desarthe, Gerard 461
Desmarets de Saint-Sorlin, Jean 434
Deutsch, Michel 443, 535
Dialogue aus dem Messingkauf [*The Messingkauf dialogues*] (Brecht) 306
Dictionnaire universel (Furetière) 68, 304
Diderot, Denis: on catharsis 334; *Entretiens sur "Le Fils naturel"* [*Interviews on "The Natural Son"*] 147, 149; *Le Fils naturel* [*The Natural Son*] 147–148, 153, 274; fourth wall 147, 148, 149, 150, 154, 159, 192, 306, 584; orality 349; *Paradoxe sur le comédien* [*Paradox of the Actor*] 185; stage directions 147, 349, 365, 366; temporality 274, 276
Didi, Evelyne 443, 444
Didi-Huberman, Georges 221, 548
diffraction: audience reception 123, 127, 135, 263, 320, 431, 499, 542, 549, 550, 551, 554; chorality 381–382, 536, 541, 542, 544; performance 137, 300, 379, 411, 426, 428, 431, 461–462, 468, 469, 546, 550; readers 357, 359; society 493; texts 356–357, 358, 392
diorama 150–151
Diot, André 425, 439

director-artists: and actors 441–446, 448–449, 450, 453; contemporary evolution 403, 489–494, 495, 496, 497, 498, 499, 509–510; emergence 415–417; image theatre 436–441; institutionalisation 415, 457, 490; meaning creation 418, 419–420, 436; previous generation 158, 162, 416; staging the classics 420–429, 430, 450–452; theatre as a relative totality 455–456, 489; triumphant theatricality 452–455, 472, 489
"discovery" 171
La Dispute [*The Dispute*] (dir. Chéreau) 211, 423, 424–425, 439, 460
distance: actors shown in their practice 202, 526; audience's awareness of other spectators 137, 138, 164, 215; Brecht's alienation and epic theatre 165, 166, 167, 168, 418, 428, 478, 504, 516, 534, 547; catharsis 333, 334; characters and actors 291, 298, 299–300, 303, 310, 311, 505–506; chorality 537, 544; cinema 327; classic and classical drama, modern staging 139, 172, 234, 420, 421, 426, 427, 430; curtain call convention 227; discontinuous engagement 305, 307, 312, 314, 315, 337; dramatic code for a long journey 100; eighteenth century theatre 112, 125, 149–150; Florentine court theatre 118; Grüber 472; in the juridical space of the theatre 137, 169, 197, 315, 337; make-up 251; musicality 544; non-illusionist captivation 547–548, 557, 562; poetic 529; reading the text 362, 366; referential offstage space 209, 218; seventeenth century theatre 164; showing process 118, 171, 195, 197, 419, 527–528, 561; showing writing 501, 504; social alienation 167, 507, 514; theatre as an individual and collective experience 42
The Distant Country [*Le Pays lointain*] (Lagarce) 407

INDEX

dithyramb 331
Doctor Faustus Lights the Lights (Stein, Gertrude) 479
Dodine, Lev 535
Dom Juan (Molière): actor's presence 58; Chéreau 423, 424; Footsbarn theatre 78, 429; indexical reading 366, 377; Jaques-Wajeman 433; referential signs 254; Tanguy and the Théâtre du Radeau 558; taste 185; Vitez 451
Donellan, Declan 235
Dort, Bernard: on emancipated representation 462–463, 464, 472, 489; on Gatti's theatre 485; on Grüber 470; on rise of *mise en scène* 416, 417, 458; on Strehler 454, 455; on Vincent's plays at the TNS 442
double cone 128
The Double-Crosser's Comeuppance [*La Fausse suivante*] (dir. Chéreau) 491
Le Dragon [*The Dragon*] (Schwartz) 450
dramatic theatre: Aristotle's *Poetics* 152–153, 165; death of 157; dramatic time 266, 274, 279; illusion box and the fourth wall 146–151, 152, 154, 157, 208, 306, 584–585; narrative principles 165–166; perspective 152; sounds and silence 222, 225
dramatic time: Brecht's episodic theatre 277; crisis of drama (late nineteenth/early twentieth century) 113, 155–156, 157; discontinuity 165, 266–275, 368, 370; episodes 152, 275, 276–277, 279, 280, 369; lighting 160, 437; Lupa's disturbing strangeness 521; readers 363–364, 370–371; stage props 238, 255, 265, 466; timelessness 279, 370; twenty four hour principle 277–278
dramaturgy: abstract theatre 519–520; and actor's play 178; Braunschweig 509, 510–511; Brechtian tradition 165, 166, 272, 280, 418, 419, 442; Chéreau 460; classic texts re-interpreted 420–425, 426, 430,

431; collective approach 442–444, 472–473, 527–528; contemporary practice 14–19, 180, 396–400, 405; *The Costume* (Brooks) 247, 248; crisis of representation 497, 498; *La Cerisaie* [*The Cherry Orchard*] (Collin) 529; Langhoff 465, 466; Marthaler 539–540; non-mimetic theatre 549, 550; props 236, 239; reading the text 353, 359, 360, 361, 370, 374, 381, 387, 391, 393, 497; rhythmic coherence 281; self-reflexivity in pre-dramatic theatre 164–165; Shakespearean 529; Strehler 455; theatre as place 179; Vitez 449
Drums on the Dyke [*Tambours sur la digue*] (dir. Mnouchkine) 186, 448
Drury Lane theatres 71, 80, 82
Du Bos, Abbé Jean-Baptiste 305
Duchamp, Marcel 475
The Duchess of Malfi (Webster) 466
Durand, Régis 459
Duroure, Jean-François 535

eccyclema 90, 91
L'Échange (T'chan'G) 495
Éden, Éden, Éden (Guyotat) 354, 411
eighteenth century theatre: actors 141–142, 143, 144; architecture 80, 81; characters 299; codes of theatrical representation 289; costumes 243–244; discontinuous performance 313; drama genre 153–154; dramatic time 276; illusion 126–127, 147, 152, 154, 303, 304–305, 306, 584; Italian-style proscenium theatres 110–111, 123, 126; lighting 214–215; in London 70–71; narrative principles 165; offstage as metonymic extension 136; Opéra Garnier 190, 191; perspective 104, 113, 127–128, 130–131; play with words and breath 293; Riccoboni 141, 144–145; scenography 111, 113, 146–147, 150–151; secularised space 122; smell and touch 182, 184; social hierarchy 110–111, 125, 129, 145; specificity 106, 124; stage

595

INDEX

directions 55, 147, 349, 365, 366; stage time, duration of 262–263; "training the audience" 124, 127, 141–142, 145, 152, 184, 225; *see also* Diderot, Denis
Einstein on the Beach (dir. Wilson) 226, 437, 479
Electra (Sophocles) 451
Elizabethan theatre: cross-dressing 251, 507; dramatic time 165, 275, 276; and medieval drama 104; *mise en abyme* 171; modern performances 57, 198–199, 434, 439, 466; sites and spaces 70, 105–106, 162; *see also* Shakespeare, William
Elsineur (dir. Lapage) 551
Elvire Jouvet 40 (dir. Jaques-Wajeman) 432–433
L'Émission de Pierre Meynard [*Pierre Meynard's Programme*] (Gatti) 487
l'Enclos [*Enclosure*] (dir. Gatti) 484
Endgame (Beckett) 122
Engel, André 44, 75–76, 77, 220, 221–222, 361, 441, 443
English language 292
Entretiens sur "Le Fils naturel" [*Interviews on "The Natural Son"*] (Diderot) 147, 149
epic theatre 164–168; *1789* (dir. Mnouchkine) 447; Brechtian 157, 165, 166, 167, 168, 270, 277, 346, 475, 527, 547; Lagarde 527; *The Mahabharata* (dir. Brook) 458; poetic dithyramb 331; Sivadier 532; time 266, 270, 279; Wilson's aesthetic 437
Eraritjaritjaka, Museum of Sentences [*Eraritjaritjaka, musée des phrases*] (Goebbels) 550, 552–553
Esnay, Christian 529, 530
L'Espérance, Théâtre de 442
Euripides 90, 92, 467, 512
Explosion of a Memory [*Bildbeschreibung/Paysage sous surveillance*] (Müller) 391–392
Extinction (dir. Lupa) 521, 522–523, 524

Fabre, Jan 185, 318, 568–569
Les Fâcheux [*The Bores*] (Molière) 313

Fang, Mei Lei 166
Fanti, Lucio 440
La Fausse suivante [*The Double-Crosser's Comeuppance*] (dir. Chéreau) 491
Faust (Goethe) 194, 233, 439–440
Faust-Salpêtrière (dir. Grüber) 470, 471
feasts 183
Feydeau, Georges 173, 247
Fiadeiro, João 570
fictional time 363; *see also* dramatic time
Fight of the Negro and the Dog [*Combat de nègre et de chiens*] (dir. Chéreau) 461
Le Fils naturel [*The Natural Son*] (Diderot) 147–148, 153, 274
Fisbach, Frédéric 503–504, 543–546
flashbacks 272–273, 368
floors 210–214; coverings for 212, 239, 248; fullness 207–208, 212–213, 238; lighting 212, 216, 217, 218; perspective 107, 108, 109, 205, 210; *Tartuffe* (dir. Allio) 422; trap doors 194–195, 196, 211, 219
fly crews 26
fly system 75, 192, 194
La Folle journée ou Le Mariage de Figaro [*The Crazy Day, or the Marriage of Figaro*] (dir. Sivadier) 531
follow-spotlights 208, 217–218
Fomenko, Piotr 415, 520
Fontana, Richard 449
Fonzo Bo, Martial di 227, 517
Footsbarn Theatre 78, 429
Forced Entertainment 571–572
Foreman, Richard 230, 477, 479
forestage 191
Forever Young (dir. Castorf) 184
Fort, Paul 182
Foucault 71 513
Foucher, Michelle 443
Four Penny Opera (Brecht) 229, 454
fourth wall: actors 138, 149, 287, 291; crisis of drama (twentieth century) 157; epic theatre 165, 168; as illusory concept 127, 173, 306; nineteenth century theatre 150–151; physical separation of the audience 111, 149, 192, 193; pre-eighteenth century 95, 208, 584; realist theatre 150–151, 159; scenography 114, 146, 150–151;

INDEX

seventeenth and eighteenth century 146–148, 154, 306, 584; touch, taste and smell 182, 184; warmth of the session 149–150
foyers 82
François, Guy-Claude 77
François, Marc 506–508, 509
Frigerio, Ezio 439, 454
Fuchs, Georg 162
Fulton, Robert 150
La Fura dels Baus 184, 200, 318
Furetière, Antoine 68, 304
the Futurists 473–474

Gabily, Didier-Georges 491–492, 495–496, 497, 500, 509, 515, 541; *see also* T'chan'G
Les Galanteries du duc d'Ossonne [*The Galanteries of the Duke of Ossonne*] (dir. Villégier) 434
García, Rodrigo 213, 226, 318, 412, 514, 568
garden side 192
Garnier, Robert 434
Garrick, David 147
Gastaldi, Jany 449
Gatti, Dante Sauveur (Armand) 411, 484–488
Gaudeamus (dir. Dodine) 535
Gay, John *see The Beggar's Opera* (Gay)
Genesi, from the Museum of Sleep (Castellucci) 259n8, 565
Genet, Jean 247, 350, 366, 411, 460, 508
Gennevilliers, Théâtre de 70, 77, 239, 425, 457
George Dandin (Molière) 421–422
Gesamtkunstwerk (total work of art) 160, 416, 462–463
The Ghosts (Ibsen) 155
Gilgamesh (dir. Rambert) 44
Giulio Cesare [*Julius Caesar*] (dir. Castellucci) 566
Giulio Cesare in Egitto (dir. Sellars) 513
Glass, Philip 437, 479
Globe theatre 105, 162, 199
Gloucester Time: Matériau Shakespeare (dir. Langhoff) 210, 238, 255, 466
Godard, Jean-Luc 327

Goebbels, Heiner 229, 550, 552
Goethe, Johann Wolfgang von 334; *see also Faust* (Goethe)
The Golden Age [*L'Âge d'or*] (dir. Mnouchkine) 442, 447
Goldoni, Carlo 21, 435, 453–454
The Good Soul of Szechuan (dir. Strehler) 454
Gorki, Maxime (Alekseï Maksimovitch Pechkovt) 454
The Government Inspector (dir. Langhoff) 182, 466, 467
grand-guignol 184, 272, 473, 532
Grant, Cary 269
Greek theatre: Aeschylus 90, 92, 274, 448, 512; chorality 89, 90, 165, 395, 512; civic and social dimension 41, 92; cross-dressing 251; Euripides 90, 92, 467, 512; and Roman theatre 92, 93; Sophocles 90, 92, 373, 451; Tanguy's montage 559; vocabulary of 89–90; *see also* Aristotle
Green, Eugène 428
Gregorio, cabaret dell'800 (dir. Bene) 563
Gropius, Walter 474
Grosz, Georg 166
Grotowski, Jerzy 99, 318, 445–446, 478
Groundings (dir. Marthaler) 539
GROUPOV 513
Grüber, Klaus Michael: art of presence 548; *Bérénice* 223–224, 420, 427, 470, 471; *Faust* 194; *Iphigenie auf Aulis* 79; *Iphigenie auf Tauris* 211, 431, 470; leading figure in postdramatic theatre 556, 557; return to proscenium style 77, 200; rise of director-artists 415, 420; scenographic collaboration with painters 440; theatricality of restraint 469–472
Grünberg, Klaus 550
Gruppetto: Impressions d'Œdipe [*Grupetto: Oedipal Impressions*] (Meyssat) 272
Guevara, Ernesto (Che) 485, 487
Guibert, Hervé 497
Guillaume Tell (Lemierre) 111, 147

597

INDEX

Guillet, Aurélia see *Penthésilée-paysage* (Guillet)
Guyotat, Pierre 350, 354, 411, 450

Hamlet (Shakespeare): *Amleto: La veemente esteriorità della morte di un mollusco* [*Hamlet: The Vehement Exteriority of the Death of a Mollusc*] (dir. Castellucci) 319–323, 564; Brook 212; Chéreau 457, 461; Kokkos' scenography 440; public crier 295; rise of the director-author 420; Tanguy's Théâtre du Radeau 560; Wilson 216–217; Zadek 215, 238
Hamletmachine (Müller) 274
Hamsun, Knut 507
happenings 47, 184, 226, 232, 473–477, 480, 537, 557
Hardy, Alexandre 385, 435
Harlequin, Servant of Two Masters [*Arlecchino servitore di due padroni*] (dir. Strehler) 202, 453
Hauptmann, Gerhart 154, 156
The Heap [*Le Tas*] (dir. Meunier) 567
Hédelin, François (abbé d'Aubignac) 124, 146, 215, 304, 584; *see also La Pratique du théâtre* [*The Practice of Theatre*] (d'Aubignac)
Hegel, Friedrich 152, 153
The Heir Apparent (dir. Ives) 269
The Heir from the Village [*L'Héritier de village*] (dir. Chéreau) 423
Henry IV (Mnouchkine) 448
Henry IV (La nuit surprise par le jour) 528–530
L'Héritier de village [*The Heir from the Village*] (dir. Chéreau) 423
Hernani (Hugo) 226, 276, 451
Heroes' Square [*Place des Héros*] (Bernhard) 237
Hersant, Philippe 550
HF microphones 230
L'Histoire terrible mais inachevée de Norodom Sihanouk roi du Cambodge [*The Terrible But Unfinished Story of Norodom Sihanouk King of Cambodia*] (Cixous, Mnouchkine) 448
The History of Tears (dir. Fabre) 568
Hitler, Adolf 99

Holocauste [*Holocaust*] (dir. Régy) 227, 516
Homeric epic 331
Horvath, Odön von 221, 578n52
Hôtel de Bourgogne 55, 109, 123, 125, 126, 183, 214
Hôtel des Fossés Saint-Germain 109, 123
Hourdin, Jean-Louis 464
House/Lights (Wooster Group) 479
Hugo, Victor 151, 452; *see also Hernani* (Hugo); *Ruy Blas* (Hugo)
Hugues de Saint-Victor 41
Human Gardening [*Jardinage humain*] (dir. García) 213
Huppert, Isabelle 284
Hynes, Gary 253

Ibsen, Henrik 154, 155, 156, 285, 299, 511
Iets op Bach (dir. Platel) 569
L'Ile des esclaves [*The Island of Slaves*] (dir. Strehler) 241–242
L'Ile du salut [*Salvation's Islands*] (dir. Langhoff) 227–228, 467
L'Illusion comique [*The Comic Illusion*] (Corneille) 39n12, 131–134, 138, 171, 196, 273, 274, 310, 312, 454
The Imaginary Invalid [*Le Malade imaginaire*] (Molière) 58, 434
I'm Blood (dir. Fabre) 568
Incertitudes de Weiner Heisenberg. Feuilles de brouillon pour recueillir les larmes des cathédrales dans la tempête et dire Jean Cavaillès sur une aire de jeu [*The Uncertainties of Weiner Heisenberg. Rough Draft for a Narrative of the Tears of the Cathedrals in the Storm and of Jean Cavaillès on a Playground*] (Gatti) 488
L'Indiade ou l'Inde de leurs rêves [*The Indiad or India of Their Dreams*] (Cixous) 448
infiltration principle 67–69
In the Penal Colony (Kafka) 75–76, 228, 467
In the Solitude of Cotton Fields [*Dans la solitude des champs de coton*] (dir. Chéreau) 218, 461
Intérieur [*Interior*] (Maeterlinck) 155, 517

INDEX

Interviews on "The Natural Son" [*Entretiens sur "Le Fils naturel"*] (Diderot) 147, 149
invisible theatre 151, 350
Ionesco, Eugène 189, 234
Iphigenie auf Tauris (dir. Grüber) 211, 431, 470
Iranian Tazieh 99–100
iron curtain 40n15, 192
I Shall Never Return (Kantor) 480
The Island of Slaves [*L'Ile des esclaves*] (dir. Strehler) 241–242
Istria, Evelyne 449, 451
Italian court theatre 65, 106, 107, 108, 117–119
Italian style (proscenium) theatres *see* proscenium (Italian-style) theatres
Italienne avec orchestre [*Cue to Cue Rehearsal, with Orchestra*] (dir. Sivadier) 531
Ives, David 269
I Was in My House and I Waited For the Rain to Come [*J'étais dans ma maison et j'attendais que la pluie vienne*] (dir. Nordey) 502

Jama'al Fna Square (Marrakech) 67
Japanese theatre: avant garde happenings 474, 476; *see also* Kabuki theatre
Jaques-Dalcroze, Émile 160
Jaques-Wajeman, Brigitte 39n12, 234, 428, 429, 432–433
Jardinage humain [*Human Gardening*] (dir. García) 213
Jarry, Alfred *see Ubu roi* [*King Ubu*] (Jarry)
Jeanneteau, Daniel 170, 233, 272, 518, 520, 548
Jelinek, Elfriede 536
Jesuit theatre 316–317, 325, 330
J'étais dans ma maison et j'attendais que la pluie vienne [*I Was in My House and I Waited For the Rain to Come*] (dir. Nordey) 502
jeu de paume, théâtre du 75, 80, 110, 123
Jourdheuil, Jean: on the art of presence 548; *Le Masque de Robespierre* [*The Mask of Robespierre*]

230; *Michel Foucault, choses dites choses vues* [*Michel Foucault, Things Said, Things Seen*] 550; non-dramatic collaboration with Peyret 549–550; opening night point of view 20–21; *La Route des Chars* [*The Road of Tanks*] 274; scenographic collaboration with painters 440, 549–550; on seating categories 83; Théâtre de l'Espérance 442
Jouvet, Louis 372, 416, 420, 421, 432, 433, 453, 458
The Joyous Apocalypse [*L'Apocalypse joyeuse*] (dir. Py) 532
Le Jugement dernier [*The Last Judgement*] (Engel) 220, 221–222
Julius Caesar [*Giulio Cesare*] (dir. Castellucci) 566

Kabuki theatre 5, 170, 201, 226, 251, 428, 448, 478, 529
Kafka-Théâtre complet (Engel) 44, 75–76, 201, 258n1, 443
Kane, Sarah *see Blasted* (Kane); *Cleansed* (Kane)
Kantor, Tadeusz 226, 232, 274, 480–484, 520, 557, 561
Karge, Manfred 465
Karpow, Allan 476
Kiesler, Friedrich 474
King Lear (Shakespeare) 390, 466
King Ubu [*Ubu roi*] (Jarry) 239, 450, 473
kissing 21, 215, 251, 269
Kleist, Heinrich von 151, 268, 350, 520
Kleist: Prince of Homburg (dir. Stein) 193
Kokkos, Yannis 439–440, 452
Koltès, Bernard-Marie 218, 220, 271, 350, 378–381, 397, 461
Konigson, Élie 96, 97, 101, 103
Kushner, Tony 433

Labiche, Eugène Marin 173
Laboratory theatre 445
Lab'ou Tansi, Sony 412
Lacascade, Eric 285
Lagarce, Luc *see J'étais dans ma maison et j'attendais que la pluie vienne* [*I Was in My House and I Waited For the Rain to Come*] (dir. Nordey);

Le Pays lointain [*The Distant Country*] (Lagarce)
Lagarde, Ludovic 526–527, 551
"landscape aesthetic" 437–438, 475
Lang, Jack 457, 490
Langhoff, Matthias: aesthetic of 465–469, 472, 556; in author's opening night point of view 13; *Gloucester Time: Matériau Shakespeare* 210, 238, 255, 466; *The Government Inspector* 182, 466, 467; *L'Ile du salut* [*Salvation's Islands*] 227–228, 467; rise of director-artists 415; use of props 182, 213, 238, 466, 467
Lassalle, Jacques 361, 399, 427, 428, 429, 490, 491
The Last Caravan Stop [*Le Dernier caravansérail*] (dir. Mnouchkine) 213, 442, 448
The Last Judgement [*Le Jugement dernier*] (Engel) 220, 221–222
The Latest News on the Plague [*Dernières nouvelles de la Peste*] (Chartreux) 444
Lauwers, Jan 570
Lavaudant, Georges 209, 438, 490, 535
LeConte, Elizabeth 230
Le Légataire universel [*The Universal Beneficiary*] (Regnard) 268–269
Lehmann, Hans-Thies 46, 438, 479, 555–556, 557, 558, 559, 562, 582, 584, 585
Leirens, Jean 325
Lemierre, Antoine-Marin 111, 147
Lenz (Büchner) 406, 468, 469
Lenz, Léonce et Léna chez Georg Büchner [*Lenz, Léonce and Léna at the Home of Georg Büchner*] (dir. Langhoff) 406, 468–469
Leonce and Lena (Büchner) 466, 468
Lepage, Robert 551
Lescot, David 559; opening night point of view 12–13
Lessing, Ephraim 150, 334
Let the Artists Die (Kantor) 480, 482
A Letter to Queen Victoria (Wilson) 437
Lichenstein, Jacqueline 433
Lichtenstein, Roy 440
The Life of Galileo (Brecht) 454, 531
The Life of Garbage Collector Auguste G. [*La Vie de l'éboueur Auguste G.*] (Gatti) 485

lighting 214–221; on a bare stage 208, 212, 440; to block the audience from the actor's view 287; court vs. city theatres (seventeenth century) 108–109, 199, 214; darkness 146, 159, 160, 215, 220, 269; *La Dispute* (dir.) Chéreau 425; electricity and realism 112; for focus 216; and the fourth wall 146; image theatre 437, 439; Lupa's disturbing strangeness 521; monologues 219; nineteenth century developments 111; opening night preparations 24, 27; panoramas and dioramas 150; *Phèdre* (dir. Chéreau, dir. Rist) 204, 218–219; side canvases 195; spotlights 208, 216–218, 440, 461; sunlight 91, 92; time 269, 273, 516–517
Liolà (dir. Pirandello) 236–237
Living Theatre 445, 476
Le Livre de Christophe Colomb [*The Book of Christopher Columbus*] (Claudel) 381
London theatres 70–71, 80, 82
Lope de Vega (Vega Carpio, Félix Lope de) 171, 434
Louÿs, Pierre 353
The Lower Depths (dir. Strehler) 454
Lucio Silla (Mozart) 460–461
Lugné-Poë, Aurélien 161–162, 416
Lumières (dir. Lavaudant) 535
Lupa, Krystian 272, 520–525
Luxembourg, Rosa 486, 487
Lynch, David 327

Macbeth (Shakespeare) 268, 466
machinery: *Amleto: La veemente esteriorità della morte di un mollusco* [*Hamlet: The Vehement Exteriority of the Death of a Mollusc*] (dir. Castellucci) 319, 320, 322, 564; denunciation of 197; depicting time 269, 270; *Dom Juan* (dir. Chéreau) 424; epic theatre 166; *Faust* (dir. Vitez) 233; *The Government Inspector* (dir. Langhoff) 467; Greek *eccyclema* 90, 91, 92; medieval theatre 95; modern scenography trends 113, 163; nineteenth century 192, 211; seventeenth and eighteenth century 107, 108, 118, 126, 127–128, 145,

INDEX

146, 192, 199–200; and spectators on the stage 127, 145; urban theatres 199–200; visibility of 118, 195, 197, 419, 528, 561; vocabulary of the traditional theatre site 192, 195, 197, 210, 211, 213
Mademoiselle Julie (dir. Schleef) 536
The Madman and the Nun (Kantor) 480
madness 245, 308–309, 310, 316, 318, 320–321, 323, 468, 470, 507, 511; *see also* delirium
Maeterlinck, Maurice 154–155, 507, 517, 553
Magritte, René 566
The Mahabharata (dir. Brook) 44, 162, 263, 457–458
Mahagonny-Songspiel (dir. Langhoff) 465
Maïakovski, Vladimir Vladimirovitch 450
Mairet, Jean 434
Maison Antoine Vitez (International Centre for Theatre Translation [Centre international de la traduction théâtrale]) 406
make-up 24, 28, 189, 240, 241, 247, 248–251, 265, 424, 561
Le Malade imaginaire [*The Imaginary Invalid*] (Molière) 58, 434
Les Mamelles de Tirésias [*The Breasts of Tiresas*] (dir. Apollinaire) 473
Mancel, Yannic 399
Man Equals Man (Brecht) 167, 527–528
Manganaro, Jean-Paul 560–561
manteau d'Arlequin 192, 193, 194
Mao Zedong 484, 487
Marais, Théâtre du 109, 123, 133, 200
Marinetti, Filippo Tommaso 473, 474
Marivaux, Pierre Carlet de Chamblain de 7, 241, 242, 423, 426, 435, 439, 450
Marleau, Denis 553
Marlowe, Christopher 434; *The Massacre at Paris* 438, 439
Marmontel, Jean-François 311, 584
Marquais, Michelle 461
The Marriage of Figaro (Beaumarchais) 58, 122, 190, 244, 432, 531
Marthaler, Christoph 537–540, 541
Martinelli, Jean-Louis 202, 203, 210, 220

Marxism 418, 419, 421, 422, 423, 498, 513
Maselli, Titina 440, 550
Le Masque de Robespierre [*The Mask of Robespierre*] (dir. Jourdheuil) 230
The Massacre at Paris (dir. Chéreau) 438, 439
Master and Margarita (dir. Lupa) 523, 524
MC 93 (Bobigny) 70, 215, 512, 535
Medea (dir. Warner) 240
Médée Matériau [*Medea Material*] (dir. Vassiliev) 228
Medici court 65, 117, 118, 119
medieval theatre: epic elements 165; infiltration principle 69; influencing the Elizabethan "wooden O" 105; mystery plays 65, 95, 98, 165, 275, 276, 279; open spaces 64, 69, 94–95, 98, 105, 106; perspectivist techniques 104; scaffold and trestle modes 95–96, 98, 103–104; scenography 94–95, 104, 107, 109, 346
Mei Lei Fang 166
Meine Schneekönigin [*My Snow Queen*] (dir. Castorf) 184, 238–239, 552
Meinhof, Ulrike 486
Mental Palace [*Palazzo mentale*] (dir. Lavaudant) 438
The Merchant of Venice (Shakespeare) 510, 513
Mercier, Louis-Sébastien 153
Mères (dir. Schleef) 536
Mesguich, Daniel 428, 461
The Messingkauf dialogues [*Dialogue aus dem Messingkauf*] (Brecht) 306
Metellus, Jean 452
metonymy 178, 235, 236, 238
Metz, Christian 324, 325
Meunier, Pierre 567
Meyerhold, Vsevolod Yemilyevich 162, 207, 251, 416, 449, 528
Meyssat, Bruno 272
Michel Foucault, choses dites choses vues [*Michel Foucault, Things Said, Things Seen*] (dir. Jourdheuil) 550
Middle Ages *see* medieval theatre
A Midsummer Night's Dream (Shakespeare) 201, 210, 558
Mikaël, Ludmilla 470

INDEX

Milhaud, Darius 503
militant theatre 65–66, 102–103, 316, 317, 323, 433, 460, 486–487
Millon, Martine 459
Minetti, Bernard 194
Minks, Wilfried 440
The Misanthrope (Molière) 58, 360–361, 373–374, 429, 443, 451, 511
Miss Julie (dir. Schleef) 537
Mitrovitsa, Redjep 309–310, 449
Mnouchkine, Ariane: *1789* and *1793* 57, 73, 74, 442, 447; and the aesthetic of Théâtre du Soleil 441; classic plays 201, 210, 429, 448, 529; *Le Dernier caravansérail [The Last Caravan Stop]* 213, 442, 448; floor clearance 213; rise of director-artists 415; *Tambours sur la digue [Drums on the Dyke]* 186, 448; use of music 229
"*moi Inga, moi Ralf, moi Dieter*" ["*I Ingo, I Ralf, I Dieter*"] (Gatti) 486
La Moitié du ciel et nous [Half of Heaven in Us] (Gatti) 486
Molière, Jean Baptiste 58; *Amphitryon* 269–270; *Le Bourgeois gentilhomme [The Bourgeois Gentleman]* 245–246; characters' space and presence 58; *La Critique de l'École des femmes* 138, 226, 451; *Les Fâcheux [The Bores]* 313; *George Dandin* (dir. Planchon) 421–422; *The Imaginary Invalid* 58, 434; lexical features 352–353; *The Misanthrope* 58, 360–361, 373–374, 429, 443, 451, 511; *Plaisirs de L'Île Enchantée [The Pleasures of the Enchanted Island]* 183; on the pleasure of tragedy 307–308; on printed text 307; as a staged classic 421–422, 426, 428–430; standard theatrical repertoire 435; symbolic use of objects 254; *see also Dom Juan* (Molière); *Tartuffe* (Molière)
Mondory (Guillaume des Gilberts) 308
Mondrian Quartet 550, 553
La Monnaie, Théâtre de 434
monologues: *Bildbeschreibung [Explosion of a Memory/Paysage sous surveillance]* (Müller) 392; and dramatic time 268, 269, 270; as highlights 313; lighting 219; Lupa 522, 524; medieval narrative 165; props 235, 236; *Quai Ouest [Quay West]* (Koltès) 379, 380; reading dialogic relationships 372, 379, 380; Tanguy's Théâtre du Radeau 561; *Victoria, la lettre* (dir. François) 507
montage: avant-garde theatre 217, 476–479, 482; *Bloody Mess* (Forced Entertainment) 571; Brechtian epic theatre 165, 166, 167; deconstructing theatricality 207, 549–550, 552; historical perspective 473–476; Langhoff 465, 466, 468; Müller's musical form 538; *Rwanda 94* 513; Tanguy's postdramatic theatre 558–559
Montalvo, José 551
Montet, Bernardo 544, 546
Montfleury (Zacharie Jacob) 285, 289, 308
The Moor of Venice (Vigny) 226
morality 141, 150, 316–317, 327–335, 338, 412
Moretti, Marcello 453
La Mort de Danton [The Death of Danton] (Büchner) 209, 532
La Mort de Pompée [The Death of Pompey] (Corneille) 375–376, 507
La Mort de Sénèque [The Death of Seneca] (Tristan L'Hermite) 434
La Mort de Tintagiles [The Death of Tintagiles] (dir. Régy) 517
Mother Courage and Her Children (Brecht) 417
Mr Puntila and his Man Matti (dir. Schleef) 536
Müller, Heiner: *Bildbeschreibung [Explosion of a Memory/Paysage sous surveillance]* 391–392; on director's role 13; dramatic time 274; *Hamletmachine* 274; lighting effects 220; *Médée Matériau [Medea Material]* 228; *Philoctète* 467; post-catastrophe diffraction 411; *Quartett* 406, 461; *Tractuer* 405
multimedia 163, 232, 404, 468, 528, 550–553, 570

Murx (dir. Marthaler) 538, 539, 540
music 228–230; avant garde theatre 473, 474, 476, 477, 478; catharsis 334; dramatic time 270–271; Fabre's *Parrots and Guinea Pigs* 568; *Hamlet* (dir. Brook) 212; in image theatre 232, 437; incidental 224, 229; Marthaler's chorality 537–538, 539–540; Milhaud's score for *L'Annonce faite à Marie* [*The Annunciation*] (dir. Fisbach) 503; for rupture and couterpoint 229–230, 550; and spectacle 313; *La Tentation de St. Antoine* [*The Temptation of St. Anthony*] (Wilson) 217; variety theatre 474; *see also* musical theatre; opera
musicality 295, 427, 455, 500, 501, 503, 504, 541, 544; *see also* rhythm
musical theatre 71, 228–229, 252, 313, 550
My Snow Queen [*Meine Schneekönigin*] (dir. Castorf) 184, 238–239, 552
mystery plays 65, 95, 98, 165, 261, 275, 276, 279

Nancy, Jean-Luc 495
Nanterre-Amandiers *see* Théâtre des Amandiers (Nanterre)
Narcisse (Rousseau) 435
narrative: actantial analysis 393–396; avant garde theatre 475; dramaturgy 396, 397, 399; for offstage events 218, 268, 364; readings of the text 343, 360, 369, 370–372; *see also* epic theatre; plot
National Conservatory of Dramatic Arts (CNSAD) 405
National Dramatic Centres (CDN) 457
naturalism: actors 296, 298, 448, 503; consciousness as stagecraft 416; contemporary theatre's denaturalisation 492, 500, 503, 514, 516, 518, 519, 520, 525, 543, 547; and the crisis of drama 113, 156; diction 295; fourth wall 151; and the *mise en scène* movement 158–159, 161–162, 272; setting 177, 253; *Tartuffe* (dir. Planchon) 423; Vitez 448, 449, 451

The Natural Son [*Le Fils naturel*] (Diderot) 147–148, 153, 274
Nevinson, Christopher Richard Wynne 474
New Criticism 426
Nietzsche, Friedrich Wilhelm 334, 558, 559
nineteenth century theatre: Boulevard du Crime, end of 71–72; catharsis 332; contemporary staging 234; costumes 243; crisis of drama and the rise of the director 154, 161–162, 181, 583; curtain to signal session time 193; fly system 192; Grand-Guignol 184; house lighting 146, 215; identification of actor and character 299–300, 306–307; narrative principles 165; naturalist theatre 177; renowned "artists' entrance" 82; scenography 111–112, 113, 150, 158, 207; *see also* Romantic era theatre
Noh theatre 163, 201, 227, 270, 428, 478
Nordey, Stanislas 353, 493, 494, 497, 500, 501–503, 509, 526, 541
El Nost Milan (dir. Strehler) 454
Nostra signora dei Turchi [*Notre-Dame of the Turks*] (dir. Bene) 563
Notebooks (Mitrovitsa) 309–310
Notorious (dir. Hitchcock) 269
Novarina, Valère 13, 294, 350, 354, 505
La Nuit des rois [*Twelfth Night*] (dir. Marthaler) 538
La nuit surprise par le jour [Night Surprised By Day] (theatre company) 527–531

Oberammergau Passion play 98–99
objects 234–240; Antoine's realism 159; *Bérénice* (dir. Grüber) 223, 471; fullness of the stage 172–173, 207–208, 212–213, 238–239, 444, 465–473; ironic use 234; Kantor's theatre of memory 481, 482–483, 561; nineteenth century developments 111; phenomenological distance 548; postdramatic aesthetic 489, 563; Py 532; temporal setting 238, 255,

265, 466; transmitting meaning 178, 189, 234–240, 252, 253, 254, 255, 257
Odéon-Berthier 76, 77, 181, 202, 203, 218
Oedipus Rex 54, 395
offstage space 53; Carstorf's use of video 552; Elizabethan theatre 105; fight scenes 268; Greek theatre 89, 90; and illusionist perspective 135–137; *The Marriage of Figaro* (Beaumarchais) 190; narrative accounts 218, 268, 364; opening/closure principle 209; scenery 195, 209; sounds and silence 223, 229; the trap room 196
olfactory signs 182, 185, 186, 467
Olmi, Véronique 433
On the Road [*Sur la grand route*] (dir. Grüber) 471
opening night points of view 7–40; actor (Scali Delpeyrat) 30–32; author (David Lescot) 12–13; director (Jean Jourdheuil) 20–21; dramaturg (Joseph Danan) 14–19; readers 33–38; set designers (Anne Surgers) 22–25; spectator 7–11; stage manager (Jeanne Piot) 26–29
open spaces: *Arrivée Gare de Bade* (dir. Marthaler) 537–538; contemporary amateur theatre 101; courtyard of Palais des Papes (Avignon) 75, 225, 457; *Faust-Salpêtrière* (dir. Grüber) 470, 471; infiltration principle 67–69; *The Mahabharata* (dir. Brook) 44, 162, 458; medieval theatre 64, 69, 94–95, 98, 105, 106; minimum theatrical requirement 59; and the naturalist aesthetic 162; need for the ultra spectacular 63; Passion plays 64, 65, 98–99; procession principle 64–66; street theatre 64, 65–66, 80, 224, 486; Tazieh plays 99–100; *Winterreise* (dir. Grüber) 470
open thrust stage 198–199, 201, 204
opera: conventional staging 253; dramatic time 270, 276; highlights 313; *Lucio Silla* (Mozart) 460–461; platform music 228; Sellars 513; stage manager's point of view 26–29; Strehler 454; video incorporation 551; Villéger 434
Opéra Garnier 80, 82, 190–192
opposite prompt side 192
orality: breath linked to words 293–294; and language (contemporary theatre) 407–408; primacy of text (contemporary theatre) 501, 502–503, 504, 505; reading, act of 37, 348–355, 359
Oresteia (Aeschylus) 448, 565
Or the Hopeless Landing [*Où bien le débarquement désastreux*] (Goebbels) 550
Orphéon 558, 559, 560
Othello (Shakespeare) 306
Où bien le débarquement désastreux [*Or the Hopeless Landing*] (Goebbels) 550

Palais-Cardinal 119, 123
Le Palais de Justice (TNS collective) 442, 444
Palais des Papes (Avignon) 55, 75, 225, 457
Palais-Royal, Théâtre du 109, 200, 290
Palazzo mentale [*Mental Palace*] (dir. Lavaudant) 438
panopticon 145
panoramas 150, 151, 170
Panoramic Sea Happening (Kantor) 480
parados 89–90
Paradoxe sur le comédien [*Paradox of the Actor*] (Diderot) 185
paraskenia 90
para-theatrical text 348
Les Paravents [*The Screens*] (Genet) 247, 411, 460
Parentheses of Blood (Sony Lab'ou Tansi) 412
Paroles du sage [*Words of the Sage*] (dir. Régy) 516–517
Parrots and Guinea Pigs (dir. Fabre) 568
Partage de midi [*Break of Noon*] (dir. Vitez) 452
parterres: Italian-style proscenium theatres 110; rhombus perspective 128; seventeenth and eighteenth

century theatre reform 130, 142, 143–144, 145, 225; social class 110; and theatre as a social space 125, 127, 129, 130, 225
Le Passage [*The Passage*] (dir. Jaques-Wajeman) 433
La Passion du Général Franco [*The Passion of General Franco*] (Gatti) 486
Passion plays 64, 65, 98–99
Pavis, Patrice 360
Paysage sous surveillance [*Bildbeschreibung/Explosion of a Memory*] (Müller) 391–392
Le Pays lointain [*The Distant Country*] (Lagarce) 407
Peduzzi, Richard 203, 425, 439, 461
Penchenat, Jean-Claude 228
Penthésilée (Kleist) 151, 268, 520
Penthésilée-paysage (Guillet) 405, 520
Perceval, Luk 570
perfect (absolute) illusion 84, 303, 304, 584
Pericles, Prince of Tyre (Shakespeare) 270, 512
peripeteia 333, 384, 385
The Perjurous City [*La Ville Parjure*] (Cixous) 448
The Persians (Aeschylus) 274, 512
perspective: actors, movement of 128–129; challenge of *mise en scène* 158; contemporary use of scenery 208; Greek theatre 91; history of 94, 104, 107, 108, 109, 113, 117–119, 126–128, 146, 152–153; and the ideal illusory space 84, 127, 232; inclined stage floor 108, 109, 205, 210; and the infinity of words 134–137; multiple points of view 118, 123, 127–134, 135, 137, 168; plays on 172; proscenium (Italian-style) theatres 114, 127, 128, 168, 192; secularised space 120–121; side canvases 195; and the stage curtain 192–193
Petit-Bourbon, Theatre-du 123
Peyret, Jean-François 274, 549–550
Phèdre (Racine): Barrault 426; Bondy 79, 181, 210, 431; Chéreau 181, 202, 203, 204, 218, 461; Delbée 260n11; Rist 181, 202, 203–204, 218–219; sword 235–236; *To You the Birdie!* adaptation 230, 479; tragic codes and conventions 385; Vitez 181, 210, 426, 450
Philipe, Gérard 285
Philoctète (dir. Langhoff) 467
Piandello, Luigi 236, 305
Picasso, Pablo Ruiz 246, 474, 475
Piccolo Teatro 73, 76, 241, 439, 453
Pierre Meynard's Programme [*L'Émission de Pierre Meynard*] (Gatti) 487
Pieta 218
Piot, Jeanne, opening night point of view 26–29
Piscator, Erwin 166–167, 305, 484, 485
Place des Héros [*Heroes' Square*] (Bernhard) 237
Les Plaisirs de L'Île Enchantée [*The Pleasures of the Enchanted Island*] 183
Planchon, Roger: classic plays 210, 259, 420, 421–423, 428, 429, 430, 439, 529; on the creation of meaning 436, 498; on scenic and dramatic writing 415–416; and Vitez 449, 450, 452; on Wilson 438
Platel, Alain 228, 569, 570
Plato 327–328, 331
The Playboy of the Western World (Synge) 253, 376–377
plot: *Blasted* (Kane) 387–391; classic tragedy 384–387; *Cleansed* (Kane) 390–391; codes and conventions 384–387, 391, 393; dramatic mimesis 154; imaginary actualisation by the reader 382–392, 393; non-mimetic/dramatic theatre 46–47, 383–384, 391–392, 549–550; *see also* narrative
Poetics (Aristotle) 91, 152
Poitrenaux, Laurent 231
Polieri, Jacques 163
political dimension: actors and the social space of the theatre 85; actors' utopias 441–442, 445; amateur theatre 101–102; American avant-garde 476, 477, 479; Braunschweig 511–512; Brecht 417, 418, 419; Cartoucherie in Vincennes 72–74; catharsis

INDEX

329, 334; chorality 536; *Cinna ou la Clémence d'Auguste* [*Cinna, or the Clemency of Caesar Augustus*] (Corneille) 374; classic texts, contemporary repertory theatre 420–427, 429–430, 433; *Cleansed* (Kane) 391; contemporary writing 407–409, 513–514; contestations (1990s) 489–490, 493, 498, 499; court theatre and the "prince's eye" 117–119, 128; Elizabethan theatre 106; Gatti 486, 486–488; *Gloucester Time: Matériau Shakespeare* (dir. Langhoff) 238, 255; *L'Ile des esclaves* [*The Island of Slaves*] (dir. Strehler) 242; Jaques-Wajeman 432–433; juridical space 338–339; Marxism 418, 419, 421, 422, 423, 498, 513; *Le Masque de Robespierre* [*The Mask of Robespierre*] (dir. Jourdheuil) 230; Piscator 166–167; play of forms 447, 449; procession principle 65–66; referential offstage space 136, 169; responding to the violence of the world 411–412; Sellars 512–513; social evils of the theatre 327–329; theatrical space, specificity of (seventeenth and eighteenth century) 80, 124; triumphant theatricality 453–454, 455, 472

Pollesh, René 514

Pommerat, Joel 520

postdramatic theatre 554–572; ambiguity and fiction/reality boundaries 557, 571; Bene 563–564; *Bloody Mess* (Forced Entertainment) 571–572; Castelluccis 564–567; displacement of the theatrical sign 555, 556, 557, 560; foregrounding of bodily presence 444–446, 514, 557, 563, 564, 566–570; historical perspective 479, 557, 583–585; and *mise en scène* 558; non-hierarchy/simultaneity 555, 556, 560; notion of neutral performance 56; printed text 582–583; rejection of the primacy of narrative and action 437–438, 555, 558, 564, 571, 583; significant figures 556, 557; spectators 46–47, 479, 555–556, 557, 562–563, 565, 581–582, 583; Tanguy and the Théâtre du Radeau 558–562; Wilsonian stage 437

La Pratique du théâtre [*The Practice of Theatre*] (d'Aubignac) 33, 142–144, 146, 306, 307, 386

"prince's eye": and the actors 116; court theatre 108, 117–119, 199; director's point of view 20; French city playhouses 109, 131; multiple points of view 123, 128, 131, 137; scenography 84, 127–128; ticket cost 81

Le Prince travesti [*The Prince in Disguise*] (Marivaux) 450

processions 64–67, 98–100, 101, 119, 183

professional theatre *see* trestle stage theatre

profile spots 216, 217

prompt side 192

proposals 496–497

props *see* objects

proscenium (Italian-style) theatres: description and vocabulary 189–197; lighting 219, 287; perspective 114, 127, 128, 168, 192; proscenium arch 162, 192, 193, 194; Roman prototypes 89–91, 93; seating categories 81; stage area 160, 191, 194–195, 198, 199; theatrical trends 60, 75, 76, 77, 78, 109, 110–111, 123, 126, 162, 200, 431

proskenion 89, 90, 91

psychoanalysis 155–156, 421, 511, 517, 521, 524

public disorder 71, 72, 143–144, 145, 215, 226, 261

Public Song In Front of Two Electric Chairs [*Chant public devant deux chaises éléctriques*] (Gatti) 411, 485–486

puppets 65–66, 450, 473, 474, 528

Pylade (dir. Nordey) 501, 541

Py, Olivier 39n20, 505, 532, 533

INDEX

Quai Ouest [Quay West] (Koltès) 378–381
Quartett (Müller) 406, 461

Racine, Jean: catharsis 333–334; on diction 295; notes on Aristotle's *Poetics* 331; punctuation and actor's breath 293; recitation, code of 295; as a staged classic 202, 426–428, 450; and the standard repertoire 7, 435; textual orality 353; *see also Andromaque* (Racine); *Bérénice* (Racine); *Phèdre* (Racine)
Radeau, Théâtre du 495, 558–562
Raimondi, Ruggero 285
Ramuz, Charles-Ferdinand 512
Rauschenberg, Robert 476
readers: actantial analysis 393–396; analytical approach to *Quai Ouest [Quay West]* (Koltès) 378–381; characters, constitution of 372–374, 382; diffracted subjects 357, 359; diversity of 3; dramaturg's role 16; haphazard reading 359–362; imaginary locus 48–49; judgement 337–338; literariness and dramatic reading 348–355; mimesis 157; multiplicity of outlooks 344; opening night point of view 33–38; perfect (absolute) illusion 303; plot 382–392, 393; reading aloud 342–343; space and time 343, 362–372; textual space 2–3, 53–54, 55, 56; the title 374–377; tragedy 304, 307; *see also* texts
reading grids 420–421, 430
realism: acting 111, 159, 230, 287, 288, 289, 291, 295, 296; contemporary deconstruction 554; costumes 159, 246; Gatti 488; Kane's *Blasted* and *Cleansed* 272, 387–390; Lupa 272, 520, 521–525; masks and make-up 249, 251; and naturalist theatre 151, 156, 158–160, 161; opera 229, 253; reading 157, 387–390; Régy's theatre of non-representation 515, 516–519; semiotic system 111–112, 172, 177, 207, 234, 253, 254–255, 265–266; spectator's complicity

287, 303; *Tartuffe* (dir. Planchon) 265, 422; television and cinema 168, 499, 500, 514; time 265–266, 272, 279; *Ubu roi [King Ubu]* (Jarry) 450, 473; Vitez 440, 449, 450, 452; *see also* dramatic theatre
Recoing, Aurélien 449
Regnard, Jean-François 268, 435
Regnault, Francois 39n12, 378, 433, 453, 460
Régy, Claude: estrangement 272, 547; as example of postdramatic theatre 556; *Holocaust* 227, 516; Jeanneteau's sets 170; lighting effects 221; and Marc François 507; rise of director-artists 415; scenic writing 492; symbolic use of props 172; tempo 282; theatre of non-representation 515, 516–519, 525, 547; *Variations sur la mort de Jon Fosse [Variations on the Death of Jon Fosse]* 233–234, 271
Reinhardt, Max 162
religious dimension: *autos sacramentales* 64, 95, 98, 122; Bread And Puppet Theatre 183; catharsis 329, 330; Greek theatre 90, 91; Iranian Tazieh 99–100; Jesuit theatre 316–317, 325, 330; medieval scaffold theatre 96, 98; mystery plays 65, 95, 98, 165, 261, 275, 276, 279; Passion plays 64, 65, 98–99; Py 532; scenography 112; secularisation 119–123; seventeenth century theatre reform 142; *Tartuffe* (Molière) 244–245, 422
Rembrandt's Anatomy Lesson (Kantor) 480
Renaissance 21, 94, 104, 107, 117–118, 153, 163, 331; *see also* sixteenth century theatre
repertory theatre 7, 255, 265, 294, 301, 384, 415, 430, 431, 432, 433–435
Retour définitif et durable de l'être aimé [Definitive and Lasting Return of the Loved One] (dir. Lagarde) 551
The Return of Ulysses (Kantor) 481
Reznikoff, Charles *see Holocaust [Holocaust]* (dir. Régy)

INDEX

rhythm: actors 282, 292; *L'Annonce faite à Marie* [*The Annunciation*] (dir. Fisbach) 503–504; Appia 160; Bene 563; to captivate the spectator 281; chorality 536, 538, 539–540; Craig 161; diction 291, 295é; and dramatic time 268, 271, 278, 280, 281; Kantor 480, 482; lighting 217, 220; Lupa 521; music and sound 217, 229, 231, 271; Nordey 502; reading 37, 349, 350, 351, 353, 355, 369; stage managers 27, 262, 281; Tanguy 560, 561; of the text 281, 352, 355, 369, 407, 408, 501, 502; Wilson 282

Riccoboni, Luigi 141, 144–145
Richard II (Shakespeare) 424, 448
Richard III (Shakespeare) 268, 466; see also Gloucester Time: Matériau Shakespeare (dir. Langhoff)
Richelieu, Armand Jean du Plessis, Cardinal de 119
Rieti, Nicky 77, 221–222, 441
Der Ring [*The Ring*] (dir. Chéreau) 457, 460
Rist, Christian 181, 202, 203–204, 218–219
Road to Damascus (Strindberg) 157, 279
The Robbers (Schiller) 440
Roberto Zucco (Koltès) 220, 271
Le Rocher, la lande, la librairie [*The Rock, the Moor, the Bookshop*] (Jourdheuil and Peyret) 549
Rodogune (Corneille) 375
Rolland, Romain 419
Le Roman comique [*Comic Novel*] (Scarron) 242
Roman drama 58, 92–94
Romantic era theatre: dramatic time 275, 276, 277; provoking the audience 226; realism 151, 207; *Ruy Blas* (Hugo) 111, 234, 235, 276; scenography 111–112, 150, 207, 214; session time 263; stage directions 111, 365; textual orality 293; twentieth and twenty-first century staging 151, 234
Romeo e Giulietta secondo Carmelo Bene [*Romeo and Juliet according to Carmelo Bene*] (dir. Bene) 563

Ronconi, Luigi 76, 490
Rond-Point, Théâtre du 407
A Room in India [*Une Chambre en Inde*] (dir. Mnouchkine) 213, 442
Rotrou, Jean 127, 171, 385, 434, 435
Rousseau, Jean-Jacques 150, 328, 334, 435
Rousset, Jean 304, 305–306
La Route des Chars [*The Road of Tanks*] (Jourdheuil and Peyret) 274
Royal Court Theatre (London) 407
Royal De Luxe 66
RUR (Capeck) 474
Russian constructivists 207, 416, 449, 474
Ruy Blas (Hugo) 111, 234, 235, 276
Rwanda 94 (Delcuvellerie) 513

Sabato, domenica e lunedì (De Filippo) 185–186
SADE (dir. Bene) 563
Saint Joan of the Stockyards (dir. Strehler) 454
Sallenave, Danièle 459
Salome (dir. Bene) 563
Salvation's Islands [*L'Ile du salut*] (dir. Langhoff) 227–228, 467
Samel, Udo 470
Sandier, Gilles 423, 424
Sarraute, Nathalie 350, 515
Satie, Eric 537
The Satin Slipper [*Le Soulier de satin*] (Claudel) 263, 452, 457, 532
satire 90, 93, 513, 514, 536, 552
Savary, Jérôme 246, 428, 429
Savoie, Paul 553
scaena 92, 93
scaffold theatre: contemporary moment 101, 102–103; infiltration principle 67–68; Iranian Tazieh 100; medieval scenography 95, 96, 97, 98–99; social location 96, 97, 98
Scarron, Paul 242, 435
scenic writing 415–416, 438, 439, 445, 446, 492, 497
Schaubühne am Lehniner Platz 77, 184, 442, 443
Schechner, Richard 5, 44, 184, 258n2, 477

INDEX

Schiaretti, Christian 434
Schiller, Friedrich von 440
Schilling, Arpád 514
Schleef, Einar 536–537, 541
Schulz, Bruno 482
Schwartz, Evgueni 450
Schweik in the Second World War (dir. Strehler) 454
The Screens [*Les Paravents*] (Genet) 247, 411, 460
The Seagull (Chekhov) 234
secularisation 119–123
Sellars, Peter 99, 163, 512–513
Seneca 93, 94
Les Sept branches de la rivière Ota [*The Seven Branches of the River Ota*] (dir. Lepage) 551
Serlo, Sebastian 107
La Servante [*The Servant*] (Py) 532–533
seventeenth century theatre: archetypes 58; catharsis 332, 333; city theatres 108–110, 124–125, 199–200, 214; classic tragedy, reading 384–387; codes of theatrical representation 289, 294–295; costumes 243–244; court theatre 64, 107–108, 214; curtain 193; dramatic time 270–271, 275, 276, 277–278; illusion and identification 308; Jesuit theatre 316–317; London theatre location 70–71; narrative principles 165; perspective 106–107, 116, 128; professional roles 181, 347; secularisation 119–123; sensory engagement 182; social and political dimension 71–72, 80, 123, 124, 141; spectators 106, 108, 109–110, 124–127, 129–130, 133–134, 142, 143, 153, 171, 199; stage time 262; theatrical precincts 57, 64–65, 68–69, 80, 106, 123; *see also* Corneille, Pierre; Corneille, Thomas; Molière, Jean Baptiste; Racine, Jean
Shakespeare, William: *As You Like It* (dir. François, Marc) 507; *Hamlet see Hamlet* (Shakespeare); *Henry IV* (Mnouchkine) 448; *Henry IV* (La nuit surprise par le jour) 528–530;

Julius Caesar see Giulio Cesare [*Julius Caesar*] (dir. Castellucci); *King Lear* 390, 466; *Macbeth* (Shakespeare) 268, 466; *The Merchant of Venice* 510, 513; *A Midsummer Night's Dream* 201, 210, 558; *Othello see The Moor of Venice* (Vigny); *Pericles, Prince of Tyre* (Shakespeare) 270, 512; *Richard II* 424, 448; *Richard III see Richard III* (Shakespeare); *Romeo and Juliet see Romeo e Giulietta secondo Carmelo Bene* [*Romeo and Juliet according to Carmelo Bene*] (dir. Bene); *Sonnets* 549; *The Tempest* (dir. Strehler) 454; *Twelfth Night* 448, 538; *The Winter's Tale* 78, 165, 510, 511
Sierens, Arne 570
silence: *Amleto: La veemente esteriorità della morte di un mollusco* [*Hamlet: The Vehement Exteriority of the Death of a Mollusc*] (dir. Castellucci) 319, 322, 323; audience attentiveness 125, 127, 129, 130, 142, 143, 145, 222, 224–225, 312; *Bloody Mess* (Forced Entertainment) 571; characters 372, 378, 379; *Deafman Glance* (Wilson) 436; dramatic time 269, 270; effecting discontinuity 293, 295, 314; to focus the spectator's attention 222–223; gaps in the text 382; Grüber's use of 223, 470, 471, 472; and the quality of audience engagement 222, 314; Régy's use of 516, 517; textual orality 349, 350
sites and buildings *see* buildings and sites
Sivadier, Jean-François 529, 531, 532, 533
sixteenth century theatre: catharsis 332, 333; court theatre 106, 107, 117, 118, 119; curtain 192; dramatic model 152, 584; Iranian Tazieh 99; lighting 182; modern performance 434; Passion plays 64; perspective 104, 107, 113, 116, 117, 118, 119; proscenium 192; reorientation from open to closed spaces 106; *see also* Elizabethan theatre

609

skene 89, 90, 91
skênographia 89–92, 112
Skiba, Piotr 522, 524
The Sleepwalkers (dir. Lupa) 521, 523, 524
Slowacki, Juliusz 446
smell 182, 185, 186, 467
Sobel, Bernard 239, 415, 425, 440, 457, 490, 509
social dimension: actor and role 285, 298, 299, 301; chorality 536; the city 61, 62, 70, 71, 74, 96–97, 98, 124–125, 327–328; classics, modern staging 421–423, 426–427, 429, 430, 433; collectives 442; contemporary society 493, 494, 495, 506, 507, 508, 512–514, 568; costumes 241, 242, 243, 244, 245; delirium 318; Diderot's "animated warmth" 149–150; Elizabethan theatre 106; experimental theatre 445; Florentine court theatre 117–118; Greek *skênographia* 90; militant theatre 65–66, 102–103, 316, 317, 323, 433, 460, 486–487; morality 141, 150, 316–317, 327–335, 338, 412; in the multiplicity of plays and spaces 138–139, 169, 314–315, 336; naturalistic aesthetic 158, 163; and perspective 127, 128, 131, 136, 138–140; public disorder 71, 72, 143–144, 145, 215, 226, 261; reading 341, 345, 359, 383; referential offstage space 136, 233, 586; scaffold and trestle theatre traditions 68, 96–103; scenery and objects 158, 177, 235, 240, 241, 255, 266; seating 81–82, 83, 110–111, 125, 129, 145; session rituals 228, 262; socialisation 82, 124, 125, 130, 138, 191, 225, 226, 263, 314; and theatre as art 114; theatre as a collective experience 41–42, 168, 584; theatre's critical function 337–338, 407–408, 419, 433, 453; theatrical establishment/ legitimacy (seventeenth and eighteenth century) 71–72, 80, 123, 124, 141; theatrical precinct 63, 66, 68, 70, 71–72, 73, 74, 80, 85, 87, 168, 504; *see also* political dimension
Societas Raffaello Sanzio 564–565
Socrates 330
Die Soldaten [*The Soldiers*] (dir. Chéreau) 423, 424
The Soldier's Tale (dir. Sellars) 512
Soleri, Ferruccio 453
soliloquies 237, 313, 379, 380, 560
The Song of Songs [*Le Cantique des Cantiques*] (dir. Fort) 182
Sophocles 90, 92, 373, 451
Sosa, Ion 487
Le Soulier de satin [*The Satin Slipper*] (Claudel) 263, 452, 457, 532
sounds 221–231; ambience 222; avant garde theatre 230; *Bérénice* (dir. Grüber) 223–224, 427; contingent noises 224–226; expressing movement 221–222; Lupa's disturbing strangeness 521; of the machinery changing scenes 224–225; marking session time 222, 226–227, 261; *Phèdre* (dir. Rist) 204; postdramatic theatre 230–231, 558–559, 565; sound effects 221–222, 229, 230, 270; Tanguy's postdramatic theatre 558; *see also* acoustics; music; silence
Spanish *corrales* 69, 162
Spanish Golden Age 104, 434
Les Spécialistes [*The Specialists*] (Marthaler) 538
spectators: abstract staging 232–233; actors (contemporary theatre) 206, 505, 508–509, 516, 517, 526, 527–528, 530–531, 532, 533, 581–582; and actors, sharing space 52, 57, 67, 199, 200, 212, 337, 530; amateur tradition 96, 103; applause 227–228, 264, 306–307; d'Aubignac's reform proposals 142, 143–144, 146; avant garde theatre 476–477, 478, 483, 486, 487, 488; beyond representation 319, 320, 322, 323; bi-frontal staging 202–204, 218; Boulevard du Crime 71; Brechtian model and emancipated representation (late twentieth century) 165, 167,

168, 418, 456, 460, 462–465, 472, 497–499; catharsis 329–335; celebrity actors 264, 284–285; and characters 61, 243, 285–286, 298, 299, 300, 302, 304, 306–311, 315, 511; chorality 537, 538, 541–542, 543, 544; cinema vs. theatre 48, 324–326, 327; classic French theatre (seventeenth century) 106, 108, 109–110, 124–127, 129–130, 133–134, 142, 143, 153, 171, 199; classic plays (modern staging) 202, 215, 421, 423, 427, 428, 430, 467; contingent noise 224–226; costumes and make-up 241, 249–250; the curtain 192–193, 222, 226; dangers of interpreting everything 252–258; and the director-artists (1960s/1970s) 421, 439; directors, renown of 181; discontinuous attention 311–314; disorderly behaviour 143–144, 145, 215, 226, 261; distance effect 137, 138, 139, 164, 169, 198, 232, 315, 317, 318, 418, 546–548; dramatic time 261, 265, 266–280, 282, 315; dramaturg as 399–400; dynamic reception 179; Elizabethan theatre 70, 105, 106; fictional space, creation of 2, 44, 47–48, 53, 54, 55, 84–85, 302–305, 314–318, 341–342; form as medium (contemporary theatre) 542, 543, 544, 545, 546; fourth wall and the frontal dynamic 60, 114–115, 146, 147–151, 152, 154, 306; Greek skênographia 89, 91; Grüber's theatricality of restraint 470, 471; interpreting the actor's body 290, 291, 292, 293, 296, 297; juridicial space 137, 140, 168, 169, 197, 256, 315, 336–337, 338; lighting effects 91, 92, 215, 216, 217, 218–219, 220, 221, 222, 430–431, 438, 516–517; medieval theatre 95, 98; minimal community (contemporary theatre) 494–495; multiple points of view 127–134, 135, 137, 139–140, 168; and notions of performance 45, 46–48;

objects/props 172–173, 178, 205, 207, 213, 234, 235, 238–239, 344, 489; opening night point of view 7–11; open space 63, 66, 67, 69, 70, 103–104, 538; origins of non-representational theatre 473, 474, 475, 583–584; pleasure of 69, 91, 187, 253, 254, 256–258, 307, 311–312, 315–316, 336; the "Prince's Eye" 84, 108, 109, 116, 117–118, 123, 128; and readers 49, 53, 307, 342, 343, 346–347, 351, 356, 358, 363, 370, 371, 375, 379; and referential offstage space 136, 209, 586; rhythm 281; Roman theatre 92, 93, 94; seating categories 81–82, 83, 110–111, 125, 129, 145; session time 226, 261, 262–265; silent reception, notion of 125, 127, 129, 130, 142, 143, 145, 222, 224–225, 312; smell, taste and touch 182–187, 467; social dangers of theatre 327–329; sounds and silence, use of 205, 221, 223, 229, 230; stage floor 198, 211, 212, 213, 214; textual primacy (late twentieth century) 500, 501, 504, 505; troubled perception (contemporary theatre) 515, 518–519, 520, 523–524, 525, 546–547, 555–556, 565, 568, 569, 571; unconventional theatre precincts 59, 72–73, 75–76, 162–163, 200–201, 457–458, 504, 538; video 232, 550, 551, 552, 553, 554; what does it mean to go to the theatre 41–49

Sportstück (dir. Schleef) 536
spotlights 208, 216–218, 440, 461
Spring Awakening (Wedekind) 440
stage benches 105, 109–110, 111, 127, 129, 130, 138, 145, 146, 184, 226
stage directions: authorial voice 356, 357; hierarchy of texts 346–348; inclusion of staging techniques 55, 56, 146–147, 235–237, 240, 347; nineteenth century romanticism 111, 146–147, 151; readers and theatrical space 53, 54, 346–347, 365, 366, 367, 368

INDEX

stage machinery *see* machinery
stage managers 26–29, 107, 111, 161, 180, 261–262, 281, 415, 439
Stanislavski [Stanislavsky], Constantin 162, 295, 310–311, 416, 453, 478
"static drama" 155, 553
Stein, Gertrude 259n5, 437, 475, 479
Stein, Peter 20, 193, 415, 442, 443, 490
Stendhal 306–307, 313
stichomythia 269, 373
Strancar, Nada 449
Stravinski, Igor 512
street theatre 64, 65–66, 80, 224, 486
Strehler, Giorgio 20–21, 196, 202, 241–242, 415, 439, 452–456, 461, 472
Strindberg, August 154, 157, 279, 300, 536
Surgers, Anne: opening night point of view 22–25
Sur la grand route [*On the Road*] (dir. Grüber) 471
surrealism 437, 474, 480
symbolism: costumes 178, 242, 247; Fabre's choreographic theatre 569; Florentine court theatre 117; and the fourth wall 151; François 507; Futurist theatre 474; Iranian Tazieh 99; Maeterlinck 154; Middle Ages 104, 107, 109; naturalism (1990s) 500; objects 173, 235–237, 239, 254; procession principle 64; Régy 172, 517; Roman *scaena* 92; stage setting 92, 104, 107, 109, 128, 163, 172–173, 178, 196, 233, 322, 530; theatrical trends (late nineteenth century) 113, 159, 161–162; verticality of the stage 211, 214
Synge, John Millington *see The Playboy of the Western World* (Synge)
Szondi, Peter 152, 154

table work 397–398, 399
Tairov, Alexander 474
Tambours sur la digue [*Drums on the Dyke*] (dir. Mnouchkine) 186, 448
Tanguy, François 170, 495, 558–562
Tartuffe (Molière): acting space 58; casting 491; costumes 244–245; delay in the appearance of the eponymous character 375; internal stage directions 365; Planchon 265, 420, 421, 422–423, 439; rise of the director-author 420; setting 177; symbolic use of objects 254; Villégier 429; Vincent 429; Vitez 451
Tasnádi, István 514
Le Tas [*The Heap*] (dir. Meunier) 567
taste 183–184, 186
Tazieh plays 99–100
T'chan'G 495–496, 527
Telefavela (Pollesh) 514
The Tempest (dir. Strehler) 454
La Tempête, Théâtre de 72, 181, 202, 203–204, 218, 218–219
Temple, Boulevard du (Boulevard du Crime) 71–72
tempo 281
La Tentation de St. Antoine [*The Temptation of St. Anthony*] (Flaubert) 201, 217, 479
The Terrible But Unfinished Story of Norodom Sihanouk King of Cambodia [*L'Histoire terrible mais inachevée de Norodom Sihanouk roi du Cambodge*] (Cixous) 448
Tertullian 328, 330
texts: actor's relationship to 141–142; appearance 343, 345–348; approval 145; Aristotle's *Poetics* 91–92, 93, 94, 347; authorial voice 349, 356, 357–358, 381–382; contemporary theatre 45, 396–400, 492–493, 499–505; critical tradition 83; diffracted emitters 356–357, 358, 392; dramaturg's role 14–15, 16; image drama and the autonomy of the stage 438; literariness 2, 348; musical model 504; and the naturalist aesthetic 162; orality and the act of reading 293, 348–355, 359; postdramatic theatre 582–583; publication 406–407; signs 180; as space and site 53, 56; systems of appropriation 4; theoretical paradox 2; Vitez on staging the classics 451; *see also* readers; stage directions
textual space 53, 56
tg STAN 181, 185, 265, 398

Théâtre-Artistic Athévains 66
Théâtre des Amandiers (Nanterre) 55, 202, 203, 214, 457, 460, 461, 490
Théâtre de l'Athénée 78, 214, 432, 434
Théâtre des Bouffes du Nord 162, 212, 235, 458
Théâtre de la Cité Universitaire 213
Théâtre de l'Espérance 442
théâtre de la foire 80, 442, 450
Théâtre Française 17, 77, 80, 190, 206, 223, 234, 313, 434–435, 468, 490
Théâtre de Gennevilliers 70, 77, 239, 425, 457
théâtre du jeu de paume 75, 80, 110, 123
Théâtre du Marais 109, 123, 133, 200
Théâtre de la Monnaie 434
Théâtre national de Chaillot 226, 233, 405, 434, 439, 449, 452, 457, 458, 490, 509, 527
Théâtre National de la Colline 233, 290, 407
Théâtre national de Strasbourg (TNS) 203, 215, 405, 442–443, 444
Théâtre des Nations 417
Théâtre de l'Odéon 80, 196, 201, 241, 259n8, 284, 319, 433, 454; see also Odéon-Berthier
Théâtre Ouvert 407
Théâtre du Palais-Royal 109, 200, 290
Théâtre-du-Petit-Bourbon 123
Théâtre populaire (magazine) 417
Théâtre/Public (journal) 406
Théâtre du Radeau 495, 558–562
Théâtre de Reims 434
Théâtre du Rond-Point 407
theatre schools 405
Théâtre du Soleil 72, 73, 74, 186, 201, 441–442, 447–448
Théâtre de la Tempête 72, 181, 202, 203–204, 218, 218–219
Théâtre des Tuileries 123
theatrical precincts *see* buildings and sites
theatrical time *see* dramatic time
theatron 89
Thibaudat, Jean-Pierre 472, 495, 521
Three Sisters (Chekhov) 156, 467
time: before the performance 8–9, 13, 20–21, 22–25, 26, 30–32, 262, 263;

celebrity theatre 264; concurrence, speaker and receiver 267; constraints on hours of operation 261; historical interpretation 238, 265–266, 466; management of the session schedule 20, 26, 28–29, 261–262; marking of (bells and curtains) 222, 226–227, 261, 309; performance duration 13, 99, 100, 226, 262–263, 266, 457–458, 513, 532–533; post-performance 226, 262, 263–264; religious constraints 261; *see also* dramatic time; rhythm
Timocrate (Corneille, Thomas) 385, 386
TNS (Théatre national de Strasbourg) 203, 215, 405, 442–444
To Damascus (Strindberg) 157, 279
Today Is My Birthday (Kantor) 480
Tomb for 500,000 Soldiers (Guyotat) 411
Tonti, Paolo 320, 323
touch 57, 182, 184, 185, 186, 187
To You, The Birdie! (*Phèdre*) 230, 479
Tractuer (dir. Bonnaud) 405
The Trade in Bread [*Le Commerce de pain*] (dir. Langhoff) 465
tragedy: catharsis 330, 331, 332, 333, 334; costumes 244, 255; epic traits in 165; of the everyday (Maeterlinck) 154, 155; Greek *skēnographia* 90, 92; in *Henry IV* (La nuit surprise par le jour [Night Surprised By Day]) 529; highlights 313; illusion 127–128, 303; *mimesis* 153, 331; narrative structure 384–385; *Othello* (Shakespeare) 306; pleasure of 307–308, 385; reading 33, 304, 307, 384–387; recitation conventions 289, 294; referential game of 139; religious belief 122; Roman *scaena* 93–94; seventeenth century session times 262; stage directions 55, 147; time 270, 273, 276–277, 279; *see also* Aeschylus; *Blasted* (Kane); *Cleansed* (Kane); Corneille, Pierre; Euripides; *Hamlet* (Shakespeare); *King Lear* (Shakespeare); Racine, Jean; Sophocles
trap doors 194–195, 196, 211, 219
trap room 75, 76, 196

INDEX

Treasure of the Humble (Maeterlinck) 154
trestle stage theatre 95, 96–97, 101, 102, 103, 106, 162, 200, 202
La Tribu des carcana en guerre contre quoi? [*The Carcana Tribe in War Against What?*] (Gatti) 487–488
La trilogia della villeggiatura (dir. Strehler) 454
Tristan l'Hermite 434
Tristan et Iseult (dir. Sellars) 513
Trojen Women (Euripedes) 467
Trottier, Patrice 440
Tudor, David 476
Tuileries, Théâtre des 123
Twelfth Night (Shakespeare) 448, 538

"uber-marionette" 161
Ubersfeld, Anne 51, 393, 395
Ubu roi [*King Ubu*] (Jarry) 239, 450, 473
The Uncertainties of Weiner Heisenberg. Rough Draft for a Narrative of the Tears of the Cathedrals in the Storm and of Jean Cavaillès on a Playground [*Incertitudes de Weiner Heisenberg. Feuilles de brouillon pour recueillir les larmes des cathédrales dans la tempête et dire Jean Cavaillès sur une aire de jeu*] (Gatti) 488
United Colors of Benetton 218
The Universal Beneficiary [*Le Légataire universel*] (Regnard) 268–269
universal time 266

Variations sur la mort de Jon Fosse [*Variations on the Death of Jon Fosse*] (Régy) 233–234, 271
variety shows 473–474
Vassiliev, Anatoly 228, 446
V comme Vietnam [*V for Vietnam*] (Gatti) 486
Le Véritable Saint Genest (Rotrou) 171, 434
verticality 211, 214
Vexations (dir. Marthaler) 537
Victoria, la lettre (dir. François) 507
video 62, 232, 404, 468, 528, 550, 551–553, 554, 570

Viebrock, Anna 538
La Vie de l'éboueur Auguste G. [*The Life of Garbage Collector Auguste G.*] (Gatti) 485
Vigny, Alfred Victor, Comte de 226
Vilar, Jean 75, 207, 415, 417, 418, 419, 426, 450, 485
Villégier, Jean-Marie 214, 426, 429, 434
La Ville Parjure [*The Perjurous City*] (Cixous) 448
Vinaver, Michel 354, 398
Vincent, Jean-Pierre 214, 415, 428, 429, 442, 443, 490
Viola, Bill 513
Les Visionnaires [*The Visionaries*] (Saint-Sorlin) 434
Vitez, Antoine: actor as interpreter 503; *Bérénice* 420; and Braunschweig 509; death of 490; estrangement effect 428; *Faust* 233, 439–440; *Hamlet* 440; *The Misanthrope* (Molière) 361, 443, 451; *mise en scène* courses 405; *mise en scène* and the rise of the director 403, 415, 420, 426–427, 457, 458–459; *Phèdre* 181, 210, 427, 450; and Planchon 449, 452; play of forms 448–452; political conceptions 498; *Le Soulier de satin* [*The Satin Slipper*] (Claudel) 263, 452, 457; table work 397, 398
Vitruvius 94, 107, 113
Vole My Dragon (Guibert) 497
Voltaire 111, 145, 147, 215, 244, 305, 435

Wagner, Richard 160, 215, 416, 457, 460, 462
Warner, Deborah 240
Watanabe, Moriaki 427–428
Wedekind, Frank 440
Wielopole, Wielopole (Kantor) 480, 481, 482
The Wild Duck (Ibsen) 155
The Wild Duck that Flies Against the Wind [*Le Canard sauvage qui vole contre le vent*] (Gatti) 487
William Tell (Lemierre) 111, 147

INDEX

Wilms, André 444, 550, 552
Wilson, Robert (Bob): aesthetic of 47, 436–438, 476–477, 557; and Castellucci's work 564; choreographic models 232; director-artists, rise of 415; *Einstein on the Beach* 226, 437, 479; image theatre 217, 260n10, 436, 437, 438, 564; lighting 197, 216–217; rhythm 282; use of the cyclorama 196
Winckler, Angela 469
Winterreise (dir. Grüber) 470

The Winter's Tale (Shakespeare) 78, 165, 510, 511
Witkiewicz, Stanistaw Ignacy 480
Wolf (dir. Platel) 569–570
"wooden O" theatre 105–106
Wooster Group 163, 230, 479
Woyzeck: Fragments Forains [*Woyzeck: Fairground Fragments*] (Büchner) 464, 558

Zadek, Peter 215, 238, 440, 466
Zola, Émile 156, 158, 159, 443

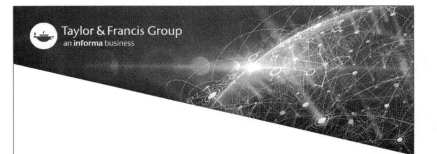